Hebrews
Preaching Verse by Verse

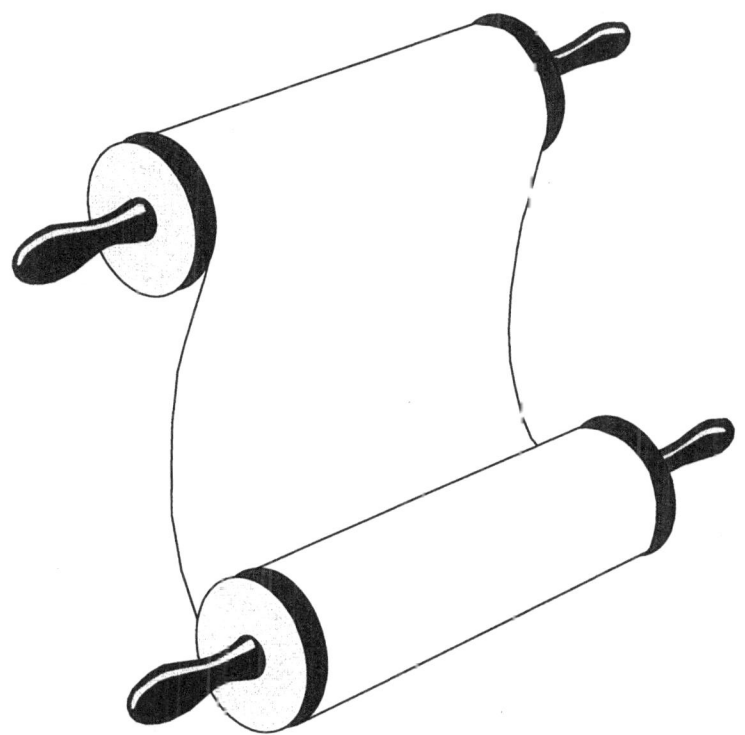

Pastor D. A. Waite, Th.D., Ph.D.

Published by
THE BIBLE FOR TODAY PRESS
900 Park Avenue
Collingswood, New Jersey 08108 U.S.A.
Pastor D. A. Waite, Th.D., Ph.D.
Bible For Today Baptist Church
Church Phone: 856-854-4747
BFT Phone: 856-854-4452
Orders: 1-800-John 10:9
e-mail: BFT@BibleForToday.org
Website: www.BibleForToday.org
fax: 856-854-2464

**We Use and Defend
the King James Bible**

Copyright, 2015
All Rights Reserved
March, 2015

BFT #4046

ISBN #978-1-56848-093-0

Publishing facilitated by
The Old Paths Publications, Inc.
142 Gold Flume Way
Cleveland, GA 30528

Acknowledgments

I wish to thank and to acknowledge the assistance of the following people:

- **The Congregation** of the **Bible For Today Baptist Church**—for whom these messages were prepared, to whom they were delivered, and by whom they were published. They listened attentively and encouraged their Pastor.
- **Yvonne Sanborn Waite**—my wife, who encouraged the publication of these sermons, read the manuscript, developed the various boxes, suggested sentences to underline, and gave other helpful suggestions and comments. The boxes help the reader to see some of the more important topics that are covered in the various chapters.
- **Patricia Canter**—a friend of Mrs. Waite who volunteered to take the cassette tapes of the verse by verse exposition of the book of Hebrews and put these words into digital format to be used for this book.
- **Anne Marie Noyle Houdyshell**—a faithful church supporter and Internet attender for many years who proofread the book and gave many useful suggestions for improvement. Though she lives in Canada, she was able to give her suggestions clearly over the phone. This took many hours of reading and correcting.
- **Tamara A. Waite**—one of our daughters-in-law, who attends our church services regularly, is a helper in many of our church projects, and has given many hours for her very detailed verse verifications, and other detailed proofreading of the book before its publication.
- **Dr. Kirk DiVietro**—a friend for many years, one of our Dean Burgon Society Vice Presidents, who is an expert on the use of computers. He has helped in various ways to make the computer work easier when performing the needed tasks.

Foreword

- **The Beginning.** This book is the **tenth** in a series of books based on my expository preaching from various books of the Bible. It is an attempt to bring to the minds of the readers two things: (1) the **meaning** of the words in the verses and (2) the practical **application** of those words to the lives of both saved and unsaved.
- **Preached Sermons.** These were messages that I preached to our **Bible For Today Baptist Church** in Collingswood, New Jersey. They were broadcast over the radio, and over the Internet by computer streaming around the world. They are now eventually all placed on the following LINK for further use for people. http://www.sermonaudio.com/search.asp?speakeronly=true&currsection=sermonsspeaker&keyword=D. A. Waite, Th.D., Ph.D. As the messages were preached, I took half a chapter each Sunday.
- **Other Verses.** In connection with both the **meaning** and **application** of the verses in this book, there are many verses from other places in the Bible that have been quoted for further elaboration on the teachings in this book. All the verses of Scripture that were used to illustrate further truth are written out in full for easy reference.
- **A Transcription.** This entire book was typed into computer format by Patricia Canter from the tape recordings of the messages as they were preached. These recordings are available in both audio and video formats (the **Audio cassettes are BFT#4046/1-13;** the **DVD Videos are BFT #4046DVD1-7.**) In addition to the words used as I preached these sermons, I have added other words for clarification as needed.
- **The Audience.** The intended audience for this book is the same as the audience that listened to the messages in the first place. These studies are not meant to be overly scholarly, though there are some references to various Greek Words used. My aim and burden is to try to help genuine Christians to understand the Words of God. It is also my hope that my children, grandchildren, great grandchildren, and many others might profit from this study of Hebrews. The 58-page INDEX takes you to any word or topic.

Yours For God's Words,

D. A. Waite

Pastor D. A. Waite, Th.D., Ph.D.
Bible For Today Baptist Church

Table of Contents

Publisher's Data	i
Acknowledgments	ii
Foreword	iii
Table of Contents	iv
Hebrews Chapter One	1
Hebrews Chapter Two	49
Hebrews Chapter Three	89
Hebrews Chapter Four	129
Hebrews Chapter Five	165
Hebrews Chapter Six	199
Hebrews Chapter Seven	233
Hebrews Chapter Eight	257
Hebrews Chapter Nine	287
Hebrews Chapter Ten	331
Hebrews Chapter Eleven	377
Hebrews Chapter Twelve	441
Hebrews Chapter Thirteen	497
Index of Words and Phrases	545
About the Author	603
Order Blank Pages	605
Defined King James Bible Orders	611

Hebrews Chapter One

Introductory Remarks

PAUL IS THE AUTHOR OF HEBREWS

In this book of Hebrews, we see **five reasons** why **Paul** is the author. It was written about 64 A.D., probably between the first and second Roman imprisonments. But many people doubt that it was **Paul**, because **Paul** did not put his name on it.

  1. **The first reason** I believe it is **Paul**, is that **Paul** wrote to the Jews in the dispersion according to 2 Peter 3:15.
- **2 Peter 3:15**
"And account *that* the longsuffering of our Lord *is* salvation; even as our beloved brother **Paul** also according to the wisdom given unto him hath written unto you;"

<u>Paul and as well as Peter wrote to the Jews who were converted to Christ.</u>

  2. **The second reason** is, the style is that of **Paul**. The words, the style, and the flow are **Pauline.**
- **Hebrews 13:23**
"Know ye that *our* brother Timothy is set at liberty; with whom, if he come shortly, I will see you."

<u>He talks about liberty. He talks about being in prison.</u> He knows about that.

  3. **The third reason** is, he talks about the saints of Italy. He knew who was there in Italy, because he was in Rome as a prisoner.
- **Hebrews 13:24**
"Salute all them that have the rule over you, and all the saints. They of Italy salute you."

<u>He is apparently writing this from Italy.</u> This could be a prison epistle itself.

  4. **The fourth reason** is, he knows something about bonds—being enslaved in bonds.

- **Hebrews 10:34**

"For ye had compassion of me in my bonds, and took joyfully the spoiling of your goods, knowing in yourselves that ye have in heaven a better and an enduring substance."

They knew that he was in prison.

- **Hebrews 13:3**

"Remember them that are in bonds, as bound with them; *and* them which suffer adversity, as being yourselves also in the body."

PAUL THE TRADITIONAL AUTHOR
5. The fifth reason is, it is the traditional authorship that is found in the Greek text. It is given in the old Scofield Bible. It is given in many places. I do not know why these newcomers say that Paul did not write Hebrews. I believe he did.

Hebrews 1:1

"God, who at sundry times and in divers manners spake in time past unto the fathers by the prophets,"

PROPHETS

Each **prophet** had his own manner—different ways of approach. Many were called **prophets** in the Old Testament. Just think of Elijah, Elisha, Nathan, Jonah, Isaiah, Jeremiah, Ezekiel, Daniel, Haggai, Zechariah, and John the Baptist.

WHAT DID PROPHETS DO?

Now what did prophets do? There were a number of things.

1. They encouraged people.
2. They predicted.
3. They preached.
4. They worried sometimes, I suppose, as when they were in prison. Jeremiah was way down in a pit.
5. They warned. They warned people of things to come.
6. They condemned sin.

THE MEANING OF "PROPHET"

Prophet is the Greek Word PROPHETES. They foretold the kingdom, the deeds, and the death of the Lord Jesus Christ. John the Baptist, the herald of the Lord Jesus Christ, was one of them. They were filled with the Spirit of God. They spoke by God's authority.

- **Jeremiah 7:23-24**

"But this thing commanded I them, saying, Obey my voice, and I will be your God, and ye shall be my people: and walk ye in all the ways that I have commanded you, that it may be well unto you. But they hearkened not, nor inclined their ear, but walked in the counsels *and* in the imagination of their evil heart, and went backward, and not forward."

They were actually disappointed, because they did not heed the prophet's warnings.

DISOBEDIENCE TO THE PROPHETS

I remember in my Bible reading this morning, the leaders said to Jeremiah, *"Please tell us what the Lord wants us to do. If you tell us, we will obey everything you say."* Jeremiah told them and they went right on and did whatever they wanted to do. They did not obey at all. How horrible!

- **Jeremiah 7:25-26**

"Since the day that your fathers came forth out of the land of Egypt unto this day I have even sent unto you all **my servants the prophets**, daily rising up early and sending *them*: Yet they hearkened not unto me, nor inclined their ear, but hardened their neck: they did worse than their fathers."

God at the first, sent the **prophets**, and the **prophets** were not listened to by the people.

- **Jeremiah 25:3-5**

"From the thirteenth year of Josiah the son of Amon king of Judah, even unto this day, that *is* the three and twentieth year, the word of the LORD hath come unto me, and I have spoken unto you, rising early and speaking; but ye have not hearkened. And the LORD hath sent unto you all **his servants the prophets**, rising early and sending *them*; but ye have not hearkened, nor inclined your ear to hear. They said, Turn ye again now every one from his evil way, and from the evil of your doings, and dwell in the land that the LORD hath given unto you and to your fathers for ever and ever:"

That is what Jeremiah wanted them to do.

> **AVOIDING 70 YEARS CAPTIVITY**
> If they would have turned, then the two tribes of Judah and Benjamin in the southern kingdom never would have gone into Babylonian captivity for 70 years. They did not turn.
>
> - Jeremiah 25:7
>
> "Yet ye have not hearkened unto me, saith the LORD; that ye might provoke me to anger with the works of your hands to your own hurt."

> **DIFFERENT PROPHETIC STYLES**
> <u>God spoke at sundry times—all different times and in different manners</u>. Each prophet had his own manner, his own way of saying it and his own way of doing it. God spoke unto the Jewish fathers—Abraham, Isaac, and Jacob, and all the Old Testament Jews—but the people refused to hearken.

Hebrews 1:2

"Hath in these last days spoken unto us by *his* Son, whom he hath appointed heir of all things, by whom also he made the worlds;"

CHRIST'S ATTRIBUTES

Prophets could not bring salvation, so God Father sent **His Son**. **The Lord Jesus Christ is God's Son.** You know and I know that people did not hearken unto **Him** either. They crucified **the Lord of Glory**. Sad, indeed.

HEIRS AND JOINT-HEIRS

His Son was virgin born, perfect Deity, perfect humanity, sinless, spotless **Lamb of God**. God the Father sent **His Son**. <u>God spoke to us by **His Son**</u>. Notice, *"whom he hath appointed **heir** of all things."* **He** is the **heir**.

> **CHRIST IS THE HEIR OF ALL THINGS**
> Everything that the Father has is the Son's. He is co-equal with the Father and co-equal with the Holy Spirit. He is the heir of all things. He is also the co-Creator. It says right here in this verse, *"by whom also he made the worlds."*

Hebrews—Preaching Verse by Verse

- **Genesis 1:1**
"In the beginning **God** created the heaven and the earth."

> **ELOHIM–THREE OR MORE**
>
> That word for God is ELOHIM. There are three numbers in Hebrew. There is the singular number. There is the dual number, two, and there is three or more, and that is ELOHIM. The Trinity is right there: Father, Son and Holy Spirit, *"by whom also he made the worlds."* He is co-Creator.

As far as appointing **the Lord Jesus Christ** *"heir of all things,"* that Greek Word for **heir** is KLERONOMOS. One of the meanings for this Word is:

> *"One who has acquired or obtained the portion allotted to him."*

The Father has given all things to **His Son**. As it says in Scripture, Christians—**genuinely saved people**—are joint-heirs with the **Lord Jesus Christ** of everything that is good in Heaven and earth.

- **Matthew 21:38**
"But when the husbandmen saw the **son**, they said among themselves, This is the **heir**; come, let us kill him, and let us seize on his inheritance."

The Lord Jesus Christ, when He was here on earth, gave an illustration. He talked about a man who had many goods. He went on a trip to a far country. He gave these goods to his servants. "Take care of them," he told his men. Instead, they beat one. They killed one. They stoned another, and so on. Then the owner of the vineyard said, "I am going to send them **my son**, maybe they will listen to him." They killed **the son** also. This was an illustration of Calvary.

In the same way, the Pharisees, knowing that **the Lord Jesus Christ** was the **heir** of all things, could not stand to be outnumbered, outvoted and outpowered by anyone other than themselves. They crucified **Him**.

- **Romans 8:17**
"And if children, then **heirs**; **heirs** of God, and **joint-heirs** with Christ; if so be that we suffer with *him*, that we may be also glorified together."

This talks about the believers that are genuinely saved and born-again. If we are children, then we are **heirs**. <u>**Everyone who is genuinely saved and born-again is a joint-heir with the Lord Jesus Christ**</u>. We have everything that **the Lord Jesus Christ** has in Heaven and earth.

- Galatians 4:7

"Wherefore thou art no more a servant, but a son; and if a son, then an **heir** of God through Christ."

The only way we can be an **heir** is through the Lord Jesus Christ.

Many people have inheritances in this earth—well-to-do people. They give to their children their multi-millions of inheritance. There are many of them—the Kennedy's and all the different ones. We have been made **heirs of God through the Lord Jesus Christ** by genuine faith if we are truly saved and born-again.

- Titus 3:7

"That being justified by his grace, we should be made **heirs** according to the hope of eternal life."

THE BEST GIFT TO YOUR CHILDREN

Now, you may not have much in the world's goods to leave to your children. I do not know your allotment. I do not know what you have in the bank and you do not know what I have in the bank. <u>Whatever we have in the bank—whatever we are going to give to our children—there is one thing that we can give to our children. That is faith in the Lord Jesus Christ, a firmness in the Words of God, stability in the things of the Lord</u>. Whatever we have in the bank, we can leave that to our children. That has always been our prayer, that the Lord Jesus Christ would bless our children, our children's children, and our children's children's children. We can leave an inheritance right down the line. That is what God is encouraging us to do as mothers, and fathers, and husbands, and wives. We are heirs of eternal life.

- Hebrews 1:14

"Are they not all ministering spirits, sent forth to minister for them who shall be **heirs** of salvation?"

The angels have a ministry to saved people.

SOME OF THE GNOSTICS' HERESIES

The Gnostics do not believe the Lord Jesus Christ was God's Son. They believe He was just a human being who needed to be saved. He was one who was just born of Joseph and Mary—just a commoner. They do not believe in the creation of the world by the Lord Jesus Christ. This verse very clearly teaches that.

CHRIST THE CREATOR

- **Mark 10:6**
"But from the beginning of the **creation** God made them male and female."

The lesbians do not like that. The male homosexuals do not like it, but **He made them** male and female in the beginning of the **creation**. **The Lord Jesus Christ** was part of that **creation**.

- **John 1:3**
"All things were made by him; and without him was not any thing made that was made."

CHRIST WAS THE CREATOR

The Lord Jesus Christ is not just a human being. He is perfect God, as well as perfect Man. He was from all eternity—God the Son—and He was the Creator. The modernists, the liberals, the apostates, the Muslims, and all the other people that do not believe the Lord Jesus Christ was perfect God, as well as perfect Man, deny that He was the Creator of anything. It is a sad thing, indeed. The Bible clearly points out our Saviour was the Creator.

- **1 Corinthians 11:9**
"Neither was the man **created** for the woman; but the woman for the man."

There is **creation** in the Bible, not evolution. Again, the lesbians and the homosexuals do not like this verse. "You mean the man was first and the woman was **created** for the man?" They say, "Not on your life!" The Scriptures are clear. The woman was **created** for the man. That is a wonderful thing. I have been married, since August, 1948, to one woman. I know it is sometimes difficult, but it is a beautiful thing. I tell you, we made it anyway. So far, so good! It is wonderful to have a godly woman.

A SPIRITUAL CREATION

There is another creation in Christ. If we are *"in Christ,"* we are a new creature—a spiritual creation that the Lord Jesus Christ can give to us if we are genuinely saved.

- **2 Corinthians 5:17**
"Therefore if any man *be* **in Christ**, *he is* a new **creature**: old things are passed away; behold, all things are become new."

- **Galatians 6:15**
"For **in Christ Jesus** neither circumcision availeth any thing, nor uncircumcision, but a new **creature**."

A new **creature** means something has been **created**. The Words of God give us information as to how we must be truly born-again. That is a new birth. That is a **creation**. That is **God giving us new life**. It is a wonderful thing. **The Lord Jesus Christ is the One—and the Father and the Holy Spirit—Who can make that true.**

- **Ephesians 2:10**

"For we are his workmanship, **created in Christ Jesus** unto good works, which God hath before ordained that we should walk in them."

This is talking about those who are genuinely saved. There is a **creation** once we are truly saved and born-again. Those that are lost and unsaved do not have that **creation.** They are not born-again. The Lord Jesus Christ has not **created** in them a new birth and a new nature.

- **Ephesians 3:9**

"And to make all *men* see what *is* the fellowship of the mystery, which from the beginning of the world hath been hid **in God, who created all things by Jesus Christ:**"

> **MODERN VERSIONS OMIT "BY JESUS CHRIST"**
>
> Those three words, *by Jesus Christ*, are gone from the modern versions, because they are gone from the Gnostic heretical Greek text. The NIV does not have them. The New American Standard, the English Standard Version, the Revised Standard, and the New Revised do not have them. All things were created *"by Jesus Christ"*—the implement of creation was the Lord Jesus Christ Himself.

- **Ephesians 4:24**

"And that ye put on the new man, which after God is **created** in righteousness and true holiness."

Here again, when we are genuinely saved, it is called a **creation.** The Lord Jesus Christ is part of that **creation**.

- **Colossians 1:16**

"For by him were all things **created**, that are in heaven, and that are in earth, visible and invisible, whether *they be* thrones, or dominions, or principalities, or powers: all things were **created** by him, and for him:"

He is the **Creator**, as well as the Father and the Holy Spirit.

> **THE THINGS CHRIST CREATED**
> Notice the things that were created by Him:
> 1. Things that are in Heaven—whether angels or whatever else that is in Heaven.
> 2. Things that are on earth—everything that is on earth, including the animals, the fish, the sea.
> 3. Things that are visible or invisible—including the atoms. They are invisible. We cannot see them.
> 4. Thrones, dominions, and principalities.
>
> All things were created by Him and for Him. The creation of the whole world—trees, shrubs, plants, animals, fish, stars, and galaxies—were created for Him, for the Lord Jesus Christ. You and I, if we are genuinely saved, are joint-heirs with the Lord Jesus Christ.

- **Colossians 3:10**

"And have put on the new *man*, which is renewed in knowledge after the image of him that **created** him:"

Again, here is the **creation** of this *new man* if we are genuinely saved.

- **James 1:18**

"Of his own will begat he us with the word of truth, that we should be a kind of firstfruits of his **creatures**."

Here again, the word *creatures* means that we were **created** by Him.

- **1 Peter 4:19**

"Wherefore let them that suffer according to the will of God commit the keeping of their souls *to him* in well doing, as unto a faithful **Creator**."

God is the **Creator**. The Lord Jesus Christ is the **Creator** as well.

- **Revelation 4:11**

"Thou art worthy, O Lord, to receive glory and honour and power: for thou hast **created** all things, and for thy pleasure they are and were **created**."

This is speaking of the Lord Jesus Christ.

- **Revelation 10:6**

"And sware by him that liveth for ever and ever, who **created** heaven, and the things that therein are, and the earth, and the things that therein are, and the sea, and the things which are therein, that there should be time no longer:"

> **EVERYTHING IN CREATION**
>
> Heaven, earth, and sea covers everything in creation. We are in the last days. If it was the last days at the time the book of Hebrews was written, we are seemingly in the last of the last days in the day in which we live.

Hebrews 1:3

"Who being the brightness of *his* glory, and the express image of his person, and upholding all things by the word of his power, when he had by himself purged our sins, sat down on the right hand of the Majesty on high;"

The Lord Jesus Christ was the **brightness of His glory**. That Greek Word, **brightness**, is APAUGASMA. Some of the meanings for that word are:

> *"Perfectly reflecting the majesty of God; a fullness shining forth of the light of a luminous body."*

That was the **brightness of His glory**.

> **THE MEANING OF "EXPRESS IMAGE"**
>
> The Greek Word for express image is CHARAKTER. We get the word *character* from it. Some of the meanings for that word are:
>
>> *"The exact impression; the expression; the image of any person or thing; marked likeness; a precise reproduction in every respect; a facsimile."*
>
> The Lord Jesus Christ told His disciples, "He that hath seen me hath seen the Father." He is the exact likeness in exact power and glory as the Father Himself.

(1) CHRIST'S GLORY

As far as His **glory** is concerned, He took upon Himself the form of a man and became obedient unto death, even the death of the cross. When the Lord Jesus Christ came from Heaven, He was a Spirit.

- **John 4:24**

"God *is* a Spirit: and they that worship him must worship *him* in spirit and in truth."

CHRIST'S GLORY WAS VEILED

When He came as Spirit into the realm of this life, through the miracle of the virgin birth, the Lord Jesus Christ became flesh and dwelt among us. We beheld His glory. He became incarnate. He came with a perfect human body and God became flesh and dwelt among us, as we see in Scripture. His glory was covered by His perfect but human flesh. Occasionally, one could see His glory, but it was veiled.

- **Matthew 25:31**

"When the Son of man shall come in his **glory**, and all the holy angels with him, then shall he sit upon the throne of his **glory**:"

THE SECOND PHASE OF CHRIST'S SECOND COMING

This is at the second phase of His coming. First of all, there will be the rapture before the Tribulation. The Lord Jesus Christ will take away those that are genuinely saved before the seven-year Tribulation. In the second phase of His coming, after the Tribulation, He will come visibly in glory to set up His millennial kingdom. Every eye shall see Him. At the rapture, nobody will see Him. The saints will be taken away. We will be caught up together with Him. The world will not see Him. When He comes in the second phase of His second coming, He will come, as it says, *"in his glory, and all the holy angels with him, then shall he sit upon the throne of his glory."* Thus the millennial reign of the Lord Jesus Christ will be set up.

- **Luke 9:32**

"But Peter and they that were with him were heavy with sleep: and when they were awake, they saw his **glory**, and the two men that stood with him."

The **glory** of the Lord Jesus Christ was shining before them.

- **John 1:14**

"And the Word was made flesh, and dwelt among us, (and we beheld his **glory**, the **glory** as of the only begotten of the Father,) full of grace and truth."

That is the Lord Jesus Christ.

- **John 2:11**

"This beginning of miracles did Jesus in Cana of Galilee, and manifested forth his **glory**; and his disciples believed on him."

He turned ordinary water into grape juice. They called it wine, but I think it was not intoxicating. It was called wine. It is the fruit of the vine.

That miracle at Canaan was a miracle that made His disciples believe.
- **John 17:5**

"And now, O Father, **glorify** thou me with thine own self with the **glory** which I had with thee before the world was."

This is the High Priestly prayer of the Lord Jesus Christ to the Father before Calvary. He knew that one day He would go back to Heaven with all the wonderful **glory** that He had before the world was.

CHRIST'S FLESH VEILED HIS GLORY

When He came on earth, His glory was veiled by His flesh. It was veiled, because we could not see it any more than Moses could see the glory of the Lord at Mount Sinai. He had to go into the cleft of the rock and let the Lord pass by. Otherwise, he would be killed. The glory was veiled.

- **John 17:22**

"And the **glory** which thou gavest me I have given them; that they may be one, even as we are one:"

He has passed on the **glory**. We have something in us, if we are genuinely saved and born-again, in our new nature—the **glory** of God, God the Holy Spirit.

- **John 17:24**

"Father, I will that they also, whom thou hast given me, be with me where I am; that they may behold my **glory**, which thou hast given me: for thou lovedst me before the foundation of the world."

If we are genuinely saved and born-again, we are going to have new bodies. In Heaven, we will see the perfect majesty and **glory** of the Lord Jesus Christ.

- **1 Corinthians 2:8**

"Which none of the princes of this world knew: for had they known *it*, they would not have crucified the **Lord of glory**."

This is talking about believing in the Lord Jesus Christ. He is called *the Lord of glory*.

- **2 Corinthians 3:18**

"But we all, with open face beholding as in a glass the **glory** of the Lord, are changed into the same image from **glory** to **glory**, *even* as by the Spirit of the Lord."

THE SCRIPTURES ARE OUR "GLASS"

The Scriptures are the glass we look into. The Scriptures can enable us see and show the *"glory of the Lord."*

- **James 2:1**

"My brethren, have not the faith of our Lord Jesus Christ, *the Lord of glory*, with respect of persons."

He is called *the Lord of glory*. That is a title for the Lord Jesus Christ.

- **1 Peter 1:21**

"Who by him do believe in God, that raised him up from the dead, and gave him **glory**; that your faith and hope might be in God."

CHRIST'S GLORY WAS GIVEN BACK
When He was raised from the dead with a resurrected body and went up to Heaven on His own, God gave Him glory back again—the glory of His heavenly location and place.

- **2 Peter 1:17**

"For he received from God the Father honour and **glory**, when there came such a voice to him from the excellent **glory**, This is my beloved Son, in whom I am well pleased."

This was at the mount of transfiguration. When Peter, James, and John went up to this mount, He just took away for a second His outer body. They could see the **glory**. They beheld the **glory**. He was manifest. His garments became whiter than snow, white as any fuller could white them. They beheld His **glory**. Peter saw it, John saw it, and James saw it as well—the **glory** of the Lord Jesus Christ.

- **Revelation 5:12**

"Saying with a loud voice, Worthy is the Lamb that was slain to receive power, and riches, and wisdom, and strength, and honour, and **glory**, and blessing."

The angelic beings said this.

(2) UPHOLDING ALL THINGS– HIS POWER

Notice also in Hebrews 1:3, *the express image of his person, and upholding all things by the word of his power*. The Lord Jesus has **power**. That is in the present tense. He is continuously upholding all things.

- **Luke 4:36**

"And they were all amazed, and spake among themselves, saying, What a word *is* this! for with authority and **power** he commandeth the unclean spirits, and they come out."

They were amazed at the **power** the Lord Jesus Christ had in His earthly ministry.

- **Luke 9:43**

"And they were all amazed at the mighty **power** of God. But while they wondered every one at all things which Jesus did, he said unto his disciples,"

They wondered at all the things which He did. <u>He had **power** and people could see it.</u>

- **Luke 21:27**

"And then shall they see the Son of man coming in a cloud with **power** and great glory."

<u>That is the second phase of His second coming—with **power** and great glory.</u>

- **Acts 10:38**

"How God anointed Jesus of Nazareth with the Holy Ghost and with **power:** who went about doing good, and healing all that were oppressed of the devil; for God was with him."

The Lord Jesus Christ has **power** and that is what is mentioned here, *by the word of his **power***.

- **Romans 1:4**

"And declared *to be* the Son of God with **power**, according to the spirit of holiness, by the resurrection from the dead:"

He has great **power** still to this day.

- **1 Corinthians 1:24**

"But unto them which are called, both Jews and Greeks, Christ the **power** of God, and the wisdom of God."

That is one of His attributes: *the **power** of God*.

- **Philippians 3:10**

"That I may know him, and the **power** of his resurrection, and the fellowship of his sufferings, being made conformable unto his death;"

THE POWER OF CHRIST'S RESURRECTION

He is resurrected. He is in Heaven's glory. Paul wanted to know the power of that resurrection.

- **Colossians 2:10**

"And ye are complete in him, which is the head of all principality and **power:**"

The Lord Jesus Christ is the Head of all the **power**.

- **Colossians 1:17**

"And he is before all things, and by him all things consist."

CHRIST PRESERVES THE BIBLE

Consist means *"to hold together."* It also means *"to be preserved."* I believe Bible preservation is part of this consisting. In Him, there is the power of holding the whole universe together. The worlds do not collide. The different parts of the universe do not collide, including the stars. He upholds all things by the word of His power.

(3) BY HIMSELF PURGED OUR SINS

Notice the next thing in Hebrews 1:3. It says, *when he had by himself purged our sins, sat down on the right hand of the Majesty on high.*

PERVERTED VERSIONS OMIT "BY HIMSELF"

Those two words, *by himself,* are gone from the Gnostic false heretical Greek New Testament of Westcott and Hort, Nestle-Aland, and the United Bible Society. Therefore, they are gone from all the versions based upon these Gnostic texts. They are gone from the NASV, the New International Version, the English Standard Version, the Revised Standard Version, and so on. The Gnostics of Alexandria did not think the Lord Jesus Christ could do anything, so they just pulled out those two words, *by himself.* He was by Himself purging our sins.

Purging means *cleansing*. There is **no purgatory** that the Roman Catholic church has believed on through the years to **purge** sins. They were all **purged** or cleansed at the cross of Calvary. It was by the Lord Jesus Christ **Himself**.

- **John 11:50**

"Nor consider that it is expedient for us, that one man should **die** for the people, and that the whole nation perish not."

The Lord Jesus Christ, **by Himself, died** for the people. Nobody else could save us from sin.

- **Romans 5:8**

"But God commendeth his love toward us, in that, while we were yet sinners, Christ **died** for us."

CHRIST SAVES ONLY "BY HIMSELF"

That is by Himself. Nobody else at that cross could save our souls. The two thieves on either side could not do it. The officers could not do it. The Pharisees could not do it. The Romans could not do it. Nobody could do it. Works could not do it. It was only by Himself.

- **Romans 8:32**

"He that spared not his own Son, but delivered him up for us all, how shall he not with him also freely give us all things?"

<u>He was delivered for all the sins of all the people of all the world</u>—not for simply a select few, but for the whole world. He **died** for us all.

- **1 Corinthians 5:7**

"Purge out therefore the old leaven, that ye may be a new lump, as ye are unleavened. For even Christ our passover is sacrificed for us:"

He was sacrificed for all of us—for everybody—the Lord Jesus Christ, **by Himself**.

- **1 Corinthians 15:3**

"For I delivered unto you first of all that which I also received, how that Christ **died** for our sins according to the scriptures;"

He **died** for the sins of the whole world. **By Himself, He died.**

- **2 Corinthians 5:21**

"For he hath made **him to be sin for us**, who knew no sin; that we might be made the righteousness of God **in him**."

<u>God the Father has made **God the Son** to be **sin for us**—all of us—in our place, in our stead.</u>

- **Galatians 1:4**

"Who **gave himself** for our sins, that he might deliver us from this present evil world, according to the will of God and our Father:"

The Lord Jesus Christ **gave Himself** for our sins, in our behalf—the sins of the whole world—**by Himself**.

- **Ephesians 5:2**

"And walk in love, as Christ also hath loved us, and hath **given himself** for us an offering and a sacrifice to God for a sweetsmelling savour."

The Lord Jesus Christ **gave Himself** in our place—the only One, (*"by Himself"*) to genuinely save us.

- **1 Thessalonians 5:10**

"Who **died** for us, that, whether we wake or sleep, we should live together with him."

This is talking about the Lord Jesus Christ, Who **died** for us—in our place—*"by Himself."*

- **Titus 2:14**

"Who **gave himself** for us, that he might redeem us from all iniquity, and purify unto **himself** a peculiar people, zealous of good works."

Again, this is speaking of the Lord Jesus Christ, Who **gave Himself** for us—"***by Himself***" alone. Nothing else could genuinely save us. No one else could truly save us.

- **1 John 2:2**

"And he is the **propitiation** for our sins: and not for ours only, but also for *the sins of* the whole world."

That is the Lord Jesus Christ.

THE MEANING OF "PROPITIATION"

Propitiation is a big word, which means *satisfaction*. God was satisfied with the work of the Son on Calvary—the propitiation for our sins.

- **1 John 4:10**

"Herein is love, not that we loved God, but that he loved us, and sent his Son *to be* the **propitiation** for our sins."

He is the **satisfaction** for our sins.

(4) SITTING ON THE RIGHT HAND

Notice also, in Hebrew 1:3, that not only did He have brightness and the express image of the Person of the Father, and upholding all things by the word of His power, and by Himself He purged our sins, but *He sat down at the right hand of the Majesty on high.* The most exalted place is the **right hand**.

That Greek Word for **right hand** is DEXIOS. It is *"a place of honor, a place of privilege."*

- **Mark 16:19**

"So then after the Lord had spoken unto them, he was received up into heaven, and sat on the **right hand** of God."

That is the only Gospel that says He is seated at the **right hand** of God.

BIBLE PERVERSIONS OMIT THE LAST OF MARK

The modern versions take out the last twelve verses of Mark. They say they do not need them. Of the four Gospels, no other Gospel but Mark has the Lord Jesus Christ seated on the right hand of God. They take out Mark 16:9-20 in every one of the new versions. They question and create doubts about them.

- **Luke 20:42**

"And David himself saith in the book of Psalms, The LORD said unto my Lord, Sit thou on my **right hand**,,"

This is a prediction of the Lord Jesus Christ sitting on the **right hand** of power and glory. Was God the Father satisfied with the Son's offering? Yes, He was. He put Him on His **right hand**. He exalted Him to the most important place of privilege.

- **Luke 22:69**

"Hereafter shall the Son of man sit on the **right hand** of the power of God."

The **right hand** is repeated over and over in Scripture.

- **Acts 2:32-33**

"This Jesus hath God raised up, whereof we all are witnesses. Therefore being by the **right hand** of God exalted, and having received of the Father the promise of the Holy Ghost, he hath shed forth this, which ye now see and hear."

CHRIST EXALTED BY GOD THE FATHER

God the Father exalted His Son, because of what He had done for the world, by His sacrifice for the sins of the world. The Lord Jesus Christ has been sacrificed and the Father was satisfied. The Father put His Son on His right hand—a place of glory and honor.

- **Acts 2:34**

"For David is not ascended into the heavens: but he saith himself, The LORD said unto my Lord, Sit thou on my **right hand**,"

- **Acts 7:55**

"But he, being full of the Holy Ghost, looked up stedfastly into heaven, and saw the glory of God, and Jesus standing on the **right hand** of God,"

When Stephen was stoned, because the people hated him, for preaching the gospel of the Lord Jesus Christ, before he died, he said, "I see Jesus standing on the **right hand** of God." <u>Now He was not seated. He was standing. People have asked, "Why was He standing?" Normally, He was seated. He was standing, waiting for Stephen to come home to Heaven.</u> I believe that is the explanation. Stephen was a godly martyr—the first martyr for the Lord Jesus Christ. The Lord Jesus Christ was standing and waiting for him to come home to Heaven. It is a wonderful picture of our Saviour waiting.

- **Acts 7:56**

"And said, Behold, I see the heavens opened, and the Son of man standing on the **right hand** of God."

- **Romans 8:34**

"Who *is* he that condemneth? *It is* Christ that died, yea rather, that is risen again, who is even at the **right hand** of God, who also maketh intercession for us."

He is at a place of power and honor at God's **right hand**.

- **Ephesians 1:20**

"Which he wrought in Christ, when he raised him from the dead, and set *him* at his own **right hand** in the heavenly *places*,"

- **Colossians 3:1**

"If ye then be risen with Christ, seek those things which are above, where Christ sitteth on the **right hand** of God."

- **Hebrews 1:13**

"But to which of the angels said he at any time, Sit on my **right hand**, until I make thine enemies thy footstool?"

- **Hebrews 8:1**

"Now of the things which we have spoken *this is* the sum: We have such an high priest, who is set on the **right hand** of the throne of the Majesty in the heavens;"

- **Hebrews 10:12**

"But this man, after he had offered one sacrifice for sins for ever, sat down on the **right hand** of God;"

- **Hebrews 12:2**

"Looking unto Jesus the author and finisher of *our* faith; who for the joy that was set before him endured the cross, despising the shame, and is set down at the **right hand** of the throne of God."

- **1 Peter 3:22**

"Who is gone into heaven, and is on the **right hand** of God; angels and authorities and powers being made subject unto him."

ROME DENIES SALVATION WAS "BY HIMSELF"

The Lord Jesus Christ died for our sins and *"by Himself"* suffered for and purged our sins. The words *"by himself"* are removed from the Greek text of the Gnostics that did not believe that the Lord Jesus Christ could do it alone. Neither does the Roman Catholic church believe that the Lord Jesus Christ can do it alone. It cannot be through the pope, or the saints, or the prayers, or the extreme unction, or church membership or anything else—nothing. It is by Himself.

> **FUNDAMENTALISTS' BIBLES DENY "BY HIMSELF"**
>
> How can the fundamentalists in this world say they agree with the Gnostic false Greek text that has over 356 doctrinal passages that are wrong? How can they praise that text and teach that text in their schools? I am thinking of Bob Jones University, Detroit Baptist, Central Baptist, and Calvary and a number of other schools. How can they teach that text in their schools? How can they push these other versions that are based upon a false text?

> **FUNDAMENTALISTS USE PERVERTED BIBLES**
>
> They have the English Revised Version, for instance, in their book stores. They have the NIV and all the others. It is beyond me. It is not that they do not know these are heretical verses in the 356 places. Many have pointed them out, but they just go ahead and say, "Well, we'll just hide our heads in the sand and just forget about them. These are nice versions." They knock the poor fellows who are against these false versions, who are against the false text, and who stand for the Textus Receptus, thus making us out to be some sort of lower animals on the totem pole of scholastic achievement and advantage.

"_By himself_" are two precious words, important doctrinally. All "_by Himself_" He did it, alone at Calvary's cross, dying for you and for me. In fact, the Father knowing that sin was upon His own Son, put out the lights of Heaven. Darkness was over the earth—pitch darkness from twelve o'clock until three, while the Son of God was taking the blackness, wickedness, and guilt of the sins of the world upon Himself.

Hebrews 1:4

"Being made so much better than the angels, as he hath by inheritance obtained a more excellent name than they."

Notice, **so much better**. In the book of Hebrews, we will see in different places that the Lord Jesus Christ is **so much better**. First, He is **better** than the prophets. He is better than the angels. We are going to see that He is **better** than Moses. He is **better** than all of them.

ANGELS

- **Psalm 68:17**
"The chariots of God *are* twenty thousand, *even* thousands of **angels**: the Lord *is* among them, *as in* Sinai, in the holy *place*."

He is **better** than any angel that ever was created. The Lord Jesus Christ was not a created being. He was from all eternity. He always was-- from everlasting to everlasting. He was always in existence, the same as God the Father, and God the Holy Spirit. The **angels** were created beings. Lucifer, the Devil himself, was a created being.

- **Matthew 26:53**
"Thinkest thou that I cannot now pray to my Father, and he shall presently give me more than twelve legions of **angels**?"

It was the will of God that the Lord Jesus Christ should go to the cross "*by Himself.*" The **angels** could have helped Him.

- **Mark 1:13**
"And he was there in the wilderness forty days, tempted of Satan; and was with the wild beasts; and the **angels** ministered unto him."

The **angels** of God ministered to the Lord Jesus Christ in the wilderness being tempted of the Devil.

- **1 Peter 3:22**
"Who is gone into heaven, and is on the right hand of God; **angels** and authorities and powers being made subject unto him."

He is over the **angels**. He is **better** than the **angels**. The **angels** are nothing compared to Him.

Hebrews 1:5

"For unto which of the angels said he at any time, Thou art my Son, this day have I begotten thee? And again, I will be to him a Father, and he shall be to me a Son?"

ANGELS ARE NOT GOD'S SONS

He did not say to the angels that they are His Sons. The Lord Jesus Christ is equal with the Father. He was always the Son. At the virgin birth of Christ, when He came on this earth, He was begotten by the Holy Spirit of God. It was the miracle of the virgin birth of Christ. He became the Son of Man, and begotten in that sense.

John MacArthur does not believe that the Lord Jesus Christ had eternal Sonship. (At least, for many years he did not believe that. He claims he has changed his belief. I do not know whether he has or not.)

He said the Lord had Sonship in different ways: Sonship when He was born; Sonship when He was resurrected, but He was not eternally the Son of God. MacArthur had to go over and preach in a church in England, I understand, so just before he went, he changed his views. Now, he claims that he believes in the eternal Sonship of the Lord Jesus Christ. My question, simply, is this, "How could God so love the world that He gave His only begotten Son, if His Son was not already in existence before He was sent by the Father?" He was eternally the Son of God.

THIS DAY HAVE I BEGOTTEN THEE
- **Psalm 2:7**

"I will declare the decree: the LORD hath said unto me, Thou art my Son; this day have I **begotten** thee."

- **Acts 13:33**

"God hath fulfilled the same unto us their children, in that he hath raised up Jesus again; as it is also written in the second psalm, Thou art my Son, this day have I **begotten** thee."

- **Hebrews 5:5**

"So also Christ glorified not himself to be made an high priest; but he that said unto him, Thou art my Son, to day have I **begotten** thee."

CHRIST BECAME THE SON OF MAN

When He took upon Himself flesh—perfect human flesh with a human soul and a human body—He became the Son of Man. He was always eternally the Son of God. This *day have I begotten thee*, I think, is talking about the virgin birth of the Lord Jesus Christ at that time.

Hebrews 1:6

"And again, when he bringeth in the firstbegotten into the world, he saith, And let all the angels of God worship him."

ANGELS WORSHIPPING
- **Psalm 97:7**

"Confounded be all they that serve graven images, that boast themselves of idols: **worship** him, all *ye* gods." ("GODS" ARE "**ANGELS**" IN THIS INSTANCE)

ANGELS WERE TO WORSHIP CHRIST

You see, the angels were to worship Him. They were not to be equal with Him. He is *so much better* than the angels. That word *firstbegotten* does not mean that He was the first thing that was created. No, *firstbegotten* is in the sense of primacy in hierarchy. Nobody is higher than the Lord Jesus Christ. He is firstbegotten, primary, top of the line. No one is greater than the Lord Jesus Christ.

The **angels** were there at His birth.
- **Luke 2:9-11**

"And, lo, the **angel** of the Lord came upon them, and the glory of the Lord shone round about them: and they were sore afraid. And the **angel** said unto them, Fear not: for, behold, I bring you good tidings of great joy, which shall be to all people. For unto you is born this day in the city of David a Saviour, which is Christ the Lord."

The **angels** were not anywhere near being saviors. The Lord Jesus Christ was the Saviour. He is above the **angels**. He came into the world to seek and to save that which was lost.
- **Luke 2:13-14**

"And suddenly there was with the **angel** a multitude of the heavenly host praising God, and saying, Glory to God in the highest, and on earth peace, good will toward men."

The **angels** were there at His birth. They **worship** Him. Certainly, the Lord Jesus Christ is much better than the **angels**.

In Hebrews 1:6, the Greek Word for **worship** is PROSKUNEO. Some of the meanings for this word are:

> "*To bow down with the forehead to the ground; an expression of profound reverence.* [In the New Testament it is] *kneeling; prostration; to do homage to one; or to make obeisance.*"

This is an important thing.

NEW VERSIONS OMIT "WORSHIP" OF CHRIST

Many times, in these new versions, when it says they worship the Lord Jesus Christ, they change it completely. Some of these new versions do not believe that the Lord Jesus Christ was God the Son—perfect God and perfect Man—but just a human being.

Hebrews 1:7

"And of the angels he saith, Who maketh his angels spirits, and his ministers a flame of fire."

ANGELS AS MINISTERS

- Psalm 104:3-4

"Who layeth the beams of his chambers in the waters: who maketh the clouds his chariot: who walketh upon the wings of the wind: Who **maketh his angels** spirits; his **ministers** a flaming fire:"

Again, He is better than the **angels**. The **angels** are spirits. Sometimes the Lord gave these **angels** bodies so that people could see them for certain missions. The **angel** was there at the tomb at the Lord Jesus Christ's resurrection. The **angels** appeared to Abraham before the Lord judged Sodom and Gomorrah.

SOMETIMES ANGELS WERE VISIBLE

In different places, God used angels and made them visible to people, but basically, angels are spirits. They do not have bodies. They do not have wings either like people portray them. Nowhere in scripture does it say anything about the angels having wings. They are spirits.

ANGELS ARE SERVANTS

Angels are ministers or servants. That word is a different word for servant.

> The Greek Word for "Servant" is LEITOURGOS. It means *"a servant of the state or a servant that has to do with ministry of some kind in a spiritual realm."*

We saw just the other day, in the book of Daniel, I believe it was, thousands upon thousands of **angels**, perhaps 100 million. That was just one reference. We cannot count the **angels**. They are spirits ministering to those that will be heirs of salvation.

CHRIST IS BETTER THAN ANY ANGEL

The Lord Jesus Christ is much better than any angel that ever was created, in any way, shape or form. He is better than prophets. He is better than Moses. He is better than all these other things. He is the best. He is the One that God has chosen to be sent into this world.

The most important part of these first seven verses in Hebrews 1, I believe, is the part in Hebrews 1:3 that says, *"when he had by himself purged our sins."* Sins must be purged. Sins must be cleansed. God has to deal with our sins.

> **A VITALLY IMPORTANT QUESTION FOR YOU**
>
> The only thing now that separates us between eternal life and eternal death is, *"What are we going to do with that One who has purged and cleansed the sins of the world?"* <u>Are we going to accept that One, the Lord Jesus Christ, and say, "Yes, I believe You purged my sins. You have cleansed my sins."</u> Are we going to receive Him genuinely, really? Or are we going to reject the Lord Jesus Christ? *"By Himself,"* He purged our sins.

There are people that think they can just do a few good works here and a few good works there. Many people go to funerals because they think maybe God is going to take them to Heaven because of that. That will not do it. Going to church will not do it. <u>Nothing will do it. Baptism will not do it, nor going to the priest for confession—none of these things—but by the Lord Jesus Christ Himself.</u>

That is what Roman Catholicism has to learn. They should throw away all the other trappings, things of apostasy, idolatry, and just keep the Lord Jesus Christ Himself alone. <u>We have to *"come out from among them"* and be separate</u> (2 Corinthians 6:17). It is *"by Himself"* that our sins are purged at the cross of Calvary. It is for all sins of all people, but that does not mean that everybody is going to be genuinely saved. <u>You must receive that salvation and trust in that Saviour honestly and confidently, and you can be genuinely saved.</u>

Hebrews 1:8

"But unto the Son *he saith*, Thy throne, O God, *is* for ever and ever: a sceptre of righteousness *is* the sceptre of thy kingdom."

THE DEITY AND RIGHTEOUSNESS OF CHRIST

There are two main things in this verse that we want to see.

1. First, the Lord God of Heaven, <u>God the Father is speaking to His Son, the Lord Jesus Christ.</u>
2. Notice what He says about Him: *<u>Thy throne, O God.</u>* This is the **Deity** of the Lord Jesus Christ. He is addressing the Lord Jesus Christ as **God**. He is **God** the Son, as well as the Son of **God** and Son of man.

THE LORD JESUS CHRIST'S THRONE

The Greek Word for *throne*, is THRONOS, which is *"the chair of state having a footstool usually."* It is assigned in the New Testament to kings with kingly power. The Lord Jesus Christ has a throne. The Greek Word for sceptre is RHABDOS. That is *"a staff or a walking stick,"* but it is used when applied to kings as *"a rod of iron."* A rod of iron indicates the severest, most rigorous rule. The Lord Jesus Christ in His millennial reign will be a rigorous Ruler over the nations with a rod of iron.

- Psalm 45:6

"Thy **throne**, O **God**, *is* for ever and ever: the **sceptre** of thy kingdom *is* a right **sceptre**."

THE LORD JESUS CHRIST IS DEITY

This Psalm is where this Hebrews 1:8 comes from. Instead of accurately translating it *"Thy throne, O God"* (meaning that the Lord Jesus Christ is God), Westcott and Hort changed this. They said, *"God is thy throne."* This is because they did not believe in the Deity of the Lord Jesus Christ. Bishops Westcott and Hort were the founders of the false Gnostic Critical Greek text.

Notice, there are two things: His Deity, and the sceptre of righteousness. There is not a single person in the world who can accuse the Lord Jesus Christ of being unrighteous. He is righteous. There are a number of verses I want to use to illustrate righteousness and the Deity of the Lord Jesus Christ.

- Psalm 9:8

"And he shall judge the world in **righteousness**, he shall minister judgment to the people in **uprightness**."

Righteousness is mentioned over and over again in Scripture. Our God is **righteous**. Hebrews 1:8 shows us a *sceptre of righteousness*.

- Psalm 11:7

"For the **righteous** LORD loveth **righteousness**; his countenance doth behold the upright.."

GOD'S PERFECT RIGHTEOUSNESS

God is righteous. He loves righteousness. He is perfectly righteous and without sin.

Hebrews—Preaching Verse by Verse

- **Psalm 23:3**

"He restoreth my soul: he leadeth me in the paths of **righteousness** for his name's sake."

This is that great psalm that the Old Testament people loved, and we love it as well. **Righteous** is our Lord Jesus Christ. Never does He do anything that is unrighteous.

- **Psalm 45:7**

"Thou lovest **righteousness**, and hatest wickedness: therefore God, thy God, hath anointed thee with the oil of gladness above thy fellows."

Over and over again, we see this word, *"righteousness."*

- **Matthew 6:33**

"But seek ye first the kingdom of God, and his **righteousness**; and all these things shall be added unto you."

The Lord Jesus Christ taught the disciples. Again, **righteousness** is the standard of God that God would have for us.

- **John 20:25**

"The other disciples therefore said unto him, We have seen the Lord. But he said unto them, Except I shall see in his hands the print of the nails, and put my finger into the print of the nails, and thrust my hand into his side, I will not believe."

Thomas, who was absent at the first evening service, was there at the second evening service. The Lord Jesus Christ appeared the second Sunday night.

- **John 20:27**

"Then saith he to Thomas, Reach hither thy finger, and behold my hands; and reach hither thy hand, and thrust *it* into my side: and be not faithless, but believing."

Then Thomas answered, *"My Lord and my God."* This is the **Deity** of the Lord Jesus Christ.

- **John 20:28**

"And Thomas answered and said unto him, **My Lord and my God.**"

This verse reinforces the **Deity** of the Lord Jesus Christ.

- **Acts 17:31**

"Because he hath appointed a day, in the which he will judge the world in **righteousness** by *that* man whom he hath ordained; *whereof* he hath given assurance unto all *men*, in that he hath raised him from the dead."

Here is another verse on **righteousness**. The Lord Jesus Christ will be the One to judge. The Father has given to the Son all judgment. It will be in **righteousness**. You might say, "Can anybody send a person to Hell, the lake of fire, to burn up for eternity?" Yes, in **righteousness**, the Lord Jesus Christ will send to that place those who do not receive Him.

- Matthew 11:28

"Come unto me, all *ye* that labour and are heavy laden, and I will give you rest."

Those that reject that invitation, God **righteously** sends to the lake of fire. He will judge in **righteousness**.

- Romans 3:22

"Even the **righteousness** of God *which is* by faith of Jesus Christ unto all and upon all them that believe: for there is no difference:"

GETTING THE RIGHTEOUSNESS OF GOD

We can get the righteousness of God if we are redeemed and genuinely trusting the Lord Jesus Christ as our Saviour. He becomes our righteousness. This is tremendously important.

- Romans 3:25

"Whom God hath set forth *to be* a propitiation through faith in his blood, to declare his **righteousness** for the remission of sins that are past, through the forbearance of God;"

ONLY CHRIST CAN FORGIVE OUR SINS

The Lord Jesus Christ can forgive sin, because He took upon Himself the sins of the world. Those who will genuinely trust Him, those of us who have really trusted Him, have accepted Him, and are redeemed by true faith in His precious blood, have remission and forgiveness of sins. God is righteous. We are sinners, but the Lord Jesus Christ, if we genuinely trust Him, has taken our sins in His own body. Therefore, He righteously can bring us to Heaven instead of sending us to Hell.

- Romans 3:26

"To declare, *I say*, at this time his **righteousness**: that he might be just, and the justifier of him which believeth in Jesus."

GOD JUSTIFIES GENUINE CHRISTIANS

God is the justifier of those that believe and He is just in doing it, because the Lord Jesus Christ took all of our sins upon Himself on the cross of Calvary. When we genuinely trust Him as our Saviour, He is just in forgiving us.

- **Romans 4:5**
"But to him that worketh not, but believeth on him that justifieth the ungodly, his faith is counted for **righteousness**."

Righteousness is counted by faith in the Lord Jesus Christ. Our righteous standing before God is only by genuine faith.

- **1 Corinthians 1:30**
"But of him are ye in Christ Jesus, who of God is made unto us wisdom, and **righteousness**, and sanctification, and redemption:"

RIGHTEOUS IN GOD'S EYES

In God's eyes, when we genuinely trust the Lord Jesus Christ, we become righteous.

- **2 Timothy 2:22**
"Flee also youthful lusts: but follow **righteousness**, faith, charity, peace, with them that call on the Lord out of a pure heart."

If we have been declared **righteous** before God, we ought to follow **righteousness** in our life today.

- **2 Timothy 3:16**
"All scripture *is* given by inspiration of God, and *is* profitable for doctrine, for reproof, for correction, for instruction in **righteousness**:"

We read this every Sunday morning in our service.

- **Titus 2:13**
"Looking for that blessed hope, and the glorious appearing of the **great God and our Saviour Jesus Christ**;"

Again, here is a verse on the **Deity** of the Lord Jesus Christ. He is our great God.

Hebrews 1:9

"Thou hast loved righteousness, and hated iniquity; therefore God, *even* thy God, hath anointed thee with the oil of gladness above thy fellows."

HATING EVIL

This is speaking of the Lord Jesus Christ again. He loves righteousness. You and I should love it as well. Notice what He **hates**: He **hates** iniquity. Therefore, God has anointed Him with the oil of gladness above His fellows. For the joy that was set before Him, He suffered the cross (Hebrews 12:2). The Lord Jesus Christ was anointed with joy. I want you to see this. Many people say, "Don't **hate** anything!" The Bible says, "Yes!" The Lord Jesus Christ **hated** something and we have to **hate** something. First, He loved that which was righteous.

Second, He **hated** iniquity. That is what the Scriptures tell us to do. I want to look at some Scriptures that tell us about the **hating of evil**.

- **Psalm 45:7**

"Thou **lovest righteousness**, and **hatest wickedness**: therefore God, thy God, hath anointed thee with the oil of gladness above thy fellows."

This is the verse from where Hebrews 1:9 is taken. We have to **hate wickedness. That is Christian. That is Scripture.**

- **Psalm 97:10**

"Ye that love the LORD, **hate** evil: he preserveth the souls of his saints; he delivereth them out of the hand of the wicked."

Get your **hate** up and **hate** evil! Don't **hate** people or **hate** righteousness, but **hate** evil.

- **Psalm 119:104**

"Through thy precepts I get understanding: therefore I **hate** every false way."

We are to **hate** false ways.

- **Psalm 119:113**

"I **hate** *vain* thoughts: but thy law do I love."

We should love the Words of God.

- **Psalm 119:128**

"Therefore I esteem all *thy* precepts *concerning* all *things to be* right; *and* I **hate** every false way."

I esteem all thy precepts—that is, I love them. I **hate the false ways**.

- **Psalm 119:163**

"I hate and abhor lying: *but* thy law do I love."

We should **hate lying as well**.

- **Proverbs 8:13**

"The fear of the LORD is to **hate** evil: pride, and arrogancy, and the evil way, and the froward mouth, do I **hate**."

If you love the Lord, you have to **hate** that which is evil. Just **hate** it. Stay away from it.

- **Proverbs 13:5**

"A righteous *man* **hateth** lying: but a wicked *man* is loathsome, and cometh to shame."

If we are righteous in the Lord's sight, we should **hate** the lie.

- **Amos 5:15**

"**Hate** the evil, and love the good, and establish judgment in the gate: it may be that the LORD God of hosts will be gracious unto the remnant of Joseph."

Hebrews—Preaching Verse by Verse

> **WE MUST HATE EVIL AND LOVE GOOD**
>
> Hate the evil. Love the good. It is just as simple as that. That hate starts with ourselves personally—our hatred of the evil that we do, and say, and think. We should hate it and confess it before the Lord. Love the good. Hate the evil.

Then there is the reverse of this. The modernists and liberals and the unbelievers reverse the love and **hate**.

- **Micah 3:2**

"Who **hate** the good, and love the evil; who pluck off their skin from off them, and their flesh from off their bones; "

Here is an example of the reversal, which is wrong. These are people who **hate** the good and love the evil. That is what the Communists do. That is what the immoral heathen do. That is what crooks do and all the other people that **hate** good and love evil. That is wrong. We have to love the good and **hate** the evil.

Hebrews 1:10

"And, Thou, Lord, in the beginning hast laid the foundation of the earth; and the heavens are the works of thine hands:"

THE CREATION OF THE EARTH'S FOUNDATION

Again, I believe He is addressing this to the Lord Jesus Christ. God the Father says, "Thy throne, O God" and in Hebrews 1:9, "Thou hast loved righteousness," speaking of the Lord Jesus Christ, His Son. In this verse, "Thou, Lord," is still speaking of the Son, the Lord Jesus Christ. He was in the beginning with the Father and He laid the **foundation** of the earth. He was the Creator, the same as the Father was the Creator. The Lord Jesus Christ was Creator.

The modernists and liberals do not believe it at all. They say, "Oh, he is just a man," and the Gnostics say, "He is just a man. He did not create anything," but He has.

> **THE EARTH HAS FOUNDATIONS**
>
> Notice, He has laid the foundation of the earth. There is a whole group of Bible-believing scientists that believe in geocentricity. The earth is the center of the universe—not the sun, heliocentricity—but geocentricity. These terms of foundation in the Bible certainly seem to bear that out.

- **Genesis 1:3**

"And God said, Let there be light: and there was light."

There is the Creation.

- **Job 38:4**

"Where wast thou when I laid the **foundations** of the earth? declare, if thou hast understanding."

- **Job 38:6**

"Whereupon are the **foundations** thereof fastened? or who laid the corner stone thereof;"

That is the world, the earth, fastened close. That is the source of the Hebrew quotation in Psalm 102:25.

- **Psalm 102:25**

"Of old hast thou laid the **foundation** of the earth: and the heavens *are* the work of thy hands."

If something has a **foundation**, it is not going to be moving. It has a **foundation**. It is **founded**.

- **Psalm 104:5**

"*Who* laid the **foundations** of the earth, *that* it should not be removed for ever."

We have **foundations**.

- **Proverbs 8:29**

"When he gave to the sea his decree, that the waters should not pass his commandment: when he appointed the **foundations** of the earth:"

These things have to mean something.

- **Isaiah 24:18**

"And it shall come to pass, *that* he who fleeth from the noise of the fear shall fall into the pit; and he that cometh up out of the midst of the pit shall be taken in the snare: for the windows from on high are open, and the **foundations** of the earth do shake."

- **Isaiah 40:21**

"Have ye not known? have ye not heard? hath it not been told you from the beginning? have ye not understood from the **foundations** of the earth?"

- **Isaiah 48:13**

"Mine hand also hath laid the **foundation** of the earth, and my right hand hath spanned the heavens: *when* I call unto them, they stand up together."

It is something that is **founded**.

- **Isaiah 51:13**

"And forgettest the LORD thy maker, that hath stretched forth the heavens, and laid the **foundations of the earth**; and hast feared continually every day because of the fury of the oppressor, as if he were ready to destroy? and where is the fury of the oppressor?"

The heavens are stretched forth, but the **foundations of the earth** have been laid.

- **Isaiah 51:16**

"And I have put my words in thy mouth, and I have covered thee in the shadow of mine hand, that I may plant the heavens, and lay the **foundations of the earth**, and say unto Zion, Thou *art* my people."

- **Jeremiah 31:37**

"Thus saith the LORD; If heaven above can be measured, and the **foundations of the earth** searched out beneath, I will also cast off all the seed of Israel for all that they have done, saith the LORD."

- **John 17:24**

"Father, I will that they also, whom thou hast given me, be with me where I am; that they may behold my glory, which thou hast given me: for thou lovedst me before the **foundation of the world**."

This is the Lord Jesus Christ's High Priestly prayer. Even before the world was created, the Lord Jesus Christ was in existence and the Father loved the Son.

- **1 Peter 1:20**

"Who verily was foreordained before the **foundation of the world**, but was manifest in these last times for you,"

The Lord Jesus Christ was foreordained from all eternity past, before the **foundation** of the world.

- **Revelation 13:8**

"And all that dwell upon the earth shall worship him, whose names are not written in the book of life of the Lamb slain from the **foundation of the world**."

GEOCENTRICITY IS BIBLICAL

The Lord Jesus Christ is the Lamb from the **foundation of the world**. Again, the world has foundations. I know that the people in the scientific world today do not believe it, but I believe the Scriptures are teaching it. Many godly scientists, Christian born-again people, believe in geocentricity—the centricity of the earth. Dr. Gerardus Bouw was a teacher for many years in Baldwin Wallace College, in Berea, Ohio, where my wife and I went to high school. He is an astronomer. He is retired now. He has written an excellent book on Bible

> subjects. He is one of the leaders in the geocentricity movement.

THE CREATOR

Then, notice it says, in Hebrews 1:10, *"and the heavens are the works of thine hands."* The Lord Jesus Christ is the **Creator**. People question this and take out some Words that refer to Him as **Creator**.

- **John 1:3**

  "All things were made by him; and without him was not any thing **made** that was made."

This talks about the Word—not the Scriptures, but the Lord Jesus Christ Himself.

- **John 1:10**

  "He was in the world, and the world was **made** by him, and the world knew him not."

> ### CHRIST THE CREATOR
>
> The Lord Jesus Christ is the Creator. Those who deny the Deity of the Lord Jesus Christ—the Gnostics and others that take it away and just make Him a man—deny that He was the Creator. He was with the Father and with the Holy Spirit through eternity.

- **Colossians 1:16**

  "For by him were all things **created**, that are in heaven, and that are in earth, visible and invisible, whether *they be* thrones, or dominions, or principalities, or powers: all things were **created** by him, and for him:"

This is very clear. It is speaking of the Lord Jesus Christ.

- **Revelation 4:11**

  "Thou art worthy, O Lord, to receive glory and honour and power: for thou hast **created** all things, and for thy pleasure they are and were **created**."

- **Ephesians 3:9**

  "And to make all *men* see what is the fellowship of the mystery, which from the beginning of the world hath been hid in God, who **created** all things by Jesus Christ:"

Hebrews—Preaching Verse by Verse

GNOSTIC OMISSION OF "BY JESUS CHRIST"

The words *"by Jesus Christ"* are left out by the Gnostic manuscripts of Westcott and Hort, because the Gnostic heretics that had those false Greek texts did not believe in the ability of the Lord Jesus Christ to create anything.

CREATION BY GOD'S "HANDS" AND "FINGERS"
- Psalm 8:3

"When I consider thy heavens, the work of thy fingers, the moon and the stars, which thou hast **ordained**;"

The **creation** of the world is His finger work. For God it is simple, but to us? Can you imagine **creating** a world and all the stars and the heavens?

Hebrews 1:11

"They shall perish; but thou remainest; and they all shall wax old as doth a garment;"

THE PERISHING EARTH

This talks about the earth and the heavens. They will **perish**. People that do not believe the Bible do not believe this will be the case. They say, "It's not going to **perish**." Look at some of the catastrophes all over the world—the thunderous floods and different things that have happened around the world, the storms and the damage that comes from hurricanes. God says, *"They shall perish; but thou remainest."*

First of all, let us look at the **perishing** of this world.
- Psalm 102:25-27

"Of old hast thou laid the foundation of the earth: and the heavens *are* the work of thy hands. They shall **perish**, but thou shalt endure: yea, all of them shall wax old like a garment; as a vesture shalt thou change them, and they shall be changed: But thou art the same, and thy years shall have no end."

This is where we get the reference in Hebrews 1:11.
- Matthew 24:35

"Heaven and earth shall **pass away**, but my words shall not **pass away**."

CHRIST'S WORDS WILL NOT PASS AWAY

Three times these Words are used in the following passages: Matthew 24:35, Mark 13:31, and Luke 21:33. The Lord Jesus Christ is speaking. This is Scripture and it is going to happen. The Lord Jesus Christ, Who created the world, says, *"Heaven and earth shall pass away."*

The next part of those three verses, *"but my words shall not pass away,"* refers to the Hebrew, Aramaic, and Greek Words that God gave us in His original manuscripts. They will not pass away. That is why we believe in the preservation of those Words. The Lord Jesus promised it and what He promises, He fulfills. That is why we believe that the Words underlying our King James Bible—the Hebrew, Aramaic, and Greek Words—are the Words that have not perished. They will not pass away, but heaven and earth *shall pass away.*

- 2 Peter 3:10

"But the day of the Lord will come as a thief in the night; in the which the heavens shall **pass away** with a great noise, and the elements shall melt with fervent heat, the earth also and the works that are therein shall be burned up."

In Noah's day, God flooded the whole earth. It was a universal flood of water. Then He promised he will no longer destroy the earth by water, but He will destroy it by fire. At a certain time, when the end of the world has come, the earth shall be burned up and the elements shall burn with fervent heat. God will create a new heavens and a new earth wherein dwelleth righteousness. The heavens shall **perish** and the earth shall perish.

THE LORD JESUS CHRIST CONTINUES

Notice, the next part in Hebrews 1:11, *"But thou remainest."* That Greek Word for *"remain"* is DIAMENO. Some of the meanings fo the word are:

"To stay permanently; remain permanently; continue."

There is a continuation for the Lord Jesus Christ. He is an everlasting God. He is not going to perish. Heavens and earth shall perish, but He remains the same.

THE LORD REMAINS THE SAME

- Psalm 90:2

"Before the mountains were brought forth, or ever thou hadst formed the earth and the world, even from **everlasting** to **everlasting**, thou *art* God."

He is **everlasting**. He does not change. That is one of His attributes. He does not change.

- Psalm 93:2

"Thy throne *is* established of old: thou *art* from **everlasting**."

He is from **everlasting to everlasting**. He is the same. He will not change.
- **Psalm 106:48**

"Blessed be the LORD God of Israel from **everlasting to everlasting**: and let all the people say, Amen. Praise ye the LORD."
- **Isaiah 9:6**

"For unto us a child is born, unto us a son is given: and the government shall be upon his shoulder: and his name shall be called Wonderful, Counsellor, The mighty God, The **everlasting** Father, The Prince of Peace."

The Lord Jesus Christ is called the *everlasting Father*.
- **Isaiah 26:4**

"Trust ye in the LORD for ever: for in the LORD JEHOVAH is **everlasting** strength:"

TRUSTING THE LORD

Why do we trust in the Lord? In the LORD JEHOVAH is *everlasting strength*—strength that will not give out. It is permanent if we genuinely trust in the Saviour, the Lord Jesus Christ, as our Lord.

- **Romans 16:26**

"But now is made manifest, and by the scriptures of the prophets, according to the commandment of the **everlasting** God, made known to all nations for the obedience of faith:"

THE LORD REMAINS THE SAME

He will not change. Heaven and earth shall perish, *but thou remainest*. Garments wax old. They get tattered and torn, especially if you wear them often. You wear them out.

- **Hebrews 13:8**

"Jesus Christ the same yesterday, and to day, and **for ever**."

The Lord Jesus Christ is always the same. He does **not change** in His righteousness, His holiness, His judgment, and His justice. It is a wonderful thing.

Hebrews 1:12

"And as a vesture shalt thou fold them up, and they shall be changed: but thou art the same, and thy years shall not fail."

THE WORLD FOLDED UP AS A GARMENT

That Greek Word for vesture is PERIBOLAION. Some of the meanings for this Word are:

"a covering thrown around; a wrap or something wrapped around; a mantle."

The Lord Jesus Christ will fold up the heavens and the earth just as a mantle. We can fold up clothes easily. We fold up towels, sheets, and pillowcases. The Lord Jesus Christ is going to fold up the heavens and the earth. He is an all-powerful, mighty God. There is going to be a new heavens and a new earth. They shall be changed. The heavens will be changed and the earth will be changed by the power of God.

THE LORD REMAINS THE SAME

Notice the negative adversative clause: *"but thou art the **same**, and thy years shall **not fail**."* He is the same. People in this world do not like things that are the **same**. They say that if you are the **same** today as yesterday, you are stuck in a rut. Well, if the rut is a right rut, keep in the right rut! Do not get in the wrong rut or the bad rut, but stay in the right rut. Righteousness does not change. Gravity does **not change**. Right and wrong do **not change**. We stick with what is true and righteous.

CHRIST REMAINS THE SAME

Thy years shall not fail means that He will be from everlasting to the future. He was from everlasting in the past. Here are more verses that talk about the Lord Jesus Christ remaining the same.

- Psalm 90:2

"Before the mountains were brought forth, or ever thou hadst formed the earth and the world, even from everlasting to everlasting, thou *art* God."

- Psalm 93:2

"Thy throne *is* established of old: thou *art* from **everlasting**."

- **Psalm 106:48**
"Blessed *be* the LORD God of Israel from **everlasting to everlasting**: and let all the people say, Amen. Praise ye the LORD."
- **Isaiah 9:6**
"For unto us a child is born, unto us a son is given: and the government shall be upon his shoulder: and his name shall be called Wonderful, Counsellor, The mighty God, The **everlasting** Father, The Prince of Peace."
- **Isaiah 26:4**
"Trust ye in the LORD for ever: for in the LORD JEHOVAH *is* **everlasting** strength:"
- **Isaiah 40:28**
"Hast thou not known? hast thou not heard, *that* the **everlasting** God, the LORD, the Creator of the ends of the earth, fainteth not, neither is weary? *there is* no searching of his understanding."
- **Micah 5:2**
"But thou, Bethlehem Ephratah, *though* thou be little among the thousands of Judah, *yet* out of thee shall he come forth unto me *that is* to be ruler in Israel; whose goings forth *have been* from of old, from **everlasting**."

This is an interesting verse. It is a prediction of the coming of the Lord Jesus Christ in Bethlehem.

THE NIV'S FIRST HERESY IN MICAH 5:2

The New International Version makes two significant changes, because of the <u>false Hebrew text and false Hebrew words</u>. <u>The King James Bible is based on the proper Hebrew.</u> It says, speaking of the Lord Jesus Christ, *"whose goings forth have been from of old, from everlasting."* In other words, He was always from everlasting to everlasting. <u>He had no beginning. He was from eternity past to eternity future</u>. That speaks of the Lord Jesus Christ. <u>What does the NIV say? Not *"whose goings forth,"* but *"whose origins."*</u> That means the <u>Lord Jesus Christ had a beginning!</u> That is pure heresy! When Haddon Heights Baptist Church had a Christmas play many years ago, they quoted the NIV and they quoted this verse. Afterwards, I went to the pastor and said, "Pastor, that is heresy! You say the Lord Jesus Christ had *origins*!" They had the wrong translation right there in the church where we were members.

> ### THE NIV'S SECOND HERESY IN MICAH 5:2
> The NIV has a second heresy in Micah 5:2. The Scripture says clearly, *"from of old, from everlasting."* That is what the Scripture says. He is from *everlasting*. He did not have an origin. What does the NIV change it to? They say, *"whose origins have been from ancient times."* My friends, that is not enough. *Ancient times* is not *from everlasting*. Ancient times is old, back to the beginning of our country in 1776, or the beginning of the world around 4000 B.C. No! He is not just from ancient times, but from everlasting. The NIV again has a second heresy, because of the false text on which it is based.

- Romans 16:26

"But now is made manifest, and by the scriptures of the prophets, according to the commandment of the **everlasting** God, made known to all nations for the obedience of faith:"

- Hebrews 13:8

"Jesus Christ the same yesterday, and to day, and **for ever**."

Hebrews 1:13

"But to which of the angels said he at any time, Sit on my right hand, until I make thine enemies thy footstool?"

Remember that in the first part of Hebrews, it says that He is better than the angels. He is better than the prophets. We will see later that He is better than Moses. He is better than all these. He is better than anything.

RIGHT HAND AND FOOTSTOOL

> #### CHRIST IS ON GOD'S RIGHT HAND
> God never set an angel on His right hand. The right hand is a place of authority, power, and honor. That Greek Word is DEXIOS, which means *"a place of honor and authority."* The only angel I can think of that wanted to be on the right hand of the Father--the place of authority--was Lucifer. This angel is Satan himself. Five times, in Isaiah 14, he said, "I will." The final one was, "I will be like the most High." The angel of God that fell because of his wickedness and his willfulness is the only one I can see that wanted to be on God's right hand. To none of the angels did He say, "Sit on my right hand, until I make thine enemies thy footstool."

> ### THE MEANING OF "FOOTSTOOL"
> By the way, that Greek Word for footstool is HUPOPODION. Some of the meanings for that Word are:
> *"in a metaphorical sense, taken from the practice of conquerors who placed their feet on the necks of their conquered enemies."*
> That is the footstool—to put your feet on what you conquered. The Lord Jesus Christ is going to be the Conqueror of all enemies.

These people that shake their fists at Him today and say, "I deny Him. I hate Him. I do not believe in Him. He is no good. He is a bum," one day, God the Father will make all these enemies the **footstool** of our Saviour. Now, He is not going to put His feet on them, but that is the picture, metaphorically speaking. He will be victorious over every enemy.

Let us take a look at this **right hand**—a place of honor. That is why when we walk, our wives (if we are husbands) should be on our **right hand**. That is why in the military, when we are walking with a senior officer, that senior officer is on our **right hand**. It is just a normal thing. Many people do not abide by it, but it is a place of honor.

- Mark 16:19

"So then after the Lord had spoken unto them, he was received up into heaven, and sat on the **right hand** of God."

The **right hand** of God is a place of honor.

- Luke 20:42

"And David himself saith in the book of Psalms, The LORD said unto my Lord, Sit thou on my **right hand**,"

> ### THE FATHER APPROVED HIS SON'S WORK
> God the Father said to God the Son, "Sit on My right hand." If God the Father was disappointed with the Lord Jesus Christ in His work on Calvary's cross, He would never have put Him on His right hand. He might say, "Go to the back of the line," or the back of the bus, as it were. He is on His right hand. That is the place of honor.

- Luke 22:69

"Hereafter shall the Son of man sit on the **right hand** of the power of God."

They spat upon Him. They did not like Him. The Lord God of Heaven and earth has placed Him on His **right hand**. He agreed with His Son. Everything He did at the cross of Calvary, dying for our sins, was pleasant to the Father. He put Him on His **right hand**—the place of honor.

- **Acts 2:33**
"Therefore being by the **right hand** of God exalted, and having received of the Father the promise of the Holy Ghost, he hath shed forth this, which ye now see and hear."

They crucified Him. God raised Him from the dead and put Him at His **right hand**. He exalted Him.

- **Acts 2:34**
"For David is not ascended into the heavens: but he saith himself, The LORD said unto my Lord, Sit thou on my **right hand**,"

Again, the Father speaks to the Son.

- **Acts 7:55**
"But he, being full of the Holy Ghost, looked up stedfastly into heaven, and saw the glory of God, and Jesus standing on the **right hand** of God,"

This was Stephen, when he was being stoned by the haters of the Saviour. Why was the Lord Jesus Christ standing? In all of these other verses, He has been seated. The Lord Jesus Christ was standing, waiting until His first martyr, Stephen, would come home to Glory. He was standing on the **right hand** of God.

- **Acts 7:56**
"And said, Behold, I see the heavens opened, and the Son of man standing on the **right hand** of God."

The Lord Jesus Christ was standing, waiting for His saint, because Stephen was killed at that time. He went home to Glory and the Lord Jesus Christ received him. He was standing and waiting for him to come.

- **Romans 8:34**
"Who *is* he that condemneth? *It is* Christ that died, yea rather, that is risen again, who is even at the **right hand** of God, who also maketh intercession for us."

CHRIST ON GOD'S RIGHT HAND

This talks about the Lord Jesus Christ, Who is at the right hand of God—the right hand of power and blessing.

- **Ephesians 1:20**
"Which he wrought in Christ, when he raised him from the dead, and set *him* at his own **right hand** in the heavenly *places*,"

Since we are in the Lord Jesus Christ, we are also placed in heavenly places at the **right hand** of glory and power. He is set on the **right hand** in the heavenly places, and we are with Him.

Hebrews—Preaching Verse by Verse

- **Colossians 3:1**

"If ye then be risen with Christ, seek those things which are above, where Christ sitteth on the **right hand** of God."

Why is this repeated? Over and over in these verses, it is repeated so that all of us will know that God the Father has completely, absolutely, and totally accepted the work that His Son did for our sins on the cross of Calvary. That is a perfect picture of God's **satisfaction**. He has been **propitiated**. That is a big word. That means He is **satisfied**. God is **satisfied** with the work of His Son. Therefore, He sets Him on the place of honor.

When the President has guests from other countries and from different places of the world, you watch the way they are seated at the table. The one that is the most-exalted and of the highest rank is on the President's **right hand**. This is a place of honor.

- **Hebrews 1:3**

"Who being the brightness of *his* glory, and the express image of his person, and upholding all things by the word of his power, when he had by himself purged our sins, sat down on the **right hand** of the Majesty on high;"

NO CHAIR IN THE TABERNACLE

When the High Priest of the Old Testament went once a year (according to Leviticus 16) into the holy place to put the blood on the altar—first for his own sins, then for the sins of the people—on the Day of Atonement, there was not a chair in the tabernacle. There was no place to sit down. He was always standing, working, walking. The Lord Jesus Christ has sat down, because His work was finished.

The High Priests could never finish their work. They had sacrifice after sacrifice. The Roman Catholic Church does the same thing—mass after mass—crucifying the Lord of Glory again and again. Our Saviour, when the work was finished, sat down. This is a wonderful picture of the finished work of the Lord Jesus Christ.

- **Hebrews 1:13**

"But to which of the angels said he at any time, Sit on my **right hand**, until I make thine enemies thy footstool?"

God never said that to an angel.

- **Hebrews 10:12**

"But this man, after he had offered one sacrifice for sins for ever, sat down on the **right hand** of God;"

This is a good verse, too. He offered one sacrifice for sins forever.

> **OVER 1,200 OBLIGATORY O.T. SACRIFICES**
>
> The Jews in the Old Testament had more than 1,200 obligatory sacrifices and offerings every year. Plus, when they sinned, everyone had to pay special offerings. The obligatory sacrifices were on the Sabbath, and weekly, and monthly, and on the feast days. The Lord Jesus had nothing to say about that. He made only one sacrifice for sins forever. The work was finished and He sat down.

- **Hebrews 12:2**

"Looking unto Jesus the author and finisher of *our* faith; who for the joy that was set before him endured the cross, despising the shame, and is set down at the **right hand** of the throne of God."

- **1 Peter 3:22**

"Who is gone into heaven, and is on the **right hand** of God; angels and authorities and powers being made subject unto him."

Next, what about the **footstool**?

- **Psalm 110:1**

"The LORD said unto my Lord, Sit thou at my **right hand**, until I make thine enemies thy **footstool**."

This is the verse from where the book of Hebrews takes verse 1:13. This is speaking of the Lord Jesus Christ—a Messianic psalm.

- **Matthew 22:44**

"The LORD said unto my Lord, Sit thou on my **right hand**, till I make thine enemies thy **footstool**?"

Again, this is quoted in Hebrews.

- **Mark 12:36**

" For David himself said by the Holy Ghost, The LORD said to my Lord, Sit thou on my **right hand**, till I make thine enemies thy **footstool**."

Over and over, this is repeated. The enemies will be defeated completely.

- **Luke 20:43**

"Till I make thine enemies thy **footstool**."

- **Acts 2:35**

"Until I make thy foes thy **footstool**."

- **Hebrews 10:13**

"From henceforth expecting till his enemies be made his **footstool**."

Over and over again, we see that the enemies of the Lord Jesus Christ will be defeated. They will be vanquished. He will be the Victor over all enemies—foreign and domestic.

Hebrews 1:14

"Are they not all ministering spirits, sent forth to minister for them who shall be heirs of salvation?"

MINISTERING ANGELS

That is what the angels are. They are not going to be at the right hand of the Father. They are just **ministering spirits**. Why are they **ministering**? It is an interesting verse.

> ### AN ANGEL FOR EVERY TRUE CHRISTIAN
> Every born-again, saved, genuine Christian has a ministering angel. That is what it says here. I believe it. That is where guardian angels come in. That is where angelic beings come in. That is what God has made them for. He has millions upon millions upon billions of them. One of them is ministering to you if you are genuinely saved and born-again. One of them is ministering to me.

I do not know how they help me. From falling? From getting in accidents? I do not know. You might wonder sometimes how you did not go into that ditch. The car is going and, all of a sudden, it pulls out. I give all the glory to the Lord Jesus Christ, but God says that we have angels whose primary duty is to **minister** to those of us who are genuinely saved and heirs of salvation.

THE ANGEL OF THE LORD--THE LORD JESUS CHRIST PRE-INCARNATE

> ### THE ANGEL OF THE LORD
> There is a special angel in the Old Testament and we are going to talk a bit about that. He is *the* Angel of the Lord. In the Old Testament, I believe the Angel of the Lord was the Lord Jesus Christ Himself, before He ever was here on earth. In the New Testament "*an* Angel of the Lord" often refers also to the Lord Jesus Christ.

Let us talk about the **Angel of the Lord** for a few minutes.
- **Genesis 22:11-13**

"And the **angel of the LORD** called unto him out of heaven, and said, Abraham, Abraham: and he said, Here *am* I. And he said, Lay not thine hand upon the lad, neither do thou any thing unto him: for now I know that thou fearest God, seeing thou hast not withheld thy son, thine only *son* from me. And Abraham lifted up his eyes, and looked, and behold behind *him* a ram caught in a thicket by his horns: and Abraham went and took the ram, and offered him up for a burnt offering in the stead of his son."

Remember, when Abraham was going to sacrifice Isaac in Mount Moriah? The **Angel of the Lord** (Who we believe is the Lord Jesus Christ in the Old Testament) was telling him, "Do not offer your son." The Lord Jesus Christ Himself, one day, was going to be the Lamb of God Who would take away the sin of the world (John 1:29b).

- **Exodus 3:2**

"And the **angel of the LORD** appeared unto him in a flame of fire out of the midst of a bush: and he looked, and, behold, the bush burned with fire, and the bush *was* not consumed."

Again, the **Angel of the Lord** comes to Moses. We believe it is the early pre-incarnate Saviour. Many believe that, as well as I.

- **Exodus 3:7-8**

"And the LORD said, I have surely seen the affliction of my people which *are* in Egypt, and have heard their cry by reason of their taskmasters; for I know their sorrows; And I am come down to deliver them out of the hand of the Egyptians, and to bring them up out of that land unto a good land and a large, unto a land flowing with milk and honey; unto the place of the Canaanites, and the Hittites, and the Amorites, and the Perizzites, and the Hivites, and the Jebusites."

- **Exodus 3:12**

"And he said, Certainly I will be with thee; and this *shall be* a token unto thee, that I have sent thee: When thou hast brought forth the people out of Egypt, ye shall serve God upon this mountain."

- **Exodus 3:17**

"And I have said, I will bring you up out of the affliction of Egypt unto the land of the Canaanites, and the Hittites, and the Amorites, and the Perizzites, and the Hivites, and the Jebusites, unto a land flowing with milk and honey."

The **Angel of the Lord** called Moses unto His service and Moses was faithful unto Him. It is amazing.

- **Judges 6:12**

"And the **angel of the LORD** appeared unto him, and said unto him, The LORD *is* with thee, thou mighty man of valour."

Again, the **Angel of the Lord** appeared to Gideon. Gideon was a great judge in the Old Testament. The **Angel of the Lord** was the pre-incarnate Saviour. The way you find that out is, every time the **Angel of the Lord** appears, we know He is Deity. He is not simply an angel, but Deity. The question is, "Which Deity is He—the Father, the Son, or the

Holy Spirit?" By process of elimination, we believe that He is the Lord Jesus Christ, God the Son.
- **1 Kings 19:5-7**
"And as he lay and slept under a juniper tree, behold, then an angel touched him, and said unto him, Arise and eat. And he looked, and, behold, there was a cake baken on the coals, and a cruse of water at his head. And he did eat and drink, and laid him down again. And <u>the **angel of the LORD** came again the second time</u>, and touched him, and said, Arise and eat; because the journey is too great for thee."

Here <u>the **Angel of the Lord** appeared unto the prophet Elijah</u>. Elijah had gone away and was lying under a juniper tree, because Jezebel, that woman that hated the Lord, was chasing him. He was afraid of a woman. Well, she had many armies. <u>The **Angel of the Lord**, the Lord Jesus Christ Himself, gave Elijah special strength to go ahead and to win the battle</u>.
- **2 Kings 19:34-35**
"For I will defend this city, to save it, for mine own sake, and for my servant David's sake. And it came to pass that night, that the **angel of the LORD** went out, and smote in the camp of the Assyrians an hundred fourscore and five thousand: and when they arose early in the morning, behold, they were all dead corpses."

<u>The **Angel of the Lord** appeared to King Hezekiah</u>. He helped Hezekiah in the battle.
- **Psalm 34:7**
"<u>The **angel of the LORD encampeth** round about them</u> that fear him, and delivereth them."
- **Matthew 1:20**
"But while he thought on these things, <u>behold, the **angel of the Lord** appeared unto him in a dream</u>, saying, Joseph, thou son of David, fear not to take unto thee Mary thy wife: for that which is conceived in her is of the Holy Ghost."
- **Matthew 2:13**
"And when they were departed, <u>behold, the **angel of the Lord** appeareth to Joseph in a dream</u>, saying, Arise, and take the young child and his mother, and flee into Egypt, and be thou there until I bring thee word: for Herod will seek the young child to destroy him."
- **Acts 5:19**
"But <u>the **angel of the Lord** by night opened the prison doors</u>, and brought them forth, and said,"

- **Acts 8:26**

"And the **angel of the Lord** spake unto Philip, saying, Arise, and go toward the south unto the way that goeth down from Jerusalem unto Gaza, which is desert."

Philip went and witnessed to the Ethiopian eunuch and led him to the Lord Jesus Christ.

- **Acts 12:7**

"And, behold, the **angel of the Lord** came upon *him*, and a light shined in the prison: and he smote Peter on the side, and raised him up, saying, Arise up quickly. And his chains fell off from *his* hands."

ANGELS DO NOT EXALT THEMSELVES

Angels have been ministering to those who are the heirs of salvation down through the corridors of time—in the Old Testament and in the New Testament. The angels' ministry is not to exalt themselves—not that the Father says to them, "Sit at my right hand," as He says to the Lord Jesus Christ, His Son—but they are ministering spirits sent forth to minister to them who shall be heirs of salvation.

These verses in Hebrews exalt the Lord Jesus Christ. They exalt Him above angels and as the Creator and as the One who laid the foundations of the world.

Notice especially in Hebrews 1:9, it tells about His love for righteousness and His hatred toward iniquity. This is what you and I must follow if we are genuinely saved and born-again. We have to follow the Lord Jesus Christ.

THE DEITY OF THE LORD JESUS CHRIST

His Deity is shown in Hebrews 1:8.

> "But unto the Son he saith, Thy throne, O God, is for ever and ever: a sceptre of righteousness is the sceptre of thy kingdom."

It is clear teaching of His Deity. One day, He is going to set things right in this wicked world. He is going to make the enemies His footstool and He will rule and reign for 1,000 years in the millennial reign of the Lord Jesus Christ. These will be the principles. The earth and the heavens will perish, but the Lord Jesus Christ endures and never changes. He is the same yesterday, today and forever. We can trust Him. We can count on Him. He is not going to let us down. He is not going to leave us in the lurch. He is always the same.

Hebrews Chapter Two

Hebrews 2:1

"Therefore we ought to give the more earnest heed to the things which we have heard, lest at any time we should let *them* slip."

We must give **earnest heed**. That Greek word for "**earnest**" is PERISSOTEROS. Some of the meanings for this Word are:
"of great degree; abundant; more exceedingly."

The Greek Word for "**heed**" is PROSECHO. Some of the meanings of this Word are:
"means to turn the mind to; to attend to."

Paul wanted these Hebrew Christians that had come from Judaism to Christ to have **earnest heed**—their minds attending to the things that he spoke to them here in this book of Hebrews. We ought to have the same **earnest heed** to the things we have heard.

TAKE HEED

- **Exodus 34:12**

"Take **heed** to thyself, lest thou make a covenant with the inhabitants of the land whither thou goest, lest it be for a snare in the midst of thee:"

Moses wrote to the Israelites. We must take **heed** to ourselves.

- **Deuteronomy 11:16**

"Take **heed** to yourselves, that your heart be not deceived, and ye turn aside, and serve other gods, and worship them;"

We must take **heed** to our hearts just as in the Old Testament.

- **Deuteronomy 12:30**

"Take **heed** to thyself that thou be not snared by following them, after that they be destroyed from before thee; and that thou enquire not after their gods, saying, How did these nations serve their gods? even so will I do likewise."

- **Psalm 39:1**

"I said, I will take **heed** to my ways, that I sin not with my tongue: I will keep my mouth with a bridle, while the wicked is before me."

Part of the taking **heed** is the tongue problem. Every one of us has a tongue. Sometimes it seems like we have more than one tongue as we talk about so many things.

A bridle usually has a bit. That bit is what controls the horse. There are two kinds of bits. The straight bit goes across the mouth. When you want them to stop, you take the bridle or reins and pull that bit. If he doesn't stop with the straight bit, then you use the curved bit. When you pull that bit, it goes right up in the roof of the horse's mouth. It pains the horse and he is going to stop. It hurts him.

- **Luke 12:15**

"And he said unto them, Take **heed, and beware of covetousness**: for a man's life consisteth not in the abundance of the things which he possesseth."

The Lord Jesus Christ is speaking here. We are to take **heed** of covetousness—"*the itch for more. I want more and more and more and am never satisfied.*"

- **Luke 21:34**

"And take **heed** to yourselves, lest at any time your hearts be overcharged with surfeiting, and drunkenness, and cares of this life, and *so* that day come upon you unawares."

The Lord Jesus is again speaking. Be careful of the cares of this life. He said that there are more important things than the cares of this life.

- **Acts 20:28**

"Take **heed** therefore unto yourselves, and to all the flock, over the which the Holy Ghost hath made you overseers, to feed the church of God, which he hath purchased with his own blood."

Paul got the elders of the church at Ephesus together. Pastors, bishops and elders are one and the same office. Take **heed, elders, pastors**! He says the same to pastors, bishops, and elders today. Take **heed**!

- **1 Corinthians 3:10**

"According to the grace of God which is given unto me, as a wise masterbuilder, I have laid the foundation, and another buildeth thereon. But let every man take **heed** how he buildeth thereupon."

It is one thing for the genuine Christian to be built upon the Lord Jesus Christ, but how are they building upon that foundation? Take **heed** how we build. Is it with gold, silver, and precious stones? Or is it with hay, wood, and stubble? Be careful how we build.

- **1 Corinthians 8:9**

"But take **heed** lest by any means this liberty of yours become a stumblingblock to them that are weak."

Again, Paul says, "Take **heed**." The Lord may allow us to do this or that,

Hebrews—Preaching Verse by Verse

but if it is a stumbling block to the weak, we have to <u>take **heed** to ourselves in what we do and what we say</u>.
- **1 Corinthians 10:12**

"Wherefore let him that thinketh he standeth *take* **heed** *lest he fall.*"
This is good for any of us. If you boast, "Oh, look! I am standing strong for the Lord," <u>take **heed** lest you fall</u>. Let us not boast about tomorrow, for we don't know what a day may bring forth. (Proverbs 27:1) <u>Take **heed** lest we fall</u>.
- **1 Timothy 4:16**

"<u>Take **heed** unto thyself, and unto the doctrine</u>; continue in them: for in doing this thou shalt both save thyself, and them that hear thee."

PASTORS MUST TAKE HEED TO THEMSELVES

Paul was speaking to Pastor Timothy of the church of Ephesus. If a pastor's heart and life is not square, he is out of line. Teachings have to be sound, but first, a pastor's life must be sound and correct as well. These are the "take heeds."

SLIPPING

THE MEANING OF "SLIPPING"

The Greek Word for "slip" is PARARRHUEO. It means *"to glide by."* It is as if you were trying to catch something in the water and as you see it going, you just let it glide by. You just let it slip. We should never let the Words of God slip or glide by, by any means. This word <u>slip</u> is used sometimes in the Scriptures. There are a few more verses on that.

- **Psalm 17:5**

"Hold up my goings in thy paths, *that* my footsteps **slip** not."
We do not want to be **slipping** or sliding as on icy paths.
- **Psalm 18:36**

"Thou hast enlarged my steps under me, that my feet did not **slip**."
- **Psalm 38:16**

"For I said, *Hear me,* lest *otherwise* they should rejoice over me: when my foot **slippeth**, they magnify *themselves* against me."
Enemies rejoice when your feet and my feet **slip**. They say, "Look at that Christian, so called! Look what he or she is doing!" They rejoice because they do not like the Lord Jesus Christ. <u>Our feet should not **slip**</u>.

- **Jude 24**

"Now unto him that is able to keep you from **falling**, and to present *you* faultless before the presence of his glory with exceeding joy,"

- **Psalm 73:2**

"But as for me, my feet were almost gone; my steps had well nigh **slipped**."

His steps had almost **slipped**. We, of course, have to be careful of **slipping** steps and **slipping** feet.

- **Psalm 94:18**

"When I said, My foot **slippeth**; thy mercy, O LORD, held me up."

THE TRULY SAVED KEPT FROM SLIPPING

<u>God is able to keep us from slipping</u>. Paul says, "<u>Do not let these things that I am talking about in the book of Hebrews slip by you</u>." Then he also says that we must give the more earnest heed. <u>Give heed. Take heed</u>. It is in the Scriptures in many places to take heed. We must be careful. That means to give earnest attention to what we are saying.

Hebrews 2:2

"For if the word spoken by angels was stedfast, and every transgression and disobedience received a just recompence of reward;"

ANGELS SPOKE IN THE BIBLE

Did you know that angels spoke some words in the Scriptures? Yes, they did speak. That word stedfast means *firm; trusty; sure.*

The Greek Word for **"transgression"** is PARABASIS. PARA is *"beside"* and BASIS is "to step." Some of the meanings of the Word are:

"a *stepping over or stepping beside.*"

That is what a **transgression** is—stepping beside, or stepping over.

THE WORD OF ANGELS

What are some of **the words of angels**? Let us take a look at what the Scriptures say.

- **Genesis 19:1**

"And there came two angels to Sodom at even; and Lot sat in the gate of Sodom: and Lot seeing *them* rose up to meet them; and he bowed himself with his face toward the ground;"

Here are some of the **words spoken by angels**. (We are living in

Sodom days right now, with all the homosexuals riding high, wide, and handsome.)
- **Genesis 19:12-13**
"And the **men said** unto Lot, Hast thou here any besides? son in law, and thy sons, and thy daughters, and whatsoever thou hast in the city, bring *them* out of this place: For we will destroy this place, because the cry of them is waxen great before the face of the LORD; and the LORD hath sent us to destroy it."

The angels were going to destroy Sodom and Gomorrah.
- **Genesis 19:15**
"And when the morning arose, then the **angels hastened** Lot, **saying**, Arise, take thy wife, and thy two daughters, which are here; lest thou be consumed in the iniquity of the city."

That was a **word spoken by angels**—It was **stedfast**.
- **Genesis 19:24-25**
"Then the LORD rained upon Sodom and upon Gomorrah brimstone and fire from the LORD out of heaven; And he overthrew those cities, and all the plain, and all the inhabitants of the cities, and that which grew upon the ground."

The **word of angels** was **stedfast**.

ANGELS SPEAK IN THE N.T.
- **Luke 1:18**
"And Zacharias said unto the angel, Whereby shall I know this? for I am an old man, and my wife well stricken in years."

The **angel said** they were going to have a baby. Zacharias was "mouthy," as they say, with backtalk to the angel.
- **Luke 1:19-20**
"And the **angel answering said** unto him, I am Gabriel, that stand in the presence of God; and am sent to speak unto thee, and to shew thee these glad tidings. And, behold, thou shalt be dumb, and not able to speak, until the day that these things shall be performed, because thou believest not my words, which shall be fulfilled in their season."

The **word** was as it was told. Zacharias questioned how God would to do this. Sure enough, when Zacharias came out of the temple, he could not speak. The **word of angels** was **stedfast**.
- **Luke 1:22**
"And when he came out, he could not speak unto them: and they perceived that he had seen a vision in the temple: for he beckoned unto them, and remained speechless."

When the baby was born, he could talk again. The **word of angels** came to pass.
- Luke 1:30-32
  "And the **angel said** unto her, Fear not, Mary: for thou hast found favour with God. And, behold, thou shalt conceive in thy womb, and bring forth a son, and shalt call his name JESUS. He shall be great, and shall be called the Son of the Highest: and the Lord God shall give unto him the throne of his father David:"

Jesus means Saviour.
- Luke 1:34-35
  "Then said Mary unto the angel, How shall this be, seeing I know not a man? And the **angel answered and said** unto her, The Holy Ghost shall come upon thee, and the power of the Highest shall overshadow thee: therefore also that holy thing which shall be born of thee shall be called the Son of God."

The **word of angels** was **stedfast** and firm. It came to pass.

Hebrews 2:3

"How shall we escape, if we neglect so great salvation; which at the first began to be spoken by the Lord, and was confirmed unto us by them that heard *him*;"

GOD'S SALVATION

This word of salvation, spoken by the Lord Jesus Christ was confirmed unto us by them that heard Him. Nothing on this earth is so great as our salvation if we are saved and born-again. Nothing matches it. Nothing comes close—not being President of the United States, not a million or a billion dollars. If we are genuinely born-again, there are seventeen things that are true of us.

CHARACTERISTICS OF GOD'S SALVATION

The following things are true if we have been genuinely born-again and saved as Christians:
1. We have gone from darkness to light.
2. We have gone from sin and its penalty to salvation.
3. We have gone from eternal death and hell into eternal life and Heaven.
4. We have gone from hell and its judgment to Heaven.
5. We have gone from judgment to justification.

> 6. We have gone from Satan and his family to the Lord Jesus Christ and His family.
> 7. We have gone from sadness in this wicked world to joy.
> 8. We have gone from emptiness to fulfillment.
> 9. We have gone from hunger to satisfaction.
> 10. We have gone from discontentment to contentment.
> 11. We have gone from godlessness to godliness.
> 12. We have gone from wretchedness to redemption.
> 13. We have gone from cruelty to kindness.
> 14. We have gone from hopelessness to hope.
> 15. We have gone from being an enemy of God to a friend.
> 16. We have gone from discouragement to encouragement.
> 17. We have gone from defeat to victory.

Let us see what the Bible tells us about His **salvation** and being saved—so great **salvation**!

- **Psalm 3:8**

"**Salvation** *belongeth* unto the LORD: thy blessing *is* upon thy people. Selah."

Nobody can give us **salvation** but the Lord. We cannot work for it ourselves.

- **Psalm 37:39**

"But the **salvation** of the righteous *is* of the LORD: *he is* their strength in the time of trouble."

Salvation is not of us—not of man, but the Lord has to accomplish it. He sent His Son to do that, dying on the cross of Calvary so that we may, by faith in Him, have everlasting life.

- **Acts 4:12**

"Neither is there **salvation** in any other: for there is none other name under heaven given among men, whereby we must be **saved**."

The apostles talked about **salvation** in the Lord Jesus Christ.

- **Romans 1:16**

"For I am not ashamed of the gospel of Christ: for it is the power of God unto **salvation** to every one that believeth; to the Jew first, and also to the Greek."

The gospel is the power of God to **salvation**.

- **Romans 10:9-10**

"That if thou shalt confess with thy mouth the Lord Jesus, and shalt believe in thine heart that God hath raised him from the dead, thou shalt be **saved**. For with the heart man believeth unto righteousness; and with the mouth confession is made unto **salvation**."

We are to confess about the **salvation** that God has given to us.
- **2 Corinthians 6:2**

"(For he saith, I have heard thee in a time accepted, and in the day of **salvation** have I succoured thee: behold, now *is* the accepted time; behold, now *is* the day of **salvation**.)"

This verse tells about the time of this great **salvation**. If anyone reading this is not **saved**, now is the day of **salvation**. Trust the Lord Jesus Christ. Do not put it off!
- **Ephesians 1:13**

"In whom ye also *trusted*, after that ye heard the word of truth, the gospel of your **salvation**: in whom also after that ye believed, ye were sealed with that holy Spirit of promise,"

The gospel brings the message that brings **salvation**. It is the good news about the Saviour.
- **2 Timothy 3:15**

"And that from a child thou hast known the holy scriptures, which are able to make thee wise unto **salvation** through faith which is in Christ Jesus."

Here is another verse on this great **salvation**. Paul is writing to Timothy, the pastor at Ephesus. What a wonderful thing, to have children know the Scriptures—the Word of God!

WISE UNTO SALVATION

You can go to grammar school and kindergarten and first grade, then junior high and high school, then college and graduate school, but you still may not know anything about salvation. In the Scriptures, you can become wise unto salvation. That is where we find salvation.

- **Titus 2:11**

"For the grace of God that bringeth **salvation** hath appeared to all men,"

It is God's grace that brings this great **salvation** to us.

There are some verses that talk about being **saved** or being **safe**, as well as the word **salvation** itself. This great **salvation** is described in that way.

SAVE OR SAVED

- **Matthew 1:21**

"And she shall bring forth a son, and thou shalt call his name JESUS: for he shall **save** his people from their sins."

Jesus means Saviour. Trusting in the Lord Jesus Christ gives us **salvation**.

- **Matthew 8:24-25**

"And, behold, there arose a great tempest in the sea, insomuch that the ship was covered with the waves: but he was asleep. And his disciples came to *him*, and awoke him, saying, Lord, **save** us: we perish."

The Lord Jesus Christ was in the back of the boat, asleep, while the disciples were wondering and worrying. Here was a physical deliverance. The Lord Jesus Christ who **saved** in that storm can save us by faith in Him, both spiritually and eternally.

- **Matthew 18:11**

"For the Son of man is come to **save** that which was lost."

> **VERSE OMITTED BY GNOSTIC BIBLES**
>
> <u>This whole verse is omitted by the false Westcott and Hort Gnostic Critical Greek text</u>. The new versions take it out—the NASV, the NIV, the ESV and all the others. It is a terrible travesty that they have believed the Gnostic heresies. Because the Gnostics did not believe the Lord Jesus Christ could save anybody, they just removed the verse. The fundamentalists that use these false versions are going right along with the Gnostics in removing this wonderful verse.

- **Matthew 27:42**

"He **saved** others; himself he cannot **save**. If he be the King of Israel, let him now come down from the cross, and we will believe him."

These mockers were at the cross of Calvary. They included both the thieves who were crucified on the right and on the left side of the Lord Jesus Christ, and also the other people who were there looking at Him. <u>It was not that He could not **save** Himself. He chose not to **save** Himself that He might **save** us</u>. They mocked Him at the cross of Calvary. He stayed on the cross, suffering for the sins of the world. Praise God for that!

- **Luke 9:56**

"For the Son of man is not come to destroy men's lives, but to **save** *them*. And they went to another village."

> **VERSE PARTLY OMITTED BY BIBLES**
>
> *"For the Son of man is not come to destroy men's lives."*
>
> <u>The whole first part of this verse is omitted by the Westcott and Hort Gnostic Critical Greek text and from the modern versions as well</u>. Some people think that is the case today. "I cannot do this and this. I have to do this and that." They do not want to be strapped down. That whole section of the verse is out of the false Greek text because the Gnostics did not believe it. The Lord Jesus Christ came, not to destroy us, but to save us.

- Luke 19:10

"For the Son of man is come to seek and to **save** that which was lost."

<u>So great **salvation**! That is why He came.</u>

- John 3:17

"For God sent not his Son into the world to condemn the world; but that the world through him might be **saved**."

That is why the Lord Jesus came. <u>So great **salvation**!</u>

- John 10:9

"I am the door: by me if any man enter in, he shall be **saved**, and shall go in and out, and find pasture."

<u>So great **salvation**</u>—He came to **save**!

- John 12:47

"And if any man hear my words, and believe not, I judge him not: for I came not to judge the world, but to **save** the world."

> **CHRIST CAME TO SAVE PEOPLE**
>
> The Lord Jesus spoke to His detractors—the Pharisees and others that were mocking Him. The world is not saved <u>just because He came</u>, but He came to save the world. If people trust Him and accept Him as their Saviour, He will save them. The Lord Jesus Christ did not come to judge. One day, He will come back to judge. The rapture will remove the believers from the earth. There will be the seven-year period of Tribulation, after which time, He will come back to judge this world at the battle of Armageddon and set up His millennial reign for a thousand years. In this second phase of His coming, He will come to judge. Now, He has come to save. Praise God for that! If He had come to judge, none of us would be saved at all.

- **Acts 4:12**
"Neither is there **salvation** in any other: for there is none other name under heaven given among men, whereby we must be **saved**."

He came with great **salvation**.

- **Acts 16:30-31**
"And brought them out, and said, Sirs, what must I do to be **saved**? And they said, Believe on the Lord Jesus Christ, and thou shalt be **saved**, and thy house."

So great **salvation**!

- **Romans 5:9**
"Much more then, being now justified by his blood, we shall be **saved** from wrath through him."

Salvation that God has given is a great **salvation**. By the way, the words "*saved from wrath*" show us that believers, the **saved** people in the church, are not going to go through the seven-year period of Tribulation. We are **saved** and delivered from wrath through Him—no wrath at all.

- **Romans 10:9**
"That if thou shalt confess with thy mouth the Lord Jesus, and shalt believe in thine heart that God hath raised him from the dead, thou shalt be **saved**."

So great **salvation**!

- **Romans 10:13**
"For whosoever shall call upon the name of the Lord shall be **saved**."

Call in genuine faith. Call and trust in the Lord Jesus as **Saviour**.

- **1 Corinthians 1:21**
"For after that in the wisdom of God the world by wisdom knew not God, it pleased God by the foolishness of preaching to **save** them that believe."

This shows us that by means of preaching, **salvation** can come. Some people say we should not preach, just talk and tell stories and big tall tales and so on. So great **salvation** is to those that trust.

- **Ephesians 2:8-9**
"For by grace are ye **saved** through faith; and that not of yourselves: *it is* the gift of God: Not of works, lest any man should boast."

Saved—so great **salvation**!

- **1 Timothy 1:15**
"This *is* a faithful saying, and worthy of all acceptation, that Christ Jesus came into the world to **save** sinners; of whom I am chief."

That is so great salvation—why He came and why He wants to have people saved.
- **1 Timothy 2:4**
"Who will have all men to be saved, and to come unto the knowledge of the truth."

His will is to have all men to be saved, not simply the elect or just some little group. He wants to have all people to be saved and to come unto the knowledge of the truth, but that does not mean that all people are saved. They must come to the Lord Jesus Christ and accept Him, but He wants to have them all saved if they would just come.
- **Matthew 11:28**
"Come unto me, all ye that labour and are heavy laden, and I will give you rest."
- **Titus 3:5**
"Not by works of righteousness which we have done, but according to his mercy he saved us, by the washing of regeneration, and renewing of the Holy Ghost;"
- **Hebrews 7:25**
"Wherefore he is able also to save them to the uttermost that come unto God by him, seeing he ever liveth to make intercession for them."

This is speaking of the Lord Jesus Christ. He is able to save to the uttermost them that come unto the Father by Him. So great salvation!

THE ONLY ESCAPE FROM HELL

How can we escape? That Greek Word for *"escape"* is EKPHEUGO. Some of the meanings of that Word are:

"to flee out of; to flee away; to seek safety."

If we do not accept the Lord Jesus Christ as so great salvation, there is no escape from hell. There is no escape. He is the only escape by faith in Him for salvation.

Hebrews 2:4

"God also bearing *them* witness, both with signs and wonders, and with divers miracles, and gifts of the Holy Ghost, according to his own will?"

When the Lord Jesus began to speak of salvation, there were witnesses—signs, **wonders**, and **miracles**—that came. **Miracles** were given to authenticate Him. There were **miracles** of healing—healing the man that was born blind, and many others. There were three people who were raised from the dead: (1) A young person, (2) a middle-aged person, and (3) an older person. The Lord Jesus Christ gave those signs to authenticate and prove that He was real, the gospel was real, and His salvation was real as well.

Hebrews 2:5

"For unto the angels hath he not put in subjection the world to come, whereof we speak."

The **angels** did not rule the world. God did not put them in charge of things. The **angels** were created beings. They were powerful. They were good, but they were not ordained to rule.

SATAN THE ANGEL OF LIGHT

Previously, Satan was one of the leading angels—perhaps an archangel. He is called Lucifer and an angel of light. He would like to have been ruler of the world and he said five times in Isaiah 14:13-14, "I will." The final "I will" was: "*I will be like the most High*." He wanted to rule the world. He wants to rule all of his children.

How do we become Satan's child? Just by being born into this world. Every single person that is born into this world is a child of Satan and he must be born again to be a child of God by faith in the Lord Jesus Christ. God did not put the world to come in subjection to the **angels**. They are not the ones that are going to hold and rule the world.

Hebrews 2:6

"But one in a certain place testified, saying, What is man, that thou art mindful of him? or the son of man, that thou visitest him?"

This is a quotation from Psalm 8:4. **Man** was to be in charge of the world. God created **man**. **Man** was visited by the Lord Himself. In the incarnation of the Lord Jesus Christ, God became **Man**. Perfect God became perfect **Man** and visited us. That is what **He** did when the Lord Jesus Christ was incarnated and made Perfect Man and Perfect God in order to save those who genuinely trust Him.

Hebrews 2:7

"Thou madest him a little lower than the angels; thou crownedst him with glory and honour, and didst set him over the works of thy hands:"

Notice, it says, *"Thou madest him."* **Creation** is taught over and over in Scripture. It is not by evolution. We did not evolve. *Thou madest him.* **Man** was a special **creation** and then created from **man**, a woman.

MAN LOWER THAN THE ANGELS

Notice, man is made a little lower than the angels. Man does not have as much power as the angels. Yet, it is not the angels that are going to rule the world. Instead, God said man is going to rule the world. Before the fall of man in the garden of Eden, that was the case. He set him over the animals and over everything that was the work of God's hands in creation. After the fall, things changed.

After the judgment of the flood, the **animals** that were once tame and ate grass, nuts, and fruit (they did not eat meat and **man** did not eat meat), all things were changed. **Animals** that were friendly to **man** became enemies of the **man**—roaring lions and tigers and bears and everything else. The sin of **man**, by the fall of **man** in the garden of Eden, caused the whole plan of God to be set aside temporarily. Now **mankind** does not have that power, nor that subjection, because of the fall of **man** in the garden of Eden.

Hebrews 2:8

"Thou hast put all things in subjection under his feet. For in that he put all in subjection under him, he left nothing *that is* not put under him. But now we see not yet all things put under him."

God's first will was to put everything in **subjection** to **man**, but that changed when man sinned. **Eve** listened to the serpent, Satan's emissary in the garden say: "Take and eat! Even though God said **you** shall not take of the fruit in the middle of the garden, go ahead! **You'll** become like God. **You'll** understand good and evil! Wonderful! Take it!" So **Eve**, following the Devil, took and then gave to **Adam**, and **he** took. The whole universe was then an inheritor of the sinful nature.

As we say, **Adam** blew the whole thing. **He** threw away the whole promise of God and it was not to be under **our** fallen state. Adam could not do it. **The Lord Jesus Christ** came in order to do it—to have the subjection.

Hebrews 2:9

"But we see Jesus, who was made a little lower than the angels for the suffering of death, crowned with glory and honour; that he by the grace of God should taste death for every man."

CHRIST TASTED DEATH FOR EVERYONE

"But," in contradiction to the other several verses, *"we see Jesus."* Who was He? Perfect God and perfect Man. Why did He come? To save sinners—all of us. He came into the world.

The Lord Jesus Christ, as a Person, was never created. The Son of God and God the Son was from all eternity. He was not a creature. He was the Creator. When God the Son took upon Himself the form of Man in a perfect human body, *"He was made a little lower than the angels."* He was not a created being, but coming down into this earth, He was made like man. He had to be made like man so He could save men and women. He had to be one of us, so He could be sympathetic to us and save us and die for our sins. In that sense, being incarnate, He was made a little lower than the angels. Why? *"For the suffering of death."*

You see, **God** could not **die**. Man—even perfect **Man**, the Lord Jesus Christ—was able to **die**. Because He could die, He could take the sins of the world upon **Himself**. He was perfect **God** and perfect **Man**. He was made for the suffering of **death**. He was crowned with glory and honour. God raised Him from the **dead** after He took our sins upon Himself. God the Father was propitiated or satisfied with the finished work of the Lord Jesus Christ at the cross of Calvary.

CHRIST TASTING DEATH

Notice, *that he* [the Lord Jesus Christ] *by the grace of God*—giving us something we do not deserve—*should taste death.* That Greek Word for taste is GEUOMAI. It is an interesting word. It means simply:

"to perceive the flavor of something; to feel; to experience.

> That is what the Lord Jesus Christ did. He tasted and experienced death.
>
> We experience death. If the Lord Jesus Christ does not come back first in the rapture, every one of us will experience death, one way or another at one time or another.

CHRIST'S UNLIMITED ATONEMENT

Notice the last three words of this verse—very vital: *"for every man."* That contradicts what hyper-Calvinists teach. Biblically, we cannot agree with them. The **Lord Jesus Christ tasted death**, not simply for the elect—some little group of people—but *"for every man."* It is up to **every man**, woman, boy and girl to trust that **Saviour** and to accept Him as **Saviour** and **Redeemer**, because **He tasted death for every man**.

I want to go over a few verses—we have gone over them before, but I want to go over them again—concerning the **Lord Jesus Christ's unlimited atonement**, that He died for the sins of the whole world. **Unlimited!** Not simply for a little group, a tiny group—the elect, and the rest of us, we cannot believe no matter how we try. That is what they teach. They teach that no matter how you try, if you are not elect, you are lost. Some of the hyper-hyper-Calvinists even teach that **God** not only elected some to go to Heaven, but He elected and chose some to go to hell. A lot of the Calvinists do not believe that. They just say that He passed over those. Here are some verses on unlimited atonement.

- **Isaiah 53:5-6**

"But he *was* wounded for our transgressions, *he was* bruised for our iniquities: the chastisement of our peace *was* upon him; and with his stripes we are healed. All we like sheep have gone astray; we have turned every one to his own way; and the LORD hath laid on him the iniquity of us all."

This is speaking of the **Lord Jesus Christ**. The word *our* is the whole world, not simply the Jews or the Gentiles. All of us have gone astray—the **whole world**, not simply the Jews. I believe that applies to all. That is **everyone—Jew, Gentile, everyone**.

- **Matthew 11:28**

"Come unto me, all *ye* that labour and are heavy laden, and I will give you rest."

The Lord Jesus Christ, while He was here on earth, was against the hyper-Calvinist position. He did not say just come because you are elect, or just the Jews, or just the Gentiles, but *all* ye that labour and are heavy laden. **He died for all. He tasted death for every man.**

- **John 1:29**

"The next day John seeth **Jesus** coming unto him, and saith, Behold the **Lamb of God**, which taketh away the **sin of the world**."

> **GOD'S LAMB TAKING AWAY SIN**
>
> John the Baptist believed that the Lord Jesus Christ did "*taste death for every man*," too. He did not say, "the sin of the elect." Instead of just a few, He said, "the sin of the world." He takes it away. As many have said, time and time again, it is no longer a <u>sin question</u>. He took away the sin of the world. It is the <u>Son question</u>. What have you done with the Lord Jesus Christ, God's Son? That is tasting death for every man.

- **John 3:14-15**

"And as Moses lifted up the serpent in the wilderness, even so must the **Son of man** be lifted up: That **whosoever believeth** in **him** should not perish, but have eternal life."

He tasted death for every man. So that *Whosoever* believeth—not just a little tiny crowd, might have everlasting life.

- **John 3:18**

"**He that believeth on him** is not condemned: but he that believeth not is condemned already, because he hath not believed in the name of the only begotten **Son of God**."

He that believeth on Him is not condemned—not just some little group, but **he that believeth**. <u>He tasted death for every man</u>.

- **Romans 5:6**

"For when **we** were yet without strength, in due time **Christ died for the ungodly**."

> **CHRIST DIED FOR ALL THE UNGODLY**
>
> Christ died for the ungodly—not simply the elect ungodly, but all of us ungodly. <u>He tasted death for every man. He died for the ungodly in the ungodly's place—your place and my place.</u>

- **2 Corinthians 5:19**

"To wit, that **God was in Christ, reconciling the world unto himself**, not imputing their trespasses **unto them**; and hath committed unto us **the word of reconciliation**."

He was reconciling the whole world, not imputing their trespasses and sins against them, so that if **they trust the Saviour, the Lord Jesus Christ, they** can have that sin forgiven. <u>He tasted death for every man—the whole world</u>.

- **1 Timothy 2:5-6**

"For *there is* one God, and one mediator between God and men, the man Christ Jesus; Who gave himself a ransom for all, to be testified in due time."

<u>He tasted death for every man—a ransom for all</u>. He died on Calvary's cross for all—everyone in the world—elect, non-elect, the whole crowd.

- **Hebrews 2:9**

"But we see **Jesus**, who was made a little lower than the angels for the suffering of death, crowned with glory and honour; that he by the grace of God **should taste death for every man**."

- **2 Peter 2:1**

"But there were **false prophets** also among the people, even as there shall be **false teachers** among you, who privily shall bring in damnable heresies, even denying **the Lord that bought them**, and bring upon themselves swift destruction."

CHRIST DIED FOR FALSE TEACHERS

This is an amazing verse that many people misinterpret. The ransom was for the unbelievers and the false teachers as well as for the ones that are not false teachers. People say that this teaches they are going to be saved. No, it does not. He bought them at Calvary's cross and died for the sins of the false teachers. If they would come to Him, they could be saved. That is a very important verse. <u>It really shows He died and tasted death for every man, even these false teachers and false prophets</u>.

- **1 John 4:14**

"And we have seen and do testify that **the Father sent the Son** *to be* **the Saviour of the world**."

Why did the **Lord Jesus Christ** come? Why did the Father send Him? **The Father sent the Son to be the Saviour of the world**. That was His mission—not simply to be **Saviour** of just a few, a little company of elect or whatever—but to be **the Saviour of the world**. It is not that the whole world is saved, but He is the Saviour of the world if they would trust Him, accept Him, and receive Him. This is very important. <u>He tasted death for every man</u>.

- **1 John 2:2**

"And he is the propitiation for our sins: and not for ours only, but also for *the sins of* the whole world."

> ### GOD THE FATHER WAS PROPITIATED
> Propitiation is a big word. It is so big that the NIV removes the whole thing. They do not even have a word there. <u>Propitiation is a good word. It means that God is satisfied with the work of His Son.</u> When God is propitious, it means He is satisfied with the work at Calvary.

> ### PROPITIATION FOR THE WORLD'S SINS
> John is writing to believers. The propitiation is for our sins—the believers—but also for the sins of the whole world. He is the satisfaction. <u>He tasted death for every man. I repeat again, the whole world is not saved until they accept this gift as their own, honestly, clearly—that must be—trusting the Lord Jesus Christ.</u> We have said many times, I can offer everyone a million dollars if I had it in my hand. Would it be yours because I offered it? No, it would not be yours because I offered it. It would be yours if you came and accepted it. God sent His Son to be the Saviour of the world. That is His wish and His will, that all would be saved, but it is only theirs if they accept that gift by faith in the Lord Jesus Christ—obedient faith.

This book of Hebrews is a tremendous book and God wants us to know all about His so great salvation. He says, "How can we escape if the word of angels was stedfast?" Everything received a just recompense of payment. <u>How shall we escape? How shall anybody in this world escape if we neglect so great **salvation**</u>?

Hebrews 2:10

"For it became him, for whom *are* all things, and by whom *are* all things, in bringing many sons unto glory, to make the captain of their salvation perfect through sufferings."

This is talking about the Lord Jesus Christ.

> ### CHRIST A FITTING CAPTAIN OF SALVATION
> The book of Hebrews was written to the Jews that were redeemed and saved. That Greek Word for *"became"* is PREPO. Some of the meanings of that Word are:
> *"conspicuous; seemly; fitting."*

> Speaking of the Lord Jesus, everything was created for Him. Everything was created by Him. The Lord Jesus Christ was the Creator. The Lord Jesus is the captain of our salvation. That Greek Word for "*captain*" is ARCHEGOS. Some of the meanings of this Word are:
> "*the chief predecessor; the pioneer*"

SUFFERINGS OF THE LORD JESUS CHRIST

Let us look at some of the **sufferings**. He was made perfect, or complete, through **sufferings**. **Sufferings** are a part of Scripture.

- **Matthew 16:21**

"From that time forth began Jesus to shew unto his disciples, how that he must go unto Jerusalem, and **suffer** many things of the elders and chief priests and scribes, and be killed, and be raised again the third day."

These are **sufferings** He predicted.

- **Luke 24:46**

"And said unto them, Thus it is written, and thus it behoved Christ to **suffer**, and to rise from the dead the third day:"

Suffering was a part of the Lord Jesus Christ's life here on earth.

- **Acts 3:18**

"But those things, which God before had shewed by the mouth of all his prophets, that Christ should **suffer**, he hath so fulfilled."

The **suffering** of the Lord Jesus was part of His coming into this world.

- **Acts 17:3**

"Opening and alleging, that Christ must needs have **suffered**, and risen again from the dead; and that this Jesus, whom I preach unto you, is Christ."

Suffering was part of the Lord Jesus' coming into this world at Calvary.

- **Acts 26:23**

"That Christ should **suffer**, *and* that he should be the first that should rise from the dead, and should shew light unto the people, and to the Gentiles."

Over and over again, Scripture tells of the **sufferings** of our Saviour.

- **Hebrews 13:12**

"Wherefore Jesus also, that he might sanctify the people with his own blood, **suffered** without the gate."

Calvary was outside the city. He **suffered** without the gate on the cross.

- **1 Peter 1:11**

"Searching what, or what manner of time the Spirit of Christ which was in them did signify, when it testified beforehand the **sufferings** of Christ, and the glory that should follow."

The early prophets did not know what they were saying. Even the prophets of the Old Testament talked about the **sufferings** of the Lord Jesus Christ.
- **1 Peter 2:21**

"For even hereunto were ye called: because Christ also **suffered** for us, leaving us an example, that ye should follow his steps:"

He **suffered** in our behalf—for those of us who are genuinely saved and also for the whole world.
- **1 Peter 2:23**

"Who, when he was reviled, reviled not again; when he **suffered**, he threatened not; but committed *himself* to him that judgeth righteously:"

That is a good thing for us. When He **suffered**, He did not threaten those terrible people that did that job.
- **1 Peter 3:18**

"For Christ also hath once **suffered** for sins, the just for the unjust, that he might bring us to God, being put to death in the flesh, but quickened by the Spirit:"

No more—just once. Not the Roman Catholic system, **suffering** every single mass. Just once, that He might bring us to God—the Just for the unjust.
- **1 Peter 4:1**

"Forasmuch then as Christ hath **suffered** for us in the flesh, arm yourselves likewise with the same mind: for he that hath **suffered** in the flesh hath ceased from sin;"
- **1 Peter 5:1**

"The elders which are among you I exhort, who am also an elder, and a witness of the sufferings of Christ, and also a partaker of the glory that shall be revealed:"

CHRIST'S MILLENNIAL REIGN

At His first coming, the Lord Jesus Christ did not come to sit on the throne as the King of kings and Lord of Lords. But He will do this one day at the second phase of His coming during His millennial reign from Jerusalem.

That Greek Word for "*perfect*" is TELEIOO. Some of the meanings of the Word are:

"*complete or entire; to carry through to completion*"

Not that He was imperfect. He could not be a faithful High Priest to understand what we go through here on earth if He Himself did not go through **sufferings**, because we go through **sufferings**. He had to be a faithful and merciful High Priest, so it became Him—it was fitting for Him—to **suffer**, and He did.

Hebrews 2:11

"For both he that **sanctifieth** and they who are **sanctified** *are* all of one: for which cause he is not ashamed to call them brethren,"

SANCTIFICATION

As far as **sanctification**, there are several verses on that. Notice, He that **sanctifieth**—He that **sets us apart** unto Himself. That Greek Word for "sanctification" is HAGIAZO. Some of the meanings for that Word are:

"*to separate from profane things; dedicate to the Lord; to cleanse.*"

That is what the Lord God of Heaven has done if we are saved today. He has **sanctified and set us apart**.

There is a unity in those that are saved and born-again and **set apart**. God is One—tri-unity, the Trinity. Notice, since we are one with the Lord once **He has sanctified and set us apart** by being saved by faith, the Lord is not ashamed to call us brethren. We are part of Him. The question is, "Are we ashamed of Him?" He is not ashamed of us if we are saved. Are we ashamed of Him as Peter was? We trust that will not be the case.

- John 17:17

"**Sanctify** them through thy truth: thy word is truth."

This was the Lord Jesus' High Priestly prayer to the Father. What is "*thy truth*"? The truth is the Word of God.

- Acts 26:18

"To open their eyes, *and* to turn *them* from darkness to light, and *from* the power of Satan unto God, that they may receive forgiveness of sins, and inheritance among them which are **sanctified** by faith that is in me."

SANCTIFICATION'S THREE TENSES

There are three tenses of sanctification: (1) past, (2) present and (3) future. At the cross of Calvary, when we are genuinely saved, (1) we are sanctified positionally and set apart immediately. (2) Then, we are sanctified practically day by day as we yield to our Lord. (3) In the future, we will be completely sanctified—set apart from sin and all that is a part of it. We are sanctified by faith.

- **1 Corinthians 6:11**

"And such were some of you: but ye are washed, but ye are **sanctified**, but ye are justified in the name of the Lord Jesus, and by the Spirit of our God."

In 1 Corinthians 6, it talks about all those wicked, evil deeds that these Corinthian Christians had done in the past. Now, Paul tells them that should be in the past. Now, you are truly saved. You are born-again.

- **Ephesians 5:26**

"That he might **sanctify** and cleanse it with the washing of water by the word,"

The Lord Jesus Christ talks about the believers, the church, the saved ones, that He might **sanctify** and cleanse it. How? With the washing of the water by the Word. The only thing that will set us apart from sin is the Word of God—not only reading, but heeding and trusting.

- **1 Thessalonians 5:23**

"And the very God of peace **sanctify** you wholly; and *I pray God* your whole spirit and soul and body be preserved blameless unto the coming of our Lord Jesus Christ."

This was Paul's prayer for the Thessalonian Christians.

- **Hebrews 10:10**

"By the which will we are **sanctified** through the offering of the body of Jesus Christ once *for all*."

SANCTIFIED BY ONE OFFERING

Just one time, we are set apart by that offering. That is past sanctification.

- **Hebrews 13:12**

"Wherefore Jesus also, that he might **sanctify** the people with his own blood, suffered without the gate."

SANCTIFIED BY CHRIST'S DEATH

That sanctifying death of the Lord Jesus Christ, on our behalf, for the sins of the whole world, was in order to set us apart and sanctify us and make us holy. Although we are once for all sanctified and set apart before the Lord, He wants us in this present time to be set apart and sanctified as well—to become as He is and to be holy in our lives, our thoughts and our deeds.

Hebrews 2:12

"Saying, I will declare thy name unto my brethren, in the midst of the church will I sing praise unto thee."

Here, He is referring back to "**my brethren**"—those whom He saved. He brought many sons unto glory. He is not ashamed to call us brethren, the saved ones. That is not the "**brethren**" of the sororities and fraternities. It is not the "**brethren**" of the unions, or the firemen or school teachers. It is the **brethren** that are related to the Lord Jesus Christ.

DECLARING GOD'S NAME
- **Psalm 22:22**

"**I will declare thy name** unto my brethren: in the midst of the congregation will I praise thee."

He is going to be praised. I do not go along with these "praise and worship" groups. They get up and have their tambourines and their guitars and all this other music. There is nothing in Scripture that says we should do that, as far as this present day, but they have it in church after church—I mean old, established churches that never had them before. All of a sudden, they are following the Pentecostal, charismatic worship type of service. We do not believe in that. **We still sing unto Him and praise Him.**

PRAISE TO THE LORD
- **Hebrews 13:15**

"By him therefore let us offer the sacrifice of **praise to God** continually, that is, the fruit of *our* lips giving thanks to his name."

We can **praise Him** through song, **praise Him** in our hearts, **praise Him** in prayer. We do not have to have the external types of activities. What is the **praise of the Lord**? "*The fruit of our lips, giving thanks to His name.*" That is the **praise** He wants. "Thank you, Lord for my health. Thank you for my home. Thank you for that Thou hast given to me." That is giving thanks to His name. That is the **praise** that He wants.

- **1 Peter 2:9**

"But ye *are* a chosen generation, a royal priesthood, an holy nation, a peculiar people; that ye should shew forth the **praises** of him who hath called you out of darkness into his marvellous light:"

Peter is talking to the Jews that had been converted. We should show forth God's **praise** in our lives. The type of songs that we sing are important.

Hebrews 2:13

"And again, I will put my trust in him. And again, Behold I and the children which God hath given me."

THE CHILDREN GOD HAS GIVEN

This first part, *I will put my trust in him*, is from Psalm 16:1. He is quoting from the Psalms. The second part, *Behold I and the children which God hath given me"* is from Isaiah 8:18, a quotation from the Old Testament. He talks about the children. He talks about the brethren. He talks about those of us who are saved. He is not ashamed to call us brethren. We are His children—not by our physical birth, but our new birth. By being born-again, we become the children of God. We are all the children of God by faith in the Lord Jesus Christ as it says in Philippians 3:25.

Hebrews 2:14

"Forasmuch then as the children are partakers of flesh and blood, he also himself likewise took part of the same; that through death he might destroy him that had the power of death, that is, the devil;"

FLESH AND BLOOD

CHRIST'S SINLESS BLOOD

Notice, He is talking about the children, the brethren. Those are normal people like you and I—ordinary human beings. We are partakers of flesh and blood. Flesh and blood usually refers to those that are people, ordinary people such as we are. The Lord Jesus Christ did take part of the same flesh and blood on His incarnation, but His flesh was perfect flesh by the miracle of the virgin birth. His blood was perfect blood, not contaminated sinful blood. He had a body that was prepared by the God the Father Himself (Hebrews 10:5). He took part and became one of us in the incarnation. This had to be in order that He would be one of us, yet perfect.

As far as the partakers of **flesh and blood**, that is we are human beings. Angels do not have **flesh and blood**. I do not believe the resurrected bodies will necessarily have **blood**, but on this earth, we are partakers of **flesh and blood**. Without the **blood** pumping through the system, we die. We have to have that **blood**. It says in Leviticus 17:14 that the life of all **flesh** is in the **blood** thereof.

- **Matthew 16:17**

"And Jesus answered and said unto him, Blessed art thou, Simon Barjona: for **flesh and blood** hath not revealed *it* unto thee, but my Father which is in heaven."

Flesh and blood, that refers to a human being, did not reveal that He was the Christ, the Son of God. It did not come from just human understanding.

- **1 Corinthians 15:50**

"Now this I say, brethren, that **flesh and blood** cannot inherit the kingdom of God; neither doth corruption inherit incorruption."

NO BLOOD IN OUR GLORIFIED BODIES

This is why I believe there will be no blood in our resurrected bodies. This is the verse that I pin my belief on.

- **Luke 24:39**

"Behold my hands and my feet, that it is I myself: handle me, and see; for a spirit hath not **flesh and bones**, as ye see me have."

They thought they had seen a spirit after He was raised from the dead. He did not say, "**flesh and blood**" but "**flesh and bones**."

- **Galatians 1:16**

"To reveal his Son in me, that I might preach him among the heathen; immediately I conferred not with **flesh and blood**:"

Paul did not go back to the apostles and say, "What will I do now? What will I say?" The Lord Himself gave him the revelation, not **flesh and blood**.

- **Ephesians 6:12**

"For we wrestle not against **flesh and blood**, but against principalities, against powers, against the rulers of the darkness of this world, against spiritual wickedness in high *places*."

Our wrestling is not with **flesh and blood**. Certainly, there are people that are against us, but that is not the main thing. It is the spiritual wickedness in high places.

DESTROYING THE POWER OF DEATH

Notice, it also says that *through death he might destroy him that had the power of death, that is, the devil.* That Greek Word for **"destroy"** is KATARGEO. Some of the meanings of that Word are:

"to render idle; to make inoperative; to cause a person to think they have no further efficiency; to deprive of force, influence or power; to cause to

cease; put an end to; do away with; annul; abolish."

The Lord Jesus Christ did this by His death on the cross of Calvary. Satan has no more efficiency if we are saved. That is what the Lord Jesus has done with the power of death. <u>Let us look at some of the verses on destroying the power of death.</u>

- **Romans 5:10**

"For if, when we were enemies, we were reconciled to God by the death of his Son, much more, being reconciled, we shall be saved by his life."

<u>The death of the Lord Jesus Christ</u> **annulled** <u>the power of Satan over death.</u>

- **Romans 6:9**

"Knowing that Christ being raised from the dead dieth no more; death hath **no more dominion** over him."

Death has **no dominion** over us either.

- **1 Corinthians 15:25-26**

"For he must reign, till he hath put <u>all enemies</u> under his feet. The last enemy *that* shall be **destroyed** *is* death."

This talks about the Lord Jesus Christ.

DEATH IS THE LAST ENEMY

Death is the last enemy. Every one of us human beings will die, unless the Lord Jesus Christ should return in the rapture before we who are truly saved die. We will face death. It is the last enemy.

- **1 Corinthians 15:54-57**

"So when this corruptible shall have put on incorruption, and this mortal shall have put on immortality, then shall be brought to pass the saying that is written, Death is **swallowed up** in **victory**. O death, where *is* thy sting? O grave, where *is* thy **victory**? The sting of death *is* sin; and the strength of sin *is* the law. But thanks *be* to God, which **giveth us the victory** through our Lord Jesus Christ."

<u>Those who are living and true Christians will be transformed at the rapture.</u> Paul quotes the Old Testament. There is **victory** in the Lord Jesus Christ.

- **John 11:25-26**

"Jesus said unto her, I am the resurrection, and the life: he that believeth in me, though he were dead, yet shall he live: And whosoever liveth and believeth in me shall **never die**. Believest thou this?"

DEATH AS A SEPARATION

Death is separation. Physical death is separation of the spirit and soul from the body. Spiritual death is separation from God spiritually. Eternal death is separation of spirit, soul, and body from God. The ones that are saved will never be separated from the Lord Jesus Christ. In that sense, we shall never die. We will never be separated from the Lord Jesus Christ. Death has no power over us.

- 2 Timothy 1:10

"But is now made manifest by the appearing of our Saviour Jesus Christ, who hath **abolished** death, and hath brought life and immortality to light through the gospel:"

NO ETERNAL DEATH FOR THE SAVED

We who are genuine Christians no longer are separated from God. That separation is death. He has abolished it. It is not that we do not die physically—we do not die eternally or spiritually if we are saved.

- Hebrews 2:9

"But we see Jesus, who was made a little lower than the angels for the suffering of death, crowned with glory and honour; that he by the grace of God should taste death for every man."

The Lord Jesus Christ **destroyed** the power of that death.

- Revelation 1:18

"I am he that liveth, and was dead; and, behold, I am alive for evermore, Amen; and have the keys of hell and of death."

CHRIST HAS THE KEYS OF DEATH

If we trust the Lord Jesus Christ as our Saviour, we are never separated from Him. He has the keys of life and death. We will go home to be with Him, which is far better. I believe Paul was taken to Heaven before he died, and then brought back to serve the Lord further. He was taken to Heaven and he knew what Heaven was like. The Lord has power over death. We are never separated from our God.

Hebrews 2:15

"**And deliver them who through fear of death were all their lifetime subject to bondage.**"

He **destroyed** the power of Satan over death. Before the Lord Jesus came, the Devil had the power of death. He was in control of everyone that was born of him by physical birth. Unless they become genuine Christians, they will have to go to the lake of fire. That lake of fire was prepared for the Devil and his angels. Now the Lord Jesus Christ has come and He has broken that. He has taken away that power of death.

ARE YOU READY FOR DEATH?

Let me ask you a question. Do you fear death? Death for the saved person is the door to Heaven. Unless the Lord Jesus Christ comes back in the rapture, the only way we get to Heaven is by death. That is the door to Heaven. You may say, "Well, I am not ready to go." I heard a person recently say (talking about Heaven), "I'm not ready!" We have to be ready. We may not want to go yet, but we had better be ready. If we are saved and born-again, we are ready.

Think of a recent head-on collision in Los Angeles with those two trains (a freight train and a passenger train) coming together. There were blood-curdling screams of those that have died. Many times, they are not ready because they are lost. Those people, I am sure, were not prepared to die that day. There were twenty or so, maybe more, who died. They did not have any fear of death, because as far as they were concerned, they were not going to die yet. They wait until they are just about ready to die with their sicknesses and on their death bed. Then they may be afraid and cry out.

CHRIST'S DELIVERANCE

That Greek word "*deliver*" is APALLASSO. Some of the meanings of this word are:

"*to remove; to depart; **to set free**.*"

That is what **deliver** means. All their lifetime they were subject to bondage—subject to the Devil, subject to Satan. The Lord Jesus Christ delivered. He is a delivering Saviour.

- **Galatians 1:4**

"Who gave himself for our sins, that he might **deliver** us from this present evil world, according to the will of God and our Father:"

He does not want genuine Christians to be wrapped up in this evil world.

- **2 Timothy 4:18**

"And the Lord shall **deliver** me from every evil work, and will preserve *me* unto his heavenly kingdom: to whom *be* glory for ever and ever. Amen."

Paul said this before he was killed by the Roman government. Even though he died physically, he is going to be preserved to the Lord's heavenly kingdom. God is in the **delivering** business.

- **2 Peter 2:9**

"The Lord knoweth how to **deliver** the godly out of temptations, and to reserve the unjust unto the day of judgment to be punished:" He knows how to **deliver** us from testings and temptations.

FEAR

THE REALITY OF FEAR

Fear is real. People who say they have no fear of anything are liars. They are just plain liars. When something is menacing against you—whether it is a gun, or a knife ready to be thrown, or some freight train coming at you and you are on the tracks and cannot move—fear is real.

- **Matthew 10:28**

"And **fear** not them which kill the body, but are not able to kill the soul: but rather **fear** him which is able to destroy both soul and body in hell."

The Lord Jesus Christ said this about **fear**. We are to **fear** our God. **Fear** the Lord. However, once we are saved by faith in the Lord Jesus Christ, there is no more **fear** of circumstances or hardships. He takes it away.

- **2 Timothy 1:7**

"For God hath not given us the spirit of **fear**; but of power, and of love, and of a sound mind."

- **Hebrews 13:6**

"So that we may boldly say, The Lord *is* my helper, and I will not **fear** what man shall do unto me."

Paul wrote to the Christians who were saved from Judaism that he was not **afraid** of what might happen to him. He was **fearless**.

That is what true Christians should be.

- **1 John 4:18**

"There is no **fear** in love; but perfect love casteth out **fear**: because **fear** hath torment. He that **feareth** is not made perfect in love."

True Christians should be not **fearful** of circumstances, but they should

always **fear** the Lord. Be sure that we can trust Him and He is going to take care of us.
- **John 14:2-3**

"In my Father's house are many mansions: if *it were* not *so,* I would have told you. I go to prepare a place for you. And if I go and prepare a place for you, I will come again, and receive you unto myself; that where I am, *there* ye may be also.'

This is where the Lord Jesus is. There should be no **fear** of death itself, maybe of dying, but not death.

BONDAGE

Without the Lord Jesus Christ, lost men and women are in **bondage**. There is no question about that.
- **2 Peter 2:19**

"While they promise them liberty, they themselves are the servants of corruption: for of whom a man is overcome, of the same is he brought in **bondage**."

VARIOUS KINDS OF BONDAGE

There are all kinds of bondage today. People are in it unless they come to the Lord Jesus Christ. Some Christians are in this kind of bondage—drugs, alcohol, nicotine, caffeine, gambling, sexual promiscuity, perversion, pornography. There are all kinds of bondage that people are in. The Lord Jesus Christ came to deliver us and that is what He did. Those of us who are saved were delivered from the fear of death. We may be afraid of the dying process. We may be in pain in the dying process, but there should be in saved, born-again Christians no fear of death beyond.

Hebrews 2:16

"For verily he took not on *him the nature of* angels; but he took on *him* the seed of Abraham."

You will notice, *"him the nature of"* is in italics, but that Greek word for *"took on him"* is EPILAMBANOMAI. It means *"to lay hold upon."* He did not take the angels' type of nature, but He took on Him the seed of Abraham. He became perfect Man as well as He was perfect God. This is very important. If He were an angel, He would not be able to die for us and to be sympathetic to us as our faithful High Priest. He took upon Himself the seed of Abraham so that He could be one of us. This is a proper thing. That seed of Abraham was taken upon Him.

Hebrews 2:17

"**Wherefore in all things it behoved him to be made like unto *his* brethren, that he might be a merciful and faithful high priest in things *pertaining* to God, to make reconciliation for the sins of the people.**"

It behoved Him to be made *like* His brethren. That Greek word *for* "*like*" is HOMOI-OO. It is a very important word. It is not come from the Greek Word HOMOU. There are two words for *like*—HOMO and HOMOI. HOMO is *"exactly the same."* That is not this word. HOMOI which means "***like or similar to, but not identical with.***" The Lord Jesus Christ took upon Himself a **similar** nature, but perfect and sinless and holy. That is the distinction. That is why it is important. He was made *like*—**similar, not the same as**—because He was sinless. He was perfect. He was perfect God and perfect Man in the incarnation by the virgin birth.

MERCIFUL

CHRIST A MERCIFUL HIGH PRIEST
The Lord Jesus Christ is a merciful High Priest.

- **Genesis 19:16**

"And while he lingered, the men laid hold upon his hand, and upon the hand of his wife, and upon the hand of his two daughters; the LORD being **merciful** unto him: and they brought him forth, and set him without the city."

- **Luke 6:36**

"Be ye therefore **merciful**, as your Father also is **merciful**."

- **Luke 18:13**

"And the publican, standing afar off, would not lift up so much as *his* eyes unto heaven, but smote upon his breast, saying, God be **merciful** to me a sinner."

- **Hebrews 8:12**

"For I will be **merciful** to their unrighteousness, and their sins and their iniquities will I remember no more."

FAITHFUL

CHRIST A FAITHFUL HIGH PRIESTS
The Lord Jesus Christ is also a faithful High Priest.

- **1 Corinthians 1:9**
"God *is* **faithful,** by whom ye were called unto the fellowship of his Son Jesus Christ our Lord."
- **1 Corinthians 10:13**
"There hath no **temptation** taken you but such as is common to man: but God *is* **faithful**, who will not suffer you to be **tempted** above that ye are able; but will with the **temptation** also make a way to escape, that ye may be able to bear *it.*"
- **1 Thessalonians 5:24**
"**Faithful** *is* he that calleth you, who also will do *it.*"
- **2 Thessalonians 3:3**
"But the Lord is **faithful,** who shall stablish you, and keep *you* from evil."
- **2 Timothy 2:13**
"If we believe not, *yet* he abideth **faithful:** he cannot deny himself."
- **Hebrews 3:2**
"Who was **faithful** to him that appointed him, as also Moses *was faithful* in all his house."
- **Hebrews 10:23**
"Let us hold fast the profession of *our* **faith** without wavering; (for he *is* **faithful** that promised;)"
- **1 Peter 4:19**
"Wherefore let them that suffer according to the will of God commit the keeping of their souls *to him* in well doing, as unto a **faithful** Creator."
- **1 John 1:9**
"If we confess our sins, he is **faithful** and just to forgive us *our* sins, and to cleanse us from all unrighteousness."
- **Revelation 1:5**
"And from Jesus Christ, *who is* the **faithful** witness, *and* the first begotten of the dead, and the prince of the kings of the earth. Unto him that loved us, and washed us from our sins in his own blood,"

CHRIST OUR HIGH PRIEST
- **Hebrews 3:1**
"Wherefore, holy brethren, partakers of the heavenly calling, consider the Apostle and **high priest** of our profession, Christ Jesus;"

- **Hebrews 4:14-15**

"Seeing then that we have a **great high priest**, that is passed into the heavens, Jesus the Son of God, let us hold fast *our* profession. For we have not an **high priest** which cannot be touched with the feeling of our infirmities; but was in all points tempted like as *we are, yet* without sin."

- **Hebrews 5:10**

"Called of God an **high priest** after the order of Melchisedec."

- **Hebrews 6:20**

"Whither the forerunner is for us entered, *even* Jesus, made an **high priest** for ever after the order of Melchisedec."

- **Hebrews 7:26**

"For such an **high priest** became us, *who is* holy, harmless, undefiled, separate from sinners, and made higher than the heavens;"

- **Hebrews 8:1**

"Now of the things which we have spoken *this is* the sum: We have such an **high priest**, who is set on the right hand of the throne of the Majesty in the heavens;"

- **Hebrews 9:11**

"But Christ being come an **high priest** of good things to come, by a greater and more perfect tabernacle, not made with hands, that is to say, not of this building;"

- **Hebrews 10:21**

"And *having* an **high priest** over the house of God;"

As far as the Lord Jesus Christ being a **High Priest**, it is one of His titles. In the past, as He came to the earth, He was a prophet. As He is at the Father's right hand today, He is our **High Priest**. One day, during the millennium, He will come back as our King of kings and Lord of lords. Right now, His office is that of **High Priest**.

- **Hebrews 8:1**

"Now of the things which we have spoken *this is* the sum: We have such an **high priest**, who is set on the right hand of the throne of the Majesty in the heavens;"

The Lord Jesus Christ is the **High Priest**. The Roman Catholic priests are not Biblical priests as the Lord Jesus Christ.

REPLACEMENT THEOLOGY

The whole Roman Catholic system is based upon a different idea as far as what the dispensations are. They hold to replacement theology. The Roman Catholic system is based upon the notion that the Jewish faith is now the Christian

> faith. Jews become Christians in their system. Going back to the Old Testament, the priests take the garments of the High Priest—the robes and all the other things—and put them into their system. That is how they get all their rigamarole. It is a terrible thing.

The Lord Jesus Christ is the **High Priest**—not as the Roman Catholic priests, not as the Episcopal priests, as they call them—but He is our **High Priest** who sits at the right hand of the throne of majesty in Heaven. That is what He is called. His present ministry is as our **High Priest**.

- **Hebrews 9:11**

"But Christ being come an **high priest** of good things to come, by a greater and more perfect tabernacle, not made with hands, that is to say, not of this building;"

> **THE HOLY OF HOLIES**
>
> As you know, in the Old Testament, there are priests and a High Priest. Aaron was the first high priest. The sons of Aaron were priests. The Levites were helpers to the priests. Only the high priest could go into the holy of holies. The priests could go into the holy place, but not into the holy of holies. The high priest went in alone, once a year, as it says in Leviticus 16 on the Day of Atonement. He had the offering of a sacrifice of blood, first for his own sins. He would take it into the holy of holies and put it upon the mercy seat. Then, he had to go out and offer another sacrifice for the sins of the people. He would then take that blood and go into the holy of holies. That was the only one that could come into the very presence of God—the high priest of the Old Testament.

The Lord Jesus Christ is our **High Priest**, not as the Old Testament **high priest**, but a completely different **High Priest** after the order of Melchizedek. He was not after the order of Aaron. Hebrew 2:17 is very important indeed.

- **Hebrews 10:21**

"And *having* an **high priest** over the house of God;"

We have a **High Priest**. The Lord Jesus Christ is our **High Priest** and we ought to praise the Lord for that.

- **Hebrews 3:2**

"Who was faithful to him that appointed him, as also Moses *was faithful* in all his house."

Notice, He is not only a **High Priest**, but He is a merciful and faithful

High Priest. He is these two different things—merciful and faithful. Merciful is *not giving us things we deserve*. Faithful is *doing all that He has promised He would do.*

Hebrews 2:18

"For in that he himself hath suffered being tempted, he is able to succour them that are tempted."

TEMPTATION & TESTING

"Succour" means *to help*. He suffered being tempted, or tested. That Greek Word for *"tempted"* is PEIRAZO. Some of the meanings for this word are:

> *"to try with the purpose of ascertaining whether it is good quality or bad quality.* In a bad sense, it means *to test one maliciously."*

Satan tempted (or tested) the Lord Jesus maliciously. He wanted to see Him fall. There are a number of verses on testings or temptations.

VERSES ON TEMPTING

- **Matthew 4:1**

"Then was Jesus led up of the Spirit into the wilderness to be **tempted** of the devil."

Adam was tempted of the Devil and Adam fell. The Lord Jesus did not fall.

- **Matthew 6:13**

"And lead us not into **temptation**, but deliver us from evil: For thine is the kingdom, and the power, and the glory, for ever. Amen."

This is the so-called "Lord's Prayer." It is the apostles' prayer.

- **Matthew 26:41**

"Watch and pray, that ye enter not into **temptation**: the spirit indeed *is* willing, but the flesh *is* weak."

This was in the garden of Gethsemane. The three apostles, Peter, James, and John, fell asleep there.

- **Luke 8:13**

"They on the rock *are they*, which, when they hear, receive the word with joy; and these have no root, which for a while believe, and in time of **temptation** fall away."

This talks about those people as the word fell on certain types of soil: the thorns, the wayside soil, the rocky soil and the good soil. The rocky soil is bad ground.

Hebrews—Preaching Verse by Verse

- **Acts 20:19**

"Serving the Lord with all humility of mind, and with many tears, and **temptations**, which befell me by the lying in wait of the Jews:"

Temptations here are in the sense of testing. Sometimes, temptation is the way we think of it today, but in Scriptures, many times, it is testings.

- **1 Corinthians 7:5**

"Defraud ye not one the other, except *it be* with consent for a time, that ye may give yourselves to fasting and prayer; and come together again, that Satan tempt you not for your incontinency."

This speaks of marriage and husband-and-wife relations. Again, temptation is testing.

- **1 Corinthians 10:13**

"There hath no temptation taken you but such as is common to man: but God *is* faithful, who will not suffer you to be tempted above that ye are able; but will with the temptation also make a way to escape, that ye may be able to bear *it*."

- **Galatians 6:1**

"Brethren, if a man be overtaken in a fault, ye which are spiritual, restore such an one in the spirit of meekness; considering thyself, lest thou also be **tempted**."

BE CAREFUL IN RESTORATION

Some Christians are overtaken in faults. Be careful when restoring others, that we may not fall into the same trap.

- **1 Timothy 6:9**

"But they that will be rich fall into **temptation** and a snare, and into many foolish and hurtful lusts, which drown men in destruction and perdition."

This is not those that *are* rich, but they that *will* be. "I want to be rich." That is the most important thing in their life. They work night and day, seven days a week. If they could, they would work 24 hours a day. They really want to be rich.

Some people are rich, but it is not their main goal in life. They just happen to have the riches. Many of them are saved and give things unto the Lord. For those that are willing—the one goal in their life is to be rich—what is going to happen when they die? They can take nothing with them. They will leave it all behind for their children to fight over and to spend like wild sailors on a binge. They can waste in a day, or a week, or a month, or a year, what their fathers and mothers have built up for a long time.

- **Hebrews 4:15**

"For we have not an high priest which cannot be touched with the feeling of our infirmities; but was in all points **tempted** like as *we are, yet* without sin."

CHRIST TESTED THOUGH SINLESS

The Lord Jesus Christ was tested in all points. That is how He can be a faithful and merciful High Priest. He knows what we are doing. He knows what we are living through. Whether a test of pain, or affliction, or people turning their backs on Him, spitting on Him, leaving Him, forsaking Him, He knows all those points. Yet, He is without sin.

- **James 1:2-3**

"My brethren, count it all joy when ye fall into divers **temptations**; Knowing *this*, that the **trying** of your faith worketh patience."

BE JOYFUL IN TESTINGS

What are we to do in testings or temptations? James says, "Count it all joy." Let it come. You get patience out of it all. People say, "Well, James must have it wrong. We don't like that." The Bible says that we ought to count it all joy.

- **James 1:12-14**

"Blessed *is* the man that endureth **temptation**: for when he is **tried**, he shall receive the crown of life, which the Lord hath promised to them that love him. Let no man say when he is **tempted**, I am **tempted** of God: for God cannot be **tempted** with evil, neither **tempteth** he any man: But every man is **tempted**, when he is drawn away of his own lust, and **enticed**."

Flip Wilson used to say, "The Devil made me do it." We ourselves make the temptation—not God, not the Devil, no one else but ourselves.

- **1 Peter 1:6-7**

"Wherein ye greatly rejoice, though now for a season, if need be, ye are in heaviness through manifold **temptations**: That the **trial** of your faith, being much more precious than of gold that perisheth, though it be **tried** with fire, might be found unto praise and honour and glory at the appearing of Jesus Christ:"

We know that sometimes we are **tested** and **tempted**. Stay firm. Do not give up, whatever it may be.

- **2 Peter 2:9**

"The Lord knoweth how to deliver the godly out of **temptations**, and to reserve the unjust unto the day of judgment to be punished:"

The Lord is good. He is faithful to us. We ought to praise His name for all that He has done for us.

> ## CHRIST BROKE SATAN'S POWER OF DEATH
>
> The main thing that we have pointed out, among the many other things that are taught here, is the Lord is able to take away the fear of death and the power of death. All our lifetimes we were subject to bondage. The Devil had the power of death before the Lord Jesus Christ came unto this earth. He died for the sins of the world. For those of us who have trusted Him and accepted Him, He has conquered death. Death hath no more dominion over Him. Those of us who are in Him (though we may die physically if He does not come in the rapture before) will go home to be with Him. <u>We will never be separated from Him—spirit, soul, and finally, in the resurrection, we will have a new body</u>—and that is a wonderful thing. We should have no more fear of death.

I know a brother who said, "Pastor, please don't pray for me that I may be healed, but that the Lord's will may be done." We should not have a fear of death. We want to stay as long as we can to serve the Lord, but the fear has been taken away by the victorious Lord Jesus Christ. That is why He said, "I have the keys of death." He has the key. <u>As I said, except for the rapture, there is no other door for the Christian to Heaven but death. If we want to go to Heaven, the only way to get there is by death.</u>
<u>That is the only way any of us genuinely saved people will get there. The unsaved will not get there at all. Let us thank God for what He has done.</u>

Hebrews Chapter Three

Hebrews 3:1

"Wherefore, holy brethren, partakers of the heavenly calling, consider the Apostle and High Priest of our profession, Christ Jesus;"

PARTAKERS

Notice Paul is talking about "*holy brethren.*" I believe the entire book of Hebrews is written to these holy brethren. I know people feel that it is written to unsaved Jews and other unsaved people. I believe it is quite clear here, that these are "*holy brethren.*" rather than unsaved people. They are "***partakers** of the heavenly calling.*" They are saved, born-again Christians. How often do we really "**consider**" our High Priest, as "***partakers** of the heavenly calling*"?

- **Colossians 1:12**

"Giving thanks unto the Father, which hath made us meet to be **partakers** of the inheritance of the saints in light:" (KJV)
This verse talks about those who are genuinely saved. They are **partakers** of the "*inheritance of the saints in light.*" They are part of that "*inheritance.*"

- **Hebrews 6:4**

"For *it is* impossible for those who were once enlightened, and have tasted of the heavenly gift, and were made **partakers** of the Holy Ghost,"

PARTAKERS OF THE HOLY SPIRIT

"*Made partakers of the Holy Ghost.*" Those people to whom Paul addressed his letter were genuinely saved people. Paul wants the readers to "*consider*" the Lord Jesus Christ. Let's look at several verses where we're told to "*consider.*"

CONSIDER

They are told to "*consider the Apostle and High Priest of our profession.*" The Greek Word is KATANOESATE. Some of the meanings of this Word are:

1. *"give careful consideration, consider closely* (Lk 12:24, 27; Heb 3:1; 10:24+); 2. *be concerned about, implying a response* (Mt 7:3; Lk 6:41+); 3. *understand completely* (Lk 20:23; Ro 4:19+); 4. *notice, discover through direct observation* (Ac 7:31, 32; 11:6; 27:39; Jas 1:23, 24+)"

- **1 Samuel 12:24**

"Only fear the LORD, and serve him in truth with all your heart: for **consider** how great *things* he hath done for you."

- **Matthew 6:28**

"And why take ye thought for raiment? **Consider** the lilies of the field, how they grow; they toil not, neither do they spin:"

- **Luke 12:24**

"**Consider** the ravens: for they neither sow nor reap; which neither have storehouse nor barn; and God feedeth them: how much more are ye better than the fowls?"

- **Hebrews 12:3**

"For **consider** him that endured such contradiction of sinners against himself, lest ye be wearied and faint in your minds."

THE LORD JESUS CHRIST THE HIGH PRIEST

- **Hebrews 2:17**

"Wherefore in all things it behoved him to be made like unto *his* brethren, that he might be a merciful and faithful **high priest** in things *pertaining* to God, to make reconciliation for the sins of the people."

- **Hebrews 4:14-15**

"Seeing then that we have a great **high priest**, that is passed into the heavens, Jesus the Son of God, let us hold fast *our* profession. For we have not an high priest which cannot be touched with the feeling of our infirmities; but was in all points tempted like as *we are*, yet without sin."

- **Hebrews 5:10**

"Called of God an **high priest** after the order of Melchisedec."

- **Hebrews 7:26**

"For such an **high priest** became us, *who is* holy, harmless, undefiled, separate from sinners, and made higher than the heavens;"

- **Hebrews 8:1**

"Now of the things which we have spoken *this is* the sum: We have such an **high priest**, who is set on the right hand of the throne of the Majesty in the heavens;"

- **Hebrews 9:11**

"But Christ being come an **high priest** of good things to come, by a greater and more perfect tabernacle, not made with hands, that is to say, not of this building;"

Hebrews 3:2

"Who was faithful to him that appointed him, as also Moses *was faithful* in all his house."

The Lord Jesus Christ was **faithful** to God the Father, and faithful in all things. Moses was also *"faithful in all his house."* He had a big task, bringing those people out of Egypt who were in slavery and bondage, and then bringing them into the land of Canaan land. There were many fights and battles among those 600,000 men plus women and children--probably 1 million, 2 million, maybe 3 million people in all that come out of Egypt. But Moses was *"faithful."*

MOSES' APPOINTMENT

- **Exodus 3:10-12**

"Come now therefore, and I will send thee unto Pharaoh, that thou mayest bring forth my people the children of Israel out of Egypt. And Moses said unto God, Who *am* I, that I should go unto Pharaoh, and that I should bring forth the children of Israel out of Egypt? And he said, Certainly I will be with thee; and this *shall be* a token unto thee, that I have sent thee: When thou hast brought forth the people out of Egypt, ye shall serve God upon this mountain."

MOSES A FAITHFUL SERVANT

- **Numbers 12:6-8**

"And he said, Hear now my words: If there be a prophet among you, *I* the LORD will make myself known unto him in a vision, *and* will speak unto him in a dream. My **servant** Moses *is* not so, who *is* **faithful** in all mine house. With him will I speak mouth to mouth, even apparently, and not in dark speeches; and the similitude of the LORD shall he behold: wherefore then were ye not afraid to speak against my **servant** Moses?"

MOSES' CLOSENESS TO THE LORD

So Moses had the privilege of being spoken to by the Lord mouth to mouth, a special kind of prophet.

- **Joshua 1:2**

"Moses my **servant** is dead; now therefore arise, go over this Jordan, thou, and all this people, unto the land which I do give to them, *even* to the children of Israel."

- **Joshua 1:7**

"Only be thou strong and very courageous, that thou mayest observe to do according to all the law, which Moses my **servant** commanded thee: turn not from it *to* the right hand or *to* the left, that thou mayest prosper whithersoever thou goest."

- **Hebrews 3:2**

"Who was **faithful** to him that appointed him, as also Moses was **faithful** in all his house."

So Moses was **faithful**. The Lord Jesus Christ, in verse 2, was "*faithful to him that* **appointed** *him*." He said "*Not my will, but thine, be done.*" Even at Calvary, as He was suffering and dying on the Cross of Calvary, the Lord Jesus Christ was **faithful** to his Father. He never flinched. He never questioned the Father.

- **John 8:29**

"And he that sent me is with me: the Father hath not left me alone; for I do always those things that please him."

And that is true about the Lord Jesus Christ. He was **faithful** to God the Father Who **appointed** Him.

Hebrews 3:3

"For this *man* was counted worthy of more glory than Moses, inasmuch as he who hath builded the house hath more honour than the house."

So the Lord Jesus Christ has "*more glory*" The Greek Word for "glory" is DOXA, meaning "*splendor and brightness*"] *than Moses*" because the one who builds the house "*hath more honor than the house.*" The Lord Jesus Christ is the Builder of this house of genuinely saved and born-again believers. He has "*more glory*" than Moses.

Hebrews 3:4

"For every house is builded by some *man*; but he that built all things *is* God."

THE CREATIVE WORK OF CHRIST

- **John 1:3**

"All things were **made by him**; and without **him** was not any thing **made** that was **made**."

- John 1:10

"He was in the world, and the world was **made by him**, and the world knew **him** not."

- Ephesians 3:9

"And to make all *men* see what *is* the fellowship of the mystery, which from the beginning of the world hath been hid in God, who **created all things by Jesus Christ:**"

OMISSION OF "BY JESUS CHRIST"

The words, "*by Jesus Christ*" are omitted from the Gnostic Critical Greek Text and therefore from the modern versions based upon it like the RSV, NRSV, ASV, NASV, NIV, ESV, and many others. The Gnostics and those who follow them deny that the Lord Jesus Christ was the Creator. The Gnostics didn't believe that the Lord Jesus Christ could create anything. The Gnostics believe the Lord Jesus Christ was a sinner. They believe Christ needed to be saved Himself. In view of their heresy, they did not believe the Lord Jesus Christ could create anything. Because of this, they just dropped out those words.

T.R. VERSUS C.T.–8,000 DIFFERENCES

The manuscripts of Vatican and Sinai were found in Alexandria, Egypt. Alexandria was also the headquarters of the Gnostic religion. When the New Testament Words did not go along with their false religion, the Gnostics either changed those Words, or eliminated them. Dr. Jack Moorman's book, *8,000 Differences Between The Received Text and The Critical Text* lists 8,000 differences between these two kinds of Greek texts. Of these 8,000 differences, there are over 356 that are doctrinal places. This is one of those places, created all things "*by Jesus Christ.*"

- Colossians 1:16

"For by **him** were **all things created**, that are in heaven, and that are in earth, visible and invisible, whether *they be* thrones, or dominions, or principalities, or powers: **all things were created by him, and for him:**"

- Revelation 4:11

"Thou art worthy, O **Lord,** to receive glory and honour and power: for **thou hast created all things,** and for **thy** pleasure they are and were **created.**"

He built all things. That is the **Lord Jesus Christ**. He was the Creator Who built all things in this world. The modernists, liberals, and apostates of all sorts deny the **Lord Jesus Christ's** deity as well as all of His miracles. They don't believe that **He** was the **founder** and **Creator** of all things. The Bible is clear on this.

Hebrews 3:5

"And Moses verily was faithful in all his house, as a servant, for a testimony of those things which were to be spoken after;"

"Those things which were to be spoken after." This *"testimony"* that Moses had for these things *"to be spoken after"* is to be found in the first five Old Testament book which Moses wrote. He was a faithful **servant** of the Lord as a *"servant"* [THERAPON] *"an attendant, or a servant."* We said that earlier about Moses' faithfulness to the Lord and as a servant.

Moses, who wrote Genesis, Exodus, Leviticus, Numbers, and Deuteronomy, used the Words given to him by the Lord Jesus Christ through the Holy Spirit. These Hebrew Words, as well as the Aramaic and Greek New Testament Words, God has preserved for us down to this day. This is called the doctrine of Bible preservation. The preservation of the Bible's original Hebrew, Aramaic, and Greek Words is doubted, not only by apostates and new-evangelicals, but also by most Fundamentalists today. Professors at Bob Jones University, for example, believe that there are "scribal errors" in the Hebrew, Aramaic, and Greek Words that we have today.

Hebrews 3:6

"But Christ as a son over his own house; whose house are we, if we hold fast the confidence and the rejoicing of the hope firm unto the end."

We don't want any fakes in this house. Some people say they are "a Christian." They include modernist liberals in that term. They include Roman Catholicism in that term. These are fake "Christians" or nominal "Christians," but not genuine "Christians."

PHONY "BELIEVERS" ARE FOUND

In this verse, it states clearly that the only ones who are in the *"house"* of the Lord Jesus Christ are those who *"hold fast the confidence and the rejoicing of the hope firm unto the end.*" It does not include those who are not genuinely saved but only think they are "Christians" and genuinely saved. "*by their fruits ye shall know them*" the Scriptures say. Sad to say, we have many phony "believers" who only say they are Christians but are not.

Hebrews 3:7

"**Wherefore (as the Holy Ghost saith, To day if ye will hear his voice,**"

- Psalm 95:7-8

"For he *is* our God; and we *are* the people of his pasture, and the sheep of his hand. To day if ye will **hear his voice**, Harden not your heart, as in the provocation, *and* as *in* the day of temptation in the wilderness:"

- Hebrews 4:7

"Again, he limiteth a certain day, saying in David, To day, after so long a time; as it is said, To day if ye will **hear his voice**, harden not your hearts."

How can a person "*hear His voice*" today? We believe that God does not speak to people face to face as He did with Moses, for example. God speaks to people today through His Words in the Bible. That is why it is so important that we have the right Bible in all the languages of the world. In English, we have our King James Bible which is an accurate translation from the proper Hebrew, Aramaic, and Greek words that underlie it. The King James Bible is God's Words kept intact in English.

YEARLY BIBLE READING

We need accurate translations in all the other languages as well. God does not want us to fail to "*hear His voice*" by reading and heeding His Words in the proper Bible, from Genesis through Revelation.

I like to read my Bible from beginning to end each year. This can be done by reading 85 verses each day, if you can. 85 verses a day will get you through the Bible in a year in order to "*hear His voice.*"

The world doesn't care about hearing God's voice by reading the Bible. They care about the voices on radio, television, the internet, and many other things. How can people stand some of the singers who come out on radio and TV day after day and night after night? Those singers who come out and sing sound very strange to me. I don't understand how anyone can stand their words and their method of worldly singing. This rock and roll and contemporary Christian music (CCM) is heard in many Christian churches all too frequently. They roll their voices around just like the world of unsaved people. But the voice of the Lord in His Words is disdained and despised.

Hebrews 3:8

"**Harden not your hearts, as in the provocation, in the day of temptation in the wilderness:**"

AVOID OF HARDENED HEARTS

The words, "*harden not your hearts*" form a prohibition, or negative command. In the Greek, it is in the present tense. As such, it means to stop an action already in process. If it were in the Greek aorist tense, it would mean to not even begin to do something. In this case, being in the present tense, it means "*Stop hardening your hearts.*" Those to whom Paul was writing were hardening their hearts. Paul told them to "*stop it.*" If any of us have hardened our hearts, we must stop it. Our hearts must be soft. Our hearts must be malleable, our hearts must be open to the will of God and the Words of God in all things.

"*As in the provocation, in the day of temptation in the wilderness*" This refers to Moses and the children of Israel for 40 years in the wilderness. They **hardened their hearts** and did not obey the Lord.

HARDENING OF HEARTS

- **Exodus 7:14**

"And the LORD said unto Moses, Pharaoh's **heart *is* hardened**, he refuseth to let the people go."

We will see about the **heart** and what it means. Pharaoh's **heart was hardened**. He did not want to let the people of Israel go. It took 10 plagues from the Lord in order for him let Israel go. After they left Egypt, he sent his soldiers to bring them back. Pharaoh wanted these slaves back to continue building his pyramids. The Lord drowned all of Pharaoh's army in the Red Sea.

- **Exodus 7:22**

"And the magicians of Egypt did so with their enchantments: and **Pharaoh's heart was hardened**, neither did he hearken unto them; as the LORD had said."

- **Exodus 8:15**

"But when Pharaoh saw that there was respite, **he hardened his heart**, and hearkened not unto them; as the LORD had said."

God took away the bad effects of various miracles. As soon as Pharaoh saw that the bad effects of the miracles were removed, and the judgment taken away, Pharaoh **hardened his heart**.

- **Exodus 9:7**

"And Pharaoh sent, and, behold, there was not one of the cattle of the Israelites dead. And the **heart of Pharaoh was hardened**, and he did not let the people go."

PHARAOH'S HARDENED HEART

The hardening of the heart to Pharaoh, is a warning that God doesn't want our hearts to be hardened, but to be soft. When God says something, in his Words, as you read the Scriptures, we should say

"Oh Lord, how can I obey them? How can I put them into practice?"

Our **hearts should never be hardened.** Our hearts should be opened to the Words of God, as we read the Scriptures. The verse refers to the *"temptation in the wilderness."* The Greek Word for *"temptation"* is PEIRASMOS. It means

"a trial or test of man's fidelity, and integrity."

It was a rebellion against God by which His power and justice were, as if it were, put to the test and challenged. In other words, these Israelites said something like this: *"You prove it to us, Lord. How are you going to get us out of this mess?"* Their **heart was hardened**. They tempted and tested God in the wilderness.

TEMPTING GOD IN THE WILDERNESS

- **Exodus 17:2**

"Wherefore the people did chide with Moses, and said, Give us water that we may drink. And Moses said unto them, Why chide ye with me? wherefore do ye **tempt** the LORD?"

- **Exodus 17:7**

"And he called the name of the place Massah, and Meribah, because of the chiding of the children of Israel, and because they **tempted** the LORD, saying, Is the LORD among us, or not?"

- **Numbers 14:22**

"Because all those men which have seen my glory, and my miracles, which I did in Egypt and in the wilderness, and have **tempted** me now these ten times, and have not hearkened to my voice;"

- **Deuteronomy 6:16**

"Ye shall not **tempt** the LORD your God, as ye **tempted** him in Massah."

- **Psalm 78:18**

"And they **tempted** God in their heart by asking meat for their lust."

LEANNESS TO THE SOUL

They doubted the Lord. They doubted that He could do what He said. They questioned God in their hearts. When they asked for "meat,"
God granted their request, but, as it says in Psalm 106:15: *"And he gave them their request; but sent leanness into their soul."*

- **Psalm 78:41**

"Yea, they turned back and **tempted** God, and limited the Holy One of Israel."

- **Psalm 78:56**

"Yet they **tempted** and provoked the most high God, and kept not his testimonies:"

- **Psalm 95:8-11**

"Harden not your heart, as in the provocation, *and* as *in* the day of **temptation in the wilderness**: When your fathers **tempted** me, proved me, and saw my work. Forty years long was I grieved with *this* generation, and said, It *is* a people that do err in their heart, and they have not known my ways: Unto whom I sware in my wrath that they should not enter into my rest."

ERRORS OF THE HEART

It was a heart error, not only the head error. The errors of the head are bad enough, but to err in the heart is far more serious. As Proverbs 4:23 says: *"Keep thy heart with all diligence; for out of it are the issues of life."*

- **Psalm 106:14**

"But lusted exceedingly in the wilderness, and **tempted** God in the desert.

They lusted, they **tempted**, they tested, and they rebelled against God in the wilderness. What Israel did was indeed a wicked thing.

Hebrews 3:9

"When your fathers tempted me, proved me, and saw my works forty years."

THE MEANING OF TEMPT

The Jewish fathers *"tempted me and proved me."* The Greek Word for "tempted" is PEIRAZO. Some of the meanings for "tempted" are:

"to try, make trial of, test: for the purpose of ascertaining his quantity, or what he thinks, or how he will behave himself."

They were trying to **tempt** Him to see if He was going to be trustworthy.

THE MEANING OF PROVE

It says they tempted and proved me. That Greek Word for *"prove"* is DOKIMAZO. Some of the meaning for *"prove"* are:

"to test, examine, prove, scrutinize (to see whether a thing is genuine or not), as metals"

They wanted to see if the Lord meant business, if the Lord's Words were correct and accurate and to recognize as genuine upon examination. Forty whole years in the wilderness is a long time to be proved and tested.

TEMPTING FOR FORTY YEARS

- Psalm 95:8-11

"Harden not your heart, as in the provocation, *and as in* the day of **temptation in the wilderness**: When your fathers **tempted** me, proved me, and saw my work. **Forty years** long was I grieved with *this* generation, and said, It *is* a people that do err in their heart, and they have not known my ways: Unto whom I sware in my wrath that they should not enter into my rest."

God said to these people that didn't believe Him, "because you do not believe me, your carcasses will fall in the wilderness." And so it happened. They went into the wilderness with 603,550 numbered (Numbers 1:46) and left the wilderness with only 601,730 numbered (Numbers 26:51). You would think they would have more people after forty years, but instead they were fewer in number because of God's judgment. Their carcasses of those twenty years old and older fell in the wilderness. They did not enter into the land of Canaan. Only those who were nineteen and younger entered in.

Hebrews 3:10

"Wherefore I was grieved with that generation, and said, They do always err in their heart; and they have not known my ways."

GOD WAS GRIEVED

God was certainly *"grieved with that generation"* because *"they have not known my ways."* That Greek Word for *"grieved"* is PROSOCHTHIZO. Some of the meanings of "grieved" are:

"to be displeased, be wroth with, to be disgusted with, to loathe, to spew out."

God was very displeased with this generation of people that didn't believe Him. The Lord was upset with His people Israel. God is not simply a God of love. With the people that don't agree with Him and His ways, He is **grieved** in His heart and displeased with them.

God said that *"They do always err in their heart."* The Greek Word for **"err"** is PLANAO. Some of the meanings for **"err"** are:

"to cause to stray, to lead astray, lead aside from the right way, to go astray, wander, roam about, and to be led into sin."

That is what God said to these people that didn't agree with Him and didn't believe in Him. They died in the wilderness.

- **Psalm 95:8-11**

"Harden not your heart, as in the provocation, *and as in* the day of temptation in the wilderness: When your fathers tempted me, proved me, and saw my work. Forty years long was I **grieved** with *this* generation, and said, It *is* a people that do err in their heart, and they have not known my ways: Unto whom I sware in my wrath that they should not enter into my rest."

GRIEVING

- **1 Samuel 2:33**

"And the man of thine, *whom* I shall not cut off from mine altar, *shall be* to consume thine eyes, and to **grieve** thine heart: and all the increase of thine house shall die in the flower of their age."

That God was **grieved in His heart** by these people.

- **Psalm 78:40**

"How oft did they provoke him in the wilderness, *and* **grieve** him in the desert!"

- **Ephesians 4:30**
"And **grieve** not the holy Spirit of God, whereby ye are sealed unto the day of redemption."

THE ISRAELITES GRIEVED THE LORD

The disbelief of the Israelites *"grieved"* the Lord because the Lord said *"They do always err in their heart."* The Greek Word for "heart" is KARDIA. It is a very important part of our body. Some of the meanings for "heart" are:

"the seat of the thoughts, passions, desires, appetites, affections, purposes, and endeavours."

To *"err"* in the *"heart"* is very serious.

IMPORTANCE OF THE HEART

- **Psalm 14:1**
"The fool hath said in his **heart**, There is no God. They are corrupt, they have done abominable works, there is none that doeth good." Not *"in his head,"* but *"in his **heart**."* The fool is absolutely and severely grounded in his unbelief. It is one thing to deny God in the head, but much more deadly to deny Him in the "**heart**".

- **Psalm 19:14**
"Let the words of my mouth, and the meditation of my **heart**, be acceptable in thy sight, O LORD, my strength, and my redeemer." The *"meditation of my heart"* is different from meditation of the *"mind."* The *"heart"* is the center core of our being.

- **Psalm 37:4**
"Delight thyself also in the LORD; and he shall give thee the desires of thine **heart**."

THE DESIRES OF THE HEART

The *"desires of thine heart"* are the things that the soul longs for. If we give ourselves to the Lord, and delight in Him, He will answer prayer.

I gave this verse to one of my friends who is now with the Lord. He was a Baptist pastor. I had cancer of the lymph glands at the time. It was called Hodgkins disease. It was at least three decades ago. I asked him to pray for me, in regard to this verse. I told him that I delighted in the Lord. I asked this pastor to pray with me that God would grant the *"desires"* of my heart and remove my cancer. God answered our prayers and took away my cancer.

I asked the Lord to remove my cancer, not for myself, but to serve Him. From that day until the present, that has been my goal and heart's desire--to serve the Lord, acceptably all these years. I am now 86. I am thankful that He answered my prayer for the *"desires of my heart."*

- **Psalm 51:10**

"Create in me a clean **heart**, O God; and renew a right spirit within me."

BEWARE OF A DIRTY HEART

Many of our **hearts** are dirty–dirty with unconfessed sin. Our **hearts** are to be clean, otherwise the whole center part of our being cannot serve the Lord Jesus Christ.

- **Psalm 55:21**

"The words of his mouth were smoother than butter, but war *was* in his **heart**: his words were softer than oil, yet *were* they drawn swords."

This is an analysis of people's **hearts** who are not clean. Do you know any people who have smooth words that are *"smoother than butter"*? When "war was in the **heart**," their words are meaningless. God doesn't look at our words. He looks at our **hearts** that are at *"war"* and like *"drawn swords."*

- **Psalm 119:11**

"Thy word have I hid in mine **heart**, that I might not sin against thee.

HIDE GOD'S WORDS IN THE HEART

That's where to hide the Words of the living God–in our hearts! It is good to have them in our hands, rather than to have them on the table. You can have God's Words into your mind. That's good. But God's will is to get His Words into your *"heart"* that you might not *"sin against Him."*

- **Psalm 139:23**

"Search me, O God, and know my **heart**: try me, and know my thoughts:"

David's prayer was to *"search"* him and to *"know his **heart**."* He also wanted the Lord to *"try"* and test him, and *"know his thoughts."* David wanted his **heart** to be searched, known, and tried. I'm sure he confessed his sin of the murder of Bathsheba's husband. I'm sure he confessed his sin of adultery with Bathsheba. That should be the daily prayer of every genuinely saved and born-again Christian. Are you afraid for God to know your thoughts? Think about it. He knows every one of them. The thought-life is important. As a man *"thinketh in his **heart**, so is he."* (Proverbs 23:7)

- **Proverbs 3:5**

"Trust in the LORD with all thine **heart**; and lean not unto thine own understanding."

TRUST WITH ALL THE HEART
The *"trust"* that the Lord desires is *"with all thine heart."* It is not with the hands, not with the head, but with the *"heart."* It is a trust and confidence in the very center of our beings. Sometimes people want to do things their own way but not the Scriptural way. We ought to say, with Paul: *"Lord, what wilt Thou have me to do?"* (Acts 9:6) We must be willing to go God's way and God's way only--not our own way.

- **Proverbs 4:23**

"Keep thy **heart** with all diligence; for out of it *are* the issues of life."

This is a command to keep and guard the **heart**. It must be that many people do not do this. The Lord tells us that we are take good care of our "**heart**." We are, *"with all diligence"* to keep it, to guard it, to make it pure, and to make it wholesome.

- **Proverbs 15:13**

"A merry **heart** maketh a cheerful countenance: but by sorrow of the **heart** the spirit is broken."

RESULTS OF A MERRY HEART
If the heart on the inside is merry and happy in the Lord, our countenance, our whole facial expression will be happy and cheerful as well.

- **Proverbs 17:22**

"A merry **heart** doeth good *like* a medicine: but a broken spirit drieth the bones."

Doctors have said that the proper condition of the **heart** and mind can sometimes make an unhealthy condition more healthy. A *"merry heart"* is just like a medicine. If our attitude is proper it will do us *"good like a medicine."* A good **heart** attitude, is many times, also used to bring cheer to sick people who are patients.

- **Proverbs 22:15**

"Foolishness *is* bound in the **heart** of a child; *but* the rod of correction shall drive it far from him."

Foolishness is in the **hearts** of children. They have the sinful nature even from birth. The Biblical answer to this is *"the rod of correction."* If Christian parents follow the Scriptural solution to this *"foolishness,"* They might be arrested by our government and put in jail. This is a very sad current development in our country and other countries. In these days, if you correct your children Biblically, you may go to jail.

DISCIPLINE OF CHILDREN

Some governmental agency might come after these parents and consider them cruel to their children. I'm very glad that they didn't have those rules while Mrs. Waite and I were bringing up our four sons and one daughter. Because of our following the Bible's principles with our children, they all turned out being genuinely saved. They love and serve the Lord today for which Mrs. Waite and I are rejoicing. If we had let go of them, so that they could do whatever the world wanted them to do, without Biblical correction, they might be *"foolish"* still. I know families like this where the parents are genuine Christians, but their children have gone astray.

Proverbs 23:26

"My son, give me thine **heart**, and let thine eyes observe my ways." If the Lord has our **heart**, our soul, our inner being, the eyes and all the other members of our body will also follow His ways. The **heart** is so important.

- **Jeremiah 17:9**

"The **heart** *is* deceitful above all *things*, and desperately wicked: who can know it?"

When we were unsaved, we had deceitfulness in our **hearts.** Now that we are redeemed, the **heart** is still the same. But the Lord has given us His Holy Spirit to live within our bodies so that we do not have to yield to our deceitful and wicked **heart.**

SPIRITUAL HEART TROUBLE

That's the problem, with the lost in the world around us. They have this heart trouble. It's not physical heart trouble but heart trouble of the soul, the spirit and their desperately wicked hearts. So, they don't care what God says. They don't care what the Bible teaches. They just do what comes naturally. It is a terrible situation.

- **Mark 7:21-23**

"For from within, out of the heart of men, proceed evil thoughts, adulteries, fornications, murders, Thefts, covetousness, wickedness, deceit, lasciviousness, an evil eye, blasphemy, pride, foolishness: All these evil things come from within, and defile the man."

The Lord Jesus Christ put His hand upon the trouble of the people that are on this earth. He said that all these evil things proceed from "*the heart.*" Many today who preach the social gospel say that the environment is the cause of bad things. They say, "just get a better environment, and things will be all right." This is wrong. The Bible teaches that sin comes from "*the heart*" rather than from the environment. I know of people who came from a bad environment. They had lost and hell-bound moms and dads. But some of their children trust the Lord Jesus Christ. He redeemed them, and they're living for Him. Environment didn't do it. The Lord Jesus Christ and the gospel can speak to the heart. The redeemed and transformed "*heart*" is the most important thing.

CLEANSED HEARTS

Genuine faith in the Lord Jesus Christ can save and redeem the heart, and give you a desire to serve and please Him.

- **John 13:2**

"And supper being ended, the devil having now put into the **heart** of Judas Iscariot, Simon's *son*, to betray him;"

In this verse, notice where the Devil placed the desire of Judas to betray the Lord Jesus Christ. It was in his "**heart**." Judas had a serious **heart** problem. The Devil knew what he was doing to effect the betrayal of the Lord Jesus Christ. He didn't put the idea of betrayal into the hands of Judas and give him something to read. He didn't put the betrayal into his mind. Satan put the betrayal desire down deep in the "**heart**" of Judas. The **heart** is the most important spiritual organ of our body. It is not the physical **heart** the Lord Jesus Christ was speaking about, but the "**heart**" where lies the deepness of our feelings, emotions, and thoughts. The Devil knew that quite well. That's why he chose to put this betrayal into Judas' **heart**.

For this reason, it is very important, as Hebrews 3:8 says: "*Harden not your hearts.*" This applies to saved, born-again Christians as well. We must stop "*hardening*" our **hearts**. God does not want any saved, born-again Christian to make his **heart** hardened against His will and Words.

Hebrews 3:11

"So I sware in my wrath, They shall not enter into my rest."

WRATH

Though the apostates do not believe it, one of the attributes of the God of the Bible is ***"wrath.***" It is necessary because of His attributes of "righteousness and justice" which are at the very center of all the other of His attributes.

This is a picture of God's **wrath**. The liberals, modernists, apostates of today, and the so called emerging church people do not believe in this attribute of God--God's **wrath**. They just say that God is a God of love, and that's it. But, we see in scripture, God is a God of **wrath** against sin. Notice what this verse of Scripture has to say about that. *"They shall not enter into my rest."*

THE REALITY OF THE WRATH OF GOD

The wrath of God is very real. It is part of the character of God. It is one of His attributes. God was talking about these Israelites in the Old Testament. They were not going to enter into the rest of Canaan. These who did not believe the Lord were condemned to die in the wilderness during the forty years of wandering. They had to move over forty different times during these forty years.

It is primarily a picture of the Israelites who were not following the Lord. But it is also a picture of those genuinely saved people today who are not following the Lord. Paul uses the name of *"carnal"* Christians for them:

"And I, brethren, could not speak unto you as unto spiritual, but as unto carnal, even as unto babes in Christ." (1 Corinthians 3:1)

So God could not have them to go into the Canaan rest at all.

As far as the wrath of God being one of His attributes, notice these verses:

- **Numbers 32:10-12**

"And the LORD'S anger was kindled the same time, and he sware, saying, Surely none of the men that came up out of Egypt, from twenty years old and upward, shall see the land which I sware unto Abraham, unto Isaac, and unto Jacob; because they have not wholly followed me: Save Caleb the son of Jephunneh the Kenezite, and Joshua the son of Nun: for they have wholly followed the LORD."

- **John 3:36**
"He that believeth on the Son hath everlasting life: and he that believeth not the Son shall not see life; but the **wrath** of God abideth on him."

> **GOD'S WRATH ON UNBELIEVERS**
>
> It is clear that *"the wrath of God"* abides on those who reject and who do not genuinely receive the Lord Jesus Christ as their Saviour. This *"wrath"* is one of His attributes. This is denied by the apostates, liberals, modernists, and emergent church people.

- **Romans 1:18**
"For the **wrath** of God is revealed from heaven against all ungodliness and unrighteousness of men, who hold the truth in unrighteousness;"

God's **wrath** is real.

- **Romans 5:9**
"Much more then, being now justified by his blood, we shall be saved from **wrath** through him."

> **TRUE CHRISTIANS SAVED FROM WRATH**
>
> I believe that genuinely saved Christians today will be saved both from the *"wrath"* of the Tribulation Period, and also from the *"wrath"* of the Lake of Fire in Hell. Saved people will be raptured to Heaven before that Tribulation Period, and will be spared from the *"wrath"* of everlasting and eternal Hell fire. He saved us from both of those wraths.

- **Romans 13:4**
"For he is the minister of God to thee for good. But if thou do that which is evil, be afraid; for he beareth not the sword in vain: for he is the minister of God, a revenger to *execute* **wrath** upon him that doeth evil."

In this verse, Paul is talking about what is truly "Biblical" government. In order for it to be "Biblical" government, here is a requirement that must be met. If it is not "Biblical" government, Christians do not have to obey it. "Biblical" government "*executes wrath upon him that doeth evil*" based upon the definitions in the Bible of what is "*evil*." If we do that which is good, we'll have the praise of "Biblical" government.

- **Ephesians 5:6**
"Let no man deceive you with vain words: for because of these things cometh the **wrath** of God upon the children of disobedience."

These are those who reject the Lord Jesus Christ as their Saviour. They are called here *"the children of disobedience."*
- **Colossians 3:6**
"For which things' sake the **wrath** of God cometh on the children of disobedience:"

<u>Again, to those who reject the Lord Jesus Christ, God's **wrath** will be upon them</u>. People don't like the Bible many times, because they don't like God's **wrath**. God is angry and wrathful against sin.
- **1 Thessalonians 1:10**
"And to wait for his Son from heaven, whom he raised from the dead, *even* Jesus, which delivered us from the **wrath** to come."

I believe that *"wrath to come"* includes both deliverance from the Tribulation period as well as deliverance from Hell and the Lake of Fire.
- **1 Thessalonians 5:9**
"For God hath not appointed us to **wrath**, but to obtain salvation by our Lord Jesus Christ,"

Again, I believe this refers to both the **(1)** <u>**wrath** of the Tribulation Period</u>, and the **(2)** <u>**wrath** of Hell</u>. He has delivered us from <u>both **wraths**</u>.
- **Revelation 6:16-17**
"And said to the mountains and rocks, Fall on us, and hide us from the face of him that sitteth on the throne, and from the **wrath** of the Lamb: For the great day of his **wrath** is come; and who shall be able to stand?"

THE WRATH OF THE LAMB

When the Lord Jesus Christ came the first time, He was not wrathful or vengeful. He did drive the moneychangers out of the temple, which evidenced His righteousness and judgment against those who had desecrated the house of God. But His main purpose during His first coming to this earth was to *"seek and to save that which was lost"* (Luke 19:10). However, during the Tribulation Period, the unbelievers will observe the *"wrath of the Lamb."*

- **Revelation 19:15**
"And out of his [THE LORD JESUS CHRIST] mouth goeth a sharp sword, that with it he should smite the nations: and he shall rule them with a rod of iron: and he treadeth the winepress of the fierceness and **wrath** of Almighty God."

And so, the Lord Jesus Christ will show His **wrath**, the *"wrath of Almighty God"* the Father. God is a God of **wrath**. Then notice, Hebrews 3:7 says that these unbelievers *"shall not enter into my rest."*

These have disobeyed the Lord and His Words. They will have no "*rest.*" The Lord Jesus Christ will gather all those who are genuinely saved into an eternal Heavenly rest.

REST

- **Matthew 11:28-29**

"Come unto me, all ye that labour and are heavy laden, and I will give you rest. Take my yoke upon you, and learn of me; for I am meek and lowly in heart: and ye shall find **rest** unto your souls."

THE REST OF ETERNAL LIFE

Do you have this rest of eternal life? I hope everyone of you who are reading this book have that rest. It is not the rest of Canaan. This is the rest of Heaven. It is offered by the Lord Jesus Christ to "*all,*" not just a little group of the "elect" that the hyper-Calvinists speak about.

- **Hebrews 3:18-19**

"And to whom sware he that they should not enter into his **rest**, but to them that believed not? So we see that they could not enter in because of unbelief."

I'll get to this aspect a little later on also. So we see that they could not enter in because of unbelief.

- **Revelation 14:11**

"And the smoke of their torment ascendeth up for ever and ever: and they have no **rest** day nor night, who worship the beast and his image, and whosoever receiveth the mark of his name."

"*No* **rest** *day nor night.*" In Hell, the Lake of Fire, there is no **rest**. Saved people have **rest** in Heaven. Praise God for that. But this is not for unbelievers.

- **Revelation 14:13**

"And I heard a voice from heaven saying unto me, Write, Blessed *are* the dead which die in the Lord from henceforth: Yea, saith the Spirit, that they may **rest** from their labours; and their works do follow them."

REST FOR THOSE WHO ARE SAVED

Those who have died in the Lord, have rest and peace. That is a wonderful assurance for those who are genuinely saved. The Greek word for "*rest*" is KATAPAUSIS. Among other things, it means:

"*1) a putting to rest; 1a) calming of the winds; 2) a resting place; 2a) metaph. the heavenly blessedness in which God*

> dwells, and of which he has promised to make persevering believers in Christ partakers after the toils and trials of life on earth are ended"

Hebrews 3:12

"Take heed, brethren, lest there be in any of you an evil heart of unbelief, in departing from the living God."

This is a warning about *"evil hearts"* that hide *"unbelief"* which would cause anyone–even those who are genuine saved Christians–to depart from the true God of the Bible.

I believe he's talking to the genuinely saved brethren, but <u>some of them are *"carnal,"* walking after the flesh. Some are spiritual and are walking after the Spirit</u>. Paul is saying to these brethren, that are saved, just like the Israelites of old, some followed the Lord and some didn't follow the Lord. He tells these brethren to *"take heed"* lest there be in any of them, *"an evil heart of unbelief, in departing from the living God."*

THE JUDGMENT SEAT OF CHRIST

There's going to be a judgment seat of Christ for genuinely saved Christians. At that judgment seat of Christ, the Lord Jesus Christ will judge all saved born-again Christians. It will depend on what kind of materials that Christian built upon Christ the Foundation. If he or she builds gold, silver, and precious stones, a reward will be given. If, on the other hand, he or she builds with hay, wood, and stubble, their works will be burned up. They will be *"saved; yet so as by fire."* If its on wood, hay and stubble, our works will be burned up. We've got to walk with the Lord Jesus Christ, take heed to God's Words, and be strongly committed to Him.

TAKE HEED

- **1 Corinthians 3:10**

"According to the grace of God which is given unto me, as a wise masterbuilder, I have laid the foundation, and another buildeth thereon. But let every man **take heed** how he buildeth thereupon."

- **1 Corinthians 10:12**

"Wherefore let him that thinketh he standeth **take heed** lest he fall."

- **1 Timothy 4:16**

"**Take heed** unto thyself, and unto the doctrine; continue in them: for in doing this thou shalt both save thyself, and them that hear thee."

> ### HEED BOTH SELF AND DOCTRINE
>
> "*Self*" and "*doctrine.*" Both of these are important. Pastors must have <u>a godly life</u>, as well as <u>proper doctrine</u>. "For in so doing this thou shalt both save thyself, and them that hear thee."

- **Jeremiah 7:24**

"But they hearkened not, nor inclined their ear, but walked in the counsels and in the imagination of their evil heart, and went backward, and not forward."

May saved people not walk backwards, as some have done.

- **Jeremiah 17:9-10**

"The heart is deceitful above all *things*, and desperately wicked: who can know it? I the LORD search the heart, *I* try the reins, even to give every man according to his ways, *and* according to the fruit of his doings."

DEPARTING

- **Daniel 9:5**

"We have sinned, and have committed iniquity, and have done wickedly, and have rebelled, even by **departing** from thy precepts and from thy judgments:"

Daniel confessed that his sin was unto the Lord at that time. That word for "***depart***" is APHISTEMI. It is important that none of us should "***depart***" from the truths of God's Words. Here are some of the meanings of this Word:

> "*1) to make stand off, cause to withdraw, to remove; 1a) to excite to revolt; 2) to stand off, to stand aloof; 2a) to go away, to depart from anyone; 2b) to desert, withdraw from one; 2c) to fall away, become faithless; 2d) to shun, flee from; 2e) to cease to vex one; 2f) to withdraw one's self from, to fall away; 2g) to keep one's self from, absent one's self from.*"

Hebrews 3:13

"But exhort one another daily, while it is called To day; lest any of you be hardened through the deceitfulness of sin."

EXHORT & EXHORTATION

THE NEED FOR PROPER EXHORTATION

It is important for born-again Christians to Scripturally *"exhort"* one another to glorify our Saviour. This is the command of God to those who are saved. *"Exhort"* is in the present tense. It implies continuous action. We are to <u>exhort continually</u>, that is, <u>we are to comfort and to take care of people</u>.

What are the qualifications to be able to *"exhort"*? He is talking to Christian believers. <u>To **exhort** biblically, a Christian must know the Bible</u>. We are to do this *"daily."* Don't wait until tomorrow. Believers need **exhortation**, they need comfort, they need encouragement. That's what this word means. We're to do this continuously, day by day.

DAILY EXHORTATION NEEDED

Why are we to do this *"daily"*? What's the purpose of exhorting one another *"daily"*? The answer is given in this verse: *"lest any of you be hardened through the deceitfulness of sin."* <u>Saved people are in danger of being hardened to sin. They can backslide. I believe that is what Paul is talking about.</u>

- Acts 14:22

"Confirming the souls of the disciples, and **exhorting** them to continue in the faith, and that we must through much tribulation enter into the kingdom of God."

That's what we must do if we are **exhorting** other believers. <u>We want them to *"continue in the faith"* of the Scriptures</u>.

- Romans 12:8

"Or he that **exhorteth**, on **exhortation**: he that giveth, *let him do it* with simplicity; he that ruleth, with diligence; he that sheweth mercy, with cheerfulness."

Paul is listing various gifts that God has given to various Christians. One gift is the gift of *"exhortation."* It should be done *"with simplicity."*

- 1 Timothy 4:13

"Till I come, give attendance to reading, to **exhortation**, to doctrine."

Paul is telling Pastor Timothy, working in a church at Ephesus, that one of things he is to give *"attendance to"* is *"to **exhortation**."* It is an important pastoral duty.
- **2 Timothy 4:2**
"Preach the word; be instant in season, out of season; reprove, rebuke, **exhort** with all longsuffering and doctrine."

Part of the preachers' duties are not only to *"rebuke"* and *"reprove,"* but also *"to **exhort**"* or encourage. This is not be done with someone's own ideas, but with *"doctrine,"* that is the teaching of the Words of God.
- **Titus 1:9**
"Holding fast the faithful word as he hath been taught, that he may be able by sound doctrine both to **exhort** and to convince the gainsayers."
- **Titus 2:15**
"These things speak, and **exhort**, and rebuke with all authority. Let no man despise thee."

I'm afraid when you start rebuking, despising comes. When you **exhort** people, they usually aren't as angry with you.
- **Hebrews 10:25**
"Not forsaking the assembling of ourselves together, as the manner of some is; but **exhorting** one another: and so much the more, as ye see the day approaching."

THE EXHORTING COMMAND
"Exhorting one another" is a command of Scripture.

- **Jude 1:3**
"Beloved, when I gave all diligence to write unto you of the common salvation, it was needful for me to write unto you, and **exhort** you that ye should earnestly contend for the faith which was once delivered unto the saints."

That's what we seek to do here at Bible For Today Baptist Church. We seek to *"earnestly contend for the faith,"* the body of doctrine and Scripture, which was *"once delivered unto the saints."*

HARDENED HEARTS & MINDS (cf. 15)
It is very easy to have our hearts *"hardened"* through the temptations that are found in this wicked world. We must be careful about this. In the book of Luke, we are reminded of the two on the road to Emmaus after the Lord's bodily resurrection. The Lord Jesus Christ met them and opened up all the Scriptures of the Old Testament. He spoke of the things concerning Himself from all the parts of the Old Testament. They remarked that their **hearts** *"burned within them"*

while He opened up to them the Scriptures. Our **hearts** should burn within us, as the Scriptures are opened up. We should not **harden our hearts or minds** as many in the following verses did.

- **Exodus 8:15**

"But when Pharaoh saw that there was respite, he **hardened his heart,** and hearkened not unto them; as the LORD had said."

- **1 Samuel 6:6**

"Wherefore then do ye **harden your hearts**, as the Egyptians and Pharaoh **hardened their hearts?** when he had wrought wonderfully among them, did they not let the people go, and they departed?"

- **2 Chronicles 36:13**

"And he [Zedekiah] also rebelled against king Nebuchadnezzar, who had made him swear by God: but he stiffened his neck, and **hardened his heart** from turning unto the LORD God of Israel."

- **Daniel 5:20**

"But when his [Nebuchadnezzar's] heart was lifted up, and **his mind hardened in pride**, he was deposed from his kingly throne, and they took his glory from him:"

- **Acts 19:9**

"But when divers were **hardened**, and believed not, but spake evil of that way before the multitude, he departed from them, and separated the disciples, disputing daily in the school of one Tyrannus."

THE PLEASANTNESS OF SIN

Sin looks so pleasant, so wonderful, if you look at it from the outside, but it is deceitful, it is desperately wicked.

DECEIT AND DECEITFULNESS

Deceit and deceitfulness are very serious defects in a person. This leads into all kinds of wickedness, corruption, and sin if not dealt with clearly.

- **Matthew 13:22**

"He also that received seed among the thorns is he that heareth the word; and the care of this world, and the **deceitfulness** of riches, choke the word, and he becometh unfruitful."

This is on unclaimed ground, the thorny ground, which is likened unto "*the deceitfulness of riches.*"

- **Proverbs 26:24-26**

"He that hateth dissembleth with his lips, and layeth up **deceit** within him; When he speaketh fair, believe him not: for *there are* seven abominations in his heart. *Whose* hatred is covered by **deceit**, his wickedness shall be shewed before the *whole* congregation."

- **Jeremiah 17:9**

"The heart is **deceitful** above all *things*, and desperately wicked: who can know it?"

- **Mark 7:21-23**

"For from within, out of the heart of men, proceed evil thoughts, adulteries, fornications, murders, Thefts, covetousness, wickedness, **deceit**, lasciviousness, an evil eye, blasphemy, pride, foolishness: All these evil things come from within, and defile the man."

DECEIT OUT OF THE HEART

One of the things that proceeds out of the heart is *"deceit,"* which is saying one thing and meaning something else. It is talking one way and meaning another way. It is smiling with your mouth, but having in you hatred, bitterness, deception, and deceitfulness.

OBAMA A GREAT DECEIVER AND LIAR

President Obama showed himself as a great deceiver and liar when he promised our nation that people could keep their health plan and their doctors under Obamacare. He promised that families could save $2,500 each year under this plan. All of these promises have proved to be total lies and deceptions. Deceitfulness is a terrible thing. It is wickedness that comes out of the heart of man. These are things that the Scriptures are clear about.

- **Colossians 2:8**

"Beware lest any man spoil you through philosophy and vain **deceit**, after the tradition of men, after the rudiments of the world, and not after Christ."

Hebrews 3:14

"For we are made partakers of Christ, if we hold the beginning of our confidence stedfast unto the end;"

PARTAKERS

I believe we who are genuinely saved are *"partakers of Christ."* The Lord Jesus Christ told His disciples: *"Abide in me."* There are Christians that *"abide"* in Christ and those who don't *"abide"* in Christ. I believe this is one of the examples. We who are saved are *"made partakers"* of all that Christ is, *"if we hold the beginning of our confidence, stedfast until the end."*

STEDFAST CHRISTIANS

I believe these are Christians that are stedfast and spiritual Christians who follow the Lord Jesus Christ all the way He leads them. Those are the Christians I believe Paul is talking about.

The Greek Word for *"partaker"* is METOCHOS. Some of the meanings of this Word are:

> "sharing in, partaking. a partner (in a work, office, dignity)."

- **2 Corinthians 1:6**

And whether we be afflicted, *it is* for your consolation and salvation, which is effectual in the enduring of the same sufferings which we also suffer: or whether we be comforted, it is for your consolation and salvation. And our hope of you is stedfast, knowing, that as ye are **partakers** of the sufferings, so *shall ye be also* of the consolation."

We have sufferings, but we are **partakers** of hope.

- **Colossians 1:12**

"Giving thanks unto the Father, which hath made us meet to be **partakers** of the inheritance of the saints in light:"

- **2 Timothy 1:8**

"Be not thou therefore ashamed of the testimony of our Lord, nor of me his prisoner: but be thou **partaker** of the afflictions of the gospel according to the power of God; "

Paul told Timothy, the pastor there at Ephesus, to be a *"partaker of the afflictions"* when the gospel is preached. There are not only blessings in the preaching, but, when you are faithful to the Lord, there will also be afflictions.

- **Hebrews 12:10**

"For they verily for a few days chastened *us* after their own pleasure; but he for *our* profit, that *we* might be **partakers** of his holiness."

That's why God chastens the genuine born-again Christians. It is in order that they might be a *"partaker of his holiness."*

- **1 Peter 4:13**

"But rejoice, inasmuch as ye are **partakers** of Christ's sufferings; that, when his glory shall be revealed, ye may be glad also with exceeding joy."

Partakers of *"sufferings,"* as well as **partakers** of *"joy."*

- **1 Peter 5:1**

"The elders which are among you I exhort, who am also an elder, and a witness of the sufferings of Christ, and also a **partaker** of the glory that shall be revealed:"

Peter saw the *"sufferings of Christ,"* but was *"also a **partaker** of the glory that shall be revealed."*

CONFIDENCE

The Greek Word for *"confidence"* that is used here is HUPOSTASIS. Some of the meanings for this Word are:

> "1) *a setting or placing under; 1a) thing put under, substructure, foundation; 2) that which has foundation, is firm; 2a) that which has actual existence; 2a1) a substance, real being; 2b) the substantial quality, nature, of a person or thing; 2c) the steadfastness of mind, firmness, courage, resolution; 2c1) confidence, firm trust, assurance"*

- **Psalm 118:8-9**

"It is better to trust in the LORD than to put **confidence** in man. *It is* better to trust in the LORD than to put **confidence** in princes."

The LORD will never let us down. Leaders will let us down and many times they do.

- **Proverbs 25:19**

"**Confidence** in an unfaithful man in time of trouble *is like* a broken tooth, and a foot out of joint."

OUT OF JOINT FEET AND BROKEN TEETH

If your going to step on a foot that is *"out of joint,"* you're going to fall. A broken tooth won't help you when you are chewing your food.

- **Ephesians 3:11-12**
"According to the eternal purpose which he purposed in Christ Jesus our Lord: In whom we have boldness and access with **confidence** by the faith of him."

Everyone who is genuinely saved has *access*" to the Father. This is a wonderful truth.

- **Philippians 3:3**
"For we are the circumcision, which worship God in the spirit, and rejoice in Christ Jesus, and have no **confidence** in the flesh."

NO CONFIDENCE IN THE FLESH

There should be no confidence in our flesh. I don't care whether it is men's flesh, women's flesh, boy's flesh, girl's flesh, or little baby's flesh-- we should have no confidence in it whatsoever. Whether that flesh is educated or uneducated, whether it is beautiful or ugly, whether it is old or young, whether it is tall or short, we must have no confidence in it. Our confidence must be in the Bible and the Holy Spirit and Our Lord and Saviour.

- **1 John 2:28**
"And now, little children, abide in him; that, when he shall appear, we may have **confidence**, and not be ashamed before him at his coming."

NOT ASHAMED AT HIS COMING

In order *"not to be ashamed before Him at his coming,"* and have *"confidence,"* we must walk with the Lord Jesus Christ day by day. We never know when He's going to return to take the saved to Heaven before the Tribulation Period. When He comes, we ought not be ashamed before Him by what we're saying, thinking, doing, or where we are.

STEDFAST

The Greek Word used here for "*stedfast*" is BEBAIOS. Some of the meanings this Word are:

"*1) stable, fast, firm; 2) metaphor--sure, trusty*"

- **Daniel 6:26**
"I make a decree, That in every dominion of my kingdom men tremble and fear before the God of Daniel: for he *is* the living God, and **stedfast** for ever, and his kingdom *that* which shall not be destroyed, and his dominion *shall be even* unto the end."

> **OUR GOD IS STEDFAST**
>
> Isn't it wonderful that our God will not move! He will not change. He will not drift. He is stedfast, permanent and firm fixed forever. This is not just in this year, but it will go on. He is stedfast.

- **1 Corinthians 15:58**

"Therefore, my beloved brethren, be ye **stedfast**, unmoveable, always abounding in the work of the Lord, forasmuch as ye know that your labour is not in vain in the Lord."

Saved Christians must always be **stedfast** in the Lord Jesus Christ.

- **Hebrews 6:18-20**

"That by two immutable things, in which it was impossible for God to lie, we might have a strong consolation, who have fled for refuge to lay hold upon the hope set before us: Which *hope* we have as an anchor of the soul, both sure and **stedfast**, and which entereth into that within the veil; Whither the forerunner is for us entered, *even* Jesus, made an high priest for ever after the order of Melchisedec."

> **ENTRANCE INTO GOD'S PRESENCE**
>
> Genuinely saved Christians have an entrance into God our Father's very presence through the Lord Jesus Christ.

- **1 Peter 5:8-9**

"Be sober, be vigilant; because your adversary the devil, as a roaring lion, walketh about, seeking whom he may devour: Whom resist **stedfast** in the faith, knowing that the same afflictions are accomplished in your brethren that are in the world."

Christians must be "***stedfast*** *in the faith.*" I believe that is what Paul is saying here. We are to be **stedfast** rather than moving around and changing our Biblical convictions. This can come through the deceitfulness of sin. Our **stedfastness** must be permanent, with confidence in the Lord Jesus Christ until the end.

Hebrews 3:15

"While it is said, To day if ye will hear his voice, harden not your hearts, as in the provocation."

HARDENING HEART AND MIND (as in v 13)

The Greek Word in this verse for "**harden**" is SKLERUNO. Some of the meanings for this Word are:

"1) to make hard, harden; 2) metaphorical: 2a) to render obstinate, stubborn; 2b) to be hardened; 2c) to become obstinate or stubborn"

This word is in the present tense in Greek. Since it is a prohibition in the present tense, it means to stop an action already in progress. Those to whom Paul was writing were *"hardening"* their hearts. Paul told them to "stop it!"

THE BIBLE-GOD'S VOICE TODAY

"To day, if ye will hear his voice." How are you going to hear His voice today except through the Bible? The Bible is the only source where God's voice can get through to us. But it must be the right Bible. In English, it is the King James Bible because it is an accurate translation from the inspired, preserved Hebrew, Aramaic. and Greek that underlies it. We must hear God's voice every day of our lives and ask the Lord how we can follow what He has given us and how can we be obedient to it. We must stop hardening our hearts as Israel did in the wilderness when they provoked the Lord continually.

- **Exodus 8:15**

"But when Pharaoh saw that there was respite, he **hardened his heart,** and hearkened not unto them; as the LORD had said."

- **1 Samuel 6:6**

"Wherefore then do ye **harden your hearts**, as the Egyptians and Pharaoh hardened their hearts? when he had wrought wonderfully among them, did they not let the people go, and they departed?"

- **2 Chronicles 36:13**

"And he [Zedekiah] also rebelled against king Nebuchadnezzar, who had made him swear by God: but he stiffened his neck, and **hardened his heart** from turning unto the LORD God of Israel."

- **Daniel 5:20**

"But when his [Nebuchadnezzar's] heart was lifted up, and **his mind hardened** in pride, he was deposed from his kingly throne, and they took his glory from him:"

- **Acts 19:9**

"But when divers were **hardened**, and believed not, but spake evil of that way before the multitude, he departed from them, and separated the disciples, disputing daily in the school of one Tyrannus".

PROVOKE OR PROVOCATION

The Greek Word in this verse for *"provocation"* is PARAPIKRAINO. Some of the meanings for this Word are:

1) *to provoke, exasperate;* 2) *to rouse to indignation;*

The root of this Greek Word is PIKRAINO. Some of the meanings for this Word are:

"1) *to make bitter; 1a) to produce a bitter taste in the stomach; 2) to embitter. exasperate; 2a) render angry, indignant; 2b) to be embittered, irritated; 2c) to visit with bitterness, to grieve (deal bitterly with)."*

The root of that word is PIKROS. It has the idea of "piercing." Some of the resultant meanings for it are:

"1) *bitter;* 2) *metaphor harsh, virulent"*

- **1 Kings 15:30**

"Because of the sins of Jeroboam which he sinned, and which he made Israel sin, by his **provocation** wherewith he **provoked** the LORD God of Israel to anger."

So Jeroboam also **provoked** the Lord. It was not only the Israelites in the Old Testament during the forty years in the wilderness who **provoked** the Lord, but other people **provoked** the Lord as well.

- **2 Kings 22:17**

"Because they have forsaken me, and have burned incense unto other gods, that they might **provoke** me to anger with all the works of their hands; therefore my wrath shall be kindled against this place, and shall not be quenched."

The sinful Israelites **provoked** the Lord to anger. They caused the Lord to be angry with them.

- **Psalm 95:8-11**

"Harden not your heart, as in the **provocation**, *and as in* the day of temptation in the wilderness: When your fathers tempted me, proved me, and saw my work. Forty years long was I grieved with *this* generation, and said, It *is* a people that do err in their heart, and they have not known my ways: Unto whom I sware in my wrath that they should not enter into my rest."

ISRAEL'S HEART-ERRING

It's a terrible thing for the Israelites to "err in their heart." What a disappointment to the Lord were the Israelites who were 20 years old and upward. Only the nineteen year olds and below entered into the land of Canaan. But the 20 year olds and older did not enter. This is a sad thing, indeed.

- **Psalm 78:40-42**

"How oft did they **provoke** him in the wilderness, *and* grieve him in the desert! Yea, they turned back and tempted God, and limited the Holy One of Israel. They remembered not his hand, *nor* the day when he delivered them from the enemy."

We today should not *"tempt"* or test the Lord. <u>This might make Him bitter against us, and might make us to be bitter against Him</u>.

Hebrews 3:16

"For some, when they had heard, did provoke: howbeit not all that came out of Egypt by Moses."

PROVOKING THE LORD

Some provoked the Lord and made Him angry against them. So he told them they would not enter into the land of Canaan, the Promised Land.

- **Numbers 26:63-65**

"These *are* they that were numbered by Moses and Eleazar the priest, who numbered the children of Israel in the plains of Moab by Jordan *near* Jericho. But among these there was not a man of them whom Moses and Aaron the priest numbered, when they numbered the children of Israel in the wilderness of Sinai. For the LORD had said of them, They shall surely die in the wilderness. And there was not left a man of them, save Caleb the son of Jephunneh, and Joshua the son of Nun."

<u>They were decimated by their sin because they did not believe in the Lord</u>. Their numbers were decreased. You would think after forty years they would multiply, no, because God took all those who were 20 years old and upward and slew them. Their carcasses fell in the wilderness and they were left, when they numbered them. There wasn't a single person left. "For the LORD had said of them, They shall surely die in the wilderness. And there was not left a man of them, save Caleb the son of Jephunneh, and Joshua the son of Nun." (Numbers 26:65)

There were only two that believed God. They reported that it as possible to slay the giants in Canaan. They gave a good report.

Hebrews 3:17

"But with whom was he grieved forty years? *was it* not with them that had sinned, whose carcases fell in the wilderness?"

WHY WAS GOD GRIEVED & WITH WHOM?

Those who obeyed the Lord were not a **grief** to Him. He was **grieved** over those who disbelieved with those who said let's not go to Canaan and go back to Egypt. He was grieved with those who did not want to follow Moses, and with those who demanded meat, and didn't like God's provision of water and manna in the wilderness. They wanted meat, but when God gave them their request, they acted in such a way that He had to slay many of them. As it says in Psalm 106:15,

"*And he gave them their request; but sent leanness into their soul.*"

That was a terrible thing.

LEANNESS TO OUR SOULS
We must be careful what we request of the Lord. Sometimes God gives us our request, but sends leanness to our soul.

- **Numbers 14:26-35**

"And the LORD spake unto Moses and unto Aaron, saying, How long *shall I bear with* this evil congregation, which murmur against me? I have heard the murmurings of the children of Israel, which they murmur against me. Say unto them, *As truly as* I live, saith the LORD, as ye have spoken in mine ears, so will I do to you: Your carcases shall fall in this wilderness; and all that were numbered of you, according to your whole number, from twenty years old and upward, which have murmured against me, Doubtless ye shall not come into the land, concerning which I sware to make you dwell therein, save Caleb the son of Jephunneh, and Joshua the son of Nun.

But your little ones, which ye said should be a prey, them will I bring in, and they shall know the land which ye have despised. But *as for* you, your carcases, they shall fall in this wilderness. And your children shall wander in the wilderness forty years, and bear your whoredoms, until your carcases be wasted in the wilderness. After the number of the days in which ye searched the land, *even* forty days, each day for a year, shall ye bear your iniquities, even forty years, and ye shall know my breach of promise. I the LORD have said, I will surely do it unto all this evil congregation, that are gathered together against me: in this wilderness they shall be consumed, and there they shall die."

ORPHANS IN THE WILDERNESS

Just think of how the children felt when their mothers and fathers died and they were left orphans in that wilderness! Yet God had to deal with the sinful ways of those who were 20 years old and above. He promised them that they would die in the wilderness. And He kept His promise.

Hebrews 3:18-19

And to whom sware he that they should not enter into his rest, but to them that believed not?

TRUST IN THE LORD

Trust in the Lord is important. When He says He will do something, He will do it. We must trust Him. It's not necessary for us always to understand what God says, but we must always believe what God says. If God says it, we must believe it. Those are the ones who did not enter into the rest of Canaan, those who did not believe what the Lord had said to them.

BELIEVED NOT THE LORD

- Psalm 78:19-22

"Yea, they spake against God; they said, Can God furnish a table in the wilderness? Behold, he smote the rock, that the waters gushed out, and the streams overflowed; can he give bread also? can he provide flesh for his people? Therefore the LORD heard *this*, and was wroth: so a fire was kindled against Jacob, and anger also came up against Israel; Because they **believed not in God**, and trusted not in his salvation:"

DISBELIEF IN THE LORD

They couldn't believe that the Lord could put manna in the wilderness. Would you be able to provide for two or three million people for forty years? No! Nor could all of the MacDonald's in the world, nor could all the other places in the world do what God did for the Israelites in the wilderness.

The manna from heaven was miraculous. Yet the same people, who saw the manna come down from Heaven six days a week for forty years asked: *"Can God furnish a table in the wilderness?"* God not only gave them bread, but also provided for them water. Later, He even gave them flesh to eat.

- **Psalm 106:24**

"Yea, they despised the pleasant land, they **believed not his word:**"

- **2 Thessalonians 2:10-12**

"And with all deceivableness of unrighteousness in them that perish; because they received not the love of the truth, that they might be saved. And for this cause God shall send them strong delusion, that they should **believe a lie**: That they all might be damned who **believed not the truth**, but had pleasure in unrighteousness."

Those who have not received Christ before the Rapture of the saved Christians, many believe (and it might be true) that they will not receive Him during the Tribulation period. Their hearts will be hardened and blinded by *"strong delusion, that they should **believe a lie**."*

BELIEVING NOT, UNBELIEF

- **Jude 1:5**

"I will therefore put you in remembrance, though ye once knew this, how that the Lord, having saved the people out of the land of Egypt, afterward destroyed them that **believed not.**"

So we see that they could not enter in because of **unbelief.**

ISRAEL'S UNBELIEVERS

The ones who came out of Egypt that God destroyed were unbelievers who did not trust in the Lord. The only thing that will keep a person out of Heaven, is unbelief in the Lord Jesus Christ.

- **Mark 16:11-14**

"And they, when they had heard that he was alive, and had been seen of her [MARY MAGDALENE], **believed not.** After that he appeared in another form unto two of them, as they walked, and went into the country. And they went and told it unto the residue: **neither believed** they them. Afterward he appeared unto the eleven as they sat at meat, and upbraided them with their **unbelief** and hardness of heart, because they **believed not** them which had seen him after he was risen."

THE DISCIPLES' UNBELIEF

The disciples didn't believe the Lord Jesus Christ either. They did not believe in His bodily resurrection. Before His death at Calvary, the Lord Jesus Christ predicted His bodily resurrection at least three different times, in Matthew, Mark, and Luke.

In Matthew 20:18-19, the Lord Jesus Christ said:

> "Behold, we go up to Jerusalem; and the Son of man shall be betrayed unto the chief priests and unto the scribes, and they shall condemn him to death, And shall deliver him to the Gentiles to mock, and to scourge, and to crucify *him*: and the third day he shall rise again."

The disciples **didn't believe** Him. After the Lord's bodily resurrection, Peter said "*I go a fishing*" (John 21:3). He was going back to his former occupation. Peter took six other disciples with him to go fishing. These disciples **didn't believe** the witnesses who told them of Christ's bodily resurrection. Peter himself only saw the empty tomb and apparently he **didn't believe** that the Saviour was risen bodily either.

This verse in Mark 16:14 also shows that the "*eleven*" disciples **did not believe** the witnesses to His bodily resurrection. He "*upbraided*" or scolded them because of "*their* **unbelief** *and hardness of heart.*" Unbelief is a terrible thing.

GOD'S MARVELOUS CREATION

There are many things in the Bible we don't understand. Perhaps the bodily resurrection of the Lord Jesus Christ is one of those things. Science has not backed it up. But science, in fact, has denied many things that we are taught in Scripture. We must believe the Bible that God has given to us. He knows the end from the beginning. Has science put the billions and billions of stars into the heavens? No. Could science create Adam and Eve and all the fish, birds, and animals in the world? No, it can't. All science (and those who agree with science) can do is fight with God, fight against His Words, and talk against His creation.

- John 3:18

"He that believeth on him is not condemned: but he that **believeth not** is condemned already, because he hath **not believed** in the name of the only begotten Son of God."

That's what sends a person to Hell—**not believing**, not trusting, not really, genuinely accepting the Lord Jesus Christ as their Saviour. Those who **believe not** are *"condemned already."*

- **John 3:36**
"He that believeth on the Son hath everlasting life: and he that **believeth not** the Son shall not see life; but the wrath of God abideth on him."

In both of these verses above, God places the results of being *"condemned already"* and having *"the wrath of God"* abiding on the person whether or not he or she genuinely *"believes"* on the Lord Jesus Christ, the Son of God. This implies that every person has the ability to believe or **not believe**. People are not *"condemned"* because they aren't one of the Hyper-Calvinist's *"elect,"* or because it was impossible for them to *"believe."* But because as being non-elect, the Lord Jesus Christ did not die for them. No. Not at all. God places the entire responsibility of whether or not a person has *"everlasting life"* upon the person's either genuinely believing or **not believing** in the Lord Jesus Christ for salvation.

THE BIBLE'S HEAVEN

The only way we know about Heaven is from the Scriptures. That is the only place we know the way to the Bible's Heaven. There are many false "Heavens" that are not Biblical such as those of the American Indians, the Hindus, the Buddhists, the Roman Catholics, the Muslims, and many other false religions. No one on this earth can go to the Bible's Heaven unless they go there in the Bible's way.

The Lord Jesus Christ told His disciples and all of us in John 14:6:
"Jesus saith unto him, I am the way, the truth, and the life: no man cometh unto the Father, but by me."

THE WAY TO HEAVEN

That's the only Bible way to get to the Bible's Heaven. I plead with you who are reading this to be sure that you are on the Bible's Way to the Bible's Heaven by genuinely accepting and trusting in the Lord Jesus Christ as your Saviour.

- **Hebrews 3:11-19**
"So I sware in my wrath, They shall not enter into my rest.) Take heed, brethren, lest there be in any of you an evil heart of unbelief, in departing from the living God. But exhort one another daily, while it is called To day; lest any of you be hardened through the

deceitfulness of sin. For we are made partakers of Christ, if we hold the beginning of our confidence stedfast unto the end; While it is said, To day if ye will hear his voice, harden not your hearts, as in the provocation. For some, when they had heard, did provoke: howbeit not all that came out of Egypt by Moses. But with whom was he grieved forty years? *was it* not with them that had sinned, whose carcases fell in the wilderness? And to whom sware he that they should not enter into his rest, but to them that believed not? So we see that they could not enter in because of **unbelief.**"

Hebrews Chapter Four

Hebrews 4:1

"Let us therefore fear, lest, a promise being left *us* of entering into his rest, any of you should seem to come short of it."

REST

> **NO REST BECAUSE OF UNBELIEF**
>
> This verse talks about *"rest."* The Israelites could not enter into Canaan rest because of unbelief. Paul says those to whom he is writing, including saved people today that we should also "fear" lest we would come short of His *"rest."*

The Greek Word used here for "rest" is KATAPAUSIS. Some of the meanings for this Word are:

> *"1) a putting to rest 1a) calming of the winds 2) a resting place; 2a) metaph. the heavenly blessedness in which God dwells, and of which he has promised to make persevering believers in Christ partakers after the toils and trials of life on earth are ended."*

I believe in the Scriptures there are **three different rests**. There are two **rests** that are on earth and there is one in Heaven, a Heavenly **rest**. The two on this earth were spoken of the Lord Jesus Christ.

1. The **first rest** is the **rest of salvation**.
   "Come unto me, all ye that labour and are heavy laden, and I will give you **rest**." (Matthew 11:28)
2. The **second rest** is the **rest of sanctification**.
   "Take my yoke upon you, and learn of me; for I am meek and lowly in heart: and ye shall find **rest** unto your souls." (Matthew 11:29)

That **rest** is found when the genuinely saved Christian is walking with the Lord moment by moment.

3. **The third rest** is the **Heavenly rest** of all saved people
"And I heard a voice from heaven saying unto me, Write, Blessed *are* the dead which die in the Lord from henceforth: yea, saith the Spirit, that they may **rest** from their labours; and their works do follow them." (Revelation 14:13)

THE REST OF SALVATION

Those of us who are genuinely saved, are in the first rest, the rest of salvation. But saved people, if they are walking after the flesh, are not in the second rest, the rest of sanctification. They are carnal Christians.

"For ye are yet carnal: for whereas *there* is among you envying, and strife, and divisions, are ye not carnal, and walk as men?" (1 Corinthians 3:3)

These are not spiritual Christians, but they are walking after the flesh rather than after God the Holy Spirit. They do not have the **rest of sanctification** that God would want them to have. They are falling "*short*."

COMING SHORT

- Romans 3:23

"For all have sinned, and **come short** of the glory of God;"

COMING SHORT OF GOD'S GLORY

Because of being humans with a sinful nature, we come "*short of the glory of God.*" Because of this, we all fall short of walking with the Lord. After we are genuinely saved, we should walk in fellowship with the Lord Jesus Christ in the power of the Holy Spirit.

Hebrews 4:2

"**For unto us was the gospel preached, as well as unto them: but the word preached did not profit them, not being mixed with faith in them that heard *it*.**"

"GOSPEL" OR GOOD NEWS

For the Israelites of old who wandered in the wilderness for forty years, the "*gospel*" or good news was they were going to Canaan. In fact, as soon as they got out of Egypt, they should have gone right to Canaan immediately, but they refused. They sent out twelve spies to survey Canaan. Ten said they couldn't go in, two said they could go in.

Because of this failure to enter when God wanted them to enter, they were condemned to wander for forty years. The **"*gospel*"** or **good news** was preached and available to the Israelites, but they didn't accept it. They didn't enter into Canaan. It didn't profit them because it wasn't mixed with faith.

TWO KINDS OF ISRAELITES
The Israelites were of two kinds, those who had faith in the Lord to do it, those who didn't have any faith, so they did not enter in. Even in the wilderness, there was no faith with most of the people.

NO FAITH IN SOME IN THE WILDERNESS
- **Deuteronomy 32:9-20**

"For the LORD'S portion *is* his people; Jacob *is* the lot of his inheritance. He found him in a desert land, and in the waste howling wilderness; he led him about, he instructed him, he kept him as the apple of his eye. As an eagle stirreth up her nest, fluttereth over her young, spreadeth abroad her wings, taketh them, beareth them on her wings: *So* the LORD alone did lead him, and *there was* no strange god with him. He made him ride on the high places of the earth, that he might eat the increase of the fields; and he made him to suck honey out of the rock, and oil out of the flinty rock; Butter of kine, and milk of sheep, with fat of lambs, and rams of the breed of Bashan, and goats, with the fat of kidneys of wheat; and thou didst drink the pure blood of the grape.

But Jeshurun waxed fat, and kicked: thou art waxen fat, thou art grown thick, thou art covered *with fatness*; then he forsook God *which* made him, and lightly esteemed the Rock of his salvation. They provoked him to jealousy with strange *gods*, with abominations provoked they him to anger. They sacrificed unto devils, not to God; to gods whom they knew not, to new *gods that* came newly up, whom your fathers feared not. Of the Rock *that* begat thee thou art unmindful, and hast forgotten God that formed thee. And when the LORD saw *it*, he abhorred *them*, because of the provoking of his sons, and of his daughters. And he said, I will hide my face from them, I will see what their end *shall be*: for they *are* a very froward generation, children in whom *is* **no faith.**"

What a wonderful blessing God gave to his people, Israel. He kept them in the wilderness for forty years. Finally Moses had faith, though he didn't have it at the beginning. God said He wanted him to take His people, Israel, out of Egypt. Moses objected, but finally Moses obeyed and led Israel out of Egypt. But they had *"no faith."*

GENUINE FAITH NECESSARY FOR SALVATION

THE REST OF ETERNAL LIFE

Faith is necessary for salvation and the *"rest"* of eternal life. That is the first type of rest, that genuinely saved people can have. Genuine faith in the Lord Jesus Christ as Saviour is necessary to bring the *"rest"* of salvation.

- **Acts 15:9**

"And put no difference between us and them, purifying their hearts by **faith.**"

Only by **genuine faith** can we come to the Lord Jesus Christ and have salvation in Him.

- **Acts 20:21**

"Testifying both to the Jews, and also to the Greeks, repentance toward God, and **faith** toward our Lord Jesus Christ."

- **Romans 3:22**

"Even the righteousness of God *which is* by **faith** of Jesus Christ unto all and upon all them that believe: for there is no difference:"

There is no other way to gain salvation than to have **genuine trust** and **faith** in the Lord Jesus Christ.

- **Romans 3:28**

"Therefore we conclude that a man is justified by **faith** without the deeds of the law."

Nothing of the works of the law can save any person. It is only by **genuine faith** in the Lord Jesus Christ.

- **Romans 4:5**

"But to him that worketh not, but believeth on him that justifieth the ungodly, his **faith is** counted for righteousness."

Not by works of any kind, but only by **genuine faith** in the Lord Jesus Christ can we receive God's righteousness.

- **Romans 5:1**

"Therefore being justified by **faith,** we have peace with God through our Lord Jesus Christ:"

- **Galatians 3:26**

"For ye are all the children of God by **faith** in Christ Jesus."

I remember I quoted this verse to a young man when I was a student at the University of Michigan, from 1945 to 1948. We were both working at the Michigan Union cafeteria. I gave him various verses to learn. He

seemed like he wanted to trust the Lord Jesus Christ and be saved, but when he got to this verse, he said :
> "*I don't believe that because it says you are all are the children of God by faith in Jesus Christ.*"

He wanted to believe that all people were the children of God, even if they did not **genuinely trust** the Lord Jesus Christ. Genuine faith in the Lord Jesus Christ is the only way to become God's child. He never wanted to learn any more verses after that.

- **Ephesians 2:8-10**

"For by grace are ye saved through **faith**; and that not of yourselves: *it is* the gift of God: Not of works, lest any man should boast. For we are his workmanship, created in Christ Jesus unto good works, which God hath before ordained that we should walk in them."

<u>Genuine faith is needed for salvation. Salvation is not of our works</u>.

- **2 Timothy 3:15**

"And that from a child thou hast known the holy scriptures, which are able to make thee wise unto salvation through **faith** which is in Christ Jesus."

SALVATION TRUTHS IN THE BIBLE

The holy Scriptures alone are where we can find the truths which can make us "*wise unto salvation through faith which is in Christ Jesus.*"

Hebrews 4:3

"**For we which have believed do enter into rest, as he said, As I have sworn in my wrath, if they shall enter into my rest: although the works were finished from the foundation of the world.**"

GOD'S REST

The Greek Word used here for "*rest*" is KATAPAUSIS. Some of the meanings for this Word are:

> "*1) a putting to rest; 1a) calming of the winds; 2) a resting place; 2a) metaphorical: the heavenly blessedness in which God dwells, and of which he has promised to make persevering believers in Christ partakers after the toils and trials of life on earth are ended.*"

CHRIST WILL GIVE YOU REST

<u>This verse refers to God's "*rest*."</u> As I've said before, there are three different "*rests*" in the Bible. I believe that this "*rest*" is referring to the "*rest*" of salvation.

> "Come unto me, all *ye* that labour and are heavy laden, and I will give you rest." (Matthew 11:28)

When you come to the Lord Jesus Christ in genuine faith, you receive the "*rest*" of God's salvation.

THE REST OF SANCTIFICATION

As I also said before, there is a second "*rest*" of sanctification or walking with the LORD:

- Matthew 11:29

  "Take my yoke upon you, and learn of me; for I am meek and lowly in heart: and ye shall find rest unto your souls."

When you follow the Lord closely and walk with Him day by day and moment by moment, you have the "*rest*" of sanctification and fellowship with the Lord.

FOUNDATION OF THE WORLD

Notice, "*the works were finished from the **foundation** of the world.*" The Greek Word for "***foundation***" is KATABOLE. Some of the meanings this Word are:

> "1) a throwing or laying down; 1a) the injection or depositing of the virile semen in the womb; 1b) of the seed of plants and animals; 2) a founding (laying down a foundation)."

This Word is referred in this verse to "*the **foundation** of the world.*" <u>This is one of the Bible references that speak of a geocentric universe rather than a heliocentric universe, meaning that the earth, not the sun, is the center of the universe and is fixed, settled, solid, and not roaming around the universe.</u> An excellent book that proves this from the Bible was written by Dr. Jack Moorman, one of our church's missionaries and a member of the Executive Committee of the Dean Burgon Society. It is called *The Biblical and Observational Case for Geocentricity* **(BFT #4054 @ $15.00 + $8.00 S&H)**.

THE BELIEVER'S REST
- **Psalm 95:11**

"Unto whom I sware in my wrath that they should not <u>enter into my rest</u>.

- **Matthew 11:28-30**

"Come unto me, all ye that labour and are heavy laden, and <u>I will give you **rest**</u>. Take my yoke upon you, and learn of me; for I am meek and lowly in heart: and ye shall <u>find **rest** unto your souls</u>. For my yoke *is* easy, and my burden is light."

- **2 Thessalonians 1:7**

"And to you who are troubled <u>**rest** with us</u>, when the Lord Jesus shall be revealed from heaven with his mighty angels,"

There will be great "***rest***," at that time.

- **Revelation 14:13**

"And I heard a voice from heaven saying unto me, Write, Blessed *are* the dead which die in the Lord from henceforth: yea, saith the Spirit, that they <u>may **rest** from their labours</u>; and their works do follow them."

DYING IN THE LORD GIVES REST

The only people who will have "*rest from their labours*" are those who "*die in the Lord*" and are thus genuinely born-again and saved. At most funerals I have viewed on television, whether for apostate Protestants, Roman Catholic priests, or others, the ministers or priests have the dead people going to Heaven, whether they are saved or lost. This universalism is not taught in the Bible, but it is strongly condemned.

Hebrews 4:4

"**For he spake in a certain place of the seventh *day* on this wise, And God did rest the seventh day from all his works.**"

GOD'S CREATION IN SIX DAYS

When Paul mentioned that God rested "*from all His works*" on the "*seventh day*," he is referring to the **works of God's creation** of all things in six days as recorded in Genesis and in other places in the Bible.

<u>We believe in **God's creation**. We deny the evolutionist's belief that the universe and all plants, fish, animals, and people came *ex nihilo* (from nothing).</u> It was not from "Big Bang" theory or anything else that unbelieving scientists have invented. We believe that God, Himself,

created the whole universe including billions of stars, as well as this earth and all the people, animals, insects, and any other things that are upon this earth.

GOD'S REST THE SEVENTH DAY FROM ALL HIS WORKS
- **Genesis 2:1-2**

"Thus the heavens and the earth were finished, and all the host of them. And on the **seventh day** God ended his work which he had made; and he rested on the **seventh day** from all his work which he had made."

The Greek word used in this verse for "**rest**" is KATAPAUO. Some of the meanings for this Word are:

"1) to make quiet, to cause to be at rest, to grant rest; 1a) to lead to a quiet abode; 1b) to still, restrain, to cause (one striving to do something); to desist; 2) to rest, take rest."

GOD RESTED AFTER HIS CREATION

So this is God's rest. God rested after He created the heaven and the earth, all the people that are in it, and all the animals that are in it. He did this in six literal days. It was an elaborate creation. I believe it is clear that these "days" were twenty-four hour days. It says in Genesis repeatedly "*the evening and the morning were the____day.*" This is repeated six times, one time for each of the days of creation. The days of creation were twenty-four hour periods like our own. God was able to create all the things that are in existence today in just six days.

But on the **seventh day**, God rested "*from all his works*" that He had made. <u>The **seventh day** is Saturday or the Sabbath on which day the Jews were told to worship the Lord. It is not the first day or Sunday when the Christians in the New Testament are to worship.</u>

SABBATH WORSHIP FOR JEWS ONLY

That commandment to "*remember the sabbath day, to keep it holy*" (Exodus 20:8) was never repeated in the New Testament. Because of this, Christians worship on the first day or Sunday. That was the day of the bodily resurrection of the Lord Jesus Christ. Unfortunately, some Christians are Sabbath worshippers. They erroneously call Sunday the "Christian Sabbath." We differ with them when they say that

> Sunday, the first day of the week, is Saturday, the seventh day of the week. These people are wrong.

Some questions have been asked, like *"What about Sunday? Why do we worship the Lord on the first day of the week?"* There are at least three different reasons.

(1) The first reason is that the Lord Jesus Christ was raised from the dead on the first day of the week.

(2) The second reason is that on the first Sunday after Christ's bodily resurrection, the apostles met in the Upper Room. Thomas was absent on that Sunday evening meeting, but was there on the next Sunday evening when they met for worship.

(3) Paul told the Christians in Corinth to lay in store their offerings on the *"first day of the week."*

> "Upon the first *day* of the week let every one of you lay by him in store, as *God* hath prospered him, that there be no gatherings when I come." (1 Corinthians 16:2)

Hebrews 4:5

"And in this *place* again, If they shall enter into my rest."

GOD'S REST

This is referring to **God's rest** once again. He wants us and the people of Israel to enter into **his rest**. They didn't follow the Lord in faith and belief, but in doubt and unbelief.

- **Psalm 95:11**

"Unto whom I sware in my wrath that they should not enter into my rest."

TWENTY YEARS AND OLDER DIED

Because of the unbelief on the part of the Israelites, from twenty years old and upwards, God judged them. They all died in the wilderness before the forty years were up. Their carcasses fell in the wilderness because of God's judgment. They did not enter Canaan. They did not believe God. However, all those from nineteen years of age and under were allowed to enter into the land of Canaan.

Hebrews 4:6

"Seeing therefore it remaineth that some must enter therein, and they to whom it was first preached entered not in because of unbelief:"

BECAUSE OF UNBELIEF

Some of the Israelites could enter into God's rest of Canaan, but others could not enter *"because of unbelief."*

- **John 1:11-12**

"He came unto his own, and his own received him not. But as many as received him, to them gave he power to become the sons of God, *even* to them that believe on his name:"

CHRIST'S OWN REJECTED HIM

And so, the Lord Jesus Christ came unto His own creation and His own people, the Jews, rejected him. In this verse, Paul said that *"some must enter therein"* to the rest of the Lord. But those to whom *"it was first preached"* did not enter in *"because of unbelief."*

This is similar to the Jews rejecting the Lord Jesus Christ and the Gentiles were receptive and the gospel was given to them as well. The Jewish rejection of the Lord opened the way for the Gentiles to come to Him by faith. I am very sorry the Jews rejected the Lord Jesus Christ as their Messiah. I wish they had all accepted him. But in a sense, I'm glad because through their rejection, the gospel was preached to the Gentiles so that we could be redeemed by genuine faith in the Lord Jesus Christ. This is a wonderful privilege.

BRANCHES

- **Romans 11:19-20**

"Thou wilt say then, The **branches were broken off,** that I might be graffed in. Well; because of unbelief they were **broken off**, and thou standest by faith. Be not highminded, but fear:"

God speaks of Israel as **broken-off branches**. The Gentiles in Rome who received the book of Romans could say of the Jews: *"The branches were broken off, that I might be grafted in."* It was because of unbelief that the **Jews were broken off** from the trunk. Then there is a warning unto the Gentiles that came to the Lord Jesus Christ. The Jews rejected and the Gentiles accepted. There is a warning about being broken off in the next verse for every one of us who are genuinely saved:

- **Romans 11:21**

"For if God spared not the **natural branches**, [that is the Jews] take heed lest he also spare not thee."

The warning is that God "*spare not thee.*" This does not mean that those who are genuinely saved can lose their salvation, but they might lose God's special blessing if they do not walk properly with Him. Though the Jews are not in the center of God's plan now, there is a glorious future for the people of Israel when the Lord Jesus Christ returns after the Tribulation period to set up His thousand year reign in Jerusalem.

JEWISH UNBELIEF

- **Romans 3:1-3**

"What advantage then hath the Jew? or what profit *is there* of circumcision? Much every way: chiefly, because that unto them were committed the oracles of God. For what if some did **not believe**? shall **their unbelief** make the faith of God without effect?"

Romans 3:2 tells us how our Bibles came into being. It is to the Jews that God gave the very Words of God ("*the oracles of God*") in Hebrew, Aramaic, and Greek. All the Old Testament writers were Jews. I believe also that all the New Testament writers were Jews.

ALL N.T. WRITERS WERE JEWS

Some teach that maybe one of them was a Gentile, but I am convinced this is not true. A Jewish man who became a genuine Christian wrote a book on this question. He convinced me very strongly that even the one they thought was not a Jew, was also a Jew. This being the case, all of the books of the Bible–Old Testament and New Testament–were written by Jews, under the direction of God the Holy Spirit Who received the Words from the Lord Jesus Christ, as it says in John 16:12-14:

"I have yet many things to say unto you, but ye cannot bear them now. Howbeit when he, the Spirit of truth, is come, he will guide you into all truth: for he shall not speak of himself; but whatsoever he shall hear, *that* shall he speak: and he will shew you things to come. He shall glorify me: for he shall receive of mine, and shall shew it unto you." (John 16:12-14)

- **Romans 3:3**

"For what if some did **not believe**? Shall **their unbelief** make the faith of God without effect?"

Unbelief, regardless of how intense, does not make the faith and truths of God "*without effect*" or useless.

- **Romans 11:30**

"For as ye in times past [he is writing to the Romans, the church of Rome, and they were Gentile people, most of them] have **not believed** God, yet have now obtained mercy through their **unbelief:**"

GENTILES OBTAINED GOD'S MERCY

Because of the unbelief of the Jews, the Gentiles obtained God's mercy. It is a wonderful blessing. It has opened up the way for Gentiles, the heathen idolatrous people all over the world, to be genuinely saved through the clear gospel message about the Lord Jesus Christ.

Hebrews 4:7

"**Again, he limiteth a certain day, saying in David, To day, after so long a time; as it is said, To day if ye will hear his voice, harden not your hearts.**"

TODAY, HEAR HIS VOICE

He's talking about King David here. But Paul is applying to the time of his writing and **today** as well. This verse mentions "*to day*" two times. It is essential we do not waste "*to day*" or any day, whether its Sunday, Monday, Tuesday, any of the days of the week. We should not squander them.

GOD'S WORDS ARE IN THE BIBLE

Then the verse mentions "*if ye will hear his voice.*" Today, the only voice we have from God is His Words. These Words must be based on the proper Hebrew, Aramaic, and Greek Words that God gave us in the original languages. These are the Words which underlie our King James Bible, but these same Words do not underlie the modern versions in most languages of the world. We believe that the King James Bible is an accurate translation of the inspired and preserved Hebrew, Aramaic, Greek Words. We can hear God's voice today by reading and heeding the words in our King James

HARDENED HEARTS

The Greek Word for "harden" is SKLERUNO. Some of the meanings of this Word are:

"1) to make hard, harden; 2) metaphorical 2a) to render obstinate, stubborn; 2b) to be hardened; 2c) to become obstinate or stubborn"

Once we read God's Words day by day, the Greek construction indicates that we are to stop **hardening our hearts**. Paul indicated by his negative prohibition in the present Greek tense, that they were to stop an action already in progress. These people read God's Words and heard His voice, but they had **hardened their hearts** against those Words. Paul tells them to stop this action and begin walking in the fellowship of the Lord Jesus Christ.

One of the things I asked the students when I was teaching recently at the Chinese seminary in Towaco, New Jersey was about their Bible reading. I gave them one of our 85-verses per day Bible reading schedule that would take them from Genesis through Revelation in one year and urged them to follow this. It is very important to know God's will which is found in the Bible's verses. I encourage people to read God's Words, day by day, from Genesis through Revelation each year.

When I was a young man, sixteen years of age, in October of 1944, I genuinely received the Lord Jesus Christ as my Saviour and was saved. In December 31st of that year, our Pastor Willetts of Berea Baptist Church, Berea, Ohio, said to all of us:

"I would like every one of you in our church, to read the entire Bible though by the end of 1945."

That sounded like a very good challenge to me. I asked Mr. Sanborn (who later became my father-in-law) how this could be done. He had been a Christian for many years, but he didn't have a daily plan to be able to do this in one year. Uncle Charlie Allen, our high school janitor who led me to Christ in October of the previous year, gave me a Bible. That Bible had the number of verses in each book and in the entire Bible. There are over 31,000 verses in all. I divided the exact amount by 365 and 1/4 days per year and arrived at 85 verses per day. On a few days, we read 86, but mostly 85.

STOP HARDENING YOUR HEARTS

If you follow that plan, today, as you hear the voice of the Lord God through reading His Words, you must, as Israel of old, stop *"hardening"* your heart. That is a difficult thing for us to do. You must ask the Lord to help us. If you are genuinely saved, you can depend on the Holy Spirit to understand God's Words and to follow them faithfully.

- **Psalm 95:7**

"For he is our God; and we *are* the people of his pasture, and the sheep of his hand. To day if ye will hear his voice, **Harden not your heart**, as in the provocation, *and as in* the day of temptation in the wilderness:"

- **2 Corinthians 6:2**

"(For he saith, I have heard thee in a time accepted, and in the day of salvation have I succoured [or helped] thee: behold, now *is* the accepted time; behold, now is the day of salvation.)"

Each day should be a day of service. Each day it should be a day of following the Lord Jesus Christ.

Hebrews 4:8

"For if Jesus had given them rest, then would he not afterward have spoken of another day."

This word for *Jesus*, refers back to Joshua in the Old Testament. Our King James Bible accurately transliterates YESOUS letter by letter, which is *"Jesus."* The translated word in the Old Testament is YOSHUA. Most modern Bible versions do not transliterate YESOUS, but interpret it as *"Joshua."* Interpretation is not translation. But the interpretation is that of *Joshua* of the Old Testament. If Joshua or Jesus had given the Israelites rest in the land of Canaan, God would not have spoken of *"another day."* That refers to God's Heavenly rest.

CANAAN WAS NOT RESTFUL

Canaan, indeed, was not very restful. The Israelites had to battle all the Canaanites, the Hivites, the Hittites, Perizzites, the Jebusites, and all the other "ites." They had to get them out of the land. This was not restful, it was involved in constant warfare.

GOD'S FUTURE "REST"

- **Hebrews 11:8-10**

"By faith Abraham, when he was called to go out into a place which he should after receive for an inheritance, obeyed; and he went out, not knowing whither he went. By faith he sojourned in the land of promise, as *in* a strange country, dwelling in tabernacles with Isaac and Jacob, the heirs with him of the same promise: For he looked for a **city** which hath foundations, whose builder and maker *is* God."

That was a great step of faith. God asked Abraham to leave his country without telling him where he was going. He obeyed the Lord and sojourned in the land of Canaan dwelling in tents. *"He looked for a city . . . whose builder and maker is God."* That's a **permanent city of Heaven** itself. As the chorus of a song goes,

"This world is not my home. I'm just a passing through. My treasures are laid up somewhere beyond the blue."

Hebrews 4:9

"There remaineth therefore a rest to the people of God."

GOD'S REST

This is the **"rest"** that remains. Remember, as we have mentioned earlier, there were three different **rests** in Scripture (1) the **rest** of salvation; (2) the **rest** of fellowship and sanctification, and (3) the **Heavenly rest**. This one is the remaining **rest**, the **Heavenly rest** that genuinely saved, born-again Christians will have for all eternity in Heaven.

The Greek Word for **"rest"** is SABBATISMOS. Some of the meanings for this Word are:

"1) a keeping sabbath; 2) the blessed rest from toils and troubles looked for in the age to come by the true worshippers of God and true Christians."

- **Matthew 11:28**

"Come unto me, all ye that labour and are heavy laden, and I will give you **rest**. Take my yoke upon you, and learn of me; for I am meek and lowly in heart: and ye shall find **rest** unto your souls."

- **Hebrews 3:18**

"And to whom sware he that they should not enter into his **rest**, but to them that believed not?"

Those who believed not were the ones who were left out of God's fellowship **rest**.

- **Revelation 14:11a**

"And the smoke of their torment ascendeth up for ever and ever: and they have **no rest** day nor night,"

God is very clear that those who are lost and have rejected the Lord Jesus Christ as their Saviour, have **no rest**, day nor night. At this time, they have received the "mark of the beast."

"And the beast was taken, and with him the false prophet that wrought miracles before him, with which he deceived them that had received the mark of the beast, and them that worshipped his image. These both were cast alive into a lake of fire burning with brimstone." (Revelation 19:20)

John MacArthur wrote an article recently and in the article stated that those who receive the "*mark of the beast*" during the Tribulation period can be saved. The above verse is very clear that these will be "*cast alive into a lake of fire burning with brimstone.*" So much for MacArthur's error on this.

- **Revelation 14:13**

". . . Blessed *are* the dead which die in the Lord from henceforth: yea, saith the Spirit, that they may **rest** from their labours; and their works do follow them."

We who are saved can **rest** in glory from our labours. But this is true only for those who are genuinely born-again.

Hebrews 4:10

"For He that is entered into his rest, he also hath ceased from his own works, as God did from *his*."

This seems to be the **rest** of fellowship and sanctification. They that enter into his **rest**, cease from their own works. We can't use works to save us and to enter into the **rest** of salvation. Works can't save us. But God wants Christians to do good works for him after they are saved in order to glorify Him and His Son, the Lord Jesus Christ.

The Greek Word for "***rest***" here is: KATAPAUSIS. Some of the meanings for this Word are:

"*1) a putting to rest; 1a) calming of the winds; 2) a resting place; 2a) metaphorical, the heavenly blessedness in which God dwells, and of which he has promised to make persevering believers in Christ partakers after the toils and trials of life on earth are ended.*"

The Greek Word for "*ceased*" is: KATAPAUO. Some of the meanings for this Word are:

"*1) to make quiet, to cause to be at **rest**, to grant **rest**; 1a) to lead to a quiet abode; 1b) to still, restrain, to cause (one striving to do something); to desist; 2) to **rest**, take **rest**"*

- **Ephesians 2:8-10**

"For by grace are ye saved through faith; and that not of yourselves: it is the gift of God: **Not of works**, lest any man should boast. For we are his workmanship, created in Christ Jesus unto good works, which God hath before ordained that we should walk in them."

We are **not saved by our good works**, but God wants every saved, born-again Christian to do works that please the Lord. That's what honors the Lord Jesus Christ in order to serve and please Him.

Hebrews 4:11

"Let us labour therefore to enter into that rest, lest any man fall after the same example of unbelief."

EXAMPLE OF UNBELIEF

WILDERNESS JEWS–EXAMPLES OF UNBELIEF

We must labor to enter into the rest of sanctification and fellowship. It doesn't come easily. We must be careful *"lest any man fall after the same example of unbelief"* as many of Israel in the wilderness. Those who were twenty and above did not serve the Lord. They followed the flesh. They were an example of unbelief. We who are genuinely saved should labour faithfully to enter into the rest of fellowship with the Lord.

The Greek Word for *"example"* is HUPODEIGMA. Some of the meanings for this Word are:

> *"1) a sign suggestive of anything, delineation of a thing, representation, figure, copy; 2) an example: for imitation; 2a) of the thing to be imitated; 2b) for a warning, of a thing to be shunned;"*

TAKING CHRIST'S YOKE

As I have quoted earlier from Matthew 11:29:

> *"**Take my yoke** upon you, and learn of me; for I am meek and lowly in heart: and ye shall find rest unto your souls."*

THE REST OF FELLOWSHIP

This "rest of fellowship" is taking the yoke of the Lord Jesus Christ and learn of Him, walking with Him step by step, without following the flesh and its depravity. It involves following the teachings of the Scriptures and walking in the power of God the Holy Spirit.

Hebrews 4:12

"For the word of God is quick, and powerful, and sharper than any two edged sword, piercing even to the dividing asunder of soul and spirit, and of the joints and marrow, and *is* a discerner of the thoughts and intents of the heart."

THE WORDS OF GOD

This section, in Hebrews 4, takes up the powerful **Words of God**. There are a total of six distinctives that the Bible has. Now this is why I named this section *"The powerful words of God."* In this verse number 12, there are a total of six distinctives that the Bible has.

    1. **The Words of God Are *"Quick"* and Living.** The first distinctive of the **Words of God** is that they are quick and living. They never fail. They refer to the Hebrew, Aramaic, and Greek Words that underlie the King James Bible primarily, but they also refer to the King James Bible that has faithfully and accurately translated these **Words** into English.

The Greek Word for *"quick"* is ZAO. <u>It is a present tense verb</u>. Some of the meanings for this Word are:

> *"1) to live, breathe, be among the living (not lifeless, not dead); 2) to enjoy real life; 2a) to have true life and worthy of the name; 2b)active, blessed, endless in the kingdom of God; 3) to live i.e. pass life, in the manner of the living and acting; 3a) of mortals or character; 4) living water, having vital power in itself and exerting the same upon the soul; 5) metaphorical, to be in full vigour; 5a) to be fresh, strong, efficient; 5b) as adj. active, powerful, efficacious."*

    2. **The Words of God Are *"Powerful."*** The second distinctive of the **Words of God** is that they are powerful. <u>They are mighty **Words**. They will break down our unbelief and give those who are genuinely saved the power to live godly lives in the midst of a wicked world around them.</u>

    3. **The Words of God Are *"Sharper Than Any Two Edged Sword."*** The third distinctive of the **Words of God** is that they are *"sharper than any two edged sword."* <u>The sharp **Words of God** get into our hearts and lives, cutting through any obstacle that would hinder Them.</u>

4. **The Words of God Are "*Piercing.*"** The fourth distinctive of the **Words of God** is that they are "*piercing.*" They are not only sharp but they pierce. They cut right into our hearts. When we are wicked, wrong, sinful, and walking in the flesh, the **Words of God** pierce through us so we can feel them trying to correct us.

5. **The Words of God Are "*Dividing.*"** The fifth distinctive of the **Words of God** is that it is "*dividing.*" They divide between the soul and the spirit of people. People classify both of them as immaterial not distinct, but the same. No, they are not the same. The **Words of God**, divide and separate between the spirit and the soul, and between the joints and marrow.

6. **The Words of God Are a "*Discerner of the Thoughts and Intents of the Heart.*"** They discern between the "*thoughts*" in our mind and the "*intents of the heart.*" We must learn to discern all things by using the **Words of God**.

The Greek Word for "*intents*" is ENNOIA. Some of the meanings for this Word are:

"*1) the act of thinking, consideration, meditation; 2) a thought, notion, conception; 3) mind, understanding, will, manner of feeling, and thinking.*"

The Greek Word for "*heart*" is KARDIA. Some of the meanings for this Word are:

"*1) the heart; 1a) that organ in the animal body which is the centre of the circulation of the blood, and hence was regarded as the seat of physical life; 1b) denotes the centre of all physical and spiritual life; 2a) the vigour and sense of physical life; 2b) the centre and seat of spiritual life; 2b1) the soul or mind, as it is the fountain and seat of the thoughts, passions, desires, appetites, affections, purposes, endeavours; 2b2) of the understanding, the faculty and seat of the intelligence; 2b3) of the will and character; 2b4) of the soul so far as it is affected and stirred in a bad way or good, or of the soul as the seat of the sensibilities, affections, emotions, desires, appetites, passions; 1c) of the middle or central or inmost part of anything, even though inanimate*"

The following are some Scriptures that discuss various aspects about I want to go over that talk about various other things about the **Words of God**.

- Psalm 119:9-11

"Wherewithal shall a young man cleanse his way? by taking heed *thereto* according to thy word. With my whole heart have I sought thee: O let me not wander from thy commandments. Thy word have I hid in mine heart, that I might not sin against thee."

THE CLEANSING OF GOD'S WORDS

Notice the cleansing of the Words of God. Nothing else in this life can cleanse our hearts and minds like the Words of God. You can wash your clothes and your body with soap, but soap cannot cleanse your heart. Only the Words of God can do that.

If this is true, why do people forsake the Words of God and not read the Scriptures from Genesis through Revelation? God's Words are cleansing Words, and, as David wrote: "*With my whole heart, have I sought thee.*" And again, he said it was the Words of God that he had hid in his heart so that he would not sin against the Lord.

- Proverbs 30:5,

"Every **word of God** *is* pure: he *is* a shield unto them that put their trust in him."

All the **Words of God** are absolutely "*pure*," and without any errors of any kind. This is in contrast to the many impurities in books, tape recordings, radio programs, Hollywood movies, and TV programs.

- Mark 7:13

"Making the **word of God** of none effect through your tradition, which ye have delivered: and many such like things do ye."

The Lord Jesus Christ had something to say about the **Words of God**. He talked to these religious Pharisees. They were hypocrites and compromisers of **God's Words**. He told them that, by their tradition, they make the **Words of God** of no effect.

GOD'S WORDS, NOT TRADITIONS

That is what the Roman Catholic church has done by their traditions which are opposed to the Words of God. In talking about purgatory, they contradict the Words of God. They do the same in their heresies about last rites, prayers for the dead, the Pope being the vicar of Christ on earth, and many other false traditions of Rome.

HERESIES IN PROTESTANT CHURCHES

> The same can be said about many of the heresies in Protestant churches that follow the traditions of men. Such heresies include: universalism that teaches all people are saved, that Hell is not real, that there is no literal fire in Hell, that the Lord Jesus Christ is not Deity, that He was not born of a virgin, that He did not performed miracles, that He was not raised bodily from the dead, that He did not ascend bodily to Heaven after His resurrection, that He is not coming back some day, and many other things.

- **Luke 4:4**

"And Jesus answered him, saying, It is written, That man shall not live by bread alone, but by **every word of God**."

Many of the **Words of God** are either removed or changed by the Gnostic Critical Greek Text that is used in most of the modern Bible versions in English and all the other languages of the world. The Saviour said that we must not live by bread alone but by "*every word of God*" That "*every*" is important. The inspired and preserved **Hebrew, Aramaic, and Greek Words** have been accurately translated into English in the King James Bible. The **Words of God** should be a vital part of everyone who is genuinely born-again and saved. It is essential.

- **Luke 8:11**

"Now the parable is this: The seed is the **word of God**."

This is the meaning of what the sower was sowing. He was sowing the seed which are the **Words of God**. The **Words of God** should be sown, as our church seeks to sow them both by our missionaries and by the Internet broadcast that are streamed to every nation of the world. That seed is sown so that people who hear it might genuinely receive the Lord Jesus Christ as their Saviour and be saved and grow in the Lord.

- **Luke 11:28**

"But he said, Yea rather, blessed *are* they that hear the **word of God**, and keep it. "

> **TWO REQUIREMENTS FOR BLESSINGS**
>
> The Lord Jesus Christ again talked about the Words of God here in this verse. He said that people would be "blessed" or "happy" if two things were true. (1) First, the people, in order to be blessed would have to "*hear the Words of God.* " In many places, and even churches, people are not able to "*hear*" God's Words proclaimed. It's wonderful to be able to hear God's Words. (2) Second, the second requirement for this blessing was, after the people heard the Words of God,

they must *"keep"* them. That is so important. And born-again genuine Christian believers must not only hear God's Words, but also *"keep"* them.

- **Acts 13:7**

"Which was with the deputy of the country, Sergius Paulus, a prudent man; who called for Barnabas and Saul, and desired to hear the **word of God**."

Here's an important and wise man of the country. He called for Barnabas and Saul. What did he want? It was not money. It was not a miracle healing. He wanted to hear the **Words of God**. What a wonderful desire that is. Many people do not have any desire at all to hear **God's Words**. I am looking for people who have a great desire to hear and keep **God's Words**. This is why in our Thursday and Sunday Bible studies as well as our Sunday morning preaching services, I attempt to allow those who attend to hear the **Words of God**, hoping that they who hear will keep those **Words**.

- **Acts 18:11**

"And he continued *there a* year and six months, teaching the **word of God** among them."

Paul continued in Corinth one year and a half. That was a long time for him to be in one place. What did Paul do there? Did he just go on a vacation, or play golf, or go swimming, or go riding on horses? Paul taught the **Words of God** to them for that entire year and a half. His ministry was, and our ministry in our church here is to teach the Words of God clearly and specifically.

- **Romans 10:17**

"So then faith *cometh* by hearing, and hearing by the **word of God**."

GOD'S WORDS–THE SOURCE OF FAITH

Genuine faith in the Lord Jesus Christ comes by hearing the Words of God. That is the source of genuine faith in the Saviour. That is why I seek to teach and preach God's Words in our services.

- **2 Corinthians 2:17**

"For we are not as many, which corrupt the **word of God**: but as of sincerity, but as of God, in the sight of God speak we in Christ."

SOME CORRUPT BIBLE VERSIONS

The new Bible versions in English and in all the languages of the world have corrupted the Bible by three methods:

(1) basing their perversions on false Hebrew, Aramaic, and Greek original Words;

(2) following false methods of translation techniques; and

(3) printing false doctrinal perversions in over 356 places.

Some of the versions using the corrupt Gnostic Critical Greek Words are:
1. the Revised Standard Version (RSV),
2. the New American Standard Version (NASV),
3. the New International Version (NIV),
4. the English Standard Version (ESV),
and many more.

By using the false Gnostic Critical Greek words and their false translation techniques, these versions either add to the Words of God, subtract from the Words of God, or change the Words of God in some other way. Paul was against all these kinds of corruptions of God's Words.

- 2 Corinthians 4:2

"But have renounced the hidden things of dishonesty, not walking in craftiness, nor handling the **word of God** deceitfully; but by manifestation of the truth commending ourselves to every man's conscience in the sight of God."

Paul said he'd "*renounced the hidden things of dishonesty.*"

DISHONEST MIS-TRANSLATIONS IN BIBLES

Modern Bible translations have not "*renounced the hidden things of dishonesty.*" They are filled with dishonest words, phrases, and mis-translations of clauses. Paul did not walk in "*craftiness*" or deceptions. Additionally, he did not believe in "*handling the word of God deceitfully*" as the modern Bible versions have been guilty of.

Gnosticism's Satanic religion is the basis of the Vatican and Sinai Critical Greek Texts. I have published a book called *GNOSTICISM The Doctrinal Foundation of the New Bible Versions* **(BFT #4088 @ $20.00 + $8.00 S&H)**. In this book are hundreds of quotations from the Gnostic sources, many of which are found in the Gnostic Critical New Testament Greek Texts. One of the things that the Gnostics do is to deceitfully handle the **Words of God**. I urge my readers to get a copy of this large documented book and study it carefully.

> **CHRISTIAN WEAPONS FOR VICTORY**
> - **Ephesians 6:17**
>
> "And take the helmet of salvation, and the sword of the Spirit, which is the word of God:"
>
> These are some of the weapons that Christians have at their disposal and should use. One of these weapons mentioned in this verse is *"the sword of the Spirit, which is the Word of God."* A sword is for offense as well as defense. The Words of God are wonderful weapons as we speak them, preach them, live them, and obey them.

- **1 Thessalonians 2:13**

"For this cause also thank we God without ceasing, because, when ye received the **word of God** which ye heard of us, ye received *it* not *as* the word of men, but as it is in truth, the **word of God**, which effectually worketh also in you that believe."

> **GOD'S WORDS EFFECTUALLY WORK**
>
> Paul thanked the Lord for, and commended the church of Thessalonica. He said that (1) they received God's Words, and (2) they received it not as the words of men, but as the Words of God. He also said that these Words *"effectually worketh"* in those who believe them. They are powerful and effective if we receive them, use them, and follow them.

- **2 Timothy 2:9**

"Wherein I suffer trouble, as an evil doer, *even* unto bonds; but the **word of God** is not bound."

Paul was not an evil doer, but was put into prison for preaching the gospel of Christ. But, though he was bound, the **Words of God** are not bound. Praise God for them. As long as we have the Bible, the right Bible, that is unshackled and not bound, it can go forth and save sinners.

- **Titus 2:5**

"*To be* discreet, chaste, keepers at home, good, obedient to their own husbands, that the **word of God** be not blasphemed."

God's words should not be blasphemed. So wives should be obedient to their own husbands to avoid this blasphemy.

Hebrews—Preaching Verse by Verse

- **Hebrews 13:7**

"Remember them which have the rule over you, who have spoken unto you the **word of God**: whose faith follow, considering the end of *their* conversation."

He's talking about the pastors/bishops/elders who preach the **Words of God**. We are to remember them. Their job is to preach and teach the **Words of God**.

- **1 Peter 1:23**

"Being born again, not of corruptible seed, but of incorruptible, by the **word of God**, which liveth and abideth for ever."

Another characteristic of the **Words of God** is that they enable us to find out how to be *"born-again" and regenerated*. It is not a natural birth, but a spiritual birth. The preservation of the **Hebrew, Aramaic, and Greek Words** is also referred to since the **Words of God** live and abide for ever. This preservation is denied by many who call themselves Fundamentalists, such as those at Bob Jones University, sad to say. It should be the correct Bible version (such as the King James Bible) to be certain that all the verses are correct to enable that new birth.

- **John 6:47**

"Verily, verily, I say unto you, He that believeth on me hath everlasting life."

NEW VERSIONS PERVERT SALVATION

The New International Version (NIV), the English Standard Version (ESV) and most of the other modern Bible versions give the false way of salvation. They all omit the essential word, "on me." Without genuine faith in the Lord Jesus Christ and in Him alone, no one can be born-again or saved. This is very, very serious doctrinal heresy against the true Words of God. It is a false gospel. If you take this verse as what the gospel is, you cannot be genuinely saved. You must be born-again only by using the accurate Words of God in this verse.

- **1 John 2:14**

"I have written unto you, fathers, because ye have known him *that is* from the beginning. I have written unto you, young men, because ye are strong, and the **word of God** abideth in you, and ye have overcome the wicked one."

The apostle John writes to the young men and says that the **Words of God** abide in them. That same **Word** should abide in all born-again Christians strongly even today.

- **Revelation 1:9**

"I John, who also am your brother, and companion in tribulation, and in the kingdom and patience of Jesus Christ, was in the isle that is called Patmos, for the **word of God**, and for the testimony of Jesus Christ."

JOHN BANISHED TO THE ISLE OF PATMOS

The apostle John was banished by Rome to the island of Patmos because of his firm stand *"for the Word of God, and for the testimony of Jesus Christ."* He stood firmly for the Words of God, and so should every truly born-again Christian today. John was faithfully preaching the Lord Jesus Christ.

- **Revelation 6:9**

"And when he had opened the fifth seal, I saw under the altar the souls of them that were slain for the **word of God**, and for the testimony which they held:"

GOVERNMENT'S 72 POTENTIAL TERRORISTS

These born-again Christians will be slain, because they hold firmly to the Words of God. Today, those of us who hold firmly to the Bible may be put in prison and possibly slain as well under the false accusation of being "terrorists." The Homeland Security of our United States government has listed 72 different beliefs of people that they brand as *"potential terrorists."* The 72nd one on that list is *"evangelical Christians."* There's not a single properly defined evangelical Bible believing Christian that is either a terrorist or a potential terrorist. This is an absolutely false untrue charge. If you want a copy of this entire list of these "72 potential terrorists," you can email me at the following email address (BFT@BibleForToday.org) and I'll be glad to send you a copy.

- **Revelation 20:4**

"And I saw thrones, and they sat upon them, and judgment was given unto them: and <u>I saw the souls of them that were beheaded for the witness of Jesus</u>, and for the **word of God**, and which had not worshipped the beast, neither his image, neither had received his mark upon their foreheads, or in their hands; and they lived and reigned with Christ a thousand years."

These <u>beheadings will take place during the seven year Tribulation period when the antichrist reigns</u>. This will take place:

(1) because they stand for the Lord Jesus Christ;
(2) because they stand for the **Words of God**;

(3) because they will not worship the Antichrist beast;
(4) because they will not worship the Antichrist beast's image; and
(5) because they will not receive the mark of this beast in their foreheads or hands.

Hebrews 4:13

"Neither is there any creature that is not manifest in his sight: but all things are naked and opened unto the eyes of him with whom we have to do."

GOD'S OMNISCIENCE AND OMNIPRESENCE

God is omniscient and knows our every thought. The Words of God tell us much, but **God knows everything. We cannot hide from Him. We cannot flee from God.** All things are **naked and opened** to the God of the Bible.

The Greek Word for "*opened*" is the verb TACHELIZO. Some of the meanings for this Word are:

> "1) to seize and twist the neck or throat; 1a) of combatants who handle thus their antagonist; 2) to bend back the neck of a victim to be slain, to lay bare or expose by bending back; 3) to lay bare, uncover, expose; 4) laid bare, laid open, made manifest to one."

- **Psalm 139:7**

"Whither shall I go from thy spirit? or whither shall I **flee from thy presence?**"

There is no way people can flee from the presence of God. There is nowhere to hide. **He is omnipresent** and can find us wherever we are. **He knows our hearts. He knows our thoughts. He knows what we do. He knows where we go. He knows where we don't go. Everything is open before Him.**

- **Jonah 1:3**

"But Jonah rose up to flee unto Tarshish from the presence of the LORD, and went down to Joppa; and he found a ship going to Tarshish: so he paid the fare thereof, and went down into it, to go with them unto Tarshish from the **presence of the LORD.**"

Jonah thought he could flee from the Lord. But Jonah found that impossible. He tried to flee unto Tarshish. God had commanded him to go and preach to Nineveh to tell them that their city was going to be torn down. Instead, Jonah went to Tarshish in a different direction. He thought he could go "*from the presence of the LORD.*" The Lord is not in one place, **He is everywhere present**. Jonah finally found that out.

Hebrews 4:14

"Seeing then that we have a great high priest, that is passed into the heavens, Jesus the Son of God, let us hold fast *our* profession."

HOLD FAST

GENUINE CHRISTIANS SHOULD HOLD FAST

Genuinely saved people have the Lord Jesus Christ as their great High Priest. Because of this, they are urged to *"hold fast our profession"* and never compromise it. This is to be continuously. They are not to wavier, not to give up, and not to change. This is true no matter how many people make fun of you and call you names. Don't ever give up your profession of your genuine faith in the Lord Jesus Christ.

The Greek Word for *"hold fast"* is KRATEO. Some of the meanings for this Word are:

> "1) to have power, be powerful; 1a) to be chief, be master of, to rule; 2) to get possession of; 2a) to become master of, to obtain; 2b) to take hold of; 2c) to take hold of, take, seize; 2c1) to lay hands on one in order to get him into one's power; 3) to hold; 3a) to hold in the hand; 3b) to hold fast, i.e. not discard or let go; 3b1) to keep carefully and faithfully; 3c) to continue to hold, to retain; 3c1) of death continuing to hold one; 3c2) to hold in check, restrain."

CHRIST OUR HIGH PRIEST

The truth about the Lord Jesus Christ being the **High Priest** of those who are genuinely saved is found in many Bible verses.

- **Hebrews 2:17**

"Wherefore in all things it behoved him to be made like unto *his* brethren, that he might be a merciful and faithful **high priest** in things *pertaining* to God, to make reconciliation for the sins of the people."

- **Hebrews 3:1**

"Wherefore, holy brethren, partakers of the heavenly calling, consider <u>the Apostle</u> and **High Priest** of our profession, Christ Jesus;"

Those who are truly saved must consider Him and never forget the Lord Jesus Christ who is at the Father's right hand as our **great High Priest**.

- **Hebrews 5:5**

"So also Christ glorified not himself to be made an **high priest**; but he that said unto him, Thou art my Son, to day have I begotten thee."

The Lord Jesus Christ did not push Himself to be our **High Priest**, but God the Father made Him our **High Priest**.

- **Hebrews 5:10**

"Called of God an **high priest** after the order of Melchisedec."

The Lord Jesus Christ has an everlasting High Priesthood. Like Melchisedec, He had no beginning of days or end of life, but is a **High Priest** forever.

- **Hebrews 6:19-20**

"Which *hope* we have as an anchor of the soul, both sure and stedfast, and which entereth into that within the veil; Whither the forerunner is for us entered, <u>even Jesus, made an **high priest** for ever after the order of Melchisedec.</u>"

CHRIST AND THE ORDER OF MELCHISEDEC

Once again, the Lord Jesus Christ's High Priesthood is called after the order of Melchisedec because it had no beginning of days nor end of life.

- **Hebrews 8:1**

"Now of the things which we have spoken *this* is the sum: We have such an **high priest**, who is set on the right hand of the throne of the Majesty in the heavens;"

THE RIGHT HAND OF GOD

The right hand of God the Father is the place of honor and blessing. The Lord Jesus Christ is seated there.

- **Hebrews 8:3**

"For every **high priest** is ordained to offer gifts and sacrifices: wherefore *it is* of necessity that this man have somewhat also to offer."

And the Lord Jesus Christ **did** offer Himself on the cross at Calvary. He shed His blood once for all to provide the basis for the forgiveness of sins for those who genuinely receive Him as their Saviour.

- **Hebrews 9:6-7**

"Now when these things were thus ordained, the priests went always into the first tabernacle, accomplishing the service *of God*. But into the second *went* the **high priest** alone once every year, not without blood, which he offered for himself, and *for* the errors of the people:"

CHRIST WAS SINLESS

Our Saviour didn't need to offer any blood for Himself. He was sinless. He offered His own blood for the sins of the world so that by truly trusting in Him, they might be saved for all eternity.

- **Hebrews 9:25-26**

"Nor yet that he should offer himself often, as the **high priest** entereth into the holy place every year with blood of others; For then must he often have suffered since the foundation of the world: but now once in the end of the world hath he appeared to put away sin by the sacrifice of himself."

CHRIST'S ONCE-FOR-ALL SACRIFICE

That is the <u>once-for-all finished work of the Lord Jesus Christ</u>. He put away sin by the sacrifice of Himself. The Roman Catholic Church which practices the repeated crucifixion of the Lord Jesus Christ in their masses all around the world are committing great and serious heresy in this practice.

- **Hebrews 9:27-28**

"And as it is appointed unto men once to die, but after this the judgment: So Christ was <u>once offered</u> to bear the sins of many; and unto them that look for him shall he appear the second time without sin unto salvation."

<u>The Roman Catholic mass is a repetition of the once-for-all offering of the Lord Jesus Christ. He is the Saviour and great **High Priest** of those who are genuinely born-again.</u>

- **Hebrews 10:19-23**

"Having therefore, brethren, boldness to enter into the holiest by the blood of Jesus, By a new and living way, which he hath consecrated for us, through the veil, that is to say, his flesh; And *having* an **high priest** over the house of God; Let us draw near with a true heart in full assurance of faith, having our hearts sprinkled from an evil conscience, and our bodies washed with pure water. Let us hold fast the profession of *our* faith without wavering; (for he *is* faithful that promised;)"

> ### A FAITHFUL HIGH PRIEST
>
> Saved, born-again Christians, have a faithful High Priest, Who is at the right hand of God the Father. The Lord Jesus Christ is sinless and faithful to help those who have trusted Him. He is not able to sin. This means He is impeccable. Some people wrongly say that He was only able not to sin (*posse non peccare*). The Bible is clear that He was not able to sin (*non posse peccare*). As the great High Priest for the genuinely saved, He is faithful in interceding for them. We should be faithful to Him as well.

Hebrews 4:15

"For we have not an high priest which cannot be touched with the feeling of our infirmities; but was in all points tempted like as *we are, yet* without sin."

The Lord Jesus Christ is an understanding **High Priest** at God the Father's right hand. In the incarnation, He took upon Himself a perfect human body by way of the miracle of His virgin birth. He was both perfect God and perfect Man. He was and still is the God-Man (THEANTHROPOS).

> ### TESTED IN ALL POINTS
>
> God the Father had to have a perfect High Priest that knew what people were like so He gave His Son a perfect human nature so He would come into this sinful world and live among us. He lived among human beings and had perfect understanding of their infirmities.
>
> He was tested in all points as humans are tested, yet he is and was without sin. I don't think the Devil knew that he was without sin or could not sin because he tried to get Him to sin three different times.

The Greek Word for "*tempted*" is PEIRAZO. Some of the meanings for this Word are:

> "*1) to try whether a thing can be done; 1a) to attempt, endeavour; 2) to try, make trial of, test: for the purpose of ascertaining his quantity, or what he thinks, or how he will behave himself; 2a) in a good sense; 2b) in a bad sense, to test one*

maliciously, craftily to put to the proof his feelings or judgments; 2c) to try or test one's faith, virtue, character, by enticement to sin; 2c1) to solicit to sin, to tempt; 2c1a) of the temptations of the devil; 2d) after the OT usage; 2d1) of God: to inflict evils upon one in order to prove his character and the steadfastness of his faith; 2d2) men are said to tempt God by exhibitions of distrust, as though they wished to try whether he is not justly distrusted; 2d3) by impious or wicked conduct to test God's justice and patience, and to challenge him, as it were to give proof of his perfections."

SATAN'S THREE TEMPTATIONS OF CHRIST
- Luke 4:1-13

"And Jesus being full of the Holy Ghost returned from Jordan, and was led by the Spirit into the wilderness, Being forty days **tempted** of the devil. And in those days he did eat nothing: and when they were ended, he afterward hungered.

First: "And the devil said unto him, If thou be the Son of God, command this stone that it be made bread. And Jesus answered him, saying, It is written, That man shall not live by bread alone, but by every word of God.

Second: "And the devil, taking him up into an high mountain, shewed unto him all the kingdoms of the world in a moment of time. And the devil said unto him, All this power will I give thee, and the glory of them: for that is delivered unto me; and to whomsoever I will I give it. If thou therefore wilt worship me, all shall be thine. And Jesus answered and said unto him, Get thee behind me, Satan: for it is written, Thou shalt worship the Lord thy God, and him only shalt thou serve.

Third: "And he brought him to Jerusalem, and set him on a pinnacle of the temple, and said unto him, If thou be the Son of God, cast thyself down from hence: For it is written, He shall give his angels charge over thee, to keep thee: And in their hands they shall bear thee up, lest at any time thou dash thy foot against a stone. And Jesus answering said unto him, It is said, Thou shalt not tempt the Lord thy God. And when the devil had ended all the **temptation**, he departed from him for a season."

Hebrews—Preaching Verse by Verse

CHRIST TESTED 40 DAYS BY SATAN

The Devil tempted and tested the Lord Jesus Christ for forty days in the wilderness. He did not eat anything for forty days. If it were us, we would pass out from hunger in a few days. The Devil knew about these conditions. He probably did not know the Lord Jesus Christ was unable to sin.

STONES INTO BREAD REFUSED

1. Temptation #1–Turning Stones Into Bread. The Devil tried to get the Lord Jesus Christ to turn stones into bread. He could have done this because, though some Fundamentalist Baptists doubt it, the Lord Jesus Christ had all the attributes of Deity. However, He did not use these attributes for His own advantage. <u>The Lord Jesus Christ had the voluntary disuse of His Divine attributes for His own purposes</u>. The Lord Jesus Christ quoted a portion of Deuteronomy 8:3 in answer to the Devil: *"It is written, That man shall not live by bread alone, but by every word of God."* Satan failed here.

WORSHIP OF SATAN REJECTED

2. Temptation #2–Worshipping Satan. The second temptation of the Lord Jesus Christ was for Him to go up to a high mountain, be shown all the kingdoms of the world, and be offered all the power and glory of these kingdoms if He would worship Satan. Again the Lord Jesus Christ quoted a portion of Deuteronomy 10:20 and said: *"for it is written, Thou shalt worship the Lord thy God, and him only shalt thou serve."* Satan failed again.

JUMPING FROM THE TEMPLE REJECTED

3. Temptation #3–Jumping From The Temple Pinnacle. The third temptation of the Lord Jesus Christ was to get him to jump from the pinnacle of the temple and have the angels catch Him. Once again the Lord Jesus Christ quoted a portion of Deuteronomy 6:16 and said: *"It is said, Thou shalt not tempt the Lord thy God."* Satan slightly misquoted the verse about the angels and failed in this temptation as well.

Hebrews 4:16

"Let us therefore come boldly unto the throne of grace, that we may obtain mercy, and find grace to help in time of need."

COME BOLDLY

Because those who are genuinely saved have a tested and true great high priest, they can "*come boldly unto the throne of grace*" in Heaven to obtain mercy and grace to help them. They have unlimited access to Heaven and to both God the Father and God the Son in prayer. Our Saviour wants to help His redeemed children.

The Greek word for "*boldly*" is PARRESIA. Some of the meanings for this Word are:

> "1) freedom in speaking, unreservedness in speech; 1a) openly, frankly, i.e without concealment; 1b) without ambiguity or circumlocution; 1c) without the use of figures and comparisons; 2) free and fearless confidence, cheerful courage, boldness, assurance; 3) the deportment by which one becomes conspicuous or secures publicity."

CHRIST'S HELP TO THE BELIEVERS

- **1 John 2:1**

"My little children, these things write I unto you, that ye sin not. And if any man sin, we have an **advocate** with the Father, Jesus Christ the righteous:"

The Lord Jesus Christ, the great **High Priest** of the genuinely saved Christians, is their **advocate or lawyer**. He is Jesus Christ the righteous One.

- **Romans 8:33-34**

"Who shall lay any thing to the charge of God's elect? *It is* God that justifieth. Who is he that condemneth? *It is* Christ that died, yea rather, that is risen again, who is even at the right hand of God, who also maketh **intercession** for us."

THE REDEEMED HAVE A GREAT HIGH PRIEST

We who are truly redeemed have a High Priest. We have a Saviour. We have a great High Priest. He is able to help us in all of our problems and difficulties. He has given us His Words in a Bible that we can read, study, and follow. We should praise God for His Bible that tells us about our Saviour and Redeemer, the Lord Jesus Christ to Whom we should live for and exalt all of our days.

Hebrews
Chapter Five

Hebrews 5:1

"For every high priest taken from among men is ordained for men in things *pertaining* to God, that he may offer both gifts and sacrifices for sins:"

THE HIGH PRIESTS & THE DAY OF ATONEMENT

This first verse tell us about the **high priests** of the Old Testament. The **high priests** were taken from **Aaron** and his sons when Aaron died. He had special clothing and special duties. A very important duty for the **high priests** was on the **Day of Atonement**, where his offerings **atoned** for the sins of Israel once a year.

Here are some twenty-seven verses that deal with the **high priest** of Israel.

- **Leviticus 16:1**

"And the LORD spake unto Moses after the death of the two sons of Aaron, when they offered before the LORD, and died;"

This entire Chapter speaks in detail about Israel's **Day of Atonement**. It gives the detailed steps taken by the **high priest** on this day each year. Aaron's two sons were slain by the Lord for offering strange fire.

- **Leviticus 16:2**

"And the LORD said unto Moses, Speak unto **Aaron** thy brother, that **he** come not at all times into the holy *place* within the vail before the mercy seat, which *is* upon the ark; that **he** die not: for I will appear in the cloud upon the mercy seat."

Anyone who would enter into the holy of holies, inside that vail, would die. God is very clear and specific on that particular point.

- **Leviticus 16:3**

"Thus shall **Aaron** come into the holy *place*: with a young bullock for a sin offering, and a ram for a burnt offering."

Aaron, the **high priest** was to bring the young bullock for a sin offering, a ram for a burnt offering for **himself** and **his** family.

- **Leviticus 16:4a**

"He shall put on the holy linen coat, and **he** shall have the linen breeches upon his flesh, and shall be girded with a linen girdle,"

AARON'S SPECIAL UNIFORM

This is Aaron's special uniform as he goes in once a year into the holy of holies on the Day of Atonement.

- **Leviticus 16:5**

"And **he** shall take of the congregation of the children of Israel two kids of the goats for a sin offering, and one ram for a burnt offering."

For the sins of the congregation, **Aaron** must take these three animals mentioned here.

- **Leviticus 16:6**

"And **Aaron** shall offer **his** bullock of the sin offering, which is for **himself**, and make an **atonement** for **himself**, and for **his** house."

PRIESTS OFFERED FOR THEIR SINS

The Lord Jesus Christ, the Great High Priest of those who are genuinely saved, did not have to offer any sin offerings for Himself. He was and is sinless and perfect. But these high priests of earth had to offer for themselves and for their families the required offerings.

- **Leviticus 16:7-8**

"And **he** shall take the two goats, and present them before the LORD at the door of the tabernacle of the congregation. And **Aaron** shall cast lots upon the two goats; one lot for the LORD, and the other lot for the scapegoat."

<u>**Aaron** is not going to kill both of these goats for the sins of the people, but just one goat.</u> The other goat will be let go as the scape goat which will live.

- **Leviticus 16:9**

"And **Aaron** shall bring the goat upon which the LORD's lot fell, and offer him *for* a sin offering."

This is the goat that will be offered for the sins of the people.

- **Leviticus 16:10**

"But the goat, on which the lot fell to be the scapegoat, shall be presented alive before the LORD, to make an **atonement** with him, *and* to let him go for a scapegoat into the wilderness."

AARON'S HANDS ON THE SCAPEGOAT

Before the scapegoat is let go, Aaron puts his hands on the head of the goat and confesses all the sins of Israel. Then he lets the goat go into the wilderness. <u>To me, the scapegoat is a picture of the Lord Jesus Christ</u> being brought back to life by His bodily resurrection, after His death on the cross for the sins of the world.

- **Leviticus 16:11**

"And **Aaron** shall bring the bullock of the sin offering, which is for **himself**, and shall make an atonement for **himself**, and for **his** house, and shall kill the bullock of the sin offering which is for **himself**:"

THE AARONIC LINE WAS IMPERFECT

It is very important to see that Aaron needed a sacrifice for his own sins. He was not perfect. No high priest in the Old Testament of the Aaronic line was perfect. Only the Lord Jesus Christ, the High Priest of those who are genuinely saved was and is perfect.

- **Leviticus 16:12**

"And **he** shall take a censer full of burning coals of fire from off the altar before the LORD, and **his** hands full of sweet incense beaten small, and bring *it* within the vail:"

Aaron had incense in **his** hands to bring into the holy of holies on the **Day of Atonement**.

- **Leviticus 16:13**

"And **he** shall put the incense upon the fire before the LORD, that the cloud of the incense may cover the mercy seat that *is* upon the testimony, that **he** die not:"

<u>Notice that the mercy seat was on top of the altar.</u>

- **Leviticus 16:14**

"And **he** shall take of the blood of the bullock, and sprinkle *it* with **his** finger upon the mercy seat eastward; and before the mercy seat shall **he** sprinkle of the blood with his finger seven times."

That mercy seat was on top of the ark of the covenant. <u>Seven times **he** sprinkled that bullock's blood for himself, for **his** own sins and for the sins of **his** family.</u>

- **Leviticus 16:15**

"Then shall **he** kill the goat of the sin offering, that *is* for the people, and bring his blood within the vail, and do with that blood as **he** did with the blood of the bullock, and sprinkle it upon the mercy seat, and before the mercy seat:"

THE BLOOD PUT ON THE MERCY SEAT

Then Aaron puts the blood of the slain goat (which is for the sins of the people) upon and before the mercy seat as he did with the blood of the bullock.

- **Leviticus 16:16**

"And he shall make an **atonement** for the holy *place*, because of the uncleanness of the children of Israel, and because of their transgressions in all their sins: and so shall he do for the tabernacle of the congregation, that remaineth among them in the midst of their uncleanness."

All this offering and placement of the blood of the goat was for the transgressions and sins of the people of Israel for the preceding year.

- **Leviticus 16:17**

"And there shall be no man in the tabernacle of the congregation when he goeth in to make an atonement in the holy *place*, until he come out, and have made an **atonement** for himself, and for his household, and for all the congregation of Israel."

When **Aaron** went in to make atonement on this **Day of Atonement** to **atone** for his sins, his family's sins, and the sins of the people, no other man could be in the tabernacle. The **high priest** must go there alone.

Christian tradition mentions that the **high priest** had bells on the hem of his garment so the bells could be heard as he was serving in the holy of holies. If the bells stopped, it meant the **high priest** had died. Then they would have to drag **his** body out either with big hooks, or by a rope previously tied to his leg. It is not certain.

THE ATONEMENT WAS FOR ALL ISRAEL

I want you to notice something important. The atonement made once a year by the high priest in the Old Testament was not made only for a certain "elect" group of people. It was made for the entire congregation of Israel. This argues against the heretical teaching of the hyper-Calvinists that the death of the Lord Jesus Christ was only for the sins of the "elect" group of people. It was rather for the sins of the entire world so that any person is encouraged to genuinely trust the Lord Jesus

> Christ as their Saviour and be redeemed and possess everlasting life.

"For God so loved the world, that he gave his only begotten Son, that whosoever believeth in him should not perish, but have everlasting life." (John 3:16)

"And the Spirit and the bride say, Come. And let him that heareth say, Come. And let him that is athirst come. And whosoever will, let him take the water of life freely." (Revelation 22:17)

- **Leviticus 16:18-19**

"And he shall go out unto the altar that *is* before the LORD, and make an **atonement** for it; and shall take of the blood of the bullock, and of the blood of the goat, and put *it* upon the horns of the altar round about. And he shall sprinkle of the blood upon it with **his** finger seven times, and cleanse it, and hallow it from the uncleanness of the children of Israel."

- **Leviticus 16:20-21**

"And when he hath made an end of reconciling the holy *place*, and the tabernacle of the congregation, and the altar, he shall bring the live goat: And **Aaron** shall lay both his hands upon the head of the live goat, and confess over him all the iniquities of the children of Israel, and all their transgressions in all their sins, putting them upon the head of the goat, and shall send *him* away by the hand of a fit man into the wilderness:"

> **THE LIVE GOAT PICTURES RESURRECTION**
>
> **Aaron** did not kill this second goat. Instead, he was to lay both his hands upon the head of the live goat, and confess over this live goat all the sins of the Israelites. After that, he was to send this goat away by a fit man into the wilderness.
>
> This goat is called the *"scape goat."* It speaks in picture of the Lord Jesus Christ when He died for the sins of the whole world, was buried for three days and three nights which is 72 hours. After this time, He rose again bodily from the dead. He was triumphant over death because all the sins of the world were atoned for. No more sins had to be paid for.

- **Leviticus 16:22**

"And the goat shall bear upon him all their iniquities unto a land not inhabited: and he shall let go the goat in the wilderness."

> **SDA--SCAPE GOAT REPRESENTS SATAN**
> One of the heresies of the <u>Seventh Day Adventists</u> is that the scape goat represents the Devil and that the Devil took away all these sins. Not at all! The scape goat is a picture of the Lord Jesus Christ bearing the sins of the world.

- **Leviticus 16:23**

"And Aaron shall come into the tabernacle of the congregation, and shall put off the linen garments, which he put on when he went into the holy *place*, and shall leave them there:"

In other words, he will leave the holy of holies and remove his linen garments. These linen garments were only for that special time when he went into the holy of holies once a year.

- **Leviticus 16:24**

"And he shall wash his flesh with water in the holy place, and put on his garments, and come forth, and offer **his** burnt offering, and the burnt offering of the people, and make an **atonement** for **himself**, and for the people."

The burnt offerings were the two rams, one ram for himself, one ram for the people of Israel. <u>Very often, we don't think of the ram in addition to the bullock for Aaron or the two goats and the ram for the children of Israel</u>.

- **Leviticus 16:32-34**

"And the **priest**, whom he shall anoint, and whom he shall consecrate to minister in the **priest's** office in his father's stead, shall make the **atonement**, and shall put on the linen clothes, *even* the holy garments: And he shall make an **atonement** for the holy sanctuary, and he shall make an **atonement** for the tabernacle of the congregation, and for the altar, and he shall make an atonement for the priests, and for all the people of the congregation. And this shall be an everlasting statute unto you, to make an **atonement** for the children of Israel for all their sins once a year. And he did as the LORD commanded Moses."

> **CHRIST--OFFERED ONLY ONCE**
> These verses summarize what the high priests of Israel were to do on the Day of Atonement once every year without fail. An important difference (among many) between the high priests of the Old Testament and the Great High Priesthood of the Lord Jesus Christ is that He did not have to offer for Himself once every year. He offered Himself, the Lamb of God, <u>only once</u>--never to be repeated forever.

The Roman Catholic Church has masses in which they presume to crucify again the Lord Jesus Christ everywhere, day by day, all around the world. This amounts to thousands and thousands of masses which they teach and believe is the death of their "Christ." This is paganism. This is serious unbiblical heresy.

Hebrews 5:2

"Who can have compassion on the ignorant, and on them that are out of the way; for that he himself also is compassed with infirmity."

COMPASSION

These high priests of the Old Testament could have **compassion** on the ignorant and the wayward because they themselves were surrounded by sin. The Lord Jesus Christ was a High Priest Who came to earth from Heaven. He also has **compassion** on all people. Sometimes those of us who are genuinely saved do not have **compassion**. There are people in mental institutions. We should have **compassion** on them as well. *"Compassion"* is used some thirty-nine times in our King James Bible.

- **Exodus 2:2-3**

"And the woman conceived, and bare a son: and when she saw him that he *was a* goodly *child*, she hid him three months. And when she could not longer hide him, she took for him an ark of bulrushes, and daubed it with slime and with pitch, and put the child therein; and she laid *it* in the flags by the river's brink."

MOSES SPARED FROM DEATH

Remember, the Egyptian king ordered all the male babies to be killed. He didn't want them to grow up and fight against the Egyptians. But the mother saw that Moses was a goodly child, so they spared Moses' life. They did not kill him.

- **Exodus 2:4-10**

"And his sister stood afar off, to wit what would be done to him. And the daughter of Pharaoh came down to wash *herself* at the river; and her maidens walked along by the river's side; and when she saw the ark among the flags, she sent her maid to fetch it. And when she had opened *it*, she saw the child: and, behold, the babe wept. And she had **compassion** on him, and said, This *is one* of the Hebrews' children. Then said his sister to Pharaoh's daughter, Shall I go and call to thee a nurse of the Hebrew women, that she may nurse the child for thee? And Pharaoh's daughter said to her,

Go. And the maid went and called the child's mother. And Pharaoh's daughter said unto her, Take this child away, and nurse it for me, and I will give *thee* thy wages. And the woman took the child, and nursed it. And the child grew, and she brought him unto Pharaoh's daughter, and he became her son. And she called his name Moses: and she said, Because I drew him out of the water."

PHARAOH'S DAUGHTER'S COMPASSION

This heathen, pagan--Pharaoh's daughter--at least had enough emotion in her soul to have compassion on this little baby whom she called *"Moses."* It is sad to see so many mothers and doctors who have no compassion on little babies, but kill them by abortion. Around one and a half million babies each year are murdered by these doctors. Where is the compassion? There is no compassion on these little babies. When Pharaoh's daughter saw this little baby weeping, she had compassion on him and spared his life. She took him into the palace and took care of him. He was in Egypt for forty years.

- **1 Kings 8:50**

"And forgive thy people that have sinned against thee, and all their transgressions wherein they have transgressed against thee, and give them **compassion** before them who carried them captive, that they may have **compassion** on them:"

This was Solomon's prayer. He prayed, that when the Israelites would be taken captive, their captors would have **compassion** on them. These captivities happened by Assyria for the ten tribes and by Babylon for the two tribes.

That's what the Lord Jesus Christ said when on the Cross:
"*. . . Father, forgive them; for they know not what they do. . .*" (Luke 23:34)

That's the attitude that Stephen, the first deacon, had when he was being stoned and killed:
"*And he kneeled down, and cried with a loud voice, Lord, lay not this sin to their charge. And when he had said this, he fell asleep.*" (Acts 7:60)

Everybody doesn't love us, let's face it. Many people can't stand us. In fact, they hate us, and despise us. So, we who are saved, should have **compassion** on those who are against us.

- **Psalm 78:38**

"But he, *being* full of **compassion**, forgave *their* iniquity, and destroyed *them* not: yea, many a time turned he his anger away, and did not stir up all his wrath."

- **Psalm 145:8**

"The Lord is gracious, and full of **compassion**; slow to anger, and of great mercy."

The Lord is **compassionate**. So the Old Testament high priests should also have **compassion** on the ignorant and on those who are out of the way. The Lord Jesus Christ Himself has **compassion** on those who are completely out of the way and lost.

- **Matthew 9:36**

"But when he saw the multitudes, he was moved with **compassion** on them, because they fainted, and were scattered abroad, as sheep having no shepherd."

> **SHEEP HAVING NO SHEPHERD**
> When the Lord Jesus Christ was on the earth, He had compassion on them because they fainted. They were like *"sheep having no shepherd."* He died for the sins of the whole world at Calvary's cross. This was His ultimate compassion.

Hebrews 5:3

"And by reason hereof he ought, as for the people, so also for himself, to offer for sins."

OLD TESTAMENT HIGH PRIESTS' OFFERINGS

Notice that it says "*as for the people, so also for himself.*" The high priest of earth had to **offer for his own sins**, as well as for the sins of the people. But the Lord Jesus Christ was sinless and did not have to **offer** for Himself. That's a great difference between the **earthly high priest** and the Lord Jesus Christ as the **Heavenly High Priest**.

- **Hebrews 7:27**

"Who needeth not daily, as those **high priests**, to **offer** up sacrifice, first for **his own sins**, and then for the people's: for this he did once, when he **offered** up himself."

This verse speaks of the once-for-all **sacrifice** of the Lord Jesus Christ at Calvary. He cried out from the cross [TETELESTAI] *"It is finished."* That atonement for the sins of the world was never to be repeated. His sacrifice was completed. It is a great and serious heresy for the priest to offer up the Lord Jesus Christ in their masses repeatedly each day all around the world!

- **Leviticus 16:5**

"And he shall take of the congregation of the children of Israel two kids of the goats for a sin **offering**, and one ram for a burnt offering."

As we read earlier, <u>all of these were the **offerings** for the sins for himself and the sins of the congregation</u> on the Day of Atonement each year.

Hebrews 5:4

"And no man taketh this honour unto himself, but he that is called of God, as *was* Aaron."

THE CALL OF AARON

Nobody can say "I want to be a priest." At one time, in Numbers 16, some of the Israelites, led by Korah, tried to take over the priesthood.

"And they gathered themselves together against Moses and against **Aaron**, and said unto them, *Ye take* too much upon you, seeing all the congregation *are* holy, every one of them, and the LORD *is* among them: wherefore then lift ye up yourselves above the congregation of the LORD?" (Numbers 16:3)

God put an end to this infighting by putting blossoms on the rod of Aaron rather than the rods of those from other tribes and families. **Aaron** was indeed *"called of God."*

We'll see a little bit later, that the Lord Jesus Christ came from a different order of priesthood. He was of the order of Melchisedec and from the tribe of Judah rather than Levi.

- **Exodus 4:14**

"And the anger of the LORD was kindled against Moses, and he said, *Is* not **Aaron** the Levite thy brother? I know that he can speak well. And also, behold, he cometh forth to meet thee: and when he seeth thee, he will be glad in his heart."

Moses told the Lord that he wasn't a good speaker. He wondered how he could take the people of Israel out of Egypt. This made the Lord angry with Moses. He told him that Aaron would be his helper.

- **Exodus 4:15**

"And thou shalt speak unto him, and put words in his mouth: and I will be with thy mouth, and with his mouth, and will teach you what ye shall do."

So **Aaron** and Moses were brought together for this important task. **Aaron** was three years older than Moses and able to speak well.

- **Exodus 4:16**

"And he shall be thy spokesman unto the people: and he shall be, *even* he shall be to thee instead of a mouth, and thou shalt be to him instead of God."

In other words, God would give Moses the words. Then Moses would give **Aaron**, his brother, the words to say and **Aaron** would speak them. In this way, God took away all the excuses that Moses offered. You and I often make excuses to the Lord as Moses did. Instead of making excuses, we should ask the Lord how we can do what the Lord wants us to do. We should look in the Bible and find in the Words of God how we can do these things He calls to do.

THE CALL OF MOSES

The task God called Moses to perform was not easy. 600,000 men plus women plus children—one or two or three million people--were under Moses' care. God said to Moses that He wanted him to take all these people out of Egypt. That was a huge task, but Moses was fitted for the task.

God also has important tasks for those He has redeemed and saved. We must say "what wilt thou have me to do"? As Moses accepted God's call and never went back, so must we.

Hebrews 5:5

"So also Christ glorified not himself to be made an high priest; but he that said unto him, Thou art my Son, to day have I begotten thee."

CHRIST'S CALL AS HIGH PRIEST

God the Father made **His Son**, the **Lord Jesus Christ** a **High Priest**. **Jesus** did not seek it **Himself**. He was **called** of the Lord to be the **High Priest**. Though John MacArthur used to teach (and maybe still believes) that the Lord Jesus Christ was not the "Son of God" from all eternity past, I believe firmly in the eternal Sonship of the Saviour. He became the Son of Man through the virgin birth, but He was the Son of God from all eternity.

- **Acts 13:33**

"God hath fulfilled the same unto us their children, in that he hath raised up Jesus again; as it is also written in the second psalm, Thou art my Son, this day have I begotten thee."

> **CHRIST'S BODILY RESURRECTION**
> "*This day have I begotten thee*" could refer to the bodily resurrection of the Lord Jesus Christ because it was then that the Lord Jesus Christ was in His resurrected, glorified body.

Hebrews 5:6

"As he saith also in another *place*, Thou *art* a priest for ever after the order of Melchisedec."

A PRIEST AFTER THE ORDER OF MELCHISEDEC

God the Father said to **His Son**: "*Thou art a priest for ever.*" **The Priesthood** of the Lord Jesus Christ was not only for many years, but for ever. His Priesthood is **after the order of Melchisedec** rather than after the order of Aaron. The **Lord Jesus Christ's eternal Priesthood** supplants that of Aaron. The entire law of Moses has been replaced by the grace of God found in **His Son**, the **Lord Jesus Christ**.

- **Genesis 14:14-16**

"And when Abram heard that his brother was taken captive, he armed his trained *servants*, born in his own house, three hundred and eighteen, and pursued *them* unto Dan. And he divided himself against them, he and his servants, by night, and smote them, and pursued them unto Hobah, which *is* on the left hand of Damascus. And he brought back all the goods, and also brought again his brother Lot, and his goods, and the women also, and the people."

> **ABRAHAM'S 318 SERVANTS**
> The Lord led these 318 servants to victory over those who had captured Abraham's nephew, Lot.

- **Genesis 14:17-18**

"And the king of Sodom went out to meet him after his return from the slaughter of Chedorlaomer, and of the kings that *were* with him, at the valley of Shaveh, which *is* the king's dale. And **Melchisedec** king of Salem brought forth bread and wine: and he *was* the **priest** of the most high God."

The king of Sodom went out to meet Abram after his victory over these kings. His nephew, Lot, was in Sodom, a very, wicked place where many Sodomites and those who committed all kinds of wickedness lived.

Melchisedec, the **Priest of the most high God**, was appointed by the Lord. He was not from Levi, but from Judah. I believe that **Melchisedec** was a **Christophany**--an appearance of the **Lord Jesus**

Christ before His incarnation. Hebrews 7:3 mentions **Melchisedec**, that he was:

> "*Without father, without mother, without descent, having neither beginning of days, nor end of life; but made like unto the Son of God; abideth a priest continually.*"

- **Genesis 14:19-20**

"And he blessed him, and said, Blessed be Abram of the most high God, possessor of heaven and earth: And blessed be the most high God, which hath delivered thine enemies into thy hand. And he gave him tithes of all."

Melchisedec blessed Abram. Then Abram gave him tithes of all the spoil that he had taken in this battle. Later, in Exodus, the Israelites were to give tithes to Levi and the priests.

MELCHISEDEC A CHRISTOPHANY

But here, Levi, who was going to be born into Abraham's family, paid tithes to Melchisedec. This shows that Melchisedec and the Lord Jesus Christ were greater than Levi. As Melchisedec, the Lord Jesus Christ had no beginning of days nor end of life. That's why I believe Melchisedec was a Christophany.

Hebrews 5:7

"Who in the days of his flesh, when he had offered up prayers and supplications with strong crying and tears unto him that was able to save him from death, and was heard in that he feared;"

CHRIST'S PRAYERS IN GETHSEMANE

According to this verse, God the Father was able to save the **Lord Jesus Christ** from death. But our **Saviour, God the Son**, did not request this of God the Father. Just like when the mob came onto the **Lord Jesus Christ**. He said:

> "*Thinkest thou that I cannot now **pray** to my Father, and he shall presently give me more than twelve legions of angels?*" (Matthew 26:53)

The **Lord Jesus Christ** said He was able to be delivered by the Father but He was not delivered because it was not the will of God the Father. The offering of the **Lord Jesus Christ** was a voluntary offering. It was not forced upon Him.

- **Matthew 26:36-38**

"Then cometh **Jesus** with them unto a place called **Gethsemane**, and saith unto the disciples, Sit ye here, while I go and **pray** yonder. And he took with him Peter and the two sons of Zebedee, and began to be sorrowful and very heavy. Then saith he unto them, My soul is exceeding sorrowful, even unto death: tarry ye here, and watch with me."

PRAYER IN GETHSEMANE

The Lord Jesus Christ was in the garden of Gethsemane. He was ready to go to Calvary. He wanted Peter, James, and John to pray with Him, but they fell asleep.

- **Luke 22:44**

"And being in an agony e **prayed** more earnestly: and his sweat was as it were great drops of blood falling down to the ground."

The **Lord Jesus Christ** was in **Gethsemane**. It was a tremendous agony. Why was he in agony? He did not want to die in **Gethsemane**. He knew His father's will was to die on the Cross at Calvary. He wanted these three disciples to watch with **Him** and **pray**, just before He went to the trial, the scourging, and the cross.

- **Matthew 26:39**

"And he went a little further, and fell on his face, and **prayed**, saying, O my father, if it be possible, let this cup pass from me: nevertheless not as I will, but as thou *wilt*."

WHAT WAS THE "CUP"?

What was the "*cup*"? Though others think it to be death at Calvary, I like the view that Dr. M. R. DeHaan, founder of the Radio Bible Class, has. He believed that the Lord Jesus Christ did not want to die in the garden, but in the place prophesied of Him—on a cross. The Lord Jesus Christ did not make any demands on God the Father. He said, "*if it be possible, let this cup pass from me.*" He also said, "*not as I will, but as Thou wilt.*" He was truly submissive to the will of God the Father.

- **Matthew 26:40-41**

"And he cometh unto the disciples, and findeth them asleep, and saith unto Peter, What, could ye not watch with me one hour? Watch and **pray**, that ye enter not into temptation: the spirit indeed is willing, but the flesh *is* weak."

Some people come to our church and say that they're a little tired. I tell them to sleep in our chairs if they wish. I tell them to get comfortable. But these disciples, who should have been ready to be with the **Lord**

Jesus Christ in His agony and sorrow before Calvary, should have been awake. Maybe they didn't get any sleep the night before, I don't know.

> **THE APOSTLES FALL ASLEEP**
> When the Lord Jesus Christ finished His first prayer, He came back to Peter, James, and John and found them asleep. He asked them if they couldn't watch with Him for one hour. He rightly stated that their *"spirit indeed is willing, but the flesh is weak."* He wanted them to watch and pray, to stay out of temptation.

- **Matthew 26:42**

"He went away again the second time, and **prayed**, saying, O my Father, if this cup may not pass away from me, except I drink it, thy will be done."

The **Lord Jesus Christ** went away from the three apostles a second time and **prayed**. He wanted God the Father's will to be done. The Saviour did not want to avoid the cross of Calvary. This is the reason God the Father sent God the Son into the world.

- **John 3:16**

"For God so loved the world, that he gave his only begotten Son, that whosoever believeth in him should not perish, but have everlasting life."

God the Father sent His only begotten Son to die for the sins of the world so that those who genuinely believe in Him might have everlasting life. Without His sacrifice on the cross at Calvary, there could be no salvation. Calvary was a necessity. This was after the Saviour's second **prayer.**

- **Matthew 26:43**

"And he came and found them asleep again: for their eyes were heavy."

Apparently these apostles didn't get enough sleep during their earlier nap, so they were sleeping again.

- **Matthew 26:44**

"And he left them, and went away again, and **prayed** the third time, saying the same words."

The Lord Jesus Christ did not wake his apostles. He just left them and **prayed** the third time. Though the words were not given, they were the "*same words*" like "*not as I will, but as Thou wilt.*"

- **Matthew 26:45**

"Then cometh he to his disciples, and saith unto them, Sleep on now, and take *your* rest: behold, the hour is at hand, and the Son of man is betrayed into the hands of sinners."

TRAITORS IN OUR MIDST?

The Lord predicted His own betrayal. It would be by one of His own apostles, Judas Iscariot. When He picked the twelve apostles, He knew that one of them would be a traitor.

That should warn all of us. In churches where it seems like many are saved, born-again Christians, there is very likely also to have a traitor or two like Judas Iscariot. Maybe one or more of them might not be genuinely saved, though they look like they are. They might look like Christians, talk like Christians, go where Christians go but maybe they are not. They might be a Judas.

Judas came to the Garden of Gethsemane a little bit later with a great multitude of Jewish leaders. They were armed with swords, staves, and spears. They asked Judas which person was the Lord Jesus Christ. Judas said it is the one he would kiss. I call it the kiss of betrayal.

Judas had professed earlier to love the Saviour. He was a hypocrite. These sinners came out to kill the Lord Jesus Christ. They took Him away to be tried in Pilate's judgment hall, and finally, to be crucified.

BARABBAS RELEASED, NOT CHRIST

Though Pilate didn't want to give the Lord to the mob to be crucified, he backed off and released murderer Barabbas, and permitted the Lord Jesus Christ to be led away to be crucified. The screaming crowds followed the leadership of the Pharisees and other Jewish leaders who hated the Saviour.

Hebrews 5:8

"Though he were a Son, yet learned he obedience by the things which he suffered;"

LEARNED

CHRIST THE "GOD-MAN"

The Lord Jesus Christ is and was the perfect Son of God through all of eternity, past, present, and all eternity future. He came into this world by the miracle of the incarnation. He was and is perfect God and perfect, sinless Man. He was and is the God-Man, the THEANTHROPOS. *"Though he were a Son, yet learned he obedience."* Obedience is a learning process. The Lord Jesus Christ learned to be obedient by the things he suffered. As God the Son, He was not inferior to God the

Father. He was not inferior to God the Holy Spirit. But there was a Divine order. He took that position of obedience to God the Father. *"Not my will but thine be done"* he said. But He learned obedience.

- **Genesis 30:27**

"And Laban said unto him, I pray thee, if I have found favour in thine eyes, *tarry: for* I have **learned** by experience that the LORD hath blessed me for thy sake."

Laban **learned** by experience. We all must **learn**.

- **Matthew 11:29**

"Take my yoke upon you, and **learn** of me; for I am meek and lowly in heart: and ye shall find rest unto your souls."

Learn of me. That's what every born-again Christian must do. <u>It's in the Bible where we find the things we are to **learn** about the Lord Jesus Christ</u>. It's in the Old Testament as well as in the New Testament.

- **John 7:15**

"And the Jews marvelled, saying, How knoweth this man letters, having never **learned**?"

CHRIST WAS OMNISCIENT

The Lord Jesus Christ knew all things, being perfect Deity as well as perfect Humanity. He was the One Who was the Author of all the Words of the Bible. But the Jews marvelled at His knowledge.

- **Philippians 4:11**

"Not that I speak in respect of want: for I have **learned**, in whatsoever state I am, *therewith* to be content."

Paul wrote this from a Roman prison. <u>Contentment is a **learning** experience</u>. You must **learn** to be content in whatever state or condition that you're in. There are many different kinds of conditions. Paul said that he had to **learn** contentment.

LEARNING IS NEEDED

Those of us who are genuinely saved must **learn** it also in whatever condition we find ourselves. The Lord is able to make us content if we trust in Him and **learn** from Him.

OBEDIENCE

- **Romans 5:19**

"For as by one man's disobedience many were made sinners, so by the **obedience** of one shall many be made righteous."

The Lord Jesus Christ was **obedient** to the will of God the Father and went to the cross of Calvary and died for the sins of the world.

SUFFERING

- **Romans 8:18**

"For I reckon that the **sufferings** of this present time *are* not worthy *to be compared* with the glory which shall be revealed in us."

SUFFERINGS AND GLORY

Paul compared the sufferings here on earth with the glory that will be revealed to the genuine Christians in Heaven.

- **Philippians 3:10**

"That I may know him, and the power of his resurrection, and the fellowship of his **sufferings**, being made conformable unto his death;"

This is quite honest of Paul to want to know the fellowship of the **sufferings** of the Lord Jesus Christ that He endured for us.

- **Hebrews 2:9**

"But we see Jesus, who was made a little lower than the angels for the **suffering** of death, crowned with glory and honour; that he by the grace of God should taste death for every man."

CHRIST TASTED DEATH FOR EVERYONE

Notice that the Lord Jesus Christ tasted death and died for "*every man*," not just for a tiny group of people called the "*elect*" as the hyper-Calvinists heretically teach.

- **Hebrews 2:10**

"For it became him, for whom *are* all things, and by whom *are* all things, in bringing many sons unto glory, to make the captain of their salvation perfect through **sufferings**."

Through His **sufferings, the Lord Jesus Christ learned full maturity in obedience**. He was and is perfect and sinless, but this learning was in practical experiences.

- **1 Peter 1:11**

"Searching what, or what manner of time the Spirit of Christ which was in them did signify, when it testified beforehand the **sufferings** of Christ, and the glory that should follow."

THE SUFFERINGS OF CHRIST
This refers to the Old Testament prophets as they wrote the Bible. They didn't understand all that they wrote, but followed the leading of the Holy Spirit. They wrote beforehand of the sufferings of Christ, and the glory that should follow.

- 1 Peter 4:13

"But rejoice, inasmuch as ye are partakers of Christ's **sufferings**; that, when his glory shall be revealed, ye may be glad also with exceeding joy."

REJOICING IN SUFFERINGS
There is joy in serving the Lord. Everyone of us who are saved, at one time or another, has some kind of sufferings, turmoil, or problems. We must realize that we can do all things through Christ which strengtheneth us (Philippians 4:13).

- 1 Peter 5:1

"The elders which are among you I exhort, who am also an elder, and a witness of the **sufferings** of Christ, and also a partaker of the glory that shall be revealed:"

Peter witnessed the **sufferings** of Christ. He saw the soldiers beat Him. He saw them put a the crown of thorns upon His head and mock Him. But Peter also saw the transfiguration glory of the Lord Jesus Christ.

Hebrews 5:9
"And being made perfect, he became the author of eternal salvation unto all them that obey him;"

THE LORD JESUS CHRIST IS PERFECT

THE PERFECTION OF CHRIST
The Lord Jesus Christ was made, in His incarnation, perfect Deity combined with perfect Humanity. No other person in all the world was perfect in his Humanity except the Lord Jesus Christ. He was and is the only One. None others on earth are perfect, even though sometimes the holiness people say they have achieved perfection. This is impossible.

The Lord Jesus Christ Himself, being made **perfect,** could also be the Author of *"eternal salvation"* for those who genuinely trust Him. Salvation is eternal. Once a person is born-again and saved, he can't ever be unborn, unsaved, or lost. Many churches teach this heresy and error.

It is taught by Pentecostals, Charismatics, the Church of Christ, the Free Methodists, the Christian And Missionary Alliance, and many other groups. John and Charles Wesley believed that once you sin, you lose your salvation. But God's salvation is *"eternal."* The Lord Jesus Christ is the author of eternal salvation.

The Greek Word for *"obey"* is HUPAKOUO. Some of the meanings of this Word are:

> *"1) to listen, to harken; 1a) of one who on the knock at the door comes to listen who it is, (the duty of a porter); 2) to harken to a command; 2a) to obey, be obedient to, submit to."*

Those who listen to, harken, and genuinely obey the Lord Jesus Christ have *"eternal salvation."*

NOT ABLE TO SIN

As far as the Lord Jesus being perfect and sinless, there are two Latin phrases that are often used to illustrate the truth. One phrase is false and the other phrase is true. The false phrase is: *"able not to sin"* (*posse non peccare*). The true phrase is: *"not able to sin"* (*non posse peccare*). <u>It was not that the Lord Jesus Christ was *"able not to sin"* that made Him perfect and sinless, but He was *"not able to sin."* He was and is absolutely perfect. In all His perfect Humanity and all his Deity, He never could sin.</u> If He could have sinned while on earth, He would be able to sin in Heaven. If that were so, those who are genuinely saved could lose their salvation and He would not any longer be the *"Author of eternal salvation."* <u>It was absolutely impossible for the Lord Jesus Christ to sin, either while on earth, or when in Heaven.</u>

- **John 8:46**

"Which of you convinceth me of sin? And if I say the truth, why do ye not believe me?"

THE IMPECCABILITY OF CHRIST

Nobody could convince Him or convict Him of sin. He was and is absolutely and totally impeccable and perfect.

- **Hebrews 4:15**

"For we have not an high priest which cannot be touched with the feeling of our infirmities; but was in all points tempted like as *we are*, *yet* without sin."

"Without sin" means that He was **perfect** and sinless.

- **2 Corinthians 5:21**

"For he hath made him *to be* sin for us, who knew no sin; that we might be made the righteousness of God in him."

God the Father made Him, the Lord Jesus Christ (Who knew no sin, but was sinless), to be made the sin offering for us, in our place, that we who genuinely trust in Him might be made the righteousness of God in Him. This is perfect righteousness and holiness as far as God is concerned in the books of heaven.

CHRIST CAME TO DIE FOR SINNERS

If the Lord Jesus Christ had not come down from Heaven to this earth and died for the sins of the world, no one would have salvation, whether Jews or Gentiles in any of the false cults or religions of the world. Eternal salvation is made available only by genuine faith in the Lord Jesus Christ.

CHRIST OUR "AUTHOR"

- **Hebrews 12:2**

"Looking unto Jesus the **author** and finisher of *our* faith; who for the joy that was set before him endured the cross, despising the shame, and is set down at the right hand of the throne of God."

Our wonderful **Author** of eternal salvation is both the **Author** and finisher of our faith. While it is true that even genuinely saved people still have the old nature--the flesh--they also have the indwelling Holy Spirit of God Who can overcome the flesh if they will continually walk in the Spirit.

"*This* I say then, Walk in the Spirit, and ye shall not fulfil the lust of the flesh." (Galatians 5:16)

ETERNAL SALVATION

- **John 3:16**

"For God so loved the world, that he gave his only begotten Son, that whosoever believeth in him should not perish, but have **everlasting life**."

Notice in this verse, God promises "*everlasting life.*" That is the life that is **everlasting** and **eternal.** It is a life that will never cease. It is for whoever genuinely believes in the Lord Jesus Christ, not only some small group called by the heretics as the "elect." All people-- "whosoever"-- are invited to and have the ability to genuinely believe in and receive the Lord Jesus Christ. The hyper-Calvinists are in serious heresy by denying this truth.

- **John 5:24**

"Verily, verily, I say unto you, He that heareth my word, and believeth on him that sent me, hath **everlasting life**, and shall not come into condemnation; but is passed from death unto life."

SALVATION CANNOT BE LOST

If you have passed from death unto life, how can you go back to death again? <u>This is the fallacy of those people that teach that you can lose your salvation.</u> It is true that saved people might be disobedient Christians at times when they sin, but they lose their fellowship with the Lord, not their salvation. They cannot be spiritually unborn-again once they are genuinely born-again by genuine faith in the Lord Jesus Christ.

My mother and father were my parents. I was born into this world on December 8, 1927. I might be a disobedient son, but I cannot be unborn physically and become a non-child. I can't be unborn. <u>So, as this verse states clearly, once we have genuinely believed on the Lord Jesus Christ, we possess **everlasting life** and pass from spiritual death to spiritual and **eternal life**</u>.

- **John 10:27-30**

"My sheep hear my voice, and I know them, and they follow me: And I give unto them **eternal life**; and they shall never perish, neither shall any *man* pluck them out of my hand. My Father, which gave *them* me, is greater than all; and no *man* is able to pluck them out of my Father's hand. I and *my* Father are one."

The Lord Jesus Christ said that. He gives **eternal life** to those who genuinely trust in Him as their Saviour. He promised that these would "*never perish*." They are safe in the Saviour's and God the Father's hands.

- **Acts 4:12**

"Neither is there **salvation** in any other: for there is none other name under heaven given among men, whereby we must be **saved**."

<u>Genuine faith in none other Name but the Name of the Lord Jesus Christ can **save** us for **all eternity**</u>.

- **Romans 1:16**

"For I am not ashamed of the gospel of Christ: for it is the power of God unto **salvation** to every one that believeth; to the Jew first, and also to the Greek."

This also speaks of an **eternal salvation**.

- **2 Corinthians 6:2**

"(For he saith, I have heard thee in a time accepted, and in the day of **salvation** have I succoured thee: behold, now *is* the accepted time; behold, now *is* the day of **salvation**.)"

The time to receive this **eternal salvation** is today. The time is now. Don't put it off. **Eternal salvation** is available right now. Don't wait until tomorrow, next month, or next year. Trust the Lord Jesus Christ as your Saviour now.

- **2 Timothy 3:15**

"And that from a child thou hast known the holy scriptures, which are able to make thee wise unto **salvation** through faith which is in Christ Jesus."

This **eternal salvation** is found in the holy Scriptures. **Salvation is only by genuine faith in the Lord Jesus Christ.**

- **Titus 2:11**

"For the grace of God that bringeth **salvation** hath appeared to all men,"

God's **eternal salvation** has appeared not only to the "elect" or a small group of people, but "*to all men.*" This **eternal salvation** is for all people in the world to receive by genuine faith in the Lord Jesus Christ. I don't understand why the hyper-Calvinists and other Calvinists heretically limit the death of the Lord Jesus Christ only to a small little group of "elect" people. He died for the sins of the whole world. This is very clear in the Bible. These people always interpret the very few verses that seem to teach otherwise to contradict the many, many clear verses that teach the truth. This is very defective hermeneutics.

Hebrews 5:10

"Called of God an high priest after the order of Melchisedec."

MELCHISEDEC

In the Old Testament, Melchisedec is spelled Melchizedek, but it is spelled differently in the New Testament. This verse is speaking of the Lord Jesus Christ. It states that he was "*called of God*" the Father. But He had a special calling after the order, not of Levi, but of **Melchisedec**. The Lord Jesus Christ was called of God to be a High Priest. But it was a High Priest after a different order. I believe **Melchisedec** was a Christophany, that is, an appearance of the Lord Jesus Christ before His incarnation.

> **SELECTION OF HIGH PRIESTS**
>
> As I have said before, the high priests of earth in the Old Testament were all from the tribe of Levi through Aaron. It was a lifetime appointment. When the high priest died, the oldest son would become the high priest. In the New Testament times, under the Roman government, they completely changed the way the high priests were appointed. They did not serve for life and they had different qualifications.

Hebrews 5:11

" **Of whom we have many things to say, and hard to be uttered, seeing ye are dull of hearing.**"

We will see a little bit later that these Hebrew Christians to whom Paul was writing were young Christians. Apparently, they were not wanting to grow at all. As such, they were dull of hearing. That doesn't mean they were lost. <u>Some Christians today are born-again and saved, and yet are dull of hearing. They don't want to hear the Words of God. It is a sad thing.</u> Paul wanted to say many things about **Melchisedec**, but he didn't do it at this time because his readers were not prepared to receive it.

- **Genesis 14:18-20**

"And **Melchizedek** king of Salem brought forth bread and wine: and he *was* the priest of the most high God. And he blessed him, and said, Blessed *be* Abram of the most high God, possessor of heaven and earth: And blessed be the most high God, which hath delivered thine enemies into thy hand. And he gave him tithes of all."

<u>It was the power of the Lord that permitted Abram to deliver his nephew, Lot.</u> **Melchisedec**, a Christophany of the Lord Jesus Christ in the Old Testament, met Abram after this victory. <u>Abram gave **Melchisedec** tithes of all the spoil.</u>

- **Hebrews 7:1-2**

"For this **Melchisedec**, king of Salem, Priest of the most high God, who met Abraham returning from the slaughter of the kings, and blessed him; To whom also Abraham gave a tenth part of all; first being by interpretation King of righteousness, and after that also King of Salem, which is, King of peace;"

ABRAHAM TITHED TO MELCHISEDEC

Now notice. Abraham was the father of Isaac and grandfather of Jacob. Jacob was the father of Levi, from whom came the Aaronic priesthood. To these, Israel was to pay the tithes. Here, however, Abraham gives tithes (10 percent of the spoils), to this king of righteousness, Melchisedec. He gave it to this Priest, Melchisedec. He is called the king of righteousness, Melchisedec and the king of peace.

- **Hebrews 7:3**

"Without father, without mother, without descent, having neither beginning of days, nor end of life; but made like unto the Son of God; abideth a priest continually."

AN OLD TESTAMENT CHRISTOPHANY

No human being can be without father, or mother, or descent. It is the Lord Jesus Christ Himself before His incarnation. Again, no human being can be without beginning of days or end of life. He is eternal. He is like to the Son of God because He was the Son of God before He came to earth in the incarnation. Melchisedec was a Christophany.

- **Hebrews 7:4**

"Now consider how great this man *was*, unto whom even the patriarch Abraham gave the tenth of the spoils."

Abraham gave a tithe or a tenth of the spoils to **Melchisedec** because of His greatness.

- **Hebrews 7:5-7**

"And verily they that are of the sons of Levi, who receive the office of the priesthood, have a commandment to take tithes of the people according to the law, that is, of their brethren, though they come out of the loins of Abraham: But he whose descent is not counted from them received tithes of Abraham, and blessed him that had the promises. And without all contradiction the less is blessed of the better."

The less is blessed by the better. Abraham was the less, and was blessed by **Melchisedec**, the better.

- **Hebrews 7:8**

"And here men that die receive tithes; but there he receiveth *them*, of whom it is witnessed that he liveth."

Melchisedec, as the Lord Jesus Christ, lives forever and ever.

- **Hebrews 7:9**

"And as I may so say, Levi also, who receiveth tithes, payed tithes in Abraham."

Abraham, the less, paid tithes to **Melchisedec** the greater.
- **Hebrews 7:10-17**

"For he was yet in the loins of his father, when **Melchisedec** met him. If therefore perfection were by the Levitical priesthood, (for under it the people received the law,) what further need was *there* that another priest should rise after the order of **Melchisedec**, and not be called after the order of Aaron? For the priesthood being changed, there is made of necessity a change also of the law. For he of whom these things are spoken pertaineth to another tribe, of which no man gave attendance at the altar. For it *is* evident that our Lord sprang out of Juda; of which tribe Moses spake nothing concerning priesthood. And it is yet far more evident: for that after the similitude of **Melchisedec** there ariseth another priest, Who is made, not after the law of a carnal commandment, but after the power of an endless life. For he testifieth, Thou *art* a priest for ever after the order of **Melchisedec**."

These verses give the rest of the story concerning the meeting of Abraham and **Melchisedec**.

DULL OF HEARING

Remember Paul said that he couldn't speak any more about Melchisedec at this time because the readers wouldn't listen to him. They were **dull, slow, or sluggish of hearing**. The Greek Word for "*dull*" is NOTHROS. Some of the meanings for this Word are:

"*1) slow, sluggish, indolent, dull, languid.*"
- **Matthew 13:15**

"For this people's heart is waxed gross, and *their* ears are **dull of hearing**, and *their* eyes they have closed; lest at any time they should see with their eyes, and hear with *their* ears, and should understand with *their* heart, and should be converted, and I should heal them."

The Lord Jesus Christ, uses that same general expression. He said the heart of the Jews to whom He was speaking was "*waxed gross*" and their ears were "***dull of hearing***." It is indeed sad when people who should listen to the truth have shut their ears away from it.
- **Acts 28:27**

"For the heart of this people is waxed gross, and their ears are **dull of hearing**, and *their* eyes have they closed; lest they should see with *their* eyes, and hear with their ears, and understand with *their* heart, and should be converted, and I should heal them."

This quotation is similar to that in Matthew 13:15. These to whom Paul was speaking, possibly even saved people, were also **dull of hearing**. They were not able to understand what Paul was speaking about.

The Lord Jesus Christ berated the Pharisees and Sadducees in Matthew 23 with eight different woes because of their hardness of heart and blindness of mind.

Hebrews 5:12

"For when for the time ye ought to be teachers, ye have need that one teach you again which *be* the first principles of the oracles of God; and are become such as have need of milk, and not of strong meat."

This is a sad situation. The people to whom Paul was writing should have been teachers by now in their Christian life. These people are not unsaved. They are just babes in Christ and not able to receive anything but milk. They only understand the *"first principles."*

The Greek Word for *"**principles**"* is STOICHEION. Some of the meanings for this Word are:

> 1) any first thing, from which the others belonging to some series or composite whole take their rise, an element, first principal; 1a) the letters of the alphabet as the elements of speech, not however the written characters, but the spoken sounds; 1b) the elements from which all things have come, the material causes of the universe; 1c) the heavenly bodies, either as parts of the heavens or (as others think) because in them the elements of man, life and destiny were supposed to reside; 1d) the elements, rudiments, primary and fundamental principles of any art, science, or discipline; 1d1) i.e. of mathematics, Euclid's geometry

TEACHERS

It is like the ABC'S of the Bible. Instead of being **teachers**, they are only students who couldn't learn very much. Like some genuine Christians today, they wouldn't read their Bibles. They needed other people to **teach** them. They should have been **teaching** others. This is a sad situation. So many Christians today are that same way.

- **Acts 13:1**

"Now there were in the church that was at Antioch certain prophets and **teachers**; as Barnabas, and Simeon that was called Niger, and Lucius of Cyrene, and Manaen, which had been brought up with Herod the tetrarch, and Saul."

There were **teachers** in the early church. The Greek Word for "*teachers*" is the word DIDASKO. Some of the meanings of that Word are:

"1) to teach; 1a) to hold discourse with others in order to instruct them, deliver didactic discourses; 1b) to be a teacher; 1c) to discharge the office of a teacher, conduct one's self as a teacher; 2) to teach one; 2a) to impart instruction; 2b) instill doctrine into one; 2c) the thing taught or enjoined; 2d) to explain or expound a thing; 2f) to teach one something"

STUDY AND TEACH GOD'S WORDS

I believe every genuinely born-again Christian, no matter what church he is from or where he is, should be reading and studying the Words of God in order that he may teach the doctrines of the faith. Every teacher must first be a student. Every teacher must know what he or she is teaching.

I **taught** language arts in junior high and high school in the school district of Philadelphia, PA, for 19 years. I had to know my subject in order to **teach** the students. The problem with the students there is that most of them do not want to listen or learn.

- **Ephesians 4:11**

"And he gave some, apostles; and some, prophets; and some, evangelists; and some, pastors and **teachers**;"

Here are some of the gifts the Lord Jesus Christ gave to the church. I believe tongues, and prophets have passed off the scene after the completion of the New Testament around 90 A.D. The gifts of evangelists, pastors and **teachers** are still with us in this age of grace. The Lord Jesus Christ gave the gift of **teachers.**

- **2 Timothy 4:3-4**

"For the time will come when they will not endure sound doctrine; but after their own lusts shall they heap to themselves **teachers**, having itching ears; And they shall turn away *their* ears from the truth, and shall be turned unto fables."

BEWARE OF WRONG TEACHERS

Paul was telling Pastor Timothy in the church at Ephesus that there will come a time when people will ask for teachers, but they are the wrong kind of teachers. They will be preaching false doctrines and fables causing people to be turned away from the truth.

- **Titus 2:3**

"The aged women likewise, that they be in behaviour as becometh holiness, not false accusers, not given to much wine, **teachers** of good things;"

The older women should know the Bible so that they can be **teachers** of good things to other women.

- **2 Timothy 2:15**

"Study to shew thyself approved unto God, a workman that needeth not to be ashamed, rightly dividing the word of truth."

Many are wrongly dividing the word of truth. Only with good Biblical **teaching** can the Words of God be rightly divided.

- **1 Timothy 4:13**

"Till I come, give attendance to reading, to exhortation, to doctrine."

Paul wanted Pastor Timothy to give himself to doctrine or proper **teaching** of the Words of God.

- **2 Peter 3:18**

"But grow in grace, and *in* the knowledge of our Lord and Saviour Jesus Christ. To him *be* glory both now and for ever. Amen."

The only way to grow in the grace and the knowledge of the Lord Jesus Christ is by studying ourselves, but also, by being helped through good and sound **teachers** in our lives.

MILK

- **1 Corinthians 3:2-3**

"I have fed you with **milk**, and not with meat: for hitherto ye were not able *to bear it*, neither yet now are ye able. For ye are yet carnal: for whereas *there is* among you envying, and strife, and divisions, are ye not carnal, and walk as men?"

CARNAL CORINTHIAN CHRISTIANS

These Christians in Corinth were genuinely saved, but they acted like spiritual babies. They were carnal and were walking after the flesh rather than after the Holy Spirit. They walked just as the unsaved men around them.

- **1 Peter 2:2**

"As newborn babes, desire the sincere **milk** of the word, that ye may grow thereby:"

<u>New Christians and even older Christians should desire the **milk** of the Words of God in order to grow up into maturity in the Lord Jesus Christ.</u>

Galatians 5:19

"Now the works of the flesh are manifest, which are *these*; Adultery, fornication, uncleanness, lasciviousness, Idolatry, witchcraft, hatred, variance, emulations, wrath, strife, seditions, heresies, Envyings, murders, drunkenness, revellings, and such like: of the which I tell you before, as I have also told *you* in time past, that they which do such things shall not inherit the kingdom of God."

Those who are babes in Christ and only able to use the **milk** of the Words of God will find themselves walking after one or more of these seventeen works of the flesh rather than after God the Holy Spirit Who indwells them. As such it is possible that they might be evidencing any one of the above works of the flesh. <u>It is a sad situation for genuinely saved Christians to be walking like the world around them in these fleshly works.</u>

<u>These genuinely saved people are fleshly and carnal.</u> They are just like babes. They need just baby **milk**. They can't eat strong meat. They must come to grips with the power of the flesh.

Hebrews 5:13

"**For every one that useth milk *is* unskilful in the word of righteousness: for he is a babe.**"

SKILL

This is the status of these Christians that Paul is addressing in this book of Hebrews. They are using only the *milk* of God's Words and no more. They can't understand the deep things of the Words of God. They are "***unskilful***" in the Word of righteousness. The Greek Word for "***unskilful***" is APEIROS. Some of the meanings for this word are:

"*1) inexperienced in, without experience of.*"

This kind of Christian is a babe. He's genuinely saved but lives and acts just like a baby in the things of the Lord Jesus Christ.

- **Daniel 1:17**

"As for these four children, God gave them knowledge and skill in all learning and wisdom: and Daniel had understanding in all visions and dreams."

All of these four Hebrews had both knowledge and **skill** in learning and wisdom. Daniel and his three friends showed this both by their words and by their actions.

BABE

- **Exodus 2:6**
"And when she had opened *it,* she saw the **child**: and, behold, the **babe** wept. And she had compassion on **him**, and said, This *is one* of the Hebrews' **children**."

Here is a picture of **Moses** when **he** was a little crying **baby**. It was the crying of this **babe** that caused Pharaoh's daughter to have compassion on **him**. She recognized **him** as one of the Hebrew **children**. Perhaps **he** was dressed like a Hebrew **child**.

- **Luke 2:12**
"And this *shall be* a sign unto you; Ye shall find the **babe** wrapped in swaddling clothes, lying in a manger."

This "**babe**" is the **Lord Jesus Christ**, the **Saviour** of those who genuinely trust in **Him**.

LYING VERSUS LAYING

It is an interesting point that so many today, including those on radio and television news programs, do not know the difference been "lying" and "laying." Our King James Bible has it correct: The babe was "*lying*" not "*laying*" in a manger.' When you lay something, you put something down. When you lie down, you assume a horizontal position.

Hebrews 5:14

"But strong meat belongeth to them that are of full age, *even* those who by reason of use have their senses exercised to discern both good and evil."

STRONG MEAT

The preceding verse talked about "*babes*" who had to use "*milk*" being unskilful in God's Words. Here, Paul speaks of the use of "*strong meat*" by way of contrast to "*milk*."

If you were just drinking milk today, I wonder what you'd look like. I wonder what you'd feel like. I wonder what your muscles would be like. I don't believe that you would be very strong with only a milk diet. Why do you think the pediatricians, after awhile, get the babies off milk? They realize that the babies must be strong and healthy. They begin with junior food and then, after a while, put them on regular adult food. But milk does not grow strong, healthy people. Right now, they're feeding the cows the GMO type of grain which contains poisons. The milk produced in this way, many say, is polluted milk. We should use some other non-GMO kind of milk to be healthy.

STRONG MEAT

But **strong meat** belongs to them that are of full age and mature in the faith. And these Hebrew Christians here were not mature. They were dull of hearing. Paul wanted to encourage them. He told these people that they ought to be teachers, but instead they needed others to teach them the ABC's of the Words of God. They that are of full age and mature can use the meat of the Bible.

EXERCISED

Strong meat is for those who <u>continuously have (Greek present tense) their senses continuously **exercised**</u> (Greek present tense) to be able to discern good and evil. The Greek Word for "*exercised*" is GUMNAZO. Some of the meanings for this Word are:

"*1) to exercise naked (in a palaestra or school of athletics); 2) to exercise vigorously, in any way, either the body or the mind.*"

Those who are genuinely born-again must continually use the Words of God by reading and study from Genesis through Revelation, to be able to have our senses **exercised**, to know what the Words of God are for our lives and to our discernment of good and evil to be effective.

DISCERNMENT

- **Leviticus 10:10**

"And that ye may put **difference** between holy and unholy, and between unclean and clean;"

DISCERNING CLEAN AND UNCLEAN

Just as those in the Old Testament, we who are genuinely saved in our days must learn to discern between the unclean and the clean. This discernment comes by continuously reading and following the Words of God.

- **2 Samuel 19:34-35**

"And Barzillai said unto the king, How long have I to live, that I should go up with the king unto Jerusalem? I *am* this day fourscore years old: *and* can I **discern** between good and evil? can thy servant taste what I eat or what I drink? can I hear any more the voice of singing men and singing women? wherefore then should thy servant be yet a burden unto my lord the king?"

Hebrews–Preaching Verse by Verse

Barzillai was so old that he couldn't any longer **discern** between good and evil. His hearing was bad at age 80.

- **1 Kings 3:9**
"Give therefore thy servant an understanding heart to judge thy people, that I may **discern** between good and bad: for who is able to judge this thy so great a people?"

God gave Solomon an understanding heart to **discern** good and evil, but in his old age, he had over 1,000 women as wives or concubines. They took away his heart and his **discernment**.

- **Ezekiel 44:23**
"And they shall teach my people the *difference* between the holy and profane, and cause them to **discern** between the unclean and the clean."

TEACHING DISCERNMENT

The priests and Levites were to teach the Israelites to discern between good and evil. We need such discernment today as well. The Words of God in the Bible teach us this discernment.

- **Malachi 3:18**
"Then shall ye return, and **discern** between the righteous and the wicked, between him that serveth God and him that serveth him not."

DISCERNMENT BADLY NEEDED TODAY

Such discernment is badly needed for the genuine Christians today as well. We must learn to discern. The Words of God give us this needed discernment.

Hebrews
Chapter Six

Hebrews 6:1

"Therefore leaving the principles of the doctrine of Christ, let us go on unto perfection; not laying again the foundation of repentance from dead works, and of faith toward God,"

The Greek Word for *"principles"* that is mentioned here is ARCHE. Some of the meanings of this Word are:

> *"1) beginning, origin; 2) the person or thing that commences, the first person or thing in a series, the leader; 3) that by which anything begins to be, the origin, the active cause; 4) the extremity of a thing; 4a) of the corners of a sail; 5) the first place, principality, rule, magistracy; 5a) of angels and demons."*

There is nothing wrong with *"principles,"* but genuine Christians must go on to full growth and maturity in the Lord Jesus Christ.

PERFECTION AND MATURITY

Remember that Paul is writing to genuine Christians in this book. Here he says he does not want these believers to stick to the baby things of the Words of God–the ABC's--but he wants them to go on to **maturity** and **full growth** in the Lord Jesus Christ, leaving the principles of the doctrine of Christ. The doctrines and teachings about the Lord Jesus Christ are important, but he does not want them to stop there.

The Greek Word for *"perfection"* is TELEIOTES. Some of the meanings of this Word are:

> *"1a) the state of the more intelligent; 1b) moral and spiritual perfection"*

The idea is completion and **maturity.** That is Paul's plea in the entire first part of Chapter Six. He does not want to lay again the various foundations of the Christian faith. These are very good but these believers must move on to **maturity.**

- **2 Corinthians 13:9**

"For we are glad, when we are weak, and ye are strong: and this also we wish, *even* your **perfection**."

This is not speaking of sinless **perfection**, but of **maturity** and **growing up** in the Lord Jesus Christ. That is what Paul wanted these Christians to do, **grow up** instead of being carnal, fleshly, and worldly.

REPENTANCE

Paul speaks also of *"repentance."* The Greek Word for **it** is METANOIA. Some of the meanings for this Word are:

> *"1) a change of mind, as it appears to one who repents, of a purpose he has formed or of something he has done."*

- **Luke 5:32**

"I came not to call the righteous, but sinners to **repentance**."

REPENT–CHANGE YOUR MIND

The Lord Jesus Christ wanted sinners to *"change their mind"* about their sin, realizing that they are considered by God as sinners. He wants all such sinners to *"change their mind"* about Him as their Saviour and their need to accept and receive by genuine faith as the One Who carried their sins in His own body on the cross.

- **Acts 20:21**

"Testifying both to the Jews, and also to the Greeks, **repentance** toward God, and faith toward our Lord Jesus Christ."

The *"change of mind"* must begin with our attitude toward God the Father, beginning with genuine faith in His Son, the Lord Jesus Christ.

- **2 Peter 3:9**

"The Lord is not slack concerning his promise, as some men count slackness; but is longsuffering to us-ward, not willing that any should perish, but that all should come to **repentance**."

As far as these basic truths, Paul said they are fine, but we ought to go on to maturity, fullness, and completion. We should not stop with these rudimentary things–needful as they are–but go on to maturity in the Saviour.

Hebrews 6:2

"Of the doctrine of baptisms, and of laying on of hands, and of resurrection of the dead, and of eternal judgment."

BAPTISMS

Here are some more basic "*principles.*" There are a total of seven "*principles.*" In verse one, there were three. In this verse, there are four more "*principles.*"

BAPTISM=IMMERSION

As far as the doctrine of baptisms, in the New Testament, it is a reference to immersion in water in obedience to the Scripture after a person has been genuinely born-again.

LAYING ON OF HANDS

When qualified men are ordained, either as pastors or deacons, there is a **laying on of hands** at the ceremony. There are various instances of this in the New Testament.

- Acts 8:16-17

"(For as yet he was fallen upon none of them: only they were baptized in the name of the Lord Jesus.) Then **laid they *their* hands** on them, and they received the Holy Ghost."

When Simon the sorcerer saw that at the **laying on of the apostles' hands**, the Holy Ghost was given, he offered them money. This was in the transitional period of Acts. Now, God the Holy Spirit enters those who are genuinely saved immediately upon their salvation.

- 1 Timothy 4:14

"Neglect not the gift that is in thee, which was given thee by prophecy, with the **laying on of the hands** of the presbytery."

Timothy was that pastor in Ephesus. This was a description of his ordination to the gospel ministry. The **laying on of hands** is a basic truth.

RESURRECTION

- Acts 24:15

"And have hope toward God, which they themselves also allow, that there shall be a **resurrection** of the dead, both of the just and unjust."

SADDUCEES AND BODILY RESURRECTION

The Sadducees didn't believe in a bodily resurrection. The Pharisees did. There was a divided house. This is another basic principle. It refers to the bodily resurrection of those who are genuinely saved. At that time, they will receive new

> bodies, like unto the resurrected body of the Lord Jesus Christ. It also refers to the bodily resurrection of the *"unjust"* or the lost prior to their being cast into Hell.

ETERNAL JUDGMENT

This speaks both of the **judgment** of the genuinely saved Christians at the **judgment** seat of Christ for their eternal rewards, and also of the **judgment** of the unsaved at the great white throne. They will be cast into the everlasting lake of fire in Hell.

- **Matthew 18:8**

"Wherefore if thy hand or thy foot offend thee, cut them off, and cast *them* from thee: it is better for thee to enter into life halt or maimed, rather than having two hands or two feet to be cast into everlasting fire."

That's the truth about the **judgment** of the lost ones in the future. Though many are doubting it, it is real and it is everlasting.

- **Matthew 25:41**

"Then shall he say also unto them on the left hand, Depart from me, ye cursed, into everlasting fire, prepared for the devil and his angels."

> ## HELL PREPARED FOR THE DEVIL AND HIS ANGELS
>
> That's why Hell was prepared. It was prepared for the Devil and his angels, not for people. People that deny and reject the Lord Jesus Christ go to this same place that was prepared for the Devil and his angels. God did not prepare everlasting fire for people, but for the Devil and his angels.

- **Matthew 25:46**

"And these shall go away into everlasting punishment: but the righteous into life eternal."

This describes the **judgment** of both the lost and the saved.

- **2 Thessalonians 1:9**

"Who shall be punished with everlasting destruction from the presence of the Lord, and from the glory of his power."

The destruction of the lost ones in Hell is everlasting, despite the fact that there are some who either deny it, or teach that it is only temporary. Billy Graham taught in the 1950's that there is not even fire in Hell. Many people today are saying that Hell is not everlasting. They say that Hell lasts only a little time and then the people get out. This is false teaching. Hell is everlasting destruction and fire.

- **Hebrews 9:27**

"And as it is appointed unto men once to die, but after this the **judgment:**"

Whether this is the **judgment** of the genuinely saved, or the **judgment** of the lost, it will be everlasting in its results.

Hebrews 6:3

"And this will we do, if God permit."

So Paul says he is going to talk about seven of these principles in the future, if time permits. God's going to permit it. He's going to go into some of the details at that time, but that's not his basic purpose at this particular time. He wants to go on to something else.

Hebrews 6:4

"For *it is* impossible for those who were once enlightened, and have tasted of the heavenly gift, and were made partakers of the Holy Ghost,"

THREE VIEWS OF HEBREWS SIX

This section of Hebrews 6:1-10 is very controversial. I believe Paul is speaking here of genuinely saved and born-again Christians. There are at least three different ways of interpreting Chapter Six, 1-10.

1. Some people say that these verses refer to saved people who can lose their salvation. I don't believe any genuinely saved Christian can lose his or her salvation.

2. Some people say that these verses refer to unsaved people. From the words used, I do not believe this view either.

3. I believe that Paul is speaking of genuinely saved Christians who are living after the flesh rather than following God the Holy Spirit Who lives within them. They are living for the world, the flesh, and the Devil rather than for the Lord Jesus Christ.

ONCE ENLIGHTENED

The first description of these people is that they were people who were *"once enlightened."* The Greek Word for *"enlightened"* is PHOTIZO. Some of the meanings of this Word are:

> *"1) to give light, to shine; 2) to enlighten, light up, illumine; 3) to bring to light, render evident; 3a) to cause something to exist and thus come to light and*

become clear to all; **4) to enlighten, spiritually, imbue with saving knowledge**; 4a) to instruct, to inform, teach; 4b) to give understanding to."

ENLIGHTENED=GENUINELY SAVED

I believe these of whom Paul is speaking were genuinely saved, as meaning #4 above would imply. They did not just get a little tiny bit of light, but they were thoroughly enlightened by God and brought to His salvation.

TASTED OF THE HEAVENLY GIFT

The second description of these people is that they have "*tasted of the heavenly gift.*" The Greek Word for "*tasted*" is GEUOMAI. Some of the meanings for this Word are:

"1) to taste, to try the flavour of; 2) to taste; 2a) i.e. perceive the flavour of, partake of, enjoy; 2b) to feel, make trial of, experience; 3) **to take food, eat**, to take nourishment, eat."

I believe that these people actually took in this Heavenly gift and consumed it like we would food.

MADE PARTAKERS OF THE HOLY GHOST

The third description of these people is that they were "*made partakers of the Holy Ghost.*" The Greek Word for "*partakers*" is: METOCHOS. Some of the meanings of this Word are:

"1) sharing in, partaking; 2) a partner (in a work, office, dignity)."

PARTAKERS=GENUINELY SAVED

I do not believe it is possible to "*partake*" of God the Holy Spirit without being genuinely born-again and saved. Unsaved people cannot share or be partakers in the Holy Spirit of God. Most of them think the entire Christian faith is foolishness.

Hebrews 6:5

"And have tasted the good word of God, and the powers of the world to come,"

TASTED THE GOOD WORD

The Greek Word for "*tasted*" is: GEUOMAI. Some of the meanings of this Word are:

"1) to taste, to try the flavour of; 2) to taste; 2a) i.e. perceive the flavour of, partake of, enjoy; 2b) to *feel, make trial of, experience; 3) **to take food, eat**, to take nourishment, eat."*

TASTED=GENUINELY SAVED

These people that Paul is writing about were genuine born-again Christians who had perceived and eaten the very Words of God. They had made these Words a part of them.

These Christians had also *"tasted"* and experienced the *"powers of the world to come."* As I mentioned in the previous Chapter, these people knew what Heaven is like; yet they were carnal. They were babes in Christ. They needed to grow up and mature.

Hebrews 6:6

"If they shall fall away, to renew them again unto repentance; seeing they crucify to themselves the Son of God afresh, and put *him* to an open shame."

FALL AWAY

Paul is speaking of these truly born-again Christians who might *"fall away."* Armenians who believe Christians can lose their salvation believe that this is the interpretation. The Greek Word for *"fall away"* is PARAPIPTO. Some of the meanings for this Word are:

*"1) to fall beside a person or thing; 2) to slip aside; 2a) **to deviate from the right path, turn aside, wander**; 2b) to error; 2c) to fall away (from the true faith): from worship of Jehovah."*

WANDERING FROM RIGHT PATH

The word means to wander away from the right path. It is those carnal Christians who are walking after the flesh rather than after God the Holy Spirit Who indwells them. They cannot lose their salvation and be unborn after they have been genuinely *"born-again."* Though these Christians knew many things about the Bible, they walked off and away from the truths of the Bible. They left the true doctrines of the faith and proper worship of the Lord.

CARNAL DEPARTURES FROM TRUTH

If these carnal, yet well-taught Christians depart from the true doctrines, they reach a point where it is impossible to change their minds (which is the meaning of *"repentance"*) about their waywardness. In this case, perhaps the Lord chastens them soundly as a Father to His children, or even might take them Home to Heaven because of their bad example. **It could be the sin unto physical death.**

The **"sin unto death"** is spoken of in 1 John 5:16:
"If any man see his brother sin a **sin** *which is* **not unto death**, he shall ask, and he shall give him life for them that **sin not unto death**. There is a **sin unto death**: I do not say that he shall pray for it."

That is referring to saved people. They **sinned so severely** against the Lord that He had to **judge them** by bringing on them **physical death**.

This is also mentioned in 1 Corinthians 11:30. Many of the Corinthians dishonored the Lord in the Lord's supper and He had to slay them in His judgment of them. The word *"sleep"* refers to the **sleep in death**.

"For this cause many *are* weak and sickly among you, and **many sleep**."

These were not unsaved people. They were genuine Christians who were **not walking with the Lord**.

- **1 Corinthians 3:1**

"And I, brethren, could not speak unto you as unto spiritual, but as unto **carnal**, even as unto **babes in Christ**."

This verse describes such genuine believers. They were both *"carnal"* and *"babes in Christ"* even though, as we will see in some later verses, they were very well taught in the Words of God.

As far as **crucifying the Son of God afresh**, this is not literally possible. What this means is that they are making a **mockery of the crucifixion of the Lord Jesus Christ. He was crucified** because **people hated him**. When a well-taught **Christian is carnal and fleshly**, people who once knew him to be a Christian--and now see him living for the world, the flesh, and the Devil put the Lord Jesus Christ **to an open shame and hate Him** all the more. They are **not lost people**. Formerly spiritual Christians who **leave the Biblical walk put their Saviour to an open shame.**

These Christians who have **left their sound Biblical walk and lifestyle**, will hear the world shame them, and also **shame the Lord Jesus Christ Who has saved them.** These Christians are no doubt producing the **works of the flesh** which are listed in Galatians 5:19-21.

"Now the works of the flesh are manifest, which are *these*; Adultery, fornication, uncleanness, lasciviousness, Idolatry, witchcraft, hatred, variance, emulations, wrath, strife, seditions, heresies, Envyings, murders, drunkenness, revellings, and such like: of the which I tell you before, as I have also told *you* in time past, that they which do such things shall not inherit the kingdom of God." (Galatians 5:19-21)

I hope that you can see how a genuine Christian producing any one or several of these **17 works of the flesh** can cause **shame** to be placed **upon the Name of the Lord Jesus Christ**. All of a sudden they see them **living for the Devil**, forsaking their original testimony and put the Lord Jesus to an open shame. Shame on them. Shame on these people that don't continue with the Lord Jesus Christ.

THE SAVED STILL HAVE THE FLESH

If we are born-again, we have the Spirit of God indwelling us, but we still have that flesh. There is a battle between the flesh and the Spirit, fighting and warring, one against the other. Can saved people manifest the works of the flesh? Yes, they can.

- **Galatians 5:17**
"For the flesh lusteth against the Spirit, and the Spirit against the flesh: and these are contrary the one to the other: so that ye cannot do the things that ye would."

THE WAR WITHIN THE SAVED PEOPLE

This verse describes the war that goes on within the saved Christian on a daily basis.

Hebrews 6:7

"For the earth which drinketh in the rain that cometh oft upon it, and bringeth forth herbs meet for them by whom it is dressed, receiveth blessing from God:"

Here is Paul's illustration of those who have *"fallen away"* from **Biblical truth and from walking with the Lord** without ever changing their minds to return to fellowship with the Lord Jesus Christ. These Christians were **not just the usual Christians**. **They were well taught**. They were like the **well watered ground** that brings forth its produce. These Christians **knew the Lord Jesus Christ as their Saviour**. **They knew the Word of God very well**. Those Words fell very often upon their ears as rain falling often upon the earth. They **should have brought forth proper fruit**. That's what God wants to produce in every saved person. **He wants fruit** that will endure and will glorify the God Who saved them. This is what the Lord expects of us who are saved.

Hebrews 6:8

"But that which beareth thorns and briers *is* rejected, and *is* nigh unto cursing; whose end *is* to be burned."

FRUIT

Those genuine Christians whose **fruit** is only thorns and briers will have that **fruit** rejected. It is cursed **fruit** which is so worthless that it is burned up in the fire. <u>It is the **fruit** that will be burned, not the people. That is very clear.</u>

- John 15:4-6

"Abide in me, and I in you. As the branch cannot bear **fruit** of itself, except it abide in the vine; no more can ye, except ye abide in me. I am the vine, ye *are* the branches: He that abideth in me, and I in him, the same bringeth forth much **fruit:** for without me ye can do nothing. If a man abide not in me, he is cast forth as a branch, and is withered; and men gather them, and cast *them* into the fire, and they are burned."

FRUITLESS CHRISTIANS

These verses describe a genuine Christian who does not abide in the Lord Jesus Christ. Therefore their works are not for the Lord Jesus Christ, but for themselves. These works-branches are burned because they are worthless. They are saved but their fruits are not. This pictures the Christians referred to in this verse.

THE JUDGMENT SEAT OF CHRIST

SUFFERING LOSS YET SAVED

Those who bear proper fruit from the repeated reception of the living Words of God receive His blessing. Those who turn down the teachings of God's Words will suffer loss at the judgment seat of Christ. Notice the words about this judgment in 1 Corinthians 3:10-15:

- 1 Corinthians 3:10-15

"*According to the grace of God which is given unto me, as a wise masterbuilder, I have laid the foundation, and another buildeth thereon. But let every man take heed how he buildeth thereupon. For other foundation can no man lay than that is* laid, which is Jesus Christ. Now *if any man build upon this foundation gold, silver, precious stones, wood, hay, stubble; Every man's work shall be made manifest: for the day shall declare it, because it shall be **revealed by fire**; and the fire shall **try every man's work** of what sort it is. If any man's work abide which he hath built thereupon, **he shall receive a reward.** If any man's **work shall be burned, he shall suffer loss**: but he himself shall be saved; yet so as **by fire**."* (1 Corinthians 3:10-15)

In these six verses, the **judgment** of the genuinely saved people is described. They are upon the Foundation—the Lord Jesus Christ. But they build upon that Foundation two different kinds of materials. Either *"gold, silver, precious stones"* or *"wood, hay, stubble."* The first set of materials are small, but very valuable. The second set of materials might be very large, but of little genuine worth. <u>These Christians in Hebrews 6 were building upon the Lord Jesus Christ merely wood, hay, and stubble. They will suffer loss when their building materials are **burned up**, yet they will be saved, but without any rewards or blessings.</u>

- **Ephesians 2:8-10**

"For by grace are ye saved through faith; and that not of yourselves: it is the gift of God: Not of works, lest any man should boast, For we are his workmanship, created in Christ Jesus **unto good works**, *which God hath before ordained that we should walk in them."*

GENUINE FAITH PRODUCES GOOD WORKS

We are not saved by our works. We are saved by God's grace through genuine faith in the Person and work of the Lord Jesus Christ. Genuine faith produces good works. God wants every saved Christian to produce good works for His honor and glory.

If a person's **works are burned** at the judgment seat of Christ, these Christians will have **no rewards**. They will suffer loss. They are going to be saved, but their **wood, hay, and stubble-works will be burned up.** <u>All those genuine Christians who have built on the Lord Jesus Christ with **gold, silver, and precious stones will receive rewards**.</u>

THORNS AND BRIERS

There are many passages that speak of **briers and thorns**. These would be some of the wood, **hay, and stubble** which would **not be useful** to the Lord as materials on which to build on the Lord Jesus Christ, our Foundation. These illustrate works that are **worthless and fruitless**.

- Isaiah 9:18a

"For wickedness burneth as the fire: it shall devour the **briers and thorns**;"

- Isaiah 27:4

"Fury *is* not in me: who would set the **briers *and* thorns** against me in battle? I would go through them, I would burn them together."

Burning the **briers and thorns** would be done because they are worthless. You can't build any buildings using them. You can't build anything from them. This is a **picture of their worthlessness**.

Hebrews 6:9

"But, beloved, we are persuaded better things of you, and things that accompany salvation, though we thus speak."

BETTER THINGS THAT ACCOMPANY SALVATION

BETTER THINGS WITH TRUE SALVATION

This verse shows clearly that those to whom Paul was speaking were genuinely saved. He hoped that this carnality would not take place in the lives of those to whom he was writing. He says to these genuine Christians that *"we are persuaded better things of you,"*–not these bad things from carnality which are worthless as thorns and briers, but the better things resulting in a walk in the power of God the Holy Spirit. These are the things that should *"accompany salvation"* that they have, rather than evil and worthless works.

Evil works should never accompany God's salvation, yet those who walk after their flesh will have evil works. If we are genuinely saved, our works should honor the Lord Jesus Christ—not ourselves, not the world, and not the Devil. Paul was persuaded of *"better things"* than the evil works mentioned earlier that were produced by carnal Christians. Paul is hopeful that none of his readers will ever be thrown into this terrible condition, spoken of earlier, where these saved Christians, though once enlightened and living for the Lord Jesus Christ, have gone back into the world, never to return to fellowship with their Saviour.

The apostle Peter was almost in this condition. He disappointed the Lord Jesus Christ on many occasions, but, fortunately, he did not fall into complete and continuous disobedience. He was restored and began again to serve his Saviour. You remember that one occasion, when Peter called the Lord Jesus Christ a liar when talking about His coming death and resurrection. He talked to Peter and said, "... *Get thee behind me, Satan...*" (Matthew 16:23)

On another occasion, after the bodily resurrection of the Lord Jesus Christ, instead of doing what he was called to do—fish for men— Peter went back to fishing for fish. He not only went himself, but also took with him six other apostles (John 21:2). Peter encouraged all six of them to stop being apostles for the Lord Jesus Christ, and rather to going back to their former occupations as fishermen. Later on, Peter went back to serving His Saviour. He was restored to fellowship with the Lord Jesus Christ and became a worthy apostle rather than a worthless one. He returned to being very faithful to the Lord. He wrote the books of First and Second Peter.

Peter had his ups and downs as many Christians have today. If you remember Galatians 2:11:

"*But when Peter was come to Antioch, I withstood him to the face, because he was to be blamed.*"

Paul had to rebuke Peter because Peter was two-faced. When no Jews were present, he had fellowship with the Gentiles. When Jews were around, he separated from the Gentiles. Paul rebuked him because "*he was to be blamed*" in this two-facedness. None of us can always walk with the Lord Jesus Christ in the power of God the Holy Spirit 100% of the time. That should be our goal, but sometimes we fail. May those of us who are genuine Christians do the **proper things** that "***accompany salvation***" rather than fleshly fruits and actions. After we are saved, **God expects us to show godly works**, as it states in Ephesians 2:10:

"*For we are his workmanship, **created in Christ Jesus unto good works**, which God hath before ordained that **we should walk in them**.*"

Hebrews 6:10

"For God *is* not unrighteous to forget your work and labour of love, which ye have shewed toward his name, in that ye have ministered to the saints, and do minister."

MINISTERING

SAVED AND SERVING OTHERS

These genuine believers worked for and loved the Name of the Lord Jesus Christ. They proved that by ministering to the saints (the born-again genuine Christians). That's what every saved Christian should do as well. We should "minister" to others, giving them the gospel of God's grace and helping them to grow in His grace. The Greek Word for "minister" is: DIAKONEO. Some of the meanings of this Word are:

"1)) to be a servant, attendant, domestic, to serve, wait upon; 1a) to minister to one, render ministering offices to: 1a1) to be served, ministered unto; 1b) to wait at a table and offer food and drink to the guests, 1b1) of women preparing food; 1c) to minister i.e. supply food and necessities of life; 1c1) to relieve one's necessities (e.g. by collecting alms), to provide take care of, distribute, the things necessary to sustain life; 1c2) to take care of the poor and the sick, who administer the office of a deacon; 1c3) in Christian churches to serve as deacons; 1d) to minister; 1d1) to attend to anything, that may serve another's interests; 1d2) to minister a thing to one, to serve one or by supplying any thing."

- **Matthew 20:28**

"Even as the Son of man came not to be **ministered unto**, but **to minister**, and to give his life a ransom for many."

We know that the Lord Jesus Christ came **to minister** and give his life a ransom for all, not just for the elect.

- **Mark 10:43-44**

"But so shall it not be among you: but whosoever will be great among you, shall be your **minister**: And whosoever of you will be the chiefest shall be servant of all."

Who is going to be chief among you? The biggest one, the best one, the brightest one? No. The greatest will be your **minister or servant**.

That's what God says--that is greatness. These Christians were **ministering** to the genuine Christians.
- **Romans 15:25**

"But now I go unto Jerusalem to **minister** unto the saints."
Paul went up there to **minister to and help the Christian believers in Jerusalem.**
- **Hebrews 1:14**

"Are they not all **ministering** spirits, sent forth to **minister** for them who shall be heirs of salvation?"
This verse is speaking about angels. God has sent angels to help and **minister** to the genuinely saved Christians. These angels keep the believers from harm and often preserve them. The angels are **ministering** and even so these Christians should have a **ministry based on love, not on money.** They helped other Christians. Paul, himself, was a good **minister** to the saints as well.

In this first part of Chapter Six, Paul talks about the Christians not wanting to bear only thorns and briers. God wants true Christians to be fruit-bearers rather than bearers of thorns and briers which will be burned up. That's all they are good for—you can't build anything with them. God wants us who are genuinely saved to be walking in the power of the Spirit of God, Who indwells us so that we do not fall into the lusts and desires of our flesh. Very important indeed.

Hebrews 6:11

"And we desire that every one of you do shew the same diligence to the full assurance of hope unto the end:"

DILIGENCE

Paul is urging these genuine Christians to walk by the Spirit of God and not in the flesh as others he has mentioned who bear only thorns and briers. He wants them to be **diligent**. The Greek Word for "***diligent***" is SPOUDE. Some of the meanings of this Word are:

"*1) haste, with haste; 2) earnestness, diligence; 2a) earnestness in accomplishing, promoting, or striving after anything; 2b) to give all diligence, interest one's self most earnestly.*"

GENUINE CHRISTIANS NEED DILIGENCE

Every genuinely born-again Christian must show all diligence in living for the Lord Jesus Christ. This should last with full assurance of hope until the entrance into Heaven.

- **Proverbs 4:23**

"Keep thy heart with all **diligence**; for out of it *are* the issues of life."

HEART DILIGENCE

We must keep our heart with all diligence because all of the issues of life proceed from it.

- **2 Corinthians 8:7**

"Therefore, as ye abound in every *thing, in* faith, and utterance, and knowledge, and *in* all **diligence**, and *in* your love to us, *see* that ye abound in this grace also."

DILIGENT LOVE FOR FELLOW CHRISTIANS

We must be diligent in our love for fellow Christians, for the Lord Jesus Christ, and for the Bible.

FULL ASSURANCE

He says we've got to have **full assurance** of hope. Not just a half hearted hope but a **full assurance**.

- **Colossians 2:2**

"That their hearts might be comforted, being knit together in love, and unto all riches of the **full assurance** of understanding, to the acknowledgment of the mystery of God, and of the Father, and of Christ."

We must have the **full assurance** of understanding of the Bible, as the Holy Spirit gives us the understanding of it.

- **Hebrews 10:22**

"Let us draw near with a true heart in **full assurance** of faith, having our hearts sprinkled from an evil conscience, and our bodies washed with pure water."

Saved people must have **full assurance** in their stand for the Lord Jesus Christ.

HOPE

Genuine Christians' **hope** in the Lord Jesus Christ is with full assurance right down to the end until the Lord calls them Home. The Greek Word for "**hope**" is ELPIS. Some of the meanings of this Word are:

> "1) expectation of evil, fear; 2) expectation of good, hope; 2a) in the Christian sense; 2a1) joyful and confident expectation of eternal salvation; 3) on hope, in hope, having hope; 3a) the author of hope,

or he who is its foundation; 3b) the thing hoped for."

> **HOPE–FUTURE BUT CERTAIN**
>
> One of the key ideas of ELPIS is that, though this *"hope"* is future, it is guaranteed and certain. It's not a *"hope"* that may or may not be true. It is future, but assured.

- **Romans 5:2**

"By whom also we have access by faith into this grace wherein we stand, and rejoice in **hope** of the glory of God."

That's future yet assured. One day saved Christians will have His glory. They will be made like unto the Lord Jesus Christ and His glorious body.

- **Romans 15:4**

"For whatsoever things were written aforetime were written for our learning, that we through patience and comfort of the scriptures might have **hope**."

The Old Testament was written for the learning, patience, and comfort of the genuine Christians in the New Testament times. These things written aforetime give **hope** for today.

- **1 Corinthians 15:19**

"If in this life only we have **hope** in Christ, we are of all men most miserable."

> **HOPE IN CHRIST FOR HEAVEN**
>
> This is a very interesting verse. Paul was being persecuted. He was being whipped and had many other harmful things happened to him. If this life is all there is, it would make him miserable. Paul knew that there is hope in Christ giving assurance and leading to Heaven for all eternity to come.

- **Colossians 1:5**

"For the **hope** which is laid up for you in heaven, whereof ye heard before in the word of the truth of the gospel;"

That's where the genuine believer's **hope** lies. It does not lie in the thought that our country or the world in general are going to get better. But the genuine and certain **hope** is laid up in Heaven.

- **Colossians 1:27**

"To whom God would make known what *is* the riches of the glory of this mystery among the Gentiles; which is Christ in you, the **hope** of glory."

What is that mystery or sacred secret? It is the Lord Jesus Christ indwelling within the truly saved Christian. He is the **hope** of glory. God the Holy Spirit is in the genuinely saved, born-again Christians but the Lord Jesus Christ is there also as well as God the Father. Notice what the Lord Jesus Christ told His apostles in John 14:23:

> *"Jesus answered and said unto him, If a man love me, he will keep my words: and my Father will love him, and we will come unto him, and make our abode with him."*

I taught the book of Colossians to some African Christians in Liberia, West Africa many years ago. Those genuine Christians were impoverished with hardly enough food to put into their bodies and with just makeshift homes, but in them dwells the Lord Jesus Christ, their **hope** of glory. What a contrast and what a **hope**!

- **1 Thessalonians 4:13**

"But I would not have you to be ignorant, brethren, concerning them which are asleep, that ye sorrow not, even as others which have **no hope**."

The world that is lost has no **hope** for Heaven, only to spend eternity in the Lake of Fire in Hell. This is sad. They are **hopeless** without our Saviour.

- **1 Thessalonians 5:8**

"But let us, who are of the day, be sober, putting on the breastplate of faith and love; and for an helmet, the **hope** of salvation."

THE CHRISTIAN'S HELMET

The hope of salvation is the genuine Christian's helmet. It protects against the blows that would hit their heads.

- **Titus 1:2**

"In **hope** of eternal life, which God, that cannot lie, promised before the world began:"

GOD KEEPS HIS PROMISES

God will keep His promise for the hope of eternal life to all those who have genuinely received the Lord Jesus Christ as their Saviour.

- **Titus 2:13**

"Looking for that blessed **hope,** and the glorious appearing of the great God and our Saviour Jesus Christ;"

> **THE RAPTURE–THE BLESSED HOPE**
> The blessed hope is the rapture of the true Christians when the Lord Jesus Christ will appear in the clouds to take them Home to Heaven.

- **Titus 3:7**

"That being justified by his grace, we should be made heirs according to the **hope** of eternal life."

Eternal life is possessed by the genuine Christian the minute he or she is saved and this life goes on for eternity in Heaven.

- **1 Peter 1:3**

"Blessed *be* the God and Father of our Lord Jesus Christ, which according to his abundant mercy hath begotten us again unto a lively **hope** by the resurrection of Jesus Christ from the dead,"

Because the Lord Jesus Christ arose from the dead, genuine Christians have a lively, living **hope**. They also shall rise. Their bodies will be just like His glorified body one day. Their bodily resurrection is indeed a wonderful **hope**.

- **1 Peter 3:15**

"But sanctify the Lord God in your hearts: and *be* ready always to *give* an answer to every man that asketh you a reason of the **hope** that is in you with meekness and fear:"

Regardless of any circumstances, there is **hope** within those who are truly born-again. The world has **no hope**. They're hopeless. Their condition is very sad indeed though they don't even know it.

Hebrews 6:12

"That ye be not slothful, but followers of them who through faith and patience inherit the promises."

SLOTHFUL

This prohibition command regarding **slothfulness** is in the Greek aorist tense. If this prohibition command were in the Greek present tense, it would mean to stop an action already in progress. However, this prohibition command in the aorist tense means don't even begin an action. Paul is saying, don't even begin to be **slothful, lazy, and doing nothing**.

On the other hand, Paul urged them to be followers of those who inherit the promises and worked hard for the Lord. Genuine Christians should be filled with patience and **not slothfulness**. A **sloth** is a very **slow moving** animal.

- **Proverbs 12:27**

"The **slothful** *man* roasteth not that which he took in hunting: but the substance of a diligent man *is* precious."

The **slothful** man is too **lazy** even to roast what he caught from his hunting.

- **Proverbs 19:15**

"**Slothfulness** casteth into a deep sleep; and an idle soul shall suffer hunger."

All the **sloth** wants to do is to sleep. He'll end up hungry. (This was written before the food stamp program that is increasing.)

- **Ecclesiastes 10:18**

"By much **slothfulness** the building decayeth; and through idleness of the hands the house droppeth through."

If a person doesn't take care of his home, it will decay.

- **Romans 12:11**

"**Not slothful** in business; fervent in spirit; serving the Lord;"

We **cannot be slothful and lazy**, especially in our service for the Lord Jesus Christ.

PATIENCE

Patience is necessary in following the Lord Jesus Christ in the lives of true Christians.

- **Psalm 37:7a**

"Rest in the LORD, and wait **patiently** for him:"

That's a difficult thing to do, but God desires it.

- **Romans 5:3-4**

"And not only *so*, but we glory in tribulations also: knowing that tribulations worketh **patience**; And **patience**, experience; and experience, hope:

PATIENT IN TRIBULATION

It is amazing how Paul could have gloried in tribulations. But that is what worked patience in his life. Paul needed patience and so do genuine Christians today. Tribulation is one way to achieve patience. Has it helped you to find patience?

- **Romans 12:12a**

"Rejoicing in hope; **patient** in tribulation:"

Though difficult, saved people must be **patient**, even in serious trouble.

- **Romans 15:4**

"For whatsoever things were written aforetime were written for our learning, that we through **patience** and comfort of the scriptures might have hope."

OLD TESTAMENT SHOWS PATIENCE

The Old Testament Scriptures, when read, give us patience as well as comfort and hope. Though the Old Testament was not written to us, it is for us and our learning. It promises to give the genuine Christian patience, comfort, and hope.

- **2 Corinthians 6:4**

"But in all *things* approving ourselves as the ministers of God, in much **patience**, in afflictions, in necessities, in distresses;"

Paul had much **patience** even in severe trials and troubles.

- **Colossians 1:11**

"Strengthened with all might, according to his glorious power, unto all **patience** and longsuffering with joyfulness;"

God the Holy Spirit Who indwells the genuine Christians gives them **patience** with joyfulness.

- **1 Timothy 3:3**

"Not given to wine, no striker, not greedy of filthy lucre; but **patient**, not a brawler, not covetous;"

The pastor/bishop/elder must be **patient**. This is one of the qualifications needed and required in the Bible. Pastoral **patience** is one of the qualification for a pastor. He must be **patient**.

- **2 Timothy 2:24**

"And the servant of the Lord must not strive; but be gentle unto all *men*, apt to teach, **patient**."

Once again, any servant of the Lord Jesus Christ must have the quality of **patience**.

- **Titus 2:2**

"That the aged men be sober, grave, temperate, sound in faith, in charity, in **patience**."

The old men who are genuinely saved should be sound in **patience**. That is not an easy thing to achieve, but it is demanded by the Lord. Some older people find it very difficult to be **patient**, much less abounding in it, but that's how God wants them to be.

- **Hebrews 6:15**

"And so, after he had **patiently** endured, he obtained the promise."

Abraham **patiently** endured and finally, after a long time, had his son, Isaac.

- **Hebrews 10:36**

"For ye have need of **patience**, that, after ye have done the will of God, ye might receive the promise."

> **PATIENCE FOR GOD'S PROMISES**
> When genuine Christians do God's will, He keeps His promises. But those promises do not always come immediately. God always keeps His promises, but patience is needed while we wait.

- **Hebrews 12:1-2**

"Wherefore seeing we also are compassed about with so great a cloud of witnesses, let us lay aside every weight, and the sin which doth so easily beset *us*, and let us run with **patience** the race that is set before us, Looking unto Jesus the author and finisher of *our* faith; who for the joy that was set before him endured the cross, despising the shame, and is set down at the right hand of the throne of God."

> **RUN THE RACE WITH PATIENCE**
> Every genuine born-again Christian has a very difficult race to run in this evil day in which they live. <u>The race must be run, but it must be run with patience</u>. That is easier said than done, however. They must rely upon the power of God the Holy Spirit Who indwells them to enable them to run that race with patience. Everyone has a different race. They have different places of service. They live on different countries and different continents.

- **James 5:11**

"Behold, we count them happy which endure. Ye have heard of the **patience** of Job, and have seen the end of the Lord; that the Lord is very pitiful, and of tender mercy."

> **JOB–A PATTERN FOR PATIENCE**
> <u>Job gives the truly saved Christians a pattern for patience.</u> Satan wanted to test him and try him. The Lord gave him that permission. Satan took away Job's children. He took away his servants. He took away all of his possessions. His wife was still with him, but she opposed him.

Job declared:

> *"Naked came I out of my mother's womb, and naked shall I return thither: the LORD gave, and the LORD hath taken away; blessed be the name of the LORD."* (Job 1:21)

Finally, Satan was given permission to touch his body with many sores and diseases. <u>Through all of these difficulties and pains, Job</u>

maintained his **patience**. May the Lord give his genuine saved ones that **patience** in all of their difficulties as well.

Hebrews 6:13

" **For when God made promise to Abraham, because he could swear by no greater, he sware by himself,**"

THE ABRAHAMIC COVENANT

There are two things mentioned here: (1) **God's promise**, and (2) **God's oath**. He made a **promise** and **He sware by Himself**. <u>Two things</u>. (We'll see it later.) Two immutable things that cannot pass away but made a **promise**. He could **sware** by no greater, "He **sware** by Himself." The **Abrahamic covenant** was a **covenant** that was unconditional. **It** was unilateral. The Lord made **it** all **by Himself**. Abraham was sleeping when God made this **Abrahamic Covenant**.

- Genesis 15:8-17

"And he said, Lord GOD, whereby shall I know that I shall inherit it? And he said unto him, Take me an heifer of three years old, and a she goat of three years old, and a ram of three years old, and a turtledove, and a young pigeon. And he took unto him all these, and divided them in the midst, and laid each piece one against another: but the birds divided he not. And when the fowls came down upon the carcases, Abram drove them away." (verses 8-11)

God told Abraham to take the animals away and divide all of them except the birds. The reason for this is that in the Old Testament, when **covenants** were made, the parties walked between the pieces of the animals.

"And when the sun was going down, a deep sleep fell upon Abram; and, lo, an horror of great darkness fell upon him. And he said unto Abram, Know of a surety that thy seed shall be a stranger in a land *that* is not theirs, and shall serve them; and they shall afflict them four hundred years;" (verses 12-13)

That refers to his going down to Egypt.

"And also that nation, whom they shall serve, will I judge: and afterward shall they come out with great substance. And thou shalt go to thy fathers in peace; thou shalt be buried in a good old age. But in the fourth generation they shall come hither again: for the iniquity of the Amorites is not yet full." (verses 14-16)

God was going to judge the Amorites in the fullness of His time. Then the Israelites would return to their land.

"And then it came to pass, that, when the sun went down, and it was dark, behold a smoking furnace, and a burning lamp that passed between those pieces." (verse 17)

ABRAHAM'S UNILATERAL COVENANT

The Lord, Himself, in the similitude of a smoking furnace and a burning lamp, passed between the pieces of the animals. Abraham was sleeping. God made a unilateral covenant. It will come to pass, no matter what might happen. It is both unilateral and unconditional.

Hebrews 6:14

"Saying, Surely blessing I will bless thee, and multiplying I will multiply thee."

GOD'S PROMISE AFTER OFFERING ISAAC

This was God's **promise** to Abraham, but before it was fulfilled, God told Abraham to **offer** up **his son, Isaac,** as a **burnt offering.** As the **offering** was to be made, God graciously stopped it.

- **Genesis 22:11-12**

"And the angel of the LORD called unto him out of heaven, and said, Abraham, Abraham: and he said, Here *am* I. And he said, Lay not thine hand upon the **lad,** neither do thou any thing unto him: for now I know that thou fearest God, seeing thou hast not withheld thy son, **thine *only* son** from me."

When God told Abraham to sacrifice his **special son, Isaac,** Abraham obeyed. He went to mount Moriah where God told him to go. He took the wood for the **sacrifice,** the knife, but **Isaac** asked his father: *"where is the lamb for a burnt offering?"* Abraham answered: *"God will provide himself a lamb for a burnt offering."* And just as Abraham was ready to raise his knife to kill his **son, Isaac,** in obedience to God, God said:

> *"Lay not thine hand upon the **lad**, neither do thou any thing unto **him**: for now I know that thou fearest God, seeing thou hast not withheld **thy son, thine only son** from me."* (Genesis 22:12)

The story continues after Abraham spared his **son, Isaac,** from death.

- **Genesis 22:13-14**

" And Abraham lifted up his eyes, and looked, and behold behind *him* a **ram** caught in a thicket by his horns: and Abraham went and took the **ram,** and offered him up for a **burnt offering** in the stead of his son. And Abraham called the name of that place Jehovahjireh: as it is said to this day, In the mount of the LORD it shall be seen." Jehovahjireh, from the Hebrew Word "*to see.*" It means, literally, "The Lord will see to it" or "The Lord will provide." And the Lord provided Himself a **ram.**

- **Genesis 22:15-18**

"And the angel of the LORD called unto Abraham out of heaven the second time, And said, By **myself have I sworn, saith the LORD,** for because thou hast done this thing, and hast not withheld **thy son, thine only** *son*: That in **blessing I will bless thee,** and in **multiplying I will multiply thy seed** as the stars of the heaven, and as the sand which *is* upon the sea shore; and **thy seed shall possess the gate of his enemies**; And **in thy seed shall all the nations of the earth be blessed;** because thou hast obeyed my voice."

God was pleased that Abraham had obeyed Him, believing (as it says in Hebrews 11) that God could have raised up **Isaac** from death after he had been **offered**:

"Accounting that God was able to raise *him* up, even from the dead; from whence also he received him in a figure." (Hebrews 11:19)

Notice how Paul translates this verse and interprets it in Galatians.

- **Galatians 3:16**

"Now to Abraham and his **seed** were the **promises** made. He saith not, And to seeds, as of many; but as of one, And to thy **seed**, which is Christ."

ACCURATE BIBLE TRANSLATIONS

Proper translation is very important, even when it comes to singular and plural nouns. That's why the King James Bible is so accurate. The other versions are not always accurate in these areas. Through genuine faith and trust in the Lord Jesus Christ, God's promised Seed, all the nations of the earth can be blessed.

Hebrews 6:15

"And so, after he had patiently endured, he obtained the promise."

ENDURANCE

It took some time, after his error with Hagar before God gave Sarah and Abraham their promised son, Isaac. Abraham patiently **endured** and then received God's promise.

- **2 Thessalonians 1:4**

"So that we ourselves glory in you in the churches of God for your patience and faith in all your persecutions and tribulations that ye **endure**:"

ENDURING FOR CHRIST

Those true Christians in Thessalonica not only had persecutions and tribulations, but they endured them faithfully and were victorious in them.

- **2 Timothy 2:3**

"Thou therefore **endure** hardness, as a good soldier of Jesus Christ."

We who are genuine Christians must **endure** hardness as good soldiers for the Lord Jesus Christ.

- **2 Timothy 4:5**

"But watch thou in all things, **endure** afflictions, do the work of an evangelist, make full proof of thy ministry."

PASTORS–WATCH IN ALL THINGS

Paul's command to Pastor Timothy at Ephesus was to watch in all things. As a pastor, I also must obey this command. Therefore, I seek to watch not only in the things of the Bible, but also in the things that are taking place in our country and in the world that are affecting true Christians. While watching, Timothy must endure any afflictions that would come because he was watching.

- **Hebrews 12:7**

"If ye **endure** chastening, God dealeth with you as with sons; for what son is he whom the father chasteneth not?"

Punishment by the Lord when true Christians are out of line and out of step should be **endured**. If this is the case, God deals with them as with sons.

Hebrews 6:16

"For men verily swear by the greater: and an oath for confirmation *is* to them an end of all strife."

OATHS

In the Old Testament, people took **oaths**, but in the New Testament genuine Christians are not to **swear** and take **oaths**.

- **Numbers 30:2**

"If a man **vow a vow** unto the LORD, or **swear an oath** to bind his soul with a bond; he shall not break his word, he shall do according to all that proceedeth out of his mouth."

In the New Testament, the Lord Jesus Christ gave us another command regarding **swearing oaths**.

- **Matthew 5:34-37**

"But I say unto you, **Swear** not at all; neither by heaven; for it is God's throne. Nor by the earth; for it is his footstool: neither by Jerusalem; for it is the city of the great King. Neither shalt thou **swear** by thy head, because thou canst not make one hair white or black. But let your communication be, Yea, yea; Nay, nay: for whatsoever is more than these cometh of evil."

CHRISTIANS SHOULD NOT SWEAR OATHS

This is very clear that true Christians in the New Testament should not swear or take oaths.

- **Acts 2:30**

"Therefore being a prophet, and knowing that God had sworn with an **oath** to him, that of the fruit of his loins, according to the flesh, he would raise up Christ to sit on his throne;"

This is referring to the Old Testament **oaths**.

- **James 5:12**

"But above all things, my brethren, **swear not**, neither by heaven, neither by the earth, neither by any other **oath**: but let your yea be yea, and your nay, nay, lest ye fall into condemnation."

CHRISTIANS CAN "AFFIRM"

I follow this when I go to court as a witness in some matter. I raise my right hand and I "affirm," but do not swear. That is possible. In fact, they usually say do you swear or affirm. I say I affirm. We are not supposed to swear or take oaths if we are following the clear New Testament teachings.

Hebrews 6:17

"Wherein God, willing more abundantly to shew unto the heirs of promise the immutability of his counsel, confirmed *it* by an oath:"

OATH PASSED TO ISAAC

God confirmed His promise with an oath and passed it on to Abraham's son, Isaac.

- **Genesis 26:3**

" Sojourn in this land, and I will be with thee, and will bless thee; for unto thee, and unto thy seed, I will give all these countries, and I will perform the **oath** which I **sware** unto **Abraham thy father;**"

God said to **Isaac** that He was going to keep **the promise He made to his father, Abraham.** God was speaking about the land of Israel and the **promised Seed.** The land does not belong to the Palestinians, but to Israel. God gave it to them exclusively. In our day, we see that politicians have diminished Israel's land and want to shrink it even further.

THE MILLENNIAL REIGN OF CHRIST

One day, in the Millennial reign of the Lord Jesus Christ, the whole land that God promised Israel will be theirs. Our Saviour will reign from that land over the entire world. And the genuinely saved Christians will reign with Him one thousand years.

Hebrews 6:18

"That by two immutable things, in which *it was* impossible for God to lie, we might have a strong consolation, who have fled for refuge to lay hold upon the hope set before us:"

LIES AND LYING

God's promise and His oath were two immutable and changeless things. It is not possible for our God to **lie**! We've seen presidents like Clinton, Obama, and others **lie** to the American people. But God does not, will not, and **cannot lie**. This gives us strong consolation and comfort.

- **Numbers 23:19**

"God *is* not a man, that he should **lie**; neither the son of man, that he should repent: hath he said, and shall he not do *it*? Or hath he spoken, and shall he not make it good?"

God always carries out what He has promised.

- **John 8:44**

"Ye are of *your* father the devil, and the lusts of your father ye will do. He was a murderer from the beginning, and **abode not in the truth,** because there is **no truth** in him. When he speaketh a **lie,** he speaketh of his own: for he is a **liar,** and the father of **it.**"

Satan is both a **liar** and the father of **lies.**

- **Acts 5:3**

"But Peter said, Ananias, why hath Satan filled thine heart to **lie** to the Holy Ghost, and to keep back *part* of the price of the land?"

Ananias and Saphira **lied** to God the Holy Spirit. God killed them because of that **lie.**

- **Colossians 3:9**

"**Lie not** one to another, seeing that ye have put off the old man with his deeds;"

LYING IN THE COLOSSE CHURCH?

I wonder if the church at Colosse was a lying church. It must have been because, according to the Greek grammatical structure used, Paul told them to stop lying. They must have been lying if they had to stop it. We must always speak the truth.

- **Titus 1:2**

"In hope of eternal life, which God, that **cannot lie,** promised before the world began;"

God **cannot lie** about anything.

REFUGE

Those who have genuinely trusted in the Lord Jesus Christ for salvation have found a safe **refuge** from Hell. In the Old Testament, there were six cities of **refuge** for a murderer to enter until a trial was held. Those who have fled to the Lord Jesus Christ for **refuge** can lay hold of the hope of Heaven that is set before them. There are a number of verses on **refuge.**

- **Numbers 35:6**

"And among the cities which ye shall give unto the Levites *there shall be* six cities for **refuge**, which ye shall appoint for the manslayer, that he may flee thither: and to them ye shall add forty and two cities."

Of the forty-eight Levitical cities, six of them were cities of **refuge**.

- **Psalm 9:9**

"The LORD also will be a **refuge** for the oppressed, a **refuge** in times of trouble."

The Lord is a **refuge** in times of trouble.

- **Psalm 46:1**

"God *is* our **refuge** and strength, a very present help in trouble."

- **Psalm 62:8**

"Trust in him at all times; *ye* people, pour out your heart before him: God *is* a **refuge** for us. Selah"

To the true Christian, the Lord Jesus Christ is a place of **refuge** and protection.

- **Isaiah 4:6**

"And there shall be a tabernacle for a shadow in the daytime from the heat, and for a place of **refuge,** and for a **covert** from storm and from rain."

God is a **refuge** and **covert** from storm and rain. He is a **shadow** from the heat and a safe **refuge** to those who have truly fled to His Son, the Lord Jesus Christ.

Hebrews 6:19

"Which *hope* we have as an anchor of the soul, both sure and stedfast, and which entereth into that within the veil;"

SURE ANCHOR

This hope is an **anchor** which holds the genuine Christian in the proper place in the storms. It is **sure** and **stedfast anchor** of the soul. This **sure Anchor** is none other than the Lord Jesus Christ Who entered within the veil into the Holy of Holies.

- **Psalm 19:7**

"The law of the LORD *is* perfect, converting the soul: the testimony of the LORD *is* **sure,** making wise the simple."

God's Words are perfect and **sure**.

- **Psalm 93:5**

"Thy testimonies are very sure: holiness becometh thine house, O LORD, for ever."

Hebrews—Preaching Verse by Verse

God's Words are very **sure**. They are not fallen or far away, but are very **sure** and **dependable**.
- **Psalm 111:7**

"The works of his hands *are* verity and judgment; all his commandments *are* **sure**."

> **GOD'S WORDS ARE AN ANCHOR**
> God's commandments don't change. They are sure just as the anchor of the soul is sure.

- **John 6:69**

"And we believe and are **sure** that thou art that Christ, the Son of living God."

The apostles were **sure**. Peter was especially **sure** because he knew for **certain** that the Lord Jesus Christ was the Son of the living God.

- **2 Timothy 2:19**

"Nevertheless the foundation of God standeth **sure**, having this seal; The Lord knoweth them that are his. And, Let every one that nameth the name of Christ depart from iniquity."

> **CHRIST IS SURE AND STEDFAST**
> God's foundation is the Lord Jesus Christ in 1 Corinthians 3:10-11. He is sure and stedfast. The Lord Jesus Christ, the true believer's Anchor has entered Heaven itself into God's eternal Holy of Holies.

VEIL

- **Matthew 27:50**

"Jesus, when he had cried again with a loud voice, yielded up the ghost. And, behold, the **veil** of the temple was rent in twain from the top to the bottom; and the earth did quake, and the rocks rent;"

During the crucifixion of the Lord Jesus Christ the **veil** of the temple was ripped in two from the top to the bottom.

- **Hebrews 10:20**

"By a new and living way, which he hath consecrated for us, through the **veil**, that is to say, his flesh;"

> **CHRIST'S FLESH WAS THE VEIL**
> When the Lord Jesus Christ died on the Cross of Calvary, His flesh was rent just like the veil between the holy place and the holy of holies. Genuine Christians can enter Heaven because of this new and living way made possible by the

shedding of the blood of the Lamb of God, the Lord Jesus Christ.

Hebrews 6:20

"Whither the forerunner is for us entered, *even* Jesus, made an high priest for ever after the order of Melchisedec."

JESUS THE HIGH PRIEST AND VEIL

The Forerunner is the Lord Jesus Christ. He has entered Heaven and was made by God the Father a **High Priest after Melchisedec's order.** The Lord Jesus Christ has entered Heaven "for us" who are genuinely saved. The Greek Word for "for" is HYPER. Some of the meanings for this Word are: *"in behalf of; for the benefit of."* That is why the Lord Jesus Christ is seated at the right hand of God the Father.

GOD MADE CHRIST A HIGH PRIEST

The Lord Jesus Christ did not ask to be a High Priest. He was made a High Priest by God the Father. By this, God dissolved the high priestly ministry of Aaron and his successors in the Old Testament. He changed the priesthood of the tribe of Levi and changed it to the tribe of Judah, from which the Lord Jesus Christ came.

The Old Testament high priest lasted only a lifetime. When the high priest died, his elder son would take over, and son through many generations. But the **Lord Jesus Christ** was made a **High Priest forever, never to change.**

This **Priesthood** was **after the order of Melchisedec.** He appeared all of a sudden to Abraham. He was a **Christophany** or an appearance of the Lord Jesus Christ in the Old Testament. At the time, Abraham was fighting a big war between five different nations. The King of Sodom and his group won the battle. The king of Sodom offered Abraham all the booty from that battle.

ABRAHAM REFUSED SODOM'S GIFTS

Abraham refused these riches lest the king of Sodom could say that he made Abraham rich. Melchisedec was there at that battle. He had no father, nor mother, no beginning of days or end of life. This was a picture, I believe, of the Lord Jesus Christ. It was a Christophany, or an appearance of the Lord Jesus Christ before He came to this earth. The Lord Jesus

> Christ's Priesthood was after the order of Melchisedec, not after the order of Aaron.

- **Matthew 27:51**

"And, behold, the **veil** of the temple was rent in twain from the top to the bottom; and the earth did quake, and the rocks rent;"

I mentioned earlier that the **veil** was rent from top to bottom. It was very thick. The **veil was a picture of the flesh of the Lord Jesus Christ that was rent at the cross.**

- **Luke 23:45**

"And the sun was darkened, and the **veil** of the temple was rent in the midst."

- **Hebrews 9:3**

"And after the second **veil**, the tabernacle which is called the Holiest of all;"

In the temple, as in the tabernacle, there was a holy place, then there was a large **veil** which separated from the holy of holies. That's where the high priest entered in once a year, with sacrifices for himself and for the sins of his people.

- **Hebrews 10:20**

"By a new and living way, which he hath consecrated for us, through the **veil**, that is to say, **his flesh**;"

> **GOD'S LIVING WAY TO HEAVEN**
>
> Through the death of the Lord Jesus Christ on the cross at Calvary there has been created <u>a living way to Heaven</u>. It is realized for all those who have genuinely trusted that Saviour and accepted Him. When a person realizes that he is a sinner and has genuinely received the Lord Jesus Christ as Saviour, he is able to enter into the presence of God, into the holiest place of all. We should be thankful that our God has made this provision for the genuine Christians.

Hebrews Chapter Seven

Hebrews 7:1

"For this Melchisedec, king of Salem, priest of the most high God, who met Abraham returning from the slaughter of the kings, and blessed him;"

BACKGROUND OF MELCHISEDEC

> **MELCHISEDEC A CHRISTOPHANY**
>
> I believe Melchisedec was a Christophany--an appearance of the Lord Jesus Christ before His incarnation. It is very important to see some of these things. In the verse before this, the Lord Jesus Christ was made a Priest according to the order of Melchisedec. It was not according to the order of Aaron but of Melchisedec.

Notice the names of **Melchisedec**. He was the **King of righteousness**, the **king of Salem or peace**, and the **priest of the most high God**. Abraham was returning from the slaughter of the kings when **Melchisedec** blessed Abraham.

- **Genesis 14:8**

"And there went out the king of Sodom, and the king of Gomorrah, and the king of Admah, and the king of Zeboiim, and the king of Bela (the same is Zoar;) and they joined battle with them in the vale of Siddim;"

There were a total of five kings that fought with four other kings in this battle.

- **Genesis 14:9**

"With Chedorlaomer the king of Elam, and with Tidal king of nations, and Amraphel king of Shinar, and Arioch king of Ellasar; four kings with five."

This is the battle that is referred to here.

- **Genesis 14:10**

"And the vale of Siddim *was full of* slimepits; and the kings of Sodom and Gomorrah fled, and fell there; and they that remained fled to the mountain."

> **LOT SHOULD NOT BE IN SODOM**
>
> Lot, a nephew of Abraham was in Sodom at this time. The four kings that won the battle took all the goods that Sodom had including plenty of money (silver and gold). They also took Lot. Lot should never have been in Sodom. He never should have gone there but he was there.

- **Genesis 14:11-13**

"And they took all the goods of Sodom and Gomorrah, and all their victuals, and went their way. And they took Lot, Abram's brother's son, who dwelt in Sodom, and his goods, and departed. And there came one that had escaped, and told Abram the Hebrew; for he dwelt in the plain of Mamre the Amorite, brother of Eshcol, and brother of Aner: and these were confederate with Abram. And when Abram heard that his brother was taken captive, he armed his trained *servants*, born in his own house, three hundred and eighteen, and pursued *them* unto Dan.

That's it. Three hundred and eighteen men to go after these kings, four different kings that had taken all this loot and Lot as well.

- **Genesis 14:15-17**

"And he divided himself against them, he and his servants, by night, and smote them, and pursued them unto Hobah, which is on the left hand of Damascus. And he brought back all the goods, and also brought again his brother Lot, and his goods, and the women also, and the people. And the king of Sodom went out to meet him after his return from the slaughter of Chedorlaomer, and of the kings that *were* with him, at the valley of Shaveh, which is the king's dale.

As soon as Abraham with his 318 servants defeated these kings, these four kings, **Melchizedek** appeared.

- **Genesis 14:18**

"And **Melchizedek king of Salem** brought forth bread and wine: and he *was* the **priest of the most high God**.

Melchizedek just seemed to appear out of nowhere. He just appeared.

- **Genesis 14:19-20**

"And he blessed him, and said, Blessed *be* Abram of the most high God, possessor of heaven and earth. And blessed be the most high God, which hath delivered thine enemies into thy hand. And he gave him tithes of all.

It was God who delivered the enemies. Even those 318 servants were better than the army of five kings. God delivered them.
- **Genesis 14:20**
"And blessed be the most high God, which hath delivered thine enemies into thy hand. And he gave him tithes of all."

> **ABRAHAM TITHED TO MELCHIZEDEK**
> Abraham gave Melchizedek ten percent of all that Abraham had taken, including silver, gold, food, and other goods.

Hebrews 7:2

"To whom also Abraham gave a tenth part of all; first being by interpretation King of righteousness, and after that also King of Salem, which is, King of peace;"

> **MELCHIZEDEK'S TWO TITLES**
> This verse shows that Abraham gave to Melchizedek a tithe of all that he received in his victorious battle. Melchizedek's two titles are also seen here: King of righteousness and King of peace. These are fitting titles for the Lord Jesus Christ as a Christophany here.

Hebrews 7:3

"Without father, without mother, without descent, having neither beginning of days, nor end of life; but made like unto the Son of God; abideth a priest continually."

This verse especially shows why I believe **Melchisedec was a Christophany—a picture of the Lord Jesus Christ before His incarnation**. Notice what this verse says about Melchisedec:

1. **He was without a father.** The Lord Jesus Christ was also without a human father.
2. **He was without a mother.** The Lord Jesus Christ had a mother, Mary, at His incarnation, but before that, He had no mother.
3. **He had no descent or pedigree.** The Lord Jesus Christ had a descent at His incarnation, but not before that.
4. **He had no beginning of days.** The Lord Jesus Christ had a beginning of days at His incarnation, but not before that. He was from eternity past.

5. **He had no end of life.** The Lord Jesus Christ had an end of life at the cross in His incarnation, after that, He arose bodily and has no end of life, but lives for eternity future.

6. **He was made like the Son of God.** The Lord Jesus Christ is the Son of God Himself. The Greek Word for *"made like"* here is APH-HOMOIOO. Some of the meanings of this Word are:

> *"1) to cause a model to pass off into an image or shape like it; 2) to express itself in it, to copy; 3) to produce a facsimile; 4) to be made like, render similar."*

Notice the part of the Word HOM<u>OI</u>--. This is merely similar or like, but not identical. HOM<u>O</u>-- would be identical.

That is similar to what is recorded when Shadrach, Meshach, and Abednego were put into the fiery furnace.

> "He answered and said, Lo, I see four men loose, walking in the midst of the fire, and they have no hurt; and the form of the fourth is like the Son of God." (Daniel 3:25)

7. **He abides a priest continually.** The Lord Jesus Christ has an eternal Priesthood.

A PRIEST CONTINUALLY

The **eternal Priesthood of the Lord Jesus Christ** is taught elsewhere as well.

- **John 12:34**

"The people answered him, We have heard out of the law that **Christ abideth for ever**: and how sayest thou, The Son of man must be lifted up? Who is this Son of man?"

Even in the Gospel of John, it talks about **the Lord Jesus Christ abiding forever.**

- **Hebrews 7:23-25**

"And they truly were many priests, because they were not suffered to continue by reason of death. But **this** *man*, because **he continueth ever**, hath an **unchangeable priesthood**. Wherefore **he** is able also to save them to the uttermost that come unto God by **him**, seeing **he ever liveth** to make intercession for them."

CHRIST A PRIEST FOREVER

The priests in the Old Testament died and their office was resumed by their eldest son. Not so with the Lord Jesus Christ. He lives and abides a Priest for ever. We who are genuinely saved can go to that High Priest in heaven at the

Father's right hand. We can ask Him to help us. Though He died for the sins of the world at Calvary, He lives for ever at the Father's right hand of honor.

Hebrews 7:4

"Now consider how great this man *was*, unto whom even the patriarch Abraham gave the tenth of the spoils."

TITHES

TITHING IN THE OLD TESTAMENT

One of the things to show how great Melchisedec was is given in this verse. Abraham, the great Jewish leader, gave Melchisedec a tithe or a tenth of all the spoils of war that he obtained by his victory. Abraham's great grandson was Levi to whom the Jews gave their tithes. Abraham's giving to Melchisedec the tithe showed how great he was. Tithing is mentioned many times in the Bible.

- **Genesis 14:20**

"And blessed be the most high God; which hath delivered thine enemies into thy hand. And he gave him **tithes** of all."

This describes what this Hebrews verse has stated.

- **Numbers 18:26**

"Thus speak unto the Levites, and say unto them, When ye take of the children of Israel the **tithes** which I have given you from them for your inheritance, then ye shall offer up an heave offering of it for the LORD, *even* a **tenth** *part* of the **tithe**."

LEVITES ALSO TITHED BACK

So even though the tithes (the ten percent) from the Israelites were given to the Levites, the Levites were to tithe or give ten percent back to the Lord. That was the practice in the Old Testament.

- **Deuteronomy 14:22**

"Thou shalt truly **tithe** all the increase of thy seed, that the field bringeth forth year by year."

That was the principle for Old Testament giving. We don't have this law of Old Testament giving anywhere repeated in the New Testament to be followed in the age of grace. Many people do **tithe** and give **ten** percent of their earnings. Some give more and some give less. The New Testament principle is given in 1 Corinthians 16:2:

> "Upon the first *day* of the week let every one of you lay by him in store, as *God* hath prospered him, that there be no gatherings when I come."

N.T.--GIVING AS GOD PROSPERS
Giving should be as God has prospered the genuine Christian. One well-known millionaire used to give 90% to the Lord's work and kept only 10% for his own needs.

Hebrews 7:5

"And verily they that are of the sons of Levi, who receive the office of the priesthood, have a commandment to take tithes of the people according to the law, that is, of their brethren, though they come out of the loins of Abraham:"

OLD TESTAMENT TITHING TO LEVITES
The Old Testament commandment was for the sons of Levi who were in the priesthood to take tithes of the people. But, in this age of grace, we are not under any part of the law of Moses. We have no Levitical priests and we have no command to pay them our tithes. It is true that all of the twelve tribes of Israel descended from Abraham, but eleven of those tribes were to give ten percent of their income to the one tribe of Levi.

Hebrews 7:6

"But he whose descent is not counted from them received tithes of Abraham, and blessed him that had the promises."

ABRAHAMIC PROMISES
This verse is describing Melchisedec, whose descent is not counted from Abraham through Levi. The Lord Jesus Christ Who was Melchisedec on this occasion as a Christophany, had His earthly descent from the tribe of Judah through Mary. Melchisedec received tithes from Abraham and blessed him who had been given **God's promises**.

God gave many **promises to Abraham** as recorded in the Old Testament Scriptures.

- **Genesis 12:1-2**

"Now the LORD had said unto Abram, Get thee out of thy country, and from thy kindred, and from thy father's house, unto a land that I will shew thee. And **I will make of thee a great nation, and I will bless thee, and make thy name great; and thou shalt be a blessing:**"

What a wonderful **promise God gave to Abraham** in these verses.

- **Genesis 12:3**

"And **I will bless them that bless thee, and curse him that curseth thee: and in thee shall all families of the earth be blessed.**"

There are many leaders who are trying to remove more and more land from the state of Israel and give it to the Ishmaelites who are constantly cursing Israel. I don't think the Israelites are going to stand for it much longer. I don't think, as President Obama has suggested, that the Jews are going to go back to the 1967 boundaries or to boundaries even less than that.

In 1967, the Jews were weaker than they are now. They could hardly defend themselves. Now, according to a former Secretary of State, they want to cut out even more land that was cut out in 1967. **God promised blessing to those who bless Israel but curses to those who curse Israel.**

MUSLIMS KILLING JEWS & CHRISTIANS

We have many Muslims that are cursing Israel, killing Jews in the same manner they are killing Christians. The Muslims are literally following the Koran which teaches them to kill all infidels, that is everyone who is not a Muslim. This includes Jews as well as Christians. Muslims are killing Christians and Jews by the thousands all over the world. I wonder when God will curse those who curse the Jews? He has brought blessing to those who have genuinely received the Lord Jesus Christ, His Son, as their Saviour.

- **Genesis 22:15-18**

"And the angel of the LORD called unto Abraham out of heaven the second time, And said, **By myself have I sworn**, saith the LORD, for because thou hast done this thing, and hast not withheld thy son, thine only *son*: That **in blessing I will bless thee, and in** multiplying I will multiply thy seed as the stars of the heaven, and as the sand which *is* upon the sea shore; and thy seed shall possess the gate of his enemies; And in thy seed shall all the nations of the earth be blessed; because thou hast obeyed my voice."

Because Abraham believed the Lord and would have sacrificed his son, Isaac, in obedience (believed God would raise him from the dead, if need be) **God promised that in his seed (the Lord Jesus Christ) all the nations of the earth would be blessed.**

- **Galatians 3:16**

"Now **to Abraham and his seed were the promises made.** He saith not, And to seeds, as of many; but as of one, And to thy seed, which is Christ."

<u>**The Lord Jesus Christ is the only Seed of Abraham** by which all the nations of the earth will be blessed</u> if they sincerely receive Him as their Saviour.

TRANSLATION TECHNIQUE IMPORTANT

This is a verse that indicates the importance of the technique of translation. This technique is one of the four superiorities of our King James Bible. Paul mentions that God did not refer to "seeds" in the plural, but to "seed" in the singular, referring to the Lord Jesus Christ. Our King James Bible pays heed to singulars and plurals, unlike the modern English versions in many cases.

Hebrews 7:7

"And without all contradiction the less is blessed of the better."

This is very true. When **Melchisedec blessed Abraham** who gave him tithes, it was shown that <u>Melchisedec was the better and Abraham was the less</u>. The Lord Jesus Christ is far superior to Abraham or any other human being who ever lived.

Hebrews 7:8

"And here men that die receive tithes; but there he *receiveth them*, of whom it is witnessed that he liveth."

TITHES

"*Here*," means on this earth, Levites who die received the **tithes** from the Israelites. But in this instance, Melchisedec (the Lord Jesus Christ in a Christophany) received **tithes** and has no end of life. This is in complete contrast to the policies that prevailed in the Old Testament during the law of Moses.

Hebrews 7:9

"And as I may so say, Levi also, who receiveth tithes, payed tithes in Abraham."

> **LEVI RECEIVED TITHES**
>
> Because Levi was the great grandson of Abraham, it makes sense to say that through Abraham, Levi paid tithes to Melchisedec. It was the reverse of what was practiced in the entire Old Testament. The Lord Jesus Christ is superior to all the Levites that ever lived.

Hebrews 7:10

"For he was yet in the loins of his father, when Melchisedec met him."

This is what Paul has repeated in other verses. Levi had not yet been born, yet by means of his grandfather, Abraham, he paid **tithes** to Melchisedec.

Hebrews 7:11

"If therefore perfection were by the Levitical priesthood, (for under it the people received the law,) what further need *was there* that another priest should rise after the order of Melchisedec, and not be called after the order of Aaron?"

AN IMPERFECT LAW

This verse shows the need to have the Lord Jesus Christ come and be the Great High Priest for genuine Christians today. The Levitical priesthood and the **law of Moses was imperfect and desperately flawed** because it rested on mere human efforts. <u>If indeed perfection were by the **law of Moses**, there would have been no need for the Lord Jesus Christ to come from a different tribe than Levi to die for the sins of the world.</u>

Though this verse shows clearly that **the law of Moses was not perfect** and therefore **has been abolished by God**, there are some Christians who still want to be under **Mosaic law**. In the book of Galatians, Paul contended with these legalistic Christians who refused to renounce the **law of Moses** completely. We must never mix these two things—**law** and grace.

- **Hebrews 7:19**

"For the **law** made nothing perfect, but the bringing in of a better hope *did*; by the which we draw nigh unto God."

It is clear that **the law of Moses made nothing perfect.** It necessitated the bringing in of the Lord Jesus Christ who is a better hope. It is unfortunate that the Messianic Jews, who profess genuine faith in the Lord Jesus Christ, seek to keep various parts of **the law of Moses.** We must never go back to **Mosaic law** (unless it is repeated in the New Testament). It is unscriptural to do so.

Hebrews 7:12

"For the priesthood being changed, there is made of necessity a change also of the law."

The priesthood has been changed and we are no longer under the priests of Levi. That means we are no longer under any part of the **law of Moses.** It is a matter of necessity that there be a **change of the law.** Saved people today are under the age of grace, not the age of the law.

Hebrews 7:13

"For he of whom these things are spoken pertaineth to another tribe, of which no man gave attendance at the altar."

ANOTHER TRIBE

It is clear from the genealogy of Mary's line, in the Gospel of Luke, that the lineage of the Lord Jesus Christ, as to His perfect Humanity, came through the line of David and the **tribe of Judah, not the tribe of Levi.** In the Old Testament, no one from the **tribe of Judah** could be a priest. By **changing the priestly tribe** in the New Testament, God made it perfectly clear, to any who are aware, that there is a **vital change in the priesthood.** (1) The Lord Jesus Christ was from **the tribe of Judah rather than the tribe of Levi,** and (2) His priesthood was eternal and without any change of any kind.

Hebrews 7:14

"For *it is* evident that our Lord sprang out of Juda; of which tribe Moses spake nothing concerning priesthood."

As I have mentioned before, **the Lord Jesus Christ**, as to His Perfect Humanity, **came out of Judah**. Matthew gives the genealogy of Joseph and Luke 3 gives the genealogy of Mary. Joseph was only the "legal" father of the Lord Jesus Christ, but Mary was the real mother.

- **Luke 3:23**

"And Jesus himself began to be about thirty years of age, being (as was supposed) the son of Joseph, which was *the son* of Heli,"

> **LUKE GIVES MARY'S GENEALOGY**
>
> The genealogy of the Lord Jesus Christ begins here at verse 23. He was (as was supposed) the son of Joseph, but this supposition was not true. God the Holy Spirit was the Divine Father of the Lord Jesus Christ, but people thought the father as Joseph. He was only his "legal" father, however.

- **Luke 3:31-32**

"Which was *the son* of Melea, which was *the son* of Menan, which was *the son* of Mattatha, which was *the son* of Nathan, which was *the son* of David, Which was *the son* of Jesse, which was *the son* of Obed, which was *the son* of Booz, which was *the son* of Salmon, which was *the son* of Naasson,"

> **MATTHEW GIVES JOSEPH'S GENEALOGY**
>
> The other genealogy, in Matthew 1, goes through a cursed line, but Mary's line, from whom our Saviour was incarnated by the miracle of a virgin birth, goes through David's son, Nathan, who was not cursed.

Hebrews 7:15

"And it is yet far more evident: for that after the similitude of Melchisedec there ariseth another priest,"

This **other Priest** is the Lord Jesus Christ Himself. Notice that He was after the *"similitude"* of Melchisedec. The Greek Word for *"similitude"* is HOMOIOTES. One of the meanings for this Word is: "1) likeness." The root, HOMOI is likeness but not identity. HOMO would mean identity and complete sameness. This separates and distinguishes Melchisedec, the Christophany, from the Lord Jesus Christ Himself.

Hebrews 7:16

"Who is made, not after the law of a carnal commandment, but after the power of an endless life."

THE "ENDLESS LIFE" OF CHRIST

The Lord Jesus Christ did not come after the law of a carnal commandment, but with the power of an **endless life**. The Priesthood of the Lord Jesus Christ had nothing to do with the Mosaic priesthood through Aaron and Levi. <u>In our Saviour, we have an **endless life** which was impossible for the Levitical priesthood.</u>

- **Psalm 90:2**

"Before the mountains were brought forth, or ever thou hadst formed the earth and the world, even **from everlasting to everlasting,** thou *art* God."

CHRIST'S ETERNALITY
The Lord Jesus Christ was from everlasting to everlasting. He has no beginning and no ending.

- **Psalm 110:4**

"The LORD hath sworn, and will not repent, Thou *art* a **priest for ever** after the order of Melchizedek."

Speaking of the Lord Jesus Christ as a **priest forever**.

- **Matthew 28:20**

"Teaching them to observe all things whatsoever I have commanded you: and, lo, I am with you **alway,** *even* unto the end of the world. Amen."

<u>The Lord Jesus Christ is with the genuine Christians **always**, to the end of the world and **into eternity**.</u>

- **John 20:28**

"And Thomas answered and said unto him, My Lord and my God."

<u>The Lord Jesus Christ is God the Son for **all eternity past and into the future**.</u>

- **Hebrews 1:8**

"But unto the Son *he saith,* Thy throne, O God, *is* **for ever and ever**: a scepter of righteousness *is* the scepter of thy kingdom."

<u>**The Lord Jesus Christ is forever and ever** as our Great High Priest.</u>

- **Hebrews 1:10-11**

"And, Thou, Lord, in the beginning hast laid the foundation of the earth; and the heavens are the works of thine hands: They shall perish; but **thou remainest**; and they all shall wax old as doth a garment;"

The Lord Jesus Christ **remains forever**.
- Hebrews 1:12

"And as a vesture shalt thou fold them up, and they shall be changed: but thou art the same, and thy **years shall not fail.**"
Our Saviour's years shall never fail. He is always the same and never changing.
- Hebrews 5:6

"As he saith also in another *place*, Thou *art* a **priest for ever** after the order of Melchisedec."
The Lord Jesus Christ is a **priest forever**.
- Hebrews 6:20

"Whither the forerunner is for us entered, *even* Jesus, made an **high priest for ever** after the order of Melchisedec."
Once more, the Lord Jesus Christ is a **high priest forever**.
- Hebrews 7:24

"But this *man*, because he **continueth ever**, hath an **unchangeable priesthood.**"
- Hebrews 7:21

("For those priests were made without an oath; but this with an oath by him that said unto him, the Lord sware and will not repent, Thou *art* a **priest for ever** after the order of Melchisedec:)"
Again, a **priest forever**.
- Hebrews 13:8

"Jesus Christ the same yesterday, and to day, and **for ever.**"
The Lord Jesus Christ and His office as **High Priest is forever**.

Hebrews 7:17

"**For he testifieth, Thou *art* a priest for ever after the order of Melchisedec.**" This verse summarizes all of the preceding verses about the eternality of the Lord Jesus Christ's priesthood.

Hebrews 7:18

"**For there is verily a disannulling of the commandment going before for the weakness and unprofitableness thereof.**"

WEAKNESS OF THE LAW

The **law of Moses** was **disannulled** because of its **weakness**. The Greek Word for "**disannulling**" is ATHETESIS. Some of the meanings of this Word are:

"*1) abolition, disannulling, put away, rejection;*"

The **law of Moses** was **weak**. It can't save anybody. No one in the Old Testament could keep it.

Hebrews 7:19

"For the law made nothing perfect, but the bringing in of a better hope *did*; by the which we draw nigh unto God."

BETTER HOPE

The law of Moses made nothing perfect. There are many people seeking to keep the law of Moses. There are even some genuine Christians who want to go back to the Old Testament and practice some of the law of Moses.

CHRIST'S BETTER HOPE

The bringing in a better hope was made possible by the death of the Lord Jesus Christ on the cross for the sins of the world. By that sacrifice, those who genuinely trust in this Saviour possess the hope of everlasting life in Heaven which the law of Moses could never offer. There are many verses that speak of this hope.

- Acts 23:6b

"I am a Pharisee, the son of a Pharisee: of the **hope** and resurrection of the dead I am called in question."

Paul has **hope** in his bodily resurrection.

- Romans 15:4

"For whatsoever things were written aforetime were written for our learning, that we through patience and comfort of the scriptures might have **hope**."

Hope can be appreciated and realized by reading the Old and the New Testament Scriptures.

- Romans 15:13

"Now the God of **hope** fill you with all joy and peace in believing, that ye may abound in **hope**, through the power of the Holy Ghost."

God is called here the "*God of hope*." The Greek Word for "*hope*" is ELPIS. It refers to something in the future yet certain to happen.

- 1 Corinthians 15:19

"If in this life only we have **hope** in Christ, we are of all men most miserable."

The **hope** in the Lord Jesus Christ extends far beyond this life. If it were not so, Paul, and others persecuted for their faith, would be miserable.

- **Ephesians 2:12**

"That at that time ye were without Christ, being aliens from the commonwealth of Israel, and strangers from the covenants of promise, having **no hope**, and without God in the world:"

> ### THE LOST ARE WITHOUT HOPE
> Before coming to true faith in the Lord Jesus Christ, these Christians at Ephesus were without hope. Every unsaved person is without hope. They are truly hopeless without the Saviour.

- **Colossians 1:5**

"For the **hope** which is laid up for you in heaven, whereof ye heard before in the word of the truth of the gospel;"

Genuine Christians have a Heavenly **hope** which is laid up for them in Heaven.

- **Colossians 1:27**

"To whom God would make known what is the riches of the glory of this mystery among the Gentiles; which is Christ in you, the **hope** of glory:"

If the Lord Jesus Christ is in a person, He is their **Hope** of glory to come in Heaven.

- **1 Thessalonians 4:13**

"But I would not have you to be ignorant, brethren, concerning them which are asleep, that ye sorrow not, even as others which have **no hope**."

> ### MANY WITH THIS HOPE
> We have friends, relatives, mothers, fathers, wives, and husbands that are born-again and have this hope. They are Home in Heaven because they are saved and have this hope.

- **Titus 2:13**

"Looking for that blessed **hope**, and the glorious appearing of the great God and our Saviour Jesus Christ;"

> ### THE BLESSED HOPE IS THE RAPTURE
> This blessed hope is the pre-Tribulation rapture of all the genuinely saved people before the seven years of Tribulation begin.

- **1 Peter 1:3**

"Blessed be the God and Father of our Lord Jesus Christ, which according to his abundant mercy hath begotten us again unto a lively **hope** by the resurrection of Jesus Christ from the dead,"

The Lord Jesus Christ is the living **Hope** because of His bodily resurrection.

Hebrews 7:20

"And inasmuch as not without an oath *he was made priest:*"

OATH

MADE A PRIEST BY AN OATH

The Lord Jesus Christ was made a Priest by an oath. It was a special contract made by God the Father concerning His Son, the Lord Jesus Christ. Levitical priests were made by birth into a family, not with a special oath or covenant.

Hebrews 7:21

"(For those priests were made without an oath; but this with an oath by him that said unto him, The Lord sware and will not repent, Thou *art* a priest for ever after the order of Melchisedec:)"

These priests of Aaron's line, these Levitical priests, were not made with a special **oath** as was the Lord Jesus Christ.
- **Psalm 110:4**

"The LORD hath **sworn**, and will not repent, Thou *art* a priest for ever after the order of Melchizedek."

The Lord of heaven and earth will not change His mind regarding His Son, the Lord Jesus Christ. **He is a priest for ever after the order of Melchisedec**, not the order of Aaron.
- **Malachi 3:6**

"For I *am* the LORD, I change not, therefore ye sons of Jacob are not consumed."

The LORD is changeless and eternal and keeps His **oaths**.

Hebrews 7:22

"By so much was Jesus made a surety of a better testament."

CHRIST OUR SURETY

This special oath that made the Lord Jesus Christ a priest for ever made Him a *"surety"* (EGGUOS) or a sponsor of a better covenant than that made with Moses. The Saviour began an entirely new testament when He came as the genuine Christian's High Priest.

Hebrews 7:23

"**And they truly were many priests, because they were not suffered to continue by reason of death:**"

There had to be a multiplicity of high priests in the Old Testament because they all eventually died and had to be replaced with their eldest son. This was not like the Priesthood of the Lord Jesus Christ Who will never be replaced as the true Christian's High Priest because **He lives forever** as stated in His **oath**.

Hebrews 7:24

"**But this *man*, because he continueth ever, hath an unchangeable priesthood.**"

But this God-Man, the Lord Jesus Christ, **continues forever**. He has a **Priesthood that is unchangeable.** He no longer needs to make any offerings because this He did when He offered up Himself on the cross of Calvary. His Priesthood is eternal.

Hebrews 7:25

"**Wherefore he is able also to save them to the uttermost that come unto God by him, seeing he ever liveth to make intercession for them.**"

SAVED AND SALVATION

CHRIST DIED FOR EVERYONE'S SINS

Because of His eternal priesthood and especially because of what the Lord Jesus Christ did when He died for the sins of the world on the cross, He is able to **save** their souls if they truly receive Him as their **Saviour.** Many verses show how the Lord Jesus Christ can **save** the souls of those who truly believe on Him.

- **Luke 19:10**

"For the Son of man is come to seek and to **save** that which was lost."

This was the purpose for the Lord Jesus Christ to come to this world, to seek and to **save** the lost people.

- **John 3:17**

"For God sent not his Son into the world to condemn the world; but that the world through him might be **saved**."

CHRIST CAME TO SAVE PEOPLE

The first coming of the Lord Jesus Christ was to save people. At His second coming, it will be for Him to judge people.

- **John 5:34**

"But I receive not testimony from man: but these things I say, that ye might be **saved**."

The purpose for the things the Lord Jesus Christ said was for people to be **saved**.

- **John 10:9**

"I am the door: by me if any man enter in, he shall be **saved**, and shall go in and out, and find pasture."

Only by the Lord Jesus Christ, the Door, can people be **saved**.

- **John 12:47**

"And if any man hear my words, and believe not, I judge him not: for I came not to judge the world, but to **save** the world."

Again, the Lord Jesus Christ said He came to **save** the world.

- **Acts 2:21**

"And it shall come to pass, that whosoever shall call on the name of the Lord shall be **saved**."

Genuine calling on the Lord Jesus Christ in faith leads to **salvation**.

- **Acts 4:12**

"Neither is there **salvation** in any other: for there is none other name under heaven given among men, whereby we must be **saved**."

No other Name but that of the Lord Jesus Christ can **save** people.

- **Acts 16:30**

"And brought them out, and said, Sirs, what must I do to be **saved**?"

The jailor asked a very important question here.

- **Acts 16:31**

"And they said, Believe on the Lord Jesus Christ, and thou shalt be **saved**, and thy house."

Genuine faith in the Lord Jesus Christ brings **salvation**.

- **Romans 5:9**

"Much more then, being now justified by his blood, we shall be **saved** from wrath through him."

Saved from wrath means saved from the everlasting fires of Hell.

- **Romans 10:1**

"Brethren, my heart's desire and prayer to God for Israel is, that they might be **saved**."

Paul wanted his people Israel to be **saved**.

- **Romans 10:9**

"That if thou shalt confess with thy mouth the Lord Jesus, and shalt believe in thine heart that God hath raised him from the dead, thou shalt be **saved**."

Belief in the Saviour must come from the heart, not only from the head.

- **Romans 10:13**

"For whosoever shall call upon the name of the Lord shall be **saved**."

- **1 Corinthians 1:18**

"For the preaching of the cross is to them that perish foolishness; but unto us which are **saved** it is the power of God."

To the really **saved** ones, the preaching of the cross is the very power of God.

- **1 Corinthians 1:21**

"For after that in the wisdom of God the world by wisdom knew not God, it pleased God by the foolishness of preaching to **save** them that believe."

God **saves** those who truly believe on His Son.

- **1 Corinthians 15:2**

"By which also ye are **saved**, if ye keep in memory what I preached unto you, unless ye have believed in vain."

Acceptance of the gospel presented makes a person to be **saved** unless this belief is in vain.

- **Ephesians 2:8**

"For by grace are ye **saved** through faith; and that not of yourselves: it is the gift of God:"

A person is **saved** by grace true through faith in the Saviour.

- **1 Timothy 1:15**

"This is a faithful saying, and worthy of all acceptation, that Christ Jesus came into the world to **save** sinners; of whom I am chief."

Saving sinners was the reason the **Saviour** came into this world.

- **1 Timothy 2:4**

"Who will have all men to be **saved**, and to come unto the knowledge of the truth."

> **GOD WOULD LIKE ALL TO BE SAVED**
>
> It is God's will that all should be saved, not just the so-called "elect" of the hyper-Calvinists. He wants all to accept His Son as their Saviour, but He will not FORCE them. They must come to the Lord Jesus Christ willingly.

- **2 Timothy 1:9**

"Who hath **saved** *us*, and called *us* with an holy calling, not according to our works, but according to his own purpose and grace, which was given us in Christ Jesus before the world began,"

Those who are genuinely **saved** were **saved** by God's grace, not by their good works.

- **Titus 3:5**

"Not by works of righteousness which we have done, but according to his mercy he **saved** us, by the washing of regeneration, and renewing of the Holy Ghost;"

God **saves** those who are truly **believe in Christ**. He does this because of His mercy and by the washing of **regeneration**.

> **ONLY GOD CAN SAVE PEOPLE**
>
> God is the One Who is able to save people who truly come to him because the Lord Jesus Christ lives for ever.

UTTERMOST

This verse declares that the Lord Jesus Christ is able to save to the very **uttermost**. The Greek Word for **"uttermost"** is PANTELES. Some of the meanings of this Word are:

"*1) all complete, perfect; 2) completely, perfectly, utterly*"

> **JUSTIFIED ONCE TRULY SAVED**
>
> Once a sinner has been saved by genuine faith in the finished work of the Lord Jesus Christ, he is justified by God and made perfect and complete in the Lord Jesus Christ. It will never be torn down or destroyed. It will last for all eternity to come.

INTERCESSION

One of the reasons that the Lord Jesus Christ saves to the uttermost when they truly receive His salvation is that <u>He ever lives as their Great High Priest</u>. In addition to this verse, **intercession** for the genuine Christians is mentioned in other places in the New Testament as well.

- **Romans 8:26**

"Likewise the Spirit also helpeth our infirmities: for we know not what we should pray for as we ought: but the Spirit itself maketh **intercession for us** with groanings which cannot be uttered."

In this case, it is God the Holy Spirit Who makes continued **intercession** for those are truly saved.

- **Romans 8:27**

"And he that searcheth the hearts knoweth what is the mind of the Spirit, because he maketh **intercession** for the saints according to the will of God."

THE HOLY SPIRIT'S INTERCESSION

This verse also refers to God the Holy Spirit Who indwells the genuine Christians. He intercedes for them according to God's will.

- **Romans 8:34**

"Who is he that condemneth? *It is* Christ that died, yea rather, that is risen again, who is even at the right hand of God, who also maketh **intercession** for us."

CHRIST INTERCEDES FOR SAVED PEOPLE

In this verse we see that the Lord Jesus Christ, who is at the right hand of God, makes intercession for truly born-again Christians.

- **Hebrews 7:25**

"Wherefore he is able also to save them to the uttermost that come unto God by him, seeing he ever liveth to make intercession for them."

Hebrews 7:26

"**For such an high priest became us,** *who is* **holy, harmless, undefiled, separate from sinners, and made higher than the heavens;**"

HARMLESS

The Lord Jesus Christ, the High Priest for true Christians has a number of attributes in this verse. He is not only holy, but He is **harmless**. The Greek Word for "**harmless**" is AKAKOS. Some of the meanings for this Word are:

> "*1) without guile or fraud, harmless, free from guilt; 2) fearing no evil from others, distrusting no one.*"

- **Matthew 10:16**

"Behold, I send you forth as sheep in the midst of wolves: be ye therefore wise as serpents, and **harmless** as doves."

Doves won't hurt anyone. They are **harmless**.

- **Philippians 2:15**

"That ye may be blameless and **harmless**, the sons of God, without rebuke, in the midst of a crooked and perverse nation, among whom ye shine as lights in the world;"

BLAMELESS AND HARMLESS LIVES
Genuine Christians should aim to be both blameless and harmless as they live their lives in this wicked world.

SEPARATE

The Lord Jesus Christ was also **separate** from sinners. That does not mean He never talked with sinners to try to bring them to Himself, but he did not have close connections with them.

- **2 Corinthians 6:17**

"Wherefore come out from among them, and be ye **separate**, saith the Lord, and touch not the unclean *thing*; and I will receive you,"

BIBLICAL SEPARATION IS VITAL
This section of 2 Corinthians, from 6:14 through 7:1 explains the Biblical doctrine of separation. Genuine Christians must follow these principles in order to please the Lord Jesus Christ. He is their example in being separate from sinners.

HIGHER THAN THE HEAVENS

Due to the **exaltation** of the Lord Jesus Christ to the Heaven of Heavens after His death on the cross and His bodily resurrection, He is made **higher than the heavens**. Paul describes this in the following verses in Philippians.

- **Philippians 2:8-11**

"And being found in fashion as a man, he humbled himself, and became obedient unto death, even the death of the cross. Wherefore God also hath **highly exalted him**, and given him a name which is above every name: That at the name of Jesus every knee should bow, of *things* in heaven, and *things* in earth, and *things* under the earth; And *that* every tongue should confess that Jesus Christ *is* Lord, to the glory of God the Father."

Hebrews 7:27

"Who needeth not daily, as those high priests, to offer up sacrifice, first for his own sins, and then for the people's: for this he did once, when he offered up himself."

The Lord Jesus Christ as the Great High Priest of all the redeemed ones of all ages did not continually offer Himself for sins. The Levitical priests had to offer daily throughout their lifetimes.

ONCE

The Saviour offered Himself just **once**. This offering will never be repeated. The Roman Catholic church wrongly consider their mass an offering of the body and blood of the Lord Jesus Christ. As such, the Roman Catholic priests make this false "offering" many times daily all around the world. The Lord Jesus Christ, on the other hand, offered Himself only **once**.

- **Hebrews 9:12**

"Neither by the blood of goats and calves, but by his own blood he entered in **once** into the holy *place*, having obtained eternal redemption *for us*."

CHRIST ENTERED THE HEAVENLY HOLY PLACE

There was only one entering into the Heavenly holy place by the Lord Jesus Christ.

- **Hebrews 9:26**

"For then must he often have suffered since the foundation of the world: but now **once** in the end of the world hath he appeared to put away sin by the sacrifice of himself."

As a sacrifice for sins, the Saviour died **only** once. He put away sin by that sacrifice.

- **Hebrews 9:28**

"So Christ was **once** offered to bear the sins of many; and unto them that look for him shall he appear the second time without sin unto salvation."

Again, our Saviour was offered only once at Calvary.

- **Hebrews 10:10**

"By the which will we are sanctified through the offering of the body of Jesus Christ **once** *for all*."

Our Lord's body was offered only **once** for the sins of the entire world.

- 1 Peter 3:18

"For Christ also hath **once** suffered for sins, the just for the unjust, that he might bring us to God, being put to death in the flesh, but quickened by the Spirit:"

CHRIST SUFFERED ONLY ONCE FOR SINS

The Lord Jesus Christ only once suffered for sins. He was the Just One, without sin of any kind. He suffered for all the people in the world, past, present, and future—all of whom were unjust.

Hebrews 7:28

"For the law maketh men high priests which have infirmity; but the word of the oath, which was since the law, *maketh* the Son, who is consecrated for evermore."

The law of Moses made high priests with infirmity and sin because they inherited imputed sin because they were in Adam's race. The contrast is made by the Word of God's oath concerning His promise to bless all the nations of the earth in Abraham's Seed, Who is the Lord Jesus Christ.

GOD'S OATH FOR CHRIST'S PRIESTHOOD

This oath, by God the Father, made the Lord Jesus Christ, God's Son, the Great and eternal High Priest Who has been consecrated, not merely for the length of a lifetime, as the Levitical priests, but for evermore. This everlasting consecration as the Great High Priest, was made possible by His once-for-all offering of Himself on the cross of Calvary as a sacrifice for the sins of the entire world. The Lord Jesus Christ will never cease to be the Great High Priest for all eternity to come.

Hebrews Chapter Eight

Hebrews 8:1

"Now of the things which we have spoken this is the sum: We have such an high priest, who is set on the right hand of the throne of the Majesty in the heavens;"

THE RIGHT HAND OF GOD

Here Paul sums up his teaching that has gone before. We who are genuinely saved and born again Christians have the Lord Jesus Christ as our high priest. He is seated in the place of honor at **God the Father's right hand** in Heaven. The Levitical priests in the Old Testament ministered daily in the tabernacle, but there was no chair in the holy place. Aaron the high priest went into the holy of holies once a year, but there was no chair there either. Their work was never completed. The Lord Jesus Christ's work was finished, so **He sat down**.

The Greek Word for "*set*" is KATHIZO. Some of the meanings of this Word are:

> "1) to make to sit down; 1a) to set, appoint, to confer a kingdom on one; 2) intransitively; 2a) to sit down; 2b) to sit; 2b1) to have fixed one's abode; 2b2) to sojourn, to settle, settle down."

CHRIST AT GOD'S RIGHT HAND

The Lord Jesus Christ, though He is omnipresent as God the Son, now has a fixed abode. He is now in Heaven. He did not sit down in just any place, but at the right hand of the Majesty in the Heavens Who is God the Father. This is the place of power and majesty.

- Matthew 20:21

"And he said unto her, What wilt thou? She said unto him, Grant that these my two sons may sit, the one **on thy right hand**, and the other on the left, in thy kingdom."

The mother of these two apostles wanted her sons to be, one **on the right hand** and the other on the left hand of the Lord Jesus Christ when He reigned upon this earth.

- **Matthew 22:44**
"The LORD said unto my Lord, **Sit thou on my right hand**, till I make thine enemies thy footstool?"

This is God the Father telling the Lord Jesus Christ **to sit on His right hand** until His enemies are conquered. One day this will come to pass.

- **Matthew 26:64**
"Jesus saith unto him, Thou hast said: nevertheless I say unto you, Hereafter shall ye see the **Son of man sitting on the right hand** of power, and coming in the clouds of heaven."

CHRIST'S COMING IN POWER

The Lord Jesus Christ told his enemies that they would one day see Him on the right hand of power and coming in the clouds.

- **Acts 2:32-33**
"This Jesus hath God raised up, whereof we all are witnesses. Therefore being **by the right hand of God** exalted, and having received of the Father the promise of the Holy Ghost, he hath shed forth this, which ye now see and hear."

Peter speaks of the Lord Jesus Christ **on God's right hand** exalted.

- **Acts 5:30-31**
"The God of our fathers raised up Jesus, whom ye slew and hanged on a tree. Him **hath God exalted with his right hand** to be a Prince and a Saviour, for to give repentance to Israel, and forgiveness of sins."

Here our Saviour is **exalted by God the Father to His right hand** after the sacrifice at Calvary was completed.

- **Acts 7:55**
"But he, being full of the Holy Ghost, looked up stedfastly into heaven, and saw the glory of God, and Jesus standing **on the right hand of God**,"

In this case, as Stephen was being stoned to death, he saw the Lord Jesus Christ standing rather than **seated on the right hand of God the Father**. He was waiting to receive Stephen to Heaven. The Savior stood up on that occasion, but now is **seated on the right hand of God**.

- **Acts 7:56**
"And said, Behold, I see the heavens opened, and the Son of man standing **on the right hand of God**."

This is another statement of Steven as he was dying. He repeated that the Lord Jesus Christ was standing **at God's right hand**.

- **Romans 8:34**
"Who is he that condemneth? It is Christ that died, yea rather, that is risen again, who is even at **the right hand of God**, who also maketh intercession for us."

Here again, the Lord Jesus Christ is in the place of honor **at the right hand of God**, making intercession for the genuinely saved Christians.

- **Ephesians 1:20**
"Which he wrought in Christ, when he raised him from the dead, and set him **at his own right hand** in the heavenly places,"

The Saviour is **at God's right hand** in Heavenly places.

- **Colossians 3:1**
"If ye then be risen with Christ, seek those things which are above, where Christ **sitteth on the right hand of God**."

The Lord Jesus Christ is **sitting at the right hand of God the Father** in this verse as well.

- **Hebrews 1:3**
"Who being the brightness of his glory, and the express image of his person, and upholding all things by the word of his power, when he had by himself purged our sins, **sat down on the right hand of the Majesty on high**;"

In this verse, the Gnostic Critical Greek texts remove "*by Himself,*" leaving room for many religions, including the Roman Catholic Church to add many things in order to obtain salvation and redemption. The Saviour is **at the right hand of the Majesty on high** in this verse.

- **Hebrews 1:13**
"But to which of the angels said he at any time, **Sit on my right hand**, until I make thine enemies thy footstool?"

This is a quotation from psalms. No angel is **on God's right hand**, only His Son.

- **Hebrews 10:12**
"But this man, after he had offered one sacrifice for sins for ever, **sat down on the right hand of God**;"

It was only after His work was finished that the Lord Jesus Christ **sat down on the right hand of God the Father**.

- **Hebrews 12:2**
"Looking unto Jesus the author and finisher of our faith; who for the joy that was set before him endured the cross, despising the shame, and is **set down at the right hand of the throne of God**."

Again, this is <u>after the cross of Calvary that our Saviour</u> **sat down at the right hand of the throne of God**.
- 1 Peter 3:21b-22

". . . by the resurrection of Jesus Christ: Who is gone into heaven, and is **on the right hand of God**; angels and authorities and powers being made subject unto him."

It was <u>after His bodily resurrection that the Lord Jesus Christ took that place of honor and power</u> **at God's right hand**.

Hebrews 8:2

"A minister of the sanctuary, and of the true tabernacle, which the Lord pitched, and not man."

CHRIST IN THE HEAVENLY SANCTUARY

What is the Lord Jesus Christ doing in Heaven at the right hand of God the Father? He is a minister and servant of the Heavenly sanctuary. It is called the true tabernacle which the Lord pitched, not man. That Heavenly sanctuary is the pattern that God gave Moses for the earthly tabernacle of the Old Testament. All the articles and details that were there on the earthly tabernacle were patterned after the tabernacle in Heaven that the Lord pitched.

THE EARTHLY TABERNACLE

MOSES' TABERNACLE

In Exodus 25, we see some of the things that are in that earthly tabernacle. Since the earthly tabernacle was made after the pattern of the Heavenly tabernacle, the things that were in that earthly tabernacle are also in the Heavenly tabernacle, where the Lord Jesus Christ ministers at this time.

- Exodus 25:1-6

"And the LORD spake unto Moses, saying, Speak unto the children of Israel, that they bring me an offering: of every man that giveth it willingly with his heart ye shall take my offering. And this is the offering which ye shall take of them, gold, silver, and brass, and blue, and purple, and scarlet, and fine linen, and goats' hair, And rams' skins dyed red, and badgers' skins, and shittim wood, Oil for the light, spices for anointing oil, and for sweet incense,"

All these different things were for **the earthly tabernacle.** The heavenly tabernacle has all these things in perfection, without any question about it.

- **Exodus 25:8**
"And let them make me a **sanctuary**; that I may dwell among them."

> **THE TABERNACLE'S SANCTUARY**
>
> **Moses was told by the Lord to make a sanctuary in the tabernacle so that He might dwell among them. That was the purpose of the tabernacle, so that the Lord might dwell among the children of Israel.**

- **Exodus 25:9**
"According to all that I shew thee, after the pattern of **the tabernacle**, and the pattern of all the instruments thereof, even so shall ye make it."

Moses had a pattern. Where did he get that pattern? God gave it to him. Where was the pattern? It was In Heaven. The Heavenly tabernacle was the pattern that God gave to Moses for **the earthly tabernacle**.

- **Exodus 25:10**
"And they shall make **an ark** of shittim wood: two cubits and a half shall be the length thereof, and a cubit and a half the breadth thereof, and a cubit and a half the height thereof."

Just as there was **an ark** for **the earthly tabernacle, I believe there is an ark in the Heavenly tabernacle**.

- **Exodus 25:11**
"And thou shalt overlay **it** with pure gold, within and without shalt thou overlay **it**, and shalt make upon **it** a crown of gold round about."

The ark was made of pure gold.

- **Exodus 25:13**
"And thou shalt make **staves** of shittim wood, and overlay them with gold."

There were **staves** that went into the rings of **the ark** to carry it. That is the way the priests were carry **the ark** whenever it was moved. In their forty years of wilderness wanderings, they moved **the ark** forty or more different times. Each time **the ark** was moved, the priests were to put **the staves** into **the rings of the ark** and to carry it on their shoulders.

King David put **the ark** on a new cart and God judged that method. They should not have done that. God judged David for that. Uzzah, who touched **the ark**, was slain by the Lord (2 Samuel 6:6-7).

- Exodus 25:16-17a

"And thou shalt put into **the ark the testimony** which I shall give thee. And thou shalt make a **mercy seat** of pure gold:"

THE WORDS OF GOD IN THE ARK

The testimony, containing the Words of God, was to be placed in the ark. There was also a mercy seat of pure gold.

- Exodus 25:18-20

"And thou shalt make **two cherubims** of gold, of beaten work shalt thou make them, in the two ends of the **mercy seat**. And make **one cherub** on the one end, and **the other cherub** on the other end: even of the **mercy seat** shall ye make the **cherubims** on the two ends thereof. And **the cherubims** shall stretch forth their wings on high, covering **the mercy seat** with their wings, and their faces shall look one to another; toward **the mercy seat** shall the faces of **the cherubims** be."

Once each year the high priest could see these **cherubims** which were in **the holy of holies**. No ordinary priest, Levite, or other Israelite could go into **the holy of holies**. Just the high priest, once a year.

- Exodus 25:21

"And thou shalt put **the mercy seat** above **upon the ark**; and in **the ark** thou shalt put **the testimony** that I shall give thee."

THE MERCY SEAT ABOVE THE ARK

The Words of God, the testimony, were in the ark and the mercy seat was above the ark. Since the Heavenly tabernacle was the pattern for the earthly tabernacle of Moses, I believe there is a Heavenly ark and a Heavenly mercy seat. After His sacrifice at Calvary was completed, I believe the Lord Jesus Christ, our Heavenly High Priest, put some of His blood on that Heavenly mercy seat. This signified that His atonement for the sins of the world was complete.

- Exodus 25:22

"And there I will meet with thee, and I will commune with thee from above **the mercy seat**, from between **the two cherubims** which are **upon the ark** of the testimony, of all things which I will give thee in commandment unto the children of Israel."

The Lord would commune with his people Israel from **above the mercy seat** between **the two cherubims** which were **upon the ark**.

That was God's place of meeting with His people Israel.
- **Exodus 25:23-24a**
"Thou shalt also make **a table of shittim wood**: two cubits shall be the length thereof, and a cubit the breadth thereof, and a cubit and a half the height thereof. And thou shalt overlay it with pure gold,"

This describes **the table** used for **the shewbread** (Exodus 25:30). <u>All these articles of the furniture in **the earthly tabernacle** are made after the pattern of the Heavenly tabernacle where the Lord Jesus Christ is now ministering in behalf of those truly saved Christians.</u>

Hebrews 8:3

"For every high priest is ordained to offer gifts and sacrifices: wherefore it is of necessity that this man have somewhat also to offer."

THE EARTHLY PRIESTS' MANY OFFERINGS

<u>Every **earthly priest** and **high priest** of this earth of the Levitical and Aaronic priesthood was ordained **to offer** gifts and sacrifices</u>. The Greek Word for "*offer*" is PROSPHERO. It is in the present tense, indicating that this was a continuous action, day in and day out, on the part of these **earthly priests**.

It was necessary for this Man, the Lord Jesus Christ also to have somewhat to **offer.** This Greek Word for "*offer*" is PROSPHERO which is the same verb as earlier in the verse. But there is a different tense that is used here. It is not in the present tense continuous action of **the earthly priest's offerings.** <u>It is in the aorist tense which indicates a once-for-all, never to be repeated, offering by the Lord Jesus Christ, the genuine Christian's Great High Priest.</u>

The repeated offerings of **the Levitical priests** are mentioned often in the Old Testament.
- **Leviticus 16:1**
"And the LORD spake unto Moses after the death of the **two sons of Aaron,** when they **offered** before the LORD, and died;"

AARON'S SONS KILLED FOR DRINKING

From the context, it seems that these two sons of Aaron had probably been drinking. They were drunk when they tried to enter the holy of holies. Only the high priest was to enter there once each year. It was no place for the ordinary priests to go.

- **Leviticus 16:2**

"And the LORD said unto Moses, Speak unto **Aaron** thy brother, that he come not at all times into the holy place within the vail"

NADAB AND ABIHU

Aaron's two sons, Nadab and Abihu, whom the Lord slew, were probably trying to enter the holy place within the vail. That was called the holy of holies or the most holy place. Even Aaron, their father, the high priest was not to enter the holy of holies any time but once a year. If a person other than the high priest would try to go into the holy of holies, he would die. If the high priest would attempt to go into the holy of holies more than once a year, he would die also.

- **Leviticus 16:3**

"Thus shall **Aaron** come into the holy place: with a **young bullock for a sin offering,** and a **ram for a burnt offering.**"

Aaron had to bring two **offerings** for the sins of himself and his household–a young bullock for a sin offering and **a ram for a burnt offering.**

- **Leviticus 16:4**

"**He** shall put on the holy linen coat, and **he** shall have the linen breeches upon his flesh, and shall be girded with a linen girdle, and with the linen mitre shall he be attired: these are holy garments; therefore shall he wash his flesh in water, and so put them on."

Aaron had to be clean before he put on his holy garments.

- **Leviticus 16:5-6**

"And **he** shall take of the congregation of the children of Israel two kids of **the goats for a sin offering,** and **one ram for a burnt offering.** And then **Aaron** shall offer **his bullock of the sin offering,** which is for himself, and make an **atonement for himself,** and **for his house.**"

AARON HAD TO ATONE FOR HIS SINS

Aaron had to make atonement for his own sins and for the sins of his household. The Lord Jesus Christ, the high priest of the genuinely saved Christians, never had to atone for His own sins because he was sinless. On the cross of Calvary, the Lord Jesus Christ took the sins of the entire world in His own body, as the Lamb of God Who taketh away the sin of the world (John 1:29).

- Leviticus 16:7

"And he shall take the two goats, and present them before the LORD at the door of the tabernacle of the congregation."

THE SCAPEGOAT IN THE WILDERNESS

One goat was the scapegoat. Aaron put his hands on the head of that scapegoat, confessed the sins of Israel, and then sent it by a fit man into the wilderness (Leviticus 16:21). Aaron slew the other goat as an atonement for the sins of Israel for the entire previous year. He put the blood of that goat upon the mercy seat.

THE HEAVENLY PRIEST'S ONE OFFERING

- Ephesians 5:2

"And walk in love, as **Christ** also hath loved us, and **hath given himself for us an offering and a sacrifice to God for a sweetsmelling savour.**"

That one and only offering by the Lord Jesus Christ at Calvary was a sweetsmelling savour to God.

- Hebrews 10:5

"Wherefore when he cometh into the world, he saith, Sacrifice and offering thou wouldest not, but **a body hast thou prepared me.**"

CHRIST'S PREPARED SPECIAL BODY

This is a prayer by the Lord Jesus Christ to God the Father. This verse tells us that God the Father prepared, by the virgin birth of His Son, every part and element of the body of the Lord Jesus Christ. This included His hair, hands, blood, legs, feet, mind and all the other parts of His perfect body.

This verse completely disproves the heresy of John MacArthur who says that the blood of the Lord Jesus Christ was just human blood. His blood was specially prepared by God the Father. It was not just human blood. MacArthur makes this false claim as a minister with a huge audience and outreach through seminaries, books, Internet, TV programs, and in many other ways. <u>To say our Saviour had merely human blood, the same as we do, is sacrilege and blasphemy. The blood of the Lord Jesus Christ was incorruptible.</u> Those of us who truly saved were not redeemed, with corruptible things, like silver and gold, but with **the precious and incorruptible blood of the Lord Jesus Christ.**

- Hebrews 10:9-11

"Then said he, Lo, I come to do thy will, O God. He taketh away the first, that he may establish the second. By the which will we are sanctified through **the offering of the body of Jesus Christ once for all.** And every priest standeth daily ministering and offering oftentimes the same sacrifices, which can never take away sins:"

<u>The sacrifices of sheep, goats, bullocks, and other animals could never take away sins.</u>

- Hebrews 10:12

"But **this man**, after he had **offered one sacrifice for sins for ever**, sat down on the right hand of God;"

CHRIST'S ONLY ONE SACRIFICE

This speaks of the finished and completed work of our Saviour on the cross of Calvary which was never to be repeated. The Roman Catholic masses (which they call the sacrifice of the Lord Jesus Christ) are offered thousands of times each day all over the world. They are heresies and blasphemies against the truth about the once for all sacrifice of our Saviour, never to be repeated.

Hebrews 8:4

"For if he were on earth, he should not be a priest, seeing that there are priests that offer gifts according to the law:"

CHRIST NOT A PRIEST FROM LEVI

If the Lord Jesus Christ were in the Old Testament times, He would be disqualified from being a priest because He did not come from the tribe of Levi, but from the tribe of Judah. No earthly priest could come from any other tribe but the tribe of Levi. The Lord Jesus Christ came after the order of Melchisedec, from a different line, from the tribe of Judah.

The gifts offered by the Levitical priests according to the law could never take away sin. Only the Lord Jesus Christ's once for all offering of Himself could take away sin. John the Baptist had it right when he called the Lord Jesus Christ, God's perfect Lamb Who alone could take away the sin of the world (John 1:29).

Hebrews 8:5

"Who serve unto the example and shadow of heavenly things, as Moses was admonished of God when he was about to make the tabernacle: for, See, saith he, that thou make all things according to the pattern shewed to thee in the mount."

EXAMPLE AND SHADOW OF HEAVENLY THINGS

These earthly Levitical priests were merely an **example and shadow of Heavenly things**. The Greek Word for *"example"* is HYPODEIGMA. Some of the meanings of this Word are:

> "1) a sign suggestive of anything, delineation of a thing, representation, figure, copy; 2) an example: for imitation; 2a) of the thing to be imitated 2b) for a warning, of a thing to be shunned."

These earthly priests were not only an **example**, but also a **shadow of Heavenly things**. The Greek Word for *"shadow"* is SKIA. Some of the meanings for this Word are:

> "1) shadow; 1a) shade caused by the interception of light; 1b) an image cast by an object and representing the form of that object; 1c) a sketch, outline, adumbration."

HEAVEN GAVE MOSES A PATTERN

The tabernacle that Moses was told to make was to be made by very closely following a pattern which was given to him. That pattern was the Heavenly tabernacle itself. The Greek Word for *"pattern"* is TUPOS.

Some of the meanings for this Greek Word are:

> "1) the mark of a stroke or blow, print; 2) a figure formed by a blow or impression; 2a) of a figure or image; 2b) of the image of the gods; 3) form; 3a) the teaching which embodies the sum and substance of religion and represents it to the mind,

manner of writing, the contents and form of a letter; 4) an example; 4a) <u>in the technical sense, the pattern in conformity to which a thing must be made</u>; 4b) in an ethical sense, a dissuasive example, a pattern of warning; 4b1) of ruinous events which serve as admonitions or warnings to others; 4c) an example to be imitated; 4c1) of men worthy of imitation; 4d) in a doctrinal sense; 4d1) of a type i.e. a person or thing prefiguring a future (Messianic) person or thing."

They were serving as **foreshadowing** of Heavenly things such as would be revealed when the Lord Jesus Christ would become God's high priest from Heaven.

The earthly tabernacle followed the **pattern** of the Heavenly tabernacle which was the real thing. The earthly priests and tabernacle were merely **shadows of Heavenly things**.

THERE IS A HEAVENLY TABERNACLE

Different Bible teachers argue and say: (1) there is no tabernacle as such in Heaven; (2) there' is no altar in Heaven; (3) there is no mercy seat in Heaven. They fight about this. If indeed Moses followed God's **pattern** for his earthly tabernacle which had an altar, a mercy seat, and all the other details, how could this be a ***"pattern"*** if none of these things existed in the Heavenly tabernacle. To have a ***"pattern,"*** there must be a reality to which the ***"pattern"*** is like.

- **Colossians 2:16-17**

"Let no man therefore judge you in meat, or in drink, or in respect of an holyday, or of the new moon, or of the Sabbath days: Which are a **shadow** of things to come; but the body is of Christ."

The entire Old Testament ordinances are but **shadows**. The true reality which casts these **shadows** is the Lord Jesus Christ.

Hebrews 8:6

"But now hath he obtained a more excellent ministry, by how much also he is the mediator of a better covenant, which was established upon better promises."

CHRIST OUR MEDIATOR

Paul is speaking about **the Lord Jesus Christ** Who has a much **more excellent ministry** than the Old Testament Levitical priests. He is a perfect, sinless high priest Who is ministering in a Heavenly tabernacle.

> **CHRIST THE MEDIATOR**
>
> The Lord Jesus Christ is, and continues to be, the Mediator of a better covenant than the Mosaic covenant of the Old Testament. This new covenant was established on better promises than any of the Old Testament covenants.

The Greek Word for *"mediator"* is MESITES. Some of the meanings for this Word are:

> *"1) one who intervenes between two, either in order to make or restore peace and friendship, or form a compact, or for ratifying a covenant; 2) a medium of communication, arbitrator."*

> **ONLY CHRIST IS GOD'S MEDIATOR**
>
> It is not Mary, or any priests, or the Pope of Rome. The Lord Jesus Christ is the only Mediator. Roman Catholicism has made up a new heresy concerning Mary. They now claim she is the Mediatrix between God and man. This is total blasphemy of the Lord Jesus Christ.

- Galatians 3:20

"Now a **mediator** is not a **mediator** of one, but God is one."
<u>The Lord Jesus Christ the Mediator of the saved Christians mediates</u> between God and the individual.

- 1 Timothy 2:5

"For there is one God, and **one mediator** between God and men, **the man Christ Jesus;**"
<u>The Lord Jesus Christ is the only Mediator between God and Man. He is both God and Perfect Man.</u> He knows all about us both by His omniscience and by His own experiences while here on earth.

- Hebrews 9:15

"And for this cause **he is the mediator** of the new testament, that by means of death, for the redemption of the transgressions that were under the first testament, they which are called might receive the promise of eternal inheritance."

> **CHRIST THE ONLY MEDIATOR**
>
> The Lord Jesus Christ is the Mediator of the New Testament. He died for the sins of the entire world and thus became the Mediator for those who truly receive Him.

- **Hebrews 12:24**

"And to **Jesus the mediator** of the new covenant, and to the blood of sprinkling, that speaketh better things than that of Abel.

The Lord Jesus Christ is the Mediator of the new covenant and New Testament by dying for the sins of the world and offering eternal life to those who genuinely trust Him.

- **Hebrews 12:22-24**

"But ye are come unto mount Sion, and unto the city of the living God, the heavenly Jerusalem, and to an innumerable company of angels, To the general assembly and church of the firstborn, which are written in heaven, and to God the Judge of all, and to the spirits of just men made perfect, And to **Jesus the mediator** of the new covenant, and to the blood of sprinkling, that speaketh better things than that of Abel."

In this passage, **the Lord Jesus Christ** is also called **the Mediator** of the New Covenant.

CHRIST'S BLOOD IN HEAVEN

Notice in these verses eight personages or objects that are in Mount Sion or Heaven:

1. The city of the living God
2. The Heavenly Jerusalem
3. An innumerable company of angels
4. The general assembly and church of the firstborn
5. God the Judge of all
6. The spirits of just men made perfect
7. Jesus the Mediator of the new covenant
8. The Lord Jesus Christ's blood of sprinkling

- **Hebrews 9:15**

"And for this cause he is the mediator of the new testament, that by means of death, for the redemption of the transgressions that were under the first testament, they which are called might receive the promise of eternal inheritance."

The Lord Jesus Christ is the Mediator of the New Testament which is based upon His sacrificial death and bodily resurrection.

MOUNT SINAI, MOUNT SION, AND HEAVEN
- **Hebrews 12:18**

"For ye are not come unto the **mount** that might be touched, and that burned with fire, nor unto blackness, and darkness, and tempest,"

WE DON'T GO TO MOUNT SINAI TODAY

Paul is referring to Mount Sinai where the law of Moses was given by the Lord. Paul says that this is not where true Christians go for instructions and comfort. They go to Heaven itself and to the Bible and to their Mediator.

- **Hebrews 12:22**

"But ye are come unto **mount Sion**, and unto the **city of the living God**, the **heavenly Jerusalem**, and to an innumerable company of angels,"

Paul is referring to the **Heavenly Mount** and the Heavenly tabernacle.

There are many who deny that, after His death and bodily resurrection, the Lord Jesus Christ placed some of His blood on the mercy seat of **Heaven** as the Levitical high priests did once a year on the Day of Atonement (Leviticus 16:14-15, 18-19). Some of His precious blood is there on the mercy seat of **Heaven** as a token of the finished and completed work of the Lord Jesus Christ. Hebrews 12:22-24 clearly teach this, as do other verses in Hebrews which we will cover later.

Hebrews 8:7

"**For if that first covenant had been faultless, then should no place have been sought for the second.**"

THE MOSAIC COVENANT OR LAW

That first covenant Paul is referring to was **the Mosaic covenant** which is also called the Mosaic law. There are many references to it in the Bible.

- **Exodus 19:3-8**

"And Moses went up unto God, and the LORD called unto him out of the mountain, saying, Thus shalt thou say to the house of Jacob, and tell the children of Israel; Ye have seen what I did unto the Egyptians, and how I bare you on eagles' wings, and brought you unto myself. Now therefore, if ye will obey my voice indeed, and keep **my covenant**, then ye shall be a peculiar treasure unto me above all people: for all the earth is mine. And ye shall be unto me a kingdom of priests, and an holy nation. These are the words which thou shalt speak unto the children of Israel. And Moses came and called for the elders of the people, and laid before their faces all these words which the LORD commanded him. And all the people answered together, and said, All the LORD hath spoken we will do. And Moses returned the words of the people unto the LORD."

The Israelites didn't obey the Words of God. Acts 7:53 mentions that the Jews received **the law** by the disposition of angels but did not kept it.

- **Acts 13:39**

"And by him all that believe are justified from all things, from which ye could not be justified by **the law of Moses**."

This is speaking about the Lord Jesus Christ. **The Law of Moses** was not able to justify anyone.

- **Romans 3:20**

"Therefore by the deeds of **the law** there shall no flesh be justified in his sight: for by **the law** is the knowledge of sin."

No flesh can be justified before God by the deeds of **the law of Moses**.

- **Romans 4:15**

"Because **the law** worketh wrath: for where no **law** is, there is no transgression."

The law of Moses defined sin and transgression.

- **Romans 5:13**

"(For until **the law** sin was in the world: but sin is not imputed when there is no **law**."

LAW DEFINES SIN

Sin was not called sin until there was a law that defined what sin is. Then the breaking of that law was clearly sin.

- **Romans 6:14**

"For sin shall not have dominion over you: for ye are not under **the law**, but under grace."

That is a very clear statement. The Christians in Rome and all genuine Christians in this age of grace are not under any part of **the law of Moses**.

- **Romans 8:3**

"For what **the law** could not do, in that it was weak through the flesh, God sending his own Son in the likeness of sinful flesh, and for sin, condemned sin in the flesh:"

The law was weak but the Lord Jesus Christ is strong.

- **Galatians 2:16**

  "Knowing that a man is not justified by the works of **the law**, but by the faith of Jesus Christ, even we have believed in Jesus Christ, that we might be justified by the faith of Christ, and not by the works of **the law**: for by the works of **the law** shall no flesh be justified."

Not a single thing that **the law of Moses** could do can justify people before God. <u>Justification before God is only accomplished by trusting truly in what the Lord Jesus Christ accomplished on the cross</u>.

- **Galatians 2:21**

  "I do not frustrate the grace of God: for if righteousness come by **the law**, then Christ is dead in vain."

<u>Righteousness before God cannot come by **the law of Moses**</u>.

- **Galatians 3:10-11**

  "For as many as are of the works of **the law** are under the curse: for it is written, Cursed is every one that continueth not in all things which are written in the book of **the law** to do them. But that no man is justified by **the law** in the sight of God, it is evident: for, The just shall live by faith."

<u>Those that tried to follow **the law** are under a curse because they could not keep it</u>.

- **Galatians 4:4-5**

  "But when the fulness of the time was come, God sent forth his Son, made of a woman, made under **the law**, To redeem them that were under **the law**, that we might receive the adoption of sons."

The Lord Jesus came to redeem those under **the law** because **the law of Moses** could not save anyone.

Hebrews 8:8

"For finding fault with them, he saith, Behold, the days come, saith the Lord, when I will make a new covenant with the house of Israel and with the house of Judah:"

THE NEW COVENANT

THE NEW COVENANT BASED ON THE CROSS

This new covenant that God says He's going to make, is mentioned in Jeremiah 31. This covenant is based on the cross of Calvary, based on the finished work of Christ.

- **Jeremiah 31:31-32**

"Behold, the days come, saith the LORD, that I will make a **new covenant** with the house of Israel, and with the house of Judah: Not according to the covenant that I made with their fathers in the day that I took them by the hand to bring them out of the land of Egypt; which my covenant they brake, although I was an husband unto them, saith the LORD:"

Not the Mosaic covenant. <u>A **new covenant** with Israel, one day</u>.

- **Jeremiah 31:33**

"But this shall be **the covenant** that I will make with the house of Israel; After those days, saith the LORD, I will put my law in their inward parts, and write it in their hearts; and will be their God, and they shall be my people."

That's almost unbelievable, but <u>what God promises, He fulfills</u>.

- **Jeremiah 31:34-35**

"And they shall teach no more every man his neighbor; and every man his brother, saying, Know the LORD: for they shall all know me, from the least of them unto the greatest of them, saith the LORD: for I will forgive their iniquity, and I will remember their sin no more. Thus saith the LORD, which giveth the sun for a light by day, and the ordinances of the moon and of the stars for a light by night, which divideth the sea when the waves thereof roar; The LORD of hosts is his name:"

<u>God promises to forgive the iniquity of those who are genuinely part of **the new covenant**</u>.

- **Jeremiah 31:36**

"If those ordinances (that is, the sun, moon and stars) depart from before me, saith the LORD, then the seed of Israel also shall cease from being a nation before me for ever."

God promised that Israel would be a nation forever.

- **Jeremiah 31:37**

"Thus saith the LORD; If heaven above can be measured, and the foundations of the earth searched out beneath, I will also cast off all the seed of Israel for all that they have done, saith the LORD."

<u>God is not going to cast off Israel</u>. They have a future with Him.

- **Hebrews 12:18-21**

"For ye are not come unto the mount that might be touched, and that burned with fire, nor unto blackness, and darkness, and tempest, And the sound of a trumpet, and the voice of words; which voice they that heard intreated that the word should not be spoken to them any more. (For they could not endure that which was commanded, And if so much as a beast touch the mountain, it shall be stoned, or thrust through with a dart: And so terrible was the sight, that Moses said, I exceedingly fear and quake:)"

When the law of Moses was given at Mount Sinai there was a frightening loudness and thunders (Exodus 19:16). If any person or animal touched the Mount, they would die.

- **Hebrews 12:22**

"But ye are come unto **mount Sion**, and unto the **city of the living God**, the **heavenly Jerusalem**, and to an innumerable company of angels,"

Eight things are in **Heaven**, the **city of the living God**. I have listed them before.

- **Luke 22:20**

"Likewise also the cup after supper, saying This cup is the **new testament** in my blood, which is shed for you."

The **New Testament** is based on the shed blood of the Lord Jesus Christ.

- **1 Corinthians 11:25**

"After the same manner also he took the cup, when he had supped, saying, This cup is the **new testament** in my blood: this do ye, as oft as ye drink it, in remembrance of me."

Again, the **New Testament** is based on the shed blood of the Lord Jesus Christ.

- **2 Corinthians 3:6**

"Who also hath made us able ministers of the **new testament**; not of the letter, but of the spirit: for the letter killeth, but the spirit giveth life."

The **new covenant** is based upon Calvary's Cross and the death of the Lord Jesus Christ on the cross for the sins of the world.

- **Hebrews 9:15**

"And for this cause he is the mediator of the **new testament**, that by means of death, for the redemption of the transgressions that were under the first testament, they which are called might receive the promise of eternal inheritance."

> **THE NEW TESTAMENT NOT THE OLD**
> This New Testament or new covenant, is not the same as the old. It has nothing to do with the old. Every part of the Mosaic covenant has passed away. Only those things that are repeated in the New Testament are to be followed, not because they're part of the Old Testament covenant, but because they are now New Testament doctrines.

Hebrews 8:9

"Not according to the covenant that I made with their fathers in the day when I took them by the hand to lead them out of the land of Egypt; because they continued not in my covenant, and I regarded them not, saith the Lord."

ISRAEL'S DISOBEDIENCE TO GOD

> **ISRAEL DID NOT FOLLOW THE LORD**
> The Israelites did not follow God's Old Testament covenant. They were disobedient to God's rules.

- 2 Kings 17:7

"For so it was, that **the children of Israel had sinned against the LORD their God,** which had brought them up out of the land of Egypt, from under the hand of Pharaoh king of Egypt, and had **feared other gods,**"

> **ISRAEL SINNED AGAINST THE LORD**
> Remember how the Israelites said they would do all that the Lord commanded of them? What prevaricators. They may have meant well, but they were liars. They sinned against the Lord God, Who brought them up out of the land of Egypt, from under the hand of Pharaoh king of Egypt, and had feared other gods. They worshipped idols in idolatry.

- 2 Kings 17:8, 9

"And **walked in the statutes of the heathen,** whom the LORD cast out from before the children of Israel, and of the kings of Israel, which they had made. And **the children of Israel did secretly those things that were not right against the LORD their God,** and **they built them high places** in all their cities, from the tower of the watchmen to the fenced city."

Hebrews–Preaching Verse by Verse

> **SECRET SINS**
> Israel committed what they thought were secret sins. There are no secrets with the Lord. They built many high places.

- 2 Kings 17:10-13

"And **they set them up images and groves in every high hill, and under every green tree: And they burnt incense in all the high places,** as did the heathen whom the LORD carried away before them; and wrought wicked things to provoke the LORD to anger: For **they served idols,** whereof the LORD had said unto them, Ye shall not do this thing. Yet the LORD testified against Israel, and against Judah, by all the prophets, and by all the seers, saying, Turn ye from your evil ways, and keep my commandments and my statues, according to all the law which I commanded your fathers, and which I sent to you by my servants the prophets."

They served many idols.

- 2 Kings 17:14-20

"Notwithstanding **they would not hear,** but **hardened their necks,** like to the neck of their fathers, that **did not believe in the LORD their God.** And **they rejected his statutes, and his covenant** that he made with their fathers, **and his testimonies** which he testified against them; and **they followed vanity,** and **became vain,** and **went after the heathen** that were round about them, concerning whom the LORD had charged them, that they should not do like them. And **they left all the commandments of the LORD their God,** and **made them molten images, even two calves,** and **made a grove,** and **worshipped all the host of heaven,** and **served Baal. And they caused their sons and their daughters to pass through the fire,** and **used divination and enchantments,** and **sold themselves to do evil in the sight of the LORD, to provoke him to anger.** Therefore, the LORD was very angry with Israel, and removed them out of his sight: there was none left but the tribe of Judah only. Also **Judah kept not the commandments of the LORD their God,** but **walked in the statues of Israel which they made:** And the LORD rejected all the seed of Israel, and afflicted them, and delivered them into the hand of spoilers, until he had cast them out of his sight."

> **ISRAEL REJECTED GOD'S COMMANDS**
> This is a picture of Israel's total rejection of the commands and covenant of the Lord. This is a very sad disobedience.

Hebrews 8:10

"For this is the covenant that I will make with the house of Israel after those days, saith the Lord; I will put my laws into their mind, and write them in their hearts: and I will be to them a God, and they shall be to me a people:"

FUTURE BLESSINGS FOR ISRAEL

Amazing though it may be, one day in the **future, Israel** that is now blinded **will turn to the Lord Jesus Christ as their true Saviour and Messiah.** A few Israelites presently have come to the Lord Jesus Christ, but the majority of them are blinded. In the future, God promised that He will put His law into their hearts and minds. Israel will return to the Lord.

- Matthew 23:37

"O Jerusalem, Jerusalem, thou that killest the prophets, [and that's exactly what the Jews did] and stonest them [and stoned them as well] which are sent unto thee, how often would I have gathered thy children together, even as a hen gathereth her chickens under her wings, and ye would not!"

> **CHRIST'S CARE FOR ISRAEL**
> The Lord Jesus Christ Himself, before he went to the Cross of Calvary, told the Jews of His day that he would have gathered them as a mother hen gathers her chickens, but they did not want to be gathered. They wanted nothing to do with the Lord Jesus Christ's gathering of them to Himself.

- Matthew 23:38-39

"Behold, your house is left unto you desolate. For I say unto you, Ye shall not see me henceforth, till **ye shall say, Blessed is he that cometh in the name of the Lord.**"

One day Israel will say blessed is he Who comes in the name of the Lord. They will say that. **They will accept the Saviour that they rejected.**

- Romans 11:26-27

"And so all Israel shall be saved: as it is written, There shall come out of Sion the Deliverer, and shall turn away ungodliness from Jacob: For this is my covenant unto them, when I shall take away their sins."

ISRAEL WILL COME TO CHRIST
The nation as a whole will one day come to the Lord Jesus Christ. There may be some that deny but as a whole, Israel will have the opportunity and will come to the Lord Jesus Christ. It may be very difficult to believe that, but God has promised it and He will fulfill His promise.

Hebrews 8:11

"And they shall not teach every man his neighbour, and every man his brother, saying, Know the Lord: for all shall know me, from the least to the greatest."

MORE FUTURE BLESSINGS FOR ISRAEL

That will be a great day when this comes to pass and Israel returns to genuine following of the Lord Jesus Christ and God the Father.

- Isaiah 11:9-11

"They shall not hurt nor destroy in all my holy mountain: for the earth shall be full of the knowledge of the LORD, as the waters cover the sea. And in that day there shall be a root of Jesse, [that's the Lord Jesus Christ] which shall stand for an ensign of the people; to it shall the Gentiles seek: and his rest shall be glorious. And it shall come to pass in that day, that the Lord shall set his hand again the second time to recover the remnant of his people, which shall be left, from Assyria, and from Egypt, and from Pathros, and from Cush, and from Elam, and from Shinar, and from Hamath, and from the islands of the sea."

> **ISRAEL WILL BE DRAWN TO JERUSALEM**
>
> The Lord put His hand on Israel and pulled them out of Egypt. For forty years they were in Egypt, but God led them out. Then they were another forty years in the wilderness. In these verses, God has promised to put His hand on Israel the second time to recover Israel from many places on this earth. It hasn't taken place yet, but one day this prophecy will be fulfilled. God will draw his people back.

- Isaiah 11:12

"And he shall set up an ensign for the nations, and shall assemble the outcasts of Israel, and gather together the dispersed of Judah from the four corners of the earth."

God will fulfill that promise. He Who created the heavens, the stars, the world, man, and all the animals, has he same power today. He will one day gather Israel back to their land.

- Habakkuk 2:14

"For the earth shall be filled with the knowledge of the glory of the LORD, as the waters cover the sea."

This is one more promise that God will bring to pass, amazing as it might sound.

Hebrews 8:12

"For I will be merciful to their unrighteousness, and their sins and their iniquities will I remember no more."

SINS NOT REMEMBERED THROUGH GOD'S MERCY

There are many verses in the Bible that speak of **forgiveness of sins** by God the Father as well as by God the Son, the Lord Jesus Christ.

> **GOD'S MERCY TO ISRAEL**
>
> God told the Israelites that He would be merciful to their unrighteousness. When God grants mercy to someone, He is not giving them something they deserve. Some day, God is going to be merciful to all the unrighteousness of his people, even the people that motivated the Romans to crucify the Lord of Lords.
>
> God also promises here that He will not remember the sins of Israel any more. That is the greatest gift that God could give to any person. There are many people in this world do not

think this is a great gift. They would far rather have money, or land, or clothes, or houses, or guns, or airplanes, or many other things. I disagree with this sentiment. I still believe that the greatest gift to any one in this world to possess is for their sins and iniquities to be remembered no more. There are a number of verses that deal with some aspect of God's forgiveness of the sins of mankind.

- **Psalm 32:1**
"Blessed is he whose transgression is forgiven, whose sin is covered."

God says <u>**forgiveness of sins is a blessing**</u>. People should be happy when their **sins have been forgiven** by genuine trust in the Lord Jesus Christ.

- **Psalm 32:2**
"**Blessed is the man unto whom the LORD imputeth not iniquity,** and in whose spirit there is no guile."

<u>Those who genuinely trust in the Lord Jesus Christ are **declared righteous by the Lord**.</u> This is a blessing.

- **Psalm 103:12**
"As far as the east is from the west, so far hath **he removed our transgressions from us.**"

This is true of true Christians. The distance from the east to the west is endless. That's how far **God has removed sins from those He has saved.**

- **Luke 5:20**
"And when he saw their faith, he said unto him, Man, **thy sins are forgiven thee.**"

CHRIST–PERFECT GOD AND MAN

The Lord Jesus Christ, perfect God and perfect Man is able to forgive sins. The greatest thing God could give to any, man, woman, or child would be to have their sins totally and completely forgiven. Only by genuine faith in the Lord Jesus Christ can this be accomplished.

- **Luke 7:48**
"And he said unto her, **Thy sins are forgiven.**"

This is a woman who was a sinner. **The Lord Jesus Christ was able to forgive all of her sins.**

- **John 1:29**

"The next day John seeth Jesus coming unto him, and saith, **Behold the Lamb of God, which taketh away the sin of the world."**

Only the Lamb of God, the Lord Jesus Christ, can take away the sin of the world when people genuinely trust Him.

- **Acts 5:31**

"Him hath God exalted with his right hand to be a Prince and a Saviour, for **to give repentance to Israel, and forgiveness of sins."**

The greatest present that God could ever give a person is the forgiveness of their sins. This is possible only through true faith in the Saviour.

- **Romans 4:7-8**

"Saying, **Blessed are they whose iniquities are forgiven, and whose sins are covered. Blessed is the man to whom the Lord will not impute sin."**

God does not impute sin to those who are really saved Christians.

- **Ephesians 1:7**

"In whom we have redemption through his blood, **the forgiveness of sins,** according to the riches of his grace;"

We who are genuine Christians **have redemption and the forgiveness of our sins.**

- **Ephesians 4:32**

"And be ye kind one to another, tenderhearted, forgiving one another, even as **God for Christ's sake hath forgiven you."**

The Lord Jesus Christ has forgiven true believers in Him.

- **Colossians 1:14**

"In whom we have redemption through his blood, even the **forgiveness of sins."**

Redemption through the blood of the Lord Jesus Christ is for those truly born-again in Him.

- **Colossians 2:13**

"And you, being dead in your sins and the uncircumcision of your flesh, hath he quickened together with him, **having forgiven you all trespasses;"**

FORGIVEN SINS OF ALL TIME

Dr. Lewis Sperry Chafer told us (his students at Dallas Seminary) years ago, when he was our teacher, something like this:

> *"Men, if you are saved and born-again, God has not simply forgiven you your sins which are past, but also sins which are present, and sins which are yet future. 'Forgiven you all trespasses' is what this verse teaches us."*

- **1 John 1:9**

"If we confess our sins, he is faithful and just to **forgive us our sins, and to cleanse us from all unrighteousness."**

When true Christians sin, they must use this verse to get back into fellowship with the Lord Jesus Christ.

- **Hebrews 10:17**

"**And their sins and iniquities will I remember no more.**"

Remembered no more is a powerful statement for those who are genuine Christians.

- **1 Peter 2:24**

"**Who his own self bare our sins in his own body on the tree,** that we, being dead to sins, should live unto righteousness: **by whose stripes ye were healed."**

CHRIST TOOK ALL SINS IN HIS BODY

The Lord Jesus Christ took the sins of all of us in His own body at Calvary. We can appropriate this if we truly trust Him as our Saviour.

- **1 John 2:12**

"I write unto you, little children, because **your sins are forgiven you for his name's sake.**"

Are your sins forgiven? They can be if you will genuinely receive the Lord Jesus Christ as your Saviour by real faith in Him. That's a great and blessed possession.

Hebrews 8:13

"In that he saith, A new covenant, he hath made the first old. Now that which decayeth and waxeth old is ready to vanish away."

THE LAW ABOLISHED

This new covenant is based on what the Lord Jesus Christ accomplished on the cross of Calvary as He died for the sins of whole world. **This new covenant made the old covenant, the law of Moses to be abolished.** The Greek Word for "*decayeth*" is PALAIOO. Some of the meanings of this Word are:

> "*1) to make ancient or old; 1a) to become old, to be worn out; 1b) of things worn out by time and use; 2) to declare a thing to be old and so about to be abrogated.*"

There is a second term used here as well. The Greek Word for "waxeth old" is GERASKO. Some of the meanings of this Word are:

> "*1) to grow old; 2) of things and institutions: to fail from age, be obsolescent.*"

MOSES LAW NOT APPLICABLE NOW

The old law of Moses was obsolescent, it was waxen old, it was no longer applicable in any way.

There is yet a third term relating to **the old Mosaic law or covenant**. The Greek Word for "*vanish*" is: APHANISMOS. This Word comes from two Greek Words, "A" (not) and "PHANISMOS" (an appearance or visibility.) Some of the meanings of this Word are:"*1) disappearance; 2) destruction"*That's exactly what the Lord Jesus Christ has done to **the law of Moses and the Mosaic old covenant**. Using a few of the meanings of these three terms in this verse, **the old covenant law of Moses** is:

> "*worn out, obsolescent, and destroyed.*"

- **John 1:17**

"**For the law was given by Moses**, but grace and truth came by Jesus Christ."

Grace and truth with the Lord Jesus Christ. **There is no more need for the law of Moses.**

- **Romans 6:14**

"For sin shall not have dominion over you: **for ye are not under the law, but under grace.**"

This is a clear statement that in this age of grace, **we are not under any part of the law of Moses**. Many people who are true Christians are law-keepers and try to keep parts of **the law of Moses**. These people in error.

In my opinion, Jews for Jesus and the Messianic Jews are not properly taught in this area. They have many songs, **old covenants, and old practices that are part of the Mosaic law. This is unscriptural and is false teaching.** This verse makes it very clear that truly saved Christians are not under any part of the Old Testament law of Moses UNLESS IT IS REPEATED IN THE NEW TESTAMENT.

There are people who keep the **Sabbath day**. That's part of **the Old Testament law and the Ten Commandments.** It is never repeated in the New Testament. Only nine of the ten commandments are repeated in the New Testament. We keep those. But **there is not a single place in the New Testament that says we are to keep the law of Moses and honor Saturday, the Jewish Sabbath day.**

SUNDAY NOT SATURDAY FOR WORSHIP

True Christians met on the first day of the week, the Lord's Day, which was the day the Lord Jesus was bodily resurrected. His disciples met on Sunday, the first day of the week (John 20:26) not on Saturday the Jewish Sabbath. Gifts were to be set aside on Sunday, the first day of the week (1 Corinthians 16:2). No part of the law should be kept UNLESS IT IS REPEATED IN THE NEW TESTAMENT.

It is wrong to call Sunday, the first day of the week, the "Christian Sabbath." It is not anything to do with the Sabbath. It is the Lord's Day. It is Sunday. It is the first day of the week.

- 2 Corinthians 3:11

"For if that which was done away [the law of Moses] was glorious, much more that which remaineth is glorious."

This which was done away refers to the law of Moses and the old covenant. That has been done away. I don't know much clearer it could be stated.

- 2 Corinthians 3:13

"And not as Moses, which put a vail over his face, that the children of Israel could not stedfastly look to the end of **that which is abolished:**"

Again, **referring to the law of Moses as that which is ABOLISHED!** What could be clearer! **The Galatians wanted to**

keep both the law and grace, mixing these two opposites together. Paul reproved them clearly for this mixture.
- Galatians 1:9

"As we said before, so say I now again, If any man preach **any other gospel** unto you than that ye have received, **let him be accursed.**"

MOSES LAW ABOLISHED

Paul was very clear that preaching law and grace was another gospel. These who mix the two should be cursed. The law of Moses was abolished, done away with, decayed, and waxed old. It should not be practiced in any form today UNLESS IT IS REPEATED IN THE NEW TESTAMENT.

- Galatians 5:18

"But if ye be led of the Spirit, **ye are not under the law.**"
Again, this is very, very clear. **Paul taught very clearly that true Christians were not under the law of Moses.**

Hebrews Chapter Nine

Hebrews 9:1

"Then verily the first *covenant* had also ordinances of divine service, and a worldly sanctuary."

ORDINANCES

This verse makes it clear that the **first covenant of the law of Moses had ordinances,** a divine service, and a worldly sanctuary.

- **Leviticus 18:4**

"Ye shall do my judgments, and keep mine **ordinances,** to walk therein: I *am* the LORD your God."

Though the Lord gave Israel His **ordinances** and told them to walk in them, they didn't walk in them.

SANCTUARY

- **Exodus 25:8-9**

"And let them make me a **sanctuary;** that I may dwell among them. According to all that I shew thee, after the pattern of the tabernacle, and the pattern of all the instruments thereof, even so shall ye make it."

MOSES' SANCTUARY

Moses was told by the Lord to make a tabernacle and a sanctuary that was to be patterned after the Heavenly tabernacle that God had and still has in Heaven.

Hebrews 9:2

"For there was a tabernacle made; the first, wherein *was* the candlestick, and the table, and the shewbread; which is called the sanctuary."

THE CANDLESTICK--CHRIST OUR LIGHT

THE CANDLESTICK

The tabernacle of Moses had many articles in it. The first

article mentioned in this verse is the candlestick. The priests had to light the candlestick each day. In addition to the candlestick, there is also the table of shewbread. This part of the tabernacle is called the sanctuary.

The **candlestick** gave light in the sanctuary. It had a core and six branches. It was a sevenfold candelabra that the Jews use even today. **The candlestick speaks of the Lord Jesus Christ as the Light of the world** as well as the **Light** for those who are genuinely saved.

- John 1:4-5

"In him was life; and the life was **the light** of men. And **the light shineth** in darkness; and the darkness comprehended it not."

The Lord Jesus Christ is shining today as the Light of the world. Many people don't care or comprehend.

- John 3:19

"And this is the condemnation, that **light** is come into the world, and men loved darkness rather than **light**, because their deeds were evil."

Nobody likes to have **light** shined upon wicked deeds and sin.

- John 8:12b

"I am the **light** of the world: he that followeth me shall not walk in darkness, but shall have the **light** of life."

Following our **Saviour's light** gives **light** in the darkness of this world.

- John 12:46

"I am come a **light** into the world, that whosoever believeth on me should not abide in darkness."

LIVE IN THE LIGHT

God does not want anyone to live in darkness and sin. This is especially important for those who have genuinely trusted the Lord Jesus Christ as their Saviour. He has become their Light. They must follow that Light.

- 2 Corinthians 4:3-4

"But if our gospel is hid, it is hid to them that are lost: In whom the god of this world hath blinded the minds of them which believe not, lest the **light of the glorious gospel of Christ**, who is the image of God, should **shine** unto them."

The Devil has blinded the minds of unsaved people so that the Light of the Lord Jesus Christ could not shine for them.

- **2 Corinthians 11:14**

"And no marvel; for Satan himself is transformed into an angel of light."

Satan is a counterfeit light. He is really darkness and blackness. He deceives people in this way in all the false religions in this world.

- **2 Corinthians 11:15**

"Therefore *it is* no great thing if his ministers also be transformed as the ministers of righteousness; whose end shall be according to their works."

Satan's has ministers and preachers in many churches who are lost and bound for Hell. They pretend to be ministers and angels of light, but, in reality, they are darkness, fake, and phony. There are many of them all around the world.

- **Colossians 1:12-13**

"Giving thanks unto the Father, which hath made us meet to be partakers of the inheritance of the saints in **light**: Who hath delivered us from the power of darkness, and hath translated us into the kingdom of his dear Son:"

DELIVERED FROM SATAN'S DARKNESS

A wonderful thing happens when a person is genuinely saved. They are delivered from Satan's darkness. They must then walk as children of the Light.

- **1 Peter 2:9**

"But ye *are* a chosen generation, a royal priesthood, an holy nation, a peculiar people; that ye should shew forth the praises of him who hath called you out of darkness into his marvelous **light**:"

The Lord Jesus Christ calls the truly saved, born-again Christians out of Satan's darkness into **His Light**. We must walk in that **Light**.

- **1 John 1:5**

"This then is the message which we have heard of him, and declare unto you, that God is **light**, and **in him** is **no darkness at all**."

The Lord Jesus Christ has no darkness of any kind.

- **1 John 1:7**

"But if we walk in the **light**, as he is in the **light**, we have fellowship one with another, and the blood of Jesus Christ his son cleanseth us from all sin."

> ## WALK IN CHRIST'S LIGHT
> When genuine Christians walk in the Light of the Lord Jesus Christ, they have fellowship and cleansing.

- **Revelation 21:23-24**

"And the city had no need of the sun, neither of the moon, to shine in it: for the **glory of God did lighten it, and the Lamb is the light thereof**. And the nations of them which are saved shall walk in the **light** of it: and the kings of the earth do bring their glory and honour into it."

It's amazing. <u>In Heaven, the Lamb of God, the Lord Jesus Christ is the Light</u>. There is no need for any sun.

THE SHEWBREAD--CHRIST OUR BREAD

> ### THE TABLE OF SHEWBREAD
> The second thing mentioned in this verse is the table of shewbread that had to be changed each Sabbath (Leviticus 24:8) to make fresh loaves. This speaks of the Lord Jesus Christ as the Bread of Life to nourish His sons and daughters in the faith. When they partake of this Bread they can be built up and made strong and healthy in the Lord Jesus Christ.

- **John 6:35**

"And **Jesus** said unto them, **I am the bread of life**: he that cometh to me shall never hunger; and he that believeth on me shall never thirst."

<u>The Lord Jesus Christ is the satisfying Bread of life</u> for those who have genuinely trusted and received Him.

- **John 6:50-51**

"This is the **bread which cometh down from heaven,** that a man may eat thereof, and not die. **I am the living bread which came down from heaven:** if any man eat of **this bread,** he shall **live for ever:** and **the bread that I will give is my flesh, which I will give for the life of the world.**"

The Lord Jesus Christ's death at Calvary made possible for the Bread of Life to be appropriated by those who genuinely trust Him as their Saviour from sin. This gives them eternal life.

- 1 Corinthians 11:23-24

"For I have received of the Lord that which also I delivered unto you, That **the Lord Jesus** the *same* night in which he was betrayed took **bread**: And when he had given thanks, he **brake it,** and said, Take, eat: **this is my body, which is broken for you: this do in remembrance of me."**

COMMUNION'S FOUR INTERPRETATIONS

"This is my body" is a metaphor. It means that this bread represents His body. Roman Catholics, Lutherans, Episcopalians, Presbyterians, and others, have a <u>distorted view</u> of the Lord's Supper.

1. <u>Roman Catholics wrongly teach that the bread and wine is transformed into the body and blood of the Lord Jesus Christ.</u> This is called "transubstantiation."

2. <u>Lutherans and possibly Episcopalians wrongly teach that in the bread and wine, the Lord Jesus Christ is literally present.</u> This is called "consubstantiation."

3. <u>Many Presbyterians and others wrongly teach that by partaking of the Lord's Supper there is some special Divine and special "grace" that is miraculously given to the ones participating.</u>

4. The true and Biblical teaching is that the Lord's Supper is to be received only by those who are genuinely born-again Christians. It is to be done in remembrance of the Lord Jesus Christ in obedience to the Bible. In the Lord's Supper, there is <u>no transubstantiation, no consubstantiation,</u> and <u>no special miraculous Divine grace given</u>. It is to be done in obedience and in remembrance of the shed blood and the broken body of the Lord Jesus Christ in His death at Calvary.

Hebrews 9:3

"And after the second veil, the tabernacle which is called the Holiest of all;"

THE MOST HOLY PLACE (OR HOLY OF HOLIES)

TWO VEILS

In the tabernacle, there were two veils. Into the first veil, the priests could go each day to take care of the lights on the candlestick, and change the bread. But after the second veil

> was the holy of holies. It is called the holiest of all. Into the holy of holies only the high priest could go once each year on the Day of Atonement. It was a special place where the presence of God dwelled with His people Israel in the tabernacle during the forty years of their wanderings in the wilderness.

- Exodus 26:33

"And thou shalt hang up **the vail** under the taches, that thou mayest bring in thither **within the vail** the ark of the testimony: and the vail shall divide unto you **between the holy** *place* and the most holy."

That special vail divided the holy place from the most holy place.

- Exodus 26:34-36

"And thou shalt put the mercy seat upon the ark of the testimony in **the most holy** *place*. And thou shalt set the table **without the vail**, and the candlestick over against the table on the side of the tabernacle toward the south: and thou shalt put the table on the north side. And thou shalt make an hanging for the door of the tent, of blue, and purple, and scarlet, and fine twined linen, wrought with needlework."

> **THE MOST HOLY PLACE**
> And so these were the two divisions of the tabernacle of Moses--the holy place where the priests could go, and the most holy place where only the high priest could go once each year.

Hebrews 9:4

"Which had the golden censer, and the ark of the covenant overlaid round about with gold, wherein *was* the golden pot that had manna, and Aaron's rod that budded, and the tables of the covenant;"

THE GOLDEN POT OF MANNA

Inside the ark of the covenant, there were these three things:
1. **the golden pot of manna,**
2. Aaron's rod that budded, and
3. the tables of the law of the covenant.

This golden pot of manna reminded them of their forty years of wandering in the wilderness and how God provided for their food.

- **Exodus 16:31**

"And the house of Israel called the name thereof **Manna: and it** *was* **like coriander seed, white; and the taste of it** *was* **like wafers made with honey.**"

> **MANNA LIKE HONEY**
>
> In Hebrew, manna means "what is it?" It was white like a coriander seed. It tasted like wafers made with honey. It was sweet. The Israelites complained about it. They wanted flesh to eat.

- **Exodus 16:32-34**

"And Moses said, This *is* the thing which the LORD commandeth, Fill an omer of it to be kept for your generations; that they may see the **bread wherewith I have fed you in the wilderness,** when I brought you forth from the land of Egypt. And Moses said unto Aaron, Take a pot, and put an omer full of **manna** therein, and lay it up before the LORD, to be kept for your generations. As the LORD commanded Moses, so Aaron laid it up before the Testimony, to be kept."

AARON'S ROD THAT BUDDED

> **AARON'S ROD IN THE ARK**
>
> In addition to the manna, the second thing in the ark was Aaron's rod that budded. The reason that Aaron's rod budded was because there was an argument as to which of the tribes should be the priestly line and should go into the tabernacle and serve. They fought about it. God settled the matter. He told them what to do.

- **Numbers 17:2-5**

"Speak unto the children of Israel, and take of every one of them a rod according to the house of *their* fathers, of all their princes according to the house of their fathers twelve rods: write thou every man's name upon his rod. And thou shalt **write Aaron's name upon the rod of Levi:** for one rod shall be for the head of the house of their fathers. And thou shalt lay them up in the tabernacle of the congregation before the testimony, where I will meet with you. And it shall come to pass, that **the man's rod, whom I shall choose, shall blossom:** and I will make to cease from me the murmurings of the children of Israel, whereby they murmur against you."

Here is what happened.
- **Numbers 17:6-8**

"And Moses spake unto the children of Israel, and every one of their princes gave him a rod apiece, for each prince one, according to their fathers' houses, even twelve rods: **and the rod of Aaron** was among their rods. And **Moses laid up the rods before the LORD** in the tabernacle of witness. And it came to pass, that on the morrow Moses went into the tabernacle of witness; and, behold, **the rod of Aaron for the house of Levi was budded, and brought forth buds, and bloomed blossoms, and yielded almonds.**"

AARON CHOSEN AS HIGH PRIEST
This was the miracle of God to show that Aaron was the one chosen to be Israel's high priest and that priests of Aaron's line were to be the priests of Israel.

- **Numbers 17:9**

"And Moses brought out all the rods from before the LORD unto all the children of Israel: and they looked, and took every man his rod."

They all had their names on their rods.
- **Numbers 17:10**

"And the LORD said unto Moses, Bring **Aaron's rod** again before the testimony, to be kept for a token against the rebels; and thou shalt quite take away their murmurings from me, that they die not."

God was ready to slay these people because they didn't trust Him to select a priest out of the tribe of Levi.

THE TABLES OF THE COVENANT

The third thing in the ark of the covenant, inside the holy of holies, were **the tables of the covenant. It was part of the law of Moses that God gave him in Mount Sinai.**
- **Deuteronomy 10:1-5**

"At that time the LORD said unto me, **Hew thee two tables of stone like unto the first**, and come up unto me into the mount, and make thee an ark of wood. And **I will write on the tables the words that were in the first tables which thou brakest**, and thou shalt put them in the ark. And I made an ark *of* shittim wood, and **hewed two tables of stone like unto the first**, and went up into the mount, having the **two tables in mine hand**. And **he wrote on** the tables, according to the first writing, the ten commandments, which the LORD spake unto you in the mount out of the midst of the fire in the day of the assembly: and the LORD gave them unto me. And I turned myself and came down from the mount, and **put the tables in the ark** which I had made; and **there they be, as the LORD commanded me."**

So, in this ark of the covenant, inside the holy of holies, there were these three things: (1) the pot of manna; (2) Aaron's rod that budded; and (3) **the tables of the covenant.** <u>Those three things are a reminder to Israel of their history and what God wanted them to do.</u>

Hebrews 9:5

"And over it the cherubims of glory shadowing the mercyseat; of which we cannot now speak particularly."

THE CHERUBIMS OVER THE ARK

On top of that ark were **the cherubims.** They had wings. They looked down towards the ark where the mercyseat was. These were cherubims of glory.

- **Exodus 25:18-22**

"And thou shalt make **two cherubims of gold,** of beaten work shalt thou make them, in the two ends of the mercy seat. And make one **cherub** on the one end, and the other **cherub** on the other end: even of the mercy seat shall ye make the **cherubims** on the two end thereof. And the **cherubims** shall stretch forth **their** wings on high, **covering the mercy seat with their wings,** and their faces shall look one to another; toward the mercy seat shall the faces of the **cherubims** be. And thou shalt put the mercy seat above upon the ark; and in the ark thou shalt put the testimony that I shall give thee. And there I will meet with thee, and I will commune with thee from above the mercy seat, from between the **two cherubims** which are upon the ark of the testimony, of all things which I will give thee in commandment unto the children of Israel."

THE CHERUBIMS OVER THE ARK

In the holy of holies, the cherubims looked down from the two ends of the mercy seat over the top of the ark of the covenant. It was on the mercy seat that Aaron could put the blood of the offerings once a year on the Day of Atonement

(Leviticus 16). He would offer first for his own sins and the sins of his family, and then for the sins of all the people of Israel.

Hebrews 9:6

"Now when these things were thus ordained, the priests went always into the first tabernacle, accomplishing the service *of God*."

THE FIRST TABERNACLE

THE OUTER TABERNACLE DIVISION

The Levitical priests were able to go into the first part of the Mosaic tabernacle to do their service for the Lord. They could not go into the holy of holies, however. That was only for the high priest once each year on the Day of Atonement.

- Exodus 26:33

"And thou shalt hang up the **vail** under the taches, that thou mayest bring in thither within the **vail the ark of the testimony**: and the **vail** shall divide unto you between the holy *place* and the most holy."

That **vail** was rent in two from the top to the bottom when the Lord Jesus Christ died for the sins of the world on the Cross of Calvary. The **vail** separated between the holy place and the holy of holies.

- Exodus 26:34

"And thou shalt put the **mercy seat upon the ark of the testimony in the most holy** *place*."

The **mercy seat** was where the sacrificial blood was placed by the high priest each year on the Day of Atonement (Leviticus 16).

- Exodus 28:42

"And thou shalt make them linen breeches to cover their nakedness; from the loins even unto the thighs they shall reach."

God provided special clothing for the priests to wear.

- Exodus 28:43

"And they shall be upon Aaron, and upon his sons, when they come in unto the **tabernacle of the congregation**, or when they come near unto the altar to minister in the **holy** *place*; that they bear not iniquity, and die: *it shall be* a statute for ever unto him and his seed after him."

> **THE PRIESTS' DRESS CODE**
> God had a dress code for the priests and for the high priest when they ministered in the tabernacle. Without the proper garments, they might die. This dress code was serious with the Lord.

Hebrews 9:7

"But into the second *went* the high priest alone once every year, not without blood, which he offered for himself, and *for* the errors of the people:"

THE HIGH PRIEST ONCE A YEAR

> **HOLY OF HOLIES ONCE A YEAR**
> Into the holy of holies only the high priest could go each year on the Day of Atonement when he offered sacrifices for himself and his family and for the errors of all the people of Israel. The Greek Word for "offered" is in the present tense. It implies continuous and repeated action because it had to be repeated each year.

- Leviticus 16:2

"And the LORD said unto Moses, **Speak unto Aaron** thy brother, that he come not at all times into the holy *place* within the vail before the mercy seat, which is upon the ark; that **he** die not: for I will appear in the cloud upon the mercy seat."

Even **Aaron the high priest could not enter the holy of holies at any time other than the Day of Atonement**. That may be one of the reasons Aaron's sons, Nadab and Abihu, were slain by the Lord. They might have tried to enter the holy of holies as well as offering strange incense.

- Leviticus 16:3

"Thus shall **Aaron** come into the holy *place*: with a young bullock for a sin offering, and a ram for a burnt offering."

Aaron had to offer these two animals on the **Day of Atonement** and bring their blood and put it on the mercy seat. This was for **his own sins and the sins of his** family.

- Leviticus 16:29

"And *this* shall be a statute for ever unto you: *that* in the **seventh month, on the tenth *day* of the month**, ye shall afflict your souls, and do no work at all, *whether it be* one of your own country, or a stranger that sojourneth among you:"

THE DAY OF ATONEMENT
The Day of Atonement was on the tenth day of the seventh month. It is called Yom Kippur today. YOM is the day and KAPHAR is to cover. It is the day of covering for sin.

Hebrews 9:8
"The Holy Ghost this signifying, that the way into the holiest of all was not yet made manifest, while as the first tabernacle was yet standing:"

THE WAY INTO THE HOLIEST OF ALL

THE VERY PRESENCE OF GOD
In other words, as long as that first Mosaic tabernacle was in existence and being used by the Jews, no one but the high priest could go into the holiest of all, into the very presence of God.

- John 14:6

"Jesus saith unto him, I am **the way**, the truth, and the life: no man cometh unto the Father, but by me."

CHRIST THE ONLY WAY
The Way into the presence of God the Father in Heaven was not available until the Lord Jesus Christ died for the sins of the world and made eternal life possible by genuine faith in Him. That is the only way into the holy of holies of Heaven today.

THE VEIL RENT IN TWO
- Matthew 27:50-51

"Jesus, when he had cried again with a loud voice, yielded up the ghost. And, behold, **the veil of the temple was rent in twain from the top to the bottom;** and the earth did quake, and the rocks rent;"

The veil was a very heavy material. It was very tall as well. No one could go through it on the other side except the high priest once a year. At the cross of Calvary, when the Lord Jesus Christ died for the sins of the world, **God Himself ripped open that veil from the top to the bottom**, showing that through the Lord Jesus Christ's sacrifice, those who genuinely trusted in Him might enter into the very presence of God the Father in Heaven.

- Mark 15:37-38

"And Jesus cried with a loud voice, and gave up the ghost. And **the veil of the temple was rent in twain from the top to the bottom.**"

This is what Matthew stated as well.

- Luke 23:45-46

"And the sun was darkened, **and the veil of the temple was rent in the midst**. And when Jesus had cried with a loud voice, he said, Father, into thy hands I commend my spirit: and having said thus, he gave up the ghost."

THE RENT VAIL AT CALVARY

Even Luke wrote about the direction of the division of this vail. It was from the top to the bottom. God the Father rent that vail. It was not torn by any man on earth. It was a miracle. Now, it is evident, that the way into the very presence of God the Father and of Heaven was made possible by the shedding of the blood of the Lord Jesus Christ in His death on the cross. The means of this entrance into Heaven is by a person's genuine faith and trust in the Lord Jesus Christ as their Saviour from sin.

Hebrews 9:9

"Which was a figure for the time then present, in which were offered both gifts and sacrifices, that could not make him that did the service perfect, as pertaining to the conscience;"

A FIGURE LOOKING FORWARD

All these gifts and offerings made by the Jewish priests and high priests could never make the one making these offerings perfect pertaining to the conscience. The offerings were a **figure or a picture looking forward** to the day when the Lord Jesus Christ would come into the world in His incarnation and, as the Lamb of God, He would make the one and only sacrifice of Himself that could bear and take away the sins of the entire world.

Hebrews 9:10

"*Which stood* only in meats and drinks, and divers washings, and carnal ordinances, imposed *on them* until the time of reformation."

TIME OF REFORMATION

CHANGES SINCE CHRIST'S COMING

All the use of the Israelites' meats, drinks, different kinds of washings, and carnal ordinances and rules were placed upon them until the time when their Messiah came. The Lord Jesus Christ would appear in His miraculous incarnation as perfect God and perfect Man and then die on the cross for the sins of the world. This is what Paul calls the time of reformation.

Hebrews 9:11

"But Christ being come an high priest of good things to come, by a greater and more perfect tabernacle, not made with hands, that is to say, not of this building;"

CHRIST A MORE PERFECT TABERNACLE

THE HEAVENLY TABERNACLE

The Lord Jesus Christ was a high priest of good things to come and of the Heavenly tabernacle. That tabernacle was the pattern that God gave to Moses in order for him to be able to make the earthly tabernacle. The Lord Jesus Christ, as the Great High Priest, is in the Heavenly tabernacle now after dying on the cross and bearing the sins of the world in His own body.

- Revelation 15:5

"And after that I looked, and, behold, **the temple of the tabernacle of the testimony in heaven was opened:**"

<u>This tabernacle in Heaven was opened.</u>

Hebrews 9:12

"Neither by the blood of goats and calves, but by his own blood he entered in once into the holy place, having obtained eternal redemption *for us*."

CHRIST'S BLOOD IS IN HEAVEN

"By His own blood" the Lord Jesus Christ entered once into the holy place of Heaven after he obtained eternal redemption for those who have truly trusted in Him. The Greek Word for "*by*" is DIA. Some of the meanings of this Word are:

> "1) through; 1a) of place; 1a1) **with**; 1a2) in; 1b) of time; 1b1) throughout; 1b2) during; 1c) of means; 1c1) by; 1c2) by the means of; 2) through; 2a) the ground or reason by which something is or is not done; 2a1) by reason of; 2a2) on account of; 2a3) because of for this reason; 2a4) therefore; 2a5) on this account."

WITH IS ONE MEANING OF "DIA"

There are many meanings for DIA, depending on the context. As noted above, "*with*" is one this Word's many meanings. I believe that "*with*" is the sense of that Greek preposition in this context. If this be true, this verse, along with others in this book of Hebrews, clearly teaches that, after the Lord Jesus Christ bare the sins of the world in His own body, took some of His blood into the holy place in the Heavenly tabernacle. This act finished His redemption for those who genuinely trust in Him, giving them eternal redemption.

THE EARTHLY AND HEAVENLY HIGH PRIESTS

I believe the **Lord Jesus Christ** put part of his shed blood on the mercy seat of Heaven, just like the **Levitical high priests** did with the blood of the animals they sacrificed every year on the Day of Atonement. This is an analogy between the earthly high priesthood and the Great High Priest in Heaven. Their offerings were yearly. His offering was only once, never to be repeated--in the Roman Catholic mass or in any other way.

Another difference between the **offerings of the Levitical high priests and the offering of the Lord Jesus Christ** is this: **their** yearly offerings were with the **blood of goats and calves**, but His once for all offering was with His own blood.

THE NATURE OF CHRIST'S BODY

CHRIST'S PERFECT PREPARED BODY

Every single part of the body of the Lord Jesus Christ, including His blood, was *"prepared"* by God the Father through the miracle of His miraculous virgin birth. In the following verse, the Lord Jesus Christ, the Son of God, was praying to God the Father:

- Hebrews 10:5

"Wherefore when he cometh into the world, he saith, Sacrifice and offering thou wouldest not, but **a body hast thou prepared me:**"

DIVINELY PREPARED BLOOD

Three days and three nights after the Lord Jesus Christ took the sins of the world in His own body, dying on the cross and shedding His specially Divinely *"prepared"* blood, He arose bodily from the tomb. It was then that ascended into Heaven and placed some of His blood on the Heavenly mercy seat. The timing of this event is alluded to in John 20. The Lord Jesus Christ entered the tabernacle in Heaven with His own pure, holy, sinless blood. When did that take place? I believe it took place after His resurrection. Here is what He told Mary at His sepulchre:

- John 20:17

"Jesus saith unto her, Touch me not; for **I am not yet ascended to my Father:** but go to my brethren, and say unto them, **I ascend unto my father, and your Father; and to my God, and your God.**"

CHRIST'S BLOOD ON THE MERCY SEAT

Mary wondered who was talking to her. She supposed He was the gardener. I believe when that took place, the Lord Jesus Christ ascended immediately after his bodily resurrection to God the Father in Heaven and put some of His Divinely *"prepared"* blood on the Heavenly mercy seat. As, on the Day of Atonement once a year, the Levitical high priests put the blood of the sacrifices on the mercy seat in the earthly tabernacle, so the Lord Jesus Christ, after His sacrifice for the sins of the world, put some of His blood on the mercy seat of the Heavenly tabernacle.

Many Bible teachers and pastors believe this is what happened (like Dr. M. R. DeHaan, the founder of the Radio Bible Class), but there are others who do not believe it such as John MacArthur.

BLOOD MEANS BLOOD

John MacArthur does not believe that *"blood"* means *"blood,"* but is only a metonym or figure of speech for *"death."* He is in error on many subjects as I have written in some of my other articles and books. [See *John MacArthur's HERESY On The Blood of Christ* (BFT #2185 @ $8.00 + $4.00 S&H].

- **Leviticus 16:14**

"And he shall take of the **blood** of the bullock, and sprinkle *it* with his finger upon the mercy seat eastward; and before the mercy seat shall he sprinkle of the **blood** with his finger seven times."

That's what Aaron and his successor high priests had to do once a year on the Day of Atonement.

- **Leviticus 16:15**

"Then shall he kill the goat of the sin offering, that *is* for the people, and bring his **blood** within the vail, and do with that **blood** as he did with the **blood** of the bullock, and sprinkle it upon the mercy seat, and before the mercy seat:"

AARON'S PLACEMENT OF BLOOD

And so that high priest, once a year, had to take the blood of the sacrifices for his own sins and the sins of his family, as well as the blood of the sacrifices for the sins of the people and placed this blood on the mercy seat upon the ark that was in the holy of holies in the tabernacle.

- **Leviticus 16:16**

"And he shall make an atonement for the holy *place*, because of the uncleanness of the children of Israel, and because of their transgressions in all their sins: and so shall he do for the tabernacle of the congregation, that remaineth among them in the midst of their uncleanness."

> ## CHRIST'S BLOOD IN HEAVEN
> As I have mentioned before, in Hebrews 8:6, some other verses that clearly teach that Christ's blood is in Heaven are Hebrews 12:22-24.

- **Hebrews 12:22-24**

"But ye are come unto mount Sion, and unto the city of the living God, the heavenly Jerusalem, and to an innumerable company of angels, To the general assembly and church of the firstborn, which are written in heaven, and to God the Judge of all, and to the spirits of just men made perfect, And to Jesus the mediator of the new covenant, and to **the blood of sprinkling**, that speaketh better things than *that of* Abel."

> ## VERSES ON CHRIST'S BLOOD IN HEAVEN
> Notice, in these verses, there are eight personages or objects that are in Heaven (mount Sion): (Hebrews 12:22-24)
> 1. The city of the living God (v. 22)
> 2. The Heavenly Jerusalem
> 3. An innumerable company of angels
> 4. The general assembly and church of the firstborn (v. 23)
> 5. God the Judge of all
> 6. The spirits of just men made perfect
> 7. Jesus the Mediator of the new covenant (v. 24)
> 8. The Lord Jesus Christ's blood of sprinkling

I think it is a clear teaching in these sections, as well as in other sections that we will come to in this book of Hebrews, that some of the **blood** of the Lord Jesus Christ was placed by Him on the mercy seat in Heaven. I say that, regardless of what many Bible-believing theologians and teachers teach on this subject. The "***blood of sprinkling***," in verse 24 above, refers to the **blood of the Lord Jesus Christ** which He placed on the mercy seat of Heaven.

GOD'S ETERNAL REDEMPTION

Notice also that this verse says *"having obtained **eternal redemption** for us."* If it is "***eternal redemption***," how could people lose it? How can this be squared with the Arminian theology of some like the Free Methodists, Pentecostals, Charismatics, and other Holiness groups? They teach that when genuine Christians sin, they can lose their "*eternal salvation*"? There are other verses that speak of "*eternal redemption*" as well.

- **John 10:27-28**
"My sheep hear my voice, and I know them, and they follow me. And I give unto them **eternal life**; and **they shall never perish, neither shall any man pluck them out of my hand.**"

If genuine Christians follow the Lord Jesus Christ, He gives them "*eternal life.*" If people can lose it, how can this life be **eternal**? How can these deniers of "*eternal redemption*" explain the words of our Saviour, "*they shall never perish*"?

- **John 10:28b-30**
"... neither shall any *man* pluck them out of my hand. My Father, which gave *them* me, is greater than all; and **no man is able to pluck *them* out of my father's hand. I and *my* Father are one.**"

Those once genuinely saved are **in the hand of the Lord Jesus Christ, and will never perish. They are also in God the Father's hand. This is double eternal security for eternal redemption.**

- **Romans 3:24**
"Being justified freely by his grace through the **redemption that is in Christ Jesus:**"

This redemption is forever.

- **1 Corinthians 1:30**
"But of him are ye in Christ Jesus, who of God is made unto us wisdom, and righteousness, and sanctification, and redemption:"

REDEMPTION FOR ETERNITY
Once a person is genuinely in Christ and is born-again, he has redemption for eternity, not just for a time.

- **Ephesians 1:7**
"In whom we have **redemption through his blood,** the forgiveness of sins, according to the riches of his grace;"

This verse speaks of those who are genuinely saved. They partake of **redemption through the blood of the Lord Jesus Christ** and forgiveness of sins.

- **1 Peter 1:18-19**
"Forasmuch as ye know that ye were not **redeemed** with corruptible things, as silver and gold, from your vain

conversation *received* by tradition from your fathers; But **with the precious blood of Christ, as of a lamb without blemish and without spot.**"

Eternal redemption, is given to us **by the Lord Jesus Christ, through His blood that was shed at the Cross of Calvary, and placed on the mercy seat of Heaven, once, never to be continued,** never to be put there again. He's at the Father's right hand even today.

- **Hebrews 9:13**

"For if the **blood** of bulls and of goats, and the ashes of an heifer sprinkling the unclean, sanctifieth to the purifying of the flesh:"

This speaks of the Levitical offerings of the **blood** of bulls and goats. This is quite different from the **blood of the Lord Jesus Christ.**

- **Hebrews 9:14**

"How much more shall the **blood of Christ,** who through the eternal Spirit offered himself without spot to God, purge your conscience from dead works to serve the living God?"

PURGING THE CONSCIENCE

The blood of bulls and goats could not purge the conscience, but the blood of the Lord Jesus Christ could do this.

This is another heresy of John MacArthur. He teaches that the **blood** of the Lord Jesus Christ is just **"human blood"** the same as yours and mine. He says that in his books and writings. This is blatant heresy! The **blood** of the Lord Jesus Christ was not the same as **human blood.** As mentioned before, this is the prayer of the Lord Jesus Christ to God the Father:

- **Hebrews 10:5b**

"Sacrifice and offering thou wouldest not, but **a body hast thou prepared me:**"

RESULTS OF THE VIRGIN BIRTH

Through the miracle of virgin birth of the Lord Jesus Christ, God the Father prepared for His Son, a specially designed and crafted human body, including every part: His head, hair, eyes, blood, muscles, bones and every part.

CHRIST'S BLOOD NOT "HUMAN"

If the Lord Jesus Christ had human blood from the line of Adam, it would have been corrupt and sinful blood, as every human being has. As such, He could never be our Saviour or atone for our sins with that sinful Adamic human blood that John MacArthur teaches that He had. If this were the case, the blood of the Lord Jesus Christ could not cleanse us from sin.

CHRIST'S SPECIAL BLOOD PROVIDED BY GOD

The blood of the Lord Jesus Christ was not common, or ordinary human blood. John MacArthur is a heretic on the blood of Christ as well as on many other doctrines, but especially on the blood of Christ. I have given many quotations from him regarding this subject in my book, *John MacArthur's HERESY on the Blood of Christ* (BFT #2185 @ $8.00 + $4.00 S&H).

Hebrews 9:13

"For if the blood of bulls and of goats, and the ashes of an heifer sprinkling the unclean, sanctifieth to the purifying of the flesh:"

THE BLOOD OF BULLS AND GOATS

All the **blood of bulls and goats** shed in the Old Testament is nothing when compared to the precious blood of the Lord Jesus Christ.

- **Numbers 19:17**
"And for an unclean *person* they shall take of the ashes of the **burnt heifer** of purification for sin, and running water shall be put thereto in a vessel:"

All these things could not atone for the sins of men and women, boys and girls. They point to and had to wait until the Lord Jesus Christ came to be the Lamb of God, Who was able to take away the sin of the world (John 1:29).

Hebrews 9:14

"How much more shall the blood of Christ, who through the eternal Spirit offered himself without spot to God, purge your conscience from dead works to serve the living God?"

THE BLOOD OF CHRIST

CHRIST'S BLOOD CAN CLEANSE

The blood of bulls and goats couldn't cleanse from sin. But the blood of the Lord Jesus Christ can cleanse from sin if a person genuinely trusts in Him as their Saviour. His blood can purge the genuinely saved Christian's conscience from dead works to serve the living God. May that be the goal and purpose of every born-again Christian today. God wants and needs His saved ones to serve Him daily.

Hebrews 9:15

"And for this cause he is the mediator of the new testament, that by means of death, for the redemption of the transgressions *that were* under the first testament, they which are called might receive the promise of eternal inheritance."

CHRIST THE MEDIATOR OF THE NEW TESTAMENT

CHRIST OUR ONLY MEDIATOR

The only way that the Lord Jesus Christ could be the Mediator was that He carried in His own body on the cross of Calvary the sins of the entire world. Then He took some of His blood and placed it on the mercy seat in Heaven. *"For this cause* [that which went before in verse 14 about the cross of Calvary] *He is the mediator of the new testament."* Paul is speaking of the New Testament of Heaven, not the Old Testament of Moses and his earthly tabernacle.

The Greek Word for *"mediator"* is MESITES. Some of the meanings of this Greek Word are:

> *"1) one who intervenes between two, either in order to make or restore peace and friendship, or form a*

compact, or for ratifying a covenant; 2) a medium of communication, arbitrator."

The Lord Jesus Christ is the only Mediator between God the Father and human beings.

ROME'S HERESY OF MARY AS MEDIATRIX

The Roman Catholic church is teaching the blatant heresy that a human being with a fallen Adamic nature, named Mary, has falsely become the mediatrix between God and human beings. In effect, this is making a woman born with a sinful, nature of flesh into almost a Deity with Divine powers. This is the height of blasphemy and heresy. She is no mediatrix, she is no mediator. She's just a person, just a human being.

The Lord Jesus Christ became the Mediator because of His substitutionary death on Calvary's cross that could even forgive the transgressions that took place under the first or Old Testament. This makes it possible for repentant sinners to become the possessors of an eternal inheritance in Heaven. Notice some of the verses on **mediators**.

- **Job 9:32-33**
"For *he is* not a man, as I *am, that* I should answer him, *and* we should come together in judgment. Neither is there any **daysman** betwixt us, *that* might lay his hand upon us both."

Job longed for a **daysman, or a mediator** who could understand both man and God. This is what **the Lord Jesus Christ** is able to do because of his miraculous incarnation and virgin birth.

- **1 Timothy 2:5**
"For *there is* one God, and **one mediator** between God and men, **the man Christ Jesus;**"

THE ONE MEDIATOR IS NOT MARY

This One Mediator is not Mary. It is not any of the Roman Catholic saints. It is not anyone else of the human race. It is the Lord Jesus Christ Who is perfect God and perfect Man. It is not any other person. It is only God the Son Himself, the Lord Jesus Christ Who is the God-Man.

- **Hebrews 8:6**
"But now hath he obtained a more excellent ministry, by how much also **he is the mediator of a better covenant,** which was established upon better promises."

The Lord Jesus Christ is the Mediator of a better covenant than that of Moses. It is based on better and eternal promises which are based on the sinless and holy blood of **the Lord Jesus Christ**.

- **Hebrews 12:24**

"And to **Jesus the mediator of the new covenant,** and to the blood of sprinkling, that speaketh better things than *that* of Abel."

This blood of sprinkling, speaking of the blood of **the Lord Jesus Christ,** is Heaven and much better than the blood of Abel.

FORGIVENESS AND ETERNAL LIFE

- **Romans 3:23-25**

"For all have sinned, and come short of the glory of God; **Being justified freely** by his grace through the **redemption** that is in Christ Jesus: Whom God hath set forth *to be* a propitiation through faith in his blood, to declare his righteousness for **the remission of sins that are past,** through the forbearance of God;"

ETERNAL INHERITANCE POSSIBLE

The forgiveness of the sins that are past include this provision from the time of Adam and Eve and into the future based upon the finished work of the Lord Jesus Christ on the cross of Calvary. This provision is for those who are genuinely saved and trusting Him as their Saviour.

He's going to be the One to give us the eternal inheritance. Now we have eternal life, if we are genuinely trusting Christ as Saviour. This is Eternal life completely.

- **John 3:14-16**

"And as Moses lifted up the serpent in the wilderness, even so must the Son of man be lifted up: That whosoever believeth in him **should not perish, but have eternal life.** For God so loved the world, that he gave his only begotten Son, that whosoever believeth in him **should not perish, but have everlasting life."**

The Lord Jesus Christ's provision is for the whosoever who truly trust Him for their **redemption**.

- **John 6:68**

"Then Simon Peter answered him, Lord, to whom shall we go? Thou has the words of **eternal life."**

The Lord Jesus Christ is the only One with these Words.

- **John 10:27-30**

"My sheep hear my voice, and I know them, and they follow me: And I give unto them **eternal life;** and they **shall never perish,** neither shall any *man* pluck them out of my hand. My

Father, which gave them me, is greater than all; and no *man* is able to pluck *them* out of my Father's hand. I and my Father are one."

That verse describes **permanent eternal life** in the Saviour's and God the Father's hands.

- Hebrews 5:9

"And being made perfect, he became the author of **eternal salvation** unto all them that obey him;"

SALVATION IS ETERNAL

Again, salvation is eternal for those who genuinely possess it. It cannot be lost once it is gained. The Bible does not agree with the Free Methodists, the Pentecostals, the Charismatics, and other holiness groups who say you can lose your salvation. Once you are born in this life you won't be unborn. Once your truly born-again you cannot be unborn-again. If you really have it, salvation is eternal.

- Hebrews 9:12

"Neither by the blood of goats and calves, but by his own blood he entered in once into the holy place, having obtained **eternal redemption** *for us*."

Genuine **redemption is eternal**. We can't lose it once we're saved.

- 1 John 5:13

"These things have I written unto you that believe on the name of the Son of God; that ye may know that ye have **eternal life**, and that ye may believe on the name of the Son of God."

Genuine salvation brings eternal life, not life only as long as a person can hang on to it by their good works. It is something to know.

Hebrews 9:16

"For where a testament is, there must also of necessity be the death of the testator."

TESTAMENT AND TESTATOR

A TESTAMENT IS A FINAL WILL

A testament is like a final will. It does not come into effect until the person who made it (the testator) dies. You must have the death of the testator for it to be valid. The Lord Jesus Christ is the Testator of the New Testament. He is the One Who made the plan of salvation (the will). He died for the sins

> of the world on the cross of Calvary thus putting into effect all of the provisions of the eternal life that it provides.

Hebrews 9:17

"For a testament *is* of force after men are dead: otherwise it is of no strength at all while the testator liveth."

Even in the provisions of a "living will" the final and complete disposition of all the effects of it cannot be determined until the death of the person [**the testator**] who made that will.

Hebrews 9:18

"Whereupon neither the first *testament* was dedicated without blood."

This **first testament**, that is, the **Old Testament**, was not carried out without the shedding of the blood of many animals who had to be offered as required under the law of Moses. Even when the law was first proposed, there was the shedding of blood.

Hebrews 9:19

"For when Moses had spoken every precept to all the people according to the law, he took the blood of calves and of goats, with water, and scarlet wool, and hyssop, and sprinkled both the book, and all the people,"

SPRINKLING BLOOD IN MOSES DAY

As soon as Moses spoke to Israel the precepts of the law, he **sprinkled the blood** of calves and goats on the book of the precepts and on all the people as well.

- Exodus 24:5-6

"And he sent young men of the children of Israel, which offered burnt offerings, and sacrificed peace offerings of oxen unto the LORD. And **Moses** took half of the blood, and put *it* in basons; and **half of the blood he sprinkled** on the altar."

This took place after **Moses** received the law. **He sprinkled blood** on the the brazen altar of the tabernacle.

- Exodus 24:7-8

"And **he** took the book of the covenant, and read in the audience of the people: and they said, All that the LORD hath said will we do, and be obedient. And **Moses took the** blood, and sprinkled *it* on the people, and said, Behold the blood of the covenant, which the LORD hath made with you concerning all these words."

> **MOSES' SPRINKLING OF THE BLOOD**
> After Moses read the book of the covenant, he took some of the blood of the offerings he had made and sprinkled it on the people. Yet the sprinkling of the blood of bulls and goats and calves by Moses could never take away sin.

Hebrews 9:20

"Saying, This is the blood of the testament which God hath enjoined unto you."

- Exodus 24:8
"And **Moses took** the blood, and sprinkled *it* on the people, and said, Behold **the blood** of the covenant, which the LORD hath made with you concerning all these words."

Before **Moses sprinkled** the Israelites **with the blood** of the offerings, he told them that this is **the blood** of the covenant that God had commanded them.

Hebrews 9:21

"Moreover he sprinkled with blood both the tabernacle, and all the vessels of the ministry."

THE THINGS SPRINKLED WITH BLOOD

Not only did Moses **sprinkle the Israelite people with the blood** of the covenant, but also all **the vessels of the ministry**. The following verses specify some of these vessels that were **sprinkled with blood**.

- Exodus 25:37-38
"And thou shalt make the **seven lamps** thereof: [they were sprinkled with blood] and they shall light **the lamps** thereof, that they may give light over against it. And **the tongs** thereof, [they were sprinkled with blood] and **the snuffdishes** thereof, [they were sprinkled with blood] *shall be* of pure gold."

These are some of **the vessels in the tabernacle** that were sprinkled with blood.

- Exodus 27:1
"And thou shalt make an **altar of shittim wood**, [that was sprinkled with blood] five cubits long, and five cubits broad;

the altar shall be foursquare: and the height thereof *shall be* three cubits."

The altar of shittim wood was sprinkled with the blood.
- **Exodus 27:3**

"And thou shalt make his **pans** to receive his ashes," [they were sprinkled with blood] and his **shovels**, [they were sprinkled with blood] and his **basons**, [they were sprinkled with blood] and his **fleshhooks**, [they were sprinkled with blood] and his **firepans**: [they were sprinkled with blood] all the **vessels** [they were sprinkled with blood] all these **vessels** thereof thou shalt make *of* brass."

THINGS SPRINKLED WITH BLOOD

The ark of the testimony was sprinkled with blood. The table was sprinkled with blood. The candlesticks were sprinkled with animal blood. The altar of burnt offering was sprinkled with blood, and all his vessels.

- **Exodus 25:13**

"And thou shalt make **staves** [they were sprinkled with blood] of shittim wood, and overlay them with gold."

"The table, and his staves, and all its vessels" were **sprinkled with blood**. We don't do that in our day and it seems very strange to us, but that's what God told Moses to do and he did it.
- **Exodus 37:16**

"And he made the **vessels** which *were* upon the **table**, his **dishes**, and his **spoons**, and his **bowls**, and his **covers** to cover withal, *of* pure gold."

All those things were **sprinkled with blood**.
- **Exodus 35:16**

"**The altar of burnt offering** [that was sprinkled with blood], with his **brasen grate**, [that was sprinkled with blood] his **staves**, [they were sprinkled with blood] and **all his vessels**, [they were sprinkled with blood] the laver and his foot."

Hebrews 9:22

"And almost all things are by the law purged with blood; and without shedding of blood is no remission."

THE IMPORTANCE OF CHRIST'S BLOOD

It is clear from this verse that all things by the law were purged or cleansed with the blood of the animals that were offered. It is also clear from this verse that **without the shedding of blood is no remission or forgiveness.** The Greek Word for *"remission"* is APHESIS. Some of the meanings for this Word are:

> *"1) release from bondage or imprisonment; 2) forgiveness or pardon, of sins (letting them go as if they had never been committed), remission of the penalty."*

JOHN MACARTHUR'S BLOOD HERESY
This is one of many verses that points out the heresy of John MacArthur on the blood of the Lord Jesus Christ. He wrongly teaches that the word, *"blood,"* does not mean literal blood, but it is a metonym or figure of speech for *"death."* What he is doing is saying that God did not know what He was doing when He wrote in the New Testament that there were at least fourteen effects about the literal blood of the Lord Jesus Christ. He is saying that God should have used the word, *"death"* (THANATOS) instead of the Word He used which was *"blood"* (HAIMA). HAIMA is not THANATOS and THANATOS is not HAIMA. God knows this and so should John MacArthur and his thousands of followers all around the world.

For an in depth study on MacArthur's heresy that I made in 1955, I suggest you get my 64-page book entitled *JOHN MACARTHUR'S HERESY ON THE BLOOD OF CHRIST* (BFT #2185 @ $10.00 + $4.00 S&H). There are scores of direct quotations by MacArthur from his own speeches or written materials which enable you to see how deep, tragic, and unBiblical his views are on this subject.

I recommend that you get my paper entitled: *"Fourteen Biblical Effects of the Literal Blood f Christ"* (BFT #2548 @ $3.00 + $2.00 S&H). Here are some of these verses that talk about the importance and the effects of the blood of the Lord Jesus Christ.

- **Acts 20:28**

"Take heed therefore unto yourselves, and to all the flock, over the which the Holy ghost hath made you overseers, to feed the church of God, which he hath **purchased with his own blood.**"

From the context in Acts 20, Paul is talking to the pastors/bishops/elders of the church of Ephesus. This shows that there is one head office in local churches with three separate functions with three separate titles for the same person.

PURCHASED WITH GOD-PROVIDED BLOOD

These overseers (pastors and elders) were to feed the church of God which He (God) has purchased with His (God's) own blood. Through the miraculous virgin birth, the Lord Jesus Christ was delivered from the sin-laden and imperfect blood-line of Adam. We have seen this before in Hebrews 10:5:

- Hebrews 10:5

"Wherefore when he cometh into the world, he saith, Sacrifice and offering thou wouldest not, but **a body hast thou prepared me:**"

CHRIST'S IMPECCABLE BLOOD

God the Son is talking with God the Father and saying that "a body hast thou (God the Father) prepared me (God the Son). As such it was a body from God the Father and was filled with God's blood, that is, blood that was from God just as His hands, feet, head, and all the members of His prepared body were from God. As such it was divine blood, perfect blood, impeccable blood. It was not merely "human blood" like we have which John MacArthur believes. This is rank heresy to say this.

- Romans 3:25

"Whom God hath set forth *to be* a propitiation [that is a satisfaction] through faith in **his blood, to declare his righteousness for the remission of sins that are past,** through the forbearance of God;"

BLOOD, NOT DEATH!

Notice, faith in His blood (not His death alone) as John MacArthur falsely teaches (though He shed His blood at His death). The blood of the Lord Jesus Christ as it was shed on the cross satisfies God the Father. That's why after His bodily resurrection God the Father could receive his Son into Heaven and seat Him at His right hand of power and authority. God the Father was totally pleased with His Son's shed blood at Calvary.

- Romans 5:9

"Much more then, being now **justified by his blood,** we shall be saved from wrath through him."

We are **justified by His blood** (not His death alone) as MacArthur falsely teaches. In his death, **the Lord Jesus Christ shed His blood, but it is the blood that God looks at as justifying us, declaring the genuine Christians righteous before Him.**

- **Ephesians 1:7**
"In whom we have **redemption through his blood**, the **forgiveness of sins**, according to the riches of his grace;"

We have **redemption through His blood** (not His death alone) as MacArthur falsely teaches. **The Lord Jesus Christ shed His blood** in his death. <u>There's no question about that.</u> We believe in His death, but **through His blood we who are truly saved have redemption and the forgiveness of sins.**

- **Ephesians 2:13**
"But now **in Christ Jesus** ye who sometimes were far off are **made nigh by the blood of Christ."**

NIGH BY CHRIST'S BLOOD

We who are truly saved are made near and close to God, by the blood of the Lord Jesus Christ (not His death alone).

- **Colossians 1:20**
"And, **having made peace through the blood of his Cross,** by him **to reconcile all things unto himself;** by him, *I say,* whether *they* be things in earth, or things in heaven."

PEACE THROUGH CHRIST'S BLOOD

Peace through the blood of His cross (not His death alone). It is the Lamb of God that taketh away the sin of the world.

- **Hebrews 9:12**
"Neither by the blood of goats and calves, but **by his own blood he entered in once into the holy place, having obtained eternal redemption *for us.*"**

The Lord Jesus Christ entered into the holy place of Heaven by His own blood (not His death alone).

- **Hebrews 9:14**
"How much more shall **the blood of Christ**, who through the eternal Spirit offered himself without spot to God, **purge your conscience from dead works to serve the living God?"**

The blood of Christ (not His death alone) **purges the consciences of those who truly trust Him as their Saviour.**

- **Hebrews 10:19**

"Having therefore, brethren, **boldness to enter into the holiest by the blood of Jesus,**"

Only the shed blood of the Lord Jesus Christ (not His death alone) can enable genuinely saved Christians to enter into the holiest of all in Heaven.

- **Hebrews 10:29**

"Of how much sorer punishment, suppose ye, shall he be thought worthy, who hath trodden under foot the Son of God, and **hath counted the blood of the covenant**, wherewith he was sanctified, an unholy thing, and hath done despite unto the Spirit of grace?"

Sorer punishment awaits one who has called **the blood** (not His death alone) **of the covenant** an unholy or common thing. The Greek Word for "**unholy**" is KOINOS. Some of the meanings of this Word are:

"**1.** LN 57.9 **mutual**, common, shared (Tit 1:4); **2.** LN 53.39 **defiled**, unclean, impure, unholy (Ac 10:14); **3.** LN 65.15 **worthless**, of little value (Heb 10:29); **4.** LN 89.118 **in common**, what is mutual between two or more persons (Jude 3); **5.** LN 57.99 ἔχω κοινός (echō koinos), share mutually, formally, have in common (Ac 2:44+)"

When John MacArthur calls **the blood of the Lord Jesus Christ** merely "*human blood,*" he is calling that blood "*unholy*," as in this verse. It talks about sore punishment for those who call the blood of the Lord Jesus Christ merely "human blood," that is, "*unholy*" (meaning common, defiled, or worthless). This is blasphemy against the blood of the Lord Jesus Christ. Anyone who refers to our Saviour's blood in this way will receive a sore punishment from the Lord Himself according to this verse.

John MacArthur does not teach this heresy on the blood of the Lord Jesus Christ to his church alone. He propagates this heresy by the thousands (1) in his books; (2) in his emails; (3) in his papers; (4) in his college and seminary in California; (5) in his radio programs; (6) in his television programs; (7) on the Internet programs, and (8) in his commentary on the whole Bible.

- **Hebrews 13:12**

"Wherefore Jesus also, that he might sanctify the **people with his own blood,** suffered without the gate."

Those truly saved have been sanctified by His blood (not His death alone).

- **Hebrews 13:20-21**
"Now the God of peace, that brought again from the dead our Lord Jesus, that great shepherd of the sheep, **through the blood of the everlasting covenant, Make you perfect in every good work to do his will, working in you that which is wellpleasing in his sight, through Jesus Christ**; to whom *be* glory for ever and ever. Amen."

   The truly saved Christians are made perfect and mature to do His will through the blood (not His death alone) **of the Lord Jesus Christ.**

- **1 Peter 1:18-19**
"Forasmuch as ye know that ye were not **redeemed** with corruptible things, *as* silver and gold, from your vain conversation *received* by tradition from your fathers; But **with the precious blood of Christ**, as of a lamb without blemish and without spot."

God says that **genuinely saved Christians have been redeemed with the precious blood** (not His death alone) **of Christ**. Not with mere "human blood" as MacArthur teaches the blood of the Lord Jesus Christ was. That would be something which is "corruptible" which could never redeem a lost person.

- **1 John 1:7**
"But if we walk in the light, as he is in the light, we have fellowship one with another, and **the blood of Jesus Christ his Son cleanseth us from all sin**."

It's **the blood** (not His death alone) **of the Lord Jesus Christ that cleanses from all sin those who are truly saved.**

- **Revelation 1:5**
"And from **Jesus Christ**, *who* is the faithful witness, *and* the first begotten of the dead, and the prince of the kings of the earth. Unto him that loved us, and **washed us from our sins in his own blood**,"

God can wash the true Christian in the blood (not His death alone) **of the Lord Jesus Christ.**

- **Revelation 5:9**
"And they sung a new song, saying, Thou art worthy to take the book, and to open the seals thereof: for thou wast slain, and hast **redeemed us to God by thy blood** out of every kindred, and tongue, and people, and nation;"

There are two parts to the death of the Lord Jesus Christ. He was slain. That's His death. And then **He redeemed the genuine Christians to God by shedding His blood** (in His death). These are two separate actions and should not be made into one as John MacArthur and others have done.

> **LAMB SLAIN–BLOOD APPLIED**
>
> In Exodus 12, was the Passover event. The lamb was slain and then its blood was applied to the top and two side posts of the doors. And so, in the case of the Lord Jesus Christ, He died and shed His blood for the sins of the world. These are also two separate things, (despite what MacArthur falsely teaches about them.)

- **Revelation 5:9b**

"for thou wast slain, and **hast redeemed us to God by thy blood** out of every kindred, and tongue, and people, and nation."

Truly saved people are redeemed to God by the blood (not His death alone) **of the Lord Jesus Christ.**

- **Revelation 7:14**

"And I said unto him, Sir, thou knowest. And he said to me, These are they which came out of great tribulation, and have **washed their robes, and made them white in the blood of the Lamb.**"

The robes were washed white in the blood (not His death alone) of the Lamb.

- **Revelation 12:10c-11**

"for the accuser of our brethren is cast down, which accused them before our God day and night. And **they overcame him by the blood of the Lamb**, and by the word of their testimony; and they loved not their lives unto the death."

They overcame Satan by the blood of the Lord Jesus Christ (not by His death alone).

Hebrews 9:23

"*It was* therefore necessary that the patterns of things in the heavens should be purified with these; but the heavenly things themselves with better sacrifices than these."

> **THE TABERNACLE PATTERN**
>
> In other words, the Old Testament tabernacle was a pattern or similar structure to the Heavenly tabernacle. God told Moses to make a tabernacle. He said to make it just like

the pattern in Heaven. It has all of the features of the earthly tabernacle only in perfection.

It was *"necessary that the patterns of things in the Heavens should be purified with these"* earthly animal blood sacrifices. But the Heavenly tabernacle was purified *"with better sacrifices than these."*

CHRIST'S BLOOD PURIFIED
It was the blood of the Lord Jesus Christ that purified the Heavenly tabernacle. This is why, as I explained earlier, I believe the Bible teaches that He took some of His blood after His bodily resurrection to Heaven and put it on the Heavenly mercy seat to purify the Heavenly things with better sacrifices than the ones used by the Levitical high priests.

Hebrews 9:24

"For Christ is not entered into the holy places made with hands, *which are* the figures of the true; but into heaven itself, now to appear in the presence of God for us."

IN HEAVEN "FOR US"
The Lord Jesus Christ did not enter the holy places made with hands, which are figures of the true, but into Heaven itself. He is there in Heaven as the great high priest for those genuine Christians. He is now in the presence of God for, and on the behalf of, those who are truly saved.

- Romans 8:34
"Who is he that condemneth? *It is* Christ that died, yea rather, that is risen again, who is even at the right hand of God, who also maketh intercession for us."

CHRIST INTERCEDING
The Lord Jesus Christ is interceding for those who are genuine Christians.

- Hebrews 6:20
"Whither the forerunner is for us entered, *even* Jesus, made an high priest for ever after the order of Melchisedec."

The Lord Jesus Christ has entered Heaven for the truly saved people.

- Hebrews 10:20

"By a new and living way, which he hath consecrated for us, through the veil, that is to say, his flesh;"

A NEW AND LIVING WAY

The Lord Jesus Christ entered Heaven by a new and living way, that is by having His flesh crucified on the cross. His crucified flesh was like the vail that separated between the holy place and the holy of holies. Now, genuinely saved Christians can enter Heaven by going through the Lord Jesus Christ in genuine faith in His shed blood.

- John 14:6

"Jesus saith unto him, I am **the way**, the truth, and the life: no man cometh unto the Father, but by me."

The only way to Heaven is through genuine faith in the Lord Jesus Christ. No one can go to Heaven except through truly trusting in this Saviour and in Him alone.

Hebrews 9:25

"Nor yet that he should offer himself often, as the high priest entereth into the holy place every year with blood of others;"

THE "ONCE" OFFERING OF CHRIST

In the Old Testament law of Moses, once a year, <u>on the tenth day of the seventh month, on the Day of Atonement, the high priest had to enter into both the holy place and the holy of holies with the blood of several animals.</u>

ONLY ONE OFFERING

By contrast, the Lord Jesus Christ does not have to offer sacrifices yearly with the blood of others, but He, at his death at Calvary, made one offering for ever (never to be repeated), and then, after His bodily resurrection, ascended to Heaven. He shed His own blood, not the blood of others.

- Romans 6:10

"For in that he died, **he died unto sin once**: but in that he liveth, he liveth unto God."

The Lord Jesus Christ died unto sin just once, but lives unto God the Father.

- **Hebrews 7:27**

"Who needeth not daily, as those high priests, to offer up sacrifice, first for his own sins, and then for the people's: for this **he did once, when he offered up himself."**

The genuine Christians' Great High Priest, Lord Jesus Christ, did not have to make any offering for His sins, (as the Aaronic high priests did), because He was the perfect, impeccable God-Man without any sin. Because He was sinless, He could take upon Himself the sins of the entire world.

- **1 Peter 2:24.**

"Who his own self bare our sins in his own body on the tree, that we, being dead to sins, should live unto righteousness: by whose stripes ye were healed."

CALVARY NEVER TO BE REPEATED

The Saviour only bore the sins of the world once, never to be repeated, unlike the Roman Catholic sacrifice of Christ hundreds of times each day all over the world in the masses they hold.

- **Hebrews 9:12**

"Neither by the blood of goats and calves, but **by his own blood he entered in once into the holy place, having obtained eternal redemption** *for us.*"

THE FINISHED WORK OF CHRIST

The Saviour entered just once into the holy of holies. He finished His work.

- **Hebrews 9:26**

"For then must he often have suffered since the foundation of the world: but now once in the end of the world hath he [the Lord Jesus Christ] appeared to **put away sin by the sacrifice of himself."**

Just once in the end of the world **our Saviour put away sin by the sacrifice of Himself.**

- **Hebrews 9:28**

"So **Christ was once offered to bear the sins of many;** and unto them that look for him shall he appear the second time without sin unto salvation."

The Lord Jesus Christ was <u>only once offered</u> to bear the sins of many.

- Hebrews 10:10

"By the which will we are sanctified **through the offering of the body of Jesus Christ once *for all*.**"

> **CHRIST'S DEATH NEVER TO BE REPEATED**
>
> Again, the Saviour's death was once for all, never to be repeated.

- 1 Peter 3:18

"For **Christ also hath once suffered for sins,** the just for the unjust, that he might bring us to God, being put to death in the flesh, but quickened by the Spirit."

It is perfectly clear that **the Lord Jesus Christ just once suffered for sins** on the cross.

Hebrews 9:26

"For then must he often have suffered since the foundation of the world: but now once in the end of the world hath he appeared to put away sin by the sacrifice of himself."

CHRIST PUT AWAY SIN BY HIS SACRIFICE

The Lord Jesus Christ did not suffer many times as the Roman Catholic Church wrongly teaches by their repeated masses. **The Saviour put away sin by the sacrifice of Himself on the cross of Calvary just one time.**

- John 1:29b

"Behold **the Lamb of God, which taketh away the sin of the world.**"

> **SINS FORGIVEN AND HEAVEN'S HOME**
>
> The Lord Jesus Christ completely took away and removed any need for any further payment for sins for ever. Every sinner in the world has the opportunity to truly believe in the Lord Jesus Christ and have their sins forgiven and be given a Home in Heaven.

Hebrews 9:27

"And as it is appointed unto men once to die, but after this the judgment:"

APPOINTMENT AND JUDGMENT

WHEN IS YOUR DEATH APPOINTMENT?

Every person has an appointment given by the God of the universe. It is an appointment to die (unless the rapture of the genuinely saved ones occurs before they die). Sometimes we have appointments with doctors or dentists, or others and we cancel them and do not keep those appointments. This appointment to die cannot be cancelled. It must be and will be kept.

The second part of that verse says that after death is the **judgment**. There are two **judgments** for people. One is for the truly saved and one is for the lost. The **truly saved judgment is the Judgment Seat of Christ** where they will receive the things done in their bodies after their salvation.

THE GREAT WHITE THRONE JUDGMENT

For those who are not genuinely saved, there is the judgment of the Great White Throne. These will be sent to an eternal lake of fire in Hell. This will include all the people of all the ages would have rejected the truth of God and His salvation. The Lord Jesus Christ will be the Judge. He will send them to that place which was prepared for the Devil and his angels. It wasn't prepared for these people who have rejected the Lord Jesus Christ, but they will go there to be with the Devil and his angels.

- 1 John 1:9

"If we confess our sins, he is faithful and just to forgive us *our* sins, and to cleanse us from all unrighteousness."

> ### RESTORING CHRISTIANS' FELLOWSHIP
> That's what the true Christians must do to keep in fellowship with the Lord Jesus Christ when they sin. They can't atone for these sins. The Lord Jesus Christ paid for them at his death on the cross. He's paid for our sins in the past, in resent, and in the future. To get back into fellowship with Him, after these true Christians sin, they must follow this verse and confess their sins unto God the Father.

The Greek Word for "confess" is HOMOLOGEO. HOMO is the same and LOGEO is to speak. The literal meaning of this word is to say the same thing about our sins as God says and therefore to AGREE with Him that we have sinned in thought, word, or deed. This restores fellowship with Him for the saved Christian. God is faithful to forgive these sins, and cleanse, and restore these people to fellowship with Him once again.

THE BREVITY OF LIFE
It's appointed unto all of us once to die. **How long is your life going to be?** You're here today. You may be gone tomorrow. I'm here today. I may be gone tomorrow. Every one of us one day will die.

- **Psalm 102:11**

"**My days *are* like a shadow that declineth**; and I am withered like grass."

Grass withers. **Our days are like a shadow.** When we're outside in an empty field, and when the sun shines, there is a shadow. In the darkness, there is no shadow. The shadows disappear. Light causes shadows, but when the light is removed, the shadow flees away. This is what our life is like. **It is very short as a shadow.** It is not permanent.

- **1 Samuel 20:3**

"And David sware moreover, and said, thy father certainly knoweth that I have found grace in thine eyes; and he saith, Let not Jonathan know this, lest he be grieved: but truly *as* the LORD liveth, and *as* thy soul liveth, **there *is* but a step between me and death**."

David was talking with Jonathan, Saul's son. He said there is **just a step between him and death**. Yes, **life is brief. Like a shadow and like just one step**.

- **Psalm 90:12**

"**So teach *us* to number our days**, that we may apply *our* hearts unto wisdom."

The psalmist asked the Lord to **teach him to number his days**. As of this writing, I am 86 years of age. I have been numbering my days for 86 years. If you multiply that by 365.25, you get 31,411 days since I turned 86 on December 8, 2013. Several times in my life I thought the Lord was going to take me Home to Heaven because of illnesses, but He didn't. He kept me back here on this earth for His own reasons unknown to me.

After we **number our days**, we must apply our hearts to the wisdom of His Words in our King James Bibles (or, if we know them, in the Hebrew, Aramaic, and Greek Words that underlie our King James Bibles). **We must live for the Lord Jesus Christ today, tomorrow, this week, this month, this year, this decade, and all the rest of the days that the Lord Jesus Christ graciously gives us.**

Some people say that when you get old, maybe it is time to stop living for the Lord Jesus Christ. They are wrong who say this. If you are a genuinely saved Christian, you should never stop living to please the Lord Jesus Christ Who redeemed you by His blood, forgave all your sins, kept you out of eternal and everlasting Hell Fire, and gave you a Home in Heaven for all eternity to come. It is always timely to live for the Lord Jesus Christ and seek to please Him. As one of the bumper stickers says so briefly and cogently for the truly saved person:

"*Only one life. 'Twill soon be past. Only what's done for Christ will last.*"

- **James 4:14**

"Whereas ye know not what *shall be* on the morrow. For **what is your life?** It is even **a vapour, that appeareth for a little time, and then vanisheth away.**"

LIFE AS A VAPOUR

James tells us our life is like a vapour that just appears for a little time and then disappears. When will your vapour and mine disappear? When will our life's shadow be no more? Only the Lord knows the answer to these questions. But while we're here, we who are redeemed by the precious blood of the Lord Jesus Christ must do our very best to live for Him and please Him in all that we think, say, and do until our appointment for death arrives.

Hebrews 9:28

"So Christ was once offered to bear the sins of many; and unto them that look for him shall he appear the second time without sin unto salvation."

CHRIST WAS OFFERED TO BEAR SINS OF MANY

Again Paul repeats to these Hebrew Christians that **our Saviour died only once to bear the sins of the entire world.** It is a heresy of the greatest sort to have the thousands and thousands of Roman Catholic masses offering the Lord Jesus Christ and killing Him over and over and over again! <u>That Greek Word for *"offered"* is in the aorist tense. That is a tense the indicates a once-for-all action never to be repeated.</u>

NOT ANY LONGER THE SIN QUESTION

Then Paul says that, for those genuine Christians who look for His return, the Lord Jesus Christ will appear the second time without having to deal with the sin question (He dealt with that at His first coming), but unto the salvation and deliverance from the Antichrist's rule during the seven-year Tribulation period. The Saviour will then take up His rule upon this entire earth for one thousand years in the millennium.

- Hebrews 10:10

"By the which will we are sanctified through **the offering of the body of Jesus Christ once *for all*.**"

The Lord Jesus Christ was offered on the cross only once.

- 1 Peter 3:18

"**For Christ also hath once suffered for sins**, the just for the unjust, that he might bring us to God, being put to death in the flesh, but quickened by the Spirit."

The Lord Jesus Christ only once suffered for the sins of the world, the Just One for all of us unjust ones.

- 1 Peter 2:24

"**Who his own self bare our sins in his own body on the tree**, that we, being dead to sins, should live unto righteousness: by whose stripes ye were healed."

This verse tells us where the Lord Jesus Christ carried our sins. It was on the tree or the cross.

- Isaiah 53:4-5

"Surely he hath borne our griefs, and carried our sorrows: yet we did esteem him stricken, smitten of God, and afflicted. But *he was* wounded for our transgressions, he was bruised for our iniquities: the chastisement of our peace was upon him; and with his stripes we are healed."

The Lord Jesus Christ is the One--the only One--Who could take care of the true Christian's sins and the sins of the whole world.

- Hebrews 9:22

"And almost all things are by the law purged with blood; and without shedding of blood is no remission."

CHRIST'S PRICELESS BLOOD

This verse sums up this Chapter very well. In the Old Testament, it was the blood of animals that looked forward and pointed to the perfect blood of the Lord Jesus Christ, the Lamb of God. His blood is not the blood of animals. It was priceless blood, incorruptible blood, perfect blood, and sinless.

APPLYING CHRIST'S BLOOD NEEDED

Without the application of the shed blood of the Lord Jesus Christ on Cavalry's cross to the heart of sinners, there can be no salvation and forgiveness. The Lord Jesus Christ must be genuinely believed and trusted. Only then can salvation and eternal life be granted by God the Father for this believing sinner. We must tell the world this story of salvation from sin that is available through the Lord Jesus Christ's death on the cross of Calvary.

Hebrews Chapter Ten

Hebrews 10:1

"For the law having a shadow of good things to come, *and* not the very image of the things, can never with those sacrifices which they offered year by year continually make the comers thereunto perfect."

SACRIFICES AS SHADOWS

The law of Moses was just a shadow of good things to come and not the things themselves. The reality is this present age of grace and the death of the Lord Jesus Christ at Calvary to shed His blood for the forgiveness of the sins of the world.

REPEATED ANIMAL SACRIFICES

The blood of animals offered yearly and repeatedly could never make the people who sacrificed them perfect or completely forgiven. This would only be possible when the Lamb of God, the Lord Jesus Christ, would come and be sacrificed on the cross of Calvary. This is the reality that the law shadow pointed to--which meant a shadow of things to come. Not the very image of the things. That shadow can never, with those sacrifices *"which they offered year by year continually," "make the comers thereunto perfect."* They could never receive salvation by those offerings of bulls and goats and doves in the Old Testament. Only the Lamb of God, the Lord Jesus Christ, who taketh away the sins of the world, can provide forgiveness.

- Hebrews 7:19a

"For the law made nothing perfect,"

This includes the **offerings** made under the law of Moses. The total of **obligatory offerings** (besides the **offerings** for various sins) numbered into the hundreds. The offering of the Lord Jesus Christ was but once and never to be repeated.

Hebrews 10:2

"For then would they not have ceased to be offered? because that the worshippers once purged should have had no more conscience of sins."

If these **offerings** could really take away sins, why did they have to **offer** them again and again and again? This is proof of their imperfection. They would have ceased to be **offered**, if they really were working and could make people perfect. True forgiveness could only come by the **one offering** of the Lord Jesus Christ Who alone is able to take away all the sins of those who genuinely trust Him.

Hebrews 10:3

"But in those *sacrifices there is* a remembrance again *made* of sins every year."

In Leviticus 16, the Jews celebrated one of their seven yearly feasts. It was called the Day of Atonement. Every single year the high priest had to **sacrifice** four animals. Two were for his sins and those of his family. Two others were for the sins of the nation of Israel. After the **sacrifices,** he had to bring the blood into the holy of holies. I have written about this in detail in earlier chapters of Hebrews.

NO MORE SACRIFICES NEEDED

In the age of grace, we do not need such continuous offerings. This is one of serious heresies of the Roman Catholic Church. Their masses represent the re-offering of the Lord Jesus Christ's body and blood. It is a pagan and Satanic procedure. The Lord Jesus Christ has made His one offering for ever for the sins of the entire world. Those who genuinely trust Him as their Saviour can have their sins forgiven.

Hebrews 10:4

"For *it is* not possible that the blood of bulls and of goats should take away sins."

There was no way for the offering of the blood of bulls and goats to be able to take away sins. That is a total impossibility. Paul emphasizes this over and over again in this book of Hebrews. He wanted the Jewish converts to Christianity to be firmly aware of this fact.

Hebrews 10:5

"Wherefore when he cometh into the world, he saith, Sacrifice and offering thou wouldest not, but a body hast thou prepared me:"

CHRIST'S BODY PREPARED BY GOD THE FATHER

This is an extremely vital verse on the incarnation and virgin birth of the Lord Jesus Christ. In this verse, we have **a prayer by the Lord Jesus Christ to God the Father**. He mentions that God the Father prepared a body for His Son, the Lord Jesus Christ. This specially prepared body by God the Father for God the Son, involved **perfect** make-up of **every detail of His body**, including His head, His hands, His blood, His feet, His brain, His heart, and every other member of that special body.

This is one proof that **the Lord Jesus Christ had perfect and incorruptible blood which was shed for the forgiveness of the sins of mankind**. It was not human blood as John MacArthur falsely claims. **It was perfect, spotless, and sinless blood** that He did not inherit from the Adamic blood line. That blood could never have atoned for sins.

BABY'S BLOOD COMES FROM THE FATHER

Most medical opinion that I have consulted agrees that, at birth, the baby's blood comes from the father. Since the Lord Jesus Christ had no human father, He escaped the sinful nature of Adam that comes through the blood line. This is very important.

This specially prepared body was for the once for all sacrifice that the Lord Jesus Christ made for the sins of the world. **His sacrificial body had to be perfect and sinless** for that special offering. This is why God the Father *"prepared"* every aspect of the body of the Lord Jesus Christ. It had to be perfect and flawless.

Hebrews 10:6

" In burnt offerings and *sacrifices* for sin thou hast had no pleasure."

This is a continuation of the prayer of the Lord Jesus Christ to His Father. It is clear that **God the Father had no pleasure in burnt offerings and sacrifices for sin that were offered under the law** of Moses in the Old Testament. They looked forward to the sacrifice of the Lord Jesus Christ on Calvary's cross.

Hebrews 10:7

"Then said I, Lo, I come (in the volume of the book it is written of me,) to do thy will, O God."

IT IS WRITTEN–BIBLE PRESERVATION

These are still the Words of the Lord Jesus Christ Who is speaking to God the Father. He tells God the Father the He has come from His Home in Heaven into this present world for the specific purpose of doing His Father's will.

WRITTEN–BIBLE PRESERVATION

This message was written concerning the Lord Jesus Christ in the Old Testament Scriptures. The Greek Word for "*is written*" is from the word, GRAPHO. The form is a perfect tense form (GEGRAPTAI). As a perfect tense, it means something that was written in the past, has been preserved unto the present, and will continue to be preserved into the future. This speaks of Bible preservation of the Hebrew and Aramaic Words of the Old Testament, and, by extension, of the New Testament Greek Words as well.

Despite the doubts of many alleged Fundamentalists, such as Bob Jones University and others, I believe very strongly, from many verses in the Bible, that **God has promised to preserve His Hebrew, Aramaic, and Greek Words of both the Old and New Testaments.**

THE WILL OF GOD

CHRIST DID THE FATHER'S WILL

The will of God the Father for God the Son was that He die on the cross of Calvary and in so doing, bear the sins of the world.

As you might remember, the Gospel of Matthew gives this report.
- **Matthew 26:39**
  "And **he** went a little further, and fell on **his** face, and prayed, saying, O my Father, if it be possible, let this cup pass from me: **nevertheless not as I will, but as thou *wilt*.**"

It was the Lord Jesus Christ's desire to please God the Father rather than Himself.

- Psalm 40:7-8

"Then said I, Lo, I come: in the volume of the book it is written of me, **I delight to do thy will, O my God**: yea, thy law is within my heart."

This verse was the one that was quoted here in Hebrews. **This prophecy was fulfilled in the New Testament by the Lord Jesus Christ.**

Hebrews 10:8

" Above when he said, Sacrifice and offering and burnt offerings and *offering* for sin thou wouldest not, neither hadst pleasure *therein*, which are offered by the law;"

Paul is repeating what he said in a previous verse. It is clear that God was not pleased with the sacrifices and the burnt offerings offered in the law of Moses. The Law of Moses is over. We of this age of grace are not under any part of that law unless it is repeated in the New Testament.

Hebrews 10:9

"Then said he, Lo, I come to do thy will, O God. He taketh away the first, that he may establish the second."

GOD THE FATHER'S WILL

ESTABLISHING THE NEW TESTAMENT

Paul is interpreting the Words of the Lord Jesus Christ mentioned in previous verses. When our Saviour told His Father that He came to do God the Father's will, He removed and took away the law of Moses. That was the *"first"* covenant. By doing His Father's will, he established the *"second"* or the New Testament age of grace.

THE LAW OF MOSES TAKEN AWAY

The Greek word for *"taketh away"* is ANAIREO. Some of the meanings of this Word are:

> "1) to take up, to lift up (from the ground); 1a) to take up for myself as mine; 1b) to own (an exposed infant); 2) to take away, abolish; 2a) <u>to do away with or abrogate</u> customs or ordinances; 2b) to put out of the way, kill slay a man."

LAW OF MOSES TOTALLY REMOVED

What could be stated more clearly than this about the total and complete removal of the law of Moses from this New Testament age of grace! When the Lord Jesus Christ was sacrificed for the sins of the world, God the Father completely took away the Old Testament law of Moses and established the New Testament age of grace.

This is one thing that the so-called "Messianic Jews" fail to understand. They are still clinging to many parts of the Old Testament law which have never been repeated in the New Testament. If they are genuinely saved, converted Jews, they should cease following the Jewish customs and practices. They should also stop separating themselves from sound, Bible-believing churches rather than going only with their own groups. They should mingle and go to other churches where saved former Gentiles worship the Lord.

- 1 Corinthians 10:32

"Give none offence, neither to the Jews, nor to the Gentiles, nor to the church of God:"

GOD'S THREE CLASSES OF PEOPLE

According to this verse, there are three kinds of people. The Jews, the Gentiles, and the Church of God. Once you're saved, even though you may be born a Jew, you're no longer considered a Jew by God. You're part of the saved, born-again body of Christ and are a Christian.

SABBATH

SUNDAY, NOT SATURDAY

Many people ask about keeping the Ten Commandments mentioned in the Old Testament in Exodus and Deuteronomy. In the New Testament, we are taught to keep nine of these ten commands because they are repeated in the New Testament. We are not to keep the Saturday Jewish Sabbath because it is never repeated for us in the New Testament. The New Testament calls for nine out of the ten to be followed and only nine.

People like the Seventh Day Baptists and others who keep the Saturday **Sabbath** are unscriptural and wrong. They might as well call themselves Seventh Day Adventists because they agree with that heresy in keeping of the seventh day, Saturday, **Sabbath**. Those people who call

Sunday the "Christian Sabbath" are also in error. **Sabbath** is Saturday and the Lord's Day is the first day of the week and is Sunday.
- **Exodus 31:17**
"It is a sign between me and the children of Israel for ever: for in six days the LORD made heaven and earth, and on the seventh day he rested, and was refreshed."

From this verse, it is clearly seen that the seventh day Saturday **Sabbath** was a "sign" between the Lord and the children of Israel, and not for the genuine Christians in the age of grace. This is one of the things of the law of Moses that the Lord Jesus Christ completely abolished as this verse in Hebrews clearly teaches. <u>Israel is not the church and the church is not Israel</u>. This should be made perfectly clear.

Hebrews 10:10

"By the which will we are sanctified through the offering of the body of Jesus Christ once *for all*."

BY THE WHICH WILL

"*By the which will*" refers back to the Lord Jesus Christ's prayer to God the Father. <u>God the Father prepared every part of the body of the Lord Jesus Christ for the express purpose of preparing a fitting and suitable sacrifice on the cross of Calvary for the sins of the world</u>. The Lord Jesus Christ came to do the **will** of God the Father and that **will** included His voluntary sacrifice on the cross.

BLOOD

If the body of the Lord Jesus Christ had not been <u>prepared by God the Father</u> through the miracle of His virgin birth, the Saviour would not have been able to bear the sins of the world on the cross. He would have partaken of Adam's **blood** line. Physicians that I have consulted have said that the **blood** of babies comes from the man, not the woman. Since the virgin birth of the Lord Jesus Christ was not made possible by any human father, the Lord Jesus Christ escaped the sinful nature and **blood** that comes through the line of Adam.

NO ADAM'S BLOOD IN THE CHRIST

Not a single drop of Adam's hereditary blood was any part of the specially prepared body of the Lord Jesus Christ. He was perfect God but He was also perfect Man. He had to be perfect in order to take upon Himself the sins of the world.

- 1 Peter 2:24

"Who his own self bare our sins in his own body on the tree, that we, being dead to sins, should live unto righteousness: by whose stripes ye were healed."

SINLESS BLOOD

Had the Saviour not been perfect, with perfect, sinless, blood that was prepared by God the Father, He could not have fulfilled the above verse. He could not bare our sins in His own body on the cross.

The death and sacrifice of the Lord Jesus Christ was once for all and was never to be repeated. As I have said before in this book, that's why it flies in the face of the masses of the Roman Catholic Church that are performed day by day all over the world. They believe the mass is a sacrifice. One of our Internet attenders told me about a funeral of a friend who died. It was a Roman Catholic service. The priest, holding the wafer said: *"This is the real body of Christ."* The priest also said of the wine: *"This is the real blood of Christ. This is a sacrifice."* They call it a sacrifice. The Roman Catholic heresy of the mass is, for them, the sacrifice of their "Christ." In reality, it is not the sacrifice of the Lord Jesus Christ. <u>This occurred only once.</u>

Hebrews 10:11

"And every priest standeth daily ministering and offering oftentimes the same sacrifices, which can never take away sins:"

OFFERING

VOLUNTARY AND OBLIGATORY OFFERINGS

This is speaking clearly of the Levitical priests and their daily offerings of the same sacrifices day by day by day. In addition to the obligatory offerings made daily, weekly, monthly, yearly, there were voluntary offerings as well as sin and trespass offerings made by the Israelites. Leviticus chapter one through chapter five outlines these five kinds of sacrifices for five different purposes.

In Leviticus one, there was the burnt **offering**. In Leviticus two, there was the meat or meal **offering**. In Leviticus three, there was the peace **offering**. In Leviticus four, there was the sin **offering**. In

Leviticus five, there was the trespass **offering**. All of these were voluntary **offerings,** but were made by the Israelites as needed.

What is emphasized once again in this verse is that these sacrifices could never take away sins. Only the Lamb of God, the Lord Jesus Christ could take away sins as mentioned in John 1:29b:

- **John 1:29b**

"Behold the Lamb of God, which taketh away the sin of the world."

THE OFFER MUST BE RECEIVED

The sacrifice of the Lamb of God, the Lord Jesus Christ, is the only sacrifice that can take away the sin of the entire world. The offer is there. Each person must genuinely receive this Saviour personally and accept God's gracious and free offer.

Hebrews 10:12

"But this man, after he had offered one sacrifice for sins for ever, sat down on the right hand of God;"

SAT DOWN AT THE RIGHT HAND OF GOD

CHRIST SAT DOWN AFTER HIS ASCENSION

This Man, referring to the Lord Jesus Christ, came to do God the Father's will. This will included the offering of just one sacrifice for sins by the Lord Jesus Christ. After that one sacrifice, the Lord Jesus Christ sat down on the right hand of God the Father. His work was finished. God the Father accepted that work and gave His only begotten Son the place of high honor at His own right hand in Heaven.

NO CHAIRS IN THE TABERNACLE

In the tabernacle there was no seat, because the priests and high priests never finished their work. They could not sit down and rest at any time they were in the tabernacle. They stood while they changed the special loaves of bread. They stood while they made sure the light in the golden candlestick was burning. They stood when they offered incense. They stood when they slew the sacrifices. They had no chair or place to rest their feet.

Even today in our society, **the right hand** is known as a place of honor. That's why wives and other ladies should be on the man's right side. That's also why, in the military services, the officer with the highest rank is always to be on the right. The junior officers and others are always on the left. **The Lord Jesus Christ at the right hand of God the Father is in the place of highest honor.**

Hebrews 10:13

"From henceforth expecting till his enemies be made his footstool."

EXPECTING OR WAITING

The One who is **expecting or waiting** is the Lord Jesus Christ. When He came to this earth the first time, He did not judge His enemies who crucified Him. His enemies, and there were many, did not trust Him as their Saviour. Instead, they mocked Him. They spit upon Him. They slapped Him. They crucified Him. They platted a crown of thorns upon His brow. They drove nails in His hands feet. They nailed Him to a cross to die in pain.

CHRIST IS WAITING

But now, the Lord Jesus Christ is expecting or waiting. He is waiting until His enemies are completely conquered and are made His footstool. This will take place at the second phase of the coming of the Lord Jesus Christ. The first phase of His second coming will be the Rapture of the Church when every genuinely born-again Christian-- whether dead and buried or alive and remaining--will be raised bodily and transformed with glorified bodies.

ENEMIES HIS FOOTSTOOL

After this will be seven years of the Tribulation period followed by the second phase of the second coming of the Lord Jesus Christ. When this takes place, He will put down Israel's opponents at the battle of Armageddon. Much blood will flow and the Lord Jesus Christ will make these **enemies His footstool**. He will then set up his millennial 1,000 year reign out of Jerusalem.

THE GREAT WHITE THRONE JUDGMENT

After the millennial reign of the Lord Jesus Christ, He will preside over the Great White Throne judgment of all the lost and unsaved people of all ages. Then will be the complete fulfillment of making His enemies His footstool for all eternity to come as they are consigned to the everlasting and literal fires of Hell. This phrase is used in other verses also.

Hebrews—Preaching Verse by Verse

- **Psalm 110:1**

"The LORD said unto my Lord, Sit thou at my right hand, until I make **thine enemies thy footstool.**"

The Lord Jesus Christ will make **His enemies His footstool.** God is longsuffering with such evil people.

- **Matthew 22:44**

"The LORD said unto my Lord, Sit thou on my right hand, till I make **thine enemies thy footstool?**"

This is a quotation of Psalm 110:1 of the Old Testament.

- **Mark 12:36**

"For David himself said by the Holy Ghost, the LORD said to my Lord, sit thou on my right hand, till I make **thine enemies thy footstool.**"

Here is another repetition of this.

- **Luke 20:42-43**

"And David himself saith in the book of Psalms, the LORD said unto my Lord, Sit thou on my right hand, Till I make **thine enemies thy footstool.**"

- **Acts 2:34-35**

"For David is not ascended into the heavens: but he saith himself, the LORD said unto my Lord, sit thou on my right hand, Until I make **thy foes thy footstool.**"

- **1 Corinthians 15:25**

"For he must reign, till he hath put **all enemies under his feet.**"

- **Philippians 3:18b**

"*They are* **enemies** of the cross of Christ."

These unbelieving pagan idolaters who have rejected genuine faith in the Lord Jesus Christ are enemies of the work He did at the cross of Calvary.

Hebrews 10:14

"For by one offering he hath perfected for ever them that are sanctified."

PERFECTED FOREVER

This verse repeats the last one about making the **enemies of the Lord Jesus Christ His footstool.** The basis of this is given here in this verse. The **victory over His enemies** will be possible because His one offering on the cross of Calvary has **perfected forever** those who have genuinely trusted the Lord Jesus Christ for His salvation and redemption. They are thus sanctified by the Saviour.

ETERNAL SECURITY OF THE SAVED

This forever perfection speaks to the eternal security of every truly saved Christian. Such individuals cannot fall away and be lost. They cannot possibly lose this salvation once given by genuine faith in the Lord Jesus Christ.

The truly saved ones, though their state on earth has problems, have a perfect slate on God's books. That slate in Heaven says they are sanctified and perfect in their standing in Heaven. They are **perfected forever**.

When I was working at the University of Michigan Union Cafeteria, while a student there, I worked with a young man that was interested in the gospel of the Lord Jesus Christ. I told him what the Saviour had done for him in dying for his sins. We read various verses of Scripture and memorized them. Everything was all right until we came to a verse he didn't agree with. This is the verse:

- **Galatians 3:26**

"For ye are all the children of God by faith in Christ Jesus."
This verse teaches clearly that the only ones who are the children of God are those who have genuine faith in the Lord Jesus Christ. He didn't agree with that and thought everyone was a child of God. He was going to a church that believed that if you sin, you lose your salvation. That is an error. Genuine salvation and redemption in the Lord Jesus Christ is for ever. It is eternal life. But this eternal salvation and everlasting life is found only in the genuine acceptance of the Lord Jesus Christ as a person's Saviour as specified in the many New Testament verses.

Hebrews 10:15

"*Whereof* the Holy Ghost also is a witness to us: for after that he had said before,"

THE JEWS WILL BE RESTORED

God the Holy Spirit is a witness of what the preceding verse has mentioned. The enemies of the Lord Jesus Christ will be placed under His footstool. In other words, they will be completely and entirely defeated by Him. The Jews will also be restored to the Lord and will honor the Lord Jesus Christ as their Messiah.

Hebrews 10:16

"This is the covenant that I will make with them after those days, saith the Lord, I will put my laws into their hearts, and in their minds will I write them;"

NEW COVENANT

This is an amazing and a miraculous promise by the Lord. It's hard to believe, in our human way of thinking that this is going to take place. The godless Jews who rejected the Lord Jesus Christ will one day, in the future, have **God's laws written in their hearts and minds.**

THE TRIBULATION AFTER THE RAPTURE

After the rapture of the genuinely saved Christians to Heaven, there will be seven years of Tribulation on this earth. It is called Daniel's 70th week or the time of Jacob's trouble. At that time, God will save 12,000 from each of the twelve tribes of Israel to be His evangelists to win people to a saving faith in the Lord Jesus Christ. This means there will be 144,000 Jewish faithful evangelists who will be soundly converted and redeemed unto the Lord Jesus Christ, their Messiah. They will, no doubt, use all the means of evangelizing that we have today and probably many others not yet invented. This would include the printed page, radio, television, the use of the Internet and many other means. God will put his laws into the hearts and minds of these 144,000 Jewish evangelists in partial fulfillment of the promise in this verse.

- **Jeremiah 31:31**

"Behold, the days come, saith the LORD, that I will make a **new covenant** with the house of Israel, and with the house of Judah:"

These days have not yet come, but they will come one day. It is an Old Testament promise by God. He is going to forgive their sins and remember them no more. He will one day **put His laws into their hearts and minds** in this **new covenant** that He will make with them.

- **Matthew 23:37**

"O Jerusalem, Jerusalem, *thou* that killest the prophets, and stonest them which are sent unto thee, how often would I have gathered thy children together, even as a hen gathereth *her* chickens under her wings, and ye would not!"

When the Lord Jesus Christ was here on earth, He would have gathered the Jews under His wings as a hen gathers her chickens, and they would not be thus gathered.

- **Matthew 23:39**
"For I say unto you, Ye shall not see me henceforth, till ye shall say, Blessed is he that cometh in the name of the Lord."

One day in the future, the Jews will say of the Lord Jesus Christ Who they crucified, *"Blessed is he that cometh in the name of the Lord."*

Hebrews 10:17

"And their sins and iniquities will I remember no more;"

SINS AND INIQUITIES REMEMBERED NO MORE

This was predicted in the Old Testament by the faithful prophet, Jeremiah.

- **Jeremiah 31:34**
"And they shall teach no more every man his neighbor, and every man his brother, saying, Know the LORD: for they shall all know me, from the least of them unto the greatest of them, saith the LORD: for I will forgive their iniquity, and I will **remember their sin no more.**"

This is a wonderful promise. This is a prophecy of Israel when they are restored and recognize their Messiah, the Lord Jesus Christ. **This will bring forgiveness of their iniquities and their sins will never be called to God's mind.**

JERUSALEM'S WAILING WALL

When Mrs. Waite and I visited the wailing wall in Jerusalem, in the 1980's, we saw multitudes of Jews putting their prayers in little holes in the wall. The men were on one side and the women on the other side of a restraining fence. We were told that they were praying for their Messiah to come. They did not believe that the Lord Jesus Christ was the Messiah. One day God will fulfill His promise and the Jews will turn to the Lord Jesus Christ as their Saviour.

When it says *"I will remember their sin no more,"* it means their **sins will never more be called to God's mind.** He will not lose His memory of their sins, but <u>will never bring them up</u> and hold them accountable for them once they have been redeemed by the Lord Jesus Christ through genuine faith in Him. Their slate will be clear and clean like that of present day born-again Christians.

Hebrews 10:18

"Now where remission of these *is, there is* no more offering for sin."

REMISSION OF SINS

That is so clear. If you have **remission and forgiveness of sins**, there is no more need for any offerings for those sins. They are removed. They are **forgiven**. They are **blotted out**. They are **gone forever**.

SINS REMEMBERED NO MORE

They are not remembered any more for ever. Forgiveness of sins was accomplished exclusively by genuine acceptance of the sacrifice of the Lord Jesus Christ at Calvary.

- Matthew 26:28

"For this is my blood of the new testament, which is shed for many for the **remission of sins**."

THE LORD'S SUPPER'S PURPOSE

The Lord's Supper represents the blood of the Lord Jesus Christ shed at Calvary for the remission and forgiveness of sins.

- Acts 10:43

"To him [that is, the Lord Jesus Christ] give all the prophets witness, that through his name whosoever believeth in him shall receive **remission of sins**."

Genuine trust in the Lord Jesus Christ brings **remission of sins, past, present, and future**.

- Acts 13:38

"Be it known unto you therefore, men *and* brethren, that through this man [the Lord Jesus Christ] is preached unto you the **forgiveness of sins:**"

The only way we have **forgiveness of sins** is through truly trusting the Lord Jesus Christ as Saviour.

One of the places where Paul gave the testimony of his salvation was in Acts 26.

- Acts 26:18

"To open their eyes, *and* to turn *them* from darkness to light, and *from* the power of Satan unto God, that they may receive **forgiveness of sins**, and inheritance among them which are sanctified by faith that is in me."

The Lord Jesus told Paul that his mission was to open the eyes of the lost ones, to turn from darkness to light, and from the power of Satan unto God in order that they might receive **forgiveness of their sins.** This is done through genuine trust and faith in the finished work of the Lord Jesus Christ.

> **PAUL WAS FAITHFUL UNTO DEATH**
>
> Paul was faithful unto death in fulfillment of this commission given him by the Lord Jesus Christ. May those who have genuinely trusted in the Lord Jesus Christ as their Saviour also be faithful to share this good news message to the lost around them, come what may!

The early church had that challenge, did they not? The emperor said, "curse Christ, accept Caesar as your God or die." There were two divisions. Some of them, no doubt cursed the Lord Jesus Christ to save their lives, but many, many, many others chose death at Caesar's hands rather than to renounce the Lord Jesus Christ their Saviour.

If that's your choice, our United States government has listed **Bible-believing Christians** among the 72 groups who are "potential terrorists." It will be their choice to deny or affirm the Lord Jesus Christ before entering the FEMA prison camps that are being constructed to imprison these 72 groups who are really not terrorists at all. If you are a genuinely saved Christian, what will your choice be? Will you stand for the Lord Jesus Christ, or will you deny Him?

- **Ephesians 1:7**

"In whom we have redemption through his blood, the **forgiveness of sins**, according to the riches of his grace;"

This is a powerful verse on the blood of the Lord Jesus Christ. The Gnostics and the critical text followers removed *"through his blood"* because they didn't believe it. It should remain in this verse.

- **Hebrews 9:22**

"And almost all things are by the law purged [cleansed] with blood; and **without shedding of blood is no remission."**

> **GENUINE TRUST IN THE SAVIOUR NEEDED**
>
> There is **no remission of sins without genuine trust in the Lord Jesus Christ Who shed His sinless blood for the forgiveness of the sins of the entire world.**

Hebrews 10:19

"Having therefore, brethren, boldness to enter into the holiest by the blood of Jesus,"
THE BLOOD OF THE LORD JESUS CHRIST

ONLY CHRIST'S BLOOD CAN CLEANSE

Paul is talking about genuinely saved brethren who are brothers and sisters in the Lord Jesus Christ. He says they have boldness to enter into the holiest of all, to heaven itself. In the Old Testament Levitical priesthood, only the high priest could enter into the holy of holies in the tabernacle and then only once per year. Into the holy of holies in Heaven, <u>every truly saved Christian can enter with boldness because of the sacrifice and shed blood of the Lord Jesus Christ</u>. It is only His blood that can cleanse from sins and give a saved person entrance into Heaven itself.

Hebrews 10:20

"By a new and living way, which he hath consecrated for us, through the veil, that is to say, his flesh;"
THE VEIL–HIS FLESH

The Lord Jesus Christ has made possible a new and living way for genuinely saved Christians to enter into the holiest of all in Heaven. He Himself was crucified for the sins of the world and **His body** was torn and rent as the **veil of the temple** was rent in two from the top to the bottom.

CHRIST'S FLESH THE RENT VEIL

The flesh of the Lord Jesus Christ is similar to the veil of the temple that separated between the holy place and the holy of holies. When the Saviour was crucified, His flesh was rent and saved people are now able to enter Heaven, as believer priests, by this new and living way made possible by the Lord Jesus Christ's finished work on the cross.

- Matthew 27:51

"And, behold, the **veil of the temple was rent** in twain from the top to the bottom; and the earth did quake, and the rocks rent;"

> **THE VEIL RENT FROM TOP TO BOTTOM**
> The veil was rent in two or split open. Notice, it was from the top to the bottom. Man didn't do it. If man would try to do it, he would probably do it from the bottom to the top unless he had a tall ladder. The veil was very heavy and thick. This veil represented the flesh of the Lord Jesus Christ. There was an earthquake and a rending of the rocks following this. These were other miraculous signs from God. This rent veil is repeated in the Gospels of Mark and Luke also.

- **Mark 15:38**

"And the **veil of the temple was rent** in twain from the top to the bottom."

- **Luke 23:45**

"And the sun was darkened, and the **veil of the temple was rent** in the midst."

- **Matthew 27:45**

"Now from the sixth hour there was darkness over all the land unto the ninth hour."

- **Luke 23:44**

"And it was about the sixth hour, and there was a darkness over all the earth until the ninth hour."

During the crucifixion, there were three hours of darkness, from the sixth hour (12 noon Jewish time) to the ninth hour (3 p.m. Jewish time). The sun was darkened when the **veil of the temple was rent.**

- **John 14:6**

"Jesus saith unto him, I am the way, the truth, and the life: no man cometh unto the Father, but by me."

The Lord Jesus Christ is the only Way to Heaven. He made a new and living way. He is the only Way. Now people try to say there are other ways to heaven. In fact, George Bush, the former U. S. President, said that there are many ways to Heaven. This is heresy! He didn't agree with the Bible that there is only one way to Heaven. He claimed to be a Christian. I really don't know if he is or is not. Only God knows the hearts of people. But I wonder about it. The only way to Heaven is not through Catholicism, not through the last rites, as the Roman Catholic Church teaches, not through the sprinkling and various other things, but only through the Lord Jesus Christ.

- **Hebrews 9:8**

"The Holy Ghost this signifying, that the way into the holiest of all was not yet made manifest, while as the first tabernacle was yet standing:"

GOD'S OPEN DOOR

While the first tabernacle of Moses was standing, the Lord Jesus Christ came to earth as Perfect God and Perfect Man. The veil separating the holy place from the most holy was like His flesh which was rent when He died for the sins of the world on the cross of Calvary. The substitutionary and vicarious death of the Lord Jesus Christ on Calvary's cross opened up a new and living way into the very presence of Heaven for those who are genuinely born-again and saved Christians. It is a Heavenly "open door policy" provided by God the Father through the work of His Son, the Lord Jesus Christ.

Hebrews 10:21

"And *having* an high priest over the house of God;"
CHRIST OUR HIGH PRIEST

This is a very strongly debated part of Hebrews 10, especially verses 26 through 29. I believe, very clearly, that Paul is writing to genuinely saved Christians yet they are out of fellowship with the **Lord Jesus Christ and God the Father**. The people Paul is addressing definitely have a **High Priest** over the house of God–**the Lord Jesus Christ**. He is their **High Priest**. They are saved and born-again Christians. None others have the **Lord Jesus Christ** as their **Great High Priest**.

Some of the characteristics of the genuine Christian's **Great High Priest** are given through this book of Hebrews.

- **Hebrews 2:17b**

"that **he might be a merciful and faithful high priest** in things *pertaining* to God, to make reconciliation for the sins of the people."

The **Lord Jesus Christ is merciful and faithful**.

- **Hebrews 3:1b**

"consider the Apostle and **High Priest of our profession, Christ Jesus;**"

Saved people have a wonderful **High Priest, the Lord Jesus Christ**.

- **Hebrews 4:14**

"Seeing then that we have a great **high priest**, that is passed into the heavens, **Jesus the Son of God, let us hold fast *our* profession.**"

He is now in Heaven, so the saved people should hold fast.

- **Hebrews 4:15**

"For we have not an **high priest** which cannot be touched with the feeling of our infirmities; but was in all points tempted like as *we are, yet* without sin."

He knew about us. **He was perfect God and perfect Man so He can be sympathetic to our needs and failings.**

- **Hebrews 5:5**

"So also **Christ** glorified not himself to be made an **high priest**; but he that said unto him, Thou art my **son**, to day have I begotten thee."

God the Father made the **Saviour our High Priest**. The **Lord Jesus Christ** did not seek this position.

- **Hebrews 5:10**

"Called of God an **high priest** after the order of Melchisedec."

> **MELCHISEDEC A CHRISTOPHANY**
> Melchisedec had neither beginning of days nor end of life. He was a picture of the Lord Jesus Christ in the Old Testament.

- **Hebrews 6:20**

"Whither the forerunner is for us entered, *even* **Jesus**, made an **high priest** for ever after the order of Melchisedec."

The **Lord Jesus Christ** is the forerunner of those who are truly saved. He entered into the very presence of God the Father for us. **He is a High Priest** forever. **He** does not die any more. He is forever living.

- **Hebrews 7:26**

"For such an **high priest** became us, *who is* holy, harmless, undefiled, separate from sinners, and made higher than the heavens;"

We who are genuinely saved have a perfect, wonderful, glorious **High Priest in** Heaven.

- **Hebrews 8:1**

"Now of the things which we have spoken *this is* the sum: We have such an **high priest**, who is set on the right hand of the throne of the Majesty in the heavens;"

He is seated at the right hand of God the Father in a place of honor.

- **Hebrews 9:11**

"But **Christ** being come an **high priest** of good things to come, by a greater and more perfect tabernacle, not made with hands, that is to say, not of this building;"

The tabernacle in Heaven is where the believer's **High Priest** is ministering.

Hebrews 9:25
"Nor yet that **he** should offer **himself** often, as the **high priest** entereth into the holy place every year with blood of others;"
The **Lord Jesus Christ** offered **Himself once.** That's all.
- **Hebrews 10:21**
"And *having* an **high priest** over the house of God;"
We who are truly saved have a **High Priest Who** takes care of us.

Hebrews 10:22

"Let us draw near with a true heart in full assurance of faith, having our hearts sprinkled from an evil conscience, and our bodies washed with pure water."

DRAWING NEAR TO THE LORD

URGED TO DRAW NEAR TO CHRIST

Truly saved Christians are urged to draw near to the Lord Jesus Christ, their High Priest in Heaven. They must have their hearts sprinkled from an evil conscience to walk with the Spirit of God. Our bodies should be spiritually washed with pure water. They must draw near in a proper fashion.

- **Psalm 73:28**
"But *it is* good for me to **draw near to God**: I have put my trust in the Lord GOD, that I may declare all thy works."
It is very important that those who are truly Christians must **draw near to the Lord Jesus Christ.**
- **Isaiah 29:13**
"Wherefore the Lord said, Forasmuch as this people **draw near** *me* with their mouth, and with their lips do honour me, but have removed their heart far from me, and their fear toward me is taught by the precept of men:"

DRAW NEAR IN HEART

The lips are not enough. True Christians must draw near to their Saviour with their hearts.

Hebrews 10:23

"Let us hold fast the profession of *our* faith without wavering; (for he is faithful that promised;)."

HOLDING FAST

The "*us*" in this verse is clearly speaking of genuinely saved people. This is an important thing to establish in view of what has been spoken of in Chapter 6 and also in this present Chapter. Paul is urging these true Christians to **hold fast** their profession of their faith. This is to be done without wavering. God is always faithful to these believers, and they should be faithful to Him. Saved people are told to "**hold fast**" in other verses as well.

- **2 Timothy 1:13**

"**Hold fast** the form of sound words, which thou hast heard of me, in faith and love which is in Christ Jesus."

The sound Words of the Bible must be **held fast**.

- **Hebrews 3:6**

"But Christ as a son over his own house; whose house are we, if we **hold fast** the confidence and the rejoicing of the hope firm unto the end."

Confidence must be **held fast**.

- **Hebrews 4:14**

"Seeing then that we have a great high priest, that is passed into the heavens, Jesus the Son of God, let us **hold fast** *our* profession."

Because the truly saved Christian's Great High Priest is in Heaven, praying for them, they should **hold fast**.

WAVERING

All of this holding fast should be **without wavering**. The Greek Word for "*wavering*" is AKLINE. The meaning of this Word is:

"*pertaining to being without change or wavering in one's faith—without wavering, firmly.*"

NO WAVERING FOR CHRISTIANS

Wavering for a truly saved Christian is a very serious thing. It should not take place, regardless of any difficult circumstances of life.

- **James 1:6**

"But let him ask in faith, **nothing wavering**. For he that **wavereth** is like a wave of the sea driven with the wind and tossed."

> **SHAME ON WAVERING CHRISTIANS**
> It is a sad thing when genuine Christians waver in the face of turmoils that come upon them. Though it is not easy, they must walk in the power of God the Holy Spirit within them and be unwavering in the things of the Lord, come what may.

THE FAITHFULNESS OF GOD

God is faithful Who has promised the truths of His Words. He always keeps the promises in His Words. What He says He will do.

- 1 Corinthians 1:9

"**God *is* faithful**, by whom ye were called unto the fellowship of **his Son Jesus Christ our Lord.**"

Those who are truly saved should be faithful in the same way that our **God is faithful.** They must do what they are supposed to do, and as they say they are going to do.

- 1 Corinthians 10:13

"There hath no temptation taken you but such as is common to man: but **God *is* faithful**, who will not suffer you to be tempted above that ye are able; but will with the temptation also make a way to escape, that ye may be able to bear it."

God is faithful to His own true Christians, even in the greatest of adversity, and makes them able to bear it.

- 1 Thessalonians 5:24

"**Faithful *is* he** that calleth you, who also will do it."

God faithfully fulfills His Words.

- 2 Thessalonians 3:3

"But the **Lord is faithful**, who shall stablish you, and keep *you* from evil."

God is faithful in keeping His people from evil.

- 2 Timothy 2:13

"If we believe not, *yet* **he abideth faithful: he cannot deny himself.**"

God is always faithful, even if his true Christians are not.

- 1 Peter 4:19

"Wherefore let them that suffer according to the will of God commit the keeping of their souls *to him* in well doing, as unto a faithful Creator."

God is a faithful Creator. He keeps His creation running as He wants it to run.

- **1 John 1:9**

"If we confess our sins, **he is faithful** and just to forgive us *our* sins, and to cleanse us from all unrighteousness."

<u>God is faithful in forgiving the sins of genuine Christians</u> when they confess them to **Him**. He restores their fellowship in this way.

- **Revelation 1:5a**

"And from **Jesus Christ**, *who* **is the faithful witness**,"

<u>The **Lord Jesus Christ is a true and faithful witness**</u>.

- **Revelation 3:14**

"And unto the angel of the church of the Laodiceans write: These things saith the **Amen, the faithful and true witness**, the beginning of the creation of **God**;"

Again, the **Lord Jesus Christ is called the faithful and true witness.**

- **Revelation 17:14**

"These shall make war with the **Lamb**, and the **Lamb** shall overcome them: for **he is Lord of lords**, and **King of kings**: and they that are with him are called, and chosen, and faithful."

VICTORY AT ARMAGEDDON

Even in the battle of Armageddon, the Lamb is faithful in winning the victory.

- **Revelation 19:11**

"And I saw heaven opened, and behold a white horse; and he that sat upon him *was* **called Faithful and True**, and in righteousness he doth judge and make war."

The **Lord Jesus Christ** is again called **Faithful and True**.

Hebrews 10:24

"And let us consider one another to provoke unto love and to good works:"

<u>Again, this is an exhortation to truly saved people, rather than to those who are unsaved and lost.</u>

Hebrews 10:25

"Not forsaking the assembling of ourselves together, as the manner of some is; but exhorting *one another*; and so much the more, as ye see the day approaching."

FORSAKING THE ASSEMBLING OF OURSELVES

How does this verse go along with the Internet ministry of our Bible For Today Baptist Church? Some people have been critical of our church's Internet ministry all around the world. They say that this is a violation of this verse. They say that those who listen and take part in our Internet services are *"forsaking"* the *"assembling of ourselves together."* The Greek Word for *"forsaking"* is ENCATALEIPO. Some of the meanings of this Word are:

"*leave progeny; forsake, leave, abandon, desert; cease, stop*"

OUR CHURCH ASSEMBLES BELIEVERS

(1) Our church does not want to *"forsake, leave, abandon, desert, cease, or stop"* the assembling together of genuine Christian believers either in our country or in countries all over the world who cannot find a <u>Bible-believing, separated, fundamental church</u> to attend. Our church is one of the very few churches around the world that stands unashamedly for these principles.

---

(2) Our church does not want to *"forsake, leave, abandon, desert, cease, or stop"* the **assembling together** of genuine Christian believers either in our country or in countries all over the world who cannot find a church that <u>stands both for the King James Bible as well as the Hebrew, Aramaic, and Greek Words that underlie that Bible</u>. Our church is one of the very few churches around the world that is that kind of church that stands unashamedly for these positions.

ASSEMBLING WITH US ON THE INTERNET

If true Christians in the USA and in other places around the world cannot find churches that unashamedly take these two positions listed above, we invite them to go to their Internet and tune into our Website at <u>www.BibleForToday.org</u>

and click on the BROWN BOX or YELLOW BOX, (24 hours a day and 7 days a week). By so doing, they can assemble together with us in our three weekly services on the Internet.

We do not want to **forsake** such Christians who are searching for these important truths from the Words of God. If they cannot find a sound Bible-believing preaching and teaching church in their area or country, they are invited to **assemble together** with us at our three services each week by way of the Internet. Without such possible fellowship, many throughout the world are totally abandoned and utterly forsaken from hearing sound Bible messages.

The Greek Word for "*assembling*" is EPISUNAGOGE. Some of the meanings of this Word are:

"*gathering together; assembling; meeting*"

We **gather together, assemble, and meet** in our church locally for our services as follows:

OUR LIVE SERVICE TIMES

LIVE SERVICES (ALL USA EASTERN TIMES)

On the BROWN BOX at BibleForToday.org

10:00 a.m. Sunday Preaching Verse By Verse Service

1:30 p.m. Sunday Verse By Verse Bible Study Discussion

8:00 p.m. Thursday Prayer and Verse By Verse Bible Study

Those all around the world who wish to **gather together** with us through the Internet streaming videos, are able to **meet** with us at the times above. If on any week people miss the LIVE services, they can view them by re-play either by clicking on www.BibleForToday.org on the **YELLOW BOX**, or going directly to www.SermonAudio.Com and go to the Bible For Today site and click on the service you missed.

Two of the features of our Bible For Today Baptist Church services that are not found in most other churches are: (1) people are able either to phone in or email in their hymn of the week which we will sing in one of our Sunday services. (2) during our 1:30 p.m. and 8:00 p.m. services, people are invited to call us at **856-261-9018** or email us at Questions@BFTBC.org with their questions or comments pertaining to the verses we are studying. This gives a close and personal fellowship between those attending our services in person and those attending our services on the Internet in this country, and all around the world.

These faithful people are **not forsaking the assembling themselves together** with us, but are taking an active part in our services–even more active a part that can be taken in most other church services. They have our hymnbook and sing with us during each of the three services. In a day when many, if not most churches, are drifting from sound Bible teachings, it is good that people have a choice to attend a church like the Bible For Today Baptist Church that stands for the old time fundamentals of the faith found in the Bible. They don't have to attend a church that has forsaken these fundamentals.

OUR CHURCH'S BIBLE DOCTRINES

Our Bible For Today Baptist Church stands strongly for the following principles:

1. A strong defense and use of the King James Bible;
2. Belief in the verbal preservation and use of the Hebrew, Aramaic, and Greek Words that underlie the King James Bible;
3. Biblical separation from apostasy in all of its forms and compromise in all of its forms;
4. The premillennial and preTribulation rapture of those who are genuinely saved and born-again;
5. A Biblical Christology including the Deity of the Lord Jesus Christ, His virgin birth, His miracles, His blood atonement and death, His bodily resurrection, His visible return for the true Christians in the rapture, His visible return after the Tribulation period to rule and reign out of Jerusalem for the 1,000-year millennium; and
6. All of the other teachings and doctrines found in the Bible.

Hebrews 10:26

"For if we sin wilfully after that we have received the knowledge of the truth, there remaineth no more sacrifice for sins,"

This is the verse where much division in understanding comes out. Many Bible teachers and those who follow them teach that Paul, after speaking to genuinely saved Christians, is all of a sudden talking about unsaved people. <u>I have made note that all the way through from the beginning of the book of Hebrews up to this point, Paul was addressing truly born-again Christians who were well-taught in the Words of God</u>. I believe firmly that those he is addressing are genuinely saved Christians as well.

WILFULLY SIN

THE RESULTS OF SINNING WILFULLY

The verse says "*if we*" sin wilfully. The "we" here is not some lost people, but those who are really saved. Paul includes himself in the word "we." Do you think Paul the apostle was a lost, Hell-bound sinner? No, as a true Christian, like all the other true Christians alive today, Paul had the old flesh which was capable of sinning wilfully. Notice that Paul says that this willful sin can be committed even after truly saved Christians have received the knowledge of the truth.

The Greek Word used for "*knowledge*" is EPIGNOSIS. Some of the meanings of this Word are:

> "1) precise and correct knowledge; 1a) used in the NT of the knowledge of things ethical and divine."

<u>These genuine Christians were not just babes in Christ</u>, but had precise and correct knowledge of the truth.

NO MORE SACRIFICE FOR SINS

CHRIST'S ONE SACRIFICE

If these true Christians sin, as all true Christians sin because they are not sinlessly perfect, there is no other sacrifice for sins except that made by the Lord Jesus Christ on the cross of Calvary. It is not as in the Old Testament where there were special sacrifices for certain kind of sins and trespasses (Leviticus 1-5 for example). There is only one offering for sins. The recourse for genuine Christians when they sin found in 1 John 1:9.

- 1 John 1:9
"If we confess our sins, he is faithful and just to forgive us *our* sins, and to cleanse us from all unrighteousness."

THE CLEANSING OF PROPER CONFESSION

When real Christians sin, they must confess (agree with God about their sin) the thoughts, words, or actions unto the Lord. He has promised both to forgive these sins and to cleanse that Christian from all unrighteousness and get him or her back into fellowship with Himself once again.

Hebrews 10:27

"But a certain fearful looking for of judgment and fiery indignation, which shall devour the adversaries."

FUTURE JUDGMENT

THE FIERY JUDGMENT OF THE LOST

Death is also something shared by both the truly saved people and unsaved people. There will be a judgment of both these groups after their physical death. For the truly saved Christians, it will be the judgment seat of the Lord Jesus Christ detailed in 1 Corinthians 3. They will be judged according to what they have done for the Lord Jesus Christ and then enjoy Heaven forever.

For the unsaved and lost people, the judgment will be at the great white throne. It will be with fiery indignation. They will be judged according to their works, including their rejection of the Lord Jesus Christ as their Saviour. They will then be cast into the Lake of Fire in Hell forever.

Hebrews 10:28

"He that despised Moses' law died without mercy under two or three witnesses:"

The Old Testament law of Moses was very strict. The **death penalty** was imposed for many infractions of that law. They **died without mercy** when two or three credible witnesses testified of their violations of the Mosaic rules.

PHYSICAL DEATH UNDER MOSES' LAW

Under the age of grace in the New Testament, sometimes born-again genuine Christians sin in such a way that God takes them away by death so they do not further ruin His testimony. This is called the sin unto physical death. It happened in Acts 5 with Ananias and Sapphira.

- Acts 5:1-11
"But a certain man named Ananias, with Sapphira his wife, sold a possession, And kept back *part* of the price, his wife also being privy *to it*, and brought a certain part, and laid *it* at the apostles' feet. But Peter said, Ananias, why hath Satan filled thine heart to lie to the Holy Ghost, and to keep back part of the price of the land? Whiles it remained, was it not thine own? and after it was sold, was it not in thine own power? why hast thou conceived this thing in thine heart? thou hast not lied unto men, but unto God. And Ananias hearing these words **fell down, and gave up the ghost**: and great fear came on all them that heard these things. And the young men arose, wound him up, and carried *him* out, and **buried** *him*. And it was about the space of three hours after, when his wife, not knowing what was done, came in. And Peter answered unto her, Tell me whether ye sold the land for so much? And she said, Yea, for so much. Then Peter said unto her, How is it that ye have agreed together to tempt the

Spirit of the Lord? behold, the feet of them which have **buried** thy husband *are* at the door, and shall carry thee out. Then **fell she down** straightway at his feet, and **yielded up the ghost**: and the young men came in, and found her **dead**, and, carrying *her* forth, **buried** *her* by her husband. And great fear came upon all the church, and upon as many as heard these things."

> ## SIN UNTO PHYSICAL DEATH
> The sin unto physical death is also mentioned in 1 John.

- 1 John 5:16-17

"If any man see his brother sin a sin *which is* not unto **death**, he shall ask, and he shall give him life for them that sin not unto **death**. There is a sin unto **death**: I do not say that he shall pray for it. All unrighteousness is sin: and there is a sin not unto **death**."

> ## LYING TO THE HOLY SPIRIT
> These two deaths were for lying to the Holy Spirit about the total price of the land that this couple sold. They pretended that they gave the entire amount to the church, but lied about it.

We do not know which sins a truly saved person may commit which are sins that might become a sin unto **physical death.** But this is a New Testament teaching which, in some senses, is similar to the Old Testament **deaths** for certain sins against the law of Moses.

- 1 Corinthians 11:28-30

"But let a man examine himself, and so let him eat of *that* bread, and drink of *that* cup. For he that eateth and drinketh unworthily, eateth and drinketh damnation to himself, not discerning the Lord's body. For this cause many *are* weak and sickly among you, and many **sleep**."

> ## THE SLEEP OF PHYSICAL DEATH
> This refers to, not the rest of sleep done at night, but the sleep of death. God judged with physical death those who were

> sinning when they partook of the Lord's Supper. These were not unsaved people, but truly saved Christians who were so out of line with the Lord that He slew them.

In the Old Testament, some of the sins that had the **death penalty** were:
1. A woman that had sex with a beast was to **die;**
2. A man that had sex with a beast was to **die**. It is sad that our military now is going to allow not only sodomy, adultery, fornication, but also bestiality. The present administration is amending the Universal Code of Military Justice (UCMJ).
3. a child who cursed his parents was to **die;**
4. those who walked too far on the Sabbath day were to **die;**
5. those who picked up sticks on the Sabbath day were to **die**.

Many other things could be listed that brought **death** under Moses' law.

Hebrews 10:29

" Of how much sorer punishment, suppose ye, shall he be thought worthy, who hath trodden under foot the Son of God, and hath counted the blood of the covenant, wherewith he was sanctified, an unholy thing, and hath done despite unto the Spirit of grace?"

TRODDEN UNDER FOOT

As the Old Testament, under Mosaic law, had punishments of death, the New Testament refers to an even sorer punishment than that meted out in the Old Testament. I believe Paul is talking about the same ones he talked about in Chapter six above. They were genuinely saved Christians who were very well taught in the things of the Words of God. The cause of this punishment in the New Testament for these well-taught Christians was because of three things:

1. **Trampling Christ.** They had, first of all, **trodden under foot**, that is, **trampled on**, despised, and showed utter disdain for the Son of God, their Saviour. The Greek Word for *"trodden under foot"* is: KATAPATEO. Some of the meanings of this Word are:

"*1. trample on; 2. despise, show utter disdain.*"

When and if this happens with well-taught Christians and they determine to follow their flesh and walk away from the fellowship of the Lord Jesus Christ, it is like **trampling on Him**. It will meet with sorer punishment than that of the Old Testament.

  2. **Believing In Unholy Blood**. These <u>well-taught and true Christians</u>, when they walk away from the Lord, count the **blood** of the New Testament, by which that person was sanctified, an **unholy thing**. These words show clearly that these people who were truly saved were also sanctified. The Greek Word for "***sanctified***" is HAGIAZO. Some of the meanings of this Word are:

> "1. dedicate, to service and loyalty to God; 2. make holy, sanctify, to cause one to have the quality of holiness 3. honor as holy, hallow, feel reverence, regard as holy."

<u>These people were truly saved, not lost.</u>

  These people **count the blood of the Lord Jesus Christ an unholy thing**. The Greek Word for "***unholy***" is: KOINOS. Some of the meanings of this Word are:

> "1. mutual, common, shared; 2. defiled, unclean, impure, unholy; 3. worthless, of little value; 4. in common, what is mutual between two or more persons; 5. share mutually, formally, have in common."

This is what John MacArthur says of the **blood of the Lord Jesus Christ**: He has taught that it is **"common" and "unholy" blood** the same as the **blood** of all human beings. This teaching is heresy. No, **our Saviour's blood was impeccable. It was sinless. It was perfect. It didn't come through the sin of Adam. It was provided through the miraculous virgin birth of the Lord Jesus Christ**. Remember Who prepared the body of the Lord Jesus Christ. As I mentioned before, in verse 5 above:

- **Hebrews 10:5**

"Wherefore when he cometh into the world, he saith, Sacrifice and offering thou wouldest not, but **a body hast thou prepared me:**"

This is a prayer by the Lord Jesus Christ to God the Father. It declares that God the Father prepared the body of His Son, the Lord Jesus Christ. That included every part of that body, including **His blood. It was not common or unholy or human blood** as John MacArthur and his many followers have believed. This heretical belief will bring "much sorer punishment" on those who hold to it.

3. **Doing Despite to the Spirit of grace.** The Greek Word for "*despite*" is: ENUBRIZO. One of the meanings for this Word is "*insult*."

These genuine well-taught, but carnal, Christians were saved by their true faith in the Lord Jesus Christ. When their salvation occurred, God the Holy Spirit ("*the Spirit of grace*") indwelled them. By their following the works of the flesh instead of the Spirit of grace, they insulted God the Holy Spirit, the Spirit of grace. It is not clear which of the works of the flesh these Christians followed, but here is the list of seventeen of them, and such like sins which are not enumerated:

- **Galatians 5:19-21**

"Now the works of the flesh are manifest, which are *these*; Adultery, fornication, uncleanness, lasciviousness, Idolatry, witchcraft, hatred, variance, emulations, wrath, strife, seditions, heresies, Envyings, murders, drunkenness, revellings, and such like: of the which I tell you before, as I have also told *you* in time past, that they which do such things shall not inherit the kingdom of God."

WALK IN THE SPIRIT

Genuinely saved Christians are ordered to "*Walk in the Spirit, and ye shall not fulfil the lust of the flesh.*" (Galatians 5:16b)

Hebrews 10:30

"**For we know him that hath said, Vengeance belongeth unto me, I will recompense, saith the Lord. And again, The Lord shall judge his people.**"

THE VENGEANCE OF THE LORD

God's vengeance and recompense will be shown for both the unsaved and the saved in utmost fairness and honesty. Various other verses also teach this part of the Lord's justice.

- **Romans 3:5a, b**
"But if our unrighteousness commend the righteousness of God, what shall we say? *Is* God unrighteous who taketh **vengeance**?"

God is not unrighteous when He takes **vengeance** against sin.

- **Romans 12:19**
"Dearly beloved, **avenge not** yourselves, but *rather* give place unto wrath; for it is written, **Vengeance** is mine; I will repay, saith the Lord."

The Lord will judge and repay in just **vengeance**.

- **2 Thessalonians 1:8**
"In flaming fire taking **vengeance** on them that know not God, and that obey not the gospel of our Lord Jesus Christ:"

This is God's **vengeance** on the unsaved who have rejected the gospel of the Lord Jesus Christ.

- **Jude 1:7**
"Even as Sodom and Gomorrha, and the cities about them in like manner, giving themselves over to fornication, and going after strange flesh, are set forth for an example, suffering the **vengeance** of eternal fire."

SODOMITES SLAIN BY GOD

Sodom and Gomorrha and the surrounding cities who were loaded with the wickedness of homosexuality suffered God's vengeance and fire that burned down their cities. When will God show His vengeance and judge the United States of America and the other nations of the world that are promoting Sodomy, homosexuality, lesbianism, and same sex marriages?

THE JUDGMENT SEAT OF CHRIST

Notice the words of this verse, *"The Lord shall judge his people."* This is further proof that Paul is speaking in Hebrews 10 concerning genuine Christians who are spoken of as God's people. The **judgment** of true Christians will take place at the **judgment seat of Christ**. This **judgment is** spoken of in detail in 1 Corinthians 3.

- **1 Corinthians 3:10-12**

"According to the grace of God which is given unto me, as a wise masterbuilder, I have laid the foundation, and another buildeth thereon. But let every man take heed how he buildeth thereupon. For other foundation can no man lay than that is laid, which is Jesus Christ. Now if any man build upon this foundation gold, silver, precious stones, wood, hay, stubble;"

There are three different building blocks that can be build upon the Lord Jesus Christ, the Christian's Foundation, that <u>will not perish</u>:

1. Gold, silver, and precious stones.

There are also three building blocks that can be built upon the Lord Jesus Christ, the Christian's Foundation, that <u>will perish</u>:

2. Wood, hay, and stubble. The first three items are small, but valuable. The second three items are large, but not valuable.

- **1 Corinthians 3:13**

"Every man's work shall be made manifest: for the day shall declare it, because it shall be revealed by fire; and the fire shall try every man's work of what sort it is."

GOD'S USE OF FIRE IN JUDGMENT

Paul is speaking of God's judgment of genuinely saved people. There will be a fire that will try or test every true Christian's works to determine what kind of works they really are. Notice, the fire will not be concerned with the size of these works, but with the kind of the works. The fire will completely consume the larger works that are likened to wood, hay, and stubble. These items will disappear in the flames.

- **1 Corinthians 3:14**

"If any man's work abide which he hath built thereupon, he shall receive a **reward**."

Those who have built upon the Foundation (the Lord Jesus Christ) with the small, but valuable, materials of gold, silver, and precious stones will discover that these works will abide the fire. In fact, the fire will purify the gold, silver, and precious stones and eliminate any impurities that might be found within them. Those who have built with these materials shall receive a **reward from the Lord Jesus Christ Himself.**

- **1 Corinthians 3:15**

"If any man's work shall be burned, he shall suffer loss: but he himself shall be saved; yet so as by fire."

THE JUDGMENT SEAT OF CHRIST

If people who are genuinely saved and born-again live for the works of the flesh (like these people Paul is writing about in Chapters six and ten in this book) all of their works will be burned. These people will suffer great loss. Yet they will not lose their eternal salvation, but will be saved, yet so as by or through the fire. These are things that will take place for genuine Christians at the judgment seat of the Lord Jesus Christ.

Hebrews 10:31

"*It is* a fearful thing to fall into the hands of the living God."

OUR SINLESS SAVIOUR

Our sinless and Perfect Saviour has nothing to do with sin. It must all be judged by Him.

If either the unsaved or the saved sin, they should be afraid of the **Lord Jesus Christ's judgment** on that sin and stay away from it. **It is a fearful thing to fall into the hands of the living God for His judgment.** It should be true for it to be a **fearful thing** (not only for the unsaved who do not know the Lord Jesus Christ as their Saviour, but also for those who are genuinely saved) to fall into the hands of the Lord Jesus Christ, the living God, in **His righteous judgment** against sin.

For the unsaved, this **fearful judgment** will take place at the Great White Throne judgment. For those who are genuinely saved, this **fearful judgment** will be at the **judgment seat of Christ. The Lord Jesus Christ Himself will be the Judge at both of these judgments**. We who are truly saved must live for our Saviour honestly and sincerely each day of our lives.

Hebrews 10:32

"But call to remembrance the former days, in which, after ye were illuminated, ye endured a great fight of afflictions;"

ILLUMINATED

Here is another verse that shows clearly that Paul is writing to genuinely saved people who were "*illuminated*." The Greek Word for "*illuminated*" is PHOTIZO. Some of the meanings of this Word are:

> "1. shine upon, give light; 2. make known; be enlightened, be illuminated."

These Christians had been given the light of the gospel of the Lord Jesus Christ. They were **illuminated and enlightened** by God the Holy Spirit.

TURMOIL WITH CHRISTIANS

Paul urged these genuine Christians to call to remembrance their former days after they were saved. In those days, they endured a great fight of affliction, turbulence, tribulation, and turmoil. This often comes after a person is genuinely converted to the Lord Jesus Christ. They should never forget that trouble often comes to those who love and serve their Saviour.

Hebrews 10:33

"Partly, whilst ye were made a gazingstock both by reproaches and afflictions; and partly, whilst ye became companions of them that were so used."

GAZINGSTOCK

These true Christians were made a "*gazingstock*." The Greek Word for "*gazingstock*" is THEATRIZO. Some of the meanings of this Word are:

> "to make a spectacle (from theatron) a theater, spectacle, show."

REPROACHES AND AFFLICTIONS

These genuine Christians were similar to being made like a theater for everyone to look at and probably make fun of. This happened partly because of having reproaches and afflictions happen to them. It happened also because they associated with other true Christians that were also participants in reproaches and afflictions.

Sometimes genuine Christians who are living for the Lord Jesus Christ are looked at by the unsaved people as a **gazingstock** spectacle and show to be looked at with disdain. These unsaved and unChristian people <u>might say</u> something like this:

> "Look at those men. Look at those women. Look what they are doing, and what they believe. They have believed that they are sinners and that the Lord Jesus Christ died for their sins. They have truly trusted Him as their Saviour and their Redeemer Who has given them everlasting life and will one day take them to Heaven to be with Him forever."

Beliefs like this make those who hold to them look like **gazingstocks,** spectacles, and fools to the unregenerated unsaved people of the world.

Hebrews 10:34

"For ye had compassion of me in my bonds, and took joyfully the spoiling of your goods, knowing in yourselves that ye have in heaven a better and an enduring substance."

COMPASSION

Those who received Paul's letter of Hebrews had **compassion** on Paul because of his bonds. This indicates that he was in prison somewhere, possibly in Rome. This is another indication that the writer was the apostle Paul. The Greek Word for *"compassion"* is SYMPATHEO. Some of the meanings of this Word are:

"1. suffer with, share in suffering, for another interp, see next; 2. have sympathy for, sympathize with."

These true Christians were joyful even when their goods and possessions were spoiled. The Greek Word for "**spoiled**" is: HARPAGE. Some of the meanings of this Word are:

"1. plunder, confiscation, robbery; something taken by force; 2. booty, that which has been taken by violence; 3. violent greed, a state of strong desire for gain by any means; greediness."

A BETTER SUBSTANCE IN HEAVEN

Apparently some people had stolen their goods. Despite the removal of the goods and the possessions of true Christians, they have in Heaven a better and an enduring substance to enjoy for all eternity to come. The Roman government, or maybe some other unsaved thieves or others, would come and steal things from their houses. It may come, sooner or later, in the United States of America just as it has in other countries all over the world.

Under the National Defense Authorization Act (NDAA) passed by both our House and Senate and signed by President Obama, any "alleged" terrorists (including on the list, "*evangelical Christians*") might undergo, as I understand the NDAA, it provides for the following things for people the government alleges are "terrorists" if they really are not:

1. They can be arrested without a trial;
2. They will be denied a lawyer to defend them;
3. They can be imprisoned anywhere in the world, including in prisons outside the United States;
4. They can have an indefinite imprisonment without appeal of any kind;
5. They can have all these happen to them in spite of the fact that this law and these actions are contrary to the provisions of the United States Constitution.

> **THE EVILS OF THE NDAA**
>
> This would result in the deprivation of everything these Christians (and others as well) owned as their possessions, including their homes, their money, their clothing, and everything else. If this comes, it is hoped that genuine Christians, as those in Paul's day, might take this oppression joyfully, looking to their better and enduring substance in Heaven.

Hebrews 10:35

"Cast not away therefore your confidence, which hath great recompence of reward."

CONFIDENCE

> **CONFIDENCE IN THE LORD IS NEEDED**
>
> The words, "*cast not away*," are a prohibition in the Greek aorist tense. Since it is in the aorist tense, it means not to begin an action. Paul is telling these genuine Christians that they are never even to begin or start to cast away their confidence in the Lord or any of His Words. If this command is obeyed, it will bring a great recompence of reward for these true believers at the judgment seat of Christ.

The Greek Word for "*confidence*" is: PARRESIA. Some of the meanings for this Word are:

"1. courage, boldness, confidence, frankness; 2. ἐν παρρησία (*en parrēsia*), in public, openness (of speech)."

Praise the Lord Jesus Christ Who can give genuine Christians courage and boldness even in the face of strong persecution and threats.

Hebrews 10:36

"For ye have need of patience, that, after ye have done the will of God, ye might receive the promise."

PATIENCE

WAITING WITHOUT GETTING UPSET

Paul says here that true Christians have a great need of patience. One definition of patience is waiting for something to happen without getting upset or angry while waiting. The fulfillment of God's promises are not always immediate. In fact, most of them take time to be fulfilled.

GOD KEEPS HIS PROMISES

This verse supposes that genuinely saved Christians are doing the will of God. God's will is found in true copies of God's Words in their own language (such as the King James Bible in English) and the Words found in the proper Hebrew, Aramaic, and Greek Words that underlie these translations. After doing God's will as found in His Words, these saved people must be patient in order to receive the promises connected with doing His will. God will fulfill His promises, but it might take a long, long time. Patience is absolutely necessary in view of this.

I know many people who are **impatient.** They have **no patience** whatsoever. They can't wait for something to happen. If it doesn't happen soon, some of them speak angrily; some of them swear; some of them throw things. These actions do not go with **patience.**

- John 3:16

"For God so loved the world, that he gave his only begotten Son, that whosoever believeth in him should not perish, but have everlasting life."

Here is one of God's promises that He fulfills the minute a sinner realizes (1) that he is a sinner, (2) that the Lord Jesus Christ died to pay for all his sins on the cross of Calvary, and (3) that he then genuinely believes on the Lord Jesus Christ. He is immediately granted everlasting life according to God's promise. Though this promise is fulfilled instantly, most of God's promises require **much patient waiting** for fulfillment.

Hebrews 10:37

"For yet a little while, and he that shall come will come, and will not tarry."

HE THAT SHALL COME

One of God's promises is that the Lord Jesus Christ will one day come again and when that time comes, He will not tarry. The Bible shows there will be two phrases of **His coming again.**

THE RAPTURE OF TRUE CHRISTIANS

1. <u>The first phase of the coming again of the Lord Jesus Christ is the rapture of all truly born-again Christians.</u> They will meet the Lord Jesus Christ in the air. This event will happen before any part of Daniel's 70th week of Tribulation occurs.

- 1 Thessalonians 4:16-17

"For the Lord himself shall descend from heaven with a shout, with the voice of the archangel, and with the trump of God: and the dead in Christ shall rise first: Then we which are alive *and* remain shall be caught up together with them in the clouds, to meet the Lord in the air: and so shall we ever be with the Lord."

CHRIST'S COMING TO JUDGE, THEN REIGN

2. <u>The second phase of the coming again of the Lord Jesus Christ</u> is when He comes to earth to judge the nations fighting at Jerusalem in the battle Armageddon followed by His thousand year millennial reign out of Jerusalem.

- Zechariah 14:1-4

"Behold, **the day of the LORD cometh**, and thy spoil shall be divided in the midst of thee. For I will gather all nations against Jerusalem to battle; and the city shall be taken, and the houses rifled, and the women ravished; and half of the city shall go forth into captivity, and the residue of the people shall not be cut off from the city. Then shall the LORD go forth, and fight against those nations, as when he fought in the day of battle. And his feet shall stand in that day upon the mount of Olives, which is before Jerusalem on the east, and the mount of Olives shall cleave in the midst thereof toward the east and toward the west, *and there shall be* a very great valley; and half of the mountain shall remove toward the north, and half of it toward the south."

- **Revelation 20:4-6**

"And I saw thrones, and they sat upon them, and judgment was given unto them: and *I saw* the souls of them that were beheaded for the witness of Jesus, and for the word of God, and which had not worshipped the beast, neither his image, neither had received *his* mark upon their foreheads, or in their hands; and they lived and reigned with Christ a thousand years. But the rest of the dead lived not again until the thousand years were finished. This is the first resurrection. Blessed and holy is he that hath part in the first resurrection: on such the second death hath no power, but they shall be priests of God and of Christ, and shall reign with him a thousand years."

THE TIMING OF CHRIST'S RETURN

Both phases of the return of the Lord Jesus Christ will take place at a time known only to God the Father, it will definitely come to pass according to God's promises.

Hebrews 10:38

"Now the just shall live by faith: but if *any man* draw back, my soul shall have no pleasure in him."

JUSTIFIED BY FAITH

Those who have been **justified by true faith** in the Lord Jesus Christ are **just** in eyes of God.

- **Romans 5:1**

"Therefore being **justified by faith**, we have peace with God through our Lord Jesus Christ:"

Every genuine born-again Christian has been declared by God as being **justified** before Him and therefore "**just**." They must live by faith in the Words of the living God.

Hebrews 10:39

"But we are not of them who draw back unto perdition; but of them that believe to the saving of the soul."

THE JUDGMENT SEAT OF CHRIST FOR SAVED

If any of these justified and just Christians draw back and fail to live by faith in God's many promises, the Lord will not be pleased with them. They will be judged by the Lord Jesus Christ at the judgment seat of Christ. <u>God expects His saved Christians to be faithful to Him, live faithfully to serve His Son, the Lord Jesus Christ, and follow the clear teachings found in the Words of the Bible. This will be the only thing that will avoid the displeasure of the Lord.</u>

Hebrews Chapter Eleven

Hebrews 11:1

"Now faith is the substance of things hoped for, the evidence of things not seen."

FAITH MENTIONED OFTEN HERE

How can you see the invisible except by faith? There are a total of ten times, in this first part of Hebrews chapter 11, where Paul talks about faith. There are also twelve times in the last part of this chapter where Paul mentions faith. This is a total of twenty-two times where faith is mentioned. Hebrews 11 can truly be called the faith chapter.

In this verse, we have a definition of **faith**. It is a **substance**. The Greek Word for *"substance"* is HYPOSTASIS. Some of the meanings of this Word are:

"1) a setting or placing under; 1a) thing put under, substructure, foundation; 2) that which has foundation, is firm; 2a) that which has actual existence; 2a1) a substance, real being; 2b) the substantial quality, nature, of a person or thing; 2c) the steadfastness of mind, firmness, courage, resolution; 2c1) confidence, firm trust, assurance."

From these definitions, it can be seen that **faith** has foundations and actual existence. Unsaved people who don't have **faith** don't believe this, but the Bible declares it. **Faith** is a **substance**, foundation, or actual existence of what?

> **FAITH AS SUBSTANCE**
> Faith is the substance of things hoped for in the future.

The Greek Word for *"hope"* is ELPIZO. Some of the meanings for this Word are:

> *"1) to hope; 1a) in a religious sense, to wait for salvation with joy and full confidence; 2) hopefully to trust in"*

> **FAITH GIVES CHRISTIANS ASSURANCE**
> The things hoped for include the assurance of genuine Christians of eternal salvation and Home in Heaven forever. The Greek Word always implies something that is not only future, but certain.
>
> Faith is also the evidence of things not seen. The Greek Word for *"evidence"* is ELEGCHOS. Some of the meanings of this Word are:
>
> > *"1) a proof, that by which a thing is proved or tested; 2) conviction."*
>
> Faith is a proof of things unseen by the true Christian. Faith gives the saved person evidence and proof that the Lord Jesus Christ has saved them and lives in Heaven to help them. They can love Him whom they have never seen.

- 1 Peter 1:8

"Whom having not seen, ye love; in whom, though now ye see *him* not, yet believing, ye rejoice with joy unspeakable and full of glory:"

Hebrews 11:2

"For by it the elders obtained a good report."

Paul is talking about the Old Testament saints such as Abraham, Isaac, Jacob, and other Jewish leaders who are called the elders. By **faith** in the Words and will of God, these Old Testament leaders obtained a **good report**. They looked forward to the Seed, the Lord Jesus Christ, Who was promised to Abraham. This **good report** was not necessarily from those around them, but a **good report** from the

Lord Himself. It is the Lord who gave them their **good report** card **by faith** in Him. Genuine Christians today can also obtain a **good report** from the Lord by doing His will as found in the Words and teachings of the Bible.

Hebrews 11:3

"Through faith we understand that the worlds were framed by the word of God, so that things which are seen were not made of things which do appear."

FAITH EXPLAINS CREATION

It's only by genuine faith in the Lord Jesus Christ and in God the Father that we understand how the worlds were framed by the Word of God and that all that things that are seen were not made by things that we can see.

In all of our secular schools—elementary, high school, college, graduate and seminary—students are taught evolution. They are also taught that **faith in God's Words** in the Bible are in error. We must have our **faith in the Words of God** concerning creation, not **faith** in the false words of the scientists who teach evolution and despise God's creation. They are walking away from **faith** in the Scriptures and into **faith** in false ideas.

THE WORLD FRAMED BY GOD'S WORD

It is only by faith that people can understand about God's creation. Those of us who are genuine Christians understand that all the universe—with its billions of galaxies and billions of stars in each of the galaxies--were framed by the Word of God. God spoke them into existence by His omnipotent creative power.

THINGS SEEN AND UNSEEN

Notice this last part of this verse, regarding **things seen and unseen**. We **see** many things. We **see** chairs; we **see** buildings; we **see** flags; we **see** cars, and many other things made by man out of things that can be **seen**. **But all the things that God created were not made of things which do appear**. They're not made by man. They are things you can **see** but the invisible God of the Bible made all these things. **The things that God created by God were not made by things which do appear. Even the things that we can see and man can make are made of unseen things.** We cannot, with our naked eyes **see** atoms, nor can we **see** the neutrons, protons or electrons that make up these atoms. Only by an electronic magnifying glass can these things be seen.

Hebrews 11:4

"By faith Abel offered unto God a more excellent sacrifice than Cain, by which he obtained witness that he was righteous, God testifying of his gifts: and by it he being dead yet speaketh."

ABEL'S MORE EXCELLENT SACRIFICE

Abel is the first of six people of faith mentioned in this first part of Hebrews chapter eleven. The six people are as follows: (1) **Abel**, (2) Enoch, (3) Noah, (4) Abraham, (5) Sarah, and (6) Isaac.

ABEL'S EXCELLENT SACRIFICE

What did Abel do by faith? He offered a more excellent sacrifice than Cain. I'm sure God had told Adam and Eve and their sons what would please Him in offerings. It was by the shedding of the blood of clean animals. Because of this knowledge, Abel took a lamb from his flock and sacrificed it unto the Lord. This was a more excellent sacrifice than Cain who merely offered some of his vegetables, thus violating God's principles for offerings.

THE FIRST BLOOD OFFERING

By this obedience of Abel in his blood offering to the Lord, Abel obtained a witness that he was righteous. God was pleased with his gifts. Abel's offering looked forward to the future coming of the Lord Jesus Christ as the Lamb of God Who was to take away the sin of the World (John 1:29).

God said that by *it*, **Abel** being dead yet speaketh. What does the "it" refer to? It could be by **his** gifts, but that would be a plural reference to a singular. <u>It must be related to the fact that **Abel** was righteous, and by this righteousness he speaks to us today.</u> The testimony of **his** being righteous by **his** proper blood offering speaks out to those in Paul's day and to us in our day.

- **Hebrews 12:24**

"And to Jesus the mediator of the new covenant, and to the blood of sprinkling, that speaketh better things than *that of Abel*."

ABEL'S OFFERING AND CHRIST'S BLOOD

In this verse it is said that the blood of the Lord Jesus Christ speaks better things than the blood that Abel offered speaks. It is a speaking story of how the shedding of blood declared Abel righteous just as the blood of the Lord Jesus Christ, when He is truly received as Saviour, declares the person righteous. Look at the Genesis account of the offering of Abel:

- **Genesis 4:1-4**

"And Adam knew Eve his wife; and she conceived, and bare Cain, and said, I have gotten a man from the LORD. And she again bare his brother **Abel**. And **Abel** was a keeper of sheep, but Cain was a tiller of the ground. And in process of time it came to pass, that Cain brought of the fruit of the ground an offering unto the LORD. And **Abel, he** also brought of the firstlings of **his** flock and of the fat thereof. And the LORD had respect unto **Abel** and to **his offering**:"

From these verses, we learn that Cain was the first-born son of Adam and Eve and **Abel** was the second-born. **Abel** was a keeper of sheep, but Cain was a farmer. He was a tiller of the ground. He was a vegetable farmer, no doubt. When the time to bring an **offering** to the Lord came, Cain brought of the fruit of the ground but **Abel** brought of the firstlings of his flock with the fat. These were two entirely different kinds of **offerings**. God's assessment of the two **offerings** was:

- **Genesis 4b-5a**

"... And the LORD had respect unto **Abel** and to **his offering**: But unto Cain and to his offering he had not respect."

> **GOD WAS PLEASED WITH BLOOD OFFERINGS**
>
> Vegetables and any other non-bloody offerings did not please the Lord in the time of Genesis and in the entire Old Testament. It is the blood of the sacrifice of the Old Testament and the blood of the Lord Jesus Christ in the New Testament that pleases the Lord. God had no respect to Cain's vegetable offering. This made Cain very angry.

- **Genesis 4:6**

"And the LORD said unto Cain, Why art thou wroth? And why is thy countenance fallen?"

When we are angry, our countenance shows it. Cain's countenance had fallen and God asked him about this and also his great anger. God talked with Cain, but it didn't do any good. He still killed his brother, **Abel**.

- **Genesis 4:7-9**

"If thou doest well, shalt thou not be accepted? And if thou doest not well, sin lieth at the door. And unto thee *shall be* his desire, and thou shalt rule over him. And Cain talked with **Abel** his brother: and it came to pass, when they were in the field, that Cain rose up against **Abel** his brother, and slew him. And the LORD said unto Cain, Where is **Abel** thy brother? And he said, I know not: *Am* I my brother's keeper?"

Cain murdered his brother because God favored **Abel's offering** more than his. Even though the Lord knew where **Abel** was, He asked a penetrating question to get Cain to thinking. Cain said *"I know not."* What a liar Cain was. All of Cain's unsaved and evil descendants are liars as well.

- **Matthew 23:35**

"That upon you may come all the righteous blood shed upon the earth, from the blood of righteous **Abel** unto the blood of Zacharias son of Barachias, whom ye slew between the temple and the altar."

In the New Testament, Matthew refers to the "*blood of righteous Abel*." Upon Israel will come all the things predicted to come to pass from the blood of righteous **Abel** to the blood of Zacharias whom they slew.

- **Luke 11:51**
  "From the blood of **Abel** unto the blood of Zacharias, which perished between the altar and the temple: verily I say unto you, It shall be required of this generation."

Luke repeats what Matthew said regarding **Abel** and Zacharias. This is a reference to the beginning and the end of the Old Testament Hebrew Bible. These two historical dates began with Genesis and ended with 2 Chronicles. **Abel's** blood was shed in Genesis and Zacharias's blood was shed in 2 Chronicles. This shows that the Hebrew Bible should be used, not the defective LXX or Septuagint. The Septuagint begins with Genesis and ends with Malachi just like our King James Bible does. Zacharias is not in Malachi, but in 2 Chronicles. All of the promises and requirements God gave to Israel in the entire Old Testament would be fulfilled by God.

- **Hebrews 12:24**
  "And to Jesus the mediator of the new covenant, and to the blood of sprinkling, [His blood is in heaven] that speaketh better things than *that of* Abel."

Abel and the blood of his offering is remembered here in the book of Hebrews.

Hebrews 11:5

"By faith Enoch was translated that he should not see death; and was not found, because God had translated him: for before his translation he had this testimony, that he pleased God."

ENOCH AND HIS TRANSLATION

Enoch is the second of the six people mentioned in this chapter. Enoch's translation is emphasized by mentioning it three times in this verse. The English word, "*translated*" comes from two Latin words, trans ["across"] and *latus* which is the past participle of *fero* ["to carry"]. It means "*to carry across.*"

> **ENOCH'S TRANSLATION TO HEAVEN**
>
> How much of Enoch was translated to Heaven? Only half of him? Only a part of him? No, not just a half or only a part, but every part of him was carried to Heaven. This definition applies to the translations of the Bible as well. As the translators of the King James Bible have done, translators should begin with the preserved Hebrew, Aramaic, and Greek Words that underlie the King James Bible. Then they should carry these Words across (just as clearly and accurately as possible) into the language they are translating. They should neither add words, subtract words, or change the words in any other way.

So **Enoch** was **taken up to Heaven.** <u>He did not see death.</u> **He** had the testimony that **he** pleased God. It's truly amazing. Here are some of the background verses about **Enoch**.

- **Genesis 5:18-19**

"And Jared lived an hundred sixty and two years, and he begot **Enoch**: And Jared lived after he begat **Enoch** eight hundred years, and begat sons and daughters."

- **Genesis 5:21**

"And **Enoch** lived sixty and five years, and begat Methuselah:" Methuselah is the oldest man mentioned in the Bible. He lived 969 years.

- **Genesis 5:24**

"And **Enoch** walked with God: and **he** *was* not; for **God took him.**"

<u>That's why **God took him**, because **he** walked with God.</u> That's an Old Testament illustration of how God will one day **take** His truly saved Christians up to Heaven in the rapture. If still living, their bodies will be transformed from mortal bodies to immortal bodies. If they have died, their bodies will be transformed from corruptible bodies to incorruptible bodies. God will **take** them up and **translate** to Heaven just like He did to **Enoch**.

Hebrews 11:6

"But without faith it is impossible to please *him*: for he that cometh to God must believe that he is, and *that* he is a rewarder of them that diligently seek him."

GENUINE FAITH IN CHRIST PLEASES GOD

Genuine faith in the Lord Jesus Christ is the only way to please God. Without true faith, it is impossible to please Him.

- John 3:16

 "For God so loved the world, that he gave his only begotten Son, that whosoever believeth in him should not perish, but have everlasting life."

EVERLASTING LIFE BY FAITH

This everlasting life is open for all who truly receive it in God's way. There must be genuine faith in the Lord Jesus Christ to receive everlasting life. God is real and exists and rewards those who diligently seek Him.

When He was here on earth, the Lord Jesus Christ invited all people to come unto Him.

- Matthew 11:28-30

 "Come unto me, all ye that labour and are heavy laden, and I will give you rest. Take my yoke upon you, and learn of me; for I am meek and lowly in heart: and ye shall find rest unto your souls. For my yoke *is* easy, and my burden is light."

God's method of coming unto the Lord Jesus Christ is by putting **genuine faith** and trust in Him and Him alone for salvation. <u>Without this **sincere faith**, it is impossible to please our God.</u>

Hebrews 11:7

"By faith Noah, being warned of God of things not seen as yet, moved with fear, prepared an ark to the saving of his house; by the which he condemned the world, and became heir of the righteousness which is by faith."

NOAH

Noah is the third of these six people mentioned in the first part of this chapter. There are a number of things that are true in this one verse.

1. <u>First, Noah was warned by God</u>. The whole world was warned about the flood. <u>Many people don't care about the warnings in Scripture</u>. God warned **Noah** about things not seen as yet. When people don't see things, it is hard for them to believe them. They believe what they can see. There is an expression, "seeing is believing." The Lord Jesus Christ told Thomas something else.

- John 20:29

"Jesus saith unto him, Thomas, because thou hast seen me, thou hast believed: blessed *are* they that have not seen, and *yet* have believed."

GOD WARNED NOAH ABOUT THE FLOOD

God warned Noah about things not seen because, in Genesis, it had never rained before. God said it was going to rain, but they never saw it before. It was unbelievable that water could come from the sky.

2. <u>Second, Noah was moved with fear</u>. **Noah** was afraid that if **he** didn't do what God told **him, he** might die also. The whole world was going to die. <u>Fear is not always bad</u>. There are things you should be afraid of. You should be afraid of a fire truck coming right down the street as you are trying to cross it. Get out of the way!

3. <u>Third, Noah prepared an ark for the saving of his house</u>. This ark was a huge ship. It took **him** many years to build it. He had helpers, I'm sure. He was a wise person. <u>He built it to save his household</u>. **He** had three sons, Shem, Ham, Japheth, and their three wives. **He** wanted to save his household.

4. **Fourth, by this Noah condemned the world.** Noah judged the world of sinful people around **him.** They didn't believe God's warning. They didn't believe God. <u>**Noah** condemned the world by his faith.</u>

5. <u>**Fifth. Noah became heir of the righteousness which is by faith.**</u>

GOD'S RIGHTEOUSNESS

In both the Old and the New Testament, **God's righteousness** is only obtained by faith in the Lord's Words.

- **Romans 3:26**

"To declare, *I say*, at this time his **righteousness**: that he might be just, and the justifier of him which believeth in Jesus."

- **Romans 4:3**

"For what saith the scripture? Abraham believed God, and it was counted unto him for **righteousness.**"

- **Romans 4:5**

"But to him that worketh not, but believeth on him that justifieth the ungodly, his faith is counted for **righteousness.**"

- **Romans 4:13**

"For the promise, that he should be the heir of the world, *was* not to Abraham, or to his seed, through the law, but through the **righteousness** of faith."

Here are some of the verses that give the background of the flood.

- **Genesis 2:5-6**

"And every plant of the field before it was in the earth, and every herb of the field before it grew: for the LORD God had not caused it to rain upon the earth, and *there was* not a man to till the ground. But there went up a mist from the earth, and watered the whole face of the ground."

<u>There was no rain before this time. There was only a mist.</u>

- **Genesis 5:28-29a**

"And Lamech lived an hundred eighty and two years, and begat a son: And he called his name **Noah**,"

In Hebrew, **Noah** means rest or comfort.

- **Genesis 5:29b**

"This *same* shall comfort us concerning our work and toil of our hands, because of the ground which the LORD hath cursed."

So Lamech named his son **Noah** because he would be a comfort to people.

- **Genesis 5:30-31**

"And Lamech lived after he begat **Noah** five hundred ninety and five years, and begat sons and daughters: And all the days of Lamech were seven hundred seventy and seven years: and he died."

- **Genesis 5:32**

"And **Noah** was five hundred years old: and **Noah** begat Shem, Ham, and Japheth."

Imagine that, begetting only three sons in 500 years!

- **Genesis 6:5**

"And GOD saw that the wickedness of man *was* great in the earth, and *that* every imagination of the thoughts of his heart *was* only evil continually."

This seems like the conditions that are in existence today. I don't know if it is as wicked now as it was back then, but it's approaching that degree.

- **Genesis 6:6-7**

"And it repented the LORD that he had made man on the earth, and it grieved him at his heart. And the LORD said, I will destroy man whom I have created from the face of the earth; both man, and beast, and the creeping thing, and the fowls of the air; for it repenteth me that I have made them."

Because of the sins of mankind, God said he was sorry He had created man on the earth.

- **Genesis 6:8**

"But **Noah** found grace in the eyes of the LORD."

NOAH FOUND GOD'S GRACE

As Noah, every one who is born-again, and genuinely trusting the Lord Jesus Christ as their Saviour has found the grace of God.

- **2 Corinthians 9:8**

"And God is able to make all grace abound toward you; that ye, always having all sufficiency in all *things*, may abound to every good work:"

Noah was a just man in his generations. **Noah** walked with God. May that be the testimony of those who are genuinely saved today. May they walk, day by day, with the Lord Jesus Christ their Saviour.

- **Genesis 6:11**

"The earth also was corrupt before God, and the earth was filled with violence."

I saw a video today that was sent to me by a friend overseas of the things that are going on in Argentina. There is great violence! Young people are rising up against the dictator. The police are shooting and killing many of these students and young people. You can see the blood in the streets. It is terrible. Talk about violence. These young people stood up against their oppressive government. They said, in essence:

> "*We want this country back in freedom. We don't like this dictatorship.*"

The Argentina military was just mowing them down--killing them.

- **Genesis 6:12-14**

"And God looked upon the earth, and, behold, it was corrupt; for all flesh had corrupted his way upon the earth. And God said unto **Noah**, The end of all flesh is come before me; for the earth is filled with violence through them; and, behold, I will destroy them with the earth. Make thee an ark of gopher wood; rooms shalt thou make in the ark, and shalt pitch it within and without with pitch."

The following are more verses in the New Testament on the relationship between **righteousness** and faith.

- **Romans 3:26**

"To declare, I *say*, at this time his **righteousness**: that he might be just, and the justifier of him which believeth in Jesus."

God declares those to be **righteous** who have genuine faith in the Lord Jesus Christ as their Saviour.

- **Romans 4:3b**

"Abraham believed God, and it was counted unto him for **righteousness**."

- **Romans 4:5**

"But to him that worketh not, but believeth on him that justifieth the ungodly, his faith is counted for **righteousness**."

- **Romans 10:4**

"For Christ *is* the end of the law for **righteousness** to every one that believeth."

- **Romans 10:10**

"For with the heart man believeth unto **righteousness**; and with the mouth confession is made unto salvation."

- **Galatians 3:6**

"Even as Abraham believed God, and it was accounted to him for **righteousness**."

- **Philippians 3:9**

"And be found in him, not having mine own **righteousness**, which is of the law, but that which is through the faith of Christ, the **righteousness** which is of God by faith."

So **Noah** is a picture here of genuine faith and the **righteousness** of God which is brought about by that genuine faith. **Noah** shows us, even in the Old Testament, the standard of God which is genuine faith in His words and commands.

NOAH'S ARK SAVED LIVES

In that case, Noah was told to build an ark to save people from a flood of waters which had never happened before but was going to happen. Noah believe God's Words and built this gigantic ark. Though Noah believed God that a flood was

> coming, all but his own family did not believe this, and perished in that flood. I'm sure they were shocked and very afraid when the flood came, but it was then too late.

Hebrews 11:8

"By faith Abraham, when he was called to go out into a place which he should after receive for an inheritance, obeyed; and he went out, not knowing whither he went."

ABRAHAM

Abraham is the fourth of these six people mentioned in the first part of this chapter. (1) The first was Abel; (2) the second was Enoch; (3) the third was Noah, and (4) the fourth is **Abraham**.

> **THREE THINGS ABOUT ABRAHAM**
>
> First, when Abraham was called by God to go out of his homeland, God told him to go to a place which he would afterwards receive for an inheritance.
>
> Second, Abraham obeyed the Lord. Obedience is doing what God says to do. For Abraham, it meant leaving his home and his friends. He went to a place that he had never seen before.
>
> Third, Abraham went out not knowing where he was going. You might call that blind faith, but it was faith in the living God, who never makes a mistake in what He tells us and He wants us to do.

We must follow what He says to us, in His Words, even though we may not understand and comprehend fully what it means. If God said it, we must obey it, even as **Abraham** did.

Abraham's story of his obedience is told in Genesis 12.

- **Genesis 12:1**

"Now the LORD had said unto **Abram**, Get thee out of thy country, and from thy kindred, and from thy father's house, unto a land that I will shew thee:"

He had to leave his country, his kindred, and his father's house and go to a land that God would show him.

- **Genesis 12:2-3**

"And I will make of **thee** a great nation, and I will bless **thee**, and make **thy** name great; and **thou** shalt be a blessing: And I will bless them that bless **thee**, and curse him that curseth **thee**: and in **thee** shall all families of the earth be blessed."

As I am writing this, many people are trying to get Israel to surrender to the ISIS and Hamas terrorist Muslims. The Muslims are trying to shrink the boundaries of Israel. Many people, including President Obama, are trying to push Israel to do this. God said clearly: *"And I will bless them that bless **thee**, and curse him that curseth **thee**: and in **thee** shall all families of the earth be blessed."*

- **Genesis 12:5**

"And **Abram** took Sarai **his** wife, and Lot **his** brother's son, and all their substance that they had gathered, and the souls that they had gotten in Haran; and they went forth to go into the land of Canaan; and into the land of Canaan they came."

- **Genesis 22:18**

"And in **thy** seed shall all the nations of the earth be blessed; because **thou** hast obeyed my voice."

The reason for God's blessing is because **Abraham** obeyed God's voice.

BLESSINGS FOR THE SAVED ONES

There is a blessing for those who are truly saved by God's grace through trusting the Lord Jesus Christ as their Saviour and obeying God's Words.

- **Genesis 26:5**

"Because that **Abraham** obeyed my voice, and kept my charge, my commandments, my statues, and my laws."

Abraham followed the Lord, obeying His voice fully. Truly saved Christians today should obey the Lord as **Abraham** and say, as the hymn says, *"Where He leads me, I will follow."*

Hebrews 11:9

"By faith he sojourned in the land of promise, as *in* a strange country, dwelling in tabernacles with Isaac and Jacob, the heirs with him of the same promise:"

Isaac and Jacob were heirs of the promise that God made to Abraham. Here are more of Abraham's moves from place to place.

- **Genesis 20:1**

"And **Abraham** journeyed from thence toward the south country, and dwelled between Kadesh and Shur, and sojourned in Gerar."

- **Genesis 21:34**

"And **Abraham** sojourned in the Philistines' land many days."

- **Genesis 23:4a**

"I *am* a stranger and a sojourner with you:"

Abraham was a sojourner. Those of us who are genuinely saved are strangers and sojourners as well. The world is not our Home. As the hymn writer has written:

> *"This world is not my home. I'm just a passing through. My treasures our laid up somewhere beyond the blue."*

Hebrews 11:10

"For he looked for a city which hath foundations, whose builder and maker *is* God."

ABRAHAM'S CITY

Abraham looked for a city. It was not just any kind of a city, but it was one that had foundations whose builder and maker is God. He wanted something that was permanent like Heaven. It was not a city with tents like he lived in which moved from place to place.

Are you who are reading this looking for that city of Heaven? **Abraham** looked for a city which had foundations and which never would be destroyed. Its builder and maker is God. He is not only the

Creator of the earth, the stars, the planets and all the galaxies, but He is the Creator of Heaven also.
- **Revelation 21:14**
  "And the wall of the city had twelve foundations, and in them the names of the twelve apostles of the Lamb."

THE NEW JERUSALEM

The New Jerusalem will be suspended above the earth. It will be a large cube with about 1,400 miles on each of its sides. It will be a huge city. From East coast to the West coast of our country is roughly 3,000 miles. This is about half the width of our country. This gives us a picture of the great size of the New Jerusalem.

Hebrews 11:11

"Through faith also Sara herself received strength to conceive seed, and was delivered of a child when she was past age, because she judged him faithful who had promised."

SARA

<u>Sara</u> is the fifth of these six people mentioned in the first part of this chapter.

(1) The first was Abel;

(2) the second was Enoch;

(3) the third was Noah;

(4) the fourth was Abraham; and

(5) the fifth is **Sara**, Abraham's **wife**.

Through faith she received strength to conceive a child. It was a miracle birth. She delivered a child when she was well past the normal age of child bearing. She was in her 90's. God performed a miracle. By faith, she believed God was going to give her a child.

Before **Sara** had this faith, she wrongly told her husband, Abraham, to take her servant, Hagar, as his wife. Abraham wrongly took **Sara's** advice and took Hagar as his wife. Hagar bare Ishmael who was a disgrace to the Lord's ways. That was not God's way. But finally, she got

Hebrews—Preaching Verse by Verse

her faith together and she conceived Isaac because she judged God to be faithful who had promised. Even in her 90's, she was going to have a child, for God fulfilled His promise.

- **Romans 9:9**
"For this is the word of promise, At this time will I come, and **Sara** shall have a son."

God told Abraham that **Sara** would have a son at the proper time.

- **Hebrews 10:23**
"Let us hold fast the profession of *our* faith without wavering; (for he *is* faithful that promised;)"

GOD KEEPS HIS PROMISES

Everything that God promises, He will carry out in every detail. This is true whether it is for salvation, whether it is for Heaven, whether it is for forgiveness, or whether it is for anything else. Because of this, those who have truly trusted in the Lord Jesus Christ as their Saviour should not waver in their faith.

JUDGMENTS

One of His promises has to do with His **judgments**.

- **Hebrews 9:27**
"And as it is appointed unto men once to die, but after this the **judgment**:"

The Bible speaks of two **judgments** for people. One **judgment** is for genuine Christians. It is the **Judgment** Seat of Christ. They will be **judged,** but will go to Heaven. The other **judgment** is for those who have not truly received the Lord Jesus Christ as their Saviour. It is the Great White Throne **judgment**. They are lost and will spend eternity in Hell, the Lake of Fire. God keeps His promises regarding good things as well as regarding bad things.

Hebrews 11:12

"Therefore sprang there even of one, and him as good as dead, *so many* as the stars of the sky in multitude, and as the sand which is by the sea shore innumerable."

ABRAHAM

ABRAHAM AND SARA'S OLD AGE

This verse says that Abraham was as good as dead. He was a hundred years old when Isaac was born. Sara was in her 90's.

- **Genesis 21:5**

"And **Abraham** was an hundred years old, when his son Isaac was born unto him."

How can you possibly have a child with these parents being so old? It was a miracle brought about because of God's promise.

- **Genesis 22:17**

"That in blessing I will bless thee, and in multiplying I will multiply thy seed as the stars of the heaven, and as the sand which *is* upon the sea shore; and thy seed shall possess the gate of his enemies;"

ABRAHAM PROMISED A MULTITUDE

God promised to make Abraham's seed as plentiful as the stars in the sky and as the sand of the sea shore. He kept that promise.

There are many verses that repeat this promise.

- **Genesis 26:4**

"And I will make thy seed to multiply as the stars of heaven, and will give unto thy seed all these countries, and in thy seed shall all the nations of the earth be blessed;"

- **Exodus 32:13**

"Remember **Abraham**, Isaac, and Israel, thy servants, to whom thou swarest by thine own self, and saidest unto them, I will multiply your seed as the stars of heaven, and all this

land that I have spoken of will I give unto your seed, and they shall inherit *it* for ever."
- **Deuteronomy 1:10**
"The LORD your God hath multiplied you, and, behold, ye *are* this day as the stars of heaven for multitude."
- **Deuteronomy 10:22**
"Thy fathers went down into Egypt with threescore and ten persons; and now the LORD thy God hath made thee as the stars of heaven for multitude."

Seventy persons went down to Egypt. Joseph and his family were already there.
- **Nehemiah 9:23**
"Their children also multipliedst thou as the stars of heaven, and broughtest them into the land, concerning which thou hadst promised to their fathers, that they should go in to possess it."

After the Jews of the southern kingdom returned to Jerusalem after their 70 years of captivity in Babylon, Nehemiah mentioned God's multiplying of them as the stars.

Hebrews 11:13

"These all died in faith, not having received the promises, but having seen them afar off, and were persuaded of *them*, and embraced *them*, and confessed that they were strangers and pilgrims on the earth."

PROMISES

All of the first five out of six mentioned in the first part of this chapter (Abel, Enoch, Noah, Abraham, and Sarah) all died. They did not receive God's **promises.** But:

(1) they saw them afar off;
(2) they embraced them; and
(3) they confessed that they were strangers and pilgrims on the earth.

> ## GOD KEEPS ALL HIS PROMISES
> God promised them many things. Though they didn't receive these promises, they still believed the Lord that He would one day fulfill them. Like those who are genuinely saved today, they have promises afar off that they have not yet received. But they must believe them, be persuaded of them, and embrace them.

The Greek Word for *"embrace"* is ASPAZOMAI. Some of the meanings of this Greek Word are:

> *"1) to draw to one's self; 1a) <u>to salute one, greet, bid welcome, wish well to</u>; 1b) to receive joyfully, welcome. It is used of those accosting anyone; of those who visit one to see him a little while, departing almost immediately afterwards; to pay respects to a distinguished person by visiting him; of those who greet one whom they meet in the way (even not in the East, Christians and Mohammedans do not greet one another); a salutation was made not merely by a slight gesture and a few words, but generally by embracing and kissing, a journey was retarded frequently by saluting."*

> ## STRANGERS AND PILGRIMS
> These Old Testament believers confessed, as the true Christians today should confess, that they were only strangers and pilgrims on the earth. This earth is not their final home.

- **2 Corinthians 5:6-7**

"Therefore *we are* always confident, knowing that, whilst we are at home in the body, we are absent from the Lord: (For we walk by faith, not by sight:)"

- **2 Corinthians 5:8-9**

"We are confident, *I say*, and willing rather to be absent from the body, and to be present with the Lord. Wherefore we labour, that, whether present or absent, we may be accepted of him."

LABORING FOR THE LORD

Those who are genuine Christians today should labor for the Lord Jesus Christ, their Saviour, that they might be accepted of Him.

- 2 Corinthians 5:10

"For we must all appear before the judgment seat of Christ; that every one may receive the things *done* in *his* body, according to that he hath done, whether *it be* good or bad."

THE JUDGMENT SEAT OF CHRIST

Every genuine born-again Christ will appear at the judgment seat of Christ to be judged by Him according to that he or she has done for the Lord Jesus Christ after having been saved.

Hebrews 11:14

"For they that say such things declare plainly that they seek a country."

THEY SEEK A COUNTRY

The testimony of these Old Testament saints declare plainly that they are **seeking a country** beyond this world. In verse 10, they looked for a city. In this verse, they **look for a country**. It is a different **country** than the **country** they have lived in on earth. Those who are truly saved should also **look for the country** of Heaven where they will one day enter. They should, as those of old, plainly declare they are looking for and seeking the **country** of Heaven that the Bible speaks about so clearly.

Hebrews 11:15

"And truly, if they had been mindful of that *country* from whence they came out, they might have had opportunity to have returned."

EGYPT

ISRAEL'S ESCAPE FROM EGYPT

God took His people out of their bondage in Egypt. If they had been constantly thinking about this country, they might have been mindful to find a way to return to it. That is exactly what many of the wicked and unbelieving Israelites wanted to do.

- Exodus 13:17

"And it came to pass, when Pharaoh had let the people go, that God led them not *through* the way of the land of the Philistines, although that *was* near; for God said, Lest peradventure the people repent when they see war, and they return to **Egypt**:"

God did not want His people to return to **Egypt** when they experienced war.

- Exodus 14:10-11

"And when Pharaoh drew nigh, the children of Israel lifted up their eyes, and, behold, the **Egyptians** marched after them; and they were sore afraid: and the children of Israel cried out unto the LORD. And they said unto Moses, Because there were no graves in **Egypt**, hast thou taken us away to die in the wilderness? Wherefore hast thou dealt thus with us, to carry us forth out of **Egypt**?"

ISRAEL'S UNBELIEF AND DOUBT

The Israelites asked the Lord why He brought them out of Egypt. They wanted to return to that land of bondage. They didn't want to die in the wilderness. The Lord asked Moses why his people were crying unto Him.

- **Exodus 14:13-17**

"And Moses said unto the people; Fear ye not, stand still, and see the salvation of the LORD, which he will shew to you to day: for the **Egyptians** whom ye have seen to day, ye shall see them again no more for ever. The LORD shall fight for you, and ye shall hold your peace. And the LORD said unto Moses, Wherefore criest thou unto me? Speak unto the children of Israel, that they go forward: But lift thou up thy rod, and stretch out thine hand over the sea, and divide it: and the children of Israel shall go on dry ground through the midst of the sea. And I, behold, I will harden the hearts of the **Egyptians**, and they shall follow them: and I will get me honour upon Pharaoh, and upon all his host, upon his chariots, and upon his horsemen."

- **Exodus 16:3**

"And the children of Israel said unto them, Would to God we had died by the hand of the LORD in the land of **Egypt**, when we sat by the flesh pots, *and* when we did eat bread to the full; for ye have brought us forth into this wilderness, to kill this whole assembly with hunger."

They wanted to go back to the **land** and return to that bad **land**. They remembered their meals, but forgot their hard bondage.

- **Exodus 17:3**

"And the people thirsted there for water; and the people murmured against Moses, and said, wherefore *is* this *that* thou hast brought us up out of **Egypt**, to kill us and our children and our cattle with thirst?"

DON'T RETURN TO WORLDLINESS

If you are a true Christian who is reading this book, I hope none of you will ever want to go back to the wicked world from which the Lord saved you. These Israelites wanted to go back to Egyptian bondage.

- **Numbers 14:1-2**

"And the congregation lifted up their voice, and cried; and the people wept that night. And all the children of Israel murmured against Moses and against Aaron: and the whole congregation said unto them, Would God that we had died in the land of **Egypt**! or would God we had died in this wilderness!"

<u>They wanted to go back and</u> stay in the land of **Egypt** rather than come into freedom.

- **Numbers 14:3**

"And wherefore hath the LORD brought us unto this land, to fall by the sword, that our wives and our children should be a prey? were it not better for us to return into **Egypt**?"

GOD AFFIRMS HIS WORDS

If the Israelites had made a vote with 600,000 men plus women and children against Aaron and Moses. They would have won the vote and would have tried to return to Egypt. But God is not a voting Person. He is not ruled and run by the votes of human beings. God wanted to stand firm in this instance, and He always stands firm on His Words. He doesn't change, no matter what the vote of the majority of people wish to do. His will and His work will stand forever, even if no human being on earth agrees with Him.

- **John 14:6**

"Jesus saith unto him, I am the way, the truth, and the life: no man cometh unto the Father, but by me."

<u>The Lord Jesus Christ and His death on Calvary to forgive the sins of the world is the only basis on which to go to Heaven and be forgiven</u>. It's God's Heaven, and those who go there must go God's way or not ever arrive there.

- **Numbers 14:4**

"And they said one to another, Let us make a captain, and let us return into **Egypt**."

They thought that if they had a captain, they could return.

- **Numbers 14:5**

"Then Moses and Aaron fell on their faces before all the assembly of the congregation of the children of Israel."

They took their problem to the Lord Himself in prayer.

- **Numbers 14:8**

"If the LORD delight in us, then he will bring us into this land, and give it us; a land which floweth with milk and honey."

These people longed to go back to **Egypt**. They were mindful of the **land** they had left and wanted to return.

ABRAHAM NEVER TURNED BACK

Abraham was different from these Israelites. He did not want to return to his former land that God told him to leave. God said, Go out, and he went out. He never turned back.

Hebrews 11:16

"But now they desire a better *country*, that is, an heavenly: wherefore God is not ashamed to be called their God: for he hath prepared for them a city."

A BETTER COUNTRY

These Old Testament heroes desired a **better country** which was **Heavenly**. Because of their desire for **God's Heaven**, He is not ashamed to be called their God. God has prepared for them a **city in Heaven** that far surpasses any city on earth.

This desire should be that of every truly born-again Christian. They should desire their **Home in Heaven** that the Lord Jesus Christ has gone to prepare for them. How many years do you have in this world? How many years do I have in this world? We do not have the answers to these questions. May God give the truly saved Christians the appreciation for their Heavenly Home and live daily to please their Saviour, the Lord Jesus Christ. God is not ashamed of true Christians, and we should never be ashamed of Him and the gospel of the Lord Jesus Christ.

DON'T BE ASHAMED

- **Romans 1:16**

"For I am **not ashamed** of the gospel of Christ: for it is the power of God unto salvation to every one that believeth; to the Jew first, and also to the Greek."

- **2 Timothy 1:12b**

"... nevertheless I am **not ashamed**: for I know whom I have believed,"

- **2 Timothy 1:16b**

"for he oft refreshed me, and was **not ashamed** of my chain:"

Paul was glad for Onesiphorus, because even when Paul was in a Roman prison, Onesiphorus was **not ashamed** of Paul's chains. We should **not be ashamed** of the chains our brothers and sisters who, in the future, may be imprisoned by those who hold Anti-Christian positions against the gospel of the Lord Jesus Christ, and the Bible and its strict moral standards. We should **not be ashamed**. We should go and visit them and see if we can help them. Onesiphorus visited Paul and was **not ashamed** of his prison chains.

- **Hebrews 2:11**

"For both he that sanctifieth and they who are sanctified *are* all of one: for which cause he is **not ashamed** to call them brethren,"

The Lord Jesus Christ is **not ashamed** of those He has truly saved. He calls them brethren. They are brothers and sisters in the Lord Jesus Christ's family.

Hebrews 11:17

"**By faith Abraham, when he was tried, offered up Isaac: and he that had received the promises offered up his only begotten *son*,**"

GOD TESTED ABRAHAM

This verse explains that **God *tried* or tested Abraham**. God told him to take his son, Isaac, and offer him up for a burnt offering. Abraham obeyed. He arrived at the mountain and told the three young men who went with him to remain at the foot of the mountain while he and Isaac would go up the mountain. He then told them: "*I and the lad will go yonder and worship, and come again to you.*" The Hebrew word for "*come*" is in the first person plural form. It means "*we will come again.*" Abraham took his son, Isaac, the fire, the wood, and the knife and went up. Isaac questioned his father.

- **Genesis 22:7b-8**

"Behold the fire and the wood: but where is lamb for a burnt offering? And Abraham said, My son, God will provide himself a lamb for a burnt offering: so they went both of them together."

ABRAHAM OFFERED UP ISAAC

They both went up the mountain. Abraham built an altar, laid the wood on the altar, bound Isaac his son, and laid his son on top of the wood. Then Abraham took the knife to slay his son.

- **Genesis 22:11-12**

"And the angel of the LORD called unto him out of heaven, and said, Abraham, Abraham: and he said, Here *am* I. And he said, Lay not thine hand upon the lad, neither do thou any thing unto him: for now I know that thou fearest God, seeing thou hast not withheld thy son, thine only son from me."

In obedience to the angel of the Lord, Abraham did not slay his son, Isaac.

- **Genesis 22:13**

"And Abraham lifted up his eyes, and looked, and behold behind *him* a ram caught in a thicket by his horns: and Abraham went and took the ram, and offered him up for a burnt offering in the stead of his son."

This is a picture of Calvary. It is a picture of the Lord Jesus Christ, our Saviour, going to the cross to die in the place of every person in the world. He is the fulfillment of the lamb that God the Father promised to provide Abraham. He is the Lamb of God Who took away the sin of the entire world (John 1:29b).

God declared that Abraham offered up his only begotten son, even though he didn't slay him. In God's eyes, it was as good as done. Also,

Abraham's faith is shown when he told the young men at the foot of the mountain, "*We will come again.*" He was certain that both He and Isaac would return, even if Abraham had slain Isaac. He believed that God was able to raise him up from the dead which He did in a figure. (Hebrews 11:19).

There are other examples in the Bible of people and things being **tried or tested**.

- **Job 23:10**

"But he knoweth the way that I take: *when* he hath **tried** me, I shall come forth as gold."

- **Psalm 12:6-7**

"The words of the LORD *are* pure words: *as* silver **tried** in a furnace of earth, purified seven times. Thou shalt keep them, O LORD, thou shalt preserve them from this generation for ever."

> **GOD PROMISED TO PRESERVE HIS WORDS**
>
> **God has promised to preserve His Hebrew, Aramaic and Greek Words from generation to generation, <u>forever</u>.**

- **Psalm 17:3**

"Thou hast proved mine heart; thou hast visited *me* in the night; thou hast **tried** me, *and* shalt find nothing; I am purposed *that* my mouth shall not transgress."

- **Psalm 66:10**

"For thou, O God, hast proved us: thou hast **tried** us, as silver is **tried**."

God does **prove**, **try**, and **test** those who have been truly born-again and saved by genuine faith in the Lord Jesus Christ.

- **Jeremiah 12:3a**

"But thou, O LORD, knowest me: thou hast seen me, and **tried** mine heart toward thee:"

- **James 1:12**

"Blessed *is* the man that endureth temptation: for when he is **tried**, he shall receive the crown of life, which the Lord hath promised to them that love him."

Hebrews 11:18

"Of whom it was said, That in Isaac shall thy seed be called:"

GOD CHOSE ISAAC

It is clear that God has chose Abraham's son, Isaac, to be his successor. It was not Ishmael.

Hebrews 11:19

"Accounting that God *was* able to raise *him* up, even from the dead; from whence also he received him in a figure."

GOD WAS ABLE TO RAISE HIM UP

Because Abraham believed that Isaac would have children and his seed would be multiplied as the stars in the heavens and as the sand of the seashore, he was going to sacrifice his son and knew that **God was able to raise him up** from the dead.

THE RESURRECTION OF ISAAC

God did raise up Isaac in a figure because, in God's sight, Abraham obeyed God and did sacrifice his only son, Isaac. This is a picture of the resurrection of the Lord Jesus Christ. It was something thought impossible, but with God all things are possible.

Hebrews 11:20

"By faith Isaac blessed Jacob and Esau concerning things to come."

ISAAC

Isaac is the sixth of the six people of faith mentioned in the first part of Hebrews 11. The other five are Abel, Enoch, Noah, Abraham, and Sara. By faith **Isaac** blessed Jacob and Esau, his two sons, concerning things to come. God used all six of these Old Testament saints. He writes about them in the New Testament. Without faith it is impossible to please Him.

> **TRUST GOD'S WORDS**
>
> <u>Those of us who are genuinely saved must also have faith and trust in God's Words.</u> We should follow the examples of these six people in the times when they wholly followed the Lord.

In the New Testament, we have much more truth than they had in the Old Testament. Those who are truly saved should follow the Lord Jesus Christ even more aggressively than those in the Old Testament followed the Lord.

Hebrews 11:21

"By faith Jacob, when he was a dying, blessed both the sons of Joseph; and worshipped, *leaning* upon the top of his staff."

JACOB

Jacob had gone to Egypt at Joseph's request. As **Jacob** was dying, **he** blessed both the sons of Joseph and worshipped the Lord. At this blessing, **Jacob** switched his hands. <u>Instead of placing **his** right hand on Manasseh's head (the firstborn son), **he** placed it on Ephraim's head (the second-born son). This indicated that Ephraim would be the favorite son rather than Manasseh.</u> Joseph objected, but **Jacob** did not change **his** hands. <u>This was fulfilled and Ephraim became the prominent son.</u>

- **Genesis 47:28-29**

"And **Jacob** lived in the land of Egypt seventeen years: so the whole age of **Jacob** was an hundred forty and seven years. And the time drew nigh that **Israel** must die: and he called his son Joseph, and said unto him, If now **I** have found grace in thy sight, put, **I** pray thee, thy hand under my thigh, and deal kindly and truly with me; bury me not, I pray thee, in Egypt:"

JACOB BURIED IN CANAAN

Jacob did not want to be buried in Egypt. He wanted to be buried in his homeland. That is what was done. Jacob's body was taken back and buried in Canaan.

- **Genesis 48:4**

"And said unto me, Behold, I will make thee fruitful, and multiply thee, and I will make of thee a multitude of people; and will give this land to thy seed after thee *for* an everlasting possession."

CANAAN IS FOR ABRAHAM'S POSTERITY

God had promised the land of Canaan to Abraham, Isaac, Jacob and their posterity. God did fulfill this promise in His own time. The battles in Palestine today are over this land which was promised to the Jewish people long ago.

Hebrews 11:22

"By faith Joseph, when he died, made mention of the departing of the children of Israel; and gave commandment concerning his bones."

JOSEPH

JOSEPH REFUSED CREMATION

If ever there was an excuse to have cremation, this was it. Here was this man, Joseph. He was in the land of Egypt. He wanted his body to be buried in the land of Canaan. It would have been much easier and cheaper to burn up his body in cremation and carry the ashes into Canaan. But that was not and is not God's way to take care of those who have died. God's way is the burial of those who die.

JOSEPH MENTIONED ISRAEL'S DEPARTING

Joseph mentioned the departing of the children of Israel from Egypt. He had faith that one day, God was going to remove the Israelites out of Egypt, the land of their bondage, back to the land of Canaan which God had promised to them.

- Genesis 50:24-25

"And **Joseph** said unto his brethren, I die: and God will surely visit you, and bring you out of this land unto the land which he sware to Abraham, to Isaac, and to Jacob. And **Joseph** took an oath of the children of Israel, saying, God will surely visit you, and ye shall carry up **my** bones from hence."

JOSEPH IN THE LAND OF PROMISE

Joseph wanted to be buried in Canaan, the land of promise. So they carried up his bones to Canaan in due time.

- Genesis 50:26

"So **Joseph** died, *being* an hundred and ten years old: and they embalmed him, and he was put in a coffin in Egypt."

At the time, when the children of Israel went up to Canaan, they did take **Joseph's** bones and buried them in Caanan. In the meantime, he was embalmed and put in a coffin in Egypt. By faith, **Joseph** believed that one day God would take His people, people of Israel, out of Egyptian bondage and back to the land of Caanan. And it came to pass.

Hebrews 11:23

"By faith Moses, when he was born, was hid three months of his parents, because they saw *he was* a proper child; and they were not afraid of the king's commandment."

MOSES AND HIS PARENTS

THE FAITH OF MOSES' PARENTS

Moses was hid three months by his mother and father. His mother and father had faith to believe that he was going to live. They might have also believed that God would use their son to lead his people out of Egypt. They saw that he was a proper child. They were not afraid of the king's commandment to kill all the male babies.

Moses' parents committed what we call civil disobedience. They disobeyed the law of Egypt because it was against the Words of God. Those who are genuine Christians today, may have to do the same when their government tells them to do what the Bible tells them they are not to do. They must do what the Bible tells them to do, even if the government forbids it.

OBEY GOD RATHER THAN MEN

Genuine Christians should speak out against homosexuality, homosexual marriages, abortions, bestiality, and other sins. On the other hand, they should speak up in favor of home schooling, Biblical marriage and other Biblical positions. If our president or any other government authority makes laws that forbid genuine Christians from following the Words of God, they should disobey those laws just like the early church did in the book Acts when they said, *"We ought to obey God rather than men"* (Acts 5:29b), regardless of the price that might be paid for this obedience.

- Exodus 1:22

"And Pharaoh charged all his people, saying, Every son that is born ye shall cast into the river, and every daughter ye shall save alive."

- Exodus 2:1-2

"And there went a **man of the house of Levi, and took** *to wife* **a daughter of Levi**. And the **woman conceived**, and **bare a son**: and when she saw him that he *was a* goodly **child**, she hid him three months."

MOSES' LIFE WAS SPARED

God miraculously spared the life of Moses after his mother put him in the Nile river in a little floating basket.

- **Exodus 2:3-9**

"And when she could not longer hide him, she took for him an ark of bulrushes, and daubed it with slime and with pitch, and put the **child** therein; and she laid *it* in the flags by the river's brink. And his sister stood afar off, to wit what would be done to him. And the daughter of Pharaoh came down to wash *herself* at the river; and her maidens walked along by the river's side; and when she saw the ark among the flags, she sent her maid to fetch it. And when she had opened it, she saw the **child**: and, behold, the **babe** wept. And she had compassion on **him**, and said, This *is one* of the **Hebrews' children**. Then said his sister to Pharaoh's daughter, Shall I go and call to thee a nurse of the **Hebrew women**, that she may nurse the **child** for thee? And Pharaoh's daughter said to her, Go. And the maid went and called the **child's mother**. And Pharaoh's daughter said unto her, Take this **child** away, and nurse it for me, and I will give *thee* thy wages. And the **woman took the child, and nursed it**."

MOSES' PARENTS DISOBEYED THE KING

By faith Moses' parents disobeyed the king's commandment and God undertook for them and saved their son, Moses. They weren't afraid of the king's commandment. They may have been afraid but did it anyway because it was right.

Hebrews 11:24

"By faith Moses, when he was come to years, refused to be called the son of Pharaoh's daughter;"

MOSES AS AN ADULT

MOSES' IMPORTANT CHOICE

When Moses was an adult, he had a choice. He could remain in Pharaoh's house and be called his daughter's son, or he could choose to be with the people of Israel who were being oppressed by the Pharaoh and his government.

- **Exodus 2:10-12**

"And the **child grew**, and she brought him unto Pharaoh's daughter, and he became her son. And she called **his name Moses**: and she said, Because I drew him out of the water. And it came to pass in those days, **when Moses was grown**, that he went out unto his brethren, and looked on their burdens: and he spied an Egyptian smiting an Hebrew, one of his brethren. And he looked this way and that way, and when he saw that there was no man, he slew the Egyptian, and hid him in the sand."

This was an sad event that happened. It was this event that made **Moses** make **his** decision to leave Pharaoh's house.

- **Exodus 2:14**

"And he said, Who made thee a prince and a judge over us? intendest thou to kill me, as thou killedst the Egyptian? And **Moses** feared, and said, Surely this thing is known."

MOSES' KILLING OF AN EGYPTIAN

Moses knew that this killing was known by the Egyptians. So he fled out of Egypt. He must have known he did wrong in killing the Egyptian.

Hebrews 11:25

"Choosing rather to suffer affliction with the people of God, than to enjoy the pleasures of sin for a season;"

AFFLICTION

MOSES' CHOICE OF AFFLICTION

Moses chose to suffer affliction with God's people of Israel rather than to continue being in Pharaoh's house in Egypt with all of the pleasures this afforded him.

The Greek Word for "*suffer affliction*" is SUGKAKOUCHEO. Some of the meanings of this Word are:

"*1) to treat ill with another; 2) to be ill treated in company with, share persecutions or come into a fellowship of ills.*"

Just as with Moses in his day, so genuine Christians in our day are often made to **suffer affliction** because of their firm position in obedience to the Words of God.

It is interesting to note that the pleasures found in Pharaoh's palace, as all the other pleasures in this world, are only for a season. They are not eternal. They do not endure. They only last for a little while. The Greek Word for "*a season*" is PROSKAIROS. Some of the meanings of this Word are:

"*1) for a season; 2) enduring only for a while; 3) temporary*"

- **Nehemiah 9:9**

"And didst see the **affliction** of our fathers in Egypt, and heardest their cry by the Red sea;"

The Israelites certainly had **affliction** both in the land of Egypt and also as they faced crossing of the Red sea.

- **Psalm 16:11**

"Thou wilt shew me the path of life: in thy presence *is* fullness of joy; at thy right hand *there are* pleasures for evermore."

God's pleasures are not only for a season, but they are for evermore.

- **Psalm 36: 8b**

"and thou shalt make them drink of the river of thy pleasures."

God has eternal pleasures that He allows those who are truly born-again to partake of. His pleasures are forever.

Hebrews 11:26

"**Esteeming the reproach of Christ greater riches than the treasures in Egypt: for he had respect unto the recompence of the reward.**"

ESTEEMED

Moses **esteemed** the reproach of Christ greater riches than all the treasures in Egypt. The Greek Word for "*esteem*" is HEGEOMAI. Some of the meanings for this word are:

"*1) to lead; 1a) to go before; 1b) to be a leader; 1b1) to rule, command 1b2) to have authority over; 1b3) a prince, of regal power, governor, viceroy, chief, leading as respects influence, controlling in counsel, overseers or leaders of the churches;*

1b4) used of any kind of leader, chief, commander; 1b5) the leader in speech, chief, spokesman; 2) to consider, deem, account, think."

> **REPROACH VERSUS TREASURES**
>
> Think of how Moses esteemed the reproach of Christ more valuable than the treasures in Egypt. Think of what Moses had in Egypt. He was the son of Pharaoh's daughter. One day he would likely have possessed all the treasures of Egypt as his very own. But Moses had a different accounting program than the world around him. Christ, His Messiah, was a far greater treasure than anything found in Egypt. He had respect to the reward that God would give him for being faithful to His cause.

- **Job 23:12**

"Neither have I gone back from the commandment of his lips; I have **esteemed** the words of his mouth more than my necessary food."

Like Moses, Job **esteemed** some things as valuable. God's Words were of more value than his necessary food.

- **Psalm 119:128**

"Therefore I **esteem** all *thy* precepts *concerning* all *things to be* right; *and* I hate every false way."

David also put great value on God's Words.

- **Matthew 6:19-20**

"Lay not up for yourselves treasures upon earth, where moth and rust doth corrupt, and where thieves break through and steal: But lay up for yourselves treasures in heaven, where neither moth nor rust doth corrupt, and where thieves do not break through nor steal: For where your treasure is, there will your heart be also."

This is a warning from the Lord Jesus Christ about the value of earthly treasures versus Heavenly treasures.

- **Colossians 2:3**

"In whom are hid all the treasures of wisdom and knowledge."

This refers to the Lord Jesus Christ. This is no doubt why Moses **esteemed** the treasures of Christ his Messiah, greater riches than the treasures of Egypt. The Lord Jesus Christ has far more treasures than anything in Egypt.

Notice, in this verse, that Moses had **"respect"** unto the recompence of the reward. The Greek Word for **"respect"** is APOBLEPO. Some of the meanings of this Word are:

"1) to turn the eyes away from other things and fix them on some one thing; 1a) to look at attentively; 2) to look with steadfast mental gaze."

LOOKING UNTO CHRIST THE MESSIAH

Being in the Greek present tense, it indicates that Moses constantly turned his eyes away from the things of Egypt, and fixed them attentively and steadfastly on the things of Christ, his Messiah, that his mother evidently had taught him about. Likewise, every truly born-again Christian should be constantly looking unto Jesus, the Author and Finisher of their faith (Hebrews 12:2a)

Hebrews 11:27

"By faith he forsook Egypt, not fearing the wrath of the king: for he endured, as seeing him who is invisible."

INVISIBLE

MOSES SAW THE INVISIBLE ONE

Moses didn't fear the wrath of the king of Egypt. He forsook Egypt and endured. He saw the invisible God of Heaven. How can you see someone who is invisible? You cannot see the unseen except by faith and that's how Moses saw the invisible God. It was by his faith.

- Exodus 2:15b

"But Moses fled from the face of Pharaoh,"
<u>Pharaoh would have killed Moses if he had not left Egypt.</u>

Hebrews—Preaching Verse by Verse

- **Romans 1:20**

"For the **invisible** things of him from the creation of the world are clearly seen, being understood by the things that are made, *even* his eternal power and Godhead; so that they are without excuse:"

INVISIBLE THINGS CLEARLY SEEN

This verse also talks about invisible things being clearly seen. I ask a third time, how can the invisible things be clearly seen? Everything that is made in this world is made up of unseen things.

- **Colossians 1:15**

"Who is the image of the **invisible** God, the firstborn of every creature:"

THE FATHER'S IMAGE MADE VISIBLE

God the Father is invisible yet, through the incarnation of the Lord Jesus Christ, God the Father's image has been made visible.

- **Colossians 1:16**

"For by him were all things created, that are in heaven, and that are in earth, visible and **invisible**, whether *they be* thrones, or dominions, or principalities, or powers: all things were created by him, and for him."

This verse refers to the Lord Jesus Christ. He created everything that was created, both the **invisible** things as well as the visible things. By faith, Moses saw Him Who is invisible.

- **1 Timothy 1:17**

"Now unto the King eternal, immortal, **invisible**, the only wise God, *be* honour and glory for ever and ever. Amen"

By faith, Moses saw the **invisible** eternal King of Heaven.

- **Titus 2:13**

"Looking for that blessed hope, and the glorious appearing of the great God and our Saviour Jesus Christ;"

> **THE RAPTURE OF THE SAVED ONES**
>
> One day, the Lord Jesus Christ, the great God and Saviour, will appear to those who are genuinely saved by faith in Him. Though He is invisible to them now, at the rapture of the saved ones, they will behold Him.

- Hebrews 12:2a

"Looking unto Jesus the author and finisher of *our* faith;"
Those who are truly saved are to look unto the Lord Jesus Christ by faith day by day. He will sustain and help them.

- 1 Peter 1:8

"Whom having **not seen**, ye love, in whom, though now ye **see him** not, yet believing, ye rejoice with joy unspeakable and full of glory:"

> **LOVE WITHOUT SEEING**
>
> Truly saved Christians today can love the Lord Jesus Christ even though they have never seen Him with their eyes. It reminds me of Thomas who had to see Him to believe in His bodily resurrection.

- John 20:25

"The other disciples therefore said unto him, We have seen the Lord. But he said unto them, Except I shall see in his hands the print of the nails, and put my finger into the print of the nails, and thrust my hand into his side, I will not believe."

> **THE DOUBT OF THOMAS**
>
> The apostle Thomas doubted the bodily resurrection of the Lord Jesus Christ. The second Sunday evening service, the disciples were gathered, and the Lord Jesus appeared through the walls, because the door was shut. He could do that because of His resurrected body.

- **John 20:26-29**

"And after eight days again his disciples were within, and Thomas with them: *then* came Jesus, the doors being shut, and stood in the midst, and said, Peace *be* unto you. Then saith he to Thomas, Reach hither thy finger, and behold my hands; and reach hither thy hand, and thrust it into my side: and be not faithless, but believing. And Thomas answered and said unto him, My Lord and my God. Jesus saith unto him, Thomas, because thou hast seen me, thou hast believed: blessed *are* they that **have not seen**, and *yet* have believed."

FAITH WITHOUT SEEING

May those of us who are genuine Christians learn the lesson that Thomas learned. We must believe, by true faith, without seeing.

Hebrews 11:28

"Through faith he kept the passover, and the sprinkling of blood, lest he that destroyed the firstborn should touch them."

PASSOVER

Moses kept the **passover** that God commanded of him. God told Moses that He was going to slay the eldest son of all the people of Egypt. He had to believe by faith that was going to happen. To prevent this from happening to His people, Israel, each household was to take a clean and perfect lamb. After a few days, they were to kill the lamb and put some of the lamb's blood on the top and side posts of their doors.

SAFETY THROUGH THE APPLIED BLOOD

God told Moses that when He sees the blood on the door, that house would be spared. God would not slay the firstborn in that home. Because Moses believed what God told him, he obeyed His commands to the letter.

- **Exodus 12:11**

"And thus shall ye eat it; *with* your loins girded, your shoes on your feet, and your staff in your hand; and ye shall eat it in haste: it is the LORD's **passover**."

- **Exodus 12:12-13**

"For I will pass through the land of Egypt this night, and will smite all the firstborn in the land of Egypt, both man and beast; and against all the gods of Egypt I will execute judgment: I am the LORD. And the blood shall be to you for a token upon the houses where ye *are*: and when I see the blood, I will **pass over** you, and the plague shall not be upon you to destroy *you*, when I smite the land of Egypt."

THE BLOOD, NOT THE LAMB SLAIN

God looked at the blood of the lamb properly applied on the door. He did not look at the lamb that was slain. This is the serious error of John MacArthur, who erroneously believes that blood doesn't mean blood. It is just a synonym for death. God said when He sees the blood applied He would pass over them. The understanding of the Word for "*pass over*" is the idea of hovering over for protection so the death angel would not slay that family.

Hebrews 11:29

"**By faith they passed through the Red sea as by dry land; which the Egyptians assaying to do were drowned.**"

GOD'S OPENING OF THE RED SEA

Moses was told by the Lord to stretch forth his hand to the Red Sea and it would part in two. He believed God, and by faith, he did it. God parted the Red Sea so that Israel could pass through it as by dry land. God fulfilled His promise to Moses.

- **Exodus 14:16**

"But lift thou up thy rod, and stretch out thine hand over the sea, and divide it and the children of Israel shall go on dry *ground* through the midst of the sea."

Moses obeyed the Lord. He did not argue with the Lord.

- **Exodus 13:18a**

"But God led the people about, *through* the way of the wilderness of the Red Sea:"

- **Exodus 14:27a**

"And Moses stretched forth his hand over the sea, and the sea returned to his strength when the morning appeared;"

After the Israelites had gone through the Red Sea, the Egyptians went into the Red Sea in pursuit of them. It was then that the Lord overthrew the Egyptians in the midst of the sea. The sea returned in full strength, covering the chariots, the horsemen, and all the host of Pharaoh. Not one remained alive.

ISRAEL SAW GOD'S MIRACLE

Israel saw the great work which the Lord did upon the Egyptians. After this miracle, the Israelites believed the Lord and his truth, at least for a while.

Hebrews 11:30

"By faith the walls of Jericho fell down, after they were compassed about seven days."

JERICHO

By faith, Joshua did exactly what God told him to do. God told Joshua that He was going to make the wall of **Jericho** to collapse. God explained to Joshua just how He was going to do it.

1. First, Joshua was to circle the city of **Jericho** seven times.
2. Second, the people were not to utter a single word.
3. Third, on the seventh time around the wall, when the priests blew the trumpets the people were to give a great shout.
4. Fourth, **Jericho's** wall fell down flat.

> **THE COLLAPSE OF JERICHO'S WALL**
> Joshua followed all the things that God told him to do and God did that which He told Joshua He would do. Jericho's wall fell down flat, defying all the known laws of physics. It was a miracle performed by God Himself.

- Joshua 6:15-16, 20

"And it came to pass on the seventh day, that they rose early about the dawning of the day, and compassed the **city** after the same manner seven times: only on that day they compassed the **city** seven times. And it came to pass at the seventh time, when the priests blew with the trumpets, Joshua said unto the people, Shout; for the LORD hath given you the **city**. . . . 6:20 So the people shouted when *the priests* blew with the trumpets: and it came to pass, when the people heard the sound of the trumpet, and the people shouted with a great shout, that the wall fell down flat, so that the people went up into the **city**, every man straight before him, and they took the **city**."

Can you imagine the people on that wall looking at the people of Israel, walking around the wall seven times? I'm sure they were wondering, what these people were doing.

Hebrews 11:31

"By faith the harlot Rahab perished not with them that believed not, when she had received the spies with peace."

RAHAB

The harlot **Rahab** was one of the inhabitants of Jericho that did not perish in the Israelites' assault on the city. This was because **she** hid the spies that came to spy out the city.

- Joshua 6:17b

"only **Rahab** the **harlot** shall live, she and all that are with her in the house, because she hid the messengers that we sent."

> **RAHAB'S THREE REQUIREMENTS**
>
> There were three things that this converted harlot had to do to preserve her life and that of her family.
>
> 1. Rahab had to let down a scarlet thread from her window
> 2. Rahab had to hide the two spies of Israel.
> 3. Rahab could not tell anyone about these spies.
>
> When those three things, by faith, were accomplished. She would be spared as well as those who were in her home.

- **Joshua 6:23**

"And the young men that were spies went in, and brought out **Rahab**, and her father, and her mother, and her brethren, and all that she had, and they brought out all her kindred, and left them without the camp of Israel."

- **Joshua 6:24-25**

"And they burnt the city with fire, and all that was therein only the silver, and the gold, and the vessels of brass and of iron, they put into the treasury of the house of the LORD. And Joshua saved **Rahab** the **harlot** alive, and her father's household, and all that she had; and she dwelled in Israel *even* unto this day, because she hid the messengers, which Joshua sent to spy out Jericho."

Notice that Joshua sent only two messengers to spy out the land rather than twelve like Moses sent. Of the ten, only two gave a true report to Moses. They urged him to go into Canaan and capture it. Joshua and Caleb were the two with a good report. Perhaps for this reason, Joshua sent out only two men.

> **RAHAB'S LIFE WAS CHANGED**
>
> I believe Rahab's heart and life was changed by the Lord at this time. Her life was spared and was changed from harlotry to following the Lord God of Israel.

Hebrews 11:32

"And what shall I more say? for the time would fail me to tell of Gedeon, and *of* Barak, and *of* Samson, and *of* Jephthae; *of* David also, and Samuel, and *of* the prophets."

Paul now sums up six and more Old Testament people of faith. Here are their names [using the Greek spellings]: (1) Gedeon; (2) Barak; (3) Samson; (4) Jephthae; (5) David; (6) Samuel and other prophets.

1. GIDEON

- **Judges 7:7**

"And the LORD said unto **Gideon**, by the three hundred men that lapped will I save you, and deliver the Midianites into **thine** hand: and let all the *other* people go every man unto his place."

Gideon started out with 22,000 men. God told him that was too many. The ones that were fearful, went home and there were 10,000 left out of the 22,000. Then God said for the 10,000 to go down to the river and drink some water. Most of them put their heads down to the water and drank. Those men were sent home.

THE TEST FOR GIDEON'S ARMY

Only those men who looked around with their heads up and lapped the water with their hands were to be part of Gideon's army.

There were only 300 of the 10,000 who drank in this cautious way. 9,700 were disqualified. By faith in the Words and commands of God, **Gideon** and his 300 men were victorious over many thousands of the enemies.

2. BARAK

- **Judges 4:2-3**

"And the LORD sold them into the hand of Jabin king of Canaan, that reigned in Hazor; the captain of whose host was Sisera, which dwelt in Harosheth of the Gentiles. And the children of Israel cried unto the LORD: for he had nine hundred chariots of iron; and twenty years he mightily oppressed the children of Israel."

Sisera was a formidable foe with 900 chariots of iron and many in his army. But **Barak**, in faith, did all that God told him to do. Because of this, God wrought a great victory over Sisera.

- **Judges 4:7**

"And I will draw unto thee to the river Kishon Sisera, the captain of Jabin's army, with his chariots and his multitude; and I will deliver him into **thine** hand."

> **BARAK'S VICTORY OVER SISERA**
>
> Because Barak was faithful in obedience to the Lord, God delivered Sisera and his great army into his hands.

3. SAMSON

There are many things the Bible mentions in the life of **Samson** in the book of Judges. The Philistines put out his eyes, bound him with chains, and was made to work in hard labor. At the feast of Dagon, **Samson** prayed that the Lord would strengthen him once more so he could bring down the pillars of the house where about three thousand men and women were worshipping Dagon. God answered **Samson's** prayer and allowed him to bring down the pillars of the house thus killing himself and also his Philistine enemies.

I believe the part of his life that evidences his faith in the Lord is mentioned in the following verses.

- **Judges 16:21-30**

"But the Philistines took him, and put out his eyes, and brought him down to Gaza, and bound him with fetters of brass; and he did grind in the prison house. Howbeit the hair of his head began to grow again after he was shaven. Then the lords of the Philistines gathered them together for to offer a great sacrifice unto Dagon their god, and to rejoice: for they said, Our god hath delivered **Samson** our enemy into our hand. And when the people saw him, they praised their god: for they said, Our god hath delivered into our hands our enemy, and the destroyer of our country, which slew many of us. And it came to pass, when their hearts were merry, that they said, Call for **Samson**, that he may make us sport. And they called for

Samson out of the prison house; and he made them sport: and they set him between the pillars. And **Samson** said unto the lad that held him by the hand, Suffer me that I may feel the pillars whereupon the house standeth, that I may lean upon them. Now the house was full of men and women; and all the lords of the Philistines were there; and *there were* upon the roof about three thousand men and women, that beheld while **Samson** made sport. And **Samson** called unto the LORD, and said, O Lord GOD, remember me, I pray thee, and strengthen me, I pray thee, only this once, O God, that I may be at once avenged of the Philistines for my two eyes. And **Samson** took hold of the two middle pillars upon which the house stood, and on which it was borne up, of the one with his right hand, and of the other with his left. And **Samson** said, Let me die with the Philistines. And he bowed himself with *all his* might; and the house fell upon the lords, and upon all the people that *were* therein. So the dead which he slew at his death were more than *they* which he slew in his life."

4. JEPHTHAH

The verses below, in Judges 11, sum up **Jephthah's** faith in the power of the Lord . He vowed a vow unto the Lord and asked God to deliver the Ammonites into his hand. The Lord answered his prayer of faith.

- **Judges 11:29-32**

"Then the Spirit of the LORD came upon **Jephthah**, and he passed over Gilead, and Manasseh, and passed over Mizpeh of Gilead, and from Mizpeh of Gilead he passed over *unto* the children of Ammon. And **Jephthah** vowed a vow unto the LORD, and said, If thou shalt without fail deliver the children of Ammon into mine hands, then it shall be, that whosoever cometh forth of the doors of my house to meet me, when I return in peace from the children of Ammon, shall surely be the LORD'S, and I will offer it up for a burnt offering. So **Jephthah** passed over unto the children of Ammon to fight against them; and the LORD delivered them into his hands."

5. DAVID

DAVID DEFEATS GOLIATH

The verses below show David's faith in the battle with the giant Goliath the Philistine. God had given David victory over a lion and a bear and he had faith that God would deliver Goliath into his hand as well. The battle is and was the Lord's on that occasion. David truly was a man of strong faith in his God. By faith, this young man, with just a sling and five smooth stones, slew that giant. David was truly a man of faith and is rightly mentioned here in this catalog of faithful people.

- 1 Samuel 17:37, 45-47, 50

"**David** said moreover, The LORD that delivered me out of the paw of the lion, and out of the paw of the bear, he will deliver me out of the hand of this Philistine. And Saul said unto **David**, Go, and the LORD be with thee. . . . (45) Then said **David** to the Philistine, Thou comest to me with a sword, and with a spear, and with a shield: but I come to thee in the name of the LORD of hosts, the God of the armies of Israel, whom thou hast defied. (46) This day will the LORD deliver thee into mine hand; and I will smite thee, and take thine head from thee; and I will give the carcases of the host of the Philistines this day unto the fowls of the air, and to the wild beasts of the earth; that all the earth may know that there is a God in Israel. (47) And all this assembly shall know that the LORD saveth not with sword and spear: for the battle *is* the LORD'S, and he will give you into our hands. . . . (50) So **David** prevailed over the Philistine with a sling and with a stone, and smote the Philistine, and slew him; but *there was* no sword in the hand of **David**."

6. SAMUEL

Samuel was the last of the judges. He was brought into the temple by his mother to serve the Lord. **He was a man of faith** and loved the Words of God as this verse indicates.

- **1 Samuel 3:19**

"And **Samuel** grew, and the LORD was with **him**, and did let none of **his** words fall to the ground."

7. OTHER PROPHETS

Other prophets are mentioned in general but not named. They would include **Daniel**, Jeremiah, Isaiah, Ezekiel, and many unnamed others. Then it mentions other prophets. **Daniel's** walk of faith with the Lord was amazing to see. <u>The verses below summarize some of **Daniel's** trials and victories.</u>

- **Daniel 6:7, 10, 16-17, 19-22**

"All the presidents of the kingdom, the governors, and the princes, the counsellors, and the captains, have consulted together to establish a royal statute, and to make a firm decree, that whosoever shall ask a petition of any God or man for thirty days, save of thee, O king, he shall be cast into the den of lions. . . . (10) Now when **Daniel** knew that the writing was signed, he went into his house; and his windows being open in his chamber toward Jerusalem, he kneeled upon his knees three times a day, and prayed, and gave thanks before his God, as he did aforetime. . . . (16-17) Then the king commanded, and they brought **Daniel**, and cast *him* into the den of lions. *Now* the king spake and said unto **Daniel,** Thy God whom thou servest continually, he will deliver thee. And a stone was brought, and laid upon the mouth of the den; and the king sealed it with his own signet, and with the signet of his lords; that the purpose might not be changed concerning **Daniel**. . . . (19-22) Then the king arose very early in the morning, and went in haste unto the den of lions. And when he came to the den, he cried with a lamentable voice unto **Daniel**: *and* the king spake and said to **Daniel**, O **Daniel**, **servant** of the living God, is thy God, whom thou servest continually, able to deliver thee from the lions? Then said **Daniel** unto the king, O king, live for ever. My God hath sent his angel, and hath shut the lions' mouths, that they have not hurt me: forasmuch as before him innocency was found in me; and also before thee, O king, have **I** done no hurt."

Hebrews 11:33

"Who through faith subdued kingdoms, wrought righteousness, obtained promises, stopped the mouths of lions,"

> ### OTHER OLD TESTAMENT MEN OF FAITH
> These Old Testament men subdued kingdoms, wrought righteousness, and obtained promises by faith.

The reference to stopping the mouths of lions was no doubt a reference to the prophet **Daniel**. The day after **Daniel** was thrown into the den of lions, the king went to the den. He couldn't sleep that night.

- **Daniel 6:20b**

"O **Daniel, servant of the living God**, is thy God, whom **thou** servest continually, able to deliver thee from the lions?" The answer is yes. God was able and is able to deliver **Daniel** or anyone else if it is His will.

- **Daniel 6:21-22**

"Then said **Daniel** unto the king, O king, live for ever. My God hath sent his angel, and hath shut the lions' mouths, that they have not hurt me: forasmuch as before him innocency was found in me; and also before thee, O king, have I done no hurt." God spared **Daniel** certain death because he continued praying unto the Lord even after the king ordered that no one should ask a request of anyone, including the Lord.

> ### DANIEL ESCAPED HUNGRY LIONS
> Some people say the lions didn't eat Daniel because they weren't hungry. This certainly a lie because when those who threw Daniel into the den were thrown in, they were killed even before they reached the bottom of the den.

Hebrews 11:34

"Quenched the violence of fire, escaped the edge of the sword, out of weakness were made strong, waxed valiant in fight, turned to flight the armies of the aliens."

SHADRACH, MESHACH, AND ABEDNEGO

Shadrach, Meshach, and Abednego were in the fiery furnace and God quenched the violence of fire. They were delivered from death.

Daniel 3:24-25

"Then Nebuchadnezzar the king was astonied, and rose up in haste, *and* spake, and said unto his counsellors, Did not we cast **three men** bound into the midst of the fire? They answered and said unto the king, True, O king. He answered and said, Lo, I see four **men** loose, walking in the midst of the fire, and they have no hurt; and the form of the fourth is like the Son of God."

The Lord Jesus Christ was there protecting these **three Hebrew children** who did not bow down to the king's image. The fire did not hurt **them**.

It is said of **these men of faith** that out of weakness they were made strong. The apostle Paul found this to be true as well.

- **2 Corinthians 12:10c**

"for when I am weak, then am I strong."

- **2 Corinthians 12:9b**

"Most gladly therefore will I rather glory in my infirmities, that the power of Christ may rest upon me."

These were **valiant men**. On many occasions in the Old Testament, God made it possible for His people Israel to defeat vastly greater and well-armed enemies. He made the armies of the aliens to flee.

Hebrews 11:35

"**Women received their dead raised to life again: and others were tortured, not accepting deliverance; that they might obtain a better resurrection:**"

A WOMAN AND HER CHILD

- **2 Kings 4:8, 17, 32-35**

"And it fell on a day, that Elisha passed to Shunem, where was a **great woman**; and she constrained him to eat bread. And *so it was, that* as oft as he passed by, he turned in thither to eat bread.... (17) And the **woman** conceived, and **bare a son** at that season that Elisha had said unto her, according to the time of life.... (32-35) And when Elisha was come into the house, behold, the **child** was dead, *and* laid upon his bed. He went in therefore, and shut the door upon them twain, and prayed unto the LORD. And he went up, and lay upon the **child**, and put his mouth upon his mouth, and his eyes upon his eyes, and his hands upon his hands: and he stretched himself upon the **child**; and the flesh of the **child** waxed warm. Then he returned, and walked in the house to and fro; and went up, and stretched himself upon him: and the **child** sneezed seven times, and the **child** opened **his** eyes."

Elisha was used of the Lord to bring this little **child** back to life once again.

JEREMIAH

Others were tortured, not accepting deliverance that they might obtain a better resurrection. **Jeremiah was one of the Old Testament prophets who was tortured by the king who despised the true words he was speaking from the Lord.** Jeremiah told Zedekiah the king the following words:

- **Jeremiah 38:3-6**

"Thus saith the LORD, This city shall surely be given into the hand of the king of Babylon's army, which shall take it. Therefore the princes said unto the king, We beseech thee, let this **man** be put to death: for thus he weakeneth the hands of the men of war that remain in this city, and the hands of all the people, in speaking such words unto them: for this **man** seeketh not the welfare of this people, but the hurt. Then Zedekiah the king said, Behold, he *is* in your hand: for the king *is* not *he that* can do *any* thing against you. Then took they **Jeremiah,** and cast him into the dungeon of Malchiah the son of Hammelech, that was in the court of the prison: and they let down **Jeremiah** with cords. And in the dungeon *there was* no water, but mire: so **Jeremiah** sunk in the mire."

Jeremiah was let down into a dungeon with no water. **Jeremiah** was sunk in the mire. This was certainly a torture for **him.**

JEREMIAH ESCAPES FROM THE PIT

Ebedmelech the Ethiopian, one of the eunuchs thought Jeremiah might die unless he was taken our of that dungeon prison.

- **Jeremiah 38:7-13**

"Now when Ebedmelech the Ethiopian, one of the eunuchs which was in the king's house, heard that they had put **Jeremiah** in the dungeon; the king then sitting in the gate of Benjamin; Ebedmelech went forth out of the king's house, and spake to the king, saying, My lord the king, these men have done evil in all that they have done to **Jeremiah** the **prophet,** whom they have cast into the dungeon; and he is like to die for hunger in the place where he is: for *there is* no more bread in the city. Then the king commanded Ebedmelech the Ethiopian, saying, Take from hence thirty men with thee, and take up **Jeremiah** the prophet out of the dungeon, before he die. So Ebedmelech took the men with him, and went into the house of the king under the treasury, and took thence old cast clouts and old rotten rags, and let them down by cords into the dungeon to **Jeremiah.** And Ebedmelech the Ethiopian said unto **Jeremiah,** Put now *these* old cast clouts and rotten rags under thine armholes under the cords. And **Jeremiah** did so. So they drew up **Jeremiah** with cords, and took him up out of the dungeon: and **Jeremiah** remained in the court of the prison."

Fortunately, God honored his men and his women of faith in the Old Testament. By faith all these things took place.

CHRISTIANS SHOULD BE FAITHFUL

Those who are genuine Christians today should take heed to themselves that they might continue faithful to the Lord Jesus Christ their Saviour, come what may.

Hebrews 11:36

"And others had trial of *cruel* mockings and scourgings, yea, moreover of bonds and imprisonment:"

CRUEL MOCKINGS

Many of the saints of the Old Testament had **cruel mockings**. Here are a few examples:

- **2 Kings 2:23**

"And he went up from thence unto Bethel: and as he was going up by the way, there came forth little children out of the city, and **mocked** him, and said unto him, Go up, thou bald head; go up, thou bald head."

- **2 Chronicles 30:10**

"So the posts passed from city to city through the country of Ephraim and Manasseh even unto Zebulun: but they laughed them to scorn, and **mocked** them."

- **2 Chronicles 36:16**

"But they **mocked** the messengers of God, and despised his words, and misused his prophets, until the wrath of the LORD arose against his people, till *there was* no remedy."

- **Jeremiah 20:7**

"O LORD, thou hast deceived me, and I was deceived: thou art stronger than I, and hast prevailed: I am in derision daily, every one **mocketh** me."

- **Jeremiah 38:19**

"And Zedekiah the king said unto Jeremiah, I am afraid of the Jews that are fallen to the Chaldeans, lest they deliver me into their hand, and they **mock** me."

- **Lamentations 1:7**

"Jerusalem remembered in the days of her affliction and of her miseries all her pleasant things that she had in the days of old, when her people fell into the hand of the enemy, and none did help her: the adversaries saw her, *and* did **mock** at her sabbaths."

PRISON

Some of the Old Testament believers were put into **prison**. Here are a few illustrations of this:

- **Genesis 39:20**

"And Joseph's master took him, and put him into the **prison**, a place where the king's **prisoners** *were* bound: and he was there in the **prison**."

- **Judges 16:21**

"But the Philistines took him, and put out his eyes, and brought him down to Gaza, and bound him with fetters of brass; and he did grind in the **prison** house."

- **1 Kings 22:27**

"And say, Thus saith the king, Put this *fellow* in the **prison**, and feed him with bread of affliction and with water of affliction, until I come in peace."

- **2 Kings 17:4**

"And the king of Assyria found conspiracy in Hoshea: for he had sent messengers to So king of Egypt, and brought no present to the king of Assyria, as *he had done* year by year: therefore the king of Assyria shut him up, and bound him in **prison**."

- **2 Chronicles 16:10**

"Then Asa was wroth with the seer, and put him in a **prison** house; for *he was* in a rage with him because of this *thing*. And Asa oppressed *some* of the people the same time."

- **2 Chronicles 18:26**

"And say, Thus saith the king, Put this *fellow* in the **prison**, and feed him with bread of affliction and with water of affliction, until I return in peace."

- **Isaiah 42:22**

"But this is a people robbed and spoiled; *they are* all of them snared in holes, and they are hid in **prison** houses: they are for a prey, and none delivereth; for a spoil, and none saith, Restore."

- **Jeremiah 29:26**

"The LORD hath made thee priest in the stead of Jehoiada the priest, that ye should be officers in the house of the LORD, for every man *that* is mad, and maketh himself a prophet, that thou shouldest put him in **prison**, and in the stocks.

- **Jeremiah 32:2**

"For then the king of Babylon's army besieged Jerusalem: and Jeremiah the prophet was shut up in the court of the **prison**, which was in the king of Judah's house."

- **Jeremiah 33:1**

"Moreover the word of the LORD came unto Jeremiah the second time, while he was yet shut up in the court of the **prison**, saying,"

Genuinely saved people today are often mocked by those who are unbelievers.

OUR GOVERNMENT'S 72 TERRORIST GROUPS

Their future could be imprisonment by the present administration in our country. The reason for this is that one of the 72 groups of people whom this administration deems to be *"potential terrorists"* are *"evangelical Christians."* The nature of their possible imprisonment is dictated by the NDAA (National Defense Authorization Act). According to this law, prisons are now able to be filled without charges filed, without a trial, without a lawyer being used, and imprisonment for an indefinite time in a prison anywhere in the world.

Despite this potential **imprisonment**, truly born-again Christians should not cease from preaching the gospel of the Lord Jesus Christ clearly and without compromise. They should also continue to expose every sin and evil contained in the Words of God, despite those who are in favor of those sins. This includes the sin of homosexuality and homosexual marriages.

> **NINE REPEATED N.T. COMMANDS**
> It includes all nine of the clear commands of the Old Testament that are repeated in the New Testament. If these things prevail with genuine Christians, they will find themselves opposed to all forms of immorality being believed and practiced by the present administration in our country.

They must faithfully obey the following verse:
- Ephesians 5:11

"And have no fellowship with the unfruitful works of darkness, but rather reprove *them*."

Hebrews 11:37

"They were stoned, they were sawn asunder, were tempted, were slain with the sword: they wandered about in sheepskins and goatskins; being destitute, afflicted, tormented;"

In these verses, Paul talks about many Old Testament saints that he did not even name. Yet they had trials of cruel mockings, scourgings, bonds, and imprisonments. Most of us who are truly saved today will not be named after we go Home to Heaven. When genuine Christians die and are buried who will remember, who they were, what they did, or what they said? But these recorded in the Old Testament walked by faith in their God. True Christians today should walk by faith as well, despite persecutions or upsets that might occur to them.

Hebrews 11:38

"(Of whom the world was not worthy:) they wandered in deserts, and *in* mountains, and *in* dens and caves of the earth."

THE WORLD WAS NOT WORTHY

Concerning all these unnamed Old Testament people who walked by true faith in the Lord God of Heaven and earth, **the world was not** worthy. Their place was in Heaven with the Lord, not on earth with the unbelieving crowd. They wandered in deserts, in mountains, in dens, and in caves of the earth. They had no certain dwelling place. Remember the gospel song that we sometimes sing says: *"Take the world, but give me Jesus."*

> **MISFITS IN THIS WORLD**
>
> These people of faith didn't rightly fit into this world. They were separated to the Lord and His causes. They looked to the Lord and saw Him who is invisible, wandering about throughout the earth.

Hebrews 11:39

"And these all, having obtained a good report through faith, received not the promise:"

FUTURE PROMISES

Paul sums up the list of all he has referred to--the named as well as the unnamed. Through faith, they all obtained a good report from the Lord, yet they didn't receive His **promise** of blessing and Heaven. These people followed God's rules about proper offerings which looked forward to and pointed to the Lamb of God, the Lord Jesus Christ Who died fo the sins of the world.

They did not see the coming of the Saviour, though they looked for Him as the **promised** Seed of Abraham. They didn't see Him. We who are genuinely saved and living today have seen Him only through eyes of faith. He came from Heaven into this world. He died for the sins of the world. We have the twenty-seven books of the New Testament that speak about His life, His death, and His coming again. The **promise** for the genuine born-again Christians today is a Home in Heaven when they die or when the Lord Jesus Christ returns in the rapture for all the truly saved ones. That is a wonderful **promise** that the Lord will fulfill in His time.

Hebrews 11:40

"God having provided some better thing for us, that they without us should not be made perfect."

SOME BETTER THING

LOOKING FOR A BETTER THING

These Old Testament heroes of faith did not see the sacrifice of our Saviour. They didn't see the cross of Calvary. They didn't see the Lamb of God Who taketh away the sins of the world. They had a good testimony by faith, but God has provided some better thing for us. Paul says we have a *better thing*. We have a Saviour. We have a Heaven that we know about from the New Testament Scriptures.

- John 14:1-3

"Let not your heart be troubled: ye believe in God, believe also in me. In my father's house are many mansions: if *it were* not *so*, I would have told you. I go to prepare a place for you. And If I go and prepare a place for you, I will come again, and receive you unto myself, that where I am, *there* ye may be also."

The disciples asked how they could know the way to Heaven.

- John 14:6

"Jesus saith unto him, I am the way, the truth, and the life: no man cometh unto the Father, but by me."

HEAVEN IS THAT BETTER THING

I believe that Heaven is that *better thing* mentioned in this verse. Genuine trust in the Lord Jesus Christ Who is the way, the truth, and the life is the only way to gain access to God the Father and His Heaven.

Paul knew about **Heaven** because after being stoned by his enemies, having died, he went to **Heaven** and saw all the glories of that **Heavenly Home**.

- **Acts 14:19**

"And there came thither *certain* Jews from Antioch and Iconium, who persuaded the people, and, having stoned Paul, drew *him* out of the city, supposing he had been dead."

- **2 Corinthians 12:2**

"I knew a man in Christ above fourteen years ago, (whether in the body, I cannot tell; or whether out of the body, I cannot tell: God knoweth;) such an one caught up to the **third heaven**."

PAUL SAW HEAVEN'S GLORIES

Paul saw all the wonderful things of Glory, but he was forbidden to reveal all of them. He know that it was better to die and go Home to Heaven than to live on this earth.

- **Philippians 1:21**

"For to me to live *is* Christ, and to die *is* gain."

He knew for certain that **Heaven** was a gain. God the **Father's House** in **Heaven** has enough room for all those who truly put their trust in His Son as their Saviour. If the whole world would truly trust in the Lord Jesus Christ as their Saviour and Redeemer, there would be room for them. Yes, God has provided **some better thing** for us who are truly saved.

We are living in these latter days. The Lord has given us all His revelation in the Bible.

OLD TESTAMENT FUTURE PROMISES

Those of the Old Testament did not have all the truth that we have today. They just had faith and some promises and revelations in the Old Testament. Whatever God told them to do, they did it. That's what true Christians should do today. They should walk by faith in strict obedience to God's revealed will in His Words.

They today must walk as they of the Old Testament. They must walk by faith in all of God's Words and promises as seeing Him Who is invisible.

Hebrews
Chapter Twelve

Hebrews 12:1

"Wherefore seeing we also are compassed about with so great a cloud of witnesses, let us lay aside every weight, and the sin which doth so easily beset us, and let us run with patience the race that is set before us,"

COMPASSED ABOUT

Paul informs these genuine Christians that they are surrounded in Heaven by a great cloud of witnesses. He mentions this in Chapter 11. Notice that we are compassed about by so great a cloud of witnesses. There are a total of eighteen different witnesses of faithful people that are mentioned in chapter 11. These people of faith **compass** believers of faith in this age also.

- **Psalm 139:5**
"Thou hast beset me behind and before, and laid thine hand upon me."

WEIGHT

The Lord Himself surrounds the true Christian. But there are also people today who are looking at them and wondering if they who are genuinely saved are able to live up to the standards set by those Old Testament people of faith. Paul makes a suggestion. He says that those true Christians he is addressing should lay aside every weight as well as every sin that so easily surrounds them. After that, they are to run with patience the races set before them.

The Greek Word for *"weight"* is ONKOS. Some of the meanings of this Word are:

> "*1) whatever is prominent, protuberance, bulk, mass; 1a) hence a burden, weight, encumbrance.*"

> **WEIGHTS TO LAY ASIDE**
>
> These weights or heavy burdens should not be found on those who are trying to run in a race. These weights hold down the runner and diminish his speed. When you are running, you don't need any extra weights or even sins that so easily surrounds even truly saved Christians. People should leave both weights and sins behind when running a race.

RUN

Then Paul says how those who are truly saved should **run** the race. This is in the Greek present tense. <u>It indicates continuous **running** without letting up.</u> The Greek Word for **"*run*"** is TRECHO. Some of the meanings for this Word are:

> *"1) to run; 1a) of persons in haste; 1b) of those who run in a race course; 2) metaph; 2a) of doctrine rapidly propagated; 2b) by a metaphor taken from runners in a race, to exert one's self, strive hard; 2c) to spend one's strength in performing or attaining something; 2d) word occurs in Greek writings denoting to incur extreme peril, which it requires the exertion of all one's effort to overcome."*

> **RUNNING OUR RACE**
>
> Every genuine Christian has a course to run. There are different courses for each one, but each must run his own race in his own race course. Not only must he continuously run that race set before him, but he must run his race with patience. That is easier said than done. Patient running is very difficult.

- **1 Corinthians 9:24**

"Know ye not that they which **run** in a race **run** all, but one receiveth the prize? So **run**, that ye may obtain."

- **1 Corinthians 9:26**

"I therefore so **run**, not as uncertainly, so fight I, not as one that beateth the air:"

- **Philippians 2:16**

"Holding forth the word of life; that I may rejoice in the day of Christ, that I have not **run** in vain, neither labored in vain."

Paul himself set up that at Philippi. He wanted each genuine Christian in that church of Philippi to hold forth the Words of life. This necessitates the right preserved Hebrew, Aramaic, and Greek Words as well as proper translation of those Words into the language of the Christian. In English, this would be the King James Bible. If the Words of God were to be no longer held forth, Paul would have **run** and labored in vain. He did not want this to happen.

Hebrews 12:2

"Looking unto Jesus the author and finisher of *our* faith; who for the joy that was set before him endured the cross, despising the shame, and is set down at the right hand of the throne of God."

JESUS THE AUTHOR AND FINISHER OF OUR FAITH

LOOKING UNTO JESUS

As true Christians run with patience the race that is set before them, they are to be looking at the finish line and the Lord Jesus Christ Who is watching the progress of each runner. He is both the Author and the Finisher of the Christian's faith. As the Author, He devised the way of salvation for all mankind. As the Finisher, He finished the basis for that salvation by taking in His own body the sins of the whole world on the cross of Calvary. This is the meaning of His Words from the cross, *"It is finished."*

The purpose of the **Lord Jesus Christ's** ignominious death on the cross was for the *joy* that was set before Him. Even in what people might call the saddest event in the world, **the Lord Jesus Christ** found it to be joy that was set before Him. He knew that through that death, those who truly trusted in Him would be made the sons and daughters of God who He would bring into the glories of Heaven. Because of this, the Lord Jesus Christ *"endured the cross, despising the shame."* After His bodily resurrection, He sat down at the right hand of God the Father, showing that His sacrifice for the sins of the world was thoroughly acceptable and approved by the Father.

LOOKING TO THE LORD
- **Psalm 34:5**

"They **looked** unto him, and were lightened: and their faces were not ashamed."

The genuine Christian should constantly **look** unto the Lord.

- **Isaiah 17:7-8**

"At that day shall a man **look** to his Maker, and his eyes shall have respect for the Holy One of Israel. And he shall not look to the altars, the work of his hands, neither shall respect *that* which his fingers have made, either the groves, or the images."

- **Isaiah 45:22**

"**Look** unto me, and be ye saved, all the ends of the earth: for I *am* God, and *there is* none else."

- **Micah 7:7**

"Therefore I will **look** unto the LORD; I will wait for the God of my salvation: my God will hear me."

- **Zachariah 12:10**

"And I will pour upon the house of David, and upon the inhabitants of Jerusalem, the spirit of grace and of supplications: and they shall **look** upon me whom they have pierced, and they shall mourn for him, as one mourneth for *his* only *son*, and shall be in bitterness for him, as one that is in bitterness for *his* firstborn."

Israel one day will **look** upon **the Lord Jesus Christ Whom** they pierced. They will truly trust in **Him** to be saved.

THE FINISHER
- **John 17:4**

"I have glorified thee on the earth: I have **finished** the work which thou gavest **me** to do."

- **John 19:30**

"When **Jesus** therefore had received the vinegar, he said, It is **finished**: and **he** bowed **his** head, and gave up the ghost."

The Greek Word for "*finished*" is in the Greek perfect tense. This tense speaks of an act begun in the past, with results right up to the present, and continued on into the future.

> **LOOKING WHILE RUNNING**
>
> Genuine Christians must look unto the Lord Jesus Christ as they run their race. They should not look to the decrees of the Pope, the traditions of Rome, to books from Christian Science, or to any other heretical doctrines or personalities. They must look exclusively and only to the Lord Jesus Christ their Saviour and His inerrant and preserved Words.

Hebrews 12:3

"For consider him that endured such contradiction of sinners against himself, lest ye be wearied and faint in your minds."

CONSIDER

The Greek Word for "*consider*" is in the present tense. It indicates that this is to be a continuous action. The Greek Word for "*consider*" is ANALOGIZOMAI. Some of the meanings of this Word are:

"*1) to think over, consider, ponder.*"

The One that genuine Christians are to think over, ponder, and consider is the Lord Jesus Christ. They are to think about Him Who endured such contradiction of sinners against Himself.

> **CHRIST OPPOSED STRONGLY**
>
> The Lord Jesus Christ did not have it easy during his three and one-half years of ministry on earth. He was continually opposed, contradicted, and condemned by the leaders of the Jews. These continuous contradictions culminated in His being crucified on the cross at Calvary.

FAINT AND WEARY

The true Christians' contradictions and oppositions cannot compare with those experienced by the Lord Jesus Christ.

> **DON'T BE WEARIED**
>
> By continuously considering the Lord Jesus Christ's enduring such persecution, the true Christians will be helped lest they be wearied and faint in their minds.

The Greek Word for *"faint"* is EKLUO. Some of the meanings of this Word are:

> *"1) to loose, unloose, to set free; 2) to dissolve, metaph., to weaken, relax, exhaust; 2a) to have one's strength relaxed, to be enfeebled through exhaustion, to grow weak, grow weary, be tired out; 2b) to despond, become faint hearted."*

The verb is in the Greek present tense which implies a continuous state of being **faint**, enfeebled, exhausted and despondent. God does not want his true Christians to continue in this condition.

He doesn't want them to be **weary** either. There a number of verses on **weariness and fainting**.

- **Job 10:1a**

"My soul is **weary** of my life;"

He was in pain and suffering. He got **weary** of his life.

- **Isaiah 40:28-29**

"Hast thou not known? Hast thou not heard, *that* the everlasting God, the LORD, the Creator of the ends of the earth, fainteth not, neither is **weary**? *There* is no searching of his understanding. He giveth power to the **faint**; and to *them that have* no might he increaseth strength."

GOD IS NOT FAINT OR WEARY

Our God does not faint nor grow weary. He has everlasting strength. He can give power and increased strength to those true Christians who put their trust in Him.

- **Isaiah 40:30-31**

"Even the youths shall **faint** and be **weary**, and the young men shall utterly fall: But they that wait upon the LORD shall renew *their* strength; they shall mount up with wings as eagles; they shall run, and not be **weary**; *and* they shall walk, and not **faint**."

Waiting upon the Lord will enable the truly born-again Christians to be able to mount up with wings as eagles and not to be **weary** or **faint**. What a glorious promise!

- **Galatians 6:9**

"And let us not be **weary** in well doing: for in due season we shall reap, if we **faint** not."

- **2 Thessalonians 3:13**

"But ye, brethren, be not **weary** in well doing."

Keep going. Don't be **weary**.

- **Proverbs 24:10**

"*If* thou **faint** in the day of adversity, thy strength *is* small."

- **Ephesians 3:13**

"Wherefore I desire that ye **faint** not at my tribulations for you, which is your glory."

Hebrews 12:4

"Ye have not yet resisted unto blood, striving against sin."

These true Christians to whom Paul was writing had not resisted and striven against sinful practices that led them to be slain.

CHRIST STROVE AGAINST MAN'S SINS

The Lord Jesus Christ, the Author and Finisher of their faith shed His sinless, incorruptible blood on the cross at Calvary because he strove against the sins of the Jewish leaders of His day.

Whatever suffering these Christians had was small in comparison to that of their Saviour.

Hebrews 12:5

"And ye have forgotten the exhortation which speaketh unto you as unto children, My son, despise not thou the chastening of the Lord, nor faint when thou art rebuked of him:"

CHASTENING AND FAINTING

In this verse, is the first of eight times the word, "*chasten*" is used in this section. These true Christians had evidently forgotten the exhortation that the Lord spoke to them as to His children. This is the background of God's teaching on **chastening**.

God's command on **chastening** is stated as *"Despise not thou the chastening of the Lord."* There are several things to point out here.

    1. **A Negative Prohibition.** The form of this command is that of a negative prohibition. It is in the Greek present tense. When a negative prohibition is in the Greek **present tense, it means to stop an action already in progress.** It means that these Christians were despising God's **chastening** and Paul told them to stop it. If the Greek negative prohibition is in the **aorist tense**, it would be not even to begin an action.

    2. **The Meaning Of Chastening.** The Greek Word for "**chastening**" is PAIDEIA. Some of the meanings of this Greek Word are:

> *"1) the whole training and education of children (which relates to the cultivation of mind and morals, and employs for this purpose now commands and admonitions, now reproof and punishment) It also includes the training and care of the body; 2) whatever in adults also cultivates the soul, esp. by correcting mistakes and curbing passions; 2a) instruction which aims at increasing virtue; 2b) chastisement, chastening, (of the evils with which God visits men for their amendment)."*

Apparently, these Christians were despising God's **chastening** because of their sin.

When the verse says "*nor faint,*" this is also a negative prohibition as before. The sense is that these persecuted true Christians were to stop their **fainting** when they are rebuked by the Lord. The Greek Word for "*faint*" is the same as in verse 4 above. The meanings are the same as well. The Lord is able to keep them from being weak, tired, and exhausted. As mentioned before, Isaiah 40 says it all.

- **Isaiah 40:30-31**

"Even the youths shall **faint** and be weary, and the young men shall utterly fall: But they that wait upon the LORD shall renew *their* strength; they shall mount up with wings as eagles;

they shall run, and not be weary; *and* they shall walk, and not faint."

CHASTENING

Chastening is not limited to this verse, but has a wide variety of uses throughout the Bible

- **Deuteronomy 8:5**

"Thou shalt also consider in thine heart, that, as a man **chasteneth** his son, *so* the LORD thy God **chasteneth** thee."

- **2 Samuel 7:14**

"I will be his father, and he shall be my son. If he commit iniquity, I will **chasten** him with the rod of men, and with the stripes of the children of men:"

- **Job 5:17**

"Behold, happy is the man whom God **correcteth**: therefore despise not thou the **chastening** of the Almighty:"

> **DON'T DESPISE GOD'S CORRECTION**
> When the Lord chastens His genuine Christians, they should be happy and not despise His correction.

- **Psalm 94:12**

"Blessed *is* the man whom thou **chastenest**, O LORD, and teachest him out of thy law;"

- **Proverbs 3:11**

"My son, despise not the **chastening** of the LORD; neither be weary of his **correction**."

- **Proverbs 13:24**

"He that spareth his rod hateth his son: but he that loveth him **chasteneth** him betimes."

It is terrible the way our government has forbidden the proper use of Scriptural **discipline** with our children. If you love your children, you will properly and Scripturally **chasten** them early, before it's too late.

- **Proverbs 19:18**

"**Chasten** thy son while there is hope, and let not thy soul spare for his crying."

> **PROPERLY DISCIPLINE YOUR CHILDREN**
>
> It's obvious that our children cry when they are disciplined. Often they cry even before the discipline begins. God says that parents are not to spare discipline because the children cry.

We have five adult children. Four are boys and one is a girl. My own policy on their **discipline** was as follows:

1. Only when they need it;
2. Always when they need it; and
3. Always in the proper Biblical manner.

All three of these policies were used on all five of our children. One of them is *with the Lord*. All those still living are born-again and walking with the Lord Jesus Christ. God honored our **discipline** of our children in this way.

- **1 Corinthians 11:32**

"But when we are judged, we are **chastened** of the Lord, that we should not be condemned with the world."

God wants us clean. He doesn't want us condemned with the world.

- **Revelation 3:19**

"As many as I love, I **rebuke and chasten**: be zealous therefore, and repent."

> **GOD CHASTENS THOSE HE LOVES**
>
> Our God loves His genuine Christian children. Because He loves them, he rebukes and chastens them. He wants them to walk properly in His path and in His will.

Hebrews 12:6

"For whom the Lord loveth he chasteneth, and scourgeth every son whom he receiveth."

The Great and Loving God of the Bible **chastens and scourges every one of His sons and daughters who genuinely are born-again as they might need it.** It is because of His love for them. That is His motivation. It was the same motivation that God the Father had when He sent His Son into the world to die for the sins of the entire world of people.

- **John 3:16**

"For God so loved the world, that he gave his only begotten Son, that whosoever believeth in him should not perish, but have everlasting life."

GOD TRAINS HIS CHILDREN

The meaning of the Greek Word for "*chasten*" was given in verse 5 previously. It is God's way of developing and training His true born-again sons and daughters to make them mature and obedient to His Words. There are many verses that speak of chastening.

- **Deuteronomy 8:5**

"Thou shalt also consider in thine heart, that, as a man **chasteneth** his son, so the LORD thy God **chasteneth** thee."

- **2 Samuel 7:14**

"I will be his father, and he shall be my son. If he commit iniquity, I will **chasten** him with the rod of men, and with the stripes of the children of men:"

- **Psalm 6:1**

"O LORD, rebuke me not in thine anger, neither **chasten** me in thy hot displeasure."

- **Psalm 38:1**

"O LORD, **rebuke** me not in thy wrath: neither **chasten** me in thy hot displeasure."

- **Proverbs 13:24**

"He that spareth his rod hateth his son: but he that loveth him **chasteneth** him betimes."

Betimes means early. Timing is important.

- **Proverbs 19:18**

"**Chasten** thy son while there is hope, and let not thy soul spare for his crying."

- **Revelation 3:19**

"As many as I love, I **rebuke and chasten**: be zealous therefore, and repent."

Genuine Christians should realize that they sometimes need God's **discipline and correction**, just like a father **disciplines** his children. They should not despise **chastening and correcting**, as a father his son. The Lord does that, as needed, to those who are truly saved and born-again. They are not to despise that **chastening** but be happy about it and welcome it.

Hebrews 12:7

"If ye endure chastening, God dealeth with you as with sons; for what son is he whom the father chasteneth not?"

ENDURE GOD'S CHASTENING

This is the fourth use of the term chastening in this portion of Scripture. Truly saved Christians should endure God's wise chastening. If God's chastening is endured, He deals with His true sons and daughters who are dealt with as sons.

Though it is not always the case (sometimes it is seldom if ever the case) that fathers **chasten** their children, the Bible assumes that that is or should be the case.

The Bible gives the father the duty to **chasten and discipline** his children. When there is no father in the home, the **discipline** is left to the mother. Sad to say, there are many fatherless homes. As a result, many of the children in these homes do not have the proper Biblical training.

- Job 5:17

"Behold, happy *is* the man whom God **correcteth**: therefore despise not thou the **chastening** of the Almighty:"

- Proverbs 3:11

"My son, despise not the **chastening** of the LORD; neither be weary of his **correction**;"

- Isaiah 26:16

"LORD, in trouble have they visited thee, they poured out a prayer *when* thy **chastening** was upon them."

Truly born-again Christians should be thankful that their Heavenly Father loves them. Because of His love, He **chastens and disciplines** them if, when, and how it's needed in order to mature them and better equip them to be good soldiers for their Lord Jesus Christ.

Hebrews 12:8

"But if ye be without chastisement, whereof all are partakers, then are ye bastards, and not sons."

This is the fifth of the eight times **chastisement** is used in this section of Hebrews. This verse teaches us that all of God's genuine Christian children are **chastened and disciplined** by Him.

WHAT IF WITHOUT CHASTENING

If any of His true Children are without such discipline, they are not his true children, but are **"bastards."**

The Greek Word for **"bastards"** is NOTHOS. Some of the meanings of this Word are:

"1) illegitimate, bastard; 2) one born, not in lawful wedlock, but of a concubine or female slave."

God does not **chasten** illegitimate children. He **chastens** only His genuine Christian sons and daughters. In the human realm, it would be entirely out of place for us to **chasten or discipline** other people's children.

DISCIPLINE OUR OWN CHILDREN

We who are genuine Christians should discipline our own children so they will grow up to obey and honor the Lord Jesus Christ.

- **Deuteronomy 11:2**

"And know ye this day: for *I speak* not with your children which have not known, and which have not seen the **chastisement** of the LORD your God, his greatness, his mighty hand, and his stretched out arm,"

God used **chastisement** of His people, Israel, in the wilderness.

- **Job 34:31**

"Surely it is meet to be said unto God, I have borne **chastisement**, I will not offend *any more*:"

Job learned his lesson.

- **Isaiah 53:5**

"But he was wounded for our transgressions, *he was* bruised for our iniquities: the **chastisement** of our peace was upon him; and with his stripes we are healed."

> **CHRIST BORE CHASTENING FOR US**
>
> The Lord Jesus Christ bore the chastening and suffering of the cross of Calvary in order to bring peace to those who sincerely trust in Him as their Saviour.

Hebrews 12:9

"Furthermore we have had fathers of our flesh which corrected us, and we gave them reverence: shall we not much rather be in subjection unto the Father of spirits, and live?"

If people who are living on this earth had their fathers **correct** them and the children reverenced and honored their fathers for it, how much more should genuine Christians honor and reverence their Heavenly Father when He **corrects and chastens** them? The analogy is very easily understood.

> **CHILDREN LACKING CORRECTION**
>
> Many children living today do not have fathers that give them correction. Many, in fact, do not even have fathers who are living with their mothers and them in the same house. This is a sad state of affairs in our nation.

For nineteen years, I taught in the school district of Philadelphia. About seventeen years were in junior high school and the other two years were in senior high school. I observed firsthand the many acts and words of disobedience by those children toward their teachers. Those children knew nothing of parental **correction**. They despised many of their teachers (including me). This was an evidence of their lack of proper fatherly **discipline** at home.

If children do not properly obey their parents, they will not willingly obey proper suggestions of their teachers and other adults with whom they come in contact. <u>Children need to learn to give respect to their</u>

parents and other adults with whom they come in contact. This applies to obedience of those who are truly saved, to their Heavenly Father. He loves them and wants them to be obedient to all of His Words that are for them in the Bible.

> **GIVE GOD REVERENCE WHEN CORRECTING**
> When the Heavenly Father corrects His born-again children, we should give Him reverence, and not yell and scream at Him for His needed correction.

Hebrews 12:10

"For they verily for a few days chastened us after their own pleasure; but he for *our* profit, that we might be partakers of his holiness."

Though our earthly fathers might have **corrected** their children because of their own pleasure and desires, not so with the Heavenly Father of genuine Christians. When they need His **correction**, He does it for their profit in order that they might be partakers of His holiness. God's **chastening** is always for their profit. God wants them pure. He wants them sanctified as they walk in their daily lives. It's true that on the books of Heaven, having been justified by genuine faith in the Lord Jesus Christ, they have a holy, and sanctified standing before God. As far as God is concerned, genuine Christians have positional holiness before God. But God desires them, in their present state, to strive for a holy life.

HOLINESS

- **Psalm 29:2**

"Give unto the LORD the glory due unto his name; worship the LORD in the beauty of **holiness.**"

- **Psalm 93:5**

"Thy testimonies are very sure: **holiness** becometh thine house, O LORD, for ever."

- **Ephesians 4:24**

"And that ye put on the new man, which after God is created in righteousness and true **holiness.**"

We who are true Christians still have the old sinful flesh with us. But we have also God the Holy Spirit indwelling us. We have are put on this "new man" which is created in righteousness and true **holiness**.

- **1 Thessalonians 3:13**

"To the end he may stablish your hearts unblameable in **holiness** before God, even our Father, at the coming of our Lord Jesus Christ with all his saints."

- **1 Thessalonians 4:7**

"For God hath not called us unto uncleanness, but unto **holiness**."

WORLDLY CHRISTIANS

Sometimes it is difficult to distinguish a truly saved "worldly" Christian from an unsaved and worldly person. That is sad indeed. Only the Lord can tell whether they are genuinely saved or lost. Carnal Christian lives are anything but holy. They must walk in the power of the Holy Spirit, not after their flesh.

Hebrews 12:11

"Now no chastening for the present seemeth to be joyous, but grievous: nevertheless afterward it yieldeth the peaceable fruit of righteousness unto them which are exercised thereby."

CHASTENING

This is the eighth and final use of **chastening** in this section of Hebrews. It is the last time the word *"chasten"* appears. No **chastening** for the present, right now, as the genuine Christians are going through it, seems to be joyous. On the other hand, it appears to be grievous, painful, and depressing while they are going through the chastening.

However, after the **chastening** is over, it brings results. What kind of results does it bring to the true Christian? This verse teaches that it brings the peaceable fruit of righteousness to just a certain kind of true

Christian. It only yields this peaceable fruit to those Christians who are *"exercised thereby."*

> **DISCIPLINE NEEDED FOR ALL**
>
> I believe this means that they who are undergoing this needed discipline from the Lord Jesus Christ must recognize their need for it and that, though it is unpleasant to undergo, it was needed in their lives to straighten them out for the Lord's further service from them.

- Acts 24:16

"And herein do I exercise myself, to have always a conscience void of offence toward God, and *toward* men."

- 1 Timothy 4:7

"But refuse profane and old wives' fables, and exercise thyself *rather* unto godliness."

- Hebrews 5:14

"But strong meat belongeth to them that are of full age, *even* those who by reason of use have their senses exercised to discern both good and evil."

> **WISDOM WHEN GOD CHASTENS**
>
> May the Lord give His genuine Christian children the wisdom to understand His purpose in chastening them so that they might reap the benefits and profit from it in their future walk with the Lord.

Hebrews 12:12

"Wherefore lift up the hands which hang down, and the feeble knees;"

HANDS THAT HANG DOWN & FEEBLE KNEES

The **hands that hang down** with no strength in them are those that are not strong. They are weak and exhausted. The Greek Word for *"hang down"* is PARIEMI. Some of the meanings for this Word are:

"1) to let pass; 1a) to pass by, neglect; 1b) to disregard, omit; 2) to relax, loose, let go; 3) relaxed, unstrung, weakened, exhausted."

> ## WE NEED STRONG HANDS
> God wants His true Christians to have strong and active hands to serve Him every day of their lives. He wants them to be able to stand up strong and not have weak and feeble knees that wiggle and totter when difficult and heavy burdens come. There are other verses about such knees and hands.

- Job 4:4

"Thy words have upholden him that was falling, and thou hast strengthened the **feeble knees**."

Job needed his **feeble knees** to be strengthened in all of his adversity that Satan made him undergo.

- Psalm 109:24

"My **knees are weak** through fasting; and my flesh faileth of fatness."

- Isaiah 35:3

"Strengthen ye the **weak hands**, and confirm the **feeble knees**."

- Ezekiel 7:17

"All **hands shall be feeble**, and all **knees shall be weak** *as* water."

- Ezekiel 21:7b

". . . and all **hands shall be feeble**, and every spirit shall faint, and all **knees shall be weak** *as* water:"

> ## HAVE STRENGTHENED KNEES
> We who are genuinely saved Christians must lift up our hands for service for the Lord Jesus Christ and <u>strengthen our feeble knees</u> so that we might stand strong for God's Words in this evil day.

Hebrews 12:13

"And make straight paths for your feet, lest that which is lame be turned out of the way; but let it rather be healed."

STRAIGHT PATHS

When genuine Christians take care of their feeble knees and stand up strong, they will be able to make **straight paths** for their feet. They will not have lame and unbalanced feet to stumble out of the proper **Biblical paths**. The only **straight paths** they will ever find is to be found in the Scriptures, the Words of God. In the English language the **straight paths** are to be found in the pages of the King James Bible which is based upon the inspired and preserved Hebrew, Aramaic, and Greek Words that God gave us.

Lessons and **straight paths** are found for these Christians by rightly dividing the books of Genesis through Revelation. **Straight paths** are there. That's where they must be found--from Genesis to Revelation. We must know what God's Words tell us.

THE WORLD'S CROOKED PATHS

The unsaved world knows nothing about straight paths. They walk in crooked paths contrary to the teachings of the Words of God in the Bible. This walking makes them sick rather than spiritually well.

Hebrews 12:14

"Follow peace with all *men*, and holiness, without which no man shall see the Lord:"

PEACE AND HOLINESS

The Greek verb for *"follow"* is in the present tense. It means this action of following should be done continuously rather than just once in a while. There are two things that are to be continuously followed: (1) **peace** with all men, and (2) **holiness** without which no person can see the Lord. **Peace** with all men has many ramifications. **Holiness** with the Lord can only be possessed by a person's having genuine faith in the

Lord Jesus Christ as their Saviour. At that time, their standing before the Lord is **holiness**. They must work on their **holy** state and condition here on earth that it might also be **holy**. There are number of verses on **peace and on holiness**.

PEACE

- **Proverbs 16:7**

"When a man's ways please the LORD, he maketh even his enemies to be at **peace** with him."

- **John 14:27**

"**Peace** I leave with you, my **peace** I give unto you: not as the world giveth, give I unto you. Let not your heart be troubled, neither let it be afraid."

This is God's **peace**.

- **John 16:33**

"These things I have spoken unto you, that in me ye might have **peace**. In the world ye shall have tribulation: but be of good cheer; I have overcome the world."

- **Romans 5:1**

"Therefore being justified by faith, we have **peace** with God through our Lord Jesus Christ."

Being justified by genuine faith brings **peace** with God.

- **Romans 14:19**

"Let us therefore follow after the things which make for **peace**, and things wherewith one may edify another."

- **Colossians 3:15**

"And let the **peace** of God rule in your hearts, to the which also ye are called in one body; and be ye thankful."

Peace with God is through being justified by genuine faith in the Lord Jesus Christ. The "**peace** of God" is found by walking in the power of God the Holy Spirit Who indwells the truly saved people.

HOLINESS

In addition to following **peace** with all men, the truly saved Christian must also continue to follow **holiness**.

Hebrews–Preaching Verse by Verse

- **Romans 6:19b**

". . . for as ye have yielded your members servants to uncleanness and to iniquity unto iniquity; even so now yield your members servants to righteousness unto **holiness**."

After people become genuine Christians they are to yield their "members" as servants to righteousness unto **holiness**. The Old Testament talks of praising the Lord on an instrument of **ten strings**.

THE CHRISTIAN'S TEN STRINGS

The ten spiritual strings that a true Christian should use for righteousness unto holiness here on earth are these: two eyes; two ears; two hands; two feet; one mouth, and one heart. All of these members should be yielded to holiness by the power of God the Holy Spirit Who dwells within them.

- **Romans 6:22**

"But now being made free from sin, and become servants to God, ye have your fruit unto **holiness**, and the end everlasting life."

- **2 Corinthians 7:1**

"Having therefore these promises, dearly beloved, let us cleanse ourselves from all filthiness of the flesh and spirit, perfecting **holiness** in the fear of God."

- **1 Thessalonians 3:13**

"To the end he may stablish your hearts unblameable in **holiness** before God, even our Father, at the coming of our Lord Jesus Christ with all his saints."

HEARTS UNBLAMEABLE

God wants the genuine Christians' hearts to be unblameable in holiness before God and also before the world in which they live.

- **1 Thessalonians 4:7**

"For God hath not called us unto uncleanness, but unto **holiness**."

- **Titus 2:3**

"The aged women likewise, that *they be* in behavior as becometh **holiness**, not false accusers, not given to much wine, teachers of good things;"

THE NEED FOR HOLINESS

God wants all of His genuine Christians to be holy in their daily living here on earth. When they walk into a room, do people see that there is something different about these Christians? It is important how these true Christians look, the way they talk, the way they walk, the way they act, and even the way they dress.

They should let their light so shine in accordance with the following verse:

- **Matthew 5:16**

"Let your light so shine before men, that they may see your good works, and glorify your Father which is in heaven."

Hebrews 12:15

"Looking diligently lest any man fail of the grace of God; lest any root of bitterness springing up trouble you, and thereby many be defiled;"

LOOKING DILIGENTLY

Paul wanted these genuine Christians to **look diligently** all around them and within them lest any of them fail from God's grace and bitterness trouble and defile them. The Greek Word for *"looking"* is EPISKOPEO. Some of the meanings of this Word are:

> *"1) to look upon, inspect, oversee, look after, care for; 1a) of the care of the church which rested upon the elders; 1b) to look carefully, beware."*

LOOKING DILIGENTLY

This Greek verb is in the present tense, showing that this looking diligently and carefully must be continuous on the part of these true Christians. They are to look at their lives in order

> to be sure to match them up with the Words of God found in the Bible.

The reason for this **diligent looking** is lest a genuine Christian might fail concerning the grace of God.

The Greek Word for *"fail"* is HUSTEREO. Some of the meanings of this Word are:

> *"1) behind; 1a) to come late or too tardily; 1a1) to be left behind in the race and so fail to reach the goal, to fall short of the end; 1a2) metaph. fail to become a partaker, fall back from; 1b) to be inferior in power, influence and rank; 1b1) of the person: to be inferior to; 1c) to fail, be wanting; 1d) to be in want of, lack; 2) to suffer want, to be devoid of, to lack (be inferior) in excellence, worth."*

God does not want His true Christian children to be in any way lacking or being in want of His marvelous grace and fail to finish their course with joy.

BITTERNESS DEFILES

Another danger of not looking carefully and following the Words of God is that a root of **bitterness** might spring up causing defilement.

The Greek Word for *"bitterness"* is PIKRIA. Some of the meanings of this Word are:

> *"1) bitter gall; 1a) extreme wickedness; 1b) a bitter root, and so producing a bitter fruit; 1c) metaph. bitterness, bitter hatred."*

ELIMINATING BITTERNESS

If God the Holy Spirit Who indwells all true Christians empowers them, there will not be bitterness within them, but only the fruit of the Spirit.

- **Galatians 5:22-23**
"But the fruit of the Spirit is love, joy, peace, longsuffering, gentleness, goodness, faith, Meekness, temperance: against such there is no law."

> ### BITTERNESS DEFILES
> Bitterness troubles and defiles the genuine Christian's heart and life.

The Greek Word for "*defile*" is MIAINO. Some of the meanings of this Word are:

> "1) to dye with another colour, to stain' 2) to defile, pollute, sully, contaminate, soil; 2a) to defile with sins."

Does that mean, if genuine Christians are not walking with the Lord Jesus Christ, they can **contaminate** others? That is part of the meaning of that Word used here.

> ### ROOT OF BITTERNESS
> If they are not walking with the Lord Jesus Christ, they are failing in the grace of God and might have a root of bitterness which defiles them and others. This bitterness produces seriously bad fruit.

- Job 10:1

"My soul is weary of my life; I will leave my complaint upon myself; I will speak in the **bitterness** of my soul."

> ### JOB WAS BITTER
> Job was wanting to die. He didn't want to live. God does not want us to be bitter. He wants us to have joy of the Lord Jesus Christ Who is our strength.

- Romans 3:14

"Whose mouth *is* full of cursing and **bitterness**:"

The ones spoken of here are unsaved people, not true Christians.

- Ephesians 4:31

"Let all **bitterness**, and wrath, and anger, and clamour, and evil speaking, be put away from you, with all malice."

Apparently those in the church at Ephesus had these problems. Paul heard about them while in the Roman prison and mentioned it in his letter to them. <u>God wants His genuine Christians to be clean and free from **bitterness** of spirit</u>.

Hebrews 12:16

"Lest there *be* any fornicator, or profane person, as Esau, who for one morsel of meat sold his birthright."

FORNICATION AND PROFANE PERSONS AS ESAU

Without this earnest diligence on the part of every genuine Christian, there might be carnal and fleshly Christians who become **fornicators or profane persons like Esau.**

> **ESAU WAS A WICKED FORNICATOR**
>
> Though the Old Testament did not name Esau as a fornicator, we find this here in our New Testament. He did not care about his birthright, but sold it for a little meat.

- **Genesis 25:29-31**

"And Jacob sod pottage: and **Esau** came from the field, and he *was* faint: And **Esau** said to Jacob, Feed me, I pray thee, with that same red *pottage*; for I *am faint*: therefore was his name called **Edom**. [**Edom** means red] And Jacob said, Sell me this day thy birthright."

The birthright was given to the firstborn. He would receive a double portion of all the father's inheritance. **Esau** didn't care about this. His life was one of debauchery.

- **Genesis 25:32-34**

"And **Esau** said; Behold, I *am* at the point to die: and what profit shall this birthright do to me?" And Jacob said, Swear to me this day; and he sware unto him: and he sold his birthright unto Jacob. Then Jacob gave **Esau** bread and pottage of lentils; and he did eat and drink, and rose up, and went his way: thus **Esau** despised *his* birthright."

FORNICATION

The Greek Word for *"fornicator"* is PORNOS. Some of the meanings of this Word are:

> *"1) a man who prostitutes his body to another's lust for hire; 2) a male prostitute; 3) a man who indulges in unlawful sexual intercourse, a fornicator."*

Another form of this sinful act is from the Greek Word PORNEIA. Some of the meanings of this Word are:

> *"fornication, sexual immorality, sexual sin of a general kind, that includes many different behaviors (Mt 5:32; 15:19; 19:9; Mk 7:21; Jn 8:41; Ac 15:20; 1Co 6:18; 7:2; 2Co 12:21; Gal 5:19; Eph 5:3; 1Th 4:3)."*

<u>The sin of **fornication** (that **Esau** committed) is found in forty different places in our King James Bible.</u> Here are some of them:

- **Mark 7:21**

"For from within, out of the heart of men, proceed evil thoughts, adulteries, **fornications**, murders,"

> **FORNICATION BEGINS IN THE HEART**
>
> **Fornication begins in the heart. Though there are other meanings of it, it is basically sexual relations on the part of those who are not married.**

- **Acts 15:29**

"That ye abstain from meats offered to idols, and from blood, and from things strangled, and from **fornication**: from which if ye keep yourselves, ye shall do well."

The church at Jerusalem was told this very clearly.

- **Romans 1:29**

"Being filled with all unrighteousness, **fornication**, wickedness, covetousness, maliciousness, full of envy, murder, debate, deceit, malignity, whispers,"

One of the things they were filled with was **fornication**.

- **1 Corinthians 5:1**

"It is reported commonly *that there* is **fornication** among you, and such **fornication** as is not so much as named among the Gentiles, that one should have his father's wife."

- **1 Corinthians 6:13**

"Meats for the belly, and the belly for meats: but God shall destroy both it and them. Now the body is not for **fornication**, but for the Lord; and the Lord for the body."

The body is not for **fornication**, but for the Lord.

SEXUAL UNION ONLY IN MARRIAGE

Only in marriage between a man and a woman is sexual relations proper and Biblical.

- **Hebrews 13:4**

"Marriage is honourable in all, and the bed undefiled: but **whoremongers** and adulterers God will judge."

- **1 Corinthians 6:18**

"Flee **fornication**. Every sin that a man doeth is without the body; but he that committeth **fornication** sinneth against his own body."

- **1 Corinthians 7:2**

"Nevertheless, *to avoid* **fornication**, let every man have his own wife, and let every woman have her own husband."

- **Galatians 5:19**

"Now the works of the flesh are manifest, which are *these*; Adultery, **fornication**, uncleanness, lasciviousness,"

- **Ephesians 5:3**

"But **fornication**, and all uncleanness, or covetousness, let it not be once named among you, as becometh saints;"

- **1 Thessalonians 4:3**

"For this is the will of God, *even* your sanctification, that ye should abstain from **fornication**:"

- **Jude 7**

"Even as Sodom and Gomorrha, and the cities about them in like manner, giving themselves over to **fornication**, and going after strange flesh, are set forth for an example, suffering the vengeance of eternal fire."

SODOM DESTROYED FOR SEXUAL SIN

If God destroyed Sodom and Gomorrha because of their fornication and homosexuality, when is He going to destroy this country for the very same sins? Fornication is committed in our country (and in all others as well) everywhere—even in some Christian churches and schools!

> **CORE CURRICULUM IS WICKED**
>
> The present Obama administration imposition of his so-called "core curriculum" teaches that sexual choices are all right for students in the public schools. They are taught that one man, one woman marriage is all right. They are taught that two men or two women marriage is all right. They have rejected the morality of God's Words in the Bible. In this curriculum, homosexuality is fine, adultery is fine, fornication is fine. Not so in the Words of God! These activities are all sins.

Hebrews 12:17

"For ye know how that afterward, when he would have inherited the blessing, he was rejected: for he found no place of repentance, though he sought it carefully with tears."

ESAU

Here are some of the verses that give a background to Jacob and **Esau's** conversation about **Esau's** birthright.

- **Genesis 27:26-28**

"And his father Isaac said unto him, come near now, and kiss me, my son. And he came near, and kissed him: and he smelled the smell of his raiment, and blessed him and said, See, the smell of my son is as the smell of a field which the LORD hath blessed: Therefore God give thee of the dew of heaven, and the fatness of the earth, and plenty of corn and wine:"

Jacob was a deceiver. His mother said to dress up as if you were **Esau**, which he did.

- **Genesis 27:29**

"Let people serve thee, and nations bow down to thee: be lord over thy brethren, and let thy mother's sons bow down to thee: cursed by every one that curseth thee, and blessed be he that blesseth thee."

As the father, Isaac, was blessing Jacob, **Esau**, after getting his venison, came in from his hunting.

- **Genesis 27:31-33**

"And **he** also had made savoury meat, and brought it unto his father, and said unto his father, Let **my** father arise, and eat of his **son's** venison, that thy soul may bless me. And Isaac **his** father said unto him, Who art thou? [He had blessed one that was claiming to be **Esau**.] And he said, I *am* thy **son**, thy firstborn **Esau**. And Isaac trembled very exceedingly, and said, Who? Where *is* he that hath taken venison, and brought *it* me, and I have eaten of all before thou camest, and have blessed him? Yea, *and* he shall be blessed."

This was God's miracle. The younger would serve the older. It's a switch in blessings.

- **Genesis 27:34**

"And when **Esau** heard the words of his father, he cried with a great and exceeding bitter cry, and said unto his father, Bless me, *even* me also, O my father."

<u>Esau didn't want his birthright or the blessing that went with it</u>. Now he missed both of these things.

- **Genesis 27:35-41**

"And he said, Thy brother came with subtilty, and hath taken away thy blessing. And he said, Is not he rightly named Jacob? For he hath supplanted me these two times: he took away my birthright; and, behold, now he hath taken away my blessing. And he said, Hast thou not reserved a blessing for me? And Isaac answered and said unto **Esau**, Behold, I have made him thy lord, and all his brethren have I given to him for servants; and with corn and wine have I sustained him: and what shall I do now unto thee, my **son**? And **Esau** said unto his father, Hast thou but one blessing, my father? Bless me, *even* me also, O my father. And **Esau** lifted up his voice, and wept. And Isaac his father answered and said unto him, Behold, thy dwelling shall be fatness of the earth, and of the dew of heaven from above; And by thy sword shalt thou live, and shalt serve thy brother, and it shall come to pass when thou shalt have the dominion, that thou shalt break his yoke from off thy neck. And **Esau** hated Jacob because of the blessing wherewith his father blessed him: and **Esau** said in his heart, The days of mourning for my father are at hand; then will I slay my brother Jacob."

<u>Esau stated that he wanted to kill his brother Jacob</u>.

Hebrews 12:18

"For ye are not come unto the mount that might be touched, and that burned with fire, nor unto blackness, and darkness, and tempest,"

MOUNT SINAI

This is the **first mount** that is mentioned here in verse eighteen. There is a second mount that is mentioned in verse 22.

THE FIRST MOUNT

The first mount is mount Sinai where the law of Moses was given by God. The second mount is Heaven itself. There is quite a contrast between these two mounts.

- Exodus 19:11-12

"And be ready against the third day: for the third day the LORD will come down in the sight of all the people upon **mount Sinai**. And thou shalt set bounds [boundaries] unto the people round about, saying, Take heed to yourselves, *that* ye go *not* up into the **mount,** or touch the border of it: whosoever toucheth the **mount** shall be surely put to death."

God gave Moses several rules for the Israelites about **mount Sinai.**

1. Don't go near **it;**
2. Don't touch the border of **it;**
3. Those who touch the **mount** will be killed.

- Exodus 19:13

"There shall not an hand touch it, but he shall surely be stoned, or shot through; whether *it be* beast or man, it shall not live: when the trumpet soundeth long, they shall come up to the **mount."**

- Exodus 19:16

"And it came to pass on the third day in the morning, that there were thunders and lightnings, and a thick cloud upon the **mount,** and the voice of the trumpet exceeding loud; so that all the people that was in the camp trembled."

The people were fearful of the Lord at **mount Sinai.**

- Exodus 19:17

"And Moses brought forth the people out of the camp to meet with God; and they stood at the nether part of the **mount."**

The people stood at the bottom of the **mount**.
- **Exodus 19:18**

"And **mount Sinai** was altogether on a smoke, because the LORD descended upon it in fire: and the smoke thereof ascended as the smoke of a furnace, and the whole **mount** quaked greatly."

- **Exodus 19:19-24**

"And when the voice of the trumpet sounded long, and waxed louder and louder, Moses spake, and God answered him by a voice. And the LORD came down upon **mount Sinai**, on the top of the **mount**: and the LORD called Moses *up* to the top of the **mount**; and Moses went up. And the LORD said unto Moses, go down, charge the people, lest they break through unto the LORD to gaze, and many of them perish. And let the priests also, which come near to the LORD, sanctify themselves, lest the LORD break forth upon them. And Moses said unto the LORD, The people cannot come up to **mount Sinai**: for thou chargedst us, saying, Set bounds about the **mount**, and sanctify it. And the LORD said unto him, Away; get thee down, and thou shalt come up, thou, and Aaron with thee: but let not the priests and the people break through to come up unto the LORD, lest he break forth upon them."

ACCESS TO GOD

Praise the Lord for those who are genuinely saved today. They have an entrance into God the Father's presence in Heaven. They can approach the Lord in prayer. They have access to God the Father through their true trust in His Son, the Lord Jesus Christ. This is the opposite of what occurred at mount Sinai.

Hebrews 12:19

"And the sound of a trumpet, and the voice of words; which voice they that heard intreated that the word should not be spoken to them any more:"

At **mount Sinai**, God spoke no words. There was just the sound of a trumpet.

- **Exodus 20:18**

"And all the people saw the thunderings, and the lightnings, and the noise of the trumpet, and the mountain smoking: and when the people saw *it*, they removed, and stood afar off."

What a fearful scene that was.

- **Exodus 20:19**

"And they said unto Moses, Speak thou with us, and we will hear: but let not God speak with us, lest we die."

ISRAEL FEARED GOD'S VOICE

They were afraid of the voice of God. Praise to God that those who are genuine Christians today do not have to be afraid of God's Words. Those Words are God's voice, in the Scriptures. Those Words must be listened to and followed.

Hebrews 12:20

"(For they could not endure that which was commanded, And if so much as a beast touch the mountain, it shall be stoned, or thrust through with a dart:)"

Not even the animals could touch **mount Sinai**. If they did, they would be killed.

- **Exodus 19:13**

"There shall not an hand touch *it*, but he shall surely be stoned, or shot through; whether *it be* beast or man, it shall not live: when the trumpet soundeth long, they shall come up to the **mount**."

This shows the excellency and holiness of God the Father. That's why no one in this world can come into the presence of God and go to Heaven unless they have truly trusted the Lord Jesus Christ as their Saviour.

Hebrews 12:21

"And so terrible was the sight, *that* Moses said, I exceedingly fear and quake:)"

MOSES WAS EXCEEDINGLY AFRAID

Because of this sight at mount Sinai, **Moses was exceedingly afraid. He trembled.** Even Moses who received the law at God's hands was **filled with fear**. Wouldn't you be **fearful** of the lightnings, the thunders, the trumpet, and all the other things that happened? The

Hebrews—Preaching Verse by Verse

Greek Word for "*fear*" is EKPHOBOS. Some of the meanings for this Word are:

> "*1) stricken with fear or terror, exceedingly, frightened, terrified.*"

The Greek Word for "**quake**" is ENTROMOS. Some of the meanings for this Word are:

> "*1) trembling, terrified.*"

MOSES GREATLY FEARED

At this terrible sight, Moses was very much afraid and began shaking as he beheld it.

Hebrews 12:22

"**But ye are come unto mount Sion, and unto the city of the living God, the heavenly Jerusalem, and to an innumerable company of angels,**"

MOUNT SION

This is the **other mount** which is in contrast to mount Sinai where Moses met the Lord. It is the **Heavenly mount**. The first three of the eight things that are in **Heaven** are mentioned in this verse. #1 <u>**Mount Sion is in Heaven**</u>. #2 <u>**The City of the living God, the New Jerusalem is in Heaven**</u>. #3 <u>**The innumerable company of angels are in Heaven**</u>.

In verses 22-24, I count eight different persons or things that are in this **new mount in Heaven**. Here is the entire list of these eight.

EIGHT PERSONS AND THINGS IN HEAVEN

- Hebrews 12:22-24

"But ye are come unto mount Sion, and unto the city of the living God, the heavenly Jerusalem, and to an innumerable company of angels, To the general assembly and church of the firstborn, which are written in heaven, and to God the Judge of all, and to the spirits of just men made perfect, And to Jesus the mediator of the new covenant, and to the blood of sprinkling, that speaketh better things than that of Abel."

1. Mount Sion is in Heaven. (12:22)
2. The city of the living God, the Heavenly Jerusalem is in Heaven. (12:22)

> 3. An innumerable company of angels are in Heaven. (12:22)
> 4. The general assembly and church of the firstborn which are written in Heaven is in Heaven. (12:23)
> 5. God, the Judge of all is in Heaven. (12:23)
> 6. The spirits of just men made perfect are in Heaven. (12:23)
> 7. Jesus, the Mediator of the new covenant is in Heaven. (12:24)
> 8. The blood of sprinkling (referring to the blood of the Lord Jesus Christ) is in Heaven. (12:24)

Hebrews 12:23

"To the general assembly and church of the firstborn, which are written in heaven, and to God the Judge of all, and to the spirits of just men made perfect,"

In this verse, there are listed #4, #5, and #6 of the things that are in Heaven. #4 The fourth thing is **the general assembly and church of the firstborn which are in Heaven**. I believe this refers to the church which is Christ's body.

- **Ephesians 1:22-23**

"And hath put all *things* under his feet, and gave him *to be* the head over all *things* to the church, Which is his body, the fulness of him that filleth all in all."

- **Colossians 1:24**

"Who now rejoice in my sufferings for you, and fill up that which is behind of the afflictions of Christ in my flesh for his body's sake, which is the church:"

> **THE CHURCH WHICH IS HIS BODY**
>
> The church which is His body includes every person who is a genuinely saved, born-again Christian. They are all in the church of the firstborn, *"the church which is His body."* Their names are written in Heaven.

The *"church which is His body"* is not to be defined as merely certain kinds of Baptists. That is the heresy that is being steadily promulgated by Dr. Thomas Strouse and others. He is presently a pastor in Connecticut.

He now has a theological seminary over the Internet with many followers of this false teaching in our country and in other countries of the world.

#5 <u>The fifth thing that is in **Heaven** is **God Himself, Who is the Judge of all**</u>. Heaven is His Home. He's everywhere present, but His **City**, His **Home**, His **Base**, is in **Heaven**.

#6 <u>The sixth thing that is in **Heaven** are the spirits of just men made perfect</u>. These are genuinely saved people both in the Old Testament and in the New Testament. They are just men made perfect. They're not perfected by themselves. No one can be perfect himself. Those people who are genuinely saved and born-again, God has constituted perfect on the books of **Heaven**. <u>Those genuinely saved, in the sight of God, are absolutely perfect and righteous</u>. This is not because of anything they have done. It is because of what the Lord Jesus Christ has done at the cross of Calvary. God the Father, made God the Son, to be sin for us that we might be made the righteousness of God in Him. <u>The spirits of just men made perfect are also in **Heaven** as well</u>.

Hebrews 12:24

"And to Jesus the mediator of the new covenant, and to the blood of sprinkling, that speaketh better things than *that of* Abel."

JESUS THE MEDIATOR IN HEAVEN

In this verse, there are listed #7 and #8 things that are in **Heaven**. Here are the seventh and eighth things that are in **Heaven**.

CHRIST OUR MEDIATOR

#7 <u>The seventh thing that is in Heaven is Jesus, the Mediator of the new covenant</u>. Our Lord Jesus Christ has gone to Heaven and is seated at the right hand of God the Father. This seat of authority is His because His Father had accepted His work at Calvary for the sins of the world. It is an evidence of God the Father's hand of blessing, power, and majesty. The Lord Jesus Christ is the Mediator of the new covenant of God's grace.

The Greek Word for "*mediator*" is MESITES. Some of the meanings of this Word are:

"*1) one who intervenes between two, either in order to make or restore peace and friendship, or form a compact, or for ratifying a covenant; 2) a medium of communication, arbitrator."*

The **Lord Jesus Christ was perfect Man as well as perfect God.** **He** came to this earth by the miracle of the virgin birth. **He** knew what human beings were because **He** was a **perfect Human without sin** of any kind. **He** understands human imperfections. **He** is the **Mediator** between God and man, as it says in 1 Timothy 2:5.

- 1 Timothy 2:5

"For *there is* one God, and one **mediator** between God and men, **the man Christ Jesus;**"

MARY IS NOT OUR MEDIATRIX

The Roman Catholic Church teaches that Mary is a mediatrix. That is a false and apostate theology. There is only one Mediator between God and man.

He is the **Lord Jesus Christ**, the **Saviour** of those who genuinely trust **Him**. **He** can understand, fellowship, and communicate with God the Father, and with human beings.

THE BLOOD OF CHRIST IN HEAVEN

CHRIST'S BLOOD OF SPRINKLING

#8 The eighth thing that is in Heaven is the blood of sprinkling.

- Hebrews 9:12

"Neither by the blood of goats and calves, but by **his own blood he** entered in once into the holy place, having obtained eternal redemption *for us.*"

CHRIST'S BLOOD ON THE MERCY SEAT

I believe this blood of sprinkling refers to the blood of the Lord Jesus Christ which is in Heaven. This verse (and others in the book of Hebrews) refers to the Lord Jesus Christ's entering Heaven after His substitutionary death and bodily resurrection, to put some of His blood on the Heavenly mercy seat as the Great High Priest of the true Christians.

Many Bible teachers don't believe this. Dr. John Walvoord, former President of Dallas Theological Seminary, didn't believe it. However, Bible teacher and radio minister, Dr. M. R. DeHaan believed it. Dr. John R. Rice agreed with Dr. DeHaan on this. Many others believe this. I believe it is very clear from the book of Hebrews that **some of the blood of the Lord Jesus Christ is on the Heavenly mercy seat.**

- **Leviticus 16:14-15**

"And he shall take of the blood of the bullock, and sprinkle it with his finger upon the mercy seat eastward; and before the mercy seat shall he sprinkle of the blood with his finger seven times. Then shall he kill the goat of the sin offering, that is for the people, and bring his blood within the vail, and do with that blood as he did with the blood of the bullock, and sprinkle it upon the mercy seat, and before the mercy seat:"

THE DAY OF ATONEMENT

Once a year, on the day of atonement, the Old Testament high priest, took the blood of the bullock and the blood of the goat and put it on the mercy seat in the holy of holies. So the Lord Jesus Christ, the Great High Priest of genuine Christians did the same with His own blood.

- **John 20:17**

"Jesus saith unto her, Touch me not; for I am not yet ascended to my Father: but go to my brethren, and say unto them, I ascend unto my Father, and your Father; and *to* my God, and your God."

WHEN CHRIST PUT HIS BLOOD IN HEAVEN

This verse tells us of the time when the Lord Jesus Christ ascended back to His Father to put His blood on the Heavenly mercy seat.

Hebrews 12:25

"See that ye refuse not him that speaketh. For if they escaped not who refused him that spake on earth, much more *shall not* we *escape*, if we turn away from him that *speaketh* from heaven:"

DID NOT ESCAPE

The Old Testament Israelites didn't listen to the Words of God for a long time. When the Israelites were forty years in the wilderness, they sinned repeatedly. God slew many of them because of their repeated complaining. All those from twenty years old and up died in the wilderness as God had promised. Only those people who were nineteen years old and under went into the land of Canaan.

GOD PUNISHED SINNING ISRAEL

In the second giving of the law in the book of Deuteronomy, Moses told the new generation of Israelites all about God's wonders and miracles that He had performed in their behalf. He told them he knew after his death they were going to sin--doing that which is evil and worshipping idols. They denied this, but it was true as Moses had stated. These people forsook the Lord Who had spoken to them.

They **didn't escape** God's penalty for their sins. God put before them the Palestinian covenant. He told them of the blessings and the curses. If they didn't follow Him, all these curses would take place. They acted like this in the book of Judges.

- **Judges 21:25**

"In those days *there was* no king in Israel: every man did *that which* was right in his own eyes."

That's what is happening today in our country, and in the world. The Jews were judged by the Lord. **They didn't escape.** The northern ten tribes went into Assyrian captivity because of their sins. The southern two tribes were taken into Babylon for seventy years. Perhaps this is what is meant by Him that spake on earth, referring to His earthly people, Israel. Those who were living in Paul's day who were Christians and true Christians today will **not escape** God's judgments either. If they do not follow what God tells them to follow in His Words, they will be judged also. They will be judged at the judgment seat of Christ.

- **2 Corinthians 5:10**

"For we must all appear before the judgment seat of Christ; that every one may receive the things *done* in *his* body, according to that he hath done, whether *it be* good or bad."

The details of the Judgment seat are given in 1 Corinthians 3:10-15.

- **1 Corinthians 3:10-15**

"According to the grace of God which is given unto me, as a wise masterbuilder, I have laid the foundation, and another buildeth thereon. But let every man take heed how he buildeth thereupon. For other foundation can no man lay than that is laid, which is Jesus Christ. Now if any man build upon this foundation gold, silver, precious stones, wood, hay, stubble; Every man's work shall be made manifest: for the day shall declare it, because it shall be revealed by fire; and the fire shall try every man's work of what sort it is. If any man's work abide which he hath built thereupon, he shall receive a reward. If any man's work shall be burned, he shall suffer loss: but he himself shall be saved; yet so as by fire."

THE JUDGMENT SEAT OF CHRIST

Genuine Christians will be judged at the Judgment Seat of Christ for the things that they have done in their body after they have been saved.

Saved, born again Christians are built on the Foundation, Who is the Lord Jesus Christ. They should build upon Him with gold, silver, and precious stones. They will be purified by fire. Though they are small in size, they are very precious and valuable. If they, with their works and attitudes, build upon the Lord Jesus Christ, their Foundation, wood, hay and stubble, the fire will burn these things up, though they might be very large. Compared to gold, silver, and precious stones, they are not worth much. Because God will judge every sin that these true Christians commit in either thought, word, or deed, they must repeatedly use the cleansing truth found in 1 John 1:9.

AGREEING WITH GOD ABOUT OUR SINS

- 1 John 1:9

"If we **confess our sins**, he is faithful and just to forgive us *our* sins, and to cleanse us from all unrighteousness."

The "we" in this verse means those who are genuine Christians. This is the way they can get back into fellowship with the Lord after they have sinned in thought, word, or deed. They can never lose their salvation, but they can lose their fellowship with the Lord Jesus Christ when they sin.

THE MEANING OF CONFESS IN 1 JOHN 1:9

The Greek Word for "*confess*" is HOMOLOGEO. HOMO is "*same*" and LOGEO is "*to say.*" For the true Christian, it means to say the same thing about their sin in thought, word, or deed, that God says about it. It means to agree with God about our sins. When should this Biblical confession of sin and agreement with the Lord about it take place? It should take place immediately upon the commission of any sin of thought, word, or deed. If genuine Christians agree with God about their sin in this confession, God has promised to be faithful and just to forgive their sin and to cleanse them from all unrighteousness.

RESTORE FELLOWSHIP WITH GOD IMMEDIATELY

God is just in forgiving their sin because all of their sins were paid for at the cross of Calvary by the Lord Jesus Christ. As I said before, this confession or agreement with God must not wait a minute, an hour, a day, a week, a month, or a year—it must be immediate so that there will not be one second in their broken fellowship with the Lord Jesus Christ. Don't turn away from Him Who has spoken from Heaven, the Lord Jesus Christ.

- John 16:13

"Howbeit when he, the Spirit of truth, is come, he will guide you into all truth: for he shall not speak of himself; but whatsoever he shall hear, *that* shall he speak: and he will shew you things to come."

Hebrews 12:26

"Whose voice then shook the earth: but now he hath promised, saying, Yet once more I shake not the earth only, but also heaven."

SHAKING THE EARTH AND HEAVEN

The voice of the Lord **shook the earth** at mount Sinai, He has promised that one day He will **shake not only the earth but also the heaven.** There was an earthquake at mount Sinai. There was also an earthquake at the crucifixion (Matthew 27:54) and also one when the angel of the Lord rolled away the stone from the tomb where they had laid crucified body of the Lord Jesus Christ (Matthew 28:2). The **shaking of the heavens** is promised in Isaiah.

- Isaiah 13:13

"Therefore I will **shake the heavens, and the earth** shall remove out of her place, in the wrath of the LORD of hosts, and in the day of his fierce anger."

The apostle Peter also reminds us of this.

- 2 Peter 3:7

"But the **heavens and the earth**, which are now, by the same word are kept in store, **reserved unto fire** against the day of judgment and perdition of ungodly men."

> ### HEAVEN AND EARTH KEPT IN STORE
>
> Both the heavens and the earth are kept in store by the powerful Word of God. They are now kept without fire and destruction, but one day they will burn up with fire in the day of judgment of ungodly men. No one knows when this event will take place. We know that God has promised to renovate the earth and make a new heaven and a new earth (Isaiah 65:17; 66:22; 2 Peter 3:13; and Revelation 21:1).

Hebrews 12:27

"And this *word*, Yet once more, signifieth the removing of those things that are shaken, as of things that are made, that those things which cannot be shaken may remain."

The *"things that are made"* refers to the **present earth**, sky, stars and all things that God created. These things did not evolve, they were made by the Triune God of the Bible. These **things will be shaken and removed** one day. But the *"things that cannot be shaken will remain."* This is speaking of the Heaven of Heavens where God dwells. That is permanent and will not perish or be changed.

- Hebrews 1:10

"And, Thou, Lord, in the beginning hast laid the **foundation of the earth**, and the heavens are the works of thine hands:"

> ### GEOCENTRICITY IS BIBLICAL
>
> That's one of over one hundred verses in the King James Bible that clearly shows that geocentricity is Biblical. A foundation indicates permanency. That means that the earth is unmovable and the center of the universe rather than the sun being the center. The modern erroneous and unscriptural position holds that the sun is the center of the universe. It is called heliocentricity. For a sound, Biblical, and convincing proof of geocentricity, you should get a copy of Dr. Jack Moorman's book, *Geocentricity–The Biblical And Observational Case* (BFT #4054 @ $19.00 + $8.00 S&H).

THINGS PERISH, BUT GOD REMAINS THE SAME

- Hebrews 1:11

"They shall **perish**; but thou remainest; and they all shall wax old as doth a garment;"

All the beautiful things that God has created will **perish** one day. God has promised this in His Words. Many people don't believe that, but their unbelief does not change what the Bible predicts will happen. <u>One day, all that God created will **perish**. It will become old like a worn out garment</u>. But **God remains the same, unchangeable. He will never change.**

- Hebrews 13:8

"Jesus Christ **the same** yesterday, and to day, and for ever."

<u>The Lord Jesus Christ does not change</u>. **He is the same yesterday, today, and forever.** I'm glad that God is not like many people who are fickle and changeable.

- Hebrews 1:12

"And as a vesture shalt thou fold them up, and they shall be changed: but **thou art the same**, and thy years shall not fail."

THE EARTH TO BE FOLDED UP

The Lord Jesus Christ will one day fold up the old earth and create a new earth. It will be folded up as someone folds a garment.

He does not change. Though man changes daily on many issues, **our God remains the same. His years shall not fail.**

Hebrews 12:28

"Wherefore we receiving a kingdom which cannot be moved, let us have grace, whereby we may serve God acceptably with reverence and godly fear:"

SERVE GOD ACCEPTABLY

Though things of this earth are going to be changed, moved, shaken, and destroyed, those who are genuinely saved Christians have ben given the gift of Heaven that can never be moved. Because of this, the saved, born-again Christians should have grace to **serve their God acceptably** with both reverence and godly fear. <u>That word "*serve*" is a Greek continuous action, present tense. There should be no letup in their **Biblical and fervent service for the Lord Jesus Christ**</u>.

You might say that you've been **serving the Lord Jesus Christ** since you were saved. How long have you been genuinely saved? One year? Ten years? Fifteen, twenty, thirty, fifty, sixty, seventy, eighty years? **Proper, godly, Scriptural, Christ-honoring service** must be continuous. Those of us who are truly saved must never be moved away from this **godly service for our Saviour**. We must **continuously serve our Saviour** right up unto and including at our death bed! There should be no let up in this service. We must **serve** even when facing trouble, temptation, or evil people who hate us and don't agree with us.

GOD'S SERVICE MUST BE ACCEPTABLE

All such service must be acceptable before the Lord. There are two parts of this acceptable service mentioned in this verse. (1) it must be with reverence and (2) it must be with godly fear.

Those who are genuine Christians should **reverence their God and their Saviour** no matter what might come, even when He brings needed chastening upon them. The **Biblical service** for the true Christian should also be done with **godly fear**. God is powerful. Those genuinely saved should love Him, but should also **fear Him**. They should never underestimate His power. As the Lord Jesus Christ said in Matthew 10:28:

- **Matthew 10:28**

"And fear not them which kill the body, but are not able to kill the soul: but rather **fear him** which is able to destroy both soul and body in hell."

CHARACTERISTICS OF HEAVEN

HEAVEN FOR ALL ETERNITY

Now, we who are true Christians, have received a kingdom that cannot be moved. It is not something that Moses received at mount Sinai which shook and was moved greatly. We have, by our genuine faith in the Lord Jesus Christ as our Saviour, God's gift of Heaven for all eternity.

Heaven has **many characteristics** that are mentioned in the book of Revelation. Some are mentioned in Revelation 21:4:

- **Revelation 21:4**

"And God shall wipe away all tears from their eyes; and there shall be no more death, neither sorrow, nor crying, neither shall there be any more pain: for the former things are passed away."

FORMER THINGS PASS AWAY IN HEAVEN

All of these former things will have passed away when the genuine Christians are dwelling in their Home in Heaven.

- John 3:16

"For God so loved the world, that he gave his only begotten son, that whosoever believeth in him should not perish, but have **everlasting life.**"

That's why there is no **death in Heaven.** Because everyone who goes there will have truly trusted the Lord Jesus Christ as their Saviour. Their **life is everlasting.** There will be **no more death.**

- John 11:25-26

"I am the **resurrection,** and the **life:** he that believeth in me, though he were dead, yet shall he **live.** And whosoever **liveth** and believeth in me **shall never die.** Believeth thou this?"

The Lord Jesus Christ promised those who truly believed on him would never die.

THREE KINDS OF "DEATH"

Death is a separation. (1) spiritual death is the present separation of those who are not truly saved from God. (2) physical death is the separation of a person's spirit and soul from the body. (3) eternal death is the separation of the lost people's spirit, soul, and body from God for all eternity. <u>Those who are genuinely saved will never die spiritually, even though they may die physically.</u>

In Heaven, where true Christians will be for **all eternity,** there will be **no more sorrow.** No more death. **Sorrow will be passed away forever.**

In Heaven there will **no more crying.** Even true Christians sometimes cry. They have reasons to cry. Their crying is usually because they are sad, but sometimes they cry when they are glad.

IN HEAVEN PAIN IS REMOVED

In Heaven there will be no more pain.

Many people today are living on pain killers because of their pain. There are all kinds of drugs such as morphine and others to deaden the pain that many undergo. I remember what Dr. Lewis Sperry Chafer (founder of Dallas Theological Seminary and my teacher for four years) said to our class one time in seminary. He said, as best I can remember, words like this:

> "Worldliness, the lusts of the flesh, and various kinds of entertainment are often pursued to deaden the pain of an empty heart and life."

NO MORE FORMER THINGS IN HEAVEN

Praise God that, for those who are genuinely saved Christians in Heaven, all the former sorrowful, tearful, and painful things will be passed away.

Hebrews 12:29

"For our God *is* a consuming fire."

FIRE

The word, "*for,*" connects this verse with the previous verse 28.

GOD A CONSUMING FIRE

Godly fear must be a part of our service because of the holiness and purity of the God that true Christians must serve continually. They must realize that His nature is that of a consuming fire.

Fire was used by the Lord in various judgments that He brought to bear on sinful people.

Here are a few of the 515 uses of "*fire*" in our King James Bible that refer to God's nature and also of His punishments on sin.

- **Genesis 19:24**

"Then the LORD rained upon Sodom and upon Gomorrah brimstone and **fire** from the LORD out of heaven;"

- **Exodus 3:2**

"And the angel of the LORD appeared unto him in a flame of **fire** out of the midst of a bush: and he looked, and, behold, the bush burned with **fire**, and the bush was not consumed."

- **Exodus 9:23**

"And Moses stretched forth his rod toward heaven: and the LORD sent thunder and hail, and the **fire** ran along upon the ground; and the LORD rained hail upon the land of Egypt."

- **Exodus 13:21**

"And the LORD went before them by day in a pillar of a cloud, to lead them the way; and by night in a pillar of **fire**, to give them light; to go by day and night:"

- **Exodus 19:18**

"And mount Sinai was altogether on a smoke, because the LORD descended upon it in **fire**: and the smoke thereof ascended as the smoke of a furnace, and the whole mount quaked greatly."

- **Exodus 24:17**

"And the sight of the glory of the LORD *was* like devouring **fire** on the top of the mount in the eyes of the children of Israel."

- **Exodus 40:38**

"For the cloud of the LORD *was* upon the tabernacle by day, and **fire** was on it by night, in the sight of all the house of Israel, throughout all their journeys."

- **Leviticus 6:13**

"The **fire** shall ever be burning upon the altar; it shall never go out."

- **Leviticus 9:24**

"And there came a fire out from before the LORD, and consumed upon the altar the burnt offering and the fat: *which* when all the people saw, they shouted, and fell on their faces."

- **Leviticus 10:2**

"And there went out **fire** from the LORD, and devoured them, and they died before the LORD."

- **Numbers 9:16**

"So it was alway: the cloud covered it *by day*, and the appearance of **fire** by night."

- **Numbers 11:1**

"And *when* the people complained, it displeased the LORD: and the LORD heard *it;* and his anger was kindled; and the **fire** of the LORD burnt among them, and consumed *them that were* in the uttermost parts of the camp."

- **Numbers 11:3**

"And he called the name of the place Taberah: because the **fire** of the LORD burnt among them."

- **Numbers 14:14**

"And they will tell it to the inhabitants of this land: *for* they have heard that thou LORD *art* among this people, that thou LORD art seen face to face, and *that* thy cloud standeth over them, and *that* thou goest before them, by day time in a pillar of a cloud, and in a pillar of **fire** by night."

- **Numbers 16:35**

"And there came out a **fire** from the LORD, and consumed the two hundred and fifty men that offered incense."

- **Numbers 26:10**

"And the earth opened her mouth, and swallowed them up together with Korah, when that company died, what time the **fire** devoured two hundred and fifty men: and they became a sign."

- **Deuteronomy 1:33**

"Who went in the way before you, to search you out a place to pitch your tents in, in **fire** by night, to shew you by what way ye should go, and in a cloud by day."

- **Deuteronomy 4:11**

"And ye came near and stood under the mountain; and the mountain burned with **fire** unto the midst of heaven, with darkness, clouds, and thick darkness."

- **Deuteronomy 4:12**

"And the LORD spake unto you out of the midst of the **fire**: ye heard the voice of the words, but saw no similitude; only *ye heard* a voice."

- **Deuteronomy 4:15**

"Take ye therefore good heed unto yourselves; for ye saw no manner of similitude on the day *that* the LORD spake unto you in Horeb out of the midst of the **fire**:"

- **Deuteronomy 4:24**

"For the LORD thy God is a **consuming fire**, *even* a jealous God."

- **Deuteronomy 4:33**

"Did *ever* people hear the voice of God speaking out of the midst of the **fire**, as thou hast heard, and live?"

- **Deuteronomy 4:36**

"Out of heaven he made thee to hear his voice, that he might instruct thee: and upon earth he shewed thee his great **fire**; and thou heardest his words out of the midst of the **fire**."

- **Deuteronomy 5:4**

"The LORD talked with you face to face in the mount out of the midst of the **fire**,"

- **Deuteronomy 5:5**

"(I stood between the LORD and you at that time, to shew you the word of the LORD: for ye were afraid by reason of the **fire**, and went not up into the mount;) saying,"

- **Deuteronomy 5:22**

"These words the LORD spake unto all your assembly in the mount out of the midst of the **fire**, of the cloud, and of the thick darkness, with a great voice: and he added no more. And he wrote them in two tables of stone, and delivered them unto me.

- **Deuteronomy 5:23**

"And it came to pass, when ye heard the voice out of the midst of the darkness, (for the mountain did burn with **fire**,) that ye came near unto me, even all the heads of your tribes, and your elders;"

- **Deuteronomy 5:25**

"Now therefore why should we die? for this great **fire** will consume us: if we hear the voice of the LORD our God any more, then we shall die."

- **Deuteronomy 5:26**

"For who *is there of* all flesh, that hath heard the voice of the living God speaking out of the midst of the **fire**, as we *have*, and lived?"

- **Deuteronomy 9:3**

"Understand therefore this day, that the LORD thy God *is* he which goeth over before thee; *as* a consuming **fire** he shall destroy them, and he shall bring them down before thy face: so shalt thou drive them out, and destroy them quickly, as the LORD hath said unto thee."

- **Deuteronomy 9:10**

"And the LORD delivered unto me two tables of stone written with the finger of God; and on them *was written* according to all the words, which the LORD spake with you in the mount out of the midst of the **fire** in the day of the assembly."

- **Deuteronomy 9:15**

"So I turned and came down from the mount, and the mount burned with **fire**: and the two tables of the covenant *were* in my two hands."

- **Deuteronomy 10:4**

"And he wrote on the tables, according to the first writing, the ten commandments, which the LORD spake unto you in the mount out of the midst of the **fire** in the day of the assembly: and the LORD gave them unto me."

- **Deuteronomy 18:16**

"According to all that thou desiredst of the LORD thy God in Horeb in the day of the assembly, saying, Let me not hear again the voice of the LORD my God, neither let me see this great **fire** any more, that I die not."

- **Judges 6:21**

"Then the angel of the LORD put forth the end of the staff that *was* in his hand, and touched the flesh and the unleavened cakes; and there rose up **fire** out of the rock, and consumed the flesh and the unleavened cakes. Then the angel of the LORD departed out of his sight."

- **1 Kings 18:24**

"And call ye on the name of your gods, and I will call on the name of the LORD: and the God that answereth by **fire**, let him be God. And all the people answered and said, It is well spoken."

- **1 Kings 18:38**

"Then the **fire** of the LORD fell, and consumed the burnt sacrifice, and the wood, and the stones, and the dust, and licked up the water that *was* in the trench."

- **2 Kings 1:10**

"And Elijah answered and said to the captain of fifty, If I *be* a man of God, then let **fire** come down from heaven, and consume thee and thy fifty. And there came down **fire** from heaven, and consumed him and his fifty."

- **2 Kings 1:12**

"And Elijah answered and said unto them, If I *be* a man of God, let **fire** come down from heaven, and consume thee and thy fifty. And the **fire** of God came down from heaven, and consumed him and his fifty.

- **2 Kings 1:14**

"Behold, there came **fire** down from heaven, and burnt up the two captains of the former fifties with their fifties: therefore let my life now be precious in thy sight.

- **2 Kings 2:11**

"And it came to pass, as they still went on, and talked, that, behold, *there appeared* a chariot of **fire**, and horses of **fire**, and parted them both asunder; and Elijah went up by a whirlwind into heaven."

- **2 Kings 6:17**

"And Elisha prayed, and said, LORD, I pray thee, open his eyes, that he may see. And the LORD opened the eyes of the young man; and he saw: and, behold, the mountain *was* full of horses and chariots of **fire** round about Elisha."

- **1 Chronicles 21:26**

"And David built there an altar unto the LORD, and offered burnt offerings and peace offerings, and called upon the LORD; and he answered him from heaven by **fire** upon the altar of burnt offering."

- **2 Chronicles 7:1**

"Now when Solomon had made an end of praying, the **fire** came down from heaven, and consumed the burnt offering and the sacrifices; and the glory of the LORD filled the house."

- **2 Chronicles 7:3**

"And when all the children of Israel saw how the **fire** came down, and the glory of the LORD upon the house, they bowed themselves with their faces to the ground upon the pavement, and worshipped, and praised the LORD, *saying*, For *he is* good; for his mercy *endureth* for ever."

- **Nehemiah 9:12**

"Moreover thou leddest them in the day by a cloudy pillar; and in the night by a pillar of **fire**, to give them light in the way wherein they should go."

- **Nehemiah 9:19**

"Yet thou in thy manifold mercies forsookest them not in the wilderness: the pillar of the cloud departed not from them by day, to lead them in the way; neither the pillar of **fire** by night, to shew them light, and the way wherein they should go."

- **Job 1:16**

"While he *was* yet speaking, there came also another, and said, The **fire** of God is fallen from heaven, and hath burned up the sheep, and the servants, and consumed them; and I only am escaped alone to tell thee."

- **Job 41:19**

"Out of his mouth go burning lamps, *and* sparks of **fire** leap out.

- **Psalm 11:6**

"Upon the wicked he shall rain snares, **fire** and brimstone, and an horrible tempest: *this shall be* the portion of their cup."

- **Psalm 18:8**

"There went up a smoke out of his nostrils, and **fire** out of his mouth devoured: coals were kindled by it."

Psalm 18:12

"At the brightness *that was* before him his thick clouds passed, hail *stones* and coals of **fire**."

- **Psalm 18:13**

"The LORD also thundered in the heavens, and the Highest gave his voice; hail *stones* and coals of **fire**."

- **Psalm 21:9**

"Thou shalt make them as a fiery oven in the time of thine anger: the LORD shall swallow them up in his wrath, and the **fire** shall devour them."

- **Psalm 29:7**

"The voice of the LORD divideth the flames of **fire**."

- **Psalm 50:3**

"Our God shall come, and shall not keep silence: a **fire** shall devour before him, and it shall be very tempestuous round about him."

- **Psalm 78:14**

"In the daytime also he led them with a cloud, and all the night with a light of **fire**."

- **Psalm 97:3**

"A **fire** goeth before him, and burneth up his enemies round about."

- **Psalm 105:39**

"He spread a cloud for a covering; and **fire** to give light in the night."

- **Isaiah 4:5**

"And the LORD will create upon every dwelling place of mount Zion, and upon her assemblies, a cloud and smoke by day, and the shining of a flaming **fire** by night: for upon all the glory *shall be* a defence."

- **Isaiah 10:16**

"Therefore shall the Lord, the Lord of hosts, send among his fat ones leanness; and under his glory he shall kindle a burning like the burning of a **fire**."

- **Isaiah 29:6**

"Thou shalt be visited of the LORD of hosts with thunder, and with earthquake, and great noise, with storm and tempest, and the flame of devouring **fire**."

- **Isaiah 30:27**

"Behold, the name of the LORD cometh from far, burning with his anger, and the burden *thereof* is heavy: his lips are full of indignation, and his tongue as a devouring **fire**:"

- **Isaiah 30:30**

"And the LORD shall cause his glorious voice to be heard, and shall shew the lighting down of his arm, with the indignation of *his* anger, and *with* the flame of a devouring **fire**, *with* scattering, and tempest, and hailstones."

- **Isaiah 31:9**

"And he shall pass over to his strong hold for fear, and his princes shall be afraid of the ensign, saith the LORD, whose **fire** is in Zion, and his furnace in Jerusalem."

- **Isaiah 33:14**

"The sinners in Zion are afraid; fearfulness hath surprised the hypocrites. Who among us shall dwell with the devouring **fire**? who among us shall dwell with everlasting burnings?"

- **Isaiah 66:15**

"For, behold, the LORD will come with **fire**, and with his chariots like a whirlwind, to render his anger with fury, and his rebuke with flames of **fire**."

- **Isaiah 66:16**

"For by **fire** and by his sword will the LORD plead with all flesh: and the slain of the LORD shall be many."

- **Jeremiah 4:4**

"Circumcise yourselves to the LORD, and take away the foreskins of your heart, ye men of Judah and inhabitants of Jerusalem: lest my fury come forth like **fire**, and burn that none can quench *it*, because of the evil of your doings."

- **Jeremiah 21:12**

"O house of David, thus saith the LORD; Execute judgment in the morning, and deliver *him that* is spoiled out of the hand of the oppressor, lest my fury go out like **fire**, and burn that none can quench *it*, because of the evil of your doings."

- **Jeremiah 21:14**

"But I will punish you according to the fruit of your doings, saith the LORD: and I will kindle a **fire** in the forest thereof, and it shall devour all things round about it."

- **Lamentations 2:3**

"He hath cut off in his fierce anger all the horn of Israel: he hath drawn back his right hand from before the enemy, and he burned against Jacob like a flaming **fire**, *which* devoureth round about."

- **Lamentations 2:4**

"He hath bent his bow like an enemy: he stood with his right hand as an adversary, and slew all *that were* pleasant to the eye in the tabernacle of the daughter of Zion: he poured out his fury like **fire**."

- **Lamentations 4:11**

"The LORD hath accomplished his fury; he hath poured out his fierce anger, and hath kindled a **fire** in Zion, and it hath devoured the foundations thereof."

- **Ezekiel 1:4**

"And I looked, and, behold, a whirlwind came out of the north, a great cloud, and a **fire** infolding itself, and a brightness *was* about it, and out of the midst thereof as the colour of amber, out of the midst of the **fire**."

- **Ezekiel 22:21**

"Yea, I will gather you, and blow upon you in the **fire** of my wrath, and ye shall be melted in the midst thereof."

- **Ezekiel 22:31**

"Therefore have I poured out mine indignation upon them; I have consumed them with the **fire** of my wrath: their own way have I recompensed upon their heads, saith the Lord GOD."

- **Ezekiel 23:25**

"And I will set my jealousy against thee, and they shall deal furiously with thee: they shall take away thy nose and thine ears; and thy remnant shall fall by the sword: they shall take thy sons and thy daughters; and thy residue shall be devoured by the **fire**."

- **Ezekiel 38:19**

"For in my jealousy *and* in the **fire** of my wrath have I spoken, Surely in that day there shall be a great shaking in the land of Israel;"

- **Daniel 7:9**

"I beheld till the thrones were cast down, and the Ancient of days did sit, whose garment *was* white as snow, and the hair of his head like the pure wool: his throne *was like* the **fiery** flame, *and* his wheels *as* burning **fire**."

- **Amos 2:5**

"But I will send a **fire** upon Judah, and it shall devour the palaces of Jerusalem."

- **Amos 7:4**

"Thus hath the Lord GOD shewed unto me: and, behold, the Lord GOD called to contend by **fire**, and it devoured the great deep, and did eat up a part."

- **Nahum 1:6**

"Who can stand before his indignation? and who can abide in the fierceness of his anger? his fury is poured out like **fire**, and the rocks are thrown down by him."

- **Zechariah 2:5**

"For I, saith the LORD, will be unto her a wall of **fire** round about, and will be the glory in the midst of her."

- **Malachi 3:2**

"But who may abide the day of his coming? and who shall stand when he appeareth? for he is like a refiner's **fire**, and like fullers' soap:"

- **Luke 9:54**

"And when his disciples James and John saw *this*, they said, Lord, wilt thou that we command **fire** to come down from heaven, and consume them, even as Elias did?"

- **Luke 17:29**

"But the same day that Lot went out of Sodom it rained **fire** and brimstone from heaven, and destroyed *them* all."

- **Acts 7:30**

"And when forty years were expired, there appeared to him in the wilderness of mount Sina an angel of the Lord in a flame of **fire** in a bush."

- **Hebrews 1:7**

"And of the angels he saith, Who maketh his angels spirits, and his ministers a flame of **fire**."

- **Hebrews 12:18**

"For ye are not come unto the mount that might be touched, and that burned with **fire**, nor unto blackness, and darkness, and tempest,"

- **Hebrews 12:29**

"For our God *is* a **consuming fire**."

- **Revelation 1:14**

"His head and *his* hairs *were* white like wool, as white as snow; and his eyes *were* as a flame of **fire**;"

- **Revelation 2:18**

"And unto the angel of the church in Thyatira write; These things saith the Son of God, who hath his eyes like unto a flame of **fire**, and his feet *are* like fine brass;"

- **Revelation 4:5**

"And out of the throne proceeded lightnings and thunderings and voices: and *there were* seven lamps of **fire** burning before the throne, which are the seven Spirits of God."

- **Revelation 19:12**

"His eyes *were* as a flame of **fire**, and on his head *were* many crowns; and he had a name written, that no man knew, but he himself."

- **Revelation 20:9**

"And they went up on the breadth of the earth, and compassed the camp of the saints about, and the beloved city: and **fire** came down from God out of heaven, and devoured them."

Hebrews

Chapter Thirteen

Hebrews 13:1

"Let brotherly love continue."

BROTHERLY LOVE

Paul commands that **brotherly love** might continue. This love is **brotherly love**, not sexual love. I would like to look over twenty three verses about **love** to the genuinely saved Christians. This does not mean that we have to agree 100 percent with our brothers and sisters in Christ. We might have very strong differences such as on Bible versions, Biblical separation, music, dress, and many other things, but we are ordered to **love** them anyway.

- John 13:34

"A new commandment I give unto you, that ye **love one another**; as I have **loved** you, that ye also **love one another**."

It's impossible, but we should aim at that.

- John 13:35

"By this shall all *men* know that ye are my disciples, if ye have **love one to another**."

- John 15:12

"This is my commandment, that ye **love one another**, as I have **loved** you."

This is impossible, but it should be our goal.

- John 15:17

"These things I command you, that ye **love one another**."

- **Romans 12:10**

"*Be* kindly affectioned one to another with **brotherly love**; in honour preferring one another."

- **Romans 13:8**

"Owe no man any thing, but to **love one another**: for he that **loveth another** hath fulfilled the law."

- **Ephesians 1:15**

"Wherefore I also, after I heard of your faith in the Lord Jesus, and **love unto all the saints**,"

Not just a few, not just the good ones, but **all the saints**.

- **Ephesians 4:2**

"With all lowliness and meekness, with longsuffering, **forbearing one another in love**;"

Paul was speaking to Christian believers at Ephesus.

- **Colossians 1:4**

"Since we heard of your faith in Christ Jesus, and of the **love** *which ye have* to **all the saints**."

- **Colossians 2:2**

"That their hearts might be comforted, being **knit together in love**, and unto all riches of the full assurance of understanding, to the acknowledgment of the mystery of God, and of the Father, and of Christ;"

- **1 Thessalonians 4:9**

"But as touching **brotherly love** ye need not that I write unto you: for ye yourselves are taught of God to **love one another**."

- **1 Peter 1:22**

"Seeing ye have purified your souls in obeying the truth through the spirit unto unfeigned [that is, un-hypocritical] **love of the brethren**, *see that ye* **love one another** with a pure heart fervently:"

- **1 Peter 2:17**

"Honour all *men*. **Love the brotherhood**. Fear God. Honour the king."

- 1 Peter 3:8

"Finally, *be ye* all of one mind, having compassion one of another, **love as brethren**, *be* pitiful, *be* courteous:"

- 1 John 3:11

"For this is the message that ye heard from the beginning, that we should **love one another**."

- 1 John 3:14

"We know that we have passed from death unto life, because we **love the brethren**. He that **loveth** not *his* brother abideth in death."

- 1 John 3:18

"My little children, let us not **love** in word, neither in tongue; but in deed and in truth."

- 1 John 3:23

"And this is his commandment, that we should believe on the name of his son Jesus Christ, and **love one another**, as he gave us commandment."

- 1 John 4:7

"Beloved, let us **love one another**: for **love** is of God; and every one that **loveth** is born of God, and knoweth God."

- 1 John 4:11

"Beloved, if God so **loved** us, we ought also to **love one another**."

LOVE FELLOW CHRISTIANS

God so loved us, who are sinners, lost, and bound for hell, before we genuinely trusted the Lord Jesus Christ. We should also love fellow Christians.

- 1 John 4:20

"If a man say, I **love** God, and hateth his brother, he is a liar: for he that **loveth** not his brother whom he hath seen, how can he **love** God whom he hath not seen?"

- 1 John 4:21

"And this commandment have we from him, that he who **loveth** God **love his brother** also."

- 1 John 5:2

"By this we know that we **love the children of God**, when we **love** God, and keep his commandments."

- 2 John 1:5

"And now I beseech thee, lady, not as though I wrote a new commandment unto thee, but that which we had from the beginning, that we **love one another**."

The Lord Jesus Christ taught His disciples to have **love for all genuine Christians**, regardless of differences that they have among them.

There are all kinds of fundamental Bible believing Christians, that differ with us, for example, on the King James Bible and its underlying inerrant and preserved Hebrew, Aramaic, and Greek Words. Many such true Christians use and encourage others to use the NKJV, the ASV, the NASV, the NIV, the ESV, the RSV, the NRSV or other Bible versions, but God has ordered us to **love** them regardless. This does not mean that we are to cooperate with them in non-Biblical practices.

LOVE THE BRETHREN

When we love our brethren (with whom we differ strongly on many of their positions), we wish they would love us back. This is seldom the case, sadly.

Hebrews 13:2

"Be not forgetful to entertain strangers: for thereby some have entertained angels unawares."

ANGELS

This verb, *"be not forgetful,"* is a negative prohibition. It is in the Greek present tense. As such, it means to stop an action already in progress.

> **ENTERTAINING OTHER CHRISTIANS**
>
> These true Christians that Paul is addressing were forgetting to entertain strangers. He is telling them to stop it. There weren't any hotels or motels in those days. True Christians had to go to other Christian's homes when they traveled from place to place.

- **Genesis 19:1-2**

"And there came two **angels** to Sodom at even; and Lot sat in the gate of Sodom: and Lot seeing *them* rose up to meet them; and he bowed himself with his face toward the ground; And he said, Behold now, **my lords**, turn in, I pray **you**, into **your** servant's house, and tarry all night, and wash **your** feet, and **ye** shall rise up early, and go on **your** ways. And **they** said, Nay; but **we** will abide in the street all night."

Here's a case where <u>Lot did not know these two men were **angels**</u>. He entertained **them** unawares.

Hebrews 13:3

"**Remember them that are in bonds, as bound with them;** *and* **them which suffer adversity, as being yourselves also in the body.**"

BONDS

Paul is concerned for those in the **bonds of a prison**. I wonder if Paul was in **prison** himself at this time. There are some other remarks in Hebrews that hint about this imprisonment as well. It is not clear, but we do know that he greeted those who were in Italy where the Roman **prison** was.

- **Hebrews 13:24**

"Salute all them that have the rule over you, and all the saints. They of Italy salute you.

Regardless of whether or not Paul was in **bonds** when he wrote this, he wanted true Christians to remember them who were in **bonds** as being

bound with them. They were to be sympathetic and even empathetic with them.

There's all kinds of **bondage**. Not only physical **bondage**, but the **bondage** of drugs, evil practices, and many others. Genuine Christians should continue to remember those in **bonds**. This is the Greek present tense which represents a continuous action.

> ### THE BODY OF CHRIST=ALL THE SAVED
> I think the words *"also in the body"* refer to the body of Christ which includes all genuine Christians.

Other true Christians should take care of fellow believers just like they would do to members of their own family who suffer adversity. There are many true Christians who are in **bondage** to dictators around the world whether these are the Communists in Russia, China, Cuba, or the ISIS terrorists in the Middle East and elsewhere. Genuine Christians should pray for them as being **bound** with them.

Hebrews 13:4

"Marriage is honourable in all, and the bed undefiled: but whoremongers and adulterers God will judge."

BIBLICAL MARRIAGE

> ### HOMOSEXUAL "MARRIAGE" NOT BIBLICAL!
> There is only one definition in the Bible for marriage. It is between a man and a woman. It is totally unBiblical to define marriage as between a man and man or between a woman and a woman. That's not Biblical marriage. It a sinful and corrupt practice of sodomy for which God judged Sodom and Gomorrha.

A few years ago, as this was being written, Congress passed the **DEFENSE OF MARRIAGE ACT (DOMA)**. This law has not been enforced by Obama or by his Attorney General. On the contrary, it has been wiped out. In fact, Obama has designated the month of June to honor Lesbian, Gay, Bisexual and Transgender (LGBT) men and women who are living <u>sinful lifestyles</u> condemned by God's Words in the Bible.

Marriage is honourable in all, even including the priests and nuns of the Roman Catholic Church. This includes the Pope and all the others in that apostate and false religion. They are not honoring that Biblical status by requiring the priests and nuns to abstain from marriage. Homosexuality prevails among the priests in many of their churches and even in some of their seminaries. Often, among the nuns, lesbianism and intercourse between the nuns and the priests occurs.

SEXUAL RELATIONS OF MARRIED UNDEFILED

The bed, that is the sexual love between a husband and a wife, is undefiled. It is not sinful or wicked in any way. It is honorable and godly. But whoremongers and adulterers God will judge.

The Greek Word for "*whoremongers*" is PORNOS. Some of the meanings of this Word are:

> "1) a man who prostitutes his body to another's lust for hire; 2) a male prostitute; 3) a man who indulges in unlawful sexual intercourse, a fornicator."

GOD WILL JUDGE ADULTERERS

In addition to these whoremongers, God is going to judge adulterers as well. Those who are married and have sexual unions with those not their spouse commit the sin of adultery. God has promised to judge all such people.

The apostle Paul tells us the purpose of **marriage** and the duties of **married** love.

- **1 Corinthians 7:1-5**

"Now concerning the things whereof ye wrote unto me: *It is good for a man not to touch a woman*. Nevertheless, *to avoid fornication*, **let every man have his own wife, and let every woman have her own husband. Let the husband render unto the wife due benevolence: and likewise also the wife unto the husband. The wife hath not power of her own body, but the husband: and likewise** also the husband hath not power of his own body, but the wife. Defraud ye not one the other, except *it be* with consent for a time, that ye may give yourselves to fasting and prayer; and come together again, that Satan **tempt** you not for your incontinency."

DON'T REFUSE YOUR MATE MARRIED LOVE

I know couples who have not had married love for years. This is a direct disobedience of the Words of God! It's contrary to 1 Corinthians 7:1-5.

You may wonder how did Paul know all this. <u>I believe Paul was married.</u> He was a member of the Jewish Sanhedrin. One of the rules for such membership was that they had to be **married.** **His wife** apparently died. He knew all about **marriage.** The Lord gave him these verses and these Words which he wrote to the Corinthian church. They needed to have this sound teaching because of their incest, fornication and other wickednesses in their church. <u>All genuine Christians need this teaching today as well.</u>

Hebrews 13:5

"*Let your* conversation be without covetousness; *and be* content with such things as ye have: for he hath said, I will never leave thee, nor forsake thee."

The Greek Word for "*conversation*" used here is TROPOS. Some of the meanings of this Greek Word are:

> "1) *a manner, way, fashion; 1a) as, even as, like as'*
> 2) *manner of life, character, deportment.*"

WITHOUT COVETOUSNESS

CHRISTIANS SHOULD NOT COVET

Paul is speaking to genuine Christians here. The first thing about their manner of life is that it should be without covetousness.

The Greek Word for *"covetousness"* is: APHILARGUROS. Some of the meanings of this Word are:

"1) not loving money, not avaricious"

They should not love and long for money. There are many verses that speak of **covetousness** as being evil.

- **Exodus 20:17**

"Thou shalt not **covet** thy neighbour's house, thou shalt not **covet** thy neighbour's wife, nor his manservant, nor his maidservant, nor his ox, nor his ass, nor any thing that is thy neighbour's."

- **Mark 7:21-22**

"For from within, out of the heart of men, proceed evil thoughts, adulteries, fornications, murders, Thefts, **covetousness**, wickedness, deceit, lasciviousness, an evil eye, blasphemy, pride, foolishness:"

COVETOUSNESS COMES FROM THE HEART

Out of the heart of man proceeds these different things and one of them is **covetousness**. It's a heart problem. The cardiologist can't help you with it. Only the Lord can help true Christians with that heart problem. It's a spiritual problem.

- **Luke 12:15**

"And he said unto them, Take heed, and beware of **covetousness**: for a man's life consisteth not in the abundance of the things which he possesseth."

- **Acts 20:33**

"I have **coveted** no man's silver, or gold, or apparel."

- **Romans 1:29**

"Being filled with all unrighteousness, fornication, wickedness, **covetousness**, maliciousness; full of envy, murder, debate, deceit, malignity, whisperers, backbiters, haters of God, despiteful, proud, boasters, inventors of evil things, disobedient to parents, Without understanding, covenant-breakers, without natural affection, implacable, unmerciful:"

This is a picture of the pagan world.

- **Ephesians 5:3**

"But fornication, and all uncleanness, or **covetousness**, let it not be once named among you, as becometh saints;"

- **Colossians 3:5**

"Mortify therefore your members which are upon the earth; fornication, uncleanness, inordinate affection, evil concupiscence, and **covetousness**, which is idolatry:"

Mortify means to put to death. In this case, it is spiritual not physical. Every person has at least ten important members of their body. They have two eyes, two ears, two hands, two feet, one mind, one heart, and one tongue.

- **1 Timothy 3:3**

"Not given to wine, no striker, not greedy of filthy lucre; but patient, not a brawler, not **covetous**;"

This is one of the pastoral qualifications. Pastor-bishop-elders were not to be **covetous**.

- **2 Timothy 3:1-2**

"This know also, that in the last days perilous times shall come. For men shall be lovers of their own selves, **covetous**, boasters, proud, blasphemers, disobedient to parents, unthankful, unholy,"

EMINENT DOMAIN IS COVETOUSNESS

Covetousness is a part of the government's use of eminent domain. They take private properties sometimes for public purposes, but sometimes for some other private person's interests.

CONTENTMENT

The second requirement for the manner of life for these true Christians is that they must **be content** with such things as they have. The Greek verb for "**be content**" is ARKEO. Some of the meanings of this Word are:

"1) to be possessed of unfailing strength; 1a) to be strong, to suffice, to be enough; 1a1) to defend, ward off; 1b) to be satisfied, to be contented."

The Greek Word is in the present tense.

> ### CONTINUING CONTENTMENT COMMANDED
> This has the idea of continuous action. There must a continuing contentment on the part of these truly saved people. The truly born-again and saved Christians must be continuously content with the things that they possess.

This is often a difficult thing for many Christians to possess. But that does not mean this command must not be obeyed. Here are some of the verses on contentment.

- **Luke 3:14**

"And the soldiers likewise demanded of him, saying, and what shall we do? And he said unto them, do violence to no man, neither accuse *any* falsely; and be **content** with your wages."

The Lord Jesus talked to the soldiers.

- **Philippians 4:11**

"Not that I speak in respect of want: for I have learned, in whatsoever state I am, *therewith* to **be content**."

The apostle Paul had many more difficulties and persecutions than any of us have had and yet he learned to **be content** in whatsoever state he found himself. So should all genuine Christians living today.

- **1 Timothy 6:6**

"But godliness with **contentment** is great gain."

Not simply godliness, but with **contentment.**

- **1 Timothy 6:8**

"And having food and raiment let us be therewith **content**."

> ### CHRIST DOESN'T FORSAKE THE SAVED
> The motivating reason for continuous contentment is the fact that the Lord Jesus Christ promised never to leave nor forsake the genuinely saved.

That Greek word for *"never"* is OU ME. This is the strongest negative in the Greek language. It means, never, never, never. Here are some of the verses that also teach this truth.

- Matthew 1:23

"Behold, a virgin shall be with child, and shall bring forth a son, and they shall call his name Emmanuel, which being interpreted is, **God with us.**"

EMMANUEL–GOD WITH US

The Hebrew Word *"Emmanuel,"* means literally "With us God" or *"God with us."* The Lord Jesus Christ is with those who are truly saved.

- Matthew 28:20

"Teaching them to observe all things whatsoever I have commanded you: and, lo, **I am with you always,** *even* unto the end of the world. Amen."

CHRIST WITH THE SAVED ALWAYS

Before the Lord Jesus Christ went home to Heaven, after His bodily resurrection, He talked with his eleven disciples. He told them He would be with them always. This promise continues with every truly saved Christian even today.

Hebrews 13:6

"So that we may boldly say, The Lord is my helper, and I will not fear what man shall do unto me."

THE LORD OUR HELPER–NO FEAR

It is interesting that both *"may boldly"* and *"say"* are verbs that are in the Greek present tense. Though it is a little difficult to express, it might be thought of having continual boldness and continuously speaking about what follows.

There are two things that the genuine Christians were to continuously and boldly say: (1) **the Lord is their Helper**, and (2) They will **not fear what man should do to them**.

When a man or woman is genuinely saved by true faith in the **Lord Jesus Christ as their Saviour,** <u>**He** has promised to be their **Helper** when they are in need of help</u>. Every one of them needs **help** at one time or another.

<u>Because of **His** being their **Helper,** they will **not fear whatever man might to do to them**</u>. I recently saw a video of a terrible slaughter by terrorist Muslims of both men and women. The terrorists thrust their knives into the chests of the victims who screamed and hollered. I thought of this statement that is in this verse.

DON'T FEAR MAN

What a difficult thing to do—not to fear what man shall do unto genuine Christians. God must give them great power to fulfill this promise in the face of what might follow them in the days in which they live.

Hebrews 13:7

"Remember them which have the rule over you, who have spoken unto you the word of God: whose faith follow, considering the end of *their* conversation."

FAITHFUL RULERS AND LEADERS

ONE OFFICE–PASTORS/BISHOPS/ELDERS

Those who have the rule over true Christians and have spoken to them the Words of God are the pastors-bishops-elders. It could also speak of moms and dads who are teaching their children the things of the Lord. Notice the topic that these leaders have spoken about. It is the Words of God—not some tiny sermonette, not some philosophy lesson, not a serious of stories, but the Words of God. That's what I seek to do at our Bible For Today Baptist Church. I seek to speak and talk about the Words of God.

These faithful preachers, faithful missionaries, and faithful teaching moms and dads should be followed, especially considering the end of **their** manner of life. **They** will receive blessings from the Lord Jesus Christ as **they** live to please Him in all ways and one day, **they** will be taken to Heaven to be with Him forever.

Hebrews 13:8

"Jesus Christ the same yesterday, and to day, and for ever."

JESUS CHRIST NEVER CHANGES

It is a wonderful truth to know that the **Lord Jesus Christ never changes,** but is the **same yesterday, today, and forever.** It is so different with our country which is constantly changing, especially under the Obama administration. <u>Obama is changing many, many provisions of our United States Constitution. But the **Saviour does not change. He won't change**</u>.

- Malachi 3:6

"For I *am* the LORD, I change not; therefore ye sons of Jacob are not consumed."

AN UNCHANGEABLE GOD

Those who are genuinely saved have an unchangeable God the Father as well as an unchangeable God the Son and God the Holy Spirit.

- Micah 5:2

"But thou, Bethlehem Ephratah, *though* thou be little among the thousands of Judah, *yet* out of thee shall he come forth unto me *that is* to be ruler in Israel; whose goings forth *have been* from of old, from everlasting."

CHRIST FROM ALL ETERNITY PAST

This a prophecy of the birth of the Lord Jesus Christ Whose goings forth have been from all eternity past.

- **Hebrews 1:12**

"As a vesture shalt thou fold them up, and they shall be changed: but **thou art the same, and thy years shall not fail.**"

This is speaking of **the Lord Jesus Christ Who is the same and Whose years shall never fail.** <u>Those who are truly saved have an everlasting and unchangeable Saviour</u>. This is a wonderful truth.

Hebrews 13:9

"Be not carried about with divers and strange doctrines. For *it is* a good thing that the heart be established with grace; not with meats, which have not profited them that have been occupied therein."

SOUND DOCTRINE

<u>Sound doctrine is of vital importance. Paul did not want his readers to be carried about with different and strange unscriptural doctrines.</u> The Greek Word for *"carried about"* is PERIPHERO. Some of the meanings for this Word are:

> *"1) to carry round, to bear about everywhere with one; 2) to carry here and there; 3) to be driven; 3a) in doubt and hesitation to be led away now to this opinion, now to that."*

<u>This Greek verb is in the present tense. Since it is a negative prohibition, it means to stop an action already in progress.</u> Paul is telling them to stop being carried here and there with different and unscriptural **doctrines**.

FALSE DOCTRINES ALL AROUND US

Today, we have false doctrines all around us. True Christians must stop getting involved with false doctrines. They must be founded and grounded on the true doctrines found in the Bible. Every doctrine or teaching that is not Biblical must be rejected and avoided. This includes out and out apostasy in doctrine and practice as well as the compromises of new evangelicalism and all the other departures from truth that are rampant all around the world.

WE NEED SOUND DOCTRINE

In addition to sound and healthy doctrine, the heart of each genuine Christian must be established with grace. God's grace must be evidenced in their hearts. <u>Externals of any kind, whether meats or any other things can never take the place of God's grace.</u>

Here are some verses that deal with **doctrine**.

- **Matthew 22:33**

"And when the multitude heard *this*, they were astonished at his **doctrine**."

<u>The Lord Jesus Christ was a **doctrinal teacher**</u>. Those who heard Him were astonished.

- **John 7:16**

"Jesus answered them, and said, **My doctrine is not mine, but his that sent me.**"

The **doctrine of the Lord Jesus Christ was from His Father**.

- **John 7:17**

"If any man will do his will, he shall know of the **doctrine**, whether it be of God, or *whether* I speak of myself."

- **Romans 16:17**

"Now I beseech you, brethren, mark them which cause divisions and offences contrary to the **doctrine** which ye have learned; and avoid them."

AVOID FALSE DOCTRINE

Anyone who teaches contrary to the doctrine of the Bible must be avoided. If it's a church that's teaching false doctrine, get out of there!

- **Ephesians 4:14**

"That we henceforth be no more children, tossed to and fro, and carried about with every wind of **doctrine**, by the sleight of men, and cunning craftiness, whereby they lie in wait to deceive;"

Modernism, compromises, and apostasy are very deceptive, whether it be from Joel Osteen, Rick Warren, or from any other false prophets that lead people astray from Bible truth.

- **1 Timothy 4:6**

"If thou put the brethren in remembrance of these things, thou shalt be a good minister of Jesus Christ, nourished up in the words of faith and **good doctrine**, whereunto thou hast attained."

- **1 Timothy 4:13**

"Till I come, give attendance to reading, to exhortation, to **doctrine**."

TEACH GOD'S WORDS!

Teaching the Words of the living God was what Paul told pastor Timothy he was to do. Doctrine is important.

Many pastors do not teach and preach **doctrine**. Instead, they tell stories or take a few verses out of context and give little vacuous homilies. Some churches and many church members hate **doctrine**.

- **1 Timothy 4:16**

"Take heed unto thyself, and unto the **doctrine**; continue in them: for in doing this thou shalt both save thyself, and them that hear thee."

First of all, pastors must take heed to themselves. This is primary. They must be certain that their lives are sound and holy before the Lord. After that, the **doctrine that they teach must be Biblical and sound**.

- **1 Timothy 6:3-5**

"If any man teach otherwise, and consent not to wholesome words, *even* the words of our Lord Jesus Christ, and to the **doctrine** which is according to godliness; He is proud, knowing nothing, but doting about questions and strifes of words, whereof cometh envy, strife, railings, evil surmising, Perverse disputing of men of corrupt minds, and destitute of the truth, supposing that gain is godliness: from such withdraw thyself."

- **2 Timothy 3:10**

"But thou hast fully known my **doctrine**, manner of life, purpose, faith, longsuffering, charity, patience"

Timothy went with Paul on many of his missionary journeys. He knew fully what Paul's **teachings and doctrine** were.

- **2 Timothy 3:16-17**

"All scripture is given by inspiration of God, and *is* profitable for **doctrine**, for reproof, for correction, for instruction in righteousness: That the man of God may be perfect, thoroughly furnished unto all good works."

The Bible is profitable for sound doctrine and teachings.

- **2 Timothy 4:2**

"Preach the word; be instant in season, out of season; reprove, rebuke, exhort with all longsuffering and **doctrine**."

Sound preaching must be rooted in sound doctrine.

- **2 Timothy 4:3**

"For the time will come when they will not endure **sound doctrine**; but after their own lusts shall they heap to themselves teachers, having itching ears;"

The time has already come for people not to endure **sound doctrine**. People are accepting false teachers and false **doctrine**.

- **Titus 1:9**

"Holding fast the faithful word as he hath been taught, that he may be able by **sound doctrine** both to exhort and to convince the gainsayers."

Hold the **faithful Words of God** and don't give up for any reason.

- **Titus 2:1**

"But speak thou the things which become **sound doctrine**:"

- **Titus 2:7**

"In all things shewing thyself a pattern of good works: in **doctrine** *shewing* uncorruptness, gravity, sincerity,"

Uncorrupt and untainted Biblical doctrine must be followed faithfully.

- **2 John 9-11**

"Whosoever transgresseth, and abideth not in the **doctrine of Christ**, hath not God. He that abideth in the **doctrine of Christ**, he hath both the Father and the Son. If there come any unto you, and bring not **this doctrine**, receive him not into *your* house, neither bid him God speed. For he that biddeth him God speed is partaker of his evil deeds."

MEANING OF THE DOCTRINE OF CHRIST

The doctrine of Christ is known by the term Christology. It is one of the ten major themes of theology. It includes the Lord Jesus Christ's Deity, virgin birth, bodily resurrection, miracles, blood atonement, return in the rapture, returning to earth to set up His millennial reign, and many other things.

DON'T LET APOSTATES INTO YOUR HOUSE

If someone like the Jehovah Witnesses come to the door of the genuine Christians, they should obey this verse and neither receive them into their house or bid them God speed. To do so would make them a partaker of their evil deeds.

I remember when I was a reporter at a meeting where Billy Graham addressed the apostate National Council of Churches. After he spoke to these apostate unbelievers, he said "God bless you." As these verses proclaim, by these words, Billy Graham was a partaker of the evil deeds of the National Council of Churches.

Hebrews 13:10

"We have an altar, whereof they have no right to eat which serve the tabernacle."

JESUS CHRIST THE ALTAR

CHRIST GIVES THE SAVED HELP

This is speaking about the Lord Jesus Christ Who is the *altar* where those who are genuinely saved can go for help and support.

The Old Testament Levitical leaders had no right to partake of **this altar** because **the Lord Jesus Christ** had not yet come. The Greek Word for "*altar*" is THUSIASTERION. Some of the meanings of this Word are:

> "1) the altar for slaying and burning of victims used of; 1a) the altar of whole burnt offerings which stood in the court of the priests in the temple at Jerusalem; 1b) the altar of incense which stood in the sanctuary or the Holy Place; 1c) any other altar; 1c1) metaph., the cross on which Christ suffered an expiatory death: to eat of this altar i.e. to appropriate to one's self the fruits of Christ's expiatory death."

CHRIST DIED FOR THE SINS OF THE WORLD

In the New Testament, we have a completely different altar than there was in the Old Testament. It is the cross of Calvary on which the Lord Jesus Christ died to atone for the sins of the entire world. Only those who have genuinely trusted the Lord Jesus Christ as their Saviour have a right to that altar.

Hebrews 13:11

"**For the bodies of those beasts, whose blood is brought into the sanctuary by the high priest for sin, are burned without the camp."**

Though the blood of the Old Testament offerings were brought into the tabernacle's sanctuary for a sin offering, the bodies of those animals were burned outside the camp of Israel. So the Lord Jesus Christ was crucified without the gate of Jerusalem. It was an ignominious death which could not have taken place in Jerusalem itself.

Hebrews 13:12

"**Wherefore Jesus also, that he might sanctify the people with his own blood, suffered without the gate."**

CHRIST SUFFERED WITHOUT THE GATE

In fulfillment of the previous verse, the **Lord Jesus Christ suffered without the gates of Jerusalem.** The purpose of His substitutionary death on the cross of Calvary was in order to sanctify and set apart those who would truly trust Him as their **Saviour.** It was **with His own blood** that this sanctification and salvation could take place. **He shed His incorruptible blood for the sins of the entire world.** I have found at least fourteen things in the New Testament that are accomplished by the **shedding of the blood of the Lord Jesus Christ.** The one here results in the sanctification of those who genuinely accept **Him as their Saviour.** For the other effects of the blood of the Lord Jesus Christ, you can get a cassette tape detailing them. [See **BFT #2803** for a cassette tape on *"Fourteen Effects of the Blood of Christ"* @ $4.00 + $2.00 S&H or write for **BFT #2548-T** which is a 5-page tract that sums up these 14 points with the Bible verses to go with them @ **$2.00 including S&H**]

Hebrews 13:13

"Let us go forth therefore unto him without the camp, bearing his reproach."

BEARING CHRIST'S REPROACH

Paul was commanding the genuine Christians to go unto **the Lord Jesus Christ** outside the secular anti-Christian groups as well as apostate or compromise so-called "Christian" groups who do not follow the Bible's doctrines and teachings. This also includes all of the major false world religions of the day, including the Muslims, the Buddhists, the Taoists and all the others. These true Christians must go forth unto **the Lord Jesus Christ** for His fellowship, going outside the general camp of false religionists. They should not go into the camp of unbelievers, modernists, apostates, followers of Roman Catholicism, and all other false teachings. **They should bear His reproach.** There are people who look upon those who believe in and follow the Bible's positions as being crazy to believe the Bible. **They call them all kinds of names.**

BEARING CHRIST'S REPROACH

No matter what happens, true Christians must bear the reproach of the Lord Jesus Christ. There are many verses that talk of reproach.

- **Psalm 42:10**

"*As* with a sword in my bones, mine enemies **reproach** me; while they say daily unto me, Where is thy God?"

- **Psalm 79:4**

"We are become a **reproach** to our neighbours, a scorn and derision to them that are round about us."

- **Luke 6:22**

"Blessed are ye, when men shall hate you, and when they shall separate you *from their company*, and shall **reproach** you, and cast out your name as evil, for the Son of man's sake."

- 1 Timothy 4:10

"For therefore we both labour and **suffer reproach**, because we trust in the living God, who is the Saviour of all men, specially of those that believe."

- Hebrews 11:26

"Esteeming the **reproach of Christ** greater riches than the treasures in Egypt: for he had respect unto the recompence of the reward."

MOSES CHOSE TO OBEY GOD

Moses could have all the wonderful things that he had in the early part of his life. He was picked up by Pharaoh's daughter from the river and brought into the palace of the king of Egypt. He had good food, fine clothes, and all kinds of the finer things of life in his day.

But when God spoke to him and told him to get out of Egypt and take the Israelites with him, he said "yes." He esteemed the reproach of Christ, his Messiah, greater riches than all the treasures in Egypt.

Hebrews 13:14

"For here have we no continuing city, but we seek one to come."

NO CONTINUING CITY

HEAVEN IS SURE AND ETERNAL

The genuinely saved Christians have no continuing city here on this earth. They seek one to come in Heaven for all eternity. Those who are not genuine Christians have no continuing city on earth and what is to come for them is the Lake of fire in Hell for all eternity. This is indeed a most horrible destiny!

- Luke 9:58

"And Jesus said unto him, Foxes have holes, and birds of the air *have* nests; but the Son of man hath not where to lay *his* head."

The Lord Jesus Christ had **no continuing city** while He was here on earth. He had no home of His own.

- Hebrews 11:10

"For he **looked for a city** which hath foundations, whose builder and maker is God."

That's an eternal city. That's Heaven itself.

- Hebrews 11:16

"But now they desire **a better** *country*, that is, an **heavenly**: wherefore God is not ashamed to be called their God: for he hath prepared for them a **city**."

The Old Testament heroes of the faith also looked for a **Heavenly city**.

- Hebrews 12:22a

"But ye are come unto **mount Sion**, and unto the **city of the living God, the heavenly Jerusalem,**"

That's **the place** which the Lord Jesus Christ said He was going to prepare.

Hebrews 13:15

"By him therefore let us offer the sacrifice of praise to God continually, that is, the fruit of *lips* giving thanks to his name."

By means of the Lord Jesus Christ, truly saved Christians are to offer four sacrifices to the Lord. The first two are listed in this verse. These are not the blood offering of the Old Testament, but God considers them to be very important for His saved people today.

1. THE SACRIFICE OF CONTINUAL PRAISE TO GOD

PRAISE GOD CONTINUALLY

The first of these sacrifices that genuine Christians are to offer is praise to God continually.

- **Luke 18:41-43**

"Saying, What wilt thou that I shall do unto thee? And he said, Lord, that I may receive my sight. And Jesus said unto him, Receive thy sight: thy faith hath saved thee. And immediately he received his sight, and followed him, glorifying God: and all the people, when they saw it, gave **praise** unto God."

<u>**Praise** is the first **sacrifice** God wants every true Christian to give to Him.</u>

- **John 12:42-43**

"Nevertheless among the chief rulers also many believed on him; but because of the Pharisees they did not confess *him*, lest they should be put out of the synagogue. For they loved the **praise** of men more than the **praise of God**."

<u>True Christians should never desire the **praise** of men more than the **praise of God**.</u>

- **Romans 15:11**

"And again, **Praise the Lord**, all ye Gentiles; and laud him, all ye people."

Revelation 19:5

"And a voice came out of the throne, saying, **Praise our God**, all ye his servants, and ye that fear him, both small and great."

2. THE SACRIFICE OF THANKS TO GOD'S NAME

THANK GOD WITH OUR LIPS

The second of these sacrifices that genuine Christians are to offer is thanks to God's Name with their lips.

- **1 Thessalonians 5:18**

"<u>In every thing give **thanks**</u>: for this is the will of God in Christ Jesus concerning you."

- **John 6:11**

"And Jesus took the loaves; and when he had given **thanks**, he distributed to the disciples, and the disciples to them that were set down; and likewise of the fishes as much as they would."

He gave **thanks** before He fed the 5,000 men plus women and children.

- **John 6:23**

"(Howbeit there came other boats from Tiberias nigh unto the place where they did eat bread, after that the Lord had given **thanks**:)"

<u>We are reminded that the Lord Jesus Christ was a **thankful** Saviour to His Father, giving **thanks**.</u>

- **Ephesians 5:4**

"Neither filthiness, nor foolish talking, nor jesting, which are not convenient: but rather giving of **thanks**."

- **Colossians 1:12**

"Giving **thanks** unto the Father, which hath made us meet to be partakers of the inheritance of the saints in light."

- **Colossians 3:17**

"And whatsoever ye do in word or deed, *do* all in the name of the Lord Jesus, giving **thanks to God and the Father** by him."

THANKFUL IN ALL THINGS

Many times genuine Christians have circumstances in their lives that are very difficult. But they are still to give thanks even in those circumstances, they should be thankful.

Hebrews 13:16

"But to do good and to communicate forget not: for with such sacrifices God is well pleased."

In this verse there are two more **sacrifices** that the true Christians are to give to the Lord.

3. THE SACRIFICE OF DOING GOOD

DO WHAT GOD CALLS "GOOD"

The third sacrifice is for them to do good. They should not do that which is bad or evil, but things that are good and pleasing to the Lord.

How do they know what is **good**? The Bible is the only place where true Christians can find what is **good**. It is not what the world thinks is **good**. The world, for example, thinks that sodomy, and the marriage of two men and two women together is acceptable. God's Words disagree with these policies.

4. THE SACRIFICE OF COMMUNICATING

> **CHRISTIANS SHOULD COMMUNICATE**
>
> The fourth sacrifice is for true Christians not to forget to communicate.

The Greek Word for "*communicate*" s KOINONIA. Some of the meanings of this Word are:

> "1) fellowship, association, community, communion, joint participation, intercourse; 1a) the share which one has in anything, participation; 1b) intercourse, fellowship, intimacy; 1b1) the right hand as a sign and pledge of fellowship (in fulfilling the apostolic office); 1c) a gift jointly contributed, a collection, a contribution, as exhibiting an embodiment and proof of fellowship."

The negative prohibition of "*forget not*" is in the Greek present tense. As such, it it means that they have been forgetting to **communicate** and they must stop it. Among the various meanings of this word, the most likely meaning of "*communicate*" here is to share something with other people who need it, including money.

> **FOUR PLEASING SACRIFICES**
>
> With these four sacrifices by genuine Christians such as are mentioned in these two previous verses, God is well pleased. These include
>
> 1. giving continuous praise to God,
> 2. giving thanks to His Name,
> 3. doing that which is good, and
> 4. communicating to others who have need.

Hebrews 13:17

"Obey them that have the rule over you, and submit yourselves: for they watch for your souls, as they that must give account, that they may do it with joy, and not with grief: for that is unprofitable for you."

PASTORS-BISHOPS-ELDERS

MINISTERS' THREEFOLD TITLE

I believe this verse is referring to the pastors-bishops-elders who minister in the local churches of those who are genuine Christians. These Christians are to submit themselves to their teachings that are Biblical and in line with the Bible. These church leaders must give an account to the Lord Jesus Christ for their ministries as they watch for the souls to whom they minister. It is hoped that they all will minister with joy not with grief and harm the people to whom they minister.

I believe the New Testament is clear that there are **three titles** for the same office of **those who lead local churches.** It is the **pastor-bishop-elder**. There are two passages in the New Testament that clearly teach this.

- 1 Peter 5:1-3

"The **elders** [PRESBYTEROS, those who are elders] which are among you I exhort, who am also an elder, and a witness of the sufferings of Christ, and also a partaker of the glory that shall be revealed: **Feed** [POIMAINO feed, shepherd, or be the pastor of] the flock of God which is among you, taking the **oversight** [EPISCOPOEO, be the bishop or take the oversight] *thereof,* not by constraint, but willingly; not for filthy lucre, but of a ready mind; Neither as being lords over *God's* heritage, but being ensamples to the flock."

- **Acts 20:17, 28-29**

"And from Miletus he sent to Ephesus, and called the **elders** [PRESBYTEROS, those who are **elders**] of the church.... (28-29) Take heed therefore unto yourselves, and to all the flock, over the which the Holy Ghost hath made you **overseers**, [EPISCOPOS, **bishop or overseer**] to feed [POIMAINO feed, shepherd, or be the **pastor** of] the church of God, which he hath purchased with his own blood. For I know this, that after my departing shall grievous wolves enter in among you, not sparing the flock."

The Word for "*obey*" is PEITHO. Some of the meanings of this Word are:

"1) persuade; 1a) to persuade, i.e. to induce one by words to believe; 1b) to make friends of, to win one's favour, gain one's good; will, or to seek to win one, strive to please one; 1c) to tranquillise; 1d) to persuade unto i.e. move or induce one to persuasion to do something; 2) be persuaded; 2a) to be persuaded, to suffer one's self to be persuaded; to be induced to believe: to have faith: in a thing; 2a1) to believe; 2a2) to be persuaded of a thing concerning a person; 2b) to listen to, obey, yield to, comply with; 3) to trust, have confidence, be confident."

This command is in the Greek present tense. As such, it is to be a continuous action.

TRUST THOSE WHO RULE BIBLICALLY

Those genuine Christians were to continue to be persuaded by, to listen to, to trust, to have confidence in those pastors-bishops-elders who had the rule over them.

The Greek Word for "*rule*" is HEGEOMAI. Some of the meanings for this Word are:

"*1) to lead; 1a) to go before; 1b) to be a leader; 1b1) to rule, command; 1b2) to have authority over; 1b3) a prince, of regal power, governor, viceroy, chief, leading; as respects influence, controlling in counsel, overseers or leaders of the churches; 1b4) used of any kind of leader, chief, commander; 1b5) the leader in speech, chief, spokesman; 2) to consider, deem, account, think."*

Once again, <u>this verb is in the Greek present tense.</u> *As such, it is to be a continuous action.* The **ruling or leadership** was continuous, not just temporary.

The Greek Word for "***submit***" is HYPEIKO. Some of the meanings for this Word are:

"1) to resist no longer, but to give way, yield (of combatants); 2) metaph. to yield to authority and admonition, to submit."

<u>This verb is in the Greek present tense.</u> The true Christians are to continually yield to the authority of and submit to these **leaders** so long as they are faithful to the doctrines and teachings of the Bible. I believe that this is assumed in this verse. Those **church leaders** to whom Paul was addressing this verse in his day were **faithful to the Bible**. Today, this is not how it is in most cases. Many **pastors-bishops-elders** today have left the Bible's teachings and doctrines, and should no longer be followed in any way. This is a sad, but true, development.

DUTIES OF RULING LEADERS

Notice what these ruling leaders were supposed to do. They were to watch for the souls of those to whom they minister.

Again, sad to say, all present day **pastors-bishops-elders** in all churches do not watch for the souls of those to whom they minister. Some watch for their own pocket books. Some watch for themselves, that is, what's good for their own interests.

LOOKING OUT FOR PEOPLE

But true pastors-bishops-elders were to look out for the welfare of those to whom they minister. It is very important that this be the case.

There are some other verses that are similar to this.

- **1 Timothy 3:5**

"(For if a man know not how to **rule** his own house, how shall he take care of the church of God?)"

RULING HIS OWN HOUSE

The pastors-bishops-elders must rule over their own house and over their children under their own roof. When their children leave the roof, they cannot any longer be controlled, but when they are under the roof, if these leaders do not control their house and children, they should get out of the ministry.

When I was a **pastor** of Faith Baptist Church in Newton, Massachusetts, I told our three sons and our daughter, after the services were over, something like this:

> "Children, if you continue to wiggle around and act up during the church services, your **dad** must leave the ministry. The Bible is clear that if I don't know how to rule you and my own house, how can I continue to be a **pastor and rule** in the house of God."

Well, the children then shaped up and behaved themselves during our services and elsewhere, so I stayed in the **pastoral ministry** in that church. They're out of the house now, (in addition to our fourth son born later) and every one of them is truly born-again and is serving the Lord Jesus Christ. One of our four sons is with the Lord now, but every one of them, three sons left and one daughter who are left, are serving the Lord. I am very thankful for this and praise the Lord for it.

- **1 Timothy 5:17**

"Let the **elders that rule** well be counted worthy of double honour, especially they who labour in the word and doctrine."

- **Hebrews 13:7**

"Remember them which have the **rule over** you, who have spoken unto you the word of God: whose faith follow, considering the end of their conversation."

> **SPEAKING THE WORDS OF GOD**
>
> Again, these pastors-bishops-elders were to be speaking the Words of God to their people. They were not to be telling story after story after story. They were not to be speaking about philosophy and vain deceit. They were not to be speaking errors and false doctrines. They were to be ministering the Words of God.

- Hebrews 13:24a

"Salute all them that have the rule over you, and all the saints."

PASTORS MUST BE WATCHFUL

One of the duties of the pastors-bishops-elders is to watch for the souls of those to whom they minister. The Greek Word for "*watch*" is AGRUPNEO. Some of the meanings of this Word are:

> "1) to be sleepless, keep awake, watch; 2) to be circumspect, attentive, ready."

> **CONTINUAL WATCHFULNESS**
>
> It is in the Greek present tense and indicates a continuous and uninterrupted action of not sleeping on the job of watching. All genuine Christians, as well as pastors-bishops-elders must be watchful.

LEADERS WATCHING

- 1 Corinthians 16:13

"**Watch ye**, stand fast in the faith, quit you like men, be strong."

- 1 Thessalonians 5:6

"Therefore let us not sleep, as *do* others; but let us **watch** and be sober."

- 2 Timothy 4:5

"But **watch** thou in all things, endure afflictions, do the work of an evangelist, make full proof of thy ministry."

> **TIMOTHY WAS TO WATCH**
>
> Paul told pastor Timothy to <u>watch</u> in all things as well as doing the work of an evangelist--even in affliction.

Hebrews 13:18

"Pray for us: for we trust we have a good conscience, in all things willing to live honestly."

GOOD CONSCIENCE

This command to pray for Paul and his companions is the Greek present tense. As such, it indicates a desire for continuous prayer without letup. Paul trusts that he has a good conscience in all things.

The Greek Word for "*conscience*" is SUNEIDESIS. Some of the meanings of this Word are:

> "1) *the consciousness of anything;* 2) *the soul as distinguishing between what is morally good and bad, prompting to do the former and shun the latter,* commending one, condemning the other; 2a) *the conscience.*"

That's what a **good conscience** should do, but the problem is that many people have their **conscience** seared with a hot iron.

- 1 Timothy 4:2

"Speaking lies in hypocrisy; having their **conscience** seared with a hot iron;"

> **NO OPERATING CONSCIENCE**
>
> The unregenerated people in the world do not follow the Words of God. They live as if they have no operating conscience, living to please the world, the flesh, and the devil. On the other hand, <u>Paul wanted to listen to his conscience so he could live his life in an honest manner</u>, rather than in thievery, or in cheating either the Lord or anyone else.

EXAMPLES OF PRAYER

- John 17:9

"I **pray** for them: I **pray** not for the world, but for them which thou hast given me; for they are thine."

<u>This is the intercessory High Priestly **prayer** of the Lord Jesus Christ to God the Father for those who are genuine Christians.</u>

- John 17:15

"I **pray** not that thou shouldest take them out of the world, but that thou shouldest keep them from the evil."

- John 17:20

"Neither **pray** I for these alone, <u>but for them also which shall believe on me</u> through their word."

- 2 Corinthians 13:7

"Now I **pray** to God that ye do no evil; not that we should appear approved, but that ye should do that which is honest, though we be as reprobates."

DO NO EVIL

That's a prayer for every true Christian that they do no evil. This is only possible when they walk in the power of God the Holy Spirit Who indwells them rather than in their fallen flesh.

- Philippians 1:9

"And this I **pray**, that your love may abound yet more and more in knowledge and *in* all judgment;"

INTERCESSORY PRAYER

This is an intercessory prayer by Paul for the true Philippian Christians. Genuine Christians don't have to agree with everybody in everything, but they are to have love for all true Christians.

Hebrews—Preaching Verse by Verse

- **Colossians 1:9**

"For this cause we also, since the day we heard *it*, do not cease to **pray** for you, and to desire that ye might be filled with the knowledge of his will in all wisdom and spiritual understanding;"

Paul interceded in **prayer** for the church at Colosse. He was in prison at the time. Even though he was in jail, he **prayed** for the people. What did he **pray** for? *"That ye might be filled with the knowledge of his will in all wisdom and spiritual understanding."*

GOD'S WILL ONLY IN GOD'S WORDS

The only way you get the knowledge of his will is in knowledge of His Words. God's will is found in there.

Paul interceded for them and he wanted other believers in the church at Colosse also to intercede and pray for him.

- **1 Thessalonians 5:23**

"And the very God of peace sanctify you wholly; and *I pray* God your whole spirit and soul and body be preserved blameless unto the coming of our Lord Jesus Christ."

- **1 Thessalonians 5:25**

"Brethren, **pray** for us."

- **2 Thessalonians 1:11**

"Wherefore also we **pray** always for you, that our God would count you worthy of *this* calling, and fulfil all the good pleasure of *his* goodness, and the work of faith with power."

- **2 Thessalonians 3:1**

"Finally, brethren, **pray** for us, that the word of the Lord may have *free* course, and be glorified, even as *it is* with you:"

FREE COURSE FOR GOD'S WORDS

Why did Paul want the prayer at that time for the church at Thessalonica? It was that the Words of God, would have free course. That was a wonderful prayer.

- **James 5:16**

"Confess *your* faults one to another, and **pray** one for another, that ye may be healed. The effectual fervent **prayer** of a righteous man availeth much."

PRAYER FOR OTHERS

Intercessory prayer is part of the things that Paul wanted these true Christians to do.

Hebrews 13:19

"But I beseech *you* the rather to do this, that I may be restored to you the sooner."

RESTORED

It seems like the most important prayer request that Paul is asking is that he might be ***"restored"*** to them sooner. The Greek Word for ***"restored"*** is APOKATHISTEMI. Some of the meanings of this Word are:

> *"1) to restore to its former state; 2) to be in its former state"*

Some have felt that Paul's *"former state"* was a time when he was not in prison. He will be **restored** again to his former state. It is not a certainty, of course. We don't often say that the Hebrews is an epistle from Paul while in prison. But notice Hebrews 13:24.

- **Hebrews 13:24**

"Salute all them that have the rule over you, and all the saints. They of Italy salute you."

WAS PAUL IN ITALY?

"They of Italy salute you." Rome is in Italy, as we know. Notice also in the note after Hebrews 13:25, it says *"written to the Hebrews from Italy."* We don't know how often Paul was in Italy, but we do know he was in Italy as a prisoner in Rome.

> When Paul said he wanted to be restored soon, it might have meant that he wanted to be a free man once again and be able once again to travel and preach the gospel of the Lord Jesus Christ.

Hebrews 13:20

"Now the God of peace, that brought again from the dead our Lord Jesus, that great shepherd of the sheep, through the blood of the everlasting covenant,"

THE GOD OF PEACE

This verse is referring both to **God the Father as well as the Lord Jesus Christ.** Notice the *God of peace*. There are two kinds of peace. The first is **peace with God**. The second, after a person has made **peace with God** after truly trusting **His Son as their Saviour,** is the **peace of God**.

- Romans 5:1

"Therefore being justified by faith, we have **peace with God through our Lord Jesus Christ:**"

> **PEACE WITH GOD**
>
> That is peace with God, justified by genuine faith in the Lord Jesus Christ, and then the peace of God, filling your minds and hearts when we live to please Him.

- Philippians 4:7

"And the **peace of God**, which passeth all understanding, shall keep your hearts and minds through Christ Jesus."

This **peace of God** comes to genuine Christians who are yielded to **God the Holy Spirit Who** indwells them.

THE RESURRECTION OF CHRIST

The verse states that **God the Father** *"brought again from the dead our Lord Jesus."* **All three Persons of the Godhead had a part in the bodily resurrection of the Lord Jesus Christ.** As for the Saviour's own part, this verse explains it.

- John 10:18

"No man taketh it from **me**, but **I** lay it down of **myself. I have power to lay it down, and I have power to take it again. This commandment have I received of my Father.**"

This verse explains how **God the Holy Spirit also had a part in the bodily resurrection of the Lord Jesus Christ:**

- Romans 8:11

"But if **the Spirit of him that raised up Jesus from the dead** dwell in you, **he that raised up Christ from the dead** shall also quicken your mortal bodies by **his Spirit** that dwelleth in you."

CHRIST THE GREAT SHEPHERD

In this verse, **the Lord Jesus Christ called "that great shepherd of the sheep."** This is one of the three **Shepherd titles for our Saviour.** (1) One is **His work as the past Shepherd**, (2) one is **His work as the present Shepherd,** and (3) one is **His work as the future Shepherd.**

CHRIST'S THREEFOLD SHEPHERD MINISTRY

1. <u>Past: Christ The Good Shepherd</u>. In the past, the Lord Jesus Christ was the Good Shepherd Who gave His life for the sins of the entire world.

2. <u>Present: Christ The Great Shepherd</u>. In the present, the Lord Jesus Christ is the Great Shepherd, Who is present in Heaven, interceding for those who are genuine Christians.

3. <u>Future: Christ The Chief Shepherd</u>. In the future, the Lord Jesus Christ will be the Chief Shepherd Who, after the Tribulation, will come back to this earth and set up His thousand year millennial reign and will continue His ministries throughout eternity in Heaven.

CHRIST'S BLOOD & BODILY RESURRECTION

There is a connection between the Great Shepherd and <u>the blood of the covenant</u>. The sacrifice of the Lord Jesus Christ by

> the shedding of His blood on the cross of Calvary coupled with His bodily resurrection makes it possible for Him to fulfill His present ministry as the Great Shepherd.

The blood of the Lord Jesus Christ is real and literal blood. Blood is not, as John MacArthur heretically speaks of it, only a metonym for death. No. Blood is not a metonym or figure of speech for death. The Greek Word for blood is HAIMA. The Greek Word for death is THANATOS. They are separate and distinct things.

It is true that in the death of the Lord Jesus Christ He shed His blood, but these two concepts are distinct and separate.

As mentioned before, I have listed fourteen effects of the literal blood of the Lord Jesus Christ taught in our Bible.

[See BFT #2803 for a cassette tape on "*Fourteen Effects of the Blood of Christ*" @ $4.00 + $2.00 S&H or write for BFT #2548-T which is a 5-page tract that sums up these 14 points with the Bible verses to go with them @ $2.00 including S&H]

There various verses about the **Lord Jesus Christ** as the **Shepherd.**

- Psalm 23:1

"**The LORD is my shepherd**; I shall not want."

> ### CHRIST DIED FOR ALL SINS
> That *is* the Saviour as the Good Shepherd in the past Who gave His life for the sins of entire world.

- Isaiah 53:6

"All we like sheep have gone astray; we have turned every one to his own way; and **the LORD** hath laid on **him** the iniquity of us all."

- Isaiah 40:11

"He shall feed his flock **like a shepherd**: he shall gather the lambs with his arm, and carry *them* in his bosom, *and* shall gently lead those that are with young."

- Matthew 9:36

"But when **he** saw the multitudes, **he** was moved with compassion on them, because they fainted, and were scattered abroad, as sheep having **no shepherd**."

> **ISRAEL HAD NO SHEPHERD**
>
> The Lord Jesus Christ longed to have these people make Him their Shepherd. He had great feeling for these people for three reasons: (1) because they fainted (2) because they were scattered abroad, and (3) they were as sheep having no shepherd. He longed to make Himself their Shepherd.

Those of us who have genuinely come to **the Lord Jesus Christ** as our **Saviour** have accepted **Him** as our **Good Shepherd Who gave His life for the all the lost sheep of the world.** <u>He longed to have all the multitudes truly to receive Him as their **Saviour and Shepherd**</u>.

- John 10:11

"I am the **good shepherd**: the **good shepherd** giveth his life for the sheep."

- John 10:14

"**I am the good shepherd**, and know my *sheep*, and am known of mine."

- 1 Peter 2:25

"For ye were as sheep going astray; but are now returned unto **the Shepherd and Bishop** of your souls."

- 1 Peter 5:4

"And when the **chief Shepherd** shall appear, ye shall receive a crown of glory that fadeth not away."

> **THE JUDGMENT SEAT OF CHRIST**
>
> He's talking about the Judgment Seat of Christ as the Chief Shepherd of the future. The Good Shepherd is past. The great shepherd in the present, is interceding for us. In the future, the <u>Chief Shepherd will appear</u>.

Hebrews 13:21

"Make you perfect in every good work to do his will, working in you that which is wellpleasing in his sight, through Jesus Christ; to whom *be* glory for ever and ever. Amen."

GOOD WORK TO DO HIS WILL

It's through the blood of the everlasting covenant that genuine Christians are perfected or matured in **every good work to do His will** and be wellpleasing in His sight. His will is found in the Words of God in the Bible.

The Greek Word for *"perfect"* is KATARTIZO. Some of the meanings of this Word are:

> *"1) to render, i.e. to fit, sound, complete; 1a) to mend (what has been broken or rent), to repair; 1a1) to complete; 1b) to fit out, equip, put in order, arrange, adjust; 1b1) to fit or frame for one's self, prepare; 1c) ethically: to strengthen, perfect, complete, make one what he ought to be."*

That's what the blood of the Lord Jesus Christ can do for those who are genuine Christians. They should be complete and sound **in every good work to do His will** in their Christian life.

GOD'S WILL FOUND ONLY IN THE BIBLE

His will is found in the Bible. This is why it so vital that genuine Christians have the accurate Bible to discern the Lord's will. In English, it is the King James Bible. The underlying Hebrew, Aramaic, and Greek Words of the King James Bible are the proper original languages that should be followed. In other versions' original Words, people might find SOME of the will of God, but in the King James Bible and its underlying Hebrew, Aramaic, and Greek Words they will find ALL of the will of God! There are many verses that deal with the will of God.

- **Romans 12:2**

"And be not conformed to this world: but be ye transformed by the renewing of your mind, that ye may prove what is that good, and acceptable, and **perfect, will of God.**"

- **2 Corinthians 13:11**

"Finally, brethren, farewell. Be perfect, be of good comfort, be of one mind, live in peace; and the God of love and peace shall be with you."

"Be perfect" means grown up and mature. Don't remain in spiritual childhood or babyhood. <u>Be mature in the things of the Lord through the proper Scriptures and the full knowledge God's Words.</u>

- **Colossians 4:12**

"Epaphras, who is *one* of you, a servant of Christ, saluteth you, always laboring fervently for you in prayers, that ye may stand perfect and complete in all the **will of God.**"

- **2 Timothy 3:17**

"That the man of God may be perfect, thoroughly furnished unto **all good works.**"

- **1 Peter 5:10**

"But the God of all grace, who hath called us unto his eternal glory by Christ Jesus, after that ye have suffered a while, make you perfect, stablish, strengthen, settle you."

<u>Suffering is often a part of making true Christians mature in the Lord.</u>

- **Mark 3:35**

"For whosoever shall do the **will of God**, the same is my brother, and my sister, and mother."

Spiritual relationship to **Him**, is doing the **will of God**.

- **Romans 12:2b**

"that ye may prove what *is* that good, and acceptable, and perfect, **will of God.**"

- **Galatians 1:4**

"Who gave himself for our sins, that he might deliver us from this present evil world, according to the **will of God** and our Father:"

This is speaking of the **Lord Jesus Christ** and **His** purpose for **giving Himself. It was for the sins of the world.**

- **Ephesians 6:6**

"Not with eyeservice, as menpleasers; but as the servants of Christ, **doing the will of God** from the heart;"

THE WILL OF GOD FROM THE HEART

Doing the will of God for genuine Christians should not be from the head. It must be from the heart. To find and do the will of God from the heart they should want to read God's Words. They should want to believe God's Words. They should want to heed and follow the Words of God in order to do the will of God from their heart.

- **Colossians 4:12b**

"always laboring fervently for you in prayers, that ye may stand perfect and complete in all the **will of God.**"

- **1 Thessalonians 4:3a**

"For this is the **will of God,** *even* your sanctification,"

- **1 Thessalonians 4:3b**

"that ye abstain from fornication."

- **2 Timothy 1:1**

"Paul, an apostle of Jesus Christ by the **will of God,** according to the promise of life which is in Christ Jesus,"

- **1 Peter 4:2**

"That he no longer should live the rest of *his* time in the flesh to the lusts of men, but to the **will of God.**"

- **1 Peter 4:19**

"Wherefore let them that suffer according to the **will of God** commit the keeping of their souls *to him* in well doing, as unto a faithful Creator."

Sometimes it is **God's will** that true Christians suffer. If they suffer, they should commit ourselves to the Lord Jesus Christ, and continue to **do His will,** even if it means suffering for Him and His cause.

Hebrews 13:22

"And I beseech you, brethren, suffer the word of exhortation: for I have written a letter unto you in few words."

EXHORTATION

Paul wanted his readers to receive his **exhortations** that he gave them in this letter to the Hebrews.

- **1 Timothy 4:13**

"Till I come, give attendance to reading, to **exhortation**, to doctrine.

- **Hebrews 12:5**

"And ye have forgotten the **exhortation** which speaketh unto you as unto children, My son, despise not thou the chastening of the Lord, nor faint when thou art rebuked of him."

CHRISTIANS NEED ENCOURAGEMENT

Genuine Christians need exhortation and encouragement. Sometimes such exhortation from the Lord comes with His chastening of them so that they might be conformed to His Son, the Lord Jesus Christ.

Hebrews 13:23

"Know ye that *our* brother Timothy is set at liberty; with whom, if he come shortly, I will see you."

SET FREE

The Greek Word for *"set at liberty"* is APOLUO. Some of the meanings of this Word are:

> "1) to set free; 2) to let go, dismiss, (to detain no longer); 2a) a petitioner to whom liberty to depart is given by a decisive answer; 2b) to bid depart, send away; 3) to let go free, release; 3a) a captive i.e. to loose his bonds and bid him depart, to give him

liberty to depart; 3b) to acquit one accused of a crime and set him at liberty; 3c) indulgently to grant a prisoner leave to depart; 3d) to release a debtor, i.e. not to press one's claim against; him, to remit his debt; 4) used of divorce, to dismiss from the house, to repudiate. The wife of a Greek or Roman may divorce her husband. 5) to send one's self away, to depart."

WAS TIMOTHY IMPRISONED SOMEWHERE?

From these various definitions of this Greek Word, <u>it seems very likely that Pastor Timothy had been or was imprisoned somewhere.</u> But as Paul writes this verse, Timothy has been set free. Paul was expecting Timothy to come to him and then both of them would come to those to whom this letter is written.

Hebrews 13:24

"**Salute all them that have the rule over you, and all the saints. They of Italy salute you.**"

<u>From this verse, it appears that Paul was in Italy. Could he have been in prison at Rome?</u> We do not know this, of course. His readers were to greet all those who had the leadership over them. This would include their pastors and others who were leading them. <u>They were also to greet all the saints, that is, all the Genuine Christians.</u> They were not to leave out any of them.

Hebrews 13:25

" **Grace** *be* **with you all. Amen.**"

GRACE

"*Grace*" is an interesting word. It's the **grace** of God that brings salvation to those who genuinely receive the Lord Jesus Christ as their Saviour. They are getting something that they do not deserve.

The Greek Word for "**grace**" is CHARIS. Some of the many meanings of this Word are:

"1) grace; 1a) that which affords joy, pleasure, delight, sweetness, charm, loveliness: grace of speech; 2) good will, loving-kindness, favour; 2a) of the merciful kindness by which God, exerting his holy influence upon souls, turns them to Christ, keeps, strengthens, increases them in Christian faith, knowledge, affection, and kindles them to the exercise of the Christian virtues; 3) what is due to grace; 3a) the spiritual condition of one governed by the power of divine grace; 3b) the token or proof of grace, benefit; 3b1) a gift of grace; 3b2) benefit, bounty; 4) thanks, (for benefits, services, favours), recompense, reward."

CHRISTIANS MUST BE GRACIOUS

When Paul writes to his readers "*Grace be with you all*," he wants them to be gracious in all of their Christian lives. True Christians must be bold against evil, but there must also be a gracious spirit motiving that boldness.

HEBREWS A BOOK OF GRACE VS. LAW

This book of Hebrews gives the great contrasts between the law of Moses and the grace of God and the Lord Jesus Christ. No longer do those who are truly born-again in this age of grace have to offer blood offerings of clean animals as they did in the Old Testament. It is only the blood of the Lord Jesus Christ, Who was once offered for the sins of the world, that is to be recognized, exalted, and made central in the lives of those He has redeemed.

EARTHLY VS. HEAVENLY TABERNACLE

The earthly tabernacle of the Old Testament whose patterns came from Heaven itself has now been obliterated. There remains a Heavenly tabernacle where the Lord Jesus Christ, the Great High Priest of those who are genuinely saved, is seated at the right hand of God the Father. They can go to Him freely.

The veil of the tabernacle and the temple has been rent in two from top to the bottom. It was the veil of the flesh of the Lord Jesus Christ which was rent when He died on the cross of Calvary. This was the most gracious gift to the entire world which should be accepted and received by all.

Index Of Words And Phrases

1 Corinthians 11:9 7
1 John 17, 66, 78, 81, 118, 153, 162, 206, 283, 289, 311,
                      319, 325, 354, 359, 361, 479, 499, 500
1 Peter 4:19 .... 9, 81, 353, 539
1967 boundaries 239
2 Corinthians 5:17 7
2 Peter 3:15 1
31,000 verses 141
356 doctrinal passages 20
4000 B.C. 40
601,730 numbered 99
603,550 numbered 99
70 years of captivity in Babylon 397
72 potential terrorists 154
85 verses each day 95
85 verses per day 141
856-261-9018 356
85-verses per day Bible reading 141
A BETTER SUBSTANCE IN HEAVEN 370
A FAITHFUL HIGH PRIEST 69, 81, 159
A FIGURE LOOKING FORWARD 299
A NEW AND LIVING WAY 158, 229, 231, 322, 347-349
A PRIEST AFTER THE ORDER OF MELCHISEDEC 176
A PRIEST CONTINUALLY 177, 189, 235, 236
A SPIRITUAL CREATION 7
A TESTAMENT IS A FINAL WILL 311
A VITALLY IMPORTANT QUESTION FOR YOU 25
Aaron 83, 122, 123, 165-170, 174-176, 188, 190, 230,
                   231, 233, 241, 244, 248, 257, 263-265, 293-297,
                   303, 402, 403, 471
AARON CHOSEN AS HIGH PRIEST 294
AARON HAD TO ATONE FOR HIS SINS 265
AARON'S HANDS ON THE SCAPEGOAT 167
AARON'S PLACEMENT OF BLOOD 303
AARON'S ROD IN THE ARK 293
AARON'S ROD THAT BUDDED 292, 293, 295
AARON'S SONS KILLED FOR DRINKING 263
AARON'S SPECIAL UNIFORM 166
ABEL'S EXCELLENT SACRIFICE 380

ABEL'S OFFERING AND CHRIST'S BLOOD 381
abiding forever 236
able not to sin 159
abolished 76, 241, 284-286, 337
About the Author iv
Abraham 4, 24, 45, 46, 79, 106, 142, 143, 188-190, 219,
        221-224, 226, 230, 233-235, 237-241, 378, 380,
        387, 390-397, 403-407, 409, 410, 437
ABRAHAM AND SARA'S OLD AGE 396
ABRAHAM NEVER TURNED BACK 403
ABRAHAM OFFERED UP ISAAC 405
ABRAHAM PROMISED A MULTITUDE 396
ABRAHAM REFUSED SODOM'S GIFTS 230
ABRAHAM TITHED TO MELCHISEDEC 189
ABRAHAM TITHED TO MELCHIZEDEK 235
Abrahamic covenant 221
ABRAHAMIC PROMISES 238
ABRAHAM'S 318 SERVANTS 176
ABRAHAM'S CITY 393
ABRAHAM'S UNILATERAL COVENANT 222
ACCESS TO GOD 438, 471
accompany salvation 210
ACCURATE BIBLE TRANSLATIONS 223
Acknowledgments .... ii, iv
Acts 14, 18, 22, 27, 42, 44, 47, 48, 50, 55, 59, 68, 70, 85,
        103, 112, 114, 120, 132, 150, 172, 175, 186, 190,
        192, 194, 200, 201, 225, 227, 246, 250, 258, 272,
        282, 315, 341, 345, 360, 411, 439, 454, 457, 466,
        495, 505, 525
Adam 62, 63, 84, 126, 307, 310, 316, 333, 337, 363, 380,
        381
adulterers 467, 502, 503
adultery 102, 194, 206, 362, 364, 467, 468, 503
advocate 162
afraid 23, 47, 77-79, 91, 102, 107, 113, 367, 386, 391,
        400, 410-412, 433, 460, 472, 473, 488, 492
African Christians in Liberia 216
AGREEING WITH GOD 479
AGREEING WITH GOD ABOUT OUR SINS 479
agreement 479, 480
AGRUPNEO 528
AKAKOS 253

AKLINE	352
all men to be saved	60, 251
ALL N.T. WRITERS WERE JEWS	139
Allen	63, 141, 201, 207, 229, 309, 382, 433, 491, 530
altar	100, 154, 167, 169, 170, 190, 242, 268, 296, 312-314, 382, 383, 405, 486, 490, 516
AN ANGEL FOR EVERY TRUE CHRISTIAN	45
AN IMPERFECT LAW	241
AN OLD TESTAMENT CHRISTOPHANY	189
AN UNCHANGEABLE GOD	510
ANALOGIZOMAI	445
Ananias	227, 360
anchor	119, 157, 228, 229
ancient times	40
angel of light	61, 289
angels	6, 9, 11, 19-24, 40, 43-45, 48, 52-54, 61-63, 66, 67, 73, 76, 77, 79, 135, 160, 161, 177, 182, 199, 202, 213, 259, 260, 270-272, 275, 289, 304, 325, 473, 474, 495, 500, 501
ANGELS ARE NOT GOD'S SONS	21
ANGELS ARE SERVANTS	24
ANGELS AS MINISTERS	24
ANGELS DO NOT EXALT THEMSELVES	48
ANGELS SPOKE IN THE BIBLE	52
ANGELS WERE TO WORSHIP CHRIST	23
ANGELS WORSHIPPING	22
anitor	141
Anne Marie	ii
Anne Marie Noyle	ii
ANOTHER TRIBE	190, 242
anti-Christian	404, 518
APAUGASMA	10
APEIROS	194
APHANISMOS	284
APHESIS	315
APOBLEPO	416
APOKATHISTEMI	532
APOLUO	540
apostates	7, 94, 106, 107, 515, 518
apostles' prayer	84
APPLYING CHRIST'S BLOOD NEEDED	329
APPOINTED UNTO MEN ONCE TO DIE	158, 203, 325,

	395
appointment	91, 121, 188, 325, 327
APPOINTMENT AND JUDGMENT	325
ARCHE	199
ARCHEGOS	68
ARE YOU READY FOR DEATH?	77
Argentina	389
ark	i, 7, 17, 21, 35, 41, 44, 91, 105, 109, 115, 125, 126, 143, 144, 148, 154, 155, 165, 167, 171, 212, 222, 261, 262, 267, 292-297, 299, 303, 314, 341, 348, 374, 386, 389, 390, 412, 466, 505, 512, 538
ASPAZOMAI	398
ASSEMBLING	113, 355-357
ASSEMBLING WITH US ON THE INTERNET	355
ATHETESIS	245
atonement	43, 64, 83, 165-170, 173, 174, 262, 264, 265, 271, 292, 295-298, 301-303, 322, 332, 357, 477, 515
attributes	4, 14, 36, 106, 107, 161, 253
Audio cassettes are BFT#3026/1-13	iii
August, 1948	7
AVOID FALSE DOCTRINE	512
AVOID OF HARDENED HEARTS	96
AVOIDING 70 YEARS CAPTIVITY	4
BABE	171, 194, 195, 412
babes in Christ	106, 191, 194, 205, 206, 358
BABY'S BLOOD COMES FROM THE FATHER	333
BACKGROUND OF MELCHISEDEC	233
BAPTISM=IMMERSION	201
BAPTISMS	201
Baptists	161, 336, 474
BARABBAS RELEASED, NOT CHRIST	180
BARAK	424, 425
BARAK'S VICTORY OVER SISERA	425
Bathsheba	102
BE CAREFUL IN RESTORATION	85
BE JOYFUL IN TESTINGS	86
Be perfect	333, 337, 475, 514, 538
BEARING CHRIST'S REPROACH	518
BECAUSE OF UNBELIEF	109, 125, 128, 129, 138
begotten	11, 21-23, 65, 81, 126, 157, 169, 175, 176, 179, 185, 217, 247, 310, 319, 339, 350, 372, 385, 404,

	405, 451, 484
BELIEVED NOT THE LORD	124
Believing In Unholy Blood	363
BELIEVING NOT, UNBELIEF	125
Berea Baptist Church	141
Berea, Ohio	33, 141
BETTER HOPE	242, 246
better things	210, 270, 304, 310, 381, 383, 473, 475
BETTER THINGS THAT ACCOMPANY SALVATION	210
BETTER THINGS WITH TRUE SALVATION	210
better.	20, 76, 189, 215, 240
BEWARE OF A DIRTY HEART	102
BEWARE OF WRONG TEACHERS	193
BFT #2185	303, 307, 315
BFT #2548	315, 517, 535
BFT #2548-T	517, 535
BFT #4046	i
BFT #4054	134, 481
BFT #4088	151
BFT Phone: 856-854-4452	i
Bible For Today Baptist Church	i, iii, 113, 355-357, 509
BIBLE FOR TODAY PRESS	i
BIBLE PERVERSIONS OMIT THE LAST OF MARK	17
Bible reading	3, 95, 141
Bible-believing churches	336
Biblical and Observational Case for Geocentricity	134
BIBLICAL MARRIAGE	411, 502
BIBLICAL SEPARATION IS VITAL	254
Biblical" government	107
Billy Graham	202, 515
bishop	219, 506, 524, 525, 536
bitterness	115, 121, 444, 462-464
BITTERNESS DEFILES	463, 464
BLAMELESS AND HARMLESS LIVES	254
BLESSINGS FOR THE SAVED ONES	392
blood	28, 43, 50, 59, 68, 71, 73, 74, 77, 81, 83, 107, 131, 147, 157, 158, 167-169, 178, 230, 250, 255, 262, 265, 266, 270, 271, 275, 282, 289, 291, 295-297, 299, 301-323, 327, 329, 331-333, 337, 338, 340, 345-347, 351, 357, 362-364, 380-383, 389, 419, 420, 447, 466, 473-477, 515, 517, 520, 525, 533-535, 537, 542

blood applied	320, 420
blood atonement	357, 515
blood of bulls and goats	306-308, 313, 332
blood of Christ	303, 306-308, 315, 317, 319, 338, 476
BLOOD OF CHRIST IN HEAVEN	476
blood of sprinkling	270, 304, 310, 381, 383, 473-476
blood on the door	419
Bob Jones University	20, 94, 153, 334
bodily resurrection	113, 126, 136, 137, 167, 176, 201, 202, 211, 217, 246, 248, 254, 260, 270, 271, 302, 316, 321, 322, 357, 418, 443, 476, 508, 515, 533-535
body	2, 10, 11, 13, 15, 16, 23, 25, 28, 55, 57, 63, 67, 71, 73, 76, 78, 101, 104, 105, 113, 147, 148, 159, 168, 172, 174, 176, 184, 196, 200, 202, 215, 217, 220, 246, 255, 265, 266, 268, 283, 288, 291, 300-302, 306, 308, 316, 323, 324, 328, 332, 333, 336-338, 347, 361, 363, 364, 398, 399, 409, 418, 439, 443, 448, 460, 465-467, 474, 478-480, 483, 484, 501-504, 506, 530, 531
boldly	78, 162, 508
bondage	77, 79, 87, 91, 315, 400, 401, 410, 502
bonds	1, 2, 152, 369, 433, 436, 501, 502, 540
bones	31, 74, 103, 306, 409, 410, 518
born-again Christians	79, 89, 105, 110, 112, 117, 143, 153, 154, 159, 180, 203, 205, 216, 253, 289, 291, 344, 349, 358, 373, 435, 437, 446, 452, 482
BRANCHES	138, 139, 208, 288
Bread of life	290
brethren	13, 70, 72-74, 80, 81, 85, 86, 89, 90, 106, 110, 119, 127, 156-158, 189, 206, 216, 225, 238, 247, 251, 302, 318, 320, 345, 347, 404, 410, 413, 423, 447, 468, 469, 477, 498-500, 512, 513, 531, 538, 540
briers	208, 210, 213
brightness,	10
BROTHERLY LOVE	497, 498
Buddhists	127, 518
burn up with fire	481
burnt offering	46, 165, 166, 170, 174, 222, 264, 297, 314, 338, 404, 405, 426, 486, 490
by	1, i-iii, 2-22, 25, 27-29, 34-38, 40-44, 46, 47, 49-55, 57-

Hebrews—Preaching Verse by Verse

    63, 66-73, 75-78, 80-83, 85, 87, 91-95, 97, 98, 100, 101, 103, 104, 107-115, 118-122, 125, 127-129, 132-134, 137-143, 145, 147-151, 153-155, 158-162, 165, 167-169, 171-174, 176, 177, 180-182, 184-191, 193-196, 199-201, 204, 206, 207, 209, 210, 212, 213, 215, 217-219, 221-226, 229-231, 234-243, 245-253, 255, 256, 258-261, 263, 265-277, 280, 281, 283, 284, 287, 290, 291, 293, 296-302, 304-311, 313-325, 327-329, 331-351, 353, 356, 359-361, 363-370, 373-375, 377-381, 383, 385-387, 389-394, 396, 398, 399, 401, 402, 404-410, 412-414, 416-424, 426, 427, 429, 431-436, 438, 439, 441-443, 445, 448, 453-457, 459-462, 468-471, 474-476, 478-483, 485-494, 497, 500, 502, 503, 509, 513-515, 517, 519, 520, 522-525, 530, 533, 534, 538-540, 542, 543

by himself 10, 15-17, 19, 21, 25, 43, 221, 259
BY HIMSELF PURGED OUR SINS 10, 15, 25, 43, 259
by Jesus Christ 8, 34, 93, 284
Calvary 5, 12, 15, 20, 25, 28, 41, 43, 55, 57, 63, 67, 68, 70, 75, 92, 126, 157, 173, 178, 179, 182, 229, 231, 237, 249, 255, 256, 258, 260, 262, 265, 266, 273, 278, 283, 284, 290, 291, 296, 298, 299, 306, 308, 310, 312, 316, 322-324, 329, 331, 334, 337, 341, 345, 349, 359, 372, 402, 405, 438, 443, 445, 447, 454, 475, 480, 516, 517, 535, 543
CALVARY NEVER TO BE REPEATED 323
Calvary, ... 41, 70, 92, 126, 178, 179, 229, 237, 265, 273, 278, 298, 306, 322, 372
Calvinists 64, 109, 168, 182, 185, 187, 252
Canaan 12, 91, 100, 106, 109, 122-124, 129-131, 137, 138, 142, 143, 392, 409, 410, 423, 424, 478
CANAAN IS FOR ABRAHAM'S POSTERITY 409
CANAAN WAS NOT RESTFUL 142
cancer 101, 102
candlestick 287, 288, 291, 292, 339
Canter, Patty iii
carnal 106, 110, 130, 190, 193, 194, 200, 205, 206, 210, 244, 300, 364, 455, 465
CARNAL CORINTHIAN CHRISTIANS 193
CARNAL DEPARTURES FROM TRUTH 205
carried about 511, 513

carry up my bones 410
CCM 96
ceased" 144
Chafer 283, 484
change of mind 200
CHANGES SINCE CHRIST'S COMING 300
CHARACTERISTICS OF HEAVEN 483
CHARIS 541
Charismatics 184, 304, 311
Charlie 141
chasten 449-453
chastening 224, 447-449, 451-457, 483, 540
CHASTENING AND FAINTING 447
chastisement 64, 329, 448, 453, 454
cherub 262, 295
cherubims 262, 295
Chief Shepherd 534, 536
CHILDREN LACKING CORRECTION 454
Chinese seminary 141
CHRIST A FITTING CAPTAIN OF SALVATION 67
CHRIST A MERCIFUL HIGH PRIEST 80
CHRIST A MORE PERFECT TABERNACLE 300
CHRIST A PRIEST FOREVER 236
CHRIST AND THE ORDER OF MELCHISEDEC 157
CHRIST AT GOD'S RIGHT HAND 257
CHRIST BECAME THE SON OF MAN 22
CHRIST BORE CHASTENING FOR US 454
CHRIST BROKE SATAN'S POWER OF DEATH 87
CHRIST CAME TO DIE FOR SINNERS 185
CHRIST CAME TO SAVE PEOPLE 58, 250
CHRIST DID THE FATHER'S WILL 334
CHRIST DIED FOR ALL SINS 535
CHRIST DIED FOR ALL THE UNGODLY 65
CHRIST DIED FOR EVERYONE'S SINS 249
CHRIST DIED FOR FALSE TEACHERS 66
CHRIST DIED FOR THE SINS OF THE WORLD 296, 298, 516
CHRIST DOESN'T FORSAKE THE SAVED 507
CHRIST ENTERED THE HEAVENLY HOLY PLACE 255
CHRIST EXALTED BY GOD THE FATHER 18
CHRIST FROM ALL ETERNITY PAST 510
CHRIST GIVES THE SAVED HELP 516

CHRIST HAS THE KEYS OF DEATH 76
CHRIST IN THE HEAVENLY SANCTUARY 260
CHRIST INTERCEDES FOR SAVED PEOPLE 253
CHRIST INTERCEDING 321
CHRIST IS BETTER THAN ANY ANGEL 24
CHRIST IS ON GOD'S RIGHT HAND 40
CHRIST IS THE HEIR OF ALL THINGS 4
CHRIST IS WAITING 340
CHRIST NOT A PRIEST FROM LEVI 266
CHRIST ON GOD'S RIGHT HAND 42, 258
CHRIST OPPOSED STRONGLY 445
CHRIST OUR HIGH PRIEST 81, 156, 349
CHRIST OUR MEDIATOR 268, 475
CHRIST OUR ONLY MEDIATOR 308
CHRIST OUR SURETY 248
CHRIST OUR "AUTHOR" 185
CHRIST PRESERVES THE BIBLE 15
CHRIST PUT AWAY SIN BY HIS SACRIFICE 324
CHRIST REMAINS THE SAME 38
CHRIST SAT DOWN AFTER HIS ASCENSION 339
CHRIST SAVES ONLY "BY HIMSELF" 16
CHRIST STROVE AGAINST MAN'S SINS 447
CHRIST SUFFERED ONLY ONCE FOR SINS 256
CHRIST SUFFERED WITHOUT THE GATE 517
CHRIST TASTED DEATH FOR EVERYONE 63, 182
CHRIST TASTING DEATH 63
CHRIST TESTED 40 DAYS BY SATAN 161
CHRIST TESTED THOUGH SINLESS 86
Christ The Chief Shepherd 534
CHRIST THE CREATOR 7, 34
Christ the Foundation 110
Christ The Good Shepherd 534
Christ The Great Shepherd 534
CHRIST THE MEDIATOR 269, 308
CHRIST THE MEDIATOR OF THE NEW TESTAMENT 308
CHRIST THE ONLY MEDIATOR 269
CHRIST THE ONLY WAY 298
CHRIST THE "GOD-MAN" 180
CHRIST TOOK ALL SINS IN HIS BODY 283
CHRIST WAS OFFERED TO BEAR SINS OF MANY 328
CHRIST WAS OMNISCIENT 181
CHRIST WAS SINLESS 158, 173

CHRIST WAS THE CREATOR 7, 68, 93
CHRIST WILL GIVE YOU REST 134
CHRIST WITH THE SAVED ALWAYS 508
CHRISTIAN WEAPONS FOR VICTORY 152
Christians . . . . iii, 28, 49, 54, 71, 75-79, 83, 85, 89, 94, 95,
104-107, 110, 112, 116, 117, 119, 125, 130, 136,
137, 143, 144, 152-154, 156, 159, 162, 180, 182,
186, 188, 191, 193, 194, 196, 197, 199, 200, 202,
203, 205-220, 224-226, 229, 231, 239, 241, 244,
246, 247, 252-254, 257, 259, 263, 265, 269, 271,
272, 281-283, 285, 286, 289-291, 304, 305, 317-
319, 321, 322, 326, 328, 337, 343, 344, 346, 347,
349, 351-360, 362-365, 367-373, 375, 378, 379,
384, 392, 395, 398, 399, 403, 411, 413, 418, 419,
433, 435-437, 439, 441-443, 445-449, 452-459, 461-
465, 472, 476-480, 482-485, 497, 499-502, 504-509,
511, 515, 518-526, 528, 530, 532-534, 537-542
CHRISTIANS CAN "AFFIRM" 225
CHRISTIANS MUST BE GRACIOUS 542
CHRISTIANS NEED ENCOURAGEMENT 540
CHRISTIANS SHOULD BE FAITHFUL 433
CHRISTIANS SHOULD COMMUNICATE 523
CHRISTIANS SHOULD NOT COVET 504
CHRISTIANS SHOULD NOT SWEAR OATHS 225
Christology 357, 515
Christophany 176, 177, 187-189, 230, 233, 235, 238,
240, 243, 350
CHRIST–PERFECT GOD AND MAN 281
CHRIST'S BETTER HOPE 246
CHRIST'S BLOOD CAN CLEANSE 308, 347
CHRIST'S BLOOD IN HEAVEN 270, 304
CHRIST'S BLOOD IS IN HEAVEN 301, 304
CHRIST'S BLOOD NOT "HUMAN" 307
CHRIST'S BLOOD OF SPRINKLING 270, 304, 476
CHRIST'S BLOOD ON THE MERCY SEAT 302, 476
CHRIST'S BLOOD PURIFIED 321
CHRIST'S BODILY RESURRECTION 126, 137, 176
CHRIST'S BODY PREPARED BY GOD THE FATHER 333
CHRIST'S CALL AS HIGH PRIEST 175
CHRIST'S CARE FOR ISRAEL 278
CHRIST'S COMING IN POWER 258
CHRIST'S COMING TO JUDGE, THEN REIGN 373

CHRIST'S DEATH NEVER TO BE REPEATED	324
Christ's deity	94, 515
CHRIST'S DELIVERANCE	77
CHRIST'S ETERNALITY	244
CHRIST'S FLESH VEILED HIS GLORY	12
CHRIST'S FLESH WAS THE VEIL	229
CHRIST'S GLORY	10, 11, 13
CHRIST'S GLORY WAS GIVEN BACK	13
CHRIST'S GLORY WAS VEILED	11
CHRIST'S HELP TO THE BELIEVERS	162
CHRIST'S IMPECCABLE BLOOD	316
CHRIST'S MILLENNIAL REIGN	69
CHRIST'S ONCE-FOR-ALL SACRIFICE	158
CHRIST'S ONE SACRIFICE	358
CHRIST'S OWN REJECTED HIM	138
CHRIST'S PERFECT PREPARED BODY	302
CHRIST'S PRAYERS IN GETHSEMANE	177
CHRIST'S PREPARED SPECIAL BODY	265
CHRIST'S PRICELESS BLOOD	329
CHRIST'S SINLESS BLOOD	73
CHRIST'S SPECIAL BLOOD PROVIDED BY GOD	307
CHRIST'S THREEFOLD SHEPHERD MINISTRY	534
CHRIST'S UNLIMITED ATONEMENT	64
CHRIST'S WORDS WILL NOT PASS AWAY	35
CHRIST--OFFERED ONLY ONCE	170
Church of Christ	184
Church Phone: 856-854-4747	i
city of the living God	270, 271, 275, 304, 473, 520
cleanse	70, 71, 81, 148, 169, 283, 307, 308, 325, 326, 347, 354, 359, 451, 479, 480
cleanse from sins	347
CLEANSED HEARTS	105
Collingswood, New Jersey	i, iii
Colossians 1:16	8, 34, 93, 417
Colossians 3:10	9
COME BOLDLY	162
COMING SHORT	130
COMING SHORT OF GOD'S GLORY	130
COMMUNION'S FOUR INTERPRETATIONS	291
Communists	31, 502
COMPASSED ABOUT	220, 421, 441
COMPASSION	2, 171-173, 195, 369, 412, 499, 536

confess 31, 56, 59, 81, 169, 251, 254, 283, 325, 326,
354, 359, 398, 479, 521, 532
confession 56, 359, 390, 479, 480
CONFIDENCE 94, 103, 116-119, 128, 162, 352, 371, 377,
378, 525
CONFIDENCE IN THE LORD IS NEEDED 371
conscience 151, 158, 214, 299, 306, 308, 317, 332, 351,
457, 529
CONSIDER 15, 35, 81, 89, 90, 104, 147, 157, 189, 237,
255, 349, 354, 415, 445, 449, 451, 526
consubstantiation 291
consuming fire 485, 487, 488, 495
contaminate. 464
contemporary Christian music (CCM) 96
contend 113, 494
contend for the faith 113
content 181, 504, 506, 507
contentment 55, 181, 506, 507
CONTINUAL WATCHFULNESS 528
continuing city 519, 520
CONTINUING CONTENTMENT COMMANDED 507
CORE CURRICULUM IS WICKED 468
correct 51, 99, 104, 147, 153, 195, 358, 454
covenant 49, 167, 221, 222, 248, 268-271, 273-279, 284,
285, 287, 292, 294, 295, 304, 309, 310, 312, 313,
318, 319, 335, 343, 362, 381, 383, 473-476, 478,
489, 505, 533, 534, 537
covet 504, 505
COVETOUSNESS COMES FROM THE HEART 505
create 17, 31, 35, 36, 93, 102, 126, 136, 482, 492
created 5, 7-9, 21, 23, 24, 33-35, 61-63, 68, 93, 133, 136,
145, 209, 211, 231, 280, 379, 380, 388, 417, 455,
456, 481, 482
created all things by Jesus Christ 8, 34, 93
creating 35
creation 6-10, 31, 32, 35, 62, 126, 135, 136, 138, 353,
354, 379, 417
Creator 4, 5, 7-9, 31, 34, 39, 48, 63, 68, 81, 93, 94, 353,
394, 446, 539
cremation 409
cross 10, 15, 16, 19-21, 25, 28, 29, 41, 43, 44, 50, 55,
57, 63, 66, 68, 70, 75, 92, 157, 167, 172, 173, 178,

179, 182, 185, 200, 220, 229, 231, 236, 246, 249, 251, 254, 256, 259, 260, 265, 266, 273, 275, 278, 284, 296, 298-300, 302, 306, 308-310, 312, 316, 317, 322, 324, 326, 328, 329, 331, 334, 337, 338, 340, 341, 347, 349, 359, 372, 383, 384, 386, 405, 438, 443, 445, 447, 454, 475, 480, 516, 517, 535, 543
cross of Calvary 331
cross of Calvary 15, 25, 28, 41, 43, 55, 57, 63, 70, 75, 92, 179, 182, 229, 249, 256, 260, 265, 266, 273, 278, 284, 296, 298, 306, 308, 310, 312, 324, 329, 334, 337, 341, 349, 359, 372, 438, 443, 454, 475, 480, 516, 517, 535, 543
crown 86, 183, 261, 340, 406, 536
crown of life 86, 406
crucifying the Son of God afresh 206
crying 177, 195, 400, 449, 451, 483, 484
DAILY EXHORTATION NEEDED 112
Dallas Theological Seminary 476, 484
DANIEL ESCAPED HUNGRY LIONS 429
DAVID 18, 23, 41, 42, 44, 47, 54, 95, 102, 140, 148, 242, 243, 261, 326, 341, 415, 424, 427, 444, 490, 493
DAVID DEFEATS GOLIATH 427
Day of Atonement 43, 83, 165-168, 170, 174, 271, 292, 295-298, 301-303, 322, 332, 477
daysman 309
deaden the pain of an empty heart and life 485
death 3, 10, 14, 25, 54, 63-67, 69, 71, 73-77, 79, 87, 126, 156, 165, 167-169, 171, 177, 178, 182, 186, 187, 206, 211, 222, 223, 231, 236, 246, 249, 254, 256, 258, 263, 269-271, 275, 290, 291, 299, 308, 309, 311, 312, 316-320, 322, 324-329, 331, 338, 346, 349, 357, 359-362, 374, 383, 384, 402, 420, 426, 429-431, 437, 443, 470, 476, 478, 483, 484, 499, 506, 516, 517, 535
DEATH AS A SEPARATION 76
DEATH IS THE LAST ENEMY 75
death penalty 360, 362
decayeth 218, 284
deceit 105, 114, 115, 466, 505, 528
DECEIT AND DECEITFULNESS 114
DECEIT OUT OF THE HEART 115

deceitfulness 104, 112, 114, 115, 119, 128
DECLARING GOD'S NAME 72
Defense of Marriage Act 502
defile 105, 115, 462, 464
defiles 463, 464
Defined King James Bible Orders iv
DeHaan, Dr. M. R. 178, 303, 476
Deity 4, 25-27, 29, 34, 46, 48, 94, 149, 161, 181, 183,
184, 309, 357, 515
deliver 16, 46, 57, 77-79, 84, 86, 108, 126, 188, 192,
328, 424-429, 431, 433, 493, 538
DELIVERED FROM SATAN'S DARKNESS 289
DEPARTING 110, 111, 127, 398, 409, 410, 525
DESTROYING THE POWER OF DEATH 74, 75
Devil 14, 21, 62, 73, 74, 77, 84, 86, 87, 105, 119, 159-
161, 170, 202, 203, 206, 207, 210, 227, 288, 325,
529
Devil and his angels 77, 202, 325
DEXIOS. 17
DIA 36, 212, 301
DIAKONEO 212
DIAMENO 36
DID NOT ESCAPE 477
DIDASKO 192
died for us all 16
DIFFERENT PROPHETIC STYLES 4
DILIGENCE 98, 103, 112, 113, 213, 214, 465
diligent 213, 214, 218, 463
DILIGENT LOVE FOR FELLOW CHRISTIANS 214
disannulling 245
DISBELIEF IN THE LORD 124
discern 147, 195-197, 457, 537
Discerner 146
DISCERNING CLEAN AND UNCLEAN 196
DISCERNMENT 196, 197
DISCERNMENT BADLY NEEDED TODAY 197
discipline 104, 191, 449, 450, 452-454, 457
DISCIPLINE NEEDED FOR ALL 457
DISCIPLINE OF CHILDREN 104
DISCIPLINE OUR OWN CHILDREN 453
DISHONEST MIS-TRANSLATIONS IN BIBLES 151
dishonesty 151

DISOBEDIENCE TO THE PROPHETS	3
Dividing	146, 193, 459
DIVINELY PREPARED BLOOD	302
Divinely "prepared" blood	302
DO NO EVIL	530
DO WHAT GOD CALLS "GOOD"	522
doctrinal heresy	153
doctrinal perversions	151
doctrinal teacher	512
doctrine	29, 51, 94, 111-113, 192, 193, 199, 201, 254, 442, 511-515, 527, 540
doctrine of Christ	199, 515
doctrine of the Bible	512
doctrines	192, 193, 199, 205, 276, 307, 357, 445, 511, 518, 526, 528
DOING GOOD	14, 522
DOKIMAZO	99
DOMA	502, 506
done away	285, 286
DON'T BE ASHAMED	404
DON'T DESPISE GOD'S CORRECTION	449
DON'T FEAR MAN	509
DON'T LET APOSTATES INTO YOUR HOUSE	515
DON'T RETURN TO WORLDLINESS	401
Dr. Jack Moorman	134
Dr. Lewis Sperry Chafer	283, 484
Dr. M. R. DeHaan	178, 303, 476
DRAW NEAR IN HEART	351
DRAWING NEAR TO THE LORD	351
drinking	195, 263
drugs	484, 502
DULL OF HEARING	188, 190, 191, 196
DUTIES OF RULING LEADERS	526
DYING IN THE LORD GIVES REST	135
earth	5, 8-10, 12, 21, 23, 31-39, 41, 45, 48, 54, 58, 63, 64, 68, 69, 73, 81, 82, 87, 93, 105, 108, 110, 127, 129, 131, 133, 134, 136, 144, 148, 166, 171, 173, 177, 182-185, 188, 189, 207, 223, 225, 229-231, 234, 239, 240, 244, 248, 254, 256, 258, 263, 266, 269, 271, 274, 279, 280, 290, 298, 299, 317, 319, 327, 328, 337, 340, 342, 343, 347-349, 373, 382, 385, 387-389, 392, 394, 396-399, 402, 403, 406,

	415, 417, 427, 436, 437, 439, 444-446, 454, 460-462, 468, 469, 476-478, 480-482, 487, 488, 496, 506, 515, 519, 520, 534

EARTHLY VS. HEAVENLY TABERNACLE 542
Ebedmelech 432
Eden 62
EGGUOS 248
Egypt 3, 46, 47, 91, 93, 96, 97, 106, 122, 123, 125, 128, 130, 132, 172, 174, 175, 221, 274, 276, 279, 280, 293, 397, 400-403, 408-411, 413-416, 419, 420, 434, 485, 519
EIGHT PERSONS AND THINGS IN HEAVEN 473
EKLUO 446
EKPHEUGO 60
EKPHOBOS 473
elders 50, 68, 69, 117, 153, 183, 272, 315, 316, 378, 462, 488, 506, 509, 524-528
elect 60, 64-66, 127, 162, 212
ELIMINATING BITTERNESS 463
Elisha 2, 431, 490
ELOHIM 5
ELOHIM–THREE OR MORE 5
ELPIS 214, 215, 246
embrace 398
Emerging church 106
EMINENT DOMAIN IS COVETOUSNESS 506
EMMANUEL–GOD WITH US 508
empty heart and life 485
ENCATALEIPO 355
ENDURANCE 224
endure 35, 192, 208, 220, 224, 275, 414, 452, 472, 514, 528
ENDURE GOD'S CHASTENING 452
ENDURING FOR CHRIST 224
English Standard Version 8, 15, 151, 153
enlightened 89, 203, 204, 211, 368
ENLIGHTENED=GENUINELY SAVED 204
ENNOIA 147
ENOCH'S TRANSLATION TO HEAVEN 384
entertain strangers 500, 501
ENTERTAINING OTHER CHRISTIANS 501
ENTRANCE INTO GOD'S PRESENCE 119

environment 105
Ephesians 2:10 . . . . 8, 211
Ephesians 3:9 . . . . 8, 34, 93
Ephesians 4:24 . . . . 8, 455
EPILAMBANOMAI 79
Episcopalians 291
EPISKOPEO 462
EPISUNAGOGE 356
err 98-101, 121
ERRORS OF THE HEART 98
Esau 407, 465, 466, 468, 469
ESAU WAS A WICKED FORNICATOR 465
escape 54, 60, 67, 81, 85, 353, 400, 477, 478
ESTABLISHING THE NEW TESTAMENT 335
esteem 30, 329, 415
ESV 57, 93, 151, 153, 500
ETERNAL INHERITANCE POSSIBLE 310
ETERNAL JUDGMENT 201, 202
eternal life 6, 25, 54, 65, 109, 132, 186, 216, 217, 227,
                                        270, 290, 298, 305, 310-312, 329, 342
ETERNAL SALVATION 183-187, 214, 311, 342, 367, 378
eternal security 305, 342
ETERNAL SECURITY OF THE SAVED 342
eternal Sonship 21, 22, 175
eternity past and into the future 244
Ethiopian 48, 432
ever liveth 60, 236, 249, 253
everlasting 21, 36-40, 55, 65, 107, 127, 153, 157, 169,
                                        170, 179, 185, 186, 202, 203, 244, 246, 250, 256,
                                        310, 319, 327, 340, 342, 369, 372, 385, 409, 446,
                                        451, 461, 484, 492, 510, 511, 533, 537
everlasting and unchangeable Saviour 511
everlasting life 55, 65, 107, 127, 153, 169, 179, 185,
                                        186, 246, 310, 342, 369, 372, 385, 451, 461, 484
everlasting to everlasting 21, 36-39, 244
EVERYTHING IN CREATION 10
evolution 7, 62, 379
example 31, 69, 94, 95, 145, 206, 254, 267, 268, 359,
                                        365, 467, 500, 523
EXAMPLE AND SHADOW OF HEAVENLY THINGS 267
EXAMPLE OF UNBELIEF 145
EXAMPLES OF PRAYER 530

EXERCISED	195, 196, 456, 457
EXHORT & EXHORTATION	112
exhort continually	112
EXPECTING OR WAITING	340
e-mail: BFT@BibleForToday.org	i
faint	90, 445-449, 458, 465, 540
FAINT AND WEARY	445
faith	6, 13, 19, 28, 29, 37, 40, 44, 55-57, 59-61, 67, 70, 73, 78, 81-83, 86, 105, 112, 113, 118, 119, 130-134, 137-140, 142, 143, 145, 150, 153, 156, 158-160, 185-187, 192, 196, 199, 200, 204, 205, 209, 214-217, 219, 220, 223, 224, 242, 246, 247, 250-252, 259, 273, 281-283, 290, 298, 299, 310, 316, 322, 341-346, 351, 352, 357, 364, 374, 375, 377-380, 383, 385-387, 389-391, 393-395, 397, 398, 404, 406-410, 412, 416-430, 433, 436-439, 441, 443, 447, 455, 459, 460, 463, 483, 498, 509, 513, 514, 520, 521, 525, 527, 528, 531, 533, 542
FAITH AS SUBSTANCE	378
FAITH EXPLAINS CREATION	379
FAITH GIVES CHRISTIANS ASSURANCE	378
FAITH MENTIONED OFTEN HERE	377
FAITH WITHOUT SEEING	419
FAITHFUL	ii, 9, 46, 59, 69, 70, 79-81, 83-87, 90-92, 94, 113, 116, 156, 159, 211, 251, 283, 319, 325, 326, 343, 344, 346, 349, 352-354, 357, 359, 375, 394, 395, 415, 425, 427, 433, 441, 479, 480, 509, 514, 526, 539
faithful high priest	69, 79-81, 84, 90, 156, 159, 349
FAITHFUL RULERS AND LEADERS	509
fake "Christians"	94
fall	32, 51, 62, 84-86, 99, 108, 110, 111, 117, 123, 130, 145, 179, 186, 205, 211, 213, 225, 342, 367, 402, 428, 446, 448, 463, 494
fall away	84, 111, 205, 342
FALSE DOCTRINES ALL AROUND US	511
fax: 856-854-2464	i
fear	23, 30, 32, 47, 54, 77-79, 87, 90, 118, 129, 138, 214, 217, 275, 351, 360, 361, 386, 401, 416, 461, 472, 473, 482, 483, 485, 492, 498, 508, 509, 521
feeble	457-459
FEEBLE KNEES	457-459

Feed	50, 315, 316, 434, 465, 524, 525, 535
fifth reason	2
FIRE	24, 28, 36, 46, 53, 77, 86, 107-110, 124, 144, 149, 165, 167, 202, 208-210, 216, 236, 271, 274, 277, 295, 325, 327, 359, 365-367, 386, 395, 405, 423, 430, 467, 470, 471, 479, 481, 485-496, 519
fire in Hell	107, 149, 202, 216, 325, 359, 519
first day	136, 137, 238, 285, 337
first mount	470
first reason	1, 137
firstbegotten	22, 23
firstborn	270, 304, 408, 417, 419, 420, 444, 465, 469, 473, 474
FLESH AND BLOOD	73, 74
flesh and bones	74
fold up	38, 482
Foolishness is in the hearts of children	103
footstool	19, 26, 40, 41, 43, 44, 48, 225, 258, 259, 340-342
for the benefit of	230
Foreword	iii, iv
forget not	522
forgive	28, 81, 172, 274, 281, 283, 309, 325, 326, 343, 344, 354, 359, 402, 479, 480
forgiven	65, 281-283, 324, 331, 332, 345, 402
FORGIVEN SINS OF ALL TIME	283
FORGIVENESS AND ETERNAL LIFE	310
former things	483-485
FORMER THINGS PASS AWAY IN HEAVEN	484
FORNICATION	194, 206, 362, 364, 365, 465-468, 503-506, 539
FORNICATION BEGINS IN THE HEART	466
fornicator	465, 503
forsaking	86, 113, 207, 355, 357
foundation	12, 31-33, 35, 50, 110, 117, 133, 134, 151, 158, 199, 208-210, 215, 229, 244, 255, 323, 324, 366, 377, 478, 479, 481
foundation of the earth	31, 32, 35, 244, 481
foundations	31-33, 48, 143, 199, 274, 377, 393, 394, 493, 520
FOUR PLEASING SACRIFICES	523
four sacrifices	520, 523

fourth reason 1
FREE COURSE FOR GOD'S WORDS 531
Free Methodists 184, 304, 311
FRUIT 11, 62, 72, 111, 207, 208, 213, 225, 381, 456,
                             457, 461, 463, 464, 493, 520
FRUITLESS CHRISTIANS 208
FULL ASSURANCE 158, 213, 214, 351, 498
Fundamentalists 20, 57, 94, 153, 334
FUNDAMENTALISTS USE PERVERTED BIBLES 20
FUNDAMENTALISTS' BIBLES DENY "BY HIMSELF" 20
Future: Christ The Chief Shepherd 534
Galatians 6:15 7
gave himself for us 17
GAZINGSTOCK 368, 369
genealogy of Joseph 243
genealogy of Mary 243
Genesis 1:1 5
Genesis through Revelation 95, 141, 148, 196, 459
GENTILES OBTAINED GOD'S MERCY 140
Genuine Christians .... iii, 28, 76, 77, 104, 156, 182, 191,
                      197, 199, 206, 208-213, 215-220, 224, 225, 229,
                      231, 241, 244, 246, 247, 252-254, 272, 282, 283,
                      290, 304, 305, 317, 319, 321, 328, 337, 353, 354,
                      358-360, 365, 367-369, 371, 378, 379, 395, 399,
                      411, 413, 419, 433, 436, 441, 445, 449, 452-456,
                      459, 461, 462, 464, 472, 477, 479, 480, 483, 484,
                      500, 502, 504, 507-509, 515, 518-525, 528, 530,
                      533, 534, 537, 539-541
GENUINE CHRISTIANS NEED DILIGENCE 213
GENUINE CHRISTIANS SHOULD HOLD FAST 156
genuine faith 6, 29, 59, 105, 132-134, 138, 150, 153,
                      156, 185-187, 200, 209, 223, 242, 250, 252, 281,
                      298, 299, 322, 341, 342, 344, 379, 385, 390, 406,
                      455, 459, 460, 483, 533
genuine faith in the Lord Jesus 105, 132, 133, 138, 150,
                      153, 156, 185-187, 242, 250, 281, 322, 341, 342,
                      379, 385, 390, 406, 455, 460, 483, 533
GENUINE FAITH NECESSARY FOR SALVATION 132
GENUINE FAITH PRODUCES GOOD WORKS 209
GENUINE TRUST IN THE SAVIOUR NEEDED 346
genuine "Christians." 94
Genuinely saved 5, 7-9, 11, 12, 25, 45, 48, 69, 70, 87,

89, 92, 95, 102, 104, 106, 107, 109, 110, 116, 118, 119, 129, 135, 130, 132, 138-140, 142, 143, 145, 146, 153, 156, 159, 162, 166, 167, 171, 180, 181, 184, 185, 193, 194, 196, 201-205, 209, 210, 213, 216, 219, 226, 230, 236, 247, 252, 257, 259, 265, 288, 289, 305, 308, 310, 318, 319, 322, 325, 327, 336, 343, 346, 347, 349, 350, 352, 357, 358, 362, 364, 366-368, 372, 389, 393, 398, 408, 418, 435, 437, 441, 456, 458, 471, 474, 475, 482-485, 497, 507, 509, 510, 516, 519, 542

geocentricity 31, 33, 34, 134, 481
geocentricity is Biblical 33, 481
Geocentricity–The Biblical And Observational Case 481
Gethsemane 84, 177, 178, 180
GETTING THE RIGHTEOUSNESS OF GOD 28
GEUOMAI 63, 204
GIDEON 46, 424
GIVE GOD REVERENCE WHEN CORRECTING 455
glory 4, 9-14, 18, 23, 33, 34, 42, 43, 45, 52, 62, 63, 66-69, 72, 76, 78, 84, 86, 92, 93, 97, 114, 117, 120, 130, 144, 160, 161, 182, 183, 193, 202, 209, 215, 216, 218, 224, 247, 254, 258, 259, 280, 290, 295, 310, 319, 378, 417, 418, 430, 439, 447, 455, 486, 490, 492, 495, 524, 536-538
Gnostic 6, 8, 15, 19, 20, 26, 31, 34, 35, 57, 58, 93, 149, 151, 259, 346
Gnostic Critical Greek text 26, 57, 58, 93, 149
Gnostic Critical Greek Words 151
Gnostic false heretical Greek New Testament 15
GNOSTIC OMISSION OF "BY JESUS CHRIST" 35
GNOSTICISM The Doctrinal Foundation 151
Gnostics 6, 15, 19, 31, 34, 57, 58, 93, 151, 346
Gnostics of Alexandria 15
GOD A CONSUMING FIRE 485
GOD AFFIRMS HIS WORDS 402
GOD CHASTENS THOSE HE LOVES 450
GOD CHOSE ISAAC 407
GOD IS NOT FAINT OR WEARY 446
GOD JUSTIFIES GENUINE CHRISTIANS 28
GOD KEEPS ALL HIS PROMISES 398
GOD KEEPS HIS PROMISES 216, 372, 395
GOD MADE CHRIST A HIGH PRIEST 230

God of peace 71, 319, 531, 533
GOD PROMISED TO PRESERVE HIS WORDS 406
GOD PUNISHED SINNING ISRAEL 478
God remains the same 482
GOD RESTED AFTER HIS CREATION 136
GOD THE FATHER WAS PROPITIATED 63, 67
GOD THE FATHER'S WILL 179, 335, 339
GOD TRAINS HIS CHILDREN 451
GOD WARNED NOAH ABOUT THE FLOOD 386
GOD WAS GRIEVED 100
GOD WAS PLEASED WITH BLOOD OFFERINGS 382
GOD WILL JUDGE ADULTERERS 503
GOD WOULD LIKE ALL TO BE SAVED 252
godly service 483
God-Man 159, 180, 249, 309, 323
God's creation 135, 379
GOD'S CREATION IN SIX DAYS 135
GOD'S ETERNAL REDEMPTION 304
GOD'S FUTURE "REST" 142
GOD'S LAMB TAKING AWAY SIN 65
GOD'S LIVING WAY TO HEAVEN 231
GOD'S MARVELOUS CREATION 126
GOD'S MERCY TO ISRAEL 280
GOD'S OATH FOR CHRIST'S PRIESTHOOD 256
GOD'S OPEN DOOR 349
GOD'S OPENING OF THE RED SEA 420
GOD'S PERFECT RIGHTEOUSNESS 26
GOD'S PROMISE AFTER OFFERING ISAAC 222
GOD'S REST THE SEVENTH DAY FROM ALL HIS WORKS 136
GOD'S SALVATION 54, 134, 184, 210
GOD'S SERVICE MUST BE ACCEPTABLE 483
GOD'S THREE CLASSES OF PEOPLE 336
GOD'S USE OF FIRE IN JUDGMENT 366
GOD'S WILL FOUND ONLY IN THE BIBLE 537
GOD'S WILL ONLY IN GOD'S WORDS 531
God's Words .... iii, 95, 102, 110, 111, 140-142, 148-152,
        192, 194, 195, 208, 228, 229, 372, 379, 390, 392,
        408, 415, 439, 458, 459, 468, 472, 503, 513, 523,
        531, 538, 539
GOD'S WORDS ARE AN ANCHOR 229
GOD'S WORDS ARE IN THE BIBLE 140
GOD'S WORDS EFFECTUALLY WORK 152

GOD'S WORDS, NOT TRADITIONS	148
GOD'S WORDS–THE SOURCE OF FAITH	150
gold, silver, and precious stones	50, 110, 209, 366, 479
gold, silver, precious stones	209, 366, 478
Gomorrha	365, 467, 502
good and evil	62, 195-197, 457
Good Shepherd	534-536
gospel	17, 18, 55, 56, 61, 76, 105, 116, 130, 138, 140, 152, 153, 186, 201, 212, 215, 236, 242, 247, 251, 286, 288, 334, 342, 365, 368, 403, 404, 435, 437, 533
government	37, 39, 78, 104, 107, 154, 188, 346, 370, 389, 411, 412, 449
GOVERNMENT'S 72 POTENTIAL TERRORISTS	154
grace	6, 11, 50, 56, 59, 63, 66, 76, 110, 133, 145, 162, 176, 182, 187, 192, 193, 208, 209, 212, 214, 215, 217, 237, 238, 242, 251, 252, 272, 273, 282, 284-286, 291, 305, 310, 317, 313, 326, 331, 332, 335-337, 346, 360, 362, 364, 366, 388, 389, 392, 408, 444, 462-464, 475, 478, 482, 511, 512, 538, 541, 542
Graham, Billy	202, 515
great God	29, 216, 247, 417, 418
great High Priest	82, 90, 156-159, 162, 163, 166, 241, 244, 252, 255, 256, 263, 300, 301, 321, 323, 349, 352, 476, 477, 542
Great Shepherd	319, 533-536
Great White Throne	202, 325, 340, 359, 367, 395
greater treasure	415
grieved	98-101, 121, 123, 128, 326, 388
GRIEVING	100
groves	277, 444
Hagar	224, 394
HAGIAZO	70, 363
HAIMA	315, 535
HANDS THAT HANG DOWN	457
hang down	457
harden	95, 114, 119, 120, 128, 140-142, 401
HARDENED HEARTS	96, 113, 141
HARDENED HEARTS & MINDS	113
HARDENING HEART AND MIND	119
HARDENING OF HEARTS	96

HARMLESS 82, 90, 253, 254, 350
HARPAGE 370
hate 29-31, 41, 172, 206, 415, 483, 513, 518
HATING EVIL 29
hatred 31, 48, 115, 194, 206, 364, 463
HAVE STRENGTHENED KNEES 458
He sat down 17, 44, 257, 443
healing 14, 150
hear his voice 95, 119, 120, 128, 140, 142, 488
heart 3, 29, 49, 51, 56, 59, 90, 95-105, 109-111, 114,
              115, 119-121, 125-127, 129, 134, 135, 141-143,
              145-148, 158, 174, 181, 190, 191, 197, 214, 227,
              228, 251, 260, 329, 333, 335, 351, 360, 385, 388,
              390, 406, 415, 423, 438, 449, 451, 460, 461, 464,
              466, 469, 485, 493, 498, 505, 506, 511, 512, 539
HEART DILIGENCE 214
HEARTS UNBLAMEABLE 456, 461
heathen 31, 74, 140, 172, 276, 277
Heaven 2, 5, 8-10, 12, 13, 17-21, 25, 28, 33, 34, 36, 37,
              41, 42, 44, 45, 53-55, 59, 64, 70, 74, 76, 77, 80, 83,
              87, 93, 107-109, 118, 124, 125, 127, 129, 130, 135,
              136, 143, 149, 162, 171, 177, 182, 184-186, 188,
              205, 206, 213, 215-217, 222, 223, 225, 227, 229-
              231, 234, 236, 239, 240, 246-248, 250, 254, 257,
              258, 260, 261, 267, 268, 270, 271, 274, 275, 277,
              287, 290, 298-302, 304, 306, 308-310, 316-318,
              321, 322, 324, 327, 334, 337, 339, 342, 343, 347-
              352, 354, 359, 369-371, 373, 378, 384, 393-397,
              399, 402, 403, 405, 415-417, 436-439, 441, 443,
              455, 462, 468-477, 480-485, 487-491, 495, 496,
              508, 510, 519, 520, 534, 542
HEAVEN AND EARTH KEPT IN STORE 481
HEAVEN FOR ALL ETERNITY 215, 327, 483, 519
HEAVEN GAVE MOSES A PATTERN 267
HEAVEN IS SURE AND ETERNAL 519
HEAVEN IS THAT BETTER THING 438
heavenly Jerusalem 270, 271, 275, 304, 473, 520
Heavenly mercy seat 262, 302, 321, 476, 477
Heavenly rest 109, 129, 130, 142, 143
Hebrew and Aramaic Words 334
Hebrew, Aramaic, and Greek 36, 94, 95, 139, 140, 146,
              149, 151, 153, 327, 334, 355, 357, 372, 384, 443,

                                    149, 151, 153, 327, 334, 355, 357, 372, 384, 443, 459, 500, 537

Hebrew, Aramaic, and Greek Words 36, 94, 95, 140, 145, 149, 153, 327, 334, 355, 357, 372, 384, 443, 459, 500, 537

Hebrews 1:14 .... 6, 45, 213
Hebrews 1:2 4
Hebrews 13:23 .... 1, 540
Hebrews 13:24 .... 1, 501, 528, 532, 541
HEBREWS A BOOK OF GRACE VS. LAW 542
Hebrews Chapter Eight iv
Hebrews Chapter Eleven .... iv, 380
Hebrews Chapter Five iv
Hebrews Chapter Four iv
Hebrews Chapter Nine iv
Hebrews Chapter One iv
Hebrews Chapter Seven iv
Hebrews Chapter Six iv
Hebrews Chapter Ten iv
Hebrews Chapter Thirteen iv
Hebrews Chapter Three iv
Hebrews Chapter Twelve iv
Hebrews Chapter Two iv
HEGEOMAI 414, 525
heir 4-6, 386, 387
HEIRS AND JOINT-HEIRS 4
heliocentricity 481
Hell 28, 54, 60, 64, 76, 78, 105, 107-109, 149, 202, 216, 227, 250, 289, 325, 327, 340, 358, 359, 395, 483, 499, 519

Hell is everlasting 202
HELL PREPARED FOR THE DEVIL AND HIS ANGELS
.... 202
heresies 6, 57, 66, 148, 149, 170, 194, 207, 266, 332, 364
HERESIES IN PROTESTANT CHURCHES 148, 149
heresy 39, 40, 93, 153, 158, 171, 173, 183, 185, 265, 269, 303, 306, 307, 309, 315, 316, 318, 328, 336, 338, 348, 363, 474
heretic 8, 15, 20, 35, 168, 182, 185, 187, 307, 364, 445, 535
heretical verses in the 356 places 20

HIDE GOD'S WORDS IN THE HEART 102
high priest 19, 22, 43, 69, 70, 79-84, 86, 89-91, 119, 156-
159, 162, 163, 165-168, 171, 173, 175, 184, 187,
188, 230, 231, 236, 241, 244, 245, 249, 252, 253,
255-257, 262-265, 268, 269, 292, 294, 296-298,
300, 301, 303, 321-323, 332, 347, 349-352, 476,
477, 517, 542
high priest forever 157, 230, 245, 350
High Priestly prayer 12, 33, 70, 530
high school janitor 141
HIGHER THAN THE HEAVENS 82, 90, 253, 254, 350
His Son 4, 5, 17, 18, 22, 25, 31, 41, 43, 46, 55, 58, 67,
74, 75, 81, 108, 144, 159, 175, 176, 200, 219, 222,
223, 228, 239, 240, 248, 250-252, 259, 265, 273,
289, 306, 316, 319, 333, 349, 353, 363, 375, 388,
396, 404, 405, 407, 408, 439, 449, 451, 452, 471,
499, 533, 540
Hodgkins disease 101
hold fast 81, 82, 90, 94, 156, 159, 349, 352, 395
HOLDING FAST 352
Holiness 8, 14, 37, 117, 183, 185, 193, 228, 304, 311,
363, 455, 456, 459-462, 472, 485
holy of holies 83, 165-168, 170, 228, 229, 231, 257, 262-
264, 291, 292, 294-298, 303, 322, 323, 332, 347,
477
HOLY OF HOLIES ONCE A YEAR 170, 257, 297
HOMO 80, 236, 243, 326, 479
HOMOI 80, 236, 243
HOMOIOO 236
HOMOIOTES 243
HOMOLOGEO 326, 479
HOMOSEXUAL "MARRIAGE" NOT BIBLICAL! 502
homosexuality 365, 411, 436, 467, 468, 503
homosexuals 7, 53
HOMOU 80
hope .... iii, 6, 13, 29, 55, 94, 109, 116, 119, 157, 201, 207,
213-219, 226-228, 242, 246-248, 352, 378, 401,
417, 449, 451
HOPE IN CHRIST FOR HEAVEN 215
HOPE–FUTURE BUT CERTAIN 215
Hort 15, 26, 35, 57, 58
human blood 265, 266, 306, 307, 333, 364

HUPAKOUO	184
HUPOPODION	41
HYPEIKO	526
HYPER	64, 109, 127, 168, 182, 185, 187, 230, 252
Hyper-Calvinist	64
hyper-Calvinists	64, 109, 168, 182, 185, 187, 252
HYPODEIGMA	267
idols	22, 276, 277, 466, 478
illuminated	368
images	22, 277, 444
immersion in water	201
IMPORTANCE OF THE HEART	101
imprisonment	315, 370, 433, 435, 501
IN HEAVEN PAIN IS REMOVED	484
IN HEAVEN "FOR US"	321
incorruptible blood	266, 329, 333, 447, 517
Index of Words and Phrases	iv, 545
intents	146, 147
intercession	19, 42, 60, 162, 236, 249, 252, 253, 259, 321
intercessory prayer	530, 532
intercourse between the nuns and the priests	503
Introductory Remarks	1
INVISIBLE THINGS CLEARLY SEEN	417
Isaac	4, 46, 106, 142, 189, 219, 222-224, 226, 240, 378, 380, 393, 395, 396, 404-407, 409, 410, 468, 469
ISRAEL DID NOT FOLLOW THE LORD	276
ISRAEL FEARED GOD'S VOICE	472
ISRAEL REJECTED GOD'S COMMANDS	278
ISRAEL SAW GOD'S MIRACLE	421
ISRAEL SINNED AGAINST THE LORD	276
ISRAEL WILL BE DRAWN TO JERUSALEM	280
ISRAEL WILL COME TO CHRIST	279
Israelites	49, 97, 101, 106, 110, 121, 124, 129-131, 137, 138, 142, 169, 172, 174, 177, 197, 221, 237, 239, 240, 272, 276, 278, 280, 293, 313, 338, 339, 400-403, 410, 414, 421, 470, 477, 478, 519
ISRAEL'S DISOBEDIENCE TO GOD	276
ISRAEL'S ESCAPE FROM EGYPT	400
ISRAEL'S HEART-ERRING	121
ISRAEL'S UNBELIEF AND DOUBT	400
ISRAEL'S UNBELIEVERS	125

It is finished 444
Jacob 4, 106, 124, 131, 142, 189, 248, 271, 279, 343,
378, 393, 407-410, 465, 468, 469, 493, 510
Jacob and Esau 407
JACOB BURIED IN CANAAN 409
James 1:18 9
Jehovah Witnesses 515
JEPHTHAH 426
Jeremiah 25:3-5 3
Jeremiah 25:7 4
Jeremiah 7:23-24 3
Jeremiah 7:25-26 3
JEREMIAH ESCAPES FROM THE PIT 432
Jericho 122, 421-423
JERUSALEM'S WAILING WALL 344
Jesus 3-29, 31, 33-39, 41-48, 50, 51, 54-61, 63-69, 71-84,
86, 87, 89-94, 102, 105, 107-110, 113, 116, 118,
119, 125-127, 129, 130, 132-145, 148-150, 153,
154, 156-163, 166-195, 199-203, 206-220, 223-231,
233, 235, 236, 238-260, 262, 263, 265-273, 275,
278-285, 288-291, 296, 298-302, 304-311, 315-329,
331-354, 357, 359, 363-369, 371-375, 378-383, 385-
387, 389, 390, 392, 395, 399, 402-408, 415-419,
430, 433, 435, 437-439, 443-445, 447, 450, 453-
458, 460, 461, 464, 471-480, 482-484, 498-500,
507-513, 515-522, 524, 527, 530, 531, 533-543
JESUS CHRIST NEVER CHANGES 510
JESUS CHRIST THE ALTAR 516
JESUS THE AUTHOR AND FINISHER OF OUR FAITH 19,
44, 185, 220, 259, 418, 443
JESUS THE HIGH PRIEST AND VEIL 230
JEWISH UNBELIEF 139
JOB–A PATTERN FOR PATIENCE 220
John 1:3 .... 7, 34, 92
JOHN BANISHED TO THE ISLE OF PATMOS 154
John MacArthur 21, 144, 175, 265, 303, 306, 307, 315,
316, 318, 320, 333, 363, 364, 420, 535
JOHN MACARTHUR'S BLOOD HERESY 315
John MacArthur's HERESY On The Blood of Christ 303,
307, 315
joint-heir with the Lord Jesus Christ 5
Jonah 2, 155, 156

Joseph	6, 30, 47, 243, 397, 408-410
JOSEPH IN THE LAND OF PROMISE	410
JOSEPH MENTIONED ISRAEL'S DEPARTING	410
JOSEPH REFUSED CREMATION	409
joy	19, 23, 29, 44, 52, 55, 84, 86, 117, 183, 185, 220, 226, 259, 378, 414, 418, 443, 463, 464, 524, 542
Judah	3, 4, 39, 174, 176, 230, 238, 242, 243, 266, 273, 274, 277, 280, 343, 493, 494, 510
Judas	105, 180
Judas Iscariot	105, 180
judgment	26, 27, 30, 37, 54, 62, 78, 86, 97, 99, 108, 110, 137, 154, 158, 180, 201-203, 206, 208, 209, 229, 309, 325, 340, 359, 365-367, 371, 374, 375, 395, 399, 420, 478, 479, 481, 493, 530, 536
Judgment Seat of Christ	110, 202, 208, 209, 325, 365, 367, 371, 375, 395, 399, 478, 479, 536
JUMPING FROM THE TEMPLE REJECTED	161
Just	2, 6, 7, 13, 15, 20, 22-25, 28, 30, 31, 34, 38, 40, 41, 45, 49, 51, 52, 57-61, 64-67, 69, 71, 74, 77, 78, 81, 85, 93, 96, 103, 104, 106, 109, 110, 119, 124, 136, 143, 150, 166, 177-179, 182, 191, 193-196, 201, 204, 207, 212, 214, 216, 217, 222, 229, 234, 252, 255-257, 261, 262, 265, 270, 273, 283, 301, 304-306, 309, 316, 320, 322-328, 331, 339, 354, 358, 359, 365, 370, 374, 375, 381, 383, 384, 387, 389, 390, 393, 411, 413, 420, 421, 427, 439, 452, 456, 459, 471, 473-475, 479, 480, 498, 502, 526
JUSTIFIED BY FAITH	132, 374, 375, 460, 533
JUSTIFIED ONCE TRULY SAVED	252
KAPHAR	298
KARDIA	101, 147
KATANOESATE	89
KATAPATEO	362
KATAPAUO	136, 144
KATAPAUSIS	109, 129, 133, 144
KATARGEO	74
KATARTIZO	537
KATHIZO	257
killing Christians	239
killing Jews	239
King James Bible	i, iv, 39, 95, 120, 140, 142, 146, 149, 153, 171, 195, 223, 240, 355, 357, 372, 383, 384,

King of peace	443, 459, 466, 481, 485, 500, 537, 188, 189, 235
king of Salem	176, 188, 233-235
KLERONOMOS	5
KOINOS	318, 363
Koran	239
KRATEO	156
LABORING FOR THE LORD	399
Lake of Fire	28, 77, 107-109, 144, 202, 216, 325, 359, 395, 519
Lamb of God	4, 46, 65, 170, 230, 265, 282, 290, 299, 307, 317, 324, 329, 331, 339, 380, 405, 437, 438
LAMB SLAIN–BLOOD APPLIED	320
lamps	313, 491, 495
law	ii, 30, 53, 75, 92, 132, 141, 176, 189, 190, 228, 236-238, 241, 242, 244-246, 256, 266, 267, 271-275, 277, 278, 284-287, 292, 294, 312, 314, 322, 329, 331, 333, 335-337, 346, 360-362, 370, 387, 390, 411, 435, 449, 463, 470, 472, 478, 498, 502, 542
LAW DEFINES SIN	272
law of Moses	176, 238, 241, 242, 245, 246, 256, 271-273, 275, 284-287, 294, 312, 322, 331, 334-337, 360, 361, 470, 542
LAW OF MOSES TOTALLY REMOVED	336
lawyer	162
LAYING ON OF HANDS	201
LEANNESS TO OUR SOULS	123
LEANNESS TO THE SOUL	98
learned	180-182, 419, 453, 507, 512
LEARNING IS NEEDED	181
LEITOURGOS	24
lesbianism	365, 503
lesbians	7
Levi	174, 176, 177, 187-190, 230, 237, 238, 241, 242, 244, 266, 293, 294, 411
LEVI RECEIVED TITHES	241
LEVITES ALSO TITHED BACK	237
liar	115, 211, 227, 382, 499
liberals	7, 31, 94, 106, 107
Liberia	216
lie	30, 119, 125, 195, 215, 216, 226, 227, 360, 429, 513
LIES AND LYING	226

LIFE AS A VAPOUR	327
light	10, 32, 48, 54, 61, 68, 70, 72, 76, 89, 116, 135, 203, 204, 260, 267, 274, 287-290, 313, 319, 326, 339, 345, 346, 368, 385, 462, 486, 490-492, 522
like	7, 24, 35, 38, 40, 41, 50, 51, 61-64, 73, 76, 80, 82, 85, 86, 90, 93, 95-97, 102-104, 108, 110, 117, 123, 133, 136, 137, 141, 148, 156, 157, 159, 173, 177-180, 184, 189, 191, 193-195, 202, 204, 205, 207, 215, 217, 226, 229, 235, 236, 249, 252, 266, 268, 277, 283, 293, 294, 301, 303, 304, 311, 316, 320, 322, 326, 327, 336, 344, 349, 350, 352, 357, 358, 363-365, 367, 369, 383, 384, 388, 389, 393, 398, 411, 415, 423, 430, 432, 452, 465, 467, 478, 482, 485, 486, 492-495, 497, 502, 504, 515, 527, 528, 532, 535
like the Son of God	236, 430
like unto the Son of God	177, 189, 235
LIVE IN THE LIGHT	288
LIVE SERVICES	356
LOGEO	326, 479
looking	57, 150, 220, 299, 359, 371, 393, 399, 416, 422, 438, 441, 443-445, 462, 463, 526
LOOKING DILIGENTLY	462
LOOKING FOR A BETTER THING	438
LOOKING OUT FOR PEOPLE	526
LOOKING TO THE LORD	444
LOOKING UNTO CHRIST THE MESSIAH	416
LOOKING WHILE RUNNING	445
LOT SHOULD NOT BE IN SODOM	234
love fellow Christians	499
love one another	497-500
LOVE THE BRETHREN	499, 500
LOVE WITHOUT SEEING	418
Lucifer	21, 40, 61
LUKE GIVES MARY'S GENEALOGY	243
Lutherans	291
LYING IN THE COLOSSE CHURCH?	227
LYING TO THE HOLY SPIRIT	361
LYING VERSUS LAYING	195
MacArthur	21, 22, 144, 175, 265, 266, 303, 306, 307, 315-320, 333, 363, 364, 420, 535
MADE A PRIEST BY AN OATH	248

made like 63, 80, 90, 156, 177, 189, 215, 235, 236, 369
MADE PARTAKERS OF THE HOLY GHOST 89, 203, 204
male and female 7
man 5, 7-11, 14, 15, 18, 19, 21, 22, 25, 27, 30, 31, 41-43,
46, 50, 53-67, 76, 78-81, 85, 86, 92, 100, 103, 105,
107, 110, 111, 113, 115, 117, 122, 126, 127, 132,
133, 139, 141, 145, 148-150, 157, 159-162, 168,
169, 174, 175, 179-182, 186, 189-192, 206, 208,
209, 212, 216-218, 225, 227, 236, 237, 242, 245,
249, 250, 254, 258-260, 263, 265, 266, 268, 269,
273, 274, 279-282, 286, 290, 294, 298-300, 305,
309-311, 322, 323, 335, 337, 339, 342, 344, 345,
348-350, 353, 360-362, 366, 374, 379-381, 384,
387-390, 402, 406, 408, 409, 411, 413, 420, 422,
424, 426-428, 431-433, 435, 438, 439, 444, 449,
451, 452, 455, 459, 462, 465, 467, 468, 470, 472,
476, 478, 482, 489, 490, 496, 498, 499, 502, 503,
505, 507-509, 512-514, 520, 527, 532-534, 538
MAN LOWER THAN THE ANGELS 62
manger 195
manna 123, 124, 292, 293, 295
MANNA LIKE HONEY 293
Mark 10:6 7
mark of the beast 144
marriage 85, 411, 467, 468, 502-504, 523
married love 503, 504
Mary 47, 54, 235, 238, 243, 269, 302, 309, 476
MARY IS NOT OUR MEDIATRIX 476
Mass 69, 97, 98, 158, 255, 301, 338, 441, 527
Masses 158, 171, 173, 266, 323, 324, 328, 332, 338
Matthew 21:38 5
MATTHEW GIVES JOSEPH'S GENEALOGY 243
mature 196, 205, 319, 451, 453, 538
maturity 182, 194, 199, 200
MEANING OF THE DOCTRINE OF CHRIST 515
meanings 5, 10, 23, 36, 38, 41, 49, 52, 60, 67-70, 74, 77,
84, 89, 99-101, 111, 116-119, 121, 129, 133, 134,
136, 141, 143-147, 155, 156, 159, 162, 184, 190-
192, 194, 196, 199, 200, 203-205, 212-214, 230,
236, 243, 245, 252, 253, 257, 267, 269, 284, 301,
308, 315, 318, 335, 355, 356, 358, 362-364, 368-
371, 377, 378, 398, 413, 414, 416, 441, 442, 445,

	511, 516, 523, 525, 526, 528, 529, 532, 537, 540, 541
mediator	66, 268-271, 275, 304, 308-310, 381, 383, 473-476
Mediatrix	269, 309, 476
Melchisedec	82, 90, 119, 157, 174, 176, 177, 187-190, 230, 231, 233, 235, 237, 238, 240, 241, 243, 245, 248, 266, 321, 350
MELCHISEDEC A CHRISTOPHANY	177, 233, 350
Melchizedek	83, 187, 188, 234, 235, 244, 248
MELCHIZEDEK'S TWO TITLES	235
merciful	70, 80, 83, 84, 86, 90, 156, 280, 349, 542
mercy	52, 60, 83, 112, 140, 162, 165, 167, 168, 173, 217, 220, 247, 252, 262, 265, 268, 271, 280, 292, 295-297, 301-304, 306, 308, 321, 360, 476, 477, 490
mercy seat	83, 165, 167, 168, 262, 265, 268, 271, 292, 295-297, 301-304, 306, 308, 321, 476, 477
MESITES	269, 308, 475
Messiah	138, 278, 300, 342-344, 415, 416, 519
Messianic Jews	242, 285
METANOIA	200
METOCHOS	116, 204
MIAINO	464
Micah 5:2	39, 40, 510
MILK	46, 131, 191, 193-196, 403
millennial reign	11, 26, 48, 58, 69, 226, 340, 373, 515, 534
minister	6, 26, 45, 48, 107, 170, 212, 213, 260, 266, 296, 476, 513, 524, 526, 528
MINISTERING	6, 24, 45, 48, 212, 213, 263, 266, 269, 338, 350, 528
ministers	24, 135, 219, 260, 275, 289, 495
MINISTERS' THREEFOLD TITLE	524
miracle birth	394
miracles	11, 60, 94, 97, 144, 149, 357, 478, 515
miraculous virgin birth	302, 316, 363
MISFITS IN THIS WORLD	437
MODERN VERSIONS OMIT "BY JESUS CHRIST"	8
moms and dads	105, 509
Moorman, Dr. Jack	134
MORE FUTURE BLESSINGS FOR ISRAEL	279

Mosaic covenant 269, 271, 274, 276
Moses 12, 20, 24, 40, 46, 49, 65, 81, 83, 91, 92, 94-97,
122, 123, 128, 131, 132, 165, 170-172, 174-176,
190, 195, 238, 241-243, 245, 246, 248, 256, 260-
264, 267, 268, 271-273, 275, 284-287, 292-294,
297, 300, 308-310, 312-314, 320, 322, 331, 334-
337, 349, 360, 361, 400-403, 410-417, 419-421,
423, 470-473, 478, 483, 485, 519, 542
MOSES CHOSE TO OBEY GOD 519
MOSES GREATLY FEARED 473
MOSES LAW ABOLISHED 286
MOSES LAW NOT APPLICABLE NOW 284
MOSES SAW THE INVISIBLE ONE 416
MOSES SPARED FROM DEATH 171
MOSES WAS EXCEEDINGLY AFRAID 472
MOSES' APPOINTMENT 91
MOSES' CHOICE OF AFFLICTION 413
MOSES' CLOSENESS TO THE LORD 91
MOSES' IMPORTANT CHOICE 412
MOSES' KILLING OF AN EGYPTIAN 413
MOSES' LIFE WAS SPARED 411
MOSES' PARENTS DISOBEYED THE KING 412
MOSES' SANCTUARY 287
MOSES' SPRINKLING OF THE BLOOD 313
MOSES' TABERNACLE 260
mount 12, 13, 36, 38, 46, 91, 108, 141, 160, 161, 222,
223, 234, 244, 267, 270, 271, 274, 275, 279, 294,
295, 304, 361, 374, 404-406, 436, 437, 446, 448,
470-473, 480, 483, 486-490, 492, 495, 520
mount Sinai 12, 271, 275, 294, 470-473, 480, 483, 486
MOUNT SINAI, MOUNT SION, AND HEAVEN 271
mount Sion 270, 271, 275, 304, 473, 520
murder 102, 466, 505
Muslims 7, 127, 239, 392, 509, 518
MUSLIMS KILLING JEWS & CHRISTIANS 239
My Lord and my God 27, 244, 419
my words shall not pass away 35, 36
N.T.--GIVING AS GOD PROSPERS 238
Nadab and Abihu 264, 297
NASV 15, 57, 93, 151, 500
National Council of Churches 515
National Defense Authorization Act 370, 435

NDAA	370, 371, 435
Nebuchadnezzar	114, 120, 430
negative prohibition	141, 448, 500, 511, 523
Nestle-Aland,	15
never perish	186, 305, 310
New American Standard Version	151
new covenant	269, 270, 273-276, 284, 304, 310, 343, 381, 383, 473-475
New International Version	15, 39, 151, 153
NEW VERSIONS OMIT "WORSHIP" OF CHRIST	23
NEW VERSIONS PERVERT SALVATION	153
new-evangelicals	94
NIGH BY CHRIST'S BLOOD	317
NINE REPEATED N.T. COMMANDS	436
NIV	8, 20, 39, 40, 57, 67, 93, 151, 153, 500
NO ADAM'S BLOOD IN THE CHRIST	337
NO BLOOD IN OUR GLORIFIED BODIES	74
NO CHAIR IN THE TABERNACLE	43
NO CHAIRS IN THE TABERNACLE	339
NO CONFIDENCE IN THE FLESH	118
NO CONTINUING CITY	519, 520
NO ETERNAL DEATH FOR THE SAVED	76
NO FAITH IN SOME IN THE WILDERNESS	131
no more crying	484
no more death	483, 484
NO MORE FORMER THINGS IN HEAVEN	485
no more pain	484
NO MORE SACRIFICE FOR SINS	358
NO MORE SACRIFICES NEEDED	332
no more sorrow	484
NO OPERATING CONSCIENCE	529
NO REST BECAUSE OF UNBELIEF	129
NO WAVERING FOR CHRISTIANS	352
Noah	380, 386-391, 394, 397, 407
NOAH FOUND GOD'S GRACE	389
NOAH'S ARK SAVED LIVES	390
nominal "Christians,"	94
non posse peccare	159, 184
non-elect	66, 127
not able to sin	159, 184
NOT ANY LONGER THE SIN QUESTION	328
NOT ASHAMED AT HIS COMING	118

not believe 6, 7, 19, 21, 23, 26, 27, 31, 33, 35, 41, 57, 58, 64, 72, 73, 93, 99, 106, 122, 124, 126, 127, 137, 139, 140, 151, 184, 203, 204, 277, 303, 344, 391, 418
Noyle ii
number 2, 5, 20, 26, 84, 99, 123, 141, 146, 227, 253, 281, 326, 327, 386, 446, 460
nuns 503
OATH 221, 225, 226, 245, 248, 249, 256, 410
OATH PASSED TO ISAAC 226
OATHS 225, 248
Obama 115, 226, 239, 370, 392, 468, 502, 510
OBAMA A GREAT DECEIVER AND LIAR 115
OBEDIENCE 37, 40, 180-182, 201, 222, 240, 291, 380, 391, 405, 411, 414, 425, 439, 455
obey 3, 96, 97, 107, 152, 183, 184, 224, 271, 272, 311, 365, 391, 392, 411, 436, 453, 454, 515, 519, 525
OBEY GOD RATHER THAN MEN 411
offer 46, 67, 72, 83, 157, 158, 165, 166, 170, 173, 212, 222, 237, 246, 255, 263, 264, 266, 296, 297, 322, 323, 332, 339, 351, 404, 425, 426, 520, 521, 542
offering 16, 18, 46, 71, 83, 158, 165-168, 170, 174, 177, 185, 222, 237, 255, 256, 260, 263-267, 270, 297, 301-303, 306, 314, 316, 322-324, 328, 331-333, 335, 337-339, 341, 345, 359, 363, 380-383, 404, 405, 426, 477, 486, 490, 517, 520
OLD TESTAMENT FUTURE PROMISES 439
OLD TESTAMENT HIGH PRIESTS' OFFERINGS 173
OLD TESTAMENT SHOWS PATIENCE 219
OLD TESTAMENT TITHING TO LEVITES 238
OMISSION OF "BY JESUS CHRIST" 35, 93
omnipresent 155, 257
omniscient 155, 181
ONCE 8, 43, 62, 69-71, 78, 83, 89, 113, 125, 137, 141, 157, 158, 161, 162, 165, 166, 168, 170, 173, 183, 184, 186, 203, 206, 211, 219, 231, 245, 252, 255-257, 262-264, 266, 267, 271, 292, 295-298, 301-303, 305, 306, 311, 317, 322-326, 328, 331-333, 336-339, 342, 344, 347, 351, 359, 395, 425, 426, 431, 459, 467, 476, 477, 480, 481, 506, 526, 533, 542
ONCE ENLIGHTENED 89, 203, 211

once suffered	69, 256, 324, 328
ONE OFFICE–PASTORS/BISHOPS/ELDERS	509
ONLY CHRIST CAN FORGIVE OUR SINS	28
ONLY CHRIST IS GOD'S MEDIATOR	269
ONLY CHRIST'S BLOOD CAN CLEANSE	347
ONLY GOD CAN SAVE PEOPLE	252
ONLY ONE OFFERING	322, 359
oracles of God	139, 191
Order Blank Pages	iv
Orders: 1-800-John 10:9	i
ORDINANCES	268, 274, 287, 300, 335
origins	39, 40
ORPHANS IN THE WILDERNESS	124
OTHER OLD TESTAMENT MEN OF FAITH	429
OTHER PROPHETS	424, 428
OUR CHURCH ASSEMBLES BELIEVERS	355
OUR CHURCH'S BIBLE DOCTRINES	357
OUR GOD IS STEDFAST	119
OUR GOVERNMENT'S 72 TERRORIST GROUPS	435
OUR LIVE SERVICE TIMES	356
OUR SINLESS SAVIOUR	367
OUT OF JOINT FEET	117
OVER 1,200 OBLIGATORY O.T. SACRIFICES	44
oversight	524
PAIDEIA	448
pain	79, 86, 340, 446, 483-485
PALAIOO	284
PANTELES	252
PARABASIS	52
PARAPIKRAINO	121
PARAPIPTO	205
PARIEMI	457
PARRESIA	162, 371
partaker	69, 116, 117, 183, 463, 515, 524
partakers	73, 81, 89, 110, 116, 117, 128, 129, 133, 144, 157, 183, 203, 204, 289, 453, 455, 522
PARTAKERS OF THE HOLY SPIRIT	89
PARTAKERS=GENUINELY SAVED	204
pass away	35, 36, 179, 221, 484
passover	16, 320, 419, 420
Past: Christ The Good Shepherd	534
pastor	1, i-iii, 39, 51, 56, 101, 113, 116, 141, 193, 201,

```
                                219, 224, 474, 506, 513, 524, 525, 527, 529, 541
Pastor D. A. Waite, Th.D.,Ph.D. ............................................. 1
Pastor Timothy .................... 51, 113, 193, 224, 513, 529, 541
Pastor Willetts, Earl ..................................................... 141
PASTORS MUST BE WATCHFUL ........................... 528
PASTORS MUST TAKE HEED TO THEMSELVES ............ 51, 513
pastors-bishops-elders .............................. 509, 524-528
PASTORS–WATCH IN ALL THINGS ......................... 224
path ................................................. 205, 414, 450
PATIENCE ............... 86, 154, 160, 215, 217-221, 224, 246, 372,
                                                                    441-443
    PATIENCE FOR GOD'S PROMISES .......................... 220
    PATIENT IN TRIBULATION ................................ 218
Patricia Canter ................................................. iii
pattern ............ 220, 260-263, 267, 268, 287, 300, 320, 321, 515
PAUL IS THE AUTHOR OF HEBREWS .......................... 1
PAUL SAW HEAVEN'S GLORIES ............................. 439
PAUL THE TRADITIONAL AUTHOR ........................... 2
PAUL WAS FAITHFUL UNTO DEATH ....................... 346
Paul was married ......................................... 504
Paul wrote to the Jews in the dispersion ......................... 1
peace ................. 23, 29, 37, 39, 64, 71, 109, 132, 188, 189, 221,
                    233, 235, 246, 269, 308, 312, 317, 319, 329, 338,
                        375, 401, 419, 422, 426, 434, 454, 456, 457, 459,
                                460, 463, 475, 490, 531, 533, 538
    PEACE AND HOLINESS ................................... 459
    PEACE THROUGH CHRIST'S BLOOD ......................... 317
    PEACE WITH GOD ............................ 132, 375, 460, 533
PEIRASMOS ................................................ 97
PEIRAZO .......................................... 84, 99, 159
PEITHO ................................................. 525
Pentecostals ........................................ 184, 304, 311
perfect ............. 4, 7, 11, 12, 23, 26, 43, 61, 63, 67, 68, 73, 78-80,
                        82, 83, 91, 159, 166, 167, 180-185, 228, 241-243,
                        246, 252, 265, 267, 269, 270, 281, 299, 300, 302,
                                304, 309, 311, 316, 319, 323, 329, 331-334, 337,
                                338, 342, 349, 350, 358, 363, 367, 419, 438, 444,
                                                                    473-476, 514, 537-539
    perfect God ............... 7, 61, 63, 79, 80, 159, 180, 281, 300, 309,
                                                                337, 349, 350, 476
    perfect God and perfect Man ............ 63, 80, 159, 281, 300, 309,
                                                                        349, 350
```

perfect Man	7, 61, 63, 79, 80, 159, 269, 281, 300, 309, 337, 349, 350, 476
PERFECTED FOREVER	341, 342
perfection	183, 190, 199, 200, 241, 261, 321, 342
PERIBOLAION	38
PERIPHERO	511
perish	15, 35-37, 48, 57, 65, 125, 169, 179, 185, 186, 200, 244, 251, 305, 310, 366, 372, 385, 422, 451, 471, 481, 482, 484
perversions	17, 151
PERVERTED VERSIONS OMIT "BY HIMSELF"	15
Peter	1, 9, 11, 13, 19, 21, 33, 36, 44, 48, 66, 68-70, 72, 78, 79, 81, 84, 86, 117, 119, 126, 153, 178, 179, 182, 183, 193, 194, 200, 211, 217, 227, 229, 247, 256, 258, 260, 283, 289, 305, 310, 319, 323, 324, 328, 338, 353, 360, 378, 418, 480, 481, 498, 499, 524, 536, 538, 539
PHANISMOS	284
Pharaoh	91, 96, 97, 114, 120, 171, 276, 400, 401, 411, 412, 416, 421
PHARAOH'S DAUGHTER'S COMPASSION	172
PHARAOH'S HARDENED HEART	97
PHONY "BELIEVERS" ARE FOUND	94
PHOTIZO	203, 368
PHYSICAL DEATH UNDER MOSES' LAW	360
Piercing	146
PIKRAINO	121
Pilate	180
PLANAO	100
Pope	19, 148, 269, 445, 503
PORNEIA	466
pornography	79
PORNOS	465, 503
posse non peccare	159, 184
potential terrorists	154
power	9, 10, 13-15, 17-19, 26, 34, 38, 40-43, 54, 55, 62, 70, 73-78, 84, 87, 93, 97, 116, 130, 138, 145, 146, 156, 160, 161, 182, 186, 188, 190, 194, 202, 210, 211, 213, 219, 220, 244, 246, 251, 257-260, 280, 289, 316, 345, 346, 353, 360, 374, 379, 404, 414, 417, 426, 430, 446, 456, 460, 461, 463, 475, 483, 503, 504, 509, 525, 530, 531, 534, 542

Powerful	38, 61, 146, 152, 156, 283, 346, 481, 483
praise	20, 37, 39, 57, 58, 72, 83, 86, 87, 107, 109, 152, 163, 371, 471, 472, 485, 520, 521, 523, 527
PRAISE GOD CONTINUALLY	520
PRAISE TO GOD	72, 472, 520, 523
PRAISE TO THE LORD	72
prayer	6, 12, 33, 70-72, 84, 85, 101, 102, 162, 172, 178, 179, 251, 265, 306, 333, 337, 356, 363, 403, 425, 426, 452, 471, 504, 529-532
PRAYER FOR OTHERS	532
PRAYER IN GETHSEMANE	178
prepared	ii, 73, 77, 188, 202, 265, 302, 306, 316, 325, 333, 337, 338, 363, 386, 403, 520
prepared body	302, 316, 333, 337
prepared for the Devil and his angels	77, 202, 325
PREPO	67
present earth	481
Present: Christ The Great Shepherd	534
President Obama	115, 239, 370, 392
priest for ever	82, 119, 157, 176, 190, 230, 236, 244, 245, 248, 321, 350
priest forever	157, 230, 236, 244, 245, 350
PRIESTS OFFERED FOR THEIR SINS	166
principles	48, 104, 191, 199, 203, 254, 355, 357, 380
prison	1, 2, 47, 48, 152, 154, 181, 346, 369, 404, 425, 426, 432, 434, 435, 464, 501, 531, 532, 541
promises	36, 115, 185, 189, 216, 217, 219, 220, 223, 238, 240, 268, 269, 274, 280, 309, 353, 372-375, 383, 395, 397, 398, 404, 429, 437, 439, 461
promises to Abraham	238
PROPERLY DISCIPLINE YOUR CHILDREN	450
PROPHETS	2-4, 20, 24, 37, 40, 66, 68, 69, 183, 192, 277, 278, 343, 345, 424, 428, 431, 433, 513
prophet's warnings	3
propitiated	43, 63, 67
propitiation	17, 28, 66, 67, 310, 316
propitiation for our sins	17, 66
PROPITIATION FOR THE WORLD'S SINS	67
PROSKAIROS	414
PROSKUNEO	23
PROSOCHTHIZO	100
PROSPHERO	263

PROSPHERO	263
prove	61, 97, 99, 160, 406, 538
provocation	95, 96, 98-100, 119, 121, 128, 142
PROVOKE OR PROVOCATION	121
PROVOKING THE LORD	122
Publisher's Data	iv
PURCHASED WITH GOD-PROVIDED BLOOD	316
purgatory	15, 148
PURGING THE CONSCIENCE	306
Questions@BFTBC.org	356
Quick	146
Radio Bible Class	178, 303
RAHAB'S LIFE WAS CHANGED	423
RAHAB'S THREE REQUIREMENTS	423
rapture	11, 58, 64, 75, 77, 87, 125, 217, 247, 325, 340, 343, 357, 373, 384, 418, 437, 515
reading	ii, 3, 56, 71, 95, 109, 112, 127, 140, 141, 192, 193, 196, 246, 393, 401, 513, 540
reading and heading	95
rebuke	113, 211, 254, 450, 451, 493, 514
reconciling the world	65
Red sea	96, 414, 420, 421
REDEMPTION FOR ETERNITY	305
REFUGE	119, 226-228
REJOICING IN SUFFERINGS	183
remain	36, 346, 373, 404, 412, 432, 481, 538
REMEMBERED NO MORE	281, 283, 344, 345
remission	28, 310, 314-316, 329, 345, 346
remission of sins	28, 310, 316, 345, 346
REPEATED ANIMAL SACRIFICES	331
REPEATED IN THE NEW TESTAMENT	136, 237, 242, 276, 285, 286, 335, 336, 436
REPENTANCE	132, 199, 200, 205, 258, 282, 468
REPENT–CHANGE YOUR MIND	200
REPLACEMENT THEOLOGY	82
reproach	414, 415, 518, 519
reproach of Christ	414, 415, 519
REPROACH VERSUS TREASURES	415
REPROACHES AND AFFLICTIONS	368, 369
reprove	113, 436, 514
reserved unto fire	481
respect	10, 13, 181, 268, 381, 382, 414, 415, 444, 454,

rest 28, 45, 60, 64, 98-100, 106, 108, 109, 121, 124, 127-130, 135, 130, 132-138, 142-145, 179, 181, 190, 222, 279, 327, 339, 361, 374, 385, 387, 396, 405, 430, 539, 507, 519
REST FOR THOSE WHO ARE SAVED 109
rest of salvation 129, 130, 143, 144
rest of sanctification 129, 130, 134, 145
RESTORE FELLOWSHIP WITH GOD IMMEDIATELY 480
restored 211, 342, 344, 532, 533
RESTORING CHRISTIANS' FELLOWSHIP 326
RESULTS OF A MERRY HEART 103
RESULTS OF THE VIRGIN BIRTH 306
resurrection 14, 24, 75, 87, 113, 126, 136, 137, 149, 167, 169, 176, 182, 201, 202, 211, 217, 246-248, 254, 260, 270, 271, 302, 316, 321, 322, 357, 374, 407, 418, 431, 443, 476, 484, 508, 515, 533-535
Revelation 10:6 9
Revelation 4:11 .... 9, 34, 93
Revised Standard Version 15, 151
RHABDOS. 26
right hand 10, 15, 17-19, 21, 32, 40-45, 48, 82, 83, 90, 92, 157, 159, 162, 185, 220, 225, 230, 237, 253, 257-260, 266, 282, 306, 316, 321, 339-341, 350, 408, 414, 426, 443, 475, 493, 523, 542
RIGHT HAND OF GOD 17-19, 21, 41-44, 157, 159, 162, 230, 253, 257-260, 266, 321, 339, 340, 350, 443, 475, 542
righteous 26-30, 38, 55, 162, 181, 197, 200, 202, 281, 317, 367, 380-383, 390, 475, 532
RIGHTEOUS IN GOD'S EYES 29
righteousness 8, 16, 25-31, 36-38, 48, 56, 60, 108, 132, 185, 188, 189, 194, 233, 235, 244, 252, 273, 283, 289, 305, 310, 316, 323, 328, 338, 354, 365, 381, 386, 387, 389, 390, 429, 455, 456, 461, 475, 514
rod 26, 103, 104, 108, 174, 292-295, 401, 421, 449, 451, 485
rod of correction 103, 104
rod of iron 26, 108
Roman Catholic 15, 19, 25, 43, 69, 82, 83, 94, 127, 135, 148, 158, 171, 255, 259, 266, 269, 291, 301, 309, 323, 324, 328, 332, 338, 348, 476, 503, 518

Roman Catholic church 15, 19, 43, 148, 158, 171, 255,
 259, 309, 324, 332, 338, 348, 476, 503
Roman Catholic heresy 338
Roman Catholicism 25, 94, 269, 518
Roman Catholics 127, 291
Romans 5, 14-16, 19, 28, 29, 37, 40, 42, 55, 56, 59, 65,
 75, 107, 112, 130, 132, 138-140, 150, 162, 181,
 182, 186, 213, 215, 218, 246, 250, 251, 253, 259,
 272, 279, 280, 282, 284, 305, 310, 316, 321, 322,
 365, 375, 387, 390, 395, 404, 417, 460, 461, 464,
 466, 498, 505, 512, 521, 533, 534, 538
Romans 8:17 5
Rome 1, 19, 138, 140, 148, 154, 269, 272, 369, 445, 532,
 541
ROME DENIES SALVATION WAS "BY HIMSELF" 19
ROME'S HERESY OF MARY AS MEDIATRIX 309
root of bitterness 462-464
rule 1, 26, 48, 61, 62, 108, 153, 156, 199, 328, 357, 382,
 414, 460, 501, 509, 524, 525, 527, 528, 532, 541
RULING HIS OWN HOUSE 527
RUN 220, 353, 402, 441-443, 445, 446, 449
RUN THE RACE WITH PATIENCE 220
Sabbath 44, 136, 143, 268, 285, 290, 336, 337, 362
SABBATH WORSHIP FOR JEWS ONLY 136
SABBATISMOS 143
SACRIFICE OF COMMUNICATING 523
SACRIFICE OF CONTINUAL PRAISE TO GOD 520
SACRIFICE OF DOING GOOD 522
SACRIFICE OF THANKS TO GOD'S NAME 521
sacrifices 44, 157, 165, 231, 263, 266, 297, 299, 302,
 303, 320-322, 331-333, 335, 338, 339, 359, 490,
 520-523
SACRIFICES AS SHADOWS 331
SADDUCEES AND BODILY RESURRECTION 201
SAFETY THROUGH THE APPLIED BLOOD 419
saints of Italy 1
salvation 1, 4, 6, 19, 24, 25, 45, 48, 54-61, 67, 68, 108,
 113, 116, 124, 127, 129-134, 139, 142-144, 152,
 153, 158, 179, 182-187, 201, 203-205, 210, 213,
 214, 216, 227, 249, 250, 252, 255, 259, 311, 323,
 325, 328, 329, 331, 341, 342, 345, 364, 367, 378,
 385, 390, 395, 401, 404, 443, 444, 479, 517, 541

SALVATION CANNOT BE LOST 186
SALVATION IS ETERNAL 183, 311
SALVATION TRUTHS IN THE BIBLE 133
SAMSON 424-426
SAMUEL 90, 100, 114, 120, 196, 261, 326, 424, 427, 428, 449, 451
Sanborn .... ii, 141
SANCTIFICATION 29, 70, 71, 129, 130, 134, 143-145, 305, 467, 517, 539
SANCTIFICATION'S THREE TENSES 70
sanctified 70, 71, 255, 266, 318, 324, 328, 337, 341, 342, 345, 362, 363, 404, 455
SANCTIFIED BY CHRIST'S DEATH 71
SANCTIFIED BY ONE OFFERING 71
sanctifieth 70, 306, 307, 404
sanctify 68, 71, 217, 318, 363, 471, 517, 531
sanctuary 170, 260, 261, 287, 288, 516, 517
Sapphira 360
Sara 224, 380, 392, 394-397, 407
Sarah 224, 380, 397
Satan 21, 40, 55, 61, 70, 75, 77, 84, 85, 105, 160, 161, 170, 211, 220, 227, 289, 320, 345, 346, 360, 458, 504
SATAN THE ANGEL OF LIGHT 61
satisfaction 17, 43, 55, 67
satisfied with 17, 18, 43, 63, 67
Saturday 136, 137, 285, 336, 337
save 15-17, 23, 47, 51, 57-61, 63, 105, 106, 108, 111, 115, 122, 123, 132, 144, 152, 177, 186, 236, 246, 249-253, 273, 343, 346, 386, 390, 411, 424, 428, 513
SAVE OR SAVED 57
saved .... iii, 5-9, 11, 12, 25, 45, 48, 52, 54-60, 66, 67, 69-73, 75-79, 85, 87, 89, 92, 93, 95, 102, 104-107, 109-112, 116, 118, 119, 125, 129, 130, 135, 130, 132, 133, 135, 138-146, 149, 153, 156-159, 162, 166, 167, 171, 172, 175, 180, 181, 183-186, 188, 191, 193, 194, 196, 201-221, 226, 230, 236, 242, 247, 249-253, 257, 259, 263, 265, 266, 269, 279, 281-283, 285, 288-290, 305, 308, 310, 311, 316-322, 325-327, 336, 342, 343, 346, 347, 349-354, 357-359, 361-364, 366-368, 372, 375, 378, 384, 389,

Hebrews—Preaching Verse by Verse

```
                      412, 418, 423, 435-437, 439, 441, 442, 444, 452,
                      455, 456, 458, 460, 471, 474, 475, 479, 482-485,
                            497, 502, 507-511, 516, 519-521, 542
```
SAVED AND SALVATION 249
SAVED AND SERVING OTHERS 212
saved Christians 107, 110, 119, 125, 162, 194, 202, 203,
                          211, 213, 215, 220, 226, 259, 263, 265, 269, 282,
                         285, 318, 319, 322, 343, 347, 349, 351, 358, 359,
                    362, 364, 372, 375, 384, 403, 418, 442, 452, 458,
                                482, 435, 497, 507, 519, 520
Saviour of the world. 66
say the same thing 326, 479
scape goat 166, 170
scapegoat 166, 167, 265
sceptre 25, 26, 48
scourges 450
Scriptural, Christ-honoring service 483
season 53, 86, 113, 160, 413, 414, 431, 447, 514
second reason 1, 137
SECRET SINS 277
Seed of Abraham 79, 240, 437
SELECTION OF HIGH PRIESTS 188
SEPARATE 25, 70, 82, 90, 147, 253, 254, 315, 319, 320,
                                                350, 518, 535
serpent 62, 65, 310
servant 6, 24, 47, 91, 92, 94, 196, 197, 212, 219, 260,
                                               394, 428, 429, 538
serve 22, 46, 49, 76, 87, 90-92, 102, 104, 105, 108, 145,
                          160, 161, 188, 211, 212, 221, 244, 267, 268, 293,
                          306, 308, 317, 368, 375, 427, 458, 468, 469, 482,
                                        483, 485, 508, 516
SERVE GOD ACCEPTABLY 482
set 1, 11, 19, 28, 29, 40, 42, 44, 48, 58, 62, 70, 71, 77,
                      80, 82, 90, 119, 139, 157, 160, 185, 209, 210, 220,
                    226, 227, 257, 259, 277, 279, 280, 285, 292, 310,
                    316, 340, 350, 365, 426, 441-443, 446, 467, 470,
                          471, 494, 515, 517, 521, 534, 540, 541
set at liberty 1, 540
seven year Tribulation period 154
seventh day 135-137, 170, 336, 337, 422
Seventh Day Adventists 170, 336
Seventh Day Baptists 336

sexual promiscuity 79
SEXUAL RELATIONS OF MARRIED UNDEFILED 503
SEXUAL UNION ONLY IN MARRIAGE 467
shadow 33, 228, 267, 268, 326, 327, 331
Shadrach, Meshach, and Abednego 236, 430
shake 32, 41, 480
shaken 481, 482
SHAKING THE EARTH AND HEAVEN 480
SHAME ON WAVERING CHRISTIANS 353
Sharper... 146
shed blood 275, 291, 301, 316, 318, 322, 329, 347
sheep having no shepherd 173, 536
shepherd 173, 319, 524, 525, 533-536
similitude 91, 190, 222, 243, 487
sin unto death 206, 361
SIN UNTO PHYSICAL DEATH 206, 360, 361
Sinai........................... 12, 122, 294, 470-472, 480
sinless blood 73, 302, 333, 338, 346
SINS NOT REMEMBERED THROUGH GOD'S MERCY 280
SINS REMEMBERED NO MORE 345
Sion 11, 211, 238, 258, 270, 271, 275, 279, 304, 427,
473, 520, 525
SITTING ON THE RIGHT HAND 17, 18, 258
six literal days 136
SKIA 267
SKILL 194, 195
SKLERUNO 119, 141
sleep 11, 16, 57, 84, 172, 178, 179, 206, 216, 218, 221,
247, 361, 429, 528
slew the Egyptian 413
sloth 217, 218
SLOTHFUL 217, 218
social gospel 105
Sodom 24, 52, 53, 176, 230, 233, 234, 365, 467, 485,
495, 501, 502
SODOM DESTROYED FOR SEXUAL SIN 467
Sodomites 176, 365
SODOMITES SLAIN BY GOD 365
SOME CORRUPT BIBLE VERSIONS 150
SOME OF THE GNOSTICS' HERESIES 6
SOMETIMES ANGELS WERE VISIBLE 24
sorrow 103, 179, 216, 247, 483, 484

sorrow 103, 179, 216, 247, 483, 484
sound and healthy doctrine 512
SOUND DOCTRINE 113, 192, 511, 512, 514
SPEAKING THE WORDS OF GOD 528
SPIRITUAL HEART TROUBLE 104
spoiled 370, 435, 493
SPOUDE 213
sprinkled 158, 167, 214, 312-314, 351
SPRINKLING BLOOD IN MOSES DAY 312
STEDFAST 52-54, 67, 116, 118, 119, 128, 157, 228, 229
STEDFAST CHRISTIANS 116
step 52, 117, 143, 145, 224, 326
Stephen 18, 42, 172, 258
STOICHEION 191
STOP HARDENING YOUR HEARTS 141
STRAIGHT PATHS 459
STRANGERS AND PILGRIMS 397, 398
STRONG MEAT 191, 194-196, 457
STUDY AND TEACH GOD'S WORDS 192
submit 184, 524, 526
suffer affliction 413, 414
suffered 19, 29, 68, 69, 71, 84, 158, 180, 236, 249, 255,
                     256, 318, 323, 324, 328, 365, 516, 517, 538
suffering 57, 63, 66, 68, 69, 76, 92, 182, 208, 365, 370,
                     446, 447, 454, 467, 538, 539
SUFFERING LOSS YET SAVED 208
SUFFERINGS AND GLORY 182
SUFFERINGS OF THE LORD JESUS CHRIST 68, 69, 182
SUGKAKOUCHEO 413
Sunday .... iii, 27, 29, 136, 137, 140, 150, 285, 336, 337,
                     356, 418
SUNDAY NOT SATURDAY FOR WORSHIP 285
SUNDAY, NOT SATURDAY 336
SUNEIDESIS 529
sure 9, 34, 52, 53, 77, 79, 93, 102, 117-119, 125, 127,
                 157, 228, 229, 271, 333, 335, 339, 374, 375, 380,
                 386, 391, 415, 422, 451, 455, 463, 519, 531, 542
SURE ANCHOR 228
surety 221, 248
SYMPATHEO 369
tabernacle 43, 82, 83, 91, 158, 166, 168-170, 228, 231,
                     257, 260-263, 265, 267-269, 271, 287, 288, 291-

	294, 296-298, 300-303, 308, 312, 313, 320, 321, 339, 347-350, 486, 493, 516, 542, 543
table	iv, 43, 102, 124, 125, 212, 263, 287, 288, 290, 292, 314
Table of Contents	iv
TACHELIZO	155
TAKE HEED	49-52, 110, 127, 139, 208, 366, 433, 470, 478, 505, 513, 525
TAKING CHRIST'S YOKE	145
Taoists	518
taste death	63, 66, 76, 182
tasted	63-67, 89, 182, 203-205, 293
tasted death for every man.	64-67
TASTED OF THE HEAVENLY GIFT	89, 203, 204
TASTED THE GOOD WORD	204
TASTED=GENUINELY SAVED	205
TEACH GOD'S WORDS!	513
teachers	66, 72, 191-193, 196, 268, 303, 304, 358, 454, 462, 476, 514
TEACHING DISCERNMENT	197
TELEIOO	69
TELEIOTES	199
temptation	81, 84-86, 95, 96, 98-100, 121, 142, 160, 161, 178, 179, 353, 406, 483
Temptation #1	161
Temptation #2	161
Temptation #3	161
TEMPTATION & TESTING	84
tempted	21, 81, 82, 84-86, 90, 97-100, 121, 122, 159-161, 184, 350, 353, 436
TEMPTING FOR FORTY YEARS	99
TEMPTING GOD IN THE WILDERNESS	97
ten major themes of theology	515
ten percent	235, 237, 238
terrorists	154, 346, 370, 502, 509
Testament	2, 4, 15, 23, 26, 27, 43-46, 48, 49, 69, 73, 75, 83, 93, 94, 106, 113, 121, 136, 139, 142, 151, 165, 167, 168, 170, 171, 173, 181, 183, 187-189, 192, 196, 201, 215, 219, 221, 225, 227, 230, 236-238, 241, 242, 246, 248, 249, 252, 257, 260, 263, 266, 268-270, 275, 276, 285, 286, 307-309, 311-313, 315, 320, 322, 329, 331, 334-336, 341-345, 347,

350, 359-363, 378, 382-384, 387, 389, 390, 398, 399, 403, 407, 408, 424, 429-431, 433, 434, 436-439, 441, 461, 465, 475, 477, 516, 517, 520, 524, 542
TESTAMENT AND TESTATOR 311
testator 311, 312
tested 84, 86, 97-99, 159, 161, 162, 378, 404, 406
TESTED IN ALL POINTS 86, 159
THANATOS 315, 535
THANK GOD WITH OUR LIPS 521
THANKFUL IN ALL THINGS 522
thanks 72, 75, 89, 116, 289, 291, 428, 520-523, 542
THANKS TO GOD'S NAME 521
THE AARONIC LINE WAS IMPERFECT 167
THE ABRAHAMIC COVENANT 221
THE ANGEL OF THE LORD 23, 45-48, 222, 223, 239, 405, 480, 485, 489
THE APOSTLES FALL ASLEEP 179
THE ATONEMENT WAS FOR ALL ISRAEL 168
THE BELIEVER'S REST 135
THE BEST GIFT TO YOUR CHILDREN 6
THE BIBLE—GOD'S VOICE TODAY 120
THE BIBLE'S HEAVEN 127
THE BLESSED HOPE IS THE RAPTURE 217, 247
THE BLOOD OF BULLS AND GOATS 306-308, 313, 332
THE BLOOD OF CHRIST 303, 306-308, 315, 317, 476
THE BLOOD PUT ON THE MERCY SEAT 168
THE BLOOD, NOT THE LAMB SLAIN 420
THE BODY OF CHRIST=ALL THE SAVED 502
THE BREVITY OF LIFE 326
THE CALL OF AARON 174
THE CALL OF MOSES 175
THE CANDLESTICK 287, 288, 291, 292
THE CANDLESTICK--CHRIST OUR LIGHT 287
THE CHERUBIMS OVER THE ARK 295
THE CHILDREN GOD HAS GIVEN 73
THE CHRISTIAN'S HELMET 216
THE CHRISTIAN'S TEN STRINGS 461
THE CHURCH WHICH IS HIS BODY 474
THE CLEANSING OF GOD'S WORDS 148
THE CLEANSING OF PROPER CONFESSION 359
THE COLLAPSE OF JERICHO'S WALL 422

The Congregation	ii, 72, 166, 168-170, 174, 264, 265, 293, 296, 303, 402, 403
THE CREATIVE WORK OF CHRIST	92
THE CREATOR	7-9, 31, 34, 39, 48, 63, 68, 93, 94, 394, 446
THE DAY OF ATONEMENT	43, 83, 165-167, 170, 174, 271, 292, 295-298, 301-303, 322, 332, 477
THE DEITY OF THE LORD JESUS CHRIST	25-27, 29, 48, 357
THE DESIRES OF THE HEART	101
THE DISCIPLES' UNBELIEF	126
THE DOUBT OF THOMAS	418
THE EARTH HAS FOUNDATIONS	31
THE EARTH TO BE FOLDED UP	482
THE EARTHLY AND HEAVENLY HIGH PRIESTS	301
THE EARTHLY PRIESTS' MANY OFFERINGS	263
THE EARTHLY TABERNACLE	260-263, 268, 300, 302, 321, 542
THE EVILS OF THE NDAA	371
THE EXHORTING COMMAND	113
THE FAITH OF MOSES' PARENTS	410
THE FATHER APPROVED HIS SON'S WORK	41
THE FATHER'S IMAGE MADE VISIBLE	417
THE FIERY JUDGMENT OF THE LOST	359
THE FINISHED WORK OF CHRIST	273, 323
THE FINISHER	443, 444
THE FIRST BLOOD OFFERING	380
THE FIRST MOUNT	470
THE FIRST TABERNACLE	158, 296, 298, 348, 349
THE GOLDEN POT OF MANNA	292
THE GREAT WHITE THRONE JUDGMENT	325, 340, 367, 395
THE HEAVENLY PRIEST'S ONE OFFERING	265
THE HEAVENLY TABERNACLE	260-263, 267, 268, 271, 287, 300, 301, 303, 320, 321
THE HIGH PRIEST ONCE A YEAR	297, 298
THE HIGH PRIESTS & THE DAY OF ATONEMENT	165
THE HOLY OF HOLIES	83, 165-168, 170, 228, 229, 231, 257, 262-264, 292, 294-298, 303, 322, 323, 332, 347, 477
THE HOLY SPIRIT'S INTERCESSION	253
THE IMPECCABILITY OF CHRIST	184

THE IMPORTANCE OF CHRIST'S BLOOD	314
THE ISRAELITES GRIEVED THE LORD	101
THE JEWS WILL BE RESTORED	342
THE JUDGMENT SEAT OF CHRIST	110, 202, 208, 209, 325, 365, 367, 371, 375, 395, 399, 478, 479, 536
THE JUDGMENT SEAT OF CHRIST FOR SAVED	375
THE LAW ABOLISHED	284
THE LAW OF MOSES TAKEN AWAY	335
THE LIVE GOAT PICTURES RESURRECTION	169
THE LORD JESUS CHRIST CONTINUES	36
THE LORD JESUS CHRIST IS DEITY	26
THE LORD JESUS CHRIST IS PERFECT	183
THE LORD JESUS CHRIST THE HIGH PRIEST	90
THE LORD JESUS CHRIST'S THRONE	26
THE LORD OUR HELPER–NO FEAR	508
THE LORD REMAINS THE SAME	36-38
THE LORD'S SUPPER'S PURPOSE	345
THE LOST ARE WITHOUT HOPE	247
THE MEANING OF CONFESS IN 1 JOHN 1:9	479
THE MEANING OF TEMPT	99
THE MEANING OF "EXPRESS IMAGE"	10
THE MEANING OF "FOOTSTOOL"	41
THE MEANING OF "PROPHET"	3
THE MEANING OF "PROPITIATION"	17
THE MEANING OF "SLIPPING"	51
THE MERCY SEAT ABOVE THE ARK	262
THE MILLENNIAL REIGN OF CHRIST	226
THE MOSAIC COVENANT OR LAW	271
THE MOST HOLY PLACE	264, 291, 292, 296
THE MOST HOLY PLACE (OR HOLY OF HOLIES)	291
THE NATURE OF CHRIST'S BODY	302
THE NEED FOR HOLINESS	462
THE NEED FOR PROPER EXHORTATION	112
THE NEW COVENANT	270, 273-275, 304, 310, 381, 383, 473-475
THE NEW COVENANT BASED ON THE CROSS	273
THE NEW JERUSALEM	394, 473
THE NEW TESTAMENT NOT THE OLD	276
THE NIV'S FIRST HERESY IN MICAH 5:2	39
THE NIV'S SECOND HERESY IN MICAH 5:2	40
THE ONE MEDIATOR IS NOT MARY	309
THE ONLY ESCAPE FROM HELL	60

THE OUTER TABERNACLE DIVISION	296
THE PERFECTION OF CHRIST	183
THE PERISHING EARTH	35
THE PLEASANTNESS OF SIN	114
THE POWER OF CHRIST'S RESURRECTION	14
THE PRIESTS' DRESS CODE	297
THE RAPTURE OF THE SAVED ONES	418
THE RAPTURE OF TRUE CHRISTIANS	373
THE RAPTURE–THE BLESSED HOPE	217
THE REALITY OF FEAR	78
THE REALITY OF THE WRATH OF GOD	106
THE REDEEMED HAVE A GREAT HIGH PRIEST	163
THE RENT VAIL AT CALVARY	299
THE REST OF ETERNAL LIFE	109, 132
THE REST OF FELLOWSHIP	143-145
THE REST OF SALVATION	129, 130, 143, 144
THE REST OF SANCTIFICATION	129, 130, 134, 145
THE RESULTS OF SINNING WILFULLY	358
THE RESURRECTION OF ISAAC	407
THE RIGHT HAND OF GOD	17-19, 21, 41-44, 157, 159, 162, 230, 253, 257-260, 266, 321, 339, 340, 350, 443, 475, 542
THE SAVED STILL HAVE THE FLESH	207
THE SCAPEGOAT IN THE WILDERNESS	265
THE SCRIPTURES ARE OUR "GLASS"	12
THE SECOND PHASE OF CHRIST'S SECOND COMING	11
THE SHEWBREAD--CHRIST OUR BREAD	290
THE SLEEP OF PHYSICAL DEATH	361
THE SUFFERINGS OF CHRIST	68, 69, 117, 182, 183, 524
THE TABERNACLE PATTERN	320
THE TABERNACLE'S SANCTUARY	261, 517
THE TABLE OF SHEWBREAD	288, 290
THE TABLES OF THE COVENANT	292, 294, 295
THE TEST FOR GIDEON'S ARMY	424
THE THINGS CHRIST CREATED	9
THE THINGS SPRINKLED WITH BLOOD	313
THE TIMING OF CHRIST'S RETURN	374
THE TRIBULATION AFTER THE RAPTURE	343
THE VEIL RENT FROM TOP TO BOTTOM	348
THE VEIL RENT IN TWO	298

Hebrews—Preaching Verse by Verse

THE VENGEANCE OF THE LORD	364
THE VERY PRESENCE OF GOD	298, 299, 350
THE WAR WITHIN THE SAVED PEOPLE	207
THE WAY INTO THE HOLIEST OF ALL	298, 348
THE WAY TO HEAVEN	127, 438
THE WILL OF GOD	9, 16, 21, 77, 81, 96, 177, 178, 182, 219, 253, 334, 337, 353, 372, 467, 521, 537-539
THE WILL OF GOD FROM THE HEART	539
THE WORDS OF GOD	iii, 6, 8, 30, 51, 96, 97, 113, 146-155, 175, 188, 192-194, 196, 197, 206, 262, 272, 356, 358, 362, 379, 411, 414, 427, 435, 443, 459, 463, 468, 477, 504, 509, 528, 529, 531, 537, 539
THE WORDS OF GOD IN THE ARK	262
THE WORLD FOLDED UP AS A GARMENT	38
THE WORLD FRAMED BY GOD'S WORD	379
THE WORLD'S CROOKED PATHS	459
THE WRATH OF THE LAMB	108
THE "ENDLESS LIFE" OF CHRIST	244
THE "ONCE" OFFERING OF CHRIST	322
THEANTHROPOS	159, 180
THERE IS A HEAVENLY TABERNACLE	268
THINGS IN HEAVEN	254, 317, 473, 485
THINGS SPRINKLED WITH BLOOD	313, 314
things that accompany salvation	210
third reason	1
this cup	178, 179, 275, 334
THIS DAY HAVE I BEGOTTEN THEE	21, 22, 175
Thomas	27, 137, 244, 386, 418, 419, 474
thorns	84, 114, 183, 208, 210, 213, 340
thorns and briers	208, 210, 213
THREE KINDS OF "DEATH"	484
THREE THINGS ABOUT ABRAHAM	391
THREE VIEWS OF HEBREWS SIX	203
throne	11, 19, 25, 26, 31, 36, 38, 44, 48, 54, 69, 82, 83, 90, 108, 114, 120, 157, 162, 185, 202, 220, 225, 244, 257, 259, 260, 325, 340, 350, 359, 367, 395, 443, 494, 495, 521
THRONOS,	26
THUSIASTERION	516
time of Jacob's trouble	343
TIME OF REFORMATION	300
Timothy	1, 29, 51, 56, 59, 60, 66, 76, 78, 81, 85, 111-

    113, 116, 133, 152, 187, 192, 193, 201, 219, 224,
    229, 251, 252, 269, 309, 352, 353, 404, 417, 457,
    476, 506, 507, 513, 514, 518, 527-529, 538-541
TIMOTHY WAS TO WATCH 529
tithe 189, 235, 237
TITHES 177, 188-190, 234, 235, 237, 238, 240, 241
TITHING IN THE OLD TESTAMENT 237
Titus 3:7 .... 6, 217
TODAY, HEAR HIS VOICE 140
took on him 79
Towaco, New Jersey 141
traditional authorship 2
TRAITORS IN OUR MIDST? 180
TRANSLATION TECHNIQUE IMPORTANT 240
translation techniques 151
transubstantiation 291
treasure 271, 415
treasures 143, 393, 414-416, 519
TRECHO 442
trespasses 65, 282, 359
tribe of Judah 174, 230, 238, 242, 266, 277
tribe of Levi 188, 230, 238, 242, 266, 294
Tribulation 11, 58, 59, 107, 108, 112, 118, 125, 139, 144,
    154, 218, 247, 320, 328, 340, 343, 357, 368, 373,
    460, 534
Tribulation Period 107, 108, 118, 125, 139, 144, 154,
    328, 340, 357
Trinity 5, 70
TRODDEN UNDER FOOT 318, 362
TRUE CHRISTIANS SAVED FROM WRATH 107
truly born-again 8, 154, 205, 217, 253, 282, 311, 358,
    373, 403, 406, 414, 416, 435, 446, 452, 507, 527,
    542
truly saved 6, 8, 52, 71, 75, 157, 216, 220, 252, 253,
    263, 266, 285, 289, 317-321, 325, 327, 342, 347,
    350-354, 358, 359, 361-363, 367, 384, 392, 399,
    403, 404, 408, 418, 436, 437, 439, 442, 452, 455,
    456, 460, 483, 484, 507, 508, 511, 520
TRUST GOD'S WORDS 408
TRUST IN THE LORD 37, 59, 117, 124, 125, 223, 281,
    299, 345, 346, 351, 438, 439
TRUST THOSE WHO RULE BIBLICALLY 525

TRUST THOSE WHO RULE BIBLICALLY	525
TRUST WITH ALL THE HEART	103
TRUSTING THE LORD	28, 37, 345, 389, 392
TUPOS	267
TURMOIL WITH CHRISTIANS	368
TWENTY YEARS AND OLDER DIED	137
TWO KINDS OF ISRAELITES	131
TWO REQUIREMENTS FOR BLESSINGS	149
TWO VEILS	291
unbelief	101, 109, 110, 125-129, 137-140, 145, 146, 400, 482
unchangeable	236, 245, 249, 482, 510, 511
unchangeable priesthood	236, 245, 249
Uncle Charlie Allen	141
unholy	196, 318, 362-364, 506
unholy thing	318, 362, 363
United Bible Society	15
Universal Code of Military Justice (UCMJ)	362
University of Michigan	132, 342
Unlimited	64, 162
UNLIMITED ATONEMENT	64
unskilful	194, 195
untainted Biblical doctrine	515
URGED TO DRAW NEAR TO CHRIST	351
UTTERMOST	60, 236, 249, 252, 253, 486
vail	iii, 131, 165, 167, 168, 185, 187, 264, 285, 292, 296-299, 303, 322, 329, 477
vanish	284
vapour	327
VARIOUS KINDS OF BONDAGE	79
VEIL	119, 157, 158, 228-231, 291, 298, 299, 322, 347-349, 543
veil of the temple	229, 231, 298, 299, 347, 348
VERSE OMITTED BY GNOSTIC BIBLES	57
VERSE PARTLY OMITTED BY BIBLES	58
VERSES ON CHRIST'S BLOOD IN HEAVEN	304
vesture	35, 38, 245, 482, 511
VICTORY AT ARMAGEDDON	354
virgin birth	11, 21, 22, 73, 80, 159, 175, 243, 265, 302, 306, 309, 316, 333, 337, 357, 363, 476, 515
virgin birth of Christ	21
VOLUNTARY AND OBLIGATORY OFFERINGS	338

Waite	1, i-iii, 104, 344
WAITING WITHOUT GETTING UPSET	372
WALK IN CHRIST'S LIGHT	290
WALK IN THE SPIRIT	185, 364
walls of Jericho	421
WANDERING FROM RIGHT PATH	205
WAS PAUL IN ITALY?	532
WAS TIMOTHY IMPRISONED SOMEWHERE?	541
washed	71, 81, 158, 214, 319, 320, 351
watch	43, 178, 179, 224, 524, 526, 528, 529
WAVERING	81, 159, 352, 353, 395
way	2-7, 11, 13, 24, 25, 30, 34-36, 41, 43, 46-48, 56, 59, 60, 63-65, 75, 77, 78, 81, 84-87, 97, 100, 101, 103, 111, 114-116, 120, 123, 127, 132, 133, 138-140, 147, 148, 151, 153, 155, 158, 159, 169-173, 175, 179, 180, 188, 190-193, 195-197, 202, 205, 218, 220, 221, 229, 231, 234, 245, 255, 261, 265-267, 276, 277, 279, 282, 284-286, 289, 294, 298, 299, 301, 307, 308, 313, 317, 318, 322-324, 326, 327, 331, 332, 335, 336, 338, 339, 342, 343, 345, 347-349, 353, 354, 356, 358, 360, 363, 367, 371, 379, 380, 384-386, 389, 394, 398, 400, 402, 405, 406, 409, 412, 413, 415, 416, 421, 424, 433, 438, 443, 449-451, 459, 462-465, 469, 471, 477, 479, 480, 483-487, 490, 491, 493, 494, 503, 504, 511, 526, 531, 535, 536, 540, 541
WE DON'T GO TO MOUNT SINAI TODAY	271
WE MUST HATE EVIL AND LOVE GOOD	31
WE NEED SOUND DOCTRINE	512
WE NEED STRONG HANDS	458
weak	50, 51, 84, 178, 179, 200, 206, 246, 272, 361, 430, 446, 448, 457, 458
WEAKNESS OF THE LAW	245
weary	39, 445-449, 452, 464
Website: www.BibleForToday.org	i
WEIGHT	220, 441
WEIGHTS TO LAY ASIDE	442
well watered ground	207
Wesley	184
West Africa	216
Westcott	15, 26, 35, 57, 58
Westcott and Hort	15, 26, 35, 57, 58

WHAT DID PROPHETS DO?	2
WHAT IF WITHOUT CHASTENING	453
WHAT WAS THE "CUP"?	178
WHEN CHRIST PUT HIS BLOOD IN HEAVEN	477
WHEN IS YOUR DEATH APPOINTMENT?	325
whoremongers	467, 502, 503
Whosoever believeth	65, 169, 179, 185, 288, 310, 345, 372, 385, 451, 484
WHY WAS GOD GRIEVED & WITH WHOM?	123
wickedness	20, 27, 30, 40, 74, 105, 114, 115, 176, 210, 365, 388, 463, 466, 505
WILDERNESS JEWS–EXAMPLES OF UNBELIEF	145
Willetts	141
WISDOM WHEN GOD CHASTENS	457
WISE UNTO SALVATION	56, 133, 187
WITH IS ONE MEANING OF "DIA"	301
without covetousness	504
without hope	247
WITHOUT THE GATE	68, 71, 318, 517
woman was created for the man	7
wonders	60, 478
wood, hay, and stubble	209, 210, 366
wood, hay, stubble	209, 366, 478
Words of God	iii, 6, 8, 30, 51, 96, 97, 113, 139, 146-155, 175, 188, 192-194, 196, 197, 205, 206, 208, 262, 272, 356, 358, 362, 379, 411, 414, 427, 435, 443, 459, 463, 468, 477, 504, 509, 514, 528, 529, 531, 537, 539
works	4, 8, 16, 17, 25, 31, 34, 36, 59, 60, 62, 99, 101, 109, 110, 121, 130, 132-136, 144, 145, 194, 199, 206-211, 229, 244, 252, 273, 289, 306, 308, 311, 317, 351, 354, 359, 364, 366, 367, 436, 462, 467, 479, 481, 514, 515, 538
works of the flesh	194, 206, 207, 364, 367, 467
WORLDLY CHRISTIANS	456
WORSHIP OF SATAN REJECTED	161
WRATH	59, 98-100, 106-108, 121, 127, 133, 135, 137, 172, 194, 206, 250, 272, 316, 364, 365, 416, 433, 451, 464, 480, 491, 494
WRITTEN–BIBLE PRESERVATION	334
YEARLY BIBLE READING	95
YESOUS	142

yesterday, and to day, and for ever 37, 40, 245, 482, 510
yesterday, today, and forever 482, 510
yoke 109, 129, 134, 135, 143, 145, 181, 385, 469
YOM 298
YOSHUA 142
ZAO 146

About the Author

The author of this book, Dr. D. A. Waite, received a B.A. (Bachelor of Arts) in classical Greek and Latin from the University of Michigan in 1948, a Th.M. (Master of Theology), with high honors, in New Testament Greek Literature and Exegesis from Dallas Theological Seminary in 1952, an M.A. (Master of Arts) in Speech from Southern Methodist University in 1953, a Th.D. (Doctor of Theology), with honors, in Bible Exposition from Dallas Theological Seminary in 1955, and a Ph.D. in Speech from Purdue University in 1961. He holds both New Jersey and Pennsylvania teacher certificates in Greek and Language Arts.

He has been a teacher in the areas of Greek, Hebrew, Bible, Speech, and English for over thirty-five years in ten schools, including one junior high, one senior high, three Bible institutes, two colleges, two universities, and one seminary. He served his country as a Navy Chaplain for five years on active duty; pastored two churches; was Chairman and Director of the Radio and Audio-Film Commission of the American Council of Christian Churches; since 1966, has been Founder, President, and Director of THE BIBLE FOR TODAY; since 1978, has been President of the DEAN BURGON SOCIETY; has produced over 700 other studies, books, cassettes, or VCR's on various topics; and is heard on the Internet 24/7 IN DEFENSE OF TRADITIONAL BIBLE TEXTS and Biblical defense. Dr. and Mrs. Waite have been married since 1948; they have four sons, one daughter, and, at present, eight grandchildren and fifteen great grandchildren. Since October 4, 1998, he founded and has been the Pastor of the Bible For Today Baptist Church in Collingswood, New Jersey. His sermons are heard both on radio and the Internet over www.BibleForToday.org on the BROWN BOX.

Order Blank (p. 1)

Name:_____
Address:_____
City & State:_____Zip:_____
Credit Card #:_____Expires:_____

Preaching Verse by Verse Books

[ ] Send Hebrews–Preaching Verse by Verse, by Pastor D. A. Waite, 616 pages ($30.00 + $10.00 S&H)
[ ] Send Revelation–Preaching Verse by Verse, by Pastor D. A. Waite, 1032 pages, ($50.00 + $10.00 S&H)
[ ] Send 1 Timothy--Preaching Verse by Verse, by Pastor D. A. Waite, 288 pages, hardback ($11+$5 S&H) fully indexed.
[ ] Send *Romans--Preaching Verse by Verse* by Pastor D. A. Waite 736 pp. Hardback ($25+$5 S&H) fully indexed
[ ] Send *Colossians & Philemon--Preaching Verse by Verse* by Pastor D. A. Waite ($12+$5 S&H) hardback, 240 pages.
[ ] Send *Philippians--Preaching Verse by Verse* by Pastor D. A. Waite ($10+$5 S&H) hardback, 176 pages.
[ ] Send *Ephesians--Preaching Verse by Verse* by Pastor D. A. Waite ($13.00 + $6.00 S&H) 224 pages
[ ] Send 2 Timothy--Preaching Verse by Verse, by Pastor D. A. Waite, 250 pages, hardback ($11+$5 S&H) fully indexed.
[ ] Send *Word-For-Word Translating of The Received Texts* by Dr. H. D. Williams, 288 pages, paperback ($10+$5 S&H).

The Most Recently Published Books

[ ] Send *Biblical Separation–1,896 Bible Verses About It* by Dr. D. A. Waite ($14.00–$7.00 S&H)
[ ] Send *Gnosticism–The Doctrinal Foundation of New Bibles* by J. Moser ($20.00+$8.00 S&H)
[ ] Send *Able To Bear It* By Gertrude Sanborn ($14.00+$7 S&H)
[ ] Send *Dean Burgon's Defense of the A.V.* by Dr. David Bennett ($14.00 + $7.00 S&H)

THE BIBLE FOR TODAY
900 Park Ave., Collingswood, NJ 08108
Phone: 856-854-4452; FAX:--2464; Orders: 1-800 JOHN 10:9
E-Mail Orders: BFT@BibleForToday.org; Credit Cards OK

Order Blank (p. 2)

Name:_____
Address:_____
City & State:_____ Zip:_____
Credit Card #:_____Expires:_____

[ ] Send *Drift in Baptist Missions, Churches & Schools* by Dr. David Bennett ($12.00 + $7.00 S&H)

[ ] Send *Studies on the Deity of Christ* (486 pp.) by Dr. Ed DeWitt   ($30.00 + $10.00 S&H)

[ ] Send *Central Seminary Refuted on Bible Versions* by Dr. Waite ($10+$4 S&H) A perfect bound book, 184 pages

[ ] Send *The Case for the King James Bible* by DAW ($7 +$3 S&H) A perfect bound book, 112 pages in length.

[ ] Send *Theological Heresies of Westcott and Hort* by Dr. D. A. Waite, ($7+$3 S&H) A printed booklet.

[ ] Send *English Standard Bible (ESV) Deficiencies* by several writers and documents ($8.00 + $7.00 S&H)

[ ] Send *Visitation In Action* By R. O. Sanborn ($10.00+ $7 S&H)

[ ] Send *Strong's Micro-Print Concordance* By Sherborne ($23.00 + $7.00 S&H)

[ ] Send *8,000 Differences Between Textus Receptus & Critical Text* by Dr. Moorman, 544 pp., hd.back ($20+$5+ S&H)

[ ] *Early Manuscripts, Church Fathers, & the Authorized Version* by Dr. Jack Moorman, $18+$5 S&H. Hardback

[ ] Send *The LIE That Changed the Modern World* by Dr. H. D. Williams ($16+$5 S&H) Hardback book

[ ] Send *With Tears in My Heart* by Gertrude G. Sanborn. Hardback 414 pp. ($25+$5 S&H) 400 Christian Poems Dr.Waite, ($8+$4 S&H), paperback, fully indexed

[ ] Send *Fundamentalist MIS-INFORMATION on Bible Versions* by Dr. Waite ($7+$4 S&H) perfect bound, 136 pages

[ ] Send *Fundamentalist Distortions on Bible Versions* by Dr. Waite ($6+$3 S&H) A perfect bound book, 80 pages

THE BIBLE FOR TODAY
900 Park Ave., Collingswood, NJ 08108
Phone: 856-854-4452; FAX:--2464; Orders: 1-800 JOHN 10:9
E-Mail Orders: BFT@BibleForToday.org; Credit Cards OK

Order Blank (p. 3)

Name:_____Address:_____
City & State:_____Zip:_____
Credit Card #:_____Expires:_____

[ ] Send *Fuzzy Facts From Fundamentalists* by Dr. D. A. Waite ($8.00 + $4.00) printed booklet

[ ] Send *Foes of the King James Bible Refuted* by DAW ($10 +$4 S&H) A perfect bound book, 164 pages in length.

Preaching Verse by Verse Books

[ ] Send *Galatians--Preaching Verse By Verse* by Pastor D. A. Waite ($12+$5 S&H) hardback, 216 pages.

[ ] Send *First Peter--Preaching Verse By Verse* by Pastor D. A. Waite ($10+$5 S&H) hardback, 176 pages.

Books on Bible Texts & Translations

[ ] Send *Defending the King James Bible* by DAW ($12+$5 S&H) A hardback book, indexed with study questions.

[ ] Send *BJU's Errors on Bible Preservation* by Dr. D. A. Waite, 110 pages, paperback ($8+$4 S&H) fully indexed

[ ] Send *Fundamentalist Deception on Bible Preservation* by

More Books on Texts & Translations

[ ] Send *Westcott's Denial of Resurrection*, Dr. Waite ($4+$3)

[ ] Send *Four Reasons for Defending KJB* by DAW ($3+$3)

[ ] Send *Holes in the Holman Christian Standard Bible* by Dr. Waite ($5+$4 S&H) booklet, 40pp.

[ ] Send *Contemporary Eng. Version Exposed*, DAW ($5+$4 S&H)

[ ] Send *NIV Inclusive Language Exposed* by DAW ($7+$5 S&H)

[ ] Send *26 Hours of KJB Seminar* (4 videos) by DAW($50.00 + $10 S&H)

Send or Call Orders to:
THE BIBLE FOR TODAY
900 Park Ave., Collingswood, NJ 08108
Phone: 856-854-4452; FAX:--2464; Orders: 1-800 JOHN 10:9
E-Mail Orders: BFT@BibleForToday.org; Credit Cards OK

Order Blank (p. 4)

Name:_____
Address:_____
City & State:_____ Zip:_____
Credit Card #:_____ Expires:_____

Books By Dr. Jack Moorman

[ ] *Early Manuscripts, Church Fathers, & the Authorized Version* by Dr. Moorman, ($19+$6 S&H)
[ ] Send *Forever Settled--Bible Documents & History Survey* by Dr. Moorman, ($21+$6 S&H)
[ ] Send *When the KJB Departs from the So-Called "Majority Text"* by Dr. Moorman, $17+$6 S&H

Books By or About Dean Burgon

[ ] Send *The Revision Revised* by Dean Burgon ($26 + $6 S&H) hardback book, 640 pages in length.
[ ] Send *The Last 12 verses of Mark* by Dean Burgon ($16+$6 S&H) A hardback book 400 pages.
[ ] Send *The Traditional Text* hardback by Burgon ($16+$5 S&H) hardback, 384 pages in length.
[ ] Send *Missing in Modern Bibles--Nestle-Aland/NIV Errors* by Dr. Moorman, ($9+$5 S&H)
[ ] Send *Doctrinal Heart of the Bible–Removed by Modern Bible Versions* By Dr. Moorman, VCR, ($16 +$5 S&H)
[ ] Send *Modern Bibles--The Dark Secret* by Dr. Jack Moorman, ($6+$4 S&H)
[ ] Send *Samuel P. Tregelles--Who Made the Critical Text Acceptable to Bible Believers* by Dr. Moorman ($4+$3 S&H)
[ ] Send *8,000 Differences Between TR & CT* by Dr. Moorman [$66 + $8 S&H] Over 500 pages
[ ] Send *356 Doctrinal Erors in the NIV & Other Modern Versions*, 100-large-pages, $10.00+$6 S&H.

Send or Call Orders to:
THE BIBLE FOR TODAY
900 Park Ave., Collingswood, NJ 08108
Phone: 856-854-4452; FAX:--2464; Orders: 1-800 JOHN 10:9
E-Mail Orders: BFT@BibleForToday.org; Credit Cards OK

Order Blank (p. 5)

Name:_____
Address:_____
City & State:_____Zip:_____
Credit Card #:_____Expires:_____

[ ] Send *Causes of Corruption* by Burgon ($16+$6 S&H) A hardback book, 360 pages in length.
[ ] Send *Inspiration and Interpretation*, Dean Burgon ($26+$6 S&H) hardback book, 610 pages
[ ] Send *Burgon's Warnings on Revision* by DAW ($8+$5 S&H) perfect bound 120 pages in length.
[ ] Send *Westcott & Hort's Greek Text & Theory Refuted by Burgon's Revision Revised--Summarized* by Dr. D. A. Waite ($8.00+$5 S&H), 120 pages
[ ] Send *Dean Burgon's Confidence in KJB* by DAW ($4+$4 S&H)
[ ] Send *Vindicating Mark 16:9-20* by Dr. Waite ($4+$4 S&H)
[ ] Send *Summary of Traditional Text* by Dr. Waite ($4 +$4 S&H)
[ ] Send *Summary of Causes of Corruption*, DAW ($4+$4 S&H)

Books by D. A. Waite, Jr.
[ ] Send *Readability of A.V. (KJB)* by D. A. Waite, Jr. ($7+$4)
[ ] Send *4,114 Definitions from the Defined King James Bible* by D. A. Waite, Jr. ($7.00+$4.00 S&H)

Send or Call Orders to:
THE BIBLE FOR TODAY
900 Park Ave., Collingswood, NJ 08108
Phone: 856-854-4452; FAX:--2464; Orders: 1-800 JOHN 10:9
E-Mail Orders: BFT@BibleForToday.org; Credit Cards OK

Order Blank (p. 6)

Name:_____
Address:_____
City & State:_____ Zip:_____
Credit Card #:_____ Expires:____

[ ] Send *Summary of Inspiration* by Dr. Waite ($4+$4 S&H)
[ ] Send *The Doctored New Testament* by D. A. Waite, Jr. ($26+$8 S&H) Greek MSS differences
[ ] Send *Defined King James Bible* lg.prt. leather ($50+$8.00)
[ ] Send *Defined King James Bible* med. prt. leather ($39+$8)

Miscellaneous Authors

[ ] Send *Guide to Textual Criticism* by Edward Miller ($7+$4) Hardback book
[ ] Send Scrivener's TBS Greek New Testament Underlying the King James Bible, hardback, ($15+$6 S&H)
[ ] Send *Scrivener's Large Print <u>Annotated</u> Greek New Testament,* by Dr. F. H. Scrivener: ($36+$8 S&H);
[ ] Send *Why Not the King James Bible?--Answer to James White's KJVO Book* by Dr. DiVietro, $12+$7 S&H
[ ] Send Brochure #1: "*1000 Titles Defending the KJB/TR*" (N.C.)

More Books by Dr. D. A. Waite

[ ] Send *Making Marriage Melodious* by Pastor D. A. Waite ($8+$5 S&H), perfect bound, 112pp.

Send or Call Orders to:
THE BIBLE FOR TODAY
900 Park Ave., Collingswood, NJ 08108
Phone: 856-854-4452; FAX:--2464; Orders: 1-800 JOHN 10:9
E-Mail Orders: BFT@BibleForToday.org; Credit Cards OK

The Defined
𝕶𝖎𝖓𝖌 𝕵𝖆𝖒𝖊𝖘 𝕭𝖎𝖇𝖑𝖊

Uncommon Words Defined Accurately

I. Deluxe Genuine Leather

✦ Large Print--Black or Burgundy ✦

1 for $50.00+$8.00 S&H

✦Case of 12 for✦

$39.00 each ($468) + $30 S&H

✦ Medium Print--Black or Burgundy ✦

1 for $39.00+$8 S&H

✦Case of 12 for✦

$29.00 each ($348) +$30 S&H

II. Deluxe Hardback Editions

1 for $25.00+$7.50 S&H (Large Print)

✦Case of 12 for✦

$17.00 each ($204)+$30 S&H (Large Print)

1 for $19.50 +$7 S&H (Medium Print)

✦Case of 12 for✦

$14.50 each ($174)+$28 S&H (Med. Print)

Order Phone: 1-800-JOHN 10:9

Pastor D. A. Waite, Th.D., Ph.D.

The Lord Jesus Christ's Superiority

Christ Better Than The Angels. Though the angels a[re] super-human and have characteristics not possessed by human being[s,] the Lord Jesus Christ was far superior to them. God the Father nev[er] said to any angel *"Thou art my beloved Son."* Satan led a host of th[e] angels to follow him into all of his perverted ways. They fell into h[is] sins with him. Not the Lord Jesus Christ! He was sinless. He not on[ly] did not sin, He could not sin!

Christ Better Than Moses. Though the Lord cho[se] Moses to lead His people out of Egypt with mighty miracles; an[d] though Moses trusted the Lord to cross through the Red Se[a;] and though he trusted the Lord to give His people manna fro[m] Heaven throughout the forty years of wilderness wandering[s;] yet, when God told him to speak to the rock, he struck it twic[e] and was angry with his people. For that sin, God replaced Mose[s] with Joshua to go into the promised land. The Lord Jesus Chris[t] will never be replaced by anyone. He is faithful in everything[.]

Christ's Sacrifice Better Than The Old Testamen[t] Sacrifices. The blood of bulls and goats could only point to th[e] Lamb of God Who would one day come to die for the sins of th[e] entire world. It could not take away those sins. Only th[e] incorruptible, spotless, perfect Blood of the Lord Jesus Chris[t] made the atonement for the sins of the whole. This sacrifice fo[r] sins was acceptable to God the Father. It was voluntarily mad[e] by the Lord Jesus Christ on Calvary's cross. It brings everlastin[g] life to all those and only to those who genuinely belief on Hi[m] and receive Him as their Saviour (John 3:16).

www.BibleForToday.org

www.ingramcontent.com/pod-product-compliance
Lightning Source LLC
Chambersburg PA
CBHW060358230426
43663CB00008B/1311